FRANKLIN

AND

WINSTON

————

"The greatest man I have ever known"

Churchill and Roosevelt atop the tower
at the La Saadia villa in Marrakech,
January 24, 1943

FRANKLIN
AND
WINSTON

AN INTIMATE PORTRAIT OF

AN EPIC FRIENDSHIP

JON MEACHAM

RANDOM HOUSE
LARGE PRINT

Distributed by Random House, Inc., New York.

Library of Congress Cataloging-in-Publication Data

Meacham, Jon.
Franklin and Winston : an intimate portrait of an epic friendship / Jon Meacham.
p. cm.
ISBN 0-375-43228-0
1. Roosevelt, Franklin D. (Franklin Delano), 1882-1945—Friends and associates.   2. Churchill, Winston, Sir, 1874-1965—Friends and associates.
3. Presidents—United States—Biography.   4. Prime ministers—Great Britain—Biography.   5. World War, 1939-1945—Biography.   6. Friendship—Case studies.
7. Large type books.   I. Title.

E807.M39 2003
909.82'1'0922—dc22
[B]
2003055554

www.randomlargeprint.com

10 9 8 7 6 5 4 3 2

This Large Print edition published in accord with the standards of the N.A.V.H.

To Keith

The future is unknowable, but the past should give us hope.

—WINSTON CHURCHILL

CONTENTS

"My thoughts are always with you all"

Aboard the USS Quincy at Malta,
February 2, 1945

A Fortunate Friendship

T HE LIGHT WAS fading. Late on the afternoon of Sunday, February 4, 1945, in the Crimean coastal town of Yalta, the three most powerful men in the world—Franklin Delano Roosevelt, Winston Churchill, and Joseph Stalin—were sitting in the Grand Ballroom of the Livadia Palace, a former summerhouse of the Russian czars. The Allies in the war against Adolf Hitler's Germany were three months and four days away from conquering the Third Reich; Imperial Japan would surrender three months after that. There were huge questions to be decided about the war's final act and its aftermath, yet Churchill's circle was horrified by the paralyzed Roosevelt's condition. "He is very thin & his face is drawn & deeply lined & he looks weary all the time and as if he might be in bad pain," British Air Chief Marshal Charles Portal wrote to Pamela Churchill, then Churchill's daughter-in-law. "Also, his brain is obviously not what it was. Altogether he looks as if Truman might be in for a job of work, but of course it may be nothing serious though none of us liked the look of it much." It was quite serious: The American president was secretly suffering from congestive heart failure and high blood pressure. The prospect of losing Roosevelt troubled Churchill, who had spent five years in a turbulent but intimate alliance with the president. "Our friendship," Churchill told Roosevelt in the early months of 1945, "is the rock on which I build for the future of the world so long as I am one of the builders."

Roosevelt veered between engagement and exhaustion. "He's really absolutely sweet—very easy to make conversation to—amusing & generally in great form," Kathleen Harriman, the daughter of the American diplomat Averell Harriman, told Pamela in a letter from Yalta. But Roosevelt could not escape the shadows. Writing to Pamela about Roosevelt, Churchill, and "Uncle Joe" Stalin, Portal said: "I am sure that FDR is completely unable to think hard about anything. He is tremendously perceptive of an atmosphere, and the most wonderful politician, but on these occasions where he meets W & U.J. he is absolutely pathetic. It is such a pity, but I suppose everyone fails in one way or another."

Churchill, however, had spent so much time and invested so much of himself in maintaining a connection with the president that he could not quite contemplate life after Roosevelt. Cabling Roosevelt from London as Germany tottered after Yalta, Churchill was nostalgic. "I remember the part our personal relations have played in the advance of the world cause now nearing its first military goal," he wrote, adding that he and his wife, Clementine, were looking forward to seeing the president and Eleanor Roosevelt in England soon. "My thoughts," Churchill said, "are always with you all."

But there was nothing he could do. Roosevelt was dying. One of the great friendships in history was coming to an end.

TO MEET ROOSEVELT the president, "with all his buoyant sparkle, his iridescence," Churchill once said, was like "opening a bottle of champagne." Theirs was an extraordinary comradeship, "forged," as Churchill put it to Eleanor Roosevelt the day the president died, "in the fire of war." Between September 11, 1939, and April 11, 1945 (the eve of Roosevelt's death), the two carried on a correspondence that pro-

duced nearly two thousand letters. From the
USS *Augusta* in Placentia Bay off Newfoundland in August 1941 to the USS *Quincy* off
Alexandria, Egypt, in February 1945, they
spent a hundred and thirteen days together. By
war's end Roosevelt and Churchill would celebrate Thanksgiving, Christmas, and New Year's
in each other's company, visit Hyde Park and
Shangri-la (the retreat in Maryland's Catoctin
Mountains that President Eisenhower rechris-
tened Camp David) together, and once slip
away from the press of business to spend a brief
holiday in Marrakech, where Roosevelt was
carried to the top of a tower to see the rays of
the setting sun reflect off the snowcapped Atlas
Mountains. An accomplished artist, Churchill
painted the view for Roosevelt—the only picture Churchill produced during the war. The
spring that Roosevelt died he was planning a
state visit to Britain.

Reflecting on her father and Roosevelt, Mary
Soames, Winston and Clementine Churchill's
youngest and last surviving child, captured the
complexities of the relationship by quoting a
French proverb: "In love, there is always one
who kisses, and one who offers the cheek."
Churchill was the suitor, Roosevelt the elusive
quarry. Their friendship mirrored their private
characters. With Roosevelt, Churchill was sentimental and shrewd. With Churchill, Roo-

sevelt was cheerful and calculating. Churchill was warmer and more anxious for reassurances about Roosevelt's affection for him; Roosevelt cooler and more confident, alternately charming and distant.

WHY REVISIT the story now? There are hundreds and hundreds of books about each man, and more than a few about the two of them together. Predictably, Churchill put the problem best. Told of a new effort to write about his life and work more than half a century ago, he remarked: "There's nothing much in *that* field left unploughed." But Roosevelt and Churchill's joint leadership in the middle of the twentieth century—a time of threats from ideologues as technology tied countries and peoples together more tightly—has a particular resonance in the early years of the twenty-first. Given the world in which they lived—a global era of attacks on civilian populations, warfare, tenuous alliances, and the mechanization of genocide—Roosevelt and Churchill merit close attention, for their world is like our world, and together they managed to bring order out of chaos.

This book is not a history of World War II, nor is it a study of the Anglo-American "special relationship." It is, instead, a portrait of what I believe to be the most fascinating friendship of modern times—a portrait that is necessarily impressionistic, since feelings are fleeting. There are libraries of excellent sources for readers seeking to find their way through the military and diplomatic forests of the war, a conflict that killed more than fifty-five million people and reordered the world. My aim was to focus tightly on the two men and tell the personal tale of what they meant to each other—and, in the end, to all of us.

IT WAS NOT a foregone conclusion that Britain and America would fight what became known as World War II. At the highest levels of the British government in May 1940, there was talk of exploring a settlement with Hitler, who was in the midst of conquering a large part of Europe. Some people in London were willing to consider further appeasement—but Churchill said no. And so, on July 16, 1940, after the fall of France, Hitler directed his generals to plan for the invasion of England. Read closely, however, the führer's order was equivocal; perhaps peace was yet possible. "Since England, despite her militarily hopeless situation, still shows no signs of willingness to come to terms," Hitler said, "I have decided to prepare a landing operation against England, and if necessary to carry it out."

Three days later, in a speech to the Reichstag, Hitler announced: "I can see no reason why this war must go on." It would not have been a sunny peace, if peace could come, but a Hitlerite one, probably sanctioning Berlin's hold over the Continent and delaying, not reversing, the ultimate spread of Nazism. In London, Churchill refused to even think it over. William Shirer, the CBS Radio correspondent, was in Berlin when Britain's reply was broadcast. A German official he talked to "seemed dazed," Shirer recalled. "Can you understand those British fools?" the German said. "To turn down peace now? They're crazy!" In these same months, stretching to the last weeks of 1941, Americans were not eager to fight a war overseas—but Roosevelt slowly nudged his nation toward engagement with the world.

Both men undertook these enormously complicated tasks of statesmanship with a vision of the other in his mind. From the beginning Churchill thought victory required Roosevelt; after an initial period of uncertainty and skepticism, Roosevelt decided that Churchill was vital to the complete defeat of Hitler. From afar, and then face-to-face, they chose to believe in each other, fighting political elements in their own countries and battles beyond their borders to ensure democracy's chances against totalitarianism and terror.

Roosevelt and Churchill helped shape the way we live now. Four of the turning points of World War II—the American decision to support Britain in its struggle against Germany in the months before Pearl Harbor; the victory over the Germans in the North African desert in 1942, which kept the Middle East out of Hitler's hands; the development and control of the atomic bomb; and the timing of the liberation of Europe—were largely products of their personal collaboration. Their partnership illuminates the human dimension of high politics and suggests that the unlikeliest of people—those who are underestimated or discounted by the conventional wisdom of their own era—can emerge as formidable leaders.

It is easy to be too cynical or too sentimental about the Roosevelt-Churchill friendship. Some historians have argued that the image of Roosevelt and Churchill as friends at work in wartime is in many ways a convenient fiction, largely created by Churchill in his memoirs in an attempt to build an enduring Anglo-American alliance. Another president and another prime minister, the clinical case continues, would have probably produced the same results in World War II. I think the Roosevelt-Churchill story, however, proves that it does matter who is in power at critical points and that politicians, for all their calculations, deceptions, disagreements, and disputes, are not immune to emotion and affection as they lead nations through tumultuous times.

"A MAN IN high public office is neither husband nor father nor friend in the commonly accepted sense of the words," Eleanor Roosevelt wrote, somewhat chillingly. By the time they met during World War II, neither Churchill nor Roosevelt could really separate their political lives from their private ones. The demands of office and ambition determined the shape of their emotional spheres. Their relationship was like many friendships among the powerful, ones in which public figures conduct statecraft within a framework of professed regard and warmth.

There is almost always a practical element in a politician's connection to other people, particularly to other politicians. "It would, however, be wrong to assume that Churchill's friendships were political, even though their inspiration might be so," wrote John Colville, a Churchill private secretary known as "Jock" who was close to the prime minister and his family. "My father's friendship and love were spontaneous and unmotivated," said Mary Soames. "He was not complicated in his approach to people. He was trusting and very genuine. He could be wily if he had to, but it did not come naturally."

Wiliness came more easily to Roosevelt. "He was the coldest man I ever met," Harry Truman said of him. "He didn't give a damn personally for me or you or anyone else in the world as far as I could see. But he was a great President. He brought this country into the twentieth century." Roosevelt's true affections and feelings were hard to gauge. "Mrs. R. used to say we all served him," recalled Trude Lash, a friend of Eleanor's who was often in the White House in the war years, "and she was right."

Roosevelt and Churchill became friends under the force of circumstance. From the invasion of Poland in 1939 to the Japanese attack on Pearl Harbor in 1941, Churchill begged for help from Roosevelt, who had to be convinced Britain was worth American trust and treasure. America's entry into the war in December 1941 threw them together in what became a spirited friendship that lasted until November 1943, when America's growing power moved Churchill away from the center of Roosevelt's thinking. The Roosevelt–Churchill connection was more nuanced in the last years of the war. In 1944 and 1945 they were like an old married couple who knew each other's vulnerabilities and foibles, yet each considered the other a permanent part of life.

During the war, Churchill would flatter, appear to defer (calling himself the "President's lieutenant" or saying, "It's up to the Boss"), but fight to give as little ground as possible. Roosevelt would be genial yet try to have his own way. Still, the two thought of each other as friends. Eleanor Roosevelt was one of the most honest women who ever lived. "You must remember Mrs. R. was brutally candid, especially with friends," recalled Trude Lash. Though they were cordial to each other, the liberal Eleanor thought Churchill too conservative. Yet here is Eleanor's postwar testimony: "I shall never cease to be grateful to Churchill for his leadership during the war. The real affection which he had for my husband and which was reciprocated, he has apparently never lost. The war would have been harder to win without it, and the two men might not have gone through it so well if they had not had that personal pleasure in meeting and confidence in each other's integrity and ability."

At Christmastime 1941, Churchill, fresh from his bath, was in his guest room at the White House, pacing about naked—"completely starkers," recalled Patrick Kinna, a Churchill assistant who was taking dictation from the dripping prime minister. There was a tap at the door, and Churchill said, "Come in." Roosevelt then appeared and, seeing the nude Churchill, apologized and began to retreat. Stopping him, Churchill said, "You see, Mr. President, I have nothing to hide from you." Roosevelt loved it. "Chuckling like a small boy, he told me about it later," said presidential secretary Grace Tully. "You know, Grace," Roosevelt said, "I just happened to think of it now. He's pink and white all over." After the 1941 holidays, Roosevelt told Churchill: "It is fun to be in the same decade with you."

There was a genuine warmth between them. "The friendship and affection between my husband and Mr. Churchill grew with every visit," Eleanor recalled, "and was something quite apart from the official intercourse." In a handwritten letter to Roosevelt in the summer of 1943, Clementine told him: "I hope you know how much your friendship means to Winston personally, quite apart from its world aspect & importance." Robert E. Sherwood, the playwright who served as a White House speechwriter and wrote the landmark biography of Roosevelt and Harry Hopkins, said Roosevelt and Churchill "established an easy intimacy, a joking informality and a moratorium on pomposity and cant—and also a degree of frankness in intercourse which, if not quite complete, was remarkably close to it."

Quoting Ralph Waldo Emerson in an essay on friendship, C. S. Lewis noted that Emerson once observed, *Do you love me?* actually means *Do you see the same truth?* "Or at least," Lewis wrote, " 'Do you *care about* the same truth?' " Though they had their differences—Churchill wanted the British empire to survive and thrive; Roosevelt largely favored self-determination for colonial peoples around the world—they cared passionately about the same overarching truth: breaking the Axis. They also shared the conviction that they were destined to play these roles. A friendship like Roosevelt and Churchill's is rightly understood as a fond relationship in which two people have an interest not just in each other (though they do) but also, as Emerson saw, in a shared external truth or mission. Victory was the common goal, and only Roosevelt and Churchill knew the uncertainties that came with ultimate power. Theirs was, for a moment, the most exclusive of clubs. During World War II, remarked Isaiah Berlin, the essayist and a British official in wartime Washington, "each appeared to the other in a romantic light high above the battles of allies or subordinates: their meetings and correspondence were occasions to which they both consciously rose: they were royal cousins and felt pride in the relationship, tempered by a sharp and sometimes amused, but never ironical, perception of the other's peculiar qualities."

ROOSEVELT WAS the better politician, Churchill the warmer human being. When Hitler dominated the Continent, staring across the English Channel, Winston Churchill stood alone and stared back. Some respectable people in Britain would have cut a deal and let Hitler rule much of Europe. Defending liberty when others wavered, Churchill held out long enough to give Roosevelt time to prepare a reluctant America for the fight and then for global leadership. Together they preserved the democratic experiment.

They were men before they were monuments. "To do justice to a great man, discriminating criticism is always necessary," Churchill once wrote. "Gush, however quenching, is always insipid." Their personal faults—Roosevelt's duplicity, Churchill's self-absorption—were at times political virtues. What could make Roosevelt a trying husband and a frustrating friend made him a great president: Sometimes politicians have to pursue different courses at the same time and deceive those closest to them about what they are doing. What could make

Churchill a tiring guest and an exasperating friend made him a great prime minister: Sometimes politicians have to talk endlessly, with boundless enthusiasm and no room for argument, in order to point the way to higher ground and convince people to make the journey. While Nazism and Japanese imperialism were on the march, the West was led by human beings prone, like anyone else, to shortcoming, jealousy, and sickness—and yet capable of historic insight and courage. The Roosevelt-Churchill connection was, Eleanor Roosevelt said, a "fortunate friendship." The world was indeed lucky that Roosevelt and Churchill rallied the forces of light when darkness fell.

PART
I

IN GOD'S GOOD TIME

Beginnings to Late Fall 1941

"Awful arrogant fellow, that Roosevelt"

FDR on a fishing excursion in Britain
during his mission to Europe in 1918

"He's pig-headed in his own way"

Churchill, circa 1918, the year
he and Roosevelt first met

CHAPTER 1

TWO LIONS ROARING AT THE SAME TIME

A Disappointing Early Encounter–Their Lives Down the Years–The Coming of World War II

In THE OPENING hours of a mission to wartime Europe in July 1918, Franklin Roosevelt, then thirty-six and working for the Navy Department, looked over a typewritten "Memorandum For Assistant Secretary" to discover what was in store for him in London. Reading the schedule's description of his evening engagement for Monday, July 29, Roosevelt learned that he was "to dine at a function given for the Allied Ministers Prosecuting the War." Hosted by F. E. Smith, a government minister and good friend of Winston Churchill's, the banquet was held in the hall of Gray's Inn in London. It was a clear evening—the wind was calm—and Roosevelt and Churchill, the forty-three-year-old former first lord of the Admiralty who was then minister of munitions, mingled among the guests below a portrait of Elizabeth I.

What were Roosevelt and Churchill like on this summer night? Frances Perkins knew them both in these early years. A progressive reformer, the first female member of a president's cabinet—Roosevelt would name her secretary of labor after he was elected in 1932—Perkins saw their strengths and their weaknesses. She first encountered Roosevelt in 1910 at a tea dance in Manhattan's Gramercy Park. Perkins was a graduate student at Columbia, already immersed in the world of social causes and settlement houses; Roosevelt was running for the state senate from Dutchess County. "There was nothing particularly interesting about the tall, thin young man with the high collar and pince-nez," Perkins recalled. They spoke briefly of Roosevelt's cousin Theodore, the former president of the United States, but Perkins did not give this Roosevelt "a second thought" until she ran across him again in Albany a few years later. She watched him work the Capitol—"tall and slender, very active and alert, moving around the floor, going in and out of committee rooms, rarely talking with the members, who more or less avoided him, not particularly charming (that came later), artificially serious of face, rarely smiling, with an unfortunate habit—so natural that he was unaware of it—of throwing his head up. This, combined with his pince-nez and great height, gave him the appearance of looking down his nose at most people." Later, the toss of the head would signal confidence and cheer. In the young Roosevelt it seemed, Perkins said, "slightly supercilious." She once heard a fellow politician say: "Awful arrogant fellow, that Roosevelt."

Perkins had also spent time with Churchill when she visited pre–World War I England. He was, she recalled, "a very interesting, alert, and vigorous individual who was an intellectual clearly." Churchill, she would tell President Roosevelt years later, "is this kind of a fellow: You want to be careful. He runs ahead of himself, or at least he used to." He was stubborn, Perkins said, "so sure of himself that he would insist upon doing the thing that he thought was a good thing to do. He was a little bit vain. He thought people were old fuddy-duds if they didn't agree with him." Her bottom line?

"He's pig-headed in his own way," Perkins said. "He's often right and brilliant, but . . ." *But.* She left the sentence unfinished.

THE GRAY'S INN dinner was a glittering occasion, with high British officials going out of their way to pay homage to Roosevelt as the representative of their American ally. Hailing Roosevelt as "the member of a glorious family," Smith, who later became the earl of Birkenhead, said, "No one will welcome Mr. Roosevelt on his visit to England with a warmer hand and heart than we do." Then Roosevelt—to his "horror," he said—was unexpectedly asked to say a few words. He stumbled a bit as he began. Uncertainly, trying to find the right note, Roosevelt said he had been "given to understand that I should not be called upon to speak" and in his nervousness, looking around at the faces of his hosts, began to talk about the importance of the personal in politics and war. Citing the need for an "intimate personal relationship" among allied nations, Roosevelt said: "It is quite impossible . . . to sit at home 3000 miles or more away and to obtain that close man-to-man, shoulder-to-shoulder touch, which today characterizes the work of the Allies in conducting the War." Warming to his point, Roosevelt concluded: "We are with you—about ninety-nine and nine-tenths of 110,000,000 of our people are with you—in the declaration that we are going to see this thing through with you."

In later years, Churchill would not recall meeting the American visitor. Roosevelt certainly recalled meeting Churchill, however, and long remembered Churchill's brusqueness. "I always disliked him since the time I went to

England in 1917 or 1918," Roosevelt said to Joseph P. Kennedy, the American ambassador to Britain, in a conversation in 1939. "At a dinner I attended he acted like a stinker." Roosevelt and Churchill would not be in contact again for another twenty-one years. When they were, Churchill, not Roosevelt, would be the one sounding the trumpet about the indispensability of an "intimate personal relationship." The man who would bring them together: Adolf Hitler, a corporal who won the Iron Cross, First Class, six days after Roosevelt and Churchill dined at Gray's Inn.

THEY HAD BEEN born eight years and an ocean apart—Winston Leonard Spencer Churchill on November 30, 1874, at Blenheim Palace in Oxfordshire; Franklin Delano Roosevelt on January 30, 1882, at Hyde Park in Dutchess County, New York. They loved tobacco, strong drink, history, the sea, battleships, hymns, pageantry, patriotic poetry, high office, and hearing themselves talk. "Being with them was like sitting between two lions roaring at the same time," said Mary Soames. With Roosevelt in his naval cape and Churchill in his service uniforms, they understood the stagecraft of statesmanship. "There was a good deal of the actor in each," said Mike Reilly, Roosevelt's

Secret Service chief, "and we Secret Service men who had to arrange their exits and their entrances found we were working for a pair of master showmen who were determined that no scenes would be stolen by the other."

They were the sons of rich American mothers. Jennie Jerome married Lord Randolph Churchill in 1874; Sara Delano became the second wife of James Roosevelt in 1880. Roosevelt, the cousin of a president, came from the Hudson Valley, Groton School, Harvard College, and Columbia Law School; Churchill, the grandson of a duke, from Blenheim, Harrow, and Sandhurst. In a sign of how small the elite Anglo-American world in which they moved was, one of the wives of Winston's cousin the duke of Marlborough was romanced by Winthrop Rutherfurd, the husband of Franklin's illicit love, Lucy Mercer Rutherfurd. As boys, Roosevelt and Churchill were obsessive collectors: stamps, birds, books, and naval prints for Roosevelt, toy soldiers and butterflies for Churchill. Cousin Theodore's legend fired young Roosevelt's political imagination; Lord Randolph's career fascinated his son. As children and young men, they read the same books: Edward Lear's *Book of Nonsense,* the naval writings of Admiral Alfred Thayer Mahan, G. A. Henty's boys' books about the glories of empire, Kipling's poems and fiction, and Macaulay's history and essays. They loved Shakespeare, the Sermon on the Mount, and movies—even bad ones.

Politics was a shared passion. "My husband always had a joy in the game of politics," Eleanor said. "It was always to him an interesting game, like chess—something in which you pitted your wits against somebody else's." Until he became president, Roosevelt was a state senator, assistant secretary of the navy, the 1920 Democratic nominee for vice president, and governor of New York—and his four White House victories are unmatched in American history. Churchill was the quintessential parliamentarian. "Westminster is his ambience—his aura, as a spiritualist would say," wrote Colin Coote, managing editor of the *Daily Telegraph*. From his first election to the House of Commons in October 1900 to his summons by King George VI to become prime minister in May 1940, Churchill would serve as parliamentary undersecretary for the Colonies, president of the Board of Trade, home secretary, first lord of the Admiralty, chancellor of the duchy of Lancaster, minister of munitions, secretary of state for war and air, secretary of state for the Colonies, and chancellor of the Exchequer. He was always looking ahead. At the Munitions Ministry in September 1917, Churchill said:

"There are only two ways left now of winning the war, and they both begin with A. One is aeroplanes and the other is America."

Their minds raced and roamed. Roosevelt loved what he called "bold, persistent experimentation" in politics and government and liked to lecture Middle Eastern leaders—from the shah of Iran to Ibn Saud of Saudi Arabia—on how they might grow trees and crops in the desert. In 1918, Felix Frankfurter was visiting Cliveden, Nancy Astor's country house in England, and listened as she attacked Churchill, who was not there, at length. At last A. J. Balfour, a former prime minister, told her: "Nancy, all you say about Winston may be true, but Winston has ideas, and to a statesman with ideas much shall be forgiven."

Ceremony fascinated them. At the height of World War II, when they were in Washington, Roosevelt and Churchill took time to confer about the music that would be played at a White House concert. With Roosevelt's approval, Churchill proposed "some . . . early American airs and suggests that the list include some of Stephen Foster's—Old Kentucky Home, and others—popular Civil War airs, and winding up with the Battle Hymn of the Republic." Roosevelt's intimates belonged to an exclusive Cuff Links Club, whose founding members had been part of Roosevelt's failed vice presidential campaign; Churchill's inner circle dined together in the Pinafore Room of the Savoy as members of the Other Club, established by Churchill and F. E. Smith in 1911. Roosevelt and Churchill were fascinated by the drama of war. Roosevelt "really had military genius, and there's where he and Churchill came closest together," said the columnist Walter Lippmann. "What they loved was the war room—the maps, deployment, deciding on where to land."

In their hearts, though, they were men of peace. To them war was a necessary evil. "I have seen war," Roosevelt once said, his remarks based on his memories of the 1918 trip to Europe. "I have seen war on land and sea. I have seen blood running from the wounded. I have seen men coughing out their gassed lungs. I have seen the dead in the mud. I have seen cities destroyed. I have seen two hundred limping, exhausted men come out of line—the survivors of a regiment of one thousand that went forward forty-eight hours before. I have seen children starving. I have seen the agony of mothers and wives. I hate war." After the bloodshed of the western front, Churchill took the same view. "War, which used to be cruel and magnificent, has now become cruel and squalid," Churchill wrote in 1930. "Instead of a small number of well-trained professionals championing their country's cause with ancient weapons and a beautiful intricacy of archaic manoeuvre, sustained at every moment by the applause of their nation, we now have entire populations, including even women and children, pitted against one another in brutish mutual extermination, and only a set of bleary-eyed clerks left to add up the butcher's bill."

Roosevelt and Churchill were courageous and cool under fire. In February 1933, in Miami, an assassin armed with a revolver fired five shots at Roosevelt, missing the president-elect but killing the mayor of Chicago, who was talking with FDR. Roosevelt never flinched. That evening, the president-elect appeared unshaken and went to bed after drinking a glass of whiskey. Facing a ferocious storm on an Atlantic cruise in 1935—a sailor on board thought the tempest looked "as if all the devils of hell were breaking loose"—Roosevelt was unruffled. "He was interested but not in the least alarmed," said Admiral Wilson Brown, a Roosevelt naval aide.

At Omdurman, Churchill rode in a fabled cavalry charge, brandishing a Mauser pistol; went to the front as a battalion commander in the trenches in World War I; refused to leave London during the Blitz; preferred rooftops to bomb shelters during air raids; and had to be forbidden by George VI to strike the beaches of Normandy on D-Day. En route to Washington aboard the *Queen Mary* for a meeting with Roosevelt in 1943, Churchill waved away reports of German submarines, saying that he had had a machine gun mounted in his lifeboat. "I won't be captured," he said. "The finest way to die is in the excitement of fighting the enemy."

THEY WERE DEEPLY driven. Seated next to Violet Bonham Carter, daughter of Prime Minister H. H. Asquith, at dinner when he was thirty-three, Churchill said, "We are all worms. But I do believe that I am a glow-worm." On his first American lecture tour in 1900, Churchill was introduced to a Boston audience by an American novelist named Winston Churchill (no relation). "Why don't you run for the Presidency of the United States?" the British Churchill asked the American Churchill. "Then I will become Prime Minister of England, and we can amaze everybody." Careening from hot spot to hot spot in the empire at the turn of the century, Churchill was aware of the impression his stark ambition made on others. Some of his critics, he wrote in a memoir, "proceeded to be actually abusive, and the expressions 'Medal-hunter' and 'Self-advertiser' were used from time to time in some high and some low military circles in a manner which would, I am sure, surprise and pain the readers of these notes."

Roosevelt was stoked by ambition, too. By the

end of his college years at Harvard, Roosevelt seems to have grasped what it would take to get what he wanted in life: a relentless drive. In an editorial addressed to the incoming freshman class at Harvard in 1903, Roosevelt, then president of the *Crimson,* wrote: "It is not so much brilliance as effort that is appreciated here— determination to accomplish something."

The young Roosevelt was openly ambitious and privately anxious, and the war between these impulses came to the surface when he slept. "Sometimes he'd have nightmares and then he'd generally do very strange things," recalled Eleanor. "He was a collector of books and so one night I woke up to see him standing at the foot of the bed reaching for something. I said, 'What on earth are you doing?' and he said, 'I can't reach that book, and if I don't get it now I may miss getting it!' " Substitute any of life's great consolations for the book—love, office, fame—and we have a glimpse of the turmoil Roosevelt kept hidden from public view.

In their youth and early adult years, Churchill and Roosevelt could be unpopular with their contemporaries. As a young member of Parliament, Churchill was often isolated. "His parents' friends found him an interesting phenomenon; men of his own age thought him brash, offensive and arrogant," said Jock Colville. Roosevelt was blackballed from Porcellian, his father's and his cousin Ted's Harvard club. "He was the kind of boy whom you invited to the dance, but not the dinner," recalled Theodore Roosevelt's daughter Alice Longworth, "a good little mother's boy whose friends were dull, who belonged to the minor clubs and who was never at the really gay parties." Roosevelt did worry about his place in this world, and in his storytelling he tended to exaggerate, as if his own formidable accomplishments were not enough, as if the boy who had been the center of his parents' universe at Hyde Park could not bear to be out of the spotlight or to come up short at anything.

Their families' histories were always part of their consciousnesses. One December 8, Grace Tully recalled, "the Boss in dating a document looked up and remarked: 'This is the anniversary of my father's birth.' " On January 24, 1945—a Wednesday late in the war—Churchill, preparing for Yalta, remarked to Colville that the day marked the fiftieth anniversary of his father's death. Later, in the 1950s, "I went to his bedroom to talk to him about some business matter while he was shaving," Colville wrote. " 'Today,' he said to me, 'is the twenty-fourth of January. It is the day my father died. It is the day that I shall die too.' And on the twenty-fourth of January 1965, he did."

As leaders they had a gift for bolstering those around them. "His capacity to inspire and encourage those who had to do tough, confused, and practically impossible jobs was beyond dispute," Frances Perkins recalled of Roosevelt. "I, and everyone else, came away from an interview with the President feeling better. It was not that he had solved my problem or given me a clear direction which I could follow blindly, but that he had made me more cheerful, stronger, more determined to do what, while I talked with him, I had clearly seen was my job and not his. It wasn't so much what he said as the spirit he conveyed." Lord Bridges, secretary to the British cabinet from 1938 to 1946, remembered Churchill's habit of calling for late-night sessions—a practice that was "not popular," Bridges recalled. "A proposition would be advanced," Bridges said. "Churchill would repeat it once or twice rather slowly, looking above him rather like a man throwing a ball into the air and catching it. Then another train of thought would occur to him. Was this really the right proposition, or should it be differently stated? He would then try it in a different form: and by degrees arguments would start: different lines of thought would emerge: and crucial points would be forced into the open." The hour would be late, the conversation tiring, but the work would get done—and Churchill's passion and confidence could be infectious. "I can see now," Bridges recalled long after World War II, "that, like a few other really great men, Churchill had the power, not only to inspire those who worked for him, but to pass on to them while they worked for him, something of his own stamina, something of his own matchless qualities of courage and endurance."

They were moving targets politically. Churchill changed parties from Conservative to Liberal and back again, and the vicissitudes of his views did not surprise those closest to him. "It was not as a crusader or a missionary that he had entered politics, but rather as a fish takes to the water or a bird to the air, because it was his natural element," recalled Violet Bonham Carter. "He had not thought it necessary to evolve or assume a conscious or coherent political philosophy. Though born and cradled in the purple of the Tory fold he was not of it. His ardent and adventurous mind, forever on the move, could not have been contained within its static bounds."

Roosevelt did not come to high office with a fixed philosophy, either. "All the members of the Brains Trust and their associates will testify, I think, to the flexibility of the Roosevelt mind even when the presidency approached," said Rexford Tugwell, a Roosevelt adviser. "He was a progressive vessel yet to be filled with content."

———

CHURCHILL WAS MOSTLY exterior, Roosevelt more elusive. When World War II was going badly, Churchill "would sometimes listen to the news and tears would roll down his face," said Kathleen Harriman. Roosevelt, however, kept a pleasant mask on virtually all the time. The mature Roosevelt appears to have been seen with tears in his eyes just once, in private, shortly after his mother died in 1941. In Roosevelt's mind, one controlled emotions; you did not allow them to control you.

The origins of their distinctive styles may partly lie in their earliest days. Young Churchill was given little that he wanted, young Roosevelt rather too much. Churchill grew into a man who openly ran an endless race to win approval and affection; Roosevelt became an emotionally distant figure with a tendency to secrecy and camouflage.

Churchill adored his parents, but they paid him little attention. "It is said that famous men are usually the product of unhappy childhood," Churchill once wrote. "The stern compression of circumstances, the twinges of adversity, the spur of slights and taunts in early years, are needed to evoke that ruthless fixity of purpose and tenacious mother-wit without which great actions are seldom accomplished."

Young Churchill had plenty of such emotional hardships to work with. "I did once ask a very old cousin who had known Jennie whether Lord and Lady Randolph were really such awful parents," recalled Mary Soames. "Mind you, this cousin was a woman of very high standards." The cousin thought for a moment, then began: "I think that even by the standards of their generation . . ." The cousin was quiet and then went on: "That they were pretty awful." Churchill had to fill the void and chose his nanny, Mrs. Everest ("Woom"). "My nurse was my confidante," Churchill later wrote. "Mrs. Everest it was who looked after me and tended all my wants. It was to her I poured out my many troubles."

When Lord Randolph did take note of his son, he found Churchill wanting. "I have told you often & you never would believe me," Lord Randolph wrote his own mother, "that he has little [claim] to cleverness, to knowledge or any capacity for settled work. He has great talent for show off exaggeration & make believe." Quoting this letter in his official biography of his father, Churchill's son, Randolph, put it in context, writing that "Lord Randolph had less than eighteen months to live. His performances alike in private and public were already causing deep concern to his friends and family. He was in the grip of the progressive mental paralysis

from which he was to die." That was true—
Lord Randolph suffered from "general paralysis" related to syphilis—but he had also put his
finger on one of Winston Churchill's chief
characteristics: He did enjoy escaping to a world
of "make believe."

Young Churchill, after all, had to do something to fill his time and thoughts. "I loved her
dearly—but at a distance," Churchill said of his
mother. Jennie moved in the glamorous and
often promiscuous circles around Edward VII,
both during his years as Prince of Wales and his
decade as king. Even the worst parents, Mary
said, "managed to put in an annual appearance
at Eton or Harrow, but Lord and Lady Randolph did not. There is a wonderful story about
Papa, which a bright, perceptive boy always
remembered. Mrs. Everest came to see Papa,
and though she was hardly a stand-in for Lady
Randolph, my father was so proud of her that
he paraded her up and down the High Street at
Harrow as though she were. The boy who
recorded it thought it a very great tribute to my
father's character."

Though Lady Randolph ultimately warmed
to Churchill, the depth of the son's professed
devotion to both his parents was at odds with
his actual experience with them. "He put her
on a pedestal and he did not want her to ever
step down from it," said Mary. "I do think Jen-

nie, on the whole, comes out much better than Lord Randolph. He was very cold and unforgiving." But Churchill revered him. "In fact to me he seemed to have the key to everything worth having," Churchill recalled. How to reconcile the gap between reality and the son's memory? Churchill's son, Randolph, offered this explanation, citing George Bernard Shaw on his own mother: "Her almost complete neglect of me had the advantage that I could idolize her to the utmost pitch of my imagination and had no sordid disillusioning contacts with her. It was a privilege to be taken for a walk or a visit with her, or an excursion." The roots of Churchill's fertile imagination may lie in the nursery and at school, where he was forced to dream things that could not be.

CHURCHILL TRIED TO get close to Lord Randolph. "But if ever I began to show the slightest idea of comradeship, he was immediately offended," Churchill recalled, "and when once I suggested that I might help his private secretary to write some of his letters, he froze me into stone."

In 1893 Churchill had, on his third try, won admission to Sandhurst. His father wrote Churchill a cruel letter. "Now it is a good thing to put this business vy plainly before you," Lord

Randolph said. "Do not think I am going to take the trouble of writing to you long letters after every folly & failure you commit & undergo. . . . I am certain that if you cannot prevent yourself from leading the idle useless unprofitable life you have had during your schooldays & later months, you will become a mere social wastrel one of the hundreds of the public school failures, and you will degenerate into a shabby unhappy & futile existence." Churchill was crushed.

Still, he did not give up. Rather than damning his father, Churchill reconfigured the relationship in his mind and became the most loyal of sons. As a young man he had, in his own words, devised "a system of believing whatever I wanted to believe." One night at dinner in 1947, his daughter Sarah asked him: "If you had the power to put someone in that chair to join us now, whom would you choose?" "Oh, my father, of course," Churchill said.

In Churchill's imagination, though, nothing—including winning World War II—would ever be quite good enough to please his distant father. In November 1947, Churchill was making a copy of a damaged portrait of his father in his studio at Chartwell, his retreat in the Kent countryside, when he fancied that the late Lord Randolph appeared to him. In the episode, which Churchill wrote about in a "Private Article" entitled *The Dream,* Lord Randolph does not realize his son has risen to the pinnacle. At one point he lectures Churchill, whom he takes to be an amateurish painter who writes for the newspapers, on parliamentary democracy.

"Give me a fair arrangement of the constituencies, a wide franchise, and free elections—say what you like, and one part of Britain will correct and balance the other," Lord Randolph says.

"Yes, you brought me up to that," Churchill replies.

"I never brought you up to anything," Lord Randolph interjects. "I was not going to talk politics with a boy like you ever. Bottom of the school! Never passed any examinations, except in the Cavalry! Wrote me stilted letters. . . ." Lord Randolph was in character: demanding and unforgiving. Yet Churchill loved him, and Churchill's capacity to move forward past almost any emotional setback—in this case his father's refusal to recognize his gifts—would be an asset in his friendship with Roosevelt, who could be cold and casually cruel and yet remain an object of Churchill's affection. From his father Churchill was accustomed to such relationships.

"WINSTON WAS OFTEN RIGHT," said F. E. Smith, "but when he was wrong, well, my God."

Churchill loved action, spectacle, and the idea that he was playing a part in the sweep of history. "Not any part that came along," said his friend and parliamentary ally Leo Amery, "but the particular part of leadership in some secular crisis; to reincarnate his great ancestor, or Chatham, or the younger Pitt; to stand out in history as the champion of English freedom against another Philip of Spain, or Louis XIV, or Napoleon." Distant centuries were as real to Churchill as the present. In 1930, at the age of fifty-six, Churchill wrote, "I passed out of Sandhurst into the world. It opened like Aladdin's Cave. From the beginning of 1895 down to the present time of writing I have never had time to turn round. I could count almost on my fingers the days when I have had nothing to do. An endless moving picture in which one was an actor. On the whole Great Fun!" In 1945, Churchill was at dinner when a woman at the table asked: "Now that it is all over, what was your worst moment in the war—the fall of France, the threat of invasion, the Blitz?" After a minute he answered: "Frankly, my dear, I enjoyed every moment of it." Like Roosevelt, he found joy in governing and in the work of his days.

During the war, when problems seemed countless and insurmountable, Churchill told Lord Beaverbrook, a press baron, politician, and longtime friend: "You must not forget in the face of petty vexations the vast scale of events & the brightly-lighted stage of history upon which we stand." Churchill relished movement. Charles Eade, the editor of the *Sunday Dispatch,* was with him one evening in early 1940 and "was amazed at the speed with which this man of 65 walked along passages and up steep staircases." Churchill never lost the urge for action. One morning during his second premiership in the 1950s, he called for Anthony Montague Browne, his private secretary. "Has anything happened?" Churchill asked. "No," replied Montague Browne. "Then let's make something happen," Churchill said with mischief in his eyes.

Churchill lived large. When he visited the White House or Hyde Park, Eleanor recalled, "we had to have, in his room, all the drinkables he might wish, at any particular time." There would be Scotch, soda, ice, French—not American—champagne, and brandy. These were, Eleanor noted dryly, the "little comforts" of Churchill's life. With Winston Churchill, what you saw was usually what you got—a big, boisterous, occasionally overbearing bundle of energy.

ROOSEVELT WAS MORE subtle and fortified. The only child of James, who was fifty-three when Roosevelt was born, and Sara, who was twenty-seven (and who followed her son to Harvard and published a book entitled *My Boy Franklin* the year he became the thirty-second president of the United States), Roosevelt was inundated with the attention Churchill longed for. Yet for all of Sara's adoration, she recalled, James "often told me I nagged the boy." To cope, Roosevelt handled his mother—and, later, most other people, including Churchill—with tactics and indirection.

When Roosevelt overtly rebelled against the prevailing order at Hyde Park—which was not often; over time he would build up nuanced psychological defenses—he did so in small but telling ways. When he was a little boy, he decided to play a practical joke on his nurse by tying a string at the top of a short flight of stairs, Eleanor recalled, "hoping his nurse would not see it. She did not see it, and she and the supper tray fell down that short flight of stairs." Roosevelt liked being in control, and he liked to win. "Mummie," the young Franklin once said after being scolded for being bossy with other children, "if I didn't give the orders, nothing would happen!"

From his first moments Roosevelt was accustomed to being heeded—even, in his own mind, by animals. He spotted a winter wren near the river at Hyde Park he wanted for his collection and came into the house to retrieve his gun. "And do you think that wren is going to oblige you by staying there?" Sara asked. "Oh, yes, he'll wait," Franklin replied—and according to Sara, the bird did.

Sara once grew frustrated when her son did not look up from his stamp collection while she was reading him a story. "Franklin, I don't think there is any point reading to you anymore. You don't hear me anyway," Sara said. Young Roosevelt quoted back the last paragraph she had just read. "Why, Mom, I would be ashamed of myself if I couldn't do at least two things at once," he said with a charming smile. In White House receiving lines as president, Roosevelt would keep up a whispered running commentary to whichever aide on whose arm he leaned. "He made amusing comments under his breath about the costumes or appearance of some of the unending throng," said Admiral Brown, "until Mrs. Roosevelt, who shared our struggles to keep a straight face, hushed him."

Roosevelt never overtly doubted the foundations on which his life was built and he exuded optimism. "The only thing we have to fear," he told a broken nation in the gloom of the Great Depression, "is fear itself." One reason for his confidence was that he himself had felt taken care of all his life. Robert Hopkins, the son of Roosevelt's close aide Harry Hopkins, remembered traveling with Roosevelt in New York City on July 11, 1936, for the opening of the Triborough Bridge. Roosevelt, then fifty-four years old, was to visit his mother on East 65th Street. The motorcycles with flashing lights roared up to the front of the house, and the Secret Service carried Roosevelt from his car, the agents forming a cat's cradle with their arms. Inside, Sara focused all her attention on Roosevelt. "She seemed completely taken with her son," said Hopkins. She brushed confetti from his shoulders and worried that he wasn't wearing a sweater. "Mama, it's summertime," Roosevelt said, but Sara insisted. "You are going to wear a sweater. You might get a chill." She had one with her, Hopkins said, and waited until Roosevelt put it on. Clean and bundled, Roosevelt then beamed at his mother. He had lived this way from the beginning: with a loving and somewhat intrusive mother at hand, watching over him, offering security in a tumultuous world—whether he needed it or not.

Roosevelt loved his mother but disliked submitting to her authority or even, sometimes, to her company. When Roosevelt was president, Trude Lash recalled, "Franklin would say to Eleanor, 'Mama is coming to tea; are you ready?' He would sit with them for a while, then claim he was very busy, which he was, and excuse himself, leaving Eleanor to entertain his mother. This happened all the time. FDR liked his mother and loved her but preferred not to be with her very much." And so Roosevelt spent decades acting one way and yet feeling, in some part of his soul, another.

Roosevelt became deft at keeping secrets, controlling the flow of information, and letting people think he agreed with them. In his twenties, he managed to court and become engaged to Eleanor without Sara suspecting a thing; in his fifties and sixties, in the White House, supplicants nearly always thought they had carried their point with the president. "People would go away thinking, 'Ah, I've won,' but they hadn't," said Kathleen Harriman. "Roosevelt was the ultimate sophisticate at soft-soaping visitors."

LESSONS ABSORBED AT their prep schools stayed with Churchill and Roosevelt. At Harrow, Churchill was placed in the lowest form, where, as he put it, "I gained an immense advantage over the cleverer boys. They all went on to learn Latin and Greek and splendid things like that. But I was taught English." There he learned, too, the canonical stories of British glory. Nelson at Trafalgar made a great impression: a heroic man, standing alone against a continental enemy, dying in the service of the nation. The lecturer was a master named Parkin, who linked the account to the birth of the empire. "He told us how at Trafalgar Nelson's signal—'England expects that every man this day will do his duty'—ran down the line of battle, and how if we and our Colonies all held together, a day would come when such a signal would run not merely along a line of ships, but along a line of nations." After a naval victory over Hitler in the first months of World War II, Churchill said in a speech: "The warrior heroes of the past may look down, as Nelson's monument looks down upon us now, without any feeling that the island race has lost its daring or that the examples which they set in bygone centuries have faded as the generations have succeeded to one another. . . . And to Nelson's immortal signal of 135 years ago, 'England expects that every man will do his duty,' there may now be added last week's not less proud reply, 'The Navy is here.' "

At age fourteen, Roosevelt arrived at Groton, the Massachusetts boarding school founded by the Reverend Endicott Peabody, an Episcopal priest known as "the Rector," two years behind many of his classmates. "The other boys had already formed their friendships," Eleanor said of her husband's years at school, and he was "always a little the outsider." Still, Roosevelt adored Peabody. The Rector—and, in turn, his "boys," including Roosevelt—had been influenced by the preaching of the Reverend Frederick W. Robertson, a celebrated Victorian cleric, who declared: "We will not say much of the wretchedness of doubt. To believe is to be *strong*. Doubt cramps energy. Belief is power. Only so far as a man believes strongly, mightily, can he act cheerfully, or do anything that is worth the doing." Roosevelt applied the lesson to his views both of religion and of life. He might be rich, young, and prone to vanity, but he had an obligation to serve others and the confidence to believe he would be good at it. In the penultimate months of World War II, he would cite Peabody in his last inaugural address: "I remember that my old schoolmaster, Dr. Peabody, said in days that seemed to us then to be secure and untroubled, 'Things in life will not always run smoothly. Sometimes we will be rising toward the heights—then all will seem to reverse itself and start downward. The great fact to remember is that the trend of civilization itself is forever upward; that a line drawn through the middle of the peaks and the valleys of the centuries always has an upward trend.' "

CHURCHILL AND ROOSEVELT each had complicated marriages, and both were dependent on their wives in the midst of the competing currents of married and political life. The first time Churchill was introduced to Clementine Hozier, he was so thunderstruck by her beauty that he—quite uncharacteristically—said not a word. As they stood together, she danced off with another man. With deft understatement, their daughter Mary would describe the meeting as "brief and unpropitious." Four years later, they found themselves seated next to each other at a dinner party. Even then it was a near miss. Clementine had been asked only after another woman dropped out, and Churchill arrived late. Still, they fell in love.

He was not an easy man to live with. Early in his career, Churchill ran with an eclectic political crowd. Churchill would telephone Clementine, Jock Colville wrote, "to say that he was bringing them all back to dinner and it would be pleasant to have some lobsters and roast duck. The problems of housekeeping on a comparatively small budget were something he never grasped." But she kept things together and was an astute adviser. "Her judgment, given after careful reflection," Colville said, "often saved her husband from unwise acts on which he had impetuously determined." All was not placid, however. A perfectionist who required rest and quiet—two things in short supply in Winston Churchill's universe—Clementine could be querulous. "When her nerves were

"Mama is coming to tea; are you ready?"

Sara Delano Roosevelt and Eleanor
Roosevelt in 1903, the year Franklin—
to his mother's consternation—proposed
marriage to his cousin

stretched, she sometimes turned on Winston with vitriol in her voice and the flashing eyes of a Fury," said Colville.

A child of a broken home, Clementine seems to have reacted to the chaos of her childhood—she was shuttled about, and her closest sibling died—by insisting on at least the appearance of order. "She had a most sensitive conscience," Mary wrote, "and suffered untold miseries if the immaculate white of her lace-edged pinafore was marred by spot or stain."

Churchill and Clementine may not always have been happy, but they were never bored. Clementine would be Churchill's strongest mainstay, a pillar of support and hope and love, and a sparring partner. He loved the sunny Riviera; she preferred skiing in the Alps. He liked gambling; she hated it. He cherished life at Chartwell; to her it was, for a long time, a source of possible financial ruin. She was, her daughter said, a worrier. "It is a great fault in me that small things should have the power to harass & agonise me," Clementine wrote Winston.

He gave her big things to fret about, too. Before they were married, Churchill was staying in a house that caught fire. At first Clementine did not know if he had survived. Frightened that the man she loved might be injured or dead, she dispatched a telegram. Churchill's reply was full of the excitement of the adventure: He had had a grand time of it. "The fire was great fun & we all enjoyed it thoroughly," Churchill wrote. "It is a strange thing to be locked in deadly grapple with that cruel element. I had no conception—except from reading—of the power & majesty of a great conflagration." Clementine wrote him back: "I have been able to think of nothing but the fire & the terrible danger you have been in—The first news I heard was a rumour that the house was burnt down—That was all—My dear my heart stood still with terror." It was the beginning of a lifetime of his taking chances and her fretting about the consequences.

Churchill's thrill at the fire was not something his future friend Roosevelt would have shared. One of Roosevelt's most disturbing memories was of a fire in his childhood. "He always remembered exactly what his father had done, and he could tell me just where the panelling and the walls were that had to be torn away," recalled Eleanor. "I think it made a tremendous impression on him, because all his life he was more afraid of a surprise fire than anything else." His paralysis exacerbated those fears.

The Churchills sometimes annoyed each other, and the pressures of political life added to the tensions. "I was stupid last night—but you know what a prey I am to nerves & prepossessions," Churchill wrote Clementine after a quarrel. "It is a great comfort to me to feel absolute confidence in your love & cherishment for your poor P. D. [Pug Dog] . . . I have no one but you to break the loneliness of a bustling & bustled existence." When they fought, they made up quickly, and she never wavered in her belief in his destiny. She watched over him and cared for him, even designing his siren suits— the zippered one-piece outfits the family called his "rompers"—in exotic shades of velvet.

Yet Clementine once, as Mary wrote, "fell romantically in love" with another man. He was Terence Philip, a London art dealer who was a fellow guest (with others) on a five-month trip to Komodo, an island in the Dutch East Indies. It was the mid-1930s. She was fifty. It must have been clear to Clementine that she would spend the rest of her days trying to manage the largely unmanageable Winston Churchill, who had remained at home. She loved him, but his ambitions and his wishes took precedence, and his pace never slackened. Nothing lasting came of the Philip connection. Later, Clementine quoted a French saying to explain it: *C'était une vraie connaissance de ville d'eau*—"a holiday romance."

Clementine grounded her impetuous husband probably as much as any woman could have. "The Prime Minister does not 'dominate' his table," recalled Charles Eade. "No one waits for him to initiate a topic of conversation. Mrs. Churchill is much noisier, talks a lot in a loud voice and laughs a great deal. . . . Mrs. Churchill is a charming and friendly personality who does a little leg-pulling at his expense." When guests were not present, however, things could get rougher. Clementine, Mary wrote, "was not a good arguer: she quickly became vehement and over-emphatic, often spoiling her case by exaggeration." Churchill would then strike a defiant pose and give no quarter. "Such discussions," Mary wrote, "sometimes ended in an explosion and a 'sweep-out': once she actually shied a dish of spinach at him: it missed, but left a tell-tale mark on the wall."

She had high standards—for their houses, for her children, and, inevitably for a family in public life, for his staff and political friends. He trusted her. "Papa once said to the President, 'You know, I tell Clemmie everything,' " Mary recalled. "And Roosevelt replied, quite candidly, 'Well, I don't do that with Eleanor because she writes a column and she might confuse what should be said and what shouldn't be.' He did not think she would do it on purpose but that she might not be clear about what was sensitive and what was not. My father was quite conscious of that distinction, too, and because he spoke very freely in private, he used to sometimes say, quite fiercely, 'Now that's secret!' And then if I or somebody else looked hurt because they thought, 'Well, of course I'm not going to leave the table and pick up the telephone and ring the papers.' If Papa saw that we were wounded, he would say, 'It isn't that I don't trust you, but I'm labeling it, I'm labeling it.' That phrase passed into family history. 'I'm labeling it!' Papa would say, quite merrily sometimes. I think the fact that my father and the President could have that kind of conversation—discussing how much they told their wives—suggests a degree of closeness and friendship."

ANNA ELEANOR ROOSEVELT was Franklin's fifth cousin. She was the daughter of Teddy's younger brother, Elliott Roosevelt (FDR's godfather), and the beautiful but distant Anna Hall. Elliott was an alcoholic who never really found his footing in the world. Eleanor's mother called her "Granny," she recalled, because "I was so old-fashioned."

Like Clementine, Eleanor did not have a happy childhood. Eleanor's parents both died before she was eleven, and she was raised by her grandmother Hall, who dispatched her to school in England, at Allenswood, where Mlle. Marie Souvestre provided demanding education for girls. Later, she returned home and joined the Junior League, which assigned her to volunteer work in a settlement house on the Lower East Side of Manhattan. She was beginning a lifetime of advocacy on behalf of those who could not make themselves heard.

Eleanor and Franklin had known each other slightly as children and teenagers, and they began courting secretly after a chance meeting on a train in the summer of 1902. On November 22, 1903, during a Sunday at Groton the day after attending the Harvard-Yale game together, Roosevelt proposed marriage to Eleanor. According to Joseph Lash, Eleanor's biographer and friend, Roosevelt asked for her hand, saying he was sure he would amount to something one day "with your help." Surprised, Eleanor replied, "Why me? I am plain. I have little to bring you."

She was wrong there. She was a favored niece of TR's—the president gave her away at the wedding—and Franklin sensed she had much to teach him, that life with her might be more interesting than with the other debutantes he flirted with. Sara was stunned at news of the engagement. Prevailing on the couple to delay announcing their plans for a year, Sara took her son on a cruise, but Roosevelt's mind was made up. He would have his way, though the Roosevelts and Sara would live in adjoining East 65th Street houses. (Internal sliding doors connected the two residences.)

Sara meant to dominate her son's married life in the way she had tried to dominate his childhood and youth. Her granddaughter Anna recalled Sara as "the matriarch of the family" and "certainly the head of the household at Hyde Park," which, in addition to the linked houses in Manhattan, was where Franklin and Eleanor raised their children. "Mother had not developed enough self-confidence in herself," Anna remembered, "to be able to tell Granny, as we called her, 'This isn't what I want done with my children,' or, 'This isn't the way I wish to live.' " Eleanor's husband was little help on this front. "And as far as Father was concerned, he grew up with this and it was all perfectly natural to him that his mother was the strong person who ran things," Anna recalled. "He'd have a run-in with her as to how the farm should be run, but very often she'd stick to her guns and she won. And Mother didn't enter into these things at all."

THE YOUNG ROOSEVELTS began their political lives in Albany and soon moved on to Washington, where Roosevelt became assistant secretary of the navy under Woodrow Wilson. The capital was a glamorous place and became the scene of the defining crisis of the Roosevelt marriage.

There was another woman. Joseph Alsop, the columnist and distant Roosevelt kinsman, recalled this story of the Roosevelts in those Washington days. Franklin and Eleanor took houseguests to a ball one evening during the First World War. Before midnight, Eleanor excused herself. "When the other three got home at last at nearly 4:00 a.m.," Alsop reported, "they found Eleanor Roosevelt impersonating patience on a monument on the doormat of the Roosevelt house. Rising from her doormat, she explained sweetly that she had 'idiotically' forgotten to bring her own door key. Her husband a bit acidly inquired why on earth she had not taken a cab back to the ball to get a key from him (for there were plenty of cabs on the street in Washington in those days). 'I knew you were all having such a *glorious time,*' she replied, 'and I didn't want to *spoil the fun.*' " Alsop's view: "The truth was, Eleanor Roosevelt was exceedingly angry, because she already suspected that her husband's late hours at the ball were entirely owing to the presence of the beautiful Lucy Mercer, later Mrs. Winthrop Rutherfurd."

What happened next says much about Roosevelt's ability to deceive those closest to him in his private life while pursuing the country's greater good in his public life. (He would do the same with Churchill—be personally elusive but professionally dedicated to large and noble goals.) Eleanor had hired the twenty-two-year-old Lucy Mercer as a social secretary in the winter of 1913–1914. A charming woman with a voice, Joseph Lash remarked, "like 'dark velvet,'" Lucy became part of the Roosevelt household. "She knew how to please a man," wrote Lash, "to make his life easy and agreeable, to bolster instead of challenge him." Roosevelt fell in love with her.

The truth emerged in September 1918, when Roosevelt arrived home from his mission to England and to Europe. He had come down with double pneumonia on the trip back, and Eleanor found letters from Lucy. "The bottom dropped out of my own particular world, and I faced myself, my surroundings, my world, honestly for the first time," Eleanor recalled of the autumn of 1918. She was crushed, but there were practical questions to be answered. "Eleanor gave him a choice—if he did not break off with Lucy, she would insist on a divorce," wrote Joseph Lash. "Franklin and Lucy agreed never to see each other again." Or so they said. The marriage would go on.

PARTLY IN REACTION to Roosevelt's betrayal, Eleanor built her own life, undertaking intense friendships with women and with men. Her work, though, would always be connected to her husband's. She would come to pursue liberal causes and report back on the specifics of a program or the mood of the country to FDR. The progressives in Roosevelt's government knew where to go first. "There was a marked tendency, when we needed something from FDR, to do it through Eleanor," recalled John Kenneth Galbraith, the Harvard economist and diplomat who served in the Roosevelt administration. "She was considered the open point of access on all humane and liberal concerns."

Eleanor never slowed down. Patrick Kinna, the Churchill assistant, remembered a visit to Hyde Park during the war. "I was going up the staircase with a bundle of papers and Mrs. Roosevelt came out all dressed in riding gear, marching ahead with such determination that she nearly ran me over," Kinna recalled. She would be that way until the end of her life. Carol R. Lubin, who knew Mrs. Roosevelt and whose husband, the labor economist Isador Lubin, was Roosevelt's White House statistician, remembered Eleanor arriving at a settlement house benefit in New York long after the war. "She shook everyone's hand, went to the dais and fell sound asleep—and that was not uncommon," said Mrs. Lubin. "The great issue was always whether to wake her up or not."

She could also exhaust Roosevelt with business, but to the end of his days Roosevelt would write Eleanor as "Dear Babs" and sign letters "With lots and lots of love." Still, he maintained contact with Lucy, who later married Winthrop Rutherfurd, and Roosevelt would see her again during World War II.

At heart, the real issue in the Roosevelt-Lucy story is not sex but romance: By conducting a long-term relationship with Lucy, sexual or not, Roosevelt was involved in something he had to take pains to keep secret. She clearly meant a great deal to him, offering affectionate comfort and company. But he had once betrayed his wife with this woman, and he knew Eleanor must never discover that Lucy was even a tangential part of his world after 1918. That took effort. Franklin Roosevelt was an infinitely complex man, and this small campaign of concealment in his private universe was just one of many levels of complexity he had to manage behind his genial exterior.

Unlike Roosevelt, Churchill seems never to have carried on a secret love affair. On the Churchills' fortieth anniversary in September 1948, while they were staying at Cap d'Antibes with the duke and duchess of Windsor, Churchill wrote Clementine to "express my gratitude to you for making my life & any work I have done possible, and for giving me so much happiness in a world of accident & storm."

GALLIPOLI AND POLIO changed their lives. In 1915, when he was forty, Churchill was blamed for the failed amphibious operation in the Dardanelles and was shunted off to become chancellor of the duchy of Lancaster, a largely ceremonial cabinet post. Feeling he should not be in "well-paid inactivity" in London while men his age were at the front, in November 1915 Churchill announced he was going to war. With three children at home, his political career in ashes, Churchill left to fight. Clementine tried to reassure him about his fall. "Do not fear," she wrote him, "your political Estate has not vanished, it is all waiting for you when the right moment comes, which (Alas for the country) may not be till after the war—If only you come safely thro'." A portrait of Churchill painted by Sir William Orpen after his return is haunting. Churchill's eyes are dark and fretful. His brave pose—hand on hip, a stark stare forward—conveys more distress than defiance. Gazing at it more than eight decades later, his grandson Winston S. Churchill remarked: "He is convinced his political career is in ruins." Churchill would eventually return to power, becoming minister of munitions, where he worked with Bernard Baruch, the American

financier who would be a significant figure in
Franklin Roosevelt's Democratic Party.

ROOSEVELT BEGAN FEELING woozy at
Campobello, his family's Maine retreat, on an
August day in 1921. He had contracted polio.
He was thirty-nine and a half years old, and he
would never walk under his own power again.
Pre-polio, Roosevelt was tireless, buoyant, ener-
getic. His daughter, Anna, remembered him in
Washington in the Wilson years, sailing a small
yacht out from the capital. "He took us on many
weekends down the Potomac, and we would go
hiking, looking up old houses, these big old
Southern homes, some of which were falling
down," Anna said. "We did a great deal of sight-
seeing and listening to his stories of the history
of the country down in Virginia. . . . Father
stands out because he was so active and he led
the way." At Campobello in the first weeks of
the crisis, he was attuned to other people's emotions, particularly his children's. "He grinned at
us, and he did his best to call out, or gasp out,
some cheery response to our tremulous, just-
this-side-of-tears greetings," said his son James.
"Terrible as it was for him, he had the mental
depth and the compassion to realize how overwhelmingly frightening it was for his children,
and he tried to lighten *our* fears."

He would not ask for pity. "He never said anything at all; he never complained," Eleanor recalled. Part of this was an innate sense of dignity. Another part may have been Roosevelt's psychological need to minimize the devastation. "He never, never gave up the idea he was going to walk again," Eleanor said.

Within his domestic sphere, the people Roosevelt liked fell roughly into two categories. There were women like Anna, Crown Princess Martha of Norway, and his cousins Margaret "Daisy" Suckley and Laura "Polly" Delano. They offered, his son James recalled, a welcome "touch of triviality." Then there were aides like Missy LeHand, his longtime secretary; Louis Howe, an Albany newspaperman who was Roosevelt's key political operative until Howe died in 1936; and Harry Hopkins, the Iowa-born social worker who played indispensable roles in both the New Deal and the war. Treasury Secretary Henry Morgenthau, Supreme Court Justice Felix Frankfurter, and Interior Secretary Harold Ickes were valued advisers, but Roosevelt rarely let his guard down with any one person, and presidential intimates learned to accept the Boss's dodginess.

One junior member of the extended Roosevelt circle, Daisy Suckley's niece Mrs. Margaret Hendrick, said she thought the future president's illness had one inadvertent advantage, speculating that it may have saved his political career. "Sometimes I wonder whether he would have ever been President if he had not had polio," said Mrs. Hendrick. "He was very good-looking and had, I think, an eye for the ladies, and I wonder if his marriage would have held up. Without his illness I think he might have gotten a divorce along the way, and his political career would have been over."

To deflect attention from his paralysis and keep a comfortable emotional distance from others, Roosevelt spent almost all of his time putting on a show for those around him. The Washington columnist Marquis Childs thought Roosevelt had "the quality of the actor, the man who could be photographed and who could speak always with just the perfect camera angle. Partly this was the politician, but it was partly a great actor." Childs remembered a powerful picture of Roosevelt taken on the deck of the USS *Houston* in 1938— Roosevelt is in his naval cape, the wind in his face, the very image of a commander in chief. "He's standing with his head thrown back—now, don't tell me this is unconscious," Childs said. According to the author and foreign correspondent John Gunther, Roosevelt was once watching himself in a newsreel and said with a grin: "That was the Garbo in me." Meeting Orson Welles, Roosevelt remarked, "You know, Orson, you and I are the two best actors in America."

Roosevelt was the center of things, and people and problems swirled around him, awaiting his verdict. The Roosevelt style could be frustrating to others. As a translator at Teheran and Yalta and as an adviser on the Soviet Union in the White House, Charles E. Bohlen, the American diplomat, spent a lot of time with Roosevelt later in the war. Bohlen said that Roosevelt was of course "a world figure of monumental proportions. . . . Yet I cannot say that he was a likable man. He preferred informal relationships which were informal merely in structure. He could not stand protocol in the accepted sense of the word but was quick to resent the slightest departure from the respect normally accorded the President of the United States, and the aura of the office was always around him."

ONE WAY OF understanding the competing impulses in Franklin Roosevelt that would partly shape how he dealt with Churchill— Roosevelt liked power yet wanted to serve—is to consider how he viewed church. Roosevelt was, his son James said, "a frustrated clergyman at heart." St. James's Episcopal Church was as much a part of his universe as the estate at Hyde Park, and Roosevelt, the church's senior warden, felt the tug of tradition in the little parish.

As James told the story, when Roosevelt was governor, the rector, the Reverend Frank R. Wilson, took sick one Saturday with appendicitis. Sara called Roosevelt to tell him the news, and Roosevelt in turn rang Mrs. Wilson. "Please tell the rector that, if he needs me, I will come from Albany to Hyde Park in time to take over the 11 o'clock services as a lay reader tomorrow morning," Roosevelt said. Wilson, however, "would not dream of imposing on the Governor" and arranged for a retired priest to take the services. "Well," Roosevelt replied, "tell him that if he ever needs me I stand ready." He *wanted* to be asked. Listening to Wilson relate this anecdote years later, James suggested that "Father must have been disappointed as he probably would have liked very much to have read the services." The rector pondered this, then said: "I never thought of that! Dammit, I should have let him do it!"

Roosevelt's urge to preside at a religious service is telling, for the drama of the priesthood is partly about authority and submission—at the altar or in the pulpit, the officiant is both the center of attention and the conduit for a larger purpose, at once in charge and at work in the service of a cause other than oneself. All eyes are on whoever is reading the ancient words; all ears are attuned to his voice.

On Easter Sunday 1934, Roosevelt finally got

his wish. He was on a cruise aboard Vincent Astor's yacht, the *Nourmahal,* escorted by two American cruisers and a British one. Roosevelt, James recalled, wanted to anchor near San Salvador, where Columbus had landed. He invited the crews of the three escorting vessels and surprised everyone by handing out printed programs he had secretly prepared for "Divine Service, Easter." He then led the prayers. "On the *Nourmahal* that day, Father delivered a simple, short sermon, stressing the religious significance of the spot where we were anchored," James recalled. "He said that Columbus had arrived there and discovered America only through his belief in divine guidance, and that this belief in a Supreme Being gave Columbus courage and confidence to sail on when threatened by disaster and mutiny." Roosevelt told his party "with some elation" that this was "the first time I have ever conducted a service and preached a sermon all by myself." He seemed delighted.

Roosevelt was a more traditional believer than Churchill, once saying that two of the most influential literary passages in his life were the Beatitudes and the thirteenth chapter of St. Paul's First Letter to the Corinthians. Roosevelt does not seem to have plumbed many theological depths but contented himself with drawing reassurance from the tenets of the faith he had known forever. He rarely ruled anything out in the political realm, and he took the same approach in the religious one as well. "Once, in talking to him about some spiritualist conversations which had been sent in to me (people were always sending me their conversations with the dead)," Eleanor recalled, "I expressed a somewhat cynical disbelief in them." Roosevelt replied, "I think it is unwise to say you do not believe in anything when you can't prove that it is either true or untrue. There is so much in the world which is always new in the way of discoveries that it is wiser to say that there may be spiritual things which we are simply unable now to fathom."

In India as a young man, Churchill read books that roiled his religious faith. "Hitherto I had dutifully accepted everything I had been told," he said. A regular churchgoer during the holidays, he had attended three services every Sunday at Harrow as well as morning and evening prayer. But while in the army he read *The Martyrdom of Man* by Winwood Reade, which led to the "depressing conclusion that we simply go out like candles." Then two books by William Edward Hartpole Lecky—*History of the Rise and Influence of the Spirit of Rationalism in Europe* and *History of European Morals from Augustus to Charlemagne*—seemed to finish off the years of Church of England upbringing. This began a brief "violent and aggressive anti-religious phase which, had it lasted, might easily have made me a nuisance. My poise was restored during the next few years by frequent contact with danger. I found that whatever I might think and argue, I did not hesitate to ask for special protection when about to come under the fire of the enemy: nor to feel sincerely grateful when I got home safe to tea." He saved his passion for the cause of Britain. "I believe that man is an immortal spirit," he often said, leading Anthony Montague Browne, his last private secretary, to call him "an optimistic agnostic." Churchill's essential view: "Whether you believe or disbelieve, it is a wicked thing to take away Man's hope." As he was retiring as prime minister in 1955, his advice to his colleagues was twofold. "Man is spirit," he said—and "Never be separated from the Americans."

BOTH HAD DEMOCRATIC instincts when it came to their inner circles. The three Americans closest to Roosevelt—Louis Howe, Henry Morgenthau, and Harry Hopkins—were, as Arthur Schlesinger Jr. observed, "a middle-class newspaperman, a Jew, and the son of a harness-maker." Churchill's friends included F. E. Smith, the grandson of a coal miner; and Max Aitken, who became Lord Beaverbrook, the Canadian son of a Scottish Presbyterian minister. There was Frederick Lindemann, a vegetarian and scientist; and Brendan Bracken, a wiry redhead who was said—falsely—to be Churchill's illegitimate son. Lindemann (later Lord Cherwell) advised on technology; Bracken was a parliamentary loyalist who would run the Ministry of Information during the war.

Churchill was largely incapable of the relentless show Roosevelt put on. "He behaved in public just as he behaved in private," Colville wrote. "There were no two faces, no mask that would drop when the audience had retired. . . . If Churchill was not in the mood, he found it difficult to put on an act of affability even when circumstances positively demanded it; and in so far as he had good manners (which many would have denied) they came from fundamental kindness of heart. They were in no way cultivated, and it was unnatural for him to display a sentiment he did not genuinely feel." What, Beaverbrook once asked himself, was Churchill's chief virtue? "Magnanimity," he answered.

Churchill could forgive almost any trespass. "He was intensely pug-nacious and never bore rancour," Beaverbrook said. The origins of Churchill's ability to overlook slights and forget sins—which would be invaluable as he spent the war years with Roosevelt, who could be a chilly friend—can be traced to his childhood, where he learned to reimagine reality that upset him, and to his chosen profession. "He enjoyed a conflict of ideas, but not a conflict between people," said Lord Chandos, a businessman whom Churchill brought into government and who became a friend. "His powers were those of imagination, experience and magnanimity. He saw man as a noble and not as a mean creature." Politicians who spend long years in the arena, as Churchill did, learn that this morning's foe may become this evening's ally. "He was a warrior, and party debate was a war," said Harold Macmillan, a Churchill colleague who served as prime minister from 1957 to 1963. "It mattered, and he brought to that war the conquering weapon of words fashioned for their purpose—to wound, never to kill; to influence, never to destroy."

Among the darkest Churchillian verdicts was that something said or done was "malicious"—to be carelessly cruel was a terrible sin. "He never sought to trample on a fallen foe, whether a political opponent or a defeated nation," said Violet Bonham Carter. "His enmity could not survive once victory was won. He never hated nations or men as such. He only hated their ideas. He would knock a man down in order to pick him up again in a better frame of mind." He put much store in moving on. "Anger is a waste of energy," Churchill said. "Steam which is used to blow off a safety valve would be better used to drive the engine." He used different metaphors to make the same point. "Opinions differ. That is why we have check waist coats." After becoming prime minister in 1940, he turned back calls for recriminations about Britain's failure to stop Hitler sooner, saying: "Of this I am certain, that if we open a quarrel between the past and the present, we shall find that we have lost the future." This view sustained him in his demanding friendship with Roosevelt, enabling Churchill to overlook large and small slights.

CHURCHILL AND ROOSEVELT enjoyed eclectic company. Albert Einstein, Lawrence of Arabia, and Charles Chaplin were guests at Chartwell in the 1930s, and Churchill always liked to hear experts on different topics—though such appointments did not always work out as the prime minister planned. During the war, Isaiah Berlin wrote weekly political reports from his post at the British embassy in Washington, and Churchill, learning Mr. Berlin was in London in early 1944, asked him to lunch. "When do you think the war will end, Mr. Berlin?" Churchill asked him earnestly, among other political questions. As it turned out, the visitor was Irving Berlin, the songwriter and author of tunes like

"God Bless America," who had been invited by mistake. At the White House for Sunday supper during the war, John Wheeler-Bennett, the future biographer of George VI, found himself at a table with the Roosevelts, General George C. Marshall, Undersecretary of State Sumner Welles, Felix Frankfurter, Errol Flynn, and an elderly Episcopal bishop.

CHURCHILL WAS ACCOMPLISHED at many things, painting impressive pictures and producing more than forty books. Roosevelt's interests were varied—the sea, stamps, trees, Christmas cards, Currier & Ives prints. After he was sick but before he reentered politics, Roosevelt tried to make money with stamp-vending machines and by flying lobsters from Maine to restaurants in New York City. ("Not very successful," was Eleanor's memory.) He played at architecture (he tried to design a "hurricane-proof" house) and toyed with becoming an author but never did. "He was a man of many thoughts," observed James MacGregor Burns, one of Roosevelt's finest biographers, "not a man of trenchant ideas." Walter Lippmann knew both Roosevelt and Churchill. "Roosevelt close to was always disappointing," Lippmann said. "Churchill was just as good when you got close to him as when you saw him at a distance."

Roosevelt liked having the last word, even referring to himself as "Judge Roosevelt" on occasion. In 1930, Felix Frankfurter, an admirer of Churchill's, was disturbed to read a tough review of Churchill's multivolume history of World War I, *The World Crisis.* The criticism of Churchill's florid style came from the writer H. M. Tomlinson, and Frankfurter discussed Tomlinson's views of Churchill with Roosevelt, who was then governor. "Is wisdom there?" Tomlinson asked of Churchill's books. "It looks to me as though there were a lack of control, which is not wise. Is light there? Yes, of a kind—the kind which comes in chromatic beams from the wings to give an object on the stage an appearance it does not own. It is, for me, eloquence in an Eton collar on Speech Day. . . . If we think we ought to be eloquent because the subject deserves it, and try to be, then we are not." According to Max Freedman, editor of the Frankfurter-Roosevelt correspondence, Frankfurter and Roosevelt weighed the evidence and "gave Churchill something better than a suspended sentence as a writer."

CHURCHILL HAD THE sharper wit. Sir David Pitblado, a Churchill private secretary, told William Manchester the following story. The Labourite Clement Attlee was at the urinal in the men's room of the House of Commons. Churchill came in and, seeing Attlee, moved away. "Feeling standoffish today, are we, Winston?" Churchill replied: "That's right. Every time you see something big, you want to nationalize it." Roosevelt was more heavy-handed and had to rely on the fact that people laugh even at a president's lamest witticisms. John Gunther picked out such a moment in this press conference exchange. "Mr. President," a reporter asked, "does the ban on the highways [as part of the national defense program] include the parking shoulders?"

"Parking shoulders?" Roosevelt said.

"Yes, widening out on the edge, supposedly to let the civilians park as the military goes by."

"You don't mean necking places?"

Roosevelt and Churchill did not fool each other. Like most friends, they sensed each other's weaknesses. Musing about Churchill's flow of "brilliant ideas," Roosevelt once light-heartedly remarked: "He has a hundred a day, and about four of them are good." Roosevelt's interest in polling data worried Churchill, who thought Roosevelt tended to "follow public opinion rather than to form it and lead it."

Churchill could exhaust Roosevelt. "My father never wanted to switch off," said Mary Soames, but Roosevelt did. "Great fellow, that Churchill, if you can keep up with him," Roosevelt said. During Churchill's wartime visits to the Roosevelt White House, Eleanor recalled, "The prime minister took a long nap every afternoon, so was refreshed for hard work in the evening and far into the night. While he was sleeping, Franklin had to catch up on all of his regular work. . . . It always took him several days to catch up on sleep after Mr. Churchill left." Roosevelt called Churchill's curious rhythms "the Winston hours."

When Roosevelt did get to bed, he slept well. At the pinnacle of their power and responsibilities during the war, both men did. They knew there would be another fight another day— probably the very next day—and that energy spent fretting about what could not be undone was wasted. "I went to bed, browsed about in the files for a while, and then slept for four or five hours," Churchill said of a bleak period of military defeats in 1942. "What a blessing is the gift of sleep!"

AT THE DINNER TABLE, Mary said, Churchill "made an effort and he would suddenly not make an effort." Roosevelt could talk too much himself, but he was better at the art of listening than Churchill was.

Lady Ottoline Morrell, a figure in London's literary and intellectual circles, encountered

Churchill one weekend in 1911: "Winston was on his way to a Court Ball and was in full dress uniform, looking like a mock Napoleon," she wrote. "He talked high politics, which sounded to me almost like high Mathematics, for he is very rhetorical, and has a volcanic, complicated way of talking which is difficult to listen to."

Very few people were neutral about him. When Theodore Roosevelt met Churchill on Churchill's 1900 American tour, TR found the young man a bit much. "I saw the Englishman, Winston Churchill here, and although he is not an attractive fellow, I was interested in some of the things he said." Nearly ten years later, TR read Churchill's biography of Lord Randolph. "I have been over Winston Churchill's life of his father," Roosevelt wrote Henry Cabot Lodge. "I dislike the father and dislike the son, so I may be prejudiced. Still, I feel that, while the biographer and his subject possess some real farsightedness . . . they both possess or possest such levity, lack of sobriety, lack of permanent principle, and an inordinate thirst for that cheap form of admiration which is given to notoriety, as to make them poor public servants." By 1910, on a trip to London, TR could not bring himself to see Churchill, then the home secretary: "I have refused to meet Winston Churchill."

Imperial, bold, prolific—Churchill and Theodore Roosevelt had much in common. Arthur

Schlesinger Jr. once asked Alice Roosevelt Longworth why Churchill had so irritated her father. "Perhaps because they were so much alike," she said. There is another element in this mix, too: American skepticism about the British. Despite the afterglow of the Anglo-American victory in World War II, the two cultures had long been wary of each other. The British tended to think of Americans as upstarts obsessed with making money and susceptible to retreating from the world when it suited them; Americans, swaggering but insecure, disliked colonialism and feared the more sophisticated mother country might take advantage of them. "I'm willing to help them all I can but I don't want them to play me for a sucker," Roosevelt once told Joseph Kennedy. On an early lecture tour to talk about his adventures in the Boer War, Churchill "found it easy to make friends with American audiences. They were cool and critical, but also urbane and good-natured"— helpful training for a man who would have to charm Franklin Roosevelt.

ROOSEVELT WAS NOT perfect. He could make contradictory promises. At other times he would go on at length while visitors tried helplessly to make their own points. Walter Lippmann understood the game. "Roosevelt was a wonderful finagler," Lippmann said. "He loved to take a complicated thing which involved a certain amount of deception—hornswoggling of people—and somehow get it done." Churchill would come to know the technique well.

Both men spawned haters and skeptics. Though he carried every state but Maine and Vermont in 1936, Roosevelt had to confront a vicious bloc of opponents throughout his time in the White House, from the rich who considered him the master of confiscatory taxes to conservatives who saw trouble in the expansion of federal powers to isolationists who thought he was secretly maneuvering the country into war. Known to his enemies as "That Man in the White House," Roosevelt was a much more divisive figure politically in real time than he is in memory, and he was aware that parts of the public were deeply opposed to anything bearing the Roosevelt touch. On a personal level, he could make people love him unreservedly— or he could provoke the coldest of reactions.

Churchill had many political foes. By moving to the Liberals, he had gone against the grain of the most commonly held politics of his class— which was not unlike Roosevelt's own situation. In 1924, Churchill had returned to the Tory fold after twenty years as a Liberal. After the Russian Revolution, he supported a military campaign against the Bolsheviks—an operation Joseph

Stalin would long remember. "I was a child of the Victorian era," Churchill wrote in 1930, "when the structure of our country seemed firmly set, when its position in trade and on the seas was unrivalled, and when the realisation of the greatness of our Empire and of our duty to preserve it was ever growing stronger." In the 1930s, Churchill was seen as an extremist—an unreconstructed imperialist on India, a hard-liner at home, a provocateur on Germany.

He would long pay a political price for his apparently tragic combination of arrogance and instability. "He has a very gloomy future," the press magnate Lord Northcliffe said of him in the years before World War II. "I take a dim view of the things Winston will do in politics." Churchill sometimes thought the same thing and would become depressed.

CHURCHILL REFERRED TO his bluer episodes with an expression that Colville told the distinguished Churchill biographer Martin Gilbert he remembered his own nanny using: "to have a black dog on one's back." Perhaps, Colville speculated, Mrs. Everest used a similar phrase. However down he could feel, Churchill always overcame his darker feelings. "He experienced a sensation of annoyance and depression," Churchill wrote of his hero in his novel, *Savrola,* a story of a young soldier-politician in the imaginary state of Laurania. "Life seemed unsatisfactory; something was lacking." What clarified the mind and lifted the gloom, Churchill wrote, was the thought of death: "When the notes of life ring false, men should correct them by referring to the tuning fork of death. It is when that clear menacing tone is heard that the love of life grows keenest in the human heart."

These thoughts are put in Savrola's head, but they were true of Churchill as well. Life was too much fun to be tossed away. Churchill believed he was meant to survive. In 1931, he was nearly killed when a car struck him in Manhattan. Back in England, sitting with his researcher Maurice Ashley in the garden at Chartwell, talking about history, Churchill "started to look pale and distraught." A doctor arrived and found that he was suffering from internal bleeding, a result of the mishap in New York. As Churchill was put on a stretcher and taken away, he said: "Don't worry, Ashley, I'm not going to die."

THOUGH RESPECTABLE OPINION in Britain and elsewhere held that Hitler was a man to do business with, Churchill watched Germany with growing concern through the 1930s. Why did he sense what so many others did not? Perhaps because he intuitively understood how powerful the thirst for vengeance could be. To Churchill, a soldier and historian, battle was the natural order of things. "The story of the human race," he said, "is War." Churchill also kept himself from falling prey to the trend toward unnuanced pacifism in the twenties and thirties. In 1929, sixty-two countries, including the United States, signed the Kellogg-Briand Pact, an instrument renouncing war as a means of international power. Over three different years—1935, 1936, and 1937—the United States passed Neutrality Acts that prevented America from engaging in conflicts overseas and from selling arms to belligerents. Those in the West who urged taking up arms against expansionist dictatorships like Germany (Hitler spoke of increasing Germany's "living space" and announced a rearmament program in 1935) or Italy (Benito Mussolini invaded Ethiopia the same year) or Japan (which had invaded China in 1931) were seen as dangerous warmongers. The climate in the United States and Britain between Versailles and the German invasion of Poland was passionately antiwar. "Mr. Chamberlain can't seem to understand that we live in a very wicked world," Churchill said as Prime Minister Neville Chamberlain's government tried time and again to find a way to manage Germany without resorting to arms. "English people want to be left alone, and I daresay a great many other people want to be left alone too. But the world is like a tired old horse plodding down a long road. Every time it strays off and tries to graze peacefully in some nice green pasture, along comes a new master to flog it a bit further along."

Churchill believed Germany would attempt to avenge November 1918. In a 1935 essay entitled "Hitler and His Choice," Churchill had held out the hope that the führer would bring Germany back "serene, helpful and strong, to the forefront of the European family circle." But the warrior-patriot in Churchill suspected what was really afoot. Hitler would arm and defy the rest of the world to stop him. "If . . . we look only at the past, which is all we have to judge by, we must indeed feel anxious," Churchill wrote. "Hitherto, Hitler's triumphant career has been borne onwards, not only by a passionate love of Germany, but by currents of hatred so intense as to sear the souls of those who swim upon them." And that was just in Europe. Eager to establish a Greater East Asia Co-Prosperity Sphere by capturing islands and parts of China rich with resources, Japan also posed a developing threat.

AS CHURCHILL walked in the political wilderness, he kept an eye on America, which he

believed to be an essential ally. At a Chartwell
dinner in 1933, one of the new American president's sons, James Roosevelt, was at the table
when Churchill initiated a guessing game. What,
the host asked, was your fondest wish? "His
guests fumbled and qualified their answers," said
Kay Halle, a young American heiress with whom
Randolph Churchill had fallen in love and once
rashly tried to marry. When his turn came,
Churchill replied: "I wish to be Prime Minister
and in close and daily communication by telephone with the President of the United States.
There is nothing we could not do if we were
together."

Churchill wrote an article about Roosevelt in
1934 and included the essay in his 1937 book
Great Contemporaries. He sensed Roosevelt's
courage and saluted it. "His lower limbs refused
their office," Churchill noted. "Crutches or
assistance were needed for the smallest movement from place to place. To ninety-nine men
out of a hundred such an affliction would have
terminated all forms of public activity except
those of the mind. He refused to accept this
sentence." Will Roosevelt, Churchill asked,
"succeed or will he fail? This is not the question
we set ourselves, and to prophesy is cheap. But
succeed or fail, his impulse is one which makes
towards the fuller life of the masses of the people in every land, and which as it glows the

brighter may well eclipse both the lurid flames of German Nordic national self-assertion and the baleful unnatural lights which are diffused from Soviet Russia."

Roosevelt's sympathies were clear. Beginning in 1938, royalty from throughout Europe came to America for visits. Amid hot dogs and martinis at Hyde Park with King George VI and Queen Elizabeth in June 1939, the Roosevelts enjoyed themselves, but Eleanor understood what was in her husband's mind during the series of lunches, dinners, and motorcades. "Convinced that bad things were going to happen in Europe, he wanted to make contacts with those he hoped would preserve and adhere to democracy and prove to be allies against fascism when the conflict came," Eleanor recalled. Yet Roosevelt faced a public that, by and large, could not see what good came of forays into the affairs of seemingly faraway places. As the train left Hyde Park to begin the king and queen's journey home, the crowd sang "Auld Lang Syne." It was a bittersweet moment. "One thought of the clouds that hung over them and the worries they were going to face," Eleanor wrote, "and turned away and left the scene with a heavy heart."

"We are fighting for our lives"

Led by an unflinching Churchill,
London prepares for a German invasion,
circa 1940

THOSE BLOODY YANKEES

*Roosevelt's Letter of September 11 –
Churchill's Anguished Pleas for Help – An Elusive
America – Britain Alone*

ROOSEVELT AND CHURCHILL both got
away for a part of August 1939—but only a
part. After a tough summer fighting with Congress over repealing elements of the Neutrality
Acts that kept him from selling arms to foreign
powers if war broke out (a skirmish he lost),
Roosevelt was looking forward to escaping
Washington. A gossipy *Newsweek* item suggested Roosevelt was "more sour and irritable"
than he had been in years. A fishing cruise
aboard the *Tuscaloosa* was on the docket, a
prospect that cheered Roosevelt, who liked the
relaxing rhythms of life at sea.

After an equally tough summer pressing the
House of Commons to prepare for war (a skirmish he also lost), Churchill decamped to France

to inspect the Maginot Line. In a broadcast over NBC to the United States on August 8, he said war was in Hitler's hands: At Eagle's Nest, the führer's mountain redoubt, "there sits one man who in a single day can release the world from the fear that now oppresses it, or in a single day can plunge all that we have and are into a volcano of smoke and flame."

Roosevelt took off for his fishing trip, heading for the waters off Campobello and then north toward Newfoundland. Trolling for salmon by day and watching movies by night, he tried to unwind. Foggy weather made it difficult for planes to drop off mail from the White House, but the crisis overseas was becoming clear anyway: Hitler's ambitions were not yet fulfilled. After the Rhineland, after the Anschluss, after Kristallnacht, after Czechoslovakia, Poland was in the crosshairs.

Churchill and Clementine spent a holiday near Dreux after his inspection tour. Mary, then seventeen, was with them. "Conscious that the sands of peace were fast running out," Mary wrote, "one's appreciation of those halcyon summer days was heightened: there was swimming and tennis (so greatly enjoyed by Clementine) and *fraises des bois;* Winston painted a lovely picture of the exquisite old rose-brick house."

Churchill put his paints away and arrived in England on August 23, the same day Roosevelt, who had cut short his fishing, headed back to Washington. The news roiling both their capitals: Hitler and Stalin had reached a nonaggression pact, which freed Germany to strike to the east without worrying about a Soviet reaction. From London Churchill called for Clementine, who had remained in France, to come home. She crossed the Channel, he remembered long afterward, through Dunkirk.

On Friday, September 1, Hitler invaded Poland. Democracy itself was in danger around the world; economies were in collapse; communism and totalitarianism seemed to have much to recommend them. There was even talk of revolution in America. John Maynard Keynes was asked if there had ever been anything like the Great Depression before. "Yes," he said, "it was called the Dark Ages, and it lasted four hundred years."

ROOSEVELT AND CHURCHILL had not crossed paths since that night in 1918. As a critic of successive prime ministers who he believed were failing to see Hitler as a genuine threat, Churchill was in Parliament but wielded little power. As president of the United States, Roosevelt was now one of the great figures in the world. Churchill sporadically tried to reach out to Roosevelt, sending him a signed copy of the first volume of his *Marlborough: His Life and Times* in October 1933. His inscription wished Roosevelt luck with his presidency, then dominated by the New Deal; Churchill called it "the greatest crusade of modern times." (Churchill liked to send his new books to friends and to those he hoped would be interested in his work. Many appreciated his thoughtfulness; a few evidently did not. After receiving the last of Churchill's *Marlborough* volumes, the duke of Windsor wrote him: "Thank you so much for sending me a copy of your latest book. I have put it on the shelf with all the others.")

With his restless mind, voluble tongue, and productive pen, Churchill had expressed different views about Roosevelt at different times in the 1930s. Like the Bible, Churchill's written and spoken record can often be cited to support opposing positions—an understandable result of a long and intellectually rich life lived in the arena. He wrote that respectful piece about Roosevelt in 1934, and, answering questions at a meeting of the Oxford University Conservative Association the same year, Churchill said: "The President is a bold fellow. I like his spirit." Churchill, however, was not averse to taking a shot or two at Roosevelt. In December 1937, Churchill wrote: "The quarrel in which President Roosevelt has become involved with Wealth and Business may produce results profoundly harmful to ideals which to him and his people are dear"—conservative talk Roosevelt would have considered hopelessly Tory compared to his own more progressive views.

The word reaching Roosevelt about Churchill on the eve of war in Europe was not reassuring. In the summer of 1939, Joseph Kennedy told Roosevelt that Neville Chamberlain believed Churchill "has developed into a fine two-handed drinker and his judgment has never been proven to be good."

Churchill, of course, had always been a controversial figure. Agnes Meyer, the wife of Eugene Meyer, who bought *The Washington Post* in 1933, spent time with Clementine in February 1932 when Churchill was in the United States for a lecture tour. "Just took Mrs. Churchill to the Freer Gallery but made no effort to see her husband when Eugene gave him a party last night after his lecture because I feel a complete lack of sympathy for him," Mrs. Meyer told her diary. "His thought is very superficial." When Churchill died, Evelyn Waugh, who had been a friend of his son Randolph's, said: "He is not a man for whom I ever had esteem. Always in the wrong . . . simply a 'Radio Personality' who outlived his prime. 'Rallied the nation' indeed! I was a serving soldier in 1940. How we despised his orations."

For those who think the Churchill of legend is

not the Churchill of fact—that admiring biographers have covered up his faults and swooned over the story of Churchill-as-hero—it is worth noting that those who lived at the same time he did knew his defects. But they also recognized his strengths. The week Hitler moved into Poland, people in Washington were reading the new issue of Henry Luce's *Time* magazine, a good measuring stick of establishment opinion in the United States. Churchill was on the cover. In the White House and elsewhere, readers trying to make sense of the crisis in Europe flipped open the magazine. In a story entitled "Vision, Vindication," *Time* wrote: "As M.P. for Epping he had no more power than an honorable member for Deptford, Huddersfield, Moss Side, Smethwick . . . or the 615 constituencies of England, Scotland and Wales. But as Winston Churchill the Elder Statesman, scarred veteran of innumerable parliamentary battles, historian of the World War, novelist, biographer of his ancestors, and the most pungent and expressive critic of Prime Minister Chamberlain, he had an influence, a possible future and a voice in affairs that made his position unique." Churchill had been in the House for more than half his life. "Britain's ruling class still considers him brilliant, erratic, unsafe," *Time* noted, but on the eve of his sixty-fifth birthday, he was, however improbably, the coming man.

AT A QUARTER past eleven on Sunday morning, September 3, 1939—London's churches were unusually full—Prime Minister Neville Chamberlain went on the radio to announce that the United Kingdom was at war with Germany. Churchill and Clementine listened to the broadcast at their London apartment. A moment later the first air-raid warning rang out across the capital. "Mr. Churchill stalked to the entrance of the flats and stared up into the sky like a war horse scenting battle," recalled Inspector W. H. Thompson, Churchill's bodyguard. With a bottle of brandy in hand, Churchill went to a nearby basement shelter. There he "prowled around like a caged animal" until the all-clear came, when, Thompson noted, Churchill "was off like a shot, back down the street and straight up to the roof of the flats, where he scanned the sky for aircraft."

Later that day, Chamberlain, who would remain prime minister for almost nine more months, offered him the post of first lord of the Admiralty: Chamberlain could no longer keep the prophetic Churchill out of the cabinet. The appointment alarmed the Germans. Hitler, Albert Speer remembered, reacted with "consternation." Speer, Hitler's architect, described the Third Reich's inner circle absorbing the news. "With this ill-omened press report in his hand," Speer wrote, "Goering stepped out of the door of Hitler's salon. He dropped into the nearest chair and said wearily: 'Churchill in the Cabinet. That means that the war is really on. Now we shall have war with England.'"

By six that evening Churchill was back at the Admiralty. He was home. Despite the burdens and the dangers—actually, because of them—Churchill was invigorated. Surveying his old haunts, he heard ancient drumbeats: "Once again defence of the rights of a weak state, outraged and invaded by unprovoked aggression, forced us to draw the sword. Once again we must fight for life and honour against all the might and fury of the valiant, disciplined, and ruthless German race. Once again! So be it."

ACROSS THE ATLANTIC, many Americans thought it still might not be. More than most—and although he and Churchill were not yet close—Franklin Roosevelt understood what was at hand. Well traveled in Europe, soaked in the vigorous tradition of his cousin Theodore, shaped by the moral vision of Woodrow Wilson, Roosevelt was an attentive commander in chief who, unlike many politicians of his day, sensed that America could not hide from foreign affairs. "It is easy for you and for me to shrug our shoulders and say that conflicts taking place thousands of miles from the continental United States, and, indeed thousands of miles from the whole American hemisphere, do not seriously affect the Americas—and that all the United States has to do is to ignore them and go about its own business," Roosevelt told the country from the White House on Sunday, September 3, 1939. "Passionately though we may desire detachment, we are forced to realize that every word that comes through the air, every ship that sails the sea, every battle that is fought, does affect the American future."

Trude Lash had been born in Germany, and Roosevelt would ask her about her homeland. "When the President found out I was so anti-Hitler, he said, 'So am I, so am I,' and this was long before the war started in September," Mrs. Lash recalled. "I think the President believed very early on that Hitler was a global concern. FDR knew Hitler could not be only defeated; he had to be removed." Roosevelt had a weakness, however, for telling people what they wanted to hear. He was tough with Mrs. Lash in their passing conversation but also played to antiwar sentiment. "Franklin always said that no leader should get too far ahead of his followers," Eleanor noted. Roosevelt had to build his arsenals and to convince his people that the United States had both a practical and a moral stake in defeating the dictatorships. On the basest level of national interest, oceans under German and Japanese control would put America at the mercy of empires whose interests would take precedence. The moral claim of the war hinged on checking the Hitlerite vision of an expanding Reich and its master race, a world in which Germany and other dictatorial powers would subjugate individual rights and civil liberties.

From the autumn of 1939 to Pearl Harbor more than two years later, Britain was Roosevelt's best hope for a bulwark against this dark future. Roosevelt needed a proxy, a firewall against the dictators. He needed, he would come to see, Winston Churchill.

WORKING LONG HOURS, Churchill loved being back at the Admiralty in the first weeks of the war in September. Charles Eade left a snapshot of the first lord in these early days of the conflict. When Eade became editor of the *Sunday Dispatch* in 1938, he discovered that Churchill liked to call the paper on Saturday nights "to ask if there was any news." Now that Churchill had been restored to the cabinet, Eade thought he might republish Churchill's *My Early Life* in serialized form in the paper. A meeting was quickly arranged. "Churchill was wearing a very easy fitting driver jacket & was walking about in his socks, having kicked off his shoes," Eade recalled. Smoking a cigar, Churchill had a whiskey and soda sitting on his desk. "He seemed to me to be a little drunk," Eade said. "I was struck by the pallor of his face, which seemed bloodless and very clean." They did their deal. "He was very affable and friendly; gave me authority to cut his stuff & said he did not want to see proofs, asked me to be careful to see the sense of his articles were not altered," Eade noted. They spoke of a speech Hitler had given that afternoon in which he called Churchill a warmonger. "Churchill said it was the speech of a conqueror & that Hitler would not get away with that," Eade recalled. Then Churchill mentioned his regular journalistic contract with the *News of the World*. Though the deal had been suspended for the duration of the conflict, Churchill thought it would mean money for him once the war was over. "If," Churchill added gloomily, "there is anything left then."

Roosevelt shared Churchill's anxiety and was trying to gauge the significance of his return to the cabinet. The president understood that it was Churchill, not Chamberlain, who was being proven right as the Germans crushed the Poles. On September 11, 1939, Joseph Kennedy, who held the darkest of views about Britain's prospects, wrote Roosevelt suggesting that "there may be a point when the President himself may work out the plan for world peace." Answering for Roosevelt, Secretary of State Cordell Hull replied to Kennedy: "The President desires me to inform you . . . that this Government, so long as present European conditions continue, sees no opportunity or occasion for any peace move to be initiated by the President of the United States. The people of the United States would not support any move for peace initiated by this Government that would consolidate or make possible a survival of a regime of force and of aggression."

This, Roosevelt believed (as did Churchill), was a time for strength, not more weakness. On that same September 11, a clear Monday in Washington, between suspending limitations on sugar marketing and dining with Eleanor, Roosevelt wrote Churchill a letter.

> My dear Churchill:—
>
> It is because you and I occupied similar positions in the World War that I want you to know how glad I am that you are back again in the Admiralty. Your problems are, I realize, complicated by new factors but the essential is not very different. What I want you and the Prime Minister to know is that I shall at all times welcome it if you will

keep me in touch personally with anything you want me to know about. You can always send sealed letters through your pouch or my pouch.

I am glad you did the Marlboro volumes before this thing started—and I much enjoyed reading them.

> With my sincere regards,
> Faithfully yours,
> *Franklin D. Roosevelt*

Churchill recalled that he "responded with alacrity." The sea formed a common theme in their first months of correspondence as the new first lord tried to keep Roosevelt, who thought of himself as a shrewd old sailor, up-to-date on British maritime activity. Their first telephone conversation was about a naval crisis in the Atlantic. It was Thursday, October 5, 1939, the same day Roosevelt's letter reached London. Churchill was having supper in his apartment with the third sea lord, Rear Admiral Bruce Fraser, and the director of naval construction, Sir Stanley Goodall. As the three men were talking, the phone rang. Frank Sawyers, Churchill's valet, answered it and came into the dining room. "Who is it?" asked Churchill, who, Fraser said, "rather disliked telephones."

"I don't know, sir."

"Well, say I can't attend to it now."

"I think you ought to come, sir."

Churchill went to the phone—"rather testily," Fraser recalled. Churchill's guests were surprised to hear him say, "Yes, sir. . . . No, sir," to the caller. There were, Fraser said, "few people whom he would address as 'sir' and we wondered who on earth that was?" In a moment, Churchill returned.

"Do you know who that was?" Churchill said. "The President of the United States. It is remarkable to think of being rung up in this little flat in Victoria Street by the President himself in the midst of a great war. This is very important and I must go and see the Prime Minister at once."

The substance of the call says a good deal about the confusion of these first days of war. The Germans had sent word to Washington that an American liner then at sea, the *Iroquois,* was to be sunk by the British or the French as it neared the United States—and the British would then blame Germany for the attack to manufacture a provocation to bring America into the war. Listening to Roosevelt on the transatlantic line, Churchill believed that Berlin could blow the ship up (possibly by having planted a time bomb on board), kill the 566 passengers, most of them American, and then say it was all Britain's fault, turning American public opinion against London and toward Germany at a critical moment. The liner was stopped, searched, and sent on safely: The rumors were unfounded.

The little episode of the *Iroquois* is largely lost to history, but the call marked the first time Winston Churchill and Franklin Roosevelt had spoken to each other in more than two decades. Churchill's summons to the telephone fore-shadowed much. Here was Roosevelt, gen-uinely concerned about the battles being fought on the Atlantic and in Europe, but far removed; here was Churchill, on the front lines, deferen-tial and intrigued by the drama of a call in the night from the president.

ON THE LAST day of October, Lord Beaver-brook wrote Roosevelt to tell him Churchill was "just the most attractive Minister who ever fought a war on the lines of bitter and unrelent-ing hatred. . . . The prophets will say that, if Chamberlain falls, Churchill will succeed him, forming a Coalition Government."

Churchill and Roosevelt each had an agenda as they corresponded while Hitler held up pushing west in the winter of 1939–1940—the months of the "phony war." Churchill, who referred to himself as "Naval Person" in his cables, noted: "I think I ought to send something more to my American friend in order to keep him interested in our affairs. . . . We must not let the liaison lapse." Roosevelt also wanted to keep different lines of communication open to a region in crisis. In December 1939, Joseph Kennedy visited Roosevelt in Washington. As Roosevelt had breakfast in bed in the White House, he made his motives for cultivating Churchill clear. "I'm giving him attention now," Roosevelt told Kennedy, "because of his possibilities of being P.M. and wanting to keep my hand in."

Beaverbrook's and Roosevelt's predictions about Churchill's path to power came true on May 10, 1940, as Hitler struck Western Europe. Roosevelt told his cabinet he "supposed Churchill was the best man that England had," Harold Ickes recalled, "even if he was drunk half of his time." It was hardly a warm endorsement.

Still, Churchill had reached the summit. He was sixty-five years old. He had long believed that his fate and his nation's were intertwined; now they were. As Churchill went to bed at about three o'clock in the morning, he was "conscious of a profound sense of relief. At last I had the authority to give directions over the whole scene. I felt as if I were walking with Destiny, and that all my past life had been but a preparation for this hour and for this trial." For a moment, it seems, there was no fear, no uncertainty. "I thought I knew a good deal about it all," Churchill recalled, "and I was sure I should not fail."

ROOSEVELT WAS NOT so sure. Hitler was striking with speed and success across the west. However movingly Churchill talked about offering "blood, toil, tears and sweat"—the evocative phrase in his first speech to the House as prime minister—American officials were worried. In early March 1940, William C. Bullitt, the American ambassador to France, had come in from Paris and given a gloomy report at a Washington dinner at Harold Ickes's house. "Bill has no use for Chamberlain, and almost none for Churchill," Ickes wrote in his diary. "He thinks that the British Government is in a bad way. There are no real leaders, as he sees it, in all of England in this time of grave crisis." Despite the good champagne, the conversation was grim. "Bill is not at all sure that England and France may not be utterly defeated in the present war," Ickes noted. Undersecretary of State Sumner Welles had seen Churchill up close a month before. They had met in London, where Churchill had talked for nearly two hours—"a cascade of oratory, brilliant and always effective, interlarded with considerable wit." Yet Churchill's drinking bothered Welles (an irony, since Welles would fall from power over a scandal in which he drunkenly propositioned a railroad porter). Churchill, Welles said, was having a whiskey and soda, and "it was obvious that he had consumed a good many whiskies before I arrived." Frances Perkins recalled Roosevelt "was so uncertain about" Churchill that he wondered "what kind of a fellow" the new prime minister was. In those bleak days, that was still an open question.

ON WEDNESDAY, MAY 15, 1940, Churchill, calling himself "Former Naval Person," cabled Roosevelt. "Although I have changed my office, I am sure you would not wish me to discontinue our intimate, private correspondence," Churchill wrote. "As you are no doubt aware," he went on,

> the scene has darkened swiftly. The enemy have a marked preponderance in the air, and their new technique is making a deep impression upon the French. . . . The small countries are simply smashed up, one by one, like matchwood. We must expect, though it is not yet certain, that Mussolini will hurry in to share the loot of civilisation. We expect to be attacked here ourselves, both from the air and by parachute and air-borne troops in

the near future, and are getting ready for them. If necessary, we shall continue the war alone, and we are not afraid of that.

Having tried to reassure Roosevelt about British resolve, Churchill raised the stakes:

But I trust you realise, Mr President, that the voice and force of the United States may count for nothing if they are withheld too long. You may have a completely subjugated Nazified Europe established with astonishing swiftness, and the weight may be more than we can bear. All I ask now is that you should proclaim non-belligerency, which would mean that you would help us with everything short of actually engaging armed forces.

Churchill then listed his "immediate needs": forty or fifty "of your older" destroyers, several hundred "of the latest types" of aircraft, along with antiaircraft equipment and ammunition, and steel. Churchill was not finished: Amid "reports of possible German parachute or airborne descents in Ireland," he asked for the "visit of a United States Squadron to Irish Ports" and "to keep that Japanese dog quiet in the Pacific, using Singapore in any way convenient." It was a long wish list from a man fighting for survival and, from Churchill's point of view, an incisive and reasonable one. "We shall go on paying dollars for as long as we can," Churchill wrote, "but I should like to feel reasonably sure that when we can pay no more, you will give us the stuff all the same."

"I have just received your message," Roosevelt cabled back on Friday, May 17, "and I am sure it is unnecessary for me to say that I am most happy to continue our private correspondence as we have in the past." Roosevelt declined, however, to grant Churchill's most urgent requests. Addressing the question of destroyers, Roosevelt reminded Churchill about the American system of government. "As you know a step of that kind could not be taken except with the specific authorization of the Congress and I am not certain that it would be wise for that suggestion to be made to the Congress at this moment," Roosevelt said. There was some encouraging news in the cable: Roosevelt would try to arrange for "anti-aircraft equipment and ammunition" and for "the purchase of steel" while promising to ponder the Irish port question and to keep the fleet in Hawaii "for the time being."

BUT IT WAS not everything Churchill wanted as France was being eviscerated. Replying to

Roosevelt's unsatisfying cable, he wrote on May 18: "I do not need to tell you about the gravity of what has happened. We are determined to persevere to the very end whatever the result of the great battle raging in France may be. We must expect in any case to be attacked here on the Dutch model before very long, and we hope to give a good account of ourselves. But if American assistance is to play any part it must be available soon."

Henry Wallace, Roosevelt's liberal vice president who served from 1941 to 1945, once told John Gunther that "what went on inside FDR's head" was all that mattered. Now the president was turning a dark prospect over in his mind: What would happen if Britain fell? On the evening of May 14, trying to reassure Joseph Kennedy, Churchill said that the nation would not surrender even if the Germans overran the island. "Why, the Government will move to Canada and take the fleet and fight on," Churchill told Kennedy.

In a subsequent talk with Lord Lothian, the British ambassador to the United States, Roosevelt pressed the point: What would Churchill do about the Royal Navy if Hitler conquered England? Would the prime minister really send his ships to America or to Canada, to keep them out of German hands? The question was a sign that for all his sympathies with London—the president and Henry Morgenthau scrounged up rifles, ammunition, and machine guns for Britain in May—Roosevelt had his doubts about Churchill's chances against Hitler.

Roosevelt was in a bind. In a Gallup poll published on October 22, 1939—seven weeks after Hitler struck Poland—95 percent of Americans wanted to stay out of the fight, but 62 percent said yes when asked if they thought "the United States should do everything possible to help England and France win the war except go to war ourselves." To that end, in November the president signed the 1939 Neutrality Act, which established the principle of "cash and carry" for belligerent countries. The law, as the historian David Reynolds put it, "was presented as a peace measure, and there is little doubt that Roosevelt genuinely believed it would not bring America into the European war. But there is also no doubt that he intended it as an unneutral act. Cash and carry was intended to benefit Britain and France—countries with substantial foreign exchange reserves and large merchant fleets." Soon, however, there were fears in the United States that aid to the Allies might come at a steep cost, leaving Washington even more unprepared in the face of a victorious Germany, which had outspent America in terms of combat munitions production six times over from 1935 to 1940.

That, then, was where the president and the prime minister stood in the middle of May 1940. Roosevelt was elusive, trying to balance America's own needs with Britain's, while Churchill was at once determined and desperate. Churchill longed for anything he could get from Roosevelt—guns, ships, whatever. He got so much less than he wanted, however, that when it came time to tell the story of the summer and fall of 1940 in his memoirs, Churchill would write that the "Theme of the Volume" was "How the British people held the fort ALONE till those who hitherto had been half blind were half ready." He was talking about Roosevelt and America. Still, the fort had to be held. While Churchill fought to keep Britain free, he had to resist pressures for a settled peace in the short term and pull Roosevelt into his camp for the long run. And in many ways the immediate future of democracy depended on how deftly Winston Churchill could simultaneously seduce Roosevelt and stonewall Hitler.

AS FRANCE CONTINUED to face overwhelming German attacks on land and from the air on May 18, Churchill's son, Randolph, was on leave from the north of England, where the young man was in military training. Going straight to see his father, Randolph found

Churchill standing nearly naked in front of a shaving mirror in a silk undershirt. "It was the only thing he would wear to sleep in, and it left nothing to the imagination," recalled Winston S. Churchill, the prime minister's grandson.

"Sit down, dear boy, and read the papers while I finish shaving," Churchill told Randolph. Here is Randolph's recollection of the ensuing conversation, dictated when he was working on his father's biography in 1963:

> I did as told. After two or three minutes of hacking away, he half turned and said: "I think I see my way through." He resumed his shaving. I was astounded, and said: "Do you mean that we can avoid defeat?" (which seemed credible) or "beat the bastards?" (which seemed incredible).
>
> He flung his Valet razor in to the basin, swung around, and said:—"Of course I mean we can beat them."
>
> Me: "Well, I'm all for it, but I don't see how you can do it."
>
> By this time he had dried and sponged his face and turning round to me, said with great intensity:—"I shall drag the United States in."

It would not prove easy. Churchill was still a mystery to Roosevelt and his circle. That summer, Sumner Welles told Henry Morgenthau that Churchill was "a drunken sot" and a "third or fourth rate man."

Churchill scheduled a broadcast for Sunday evening, May 19. When he was at his best, noted the writer and member of Parliament A. P. Herbert, Churchill could say "the fine true thing" with a force that "was like an organ filling the church, and we all went out refreshed and resolute to do or die." In his youth, Churchill had been supremely confident about his own rhetorical gifts. "Those Greeks and Romans, they are so overrated," Violet Bonham Carter remembered hearing a younger Churchill remark. "I have said just as good things myself. They owe their reputation to the fact that they got in first with everything." In 1940, there was no cockiness; the stirring passages of defiance in his wartime speeches produce chills decades later, but part of his rhetorical magic was that Churchill was no mindless cheerleader. He told his audiences the story of the war, in detail, and he made it very clear that while he did not doubt victory would come, he also had no doubt it would come only with sacrifice and blood.

He had slipped away to Chartwell earlier that May Sunday to soak up some sun and feed his swan and goldfish. He was, Colville noted, "full of fight and thrives on crisis and adversity." The courage and pluck Colville noticed informed Churchill's broadcast:

> Our task is not only to win the battle, but to win the war. After this battle in France abates its force, there will come the battle for our Islands, for all that Britain is and all that Britain means. In that supreme emergency we shall not hesitate to take every step—even the most drastic—to call forth from our people the last ounce and inch of effort of which they are capable. The interests of property, the hours of labour, are nothing compared to the struggle for life and honour, for right and freedom, to which we have vowed ourselves. . . .
>
> If this is one of the most awe-striking periods in the long history of France and Britain it is also beyond all doubt the most sublime. Side by side, unaided except by their kith and kin in the great Dominions, and by the wide Empires which rest beneath their shield, the British and French peoples have advanced to rescue not Europe only but mankind from the foulest and most soul-destroying tyranny which has ever darkened and stained the pages of history. Behind them gather a group of shattered States and bludgeoned races, the Czechs, the Poles, the Norwegians, the

Danes, the Dutch, the Belgians—upon all of whom the long night of barbarism will descend unbroken by even a star of hope, unless we conquer—as conquer we must—as conquer we shall.

Roosevelt's reaction to the performance—and to most of Churchill's wartime broadcasts—is unrecorded, but Eleanor's impression is telling. Churchill's speeches, she said, "were a tonic to us here in the United States as well as to his own people."

Her husband probably would have agreed with her on that, but not on this: Eleanor found Churchill a more honest politician than Roosevelt. "To explain to one's country that there must be a long period while the military forces are being trained and armed, during which production will be one of the most important factors, and that meanwhile people must be patient and hope at best 'to hold the line' is no easy or popular thing to do," Eleanor recalled. "I always had great admiration for the way in which Mr. Churchill did this. In some ways he was more blunt with the people of Great Britain than my husband ever was with us." She did give Roosevelt one benefit of the doubt: "The British people were closer to the danger and I suppose for that very reason could better understand the blunt approach."

———

CHURCHILL HAD BARELY finished his speech before he returned to the frustrating business of winning over Roosevelt. At Admiralty House, where the Churchills were still in residence, the prime minister worked on a message to the president. In it, Churchill painted his darkest portrait yet of the dangers he faced, mentioning Roosevelt and Lothian's exchange about the future if the Germans carried the day:

> With regard to the closing part of your talk with Lothian, our intention is, whatever happens, to fight on to the end in this Island, and, provided we can get the help for which we ask, we hope to run them very close in the air battles in view of individual superiority. Members of the present administration would likely go down during this process should it result adversely, but in no conceivable circumstances will we consent to surrender. If members of the present Administration were finished and others came in to parley amid the ruins, you must not be blind to the fact that the sole remaining bargaining counter with Germany would be the Fleet, and, if this country was left by the United States to its fate, no one would have the right to blame

those then responsible if they made the best terms they could for the surviving inhabitants. Excuse me, Mr President, putting this nightmare bluntly. Evidently I could not answer for my successors, who in utter despair and helplessness might well have to accommodate themselves to the German will.

Churchill closed on a cheerful note. "However, there is happily no need at present to dwell upon such ideas. Once more thanking you for your goodwill." The real "star of hope" Churchill had alluded to in his broadcast was Roosevelt, and though the star seemed distant, the prime minister thought assertions of confidence more likely to impress the president than expressions of gloom—even if gloom was the emotion that more closely matched the reality of the moment.

Finishing the letter, Churchill lost his temper. "Considering the soothing words he always uses to America, and in particular to the President," Colville wrote, "I was somewhat taken aback when he said to me, 'Here's a telegram for those bloody Yankees. Send it off tonight.'" His annoyance with "those bloody Yankees"—and especially with Roosevelt—is not surprising. Why, Churchill could be forgiven for thinking, can't he see what I am saying?

———

ONE OF THE reasons Roosevelt was choosing not to do more—aside from his uncertainty over whether Churchill was worth banking on—was evident the same day Churchill spoke. Over the CBS Radio network, Charles A. Lindbergh, the celebrated pilot who had become a leading spokesman for isolation, expressed the feelings of millions who did not want to intervene in another European war. "We need not fear a foreign invasion unless American peoples bring it on through their own quarreling and meddling with affairs abroad," Lindbergh told the country. Then he took a shot at the interventionist elite—men like Felix Frankfurter, Secretary of War Henry Stimson, Harold Ickes, and Henry Morgenthau—which was urging Roosevelt to engage. "The only reason that we are in danger of becoming involved in this war is because there are powerful elements in America who desire us to take part. They represent a small minority of the American people, but they control much of the machinery of influence and propaganda. They seize every opportunity to push us closer to the edge."

Despite its narrow-mindedness—the populist appeal to fear "powerful elements" who "control much of the machinery of influence"—Lindbergh's speech did not sound as far-out then as it does now. Roosevelt had been cruising on the Potomac River on the Sunday Churchill and Lindbergh spoke and was handed a copy of Lindbergh's remarks when he arrived back at the White House. Yet, *The New York Times* noted, "no comment was forthcoming from any White House source." Happy isolationists, however, were delighted to weigh in. "Colonel Lindbergh has given a message to the American people such as a patriotic American President should give," Massachusetts Congressman George Holden Tinkham told the *Times*. "No political intervention into the affairs of Europe or Asia." In many parts of America, isolation was what we would later call the conventional wisdom.

Elite public opinion ran the other way, led by the Kansas newspaper editor William Allen White's Committee to Defend America by Aiding the Allies and by the Century Group—named for members who often met at the Century Association on West 43rd Street in Manhattan. Publishing "A Summons to Speak Out" three weeks after Lindbergh's address, the Century Group declared: "The United States should immediately give official recognition to the fact and to the logic of the situation—by declaring that a state of war exists between this country and Germany. Only in this constitutional manner can the energies be massed which are indispensable to the successful prosecution of a program of defense." Strong words, but they came in the same weeks as a poll that, the historians William L. Langer and S. Everett Gleason wrote, "indicated that only 7.7 percent of the population was in favor of entering the war at once and only 19 percent believed that the country should intervene if the defeat of the Allies appeared certain, as against 40 percent that opposed American participation under any circumstances." Such numbers were among the reasons Roosevelt moved with care. "Although President is our best friend," Churchill told Canadian Prime Minister Mackenzie King in these weeks, "no practical help has been forthcoming from the United States as yet." Churchill was not wrong to put his hopes on the president, but given the scope of the task Britain faced—to defeat, or at least not lose to, a dominant Hitler—it is understandable that the prime minister would also feel his American counterpart did not quite appreciate the pressures London faced.

AS MAY WOUND DOWN, a substantial Allied force—about four hundred thousand men with all their equipment and munitions—were retreating to Dunkirk. To have lost the soldiers there, trapped between the Third Reich and the

Channel, would have cut the heart out of the Allies at the moment of Hitler's greatest strength. The House of Commons, Churchill said in the last week of May, "should prepare itself for hard and heavy tidings. I have only to add that nothing which may happen in this battle can in any way relieve us of our duty to defend the world cause to which we have vowed ourselves; nor should it destroy our confidence in our power to make our way, as on former occasions in our history, through disaster and through grief to the ultimate defeat of our enemies."

In Washington Roosevelt was grave. "Tonight there was no levity," the presidential speechwriter Sam Rosenman said of an evening gathering that week. "There was no small talk. The President was reading dispatches which were being brought in to him from time to time by a White House usher. He mixed cocktails rather mechanically, as though his mind were thousands of miles away—as, of course, it was." The reports were of the retreat to Dunkirk and the plight of France. "It was a dejected dinner group," Rosenman recalled.

On May 27 came a disturbing cable from Joseph Kennedy. "Only a miracle can save the BEF from being wiped out or, as I said yesterday, surrender," Kennedy told Roosevelt. "I suspect that the Germans would be willing to make peace with both the French and the

British now—of course on their own terms but on terms that would be a great deal better than they would be if the war continues. . . . I realize that this is a terrific telegram, but there is no question that it's in the air here. The result of that will be a row amongst certain elements in the Cabinet here; Churchill, Attlee, and others will want to fight to the death but there will be other members who realize that physical destruction of men and property in England will not be a proper offset to a loss of pride." Kennedy was a defeatist, but he was not far off the mark in his assessment of what was happening at the highest tiers of government in London. Roosevelt had been told that Churchill might not be up to the job. Perhaps the critics were right. Perhaps, once again, the British would cave in to Hitler.

In a meeting of the war cabinet in London the next day, May 28, Lord Halifax, then the foreign secretary, suggested that the time might have come to use Italy to discover what German peace terms might be. (The day before, Colville had told his diary that "there are signs that Halifax is being defeatist.") Churchill resisted; talks might be a "slippery slope," he said, to German domination. Halifax said that he did not see why the prime minister thought "trying out the possibilities of mediation . . . was so wrong."

This was a crucial moment for Churchill's leadership. He was not yet the man of myth he would become. Churchill, the solemn diplomat Alexander Cadogan said in these days, was "too rambling and romantic and sentimental and temperamental." Could he stave off a move toward a settlement?

As they debated whether to negotiate, Neville Chamberlain, who was now lord president, became an important convert to Churchill's view, weighing in against further appeasement, expressing his position with convoluted understatement. According to the minutes of the meeting, "The Lord President said that, on a dispassionate survey, it was right to remember that the alternative to fighting on nevertheless involved a considerable gamble." As usual, Churchill was more declarative, saying that "nations which went down fighting rose again, but those which surrendered tamely were finished." Halifax came back at Churchill. "The Foreign Secretary said that nothing in his suggestion could even remotely be described as ultimate capitulation," according to the minutes. Churchill stood strong, replying that "the chances of decent terms being offered to us at the present time were a thousand to one against." But the door was still open. The decision to cut off movement toward a settlement was not final.

———

AT THIS POINT the war ministers left the
room, and the full cabinet came in to meet with
the prime minister. Hugh Dalton, the minister
of economic warfare, recalled the scene with
Churchill: "He was determined to prepare public opinion for bad tidings, and it would of
course be said, and with some truth, that what
was now happening in Northern France would
be the greatest British military defeat for many
centuries. We must now be prepared for the
sudden turning of the war against this island,
and prepared also for other events of great gravity in Europe. No countenance should be given
publicly to the view that France might soon
collapse, but we must not allow ourselves to be
taken by surprise by any events. It might indeed
be said that it would be easier to defend this
island alone than to defend this island plus
France, and if it was seen throughout the world
that it was the former, there would be an
immense wave of feeling, not least in the USA
which, having done nothing much to help us so
far, might even enter the war."

Then Churchill turned to the crucial question
left hanging in the war cabinet. "It was idle to
think that, if we tried to make peace now, we
should get better terms from Germany than if
we went on and fought it out. The Germans

would demand our fleet—that would be called 'disarmament'—our naval bases, and much else. We should become a slave state, though a British Government which would be Hitler's puppet would be set up. . . . And where should we be at the end of all that? On the other side, we had immense reserves and advantages. Therefore, he said, 'We shall go on and we shall fight it out, here or elsewhere, and if at last the long story is to end, it were better it should end, not through surrender, but only when we are rolling senseless on the ground.' " He had them: "There was a murmur of approval round the table. . . . No one expressed even the faintest flicker of dissent."

Buoyed by the session, Churchill returned to the war cabinet that evening and told the ministers what had happened. "They had not expressed alarm at the position in France," the minutes reported, "but had expressed the greatest satisfaction when he had told them that there was no chance of our giving up the struggle."

The significance of the moment Dalton described is that Churchill found others shared his vision, once it was voiced, of holding fast no matter what the cost. In the closed circle of the war cabinet, pounded by terrible report after terrible report, there had been uncertainty about whether he could fend off the drift to exploring a deal with Hitler. The determination of the larger group trumped the tentativeness of the smaller, and Churchill fulfilled his role as leader by disentangling himself from defeatism—one of his singular achievements at the end of May 1940.

FROM DUNKIRK, England rescued nearly 340,000 British and French soldiers, but in truth it was only the briefest of respites from the continuing German air and land victories in France. In a speech to the House on June 4, 1940, Churchill said:

> Even though large tracts of Europe and many old and famous States have fallen or may fall into the grip of the Gestapo and all the odious apparatus of Nazi rule, we shall not flag or fail. We shall go on to the end. We shall fight in France, we shall fight on the seas and oceans, we shall fight with growing confidence and growing strength in the air, we shall defend our island, whatever the cost may be. We shall fight on the beaches, we shall fight on the landing grounds, we shall fight in the fields and in the streets, we shall fight in the hills; we shall never surrender, and even if, which I do not for a moment believe, this island or a large part of it were subjugated and starv-

"I have no one but you to break the loneliness of bustling & bustled existence"

The Churchills on the Thames during the Blitz, September 25, 1940

ing, then our Empire beyond the seas, armed and guarded by the British fleet, would carry on the struggle, until, in God's good time, the new world, with all its power and might, steps forth to the rescue and the liberation of the old.

In God's good time. Though Churchill's words on this occasion are among the most enduring in the history of oratory, the passage is in fact more a prayer than a proclamation, for it climaxes on a promise he lacks the power to fulfill on his own. In London difficult days turned into weeks, which then turned into months. Yet Churchill made progress with this address, reassuring those around Roosevelt—including Roosevelt himself. "We understood the kind of courage and tenacity that Winston Churchill was beginning to put into words," Eleanor recalled, "words that expressed the spirit of the British people in the months following Dunkirk."

LESS THAN A week later, on June 10, Italy entered the war on the German side. Though allied with Hitler since 1938 in a "Pact of Steel," Benito Mussolini had hung back during the Blitzkrieg; now Mussolini fulfilled a promise he had made to Hitler aboard a train at the

Brenner Pass in March 1940 and declared war on France and England. Roosevelt was scheduled to travel to Charlottesville to deliver the commencement address at the University of Virginia Law School, where his son Franklin Jr. was getting a degree. Eleanor thought the event strange, an example of the intermingling of the personal and the political for powerful families. "It was a curious trip: we were all there; a trip to one's son's commencement is normal; but that was not a normal and happy occasion," Eleanor recalled. "The times were fraught with promise of evil. Franklin's address was not just a commencement address; it was a speech to the nation on an event that had brought us one step nearer to total war."

A raucous crowd cheered Roosevelt as he talked tough about Europe. The day was rainy, and the president, wearing a crimson academic hood, spoke to the university in the gymnasium. "On this 10th day of June, 1940, the hand that held the dagger has struck it into the back of its neighbor," Roosevelt said, starkly portraying Italy as an aggressor in the same class as Germany. "On this 10th day of June, 1940, in this university founded by the first great American teacher of democracy, we send forth our prayers and our hopes to those beyond the seas who are maintaining with magnificent valor their battle for freedom." There were rebel yells; the crowd was with him. "In our American unity, we will pursue two obvious and simultaneous courses: we will extend to the opponents of force the material resources of this nation; and, at the same time, we will harness and speed up the use of those resources in order that we ourselves in the Americas may have equipment and training equal to the task of any emergency and every defense," Roosevelt said. "Signs and signals call for speed—full speed ahead." Listening on the radio, Churchill could hardly control himself.

Could his prayers have been answered? Cabling Roosevelt, Churchill assumed that his wooing had worked. "We all listened to you last night and were fortified by the grand scope of your declaration. Your statement that the material aid of the United States will be given to the Allies in their struggle is a strong encouragement in a dark but not unhopeful hour. Everything must be done to keep France in the fight and to prevent any idea of the fall of Paris, should it occur, becoming the occasion of any kind of parley. The hope with which you inspire them may give them the strength to persevere. . . . I send you my heartfelt thanks and those of my colleagues for all you are doing and seeking to do for what we may now, indeed, call the Common Cause."

The next day, before Roosevelt could reply to

this optimistic cable, Churchill, who had just returned from French General Headquarters, told him France was teetering. "Of course I made it clear to the French that we should continue whatever happened, and that we thought Hitler could not win the war or the mastery of the world until he has disposed of us, which has not been found easy in the past, and which perhaps will not be found easy now," Churchill wrote Roosevelt. "I made it clear to the French that we had good hopes of victory, and anyhow had no doubts whatever of what our duty was. If there is anything you can say publicly or privately to the French, now is the time."

EMBOLDENED BY HIS day at Charlottesville, Roosevelt may have read too much into the enthusiasm of his commencement audience, for the president was swept up in the spirit of Churchill's telegram and took his advice. In a message for Prime Minister Paul Reynaud, Roosevelt told the French, "As I have already stated to you and to Mr. Churchill, this Government is doing everything in its power to make available to the Allied Governments the material they so urgently require, and our efforts to do still more are being redoubled. This is so because of our faith in and our support for the ideals for which the Allies are fighting."

Flying back and forth across the Channel in a hurried series of meetings with the French, Churchill begged Roosevelt to publicize the text of his telegram to Reynaud. "Mr President," Churchill wrote in a long and carefully crafted cable, "I must tell you that it seems to me absolutely vital that this message should be published tomorrow 14th June in order that it may play the decisive part in turning the course of world history."

Roosevelt refused. Churchill was crushed. Roosevelt had slipped from his grasp. The president did seem pained about staying out of the fray as France prepared to fall, telling Churchill defensively: "I appreciate fully the significance and *weight* of the considerations set forth in your message."

In France, defeat was at hand. Writing to Roosevelt on the evening of June 15, Churchill went as far as he dared and called Roosevelt's strategy into question—respectfully, of course.

> I understand all your difficulties with American public opinion and Congress, but events are moving downward at a pace where they will pass beyond the control of American public opinion when at last it is ripened. Have you considered what offers Hitler may choose to make to France? He may say, "surrender the Fleet intact and I

will leave you Alsace-Lorraine," or alternatively, "if you do not give me your ships I will destroy your towns." I am personally convinced that America will in the end go to all lengths, but this moment is supremely critical for France. A declaration that the United States will if necessary enter the war might save France. Failing that, in a few days French resistance may have crumbled and we shall be left alone.

Although the present Government and I personally would never fail to send the Fleet across the Atlantic if resistance was beaten down here, a point may be reached in the struggle where the present ministers no longer have control of affairs and when very easy terms could be obtained for the British Islands by their becoming a vassal state of the Hitler empire. A pro-German Government would certainly be called into being to make peace and might present to a shattered or a starving nation an almost irresistible case for entire submission to the Nazi will. The fate of the British Fleet, as I have already mentioned to you, would be decisive on the future of the United States, because if it were joined to the Fleets of Japan, France and Italy and the great resources of German industry, overwhelming sea-power would be in Hitler's hands. He might, of course, use it with a merciful moderation. On the other hand, he might not. This revolution in sea-power might happen very quickly and certainly long before the United States would be able to prepare against it. If we go down you may have a United States of Europe under the Nazi command far more numerous, far stronger, far better armed than the New World.

I know well, Mr President, that your eye will already have searched these depths, but I feel I have the right to place on record the vital manner in which American interests are at stake in our battle and that of France.

Before Roosevelt could respond, it was over. Shortly after dispatching his warning, Churchill cabled again to say that unless the United States assured France America would enter the war, "the French will very quickly ask for an armistice." Which they did.

TO CHURCHILL, it seemed as though Britain would have to go it alone, and a German invasion could be at hand. One June evening at dinner with Clementine and Randolph's wife, Pamela, who was six months pregnant, Churchill seemed lost in his thoughts until suddenly his eyes locked with his daughter-in-law's. "If the

Hun comes, I am counting on each of you to take one with you before you go," the prime minister said.

"But Papa," Pamela replied, "I don't have a gun, and even if I did, I wouldn't know how to use it."

"But my dear," Churchill said, "you may go to the kitchen"—at this the prime minister raised his fist high in the air in a menacing gesture—"and grab a carving knife."

On June 18, Churchill briefed the nation on the crisis it now faced without the French in the fight.

Upon this battle depends the survival of Christian civilisation. Upon it depends our own British life and the long continuity of our institutions and our Empire. The whole fury and might of the enemy must very soon be turned on us. Hitler knows that he will have to break us in this island or lose the war. If we can stand up to him, all Europe may be free, and the life of the world may move forward into broad, sunlit uplands; but if we fail then the whole world, including the United States, and all that we have known and cared for, will sink into the abyss of a new dark age made more sinister, and perhaps more prolonged, by the lights of a perverted science. Let us therefore brace ourselves to our duty and so bear ourselves that if the British Commonwealth and Empire lasts for a thousand years, men will still say, "This was their finest hour."

After the broadcast, Churchill "was furious because the morning papers, which he likes to see before going to bed, had not arrived," Colville noted. "In his emotion he upset his whisky and soda over all his papers."

Churchill was under the severest stress. He had been prime minister for thirty-nine days. In this brief span had come the near miss with the defeatists, Dunkirk, German victories in Norway, the collapse of the Low Countries and of France, and the unsuccessful appeals to Roosevelt to intervene to keep France in the war. Given to sharp swings between optimism and pessimism, Churchill could at times be hard to work with—and for. "He was an alarming master," recalled John Martin, who came to work for him as a private secretary on the eve of Dunkirk. "For a newcomer it was often difficult to understand his instructions. His speech was hard to follow. Only after months did one acquire skill to interpret what at first seemed inarticulate grunts or single words thrown out without explanation. One had to learn his private allusions, as when he referred to 'that moon-faced man in the Foreign Office' or identified one of his own Minutes by its opening words like a Papal encyclical."

There would be explosions, then forgiveness. "On one of those early nights, when I was working alone with him long after midnight and the more experienced hands had left," Martin said, "everything went wrong: I knew none of the answers and could find none of the papers he wanted. At last he rose wearily to go upstairs to bed but not before he had laid his hand kindly on my shoulder and said he was sorry there had been no time in the rush of these days to get to know me. 'You know,' he added, 'I may seem very fierce, but I am fierce only with one man—Hitler.' " Gracious, but the pressure was always on.

Clementine was keeping a concerned eye on her husband. Mrs. Churchill, Colville noted, was "the only person who was never, in any circumstances, even the slightest bit overawed or afraid" of her husband, and she showed that at the end of June 1940 when she wrote him a candid and loving letter. "My Darling," Clementine began,

> I hope you will forgive me if I tell you something that I feel you ought to know.
>
> One of the men in your entourage (a devoted friend) has been to me & told me that there is a danger of your being generally

disliked by your colleagues & subordinates because of your rough sarcastic & overbearing manner—It seems your Private Secretaries have agreed to behave like schoolboys & "take what's coming to them" & then escape out of your presence shrugging their shoulders—Higher up, if an idea is suggested (say at a conference) you are supposed to be so contemptuous that presently no ideas, good or bad, will be forthcoming. I was astonished & upset because in all these years I have been accustomed to all those who have worked with & under you, loving you—I said this & I was told "No doubt it's the strain"—

My darling Winston—I must confess that I have noticed a deterioration in your manner; & you are not so kind as you used to be.

It is for you to give the Orders & if they are bungled—except for the King the Archbishop of Canterbury & the Speaker you can sack anyone & everyone—Therefore with this terrific power you must combine urbanity, kindness and if possible Olympic calm. You used to quote:—"On ne règne sur les âmes que par le calme" [One can only reign over souls with calmness]—I cannot bear that those who serve the Country & yourself should not love you as well as admire and respect you—

Besides you won't get the best results by irascibility & rudeness. They <u>will</u> breed either dislike or a slave mentality—(Rebellion in War time being out of the question!)

> Please forgive your loving
> devoted & watchful Clemmie

I wrote this at Chequers last Sunday, tore it up, but here it is now.

No reply exists, but Churchill may have taken his wife's words to heart, for, as Mary Soames wrote, most of the men around him then—Colville and Martin among them—became lifelong Churchillians.

AS HE WATCHED Churchill from Washington, Roosevelt had not decided whether Churchill's unflinching talk was a harbinger of greatness or eloquent bombast on the road to disaster. Churchill always sounded confident. "For forty years of public life," wrote the author and scientist C. P. Snow, "the orthodox remark in England was: 'Churchill? Brilliant, of course. But no judgment.' "

In late June, Roosevelt found himself reading a recommendation from the joint planners of the War and Navy Departments arguing that "further release of war material now in the hands of our armed forces will seriously weaken our present state of defense." General George C. Marshall, the man who had been assigned the task of transforming America's unprepared military (even the Dutch were stronger), said: "There was no doubt that we had sold so generously to the Allied Powers that our own stocks were below the safety point. One could argue that by giving more aid to Britain and Canada we would be increasing our own defensive strength. That might be true, but it was not provable, and if Britain were defeated the Army and the Administration could never justify to the American people the risk they had taken." Roosevelt would not give up the fight to get aid to Britain—far from it—but he would move slowly, and Churchill's problem was that there seemed no time to spare. And despite the prime minister's warm words of thanks for the help that did arrive, what seemed generous in Washington—sales of what arms and equipment the administration could dredge up and which often got to the Allies over isolationist objections in Congress—seemed less so in London.

IT WAS NOW JULY. London had to decide what to do about the French fleet, which the Allies could not allow to fall into German or

Italian hands. Churchill realized he had to destroy the French ships, which were in port at Oran in Algiers, in French North Africa. It was a painful moment. "The night he decided to bombard the French fleet in Oran, it was 2 o'clock in the morning before he came to his decision," recalled Lord Beaverbrook. "He had to stand alone. . . . He arrived at his own conclusion. Immediately after reaching it he went out of the Cabinet room into the garden at No. 10 Downing Street. He marched up and down the lawn and a high wind was blowing—a very high wind. The night was dark. There were no lights anywhere and he found his way up and down the lawn because he knew the ground so thoroughly. He was terribly disturbed and only recovered after a few minutes of aggressive and vigorous exercise."

Roosevelt was watching with approval. The action at Oran "served forcibly to underscore Churchill's defiant assurance that 'we will fight them in the streets' and 'never surrender,' " wrote Robert Sherwood. "It exerted a particular effect on Roosevelt." Churchill might really hold out.

Churchill kept a sharp eye on his own nation's interests. British code breakers at Bletchley Park were beginning to figure out how to decipher German radio messages sent in its "Enigma" cipher, intelligence Churchill guarded carefully.

In July Roosevelt dispatched Colonel "Wild Bill" Donovan, founder of the Office of Strategic Services (the forerunner of the Central Intelligence Agency), to assess Britain's chances, and the spymaster returned with a bullish report and an understanding to share some intelligence. Churchill, though, played his hand shrewdly, protecting several different kinds of technology. "Are we going to throw all our secrets into the American lap, and see what they give us in exchange?" he asked Lord Ismay, his liaison to the military chiefs of staff, on July 17. "If so, I am against it. It would be very much better to go slow, as we have far more to give than they."

CHURCHILL'S NOTES FOR a speech to a secret session of the House on June 20 indicate his developing strategy. He dictated them to a secretary; they are fragmentary but revealing, laying out the course of the war, his fears and his hopes.

If Hitler fails to invade
            or destroy Britain
                        he has lost the war.

I do not consider only the severities
            of the winter in Europe.

I look to superiority in Air power
                        in the future.

Transatlantic reinforcements.

If get through next 3 months
get through next 3 years.

It may well be our fine Armies
have not said goodbye to the Continent
of Europe.

If enemy coastline extends from the Arctic
to the Mediterranean

and we retain sea-power
and a growing Air power

it is evident that Hitler
master of a starving, agonized and
surging Europe;

will have his dangers as well as we.

But all depends upon winning this battle
here in Britain, now this summer.

If we do, the prospects of the future
will expand,

and we may look forward
and make our plans for 1941 and 1942

and that is what we are doing.

Attitude of United States.
Nothing will stir them like fighting
in England.

No good suggesting **to them** we are down
and out.

The heroic struggle of Britain
best chance of bringing them in.

Anyhow they have promised fullest aid
in materials, munitions.

A tribute to Roosevelt . . .

All depends upon our resolute bearing
and holding out until Election issues
are settled there.

If we can do so, I cannot doubt
a whole English-speaking world
will be in line together

THE POLITICIAN IN him had put his finger
on what was occupying the president. It would
not much matter what Roosevelt thought if he
was in retirement at Hyde Park in January 1941.
Before the war broke out, Roosevelt signaled his
intention to move aside. In 1938, he had begun
to build Top Cottage, a hideaway at Hyde Park.
(Eleanor already had a separate house on the
estate, Val-Kill.) He thought he would write
magazine pieces and arranged a $75,000 annual
deal with *Collier's.*

"I think my husband was torn," Eleanor recalled of the decision to run again. "He would often talk about the reasons against a third term," but "there was a great sense of responsibility" and "the great feeling that possibly he was the only one who was equipped and trained and cognizant not only of the people who were involved in the future, and in what was going to happen, but of every phase of the situation."

Like Churchill, Roosevelt sensed the making of a memorable chapter in history. In his speech accepting the Democratic nomination on July 19, 1940, Roosevelt said:

> In times like these—in times of great tension, of great crisis—the compass of the world narrows to a single fact. The fact which dominates our world is the fact of armed aggression, the fact of successful armed aggression, aimed at the form of Government, the kind of society that we in the United States have chosen and established for ourselves. It is a fact which no one longer doubts—which no one is longer able to ignore.
>
> It is not an ordinary war. It is a revolution imposed by force of arms, which threatens all men everywhere. It is a revolution which proposes not to set men free but to reduce

them to slavery—to reduce them to slavery in the interest of a dictatorship which has already shown the nature and the extent of the advantage which it hopes to obtain.

That is the fact which dominates our world and which dominates the lives of all of us, each and every one of us. In the face of the danger which confronts our time, no individual retains or can hope to retain, the right of personal choice which free men enjoy in times of peace. He has a first obligation to serve in the defense of our institutions of freedom—a first obligation to serve his country in whatever capacity his country finds him useful.

Like most men of my age, I had made plans for myself, plans for a private life of my own choice and for my own satisfaction, a life of that kind to begin in January, 1941. These plans, like so many other plans, had been made in a world which now seems as distant as another planet. Today all private plans, all private lives, have been in a sense repealed by an overriding public danger. In the face of that public danger all those who can be of service to the Republic have no choice but to offer themselves for service in those capacities for which they may be fitted.

Those, my friends, are the reasons why I have had to admit to myself, and now to state to you, that my conscience will not let me turn my back upon a call to service.

He and Churchill both thought in grand terms. "I think the greatest drive in Franklin's objectives in life was that he wanted to be remembered in history because he had an historical sense and he saw whatever he did in the framework of history," Eleanor said. Marquis Childs mused that Roosevelt had mastered the complexities of America's rise to world power with a kind of "feminine intuition," and now his intuition told him the country was ready to move toward engagement.

SIR WILLIAM WISEMAN, a friend of Walter Lippmann's, returned to Washington from a visit to London in midsummer and told Lippmann: "I think they'll resist. The morale is good. If they can see any light at the end of the tunnel, they'll resist. But if the tunnel is black all the way, no people can stand it, and only the Americans can provide that light."

In the last week of July, Churchill wrote Roosevelt for the first time in eight weeks.

It is some time since I ventured to cable personally to you, and many things both good and bad have happened in between. It has now become most urgent for you to give us the destroyers, motor-boats and flying-boats for which we have asked. The Germans have the whole French coastline from which to launch U-boats and dive-bomber attacks upon our trade and food, and in addition we must be constantly prepared to repel by sea action threatened invasion in the narrow waters. . . .

Latterly the Air attack on our shipping has become injurious. In the last ten days we have had the following destroyers sunk: *Brazen, Codrington, Delight, Wren,* and the following damaged: *Beagle, Boreas, Brilliant, Griffin, Montrose, Walpole,* total ten. All this in the advent of any attempt which may be made at invasion. Destroyers are frightfully vulnerable to Air bombing, and yet they must be held in the Air bombing area to prevent sea-borne invasion. We could not keep up the present rate of casualties for long, and if we cannot get a substantial reinforcement, the whole fate of the war may be decided by this minor and easily remediable factor. I cannot understand why, with the position as it is, you do not send me at least 50 or 60 of your oldest destroyers.

Then he laid it on the line. "Mr President," Churchill said, "with great respect I must tell you that in the long history of the world this is a thing to do now."

Like Churchill, Roosevelt was a student of the writings of Admiral Alfred Thayer Mahan. Mahan argued that control of the seas was essential to a nation's capacity to project power—a lesson the British knew well, since the might of the Royal Navy had been a fundamental element in building their empire. Now Roosevelt wanted mastery of the sea, and British naval bases were key to controlling the Atlantic.

The United States would send the destroyers over in exchange for a promise that the Royal Navy would dispatch the fleet to North America if the Germans overran England and for ninety-nine-year leases for air and naval rights in the British West Indies, Newfoundland, and Bermuda. When Lippmann told Wiseman about the destroyer deal, Wiseman replied: "Well, that'll do it. It will give [them] something to go on with."

Churchill knew he was not getting the best of deals. "The President, having always to consider Congress and also the Navy authorities in the United States, was of course increasingly drawn to present the transaction to his fellow-countrymen as a highly advantageous bargain whereby immense securities were gained in these dangerous times by the United States in return for a few flotillas of obsolete destroyers,"

Churchill later wrote. "This was indeed true; but not exactly a convenient statement for me."

Churchill had no choice. "We intend to fight this out here to the end, and none of us would ever buy peace by surrendering or scuttling the fleet," he wrote Roosevelt on August 15. Then, with apparent resentment, he added: "But in any use you may make of this repeated assurance you will please bear in mind the disastrous effect from our point of view, and perhaps also from yours, of allowing any impression to grow that we regard the conquest of the British Islands and its naval bases as any other than an impossible contingency. The spirit of our people is splendid."

THE AMERICAN PRESIDENT was not quite in tune with the mood Churchill had created in England. Roosevelt was thinking of darkness. Led by Churchill, the British were living in the light. Common dangers bind people together, if only for a short while. "Oddly enough, most of us were very happy in those days," wrote C. P. Snow of that English summer. "There was a kind of collective euphoria over the whole country. I don't know what we were thinking about. We were very busy. We had a purpose. We were living in constant excitement, usually, if we examined the true position, of an unpromising kind. In one's realistic moments, it was difficult to see what chance we had. But I doubt if most of us had many realistic moments, or thought much at all. We were working like mad. We were sustained by a surge of national emotion, of which Churchill was both symbol and essence, evocator and voice."

The practical politician in Roosevelt did not care how evocative Churchill was. He wanted the base leases to give himself domestic cover for sending the destroyers over. If America appeared to be getting the better end of the bargain, then Roosevelt could argue he was being shrewd, not sentimental—or stupid, since the war picture was still discouraging for the British. Confronted with a hostile Congress, Roosevelt took executive action and put the deal into effect—a brave political gamble so close to the November elections.

It was not exactly an even trade, and Churchill only grudgingly gave Roosevelt the assurance the president wanted. "You ask, Mr President, whether my statement in Parliament on June 4th, 1940, about Great Britain never surrendering or scuttling her Fleet 'represents the settled policy of His Majesty's Government,'" Churchill wrote Roosevelt on the last day of August. "It certainly does. I must, however, observe that these hypothetical contingencies seem more likely to concern the German Fleet or what is left of it than our own."

Churchill was doing what he often did with an uncomfortable reality: He was recasting it in more attractive terms. "Thus all was happily settled," he later wrote. Churchill had, he recalled, tried "to place the transaction on the highest level, where indeed it had a right to stand, because it expressed and conserved the enduring common interests of the English-speaking world." In his mind's eye Churchill saw the two nations "somewhat mixed up together," and he relished the image. "Like the Mississippi," he told the House of Commons in August, "it just keeps rolling along. Let it roll. Let it roll on full flood, inexorable, irresistible, benignant, to broader lands and better days."

A comforting prospect, but only a prospect: The destroyers were not there yet, and Churchill now had a more immediate problem. In these same August weeks, Hitler unleashed air attacks as a prelude to a possible September invasion—all while Roosevelt was driving a tough bargain for destroyers that would not appear for months (and even then would have maintenance problems).

WHILE CHURCHILL WAS negotiating with Roosevelt, the Luftwaffe attacked England on August 13; the Germans called it "the Day of the Eagle." The Battle of Britain was beginning. On August 16, Churchill and Lord Ismay went to the operations room of No. 11 Group, Fighter Command. "There had been fighting throughout the afternoon; and at one moment every single squadron in the Group was engaged; there was nothing in reserve, and the map table showed new waves of attackers crossing the coast," Ismay recalled. "I felt sick with fear." At the end of the day the British fought well. Leaving for Chequers, Churchill said to Ismay: "Don't speak to me; I have never been so moved." Five minutes passed, and the prime minister said: "Never in the field of human conflict has so much been owed by so many to so few"—a phrase he would repeat in an inspiring speech to the House and to the nation.

On August 23, the Luftwaffe bombed London; two days later Britain launched a counterstrike on Berlin. Then, on September 7, the Germans blitzed London, killing—in a single night—more than 300 people and injuring 1,337. The Luftwaffe would come day after day and night after night for eight months. Amid the terror, however, the British, bolstered by Churchill, refused to give in. "How I wish you could see the women of England, particularly the older women—it is staggering—their courage and endurance," Nancy Astor, the tart-tongued American woman who had married well, been elected to Parliament, and after a period of appeasement in the 1930s become an enthusiastic patriot during the war, wrote *The Washington Post*'s Eugene Meyer. "To see them, as I have, gazing at what was their home, now a heap of ashes, their neighbors dead, and sometimes their own families too, and yet they look at you with steadfast English eyes and say, 'Hitler won't beat us this way.' It makes you feel that war is not such a dreadful thing if it brings out this in people."

On September 17, Hitler postponed SEA LION, his code name for a full-scale invasion of Britain. After subduing much of Western Europe, he had thought he could bring Britain into line, but he had not counted on Churchill and the British people standing so fast. Frustrated in the west, Hitler began to plan a strike against Stalin in the east. But in Britain, the Blitz wore on, killing in all more than forty thousand people—at least five thousand of them children.

It was a troubling season on many fronts. The Battle of the Atlantic had long been under way between American and British ships and German U-boats. A vital factor from the first days of the war, the Atlantic lifeline was essential to keeping Britain armed and fed. Italy's declaration of war and ensuing battles for British and French possessions in Africa helped turn the Mediterranean into a critical war zone. For much of the rest of the war, the Axis and the Allies would fight along the top of the African continent. Arguably the largest strategic stake was Allied control of Egypt, which served as a bulwark against Axis moves to cut the Suez Canal and threaten the oil-rich Middle East. Meanwhile, on September 27 Japan signed the Tripartite Pact, linking Tokyo with Berlin and Rome.

IN THE UNITED STATES, the Roosevelt–Wendell Willkie race was close. "Let me say to you, if you elect me President of the United States, no American boys will ever be sent to the shambles of the European trenches," Willkie told audiences in the autumn of 1940. Roosevelt watched his opponent carefully. The critical moment came in Boston a week before the election. Playing to isolationists himself, Roosevelt declared: "I have said this before, but I shall say it again and again and again: 'Your boys are not going to be sent into any foreign wars.' " Until now, Roosevelt had also said "except in case of attack." Today he dropped it. When Sam Rosenman challenged Roosevelt about abandoning the qualifier, an irritated president replied: "Of course we'll fight if we're attacked. If somebody attacks us, then it isn't a foreign war, is it? Or do they want me to guarantee that our troops will be sent into battle only in the event of another Civil War?" But his sharp tone suggests he was uncomfortable with the late October omission.

Churchill observed the contest with "profound anxiety. . . . No newcomer into power could possess or soon acquire the knowledge and experience of Franklin Roosevelt. None could equal his commanding gifts." Those words were written after the war, when Churchill was using his memoirs to cement the Anglo-American alliance during the cold war, but it was true that he had more than a year invested in Roosevelt, and the destroyer deal suggested Roosevelt's heart was in the right place. Though some historians have argued that a Willkie administration would have had the same ultimate policies as Roosevelt's did, there is evidence he would not have been quite as open to Churchill as Roosevelt eventually was. Willkie, Henry Wallace noted after a conversation later in the war, "expressed himself as having very little use for Churchill, saying that he was altogether too self-assured, that a self-assured man made a poor planner. He said Churchill was gifted with the ability to speak like a Demosthenes and write like an angel. . . . He had no one to suggest as Churchill's substitute; nevertheless it was obvious that he has no confidence in Churchill."

In the fall of 1940, another campaign was afoot. The shrewdest men in Churchill's inner circle were building up Churchill in the eyes of the establishment in Roosevelt's capital. Replying to a letter Eugene Meyer had sent him with a clipping about British war orphans finding homes in the United States, Brendan Bracken laid out Churchill's case. "You cannot imagine how grateful the English are to your country for all you are doing for us," Bracken wrote. "In the midst of our lonely and desperate fight against the greatest military power in the world and its carrion allies, we are heartened by the great help and sympathy given us by the United States." Echoing Churchill's tone with Roosevelt—one of determination and disproportionate gratitude—Bracken wrote Meyer: "England will never forget what America is doing for her. And I believe that this War will not have been in vain if it ends by welding the foreign naval and military policies of England and America into an instrument which can stifle the rebirth of tyranny, race prejudice, and all the other beastly systems bred by Nazis and Fascists. We are having a rough time, but our people are very cheerful, and inflexible in their determination to carry this War through to a successful conclusion. Grief, destruction, and death must be our lot for many months, and perhaps years, to come. But we shall never surrender. And we are getting stronger and our people are adapting themselves to bombing and all the other hardships created by War."

Bracken hoped that such letters—Meyer was the publisher of one of the newspapers Roosevelt read over breakfast in his bed in the White House every morning—would reassure influential Americans at a critical time. Meyer, who was prointervention, was delighted by Bracken's message, writing back: "America is profoundly impressed by the splendid defense put up by your people by air warfare and the high morale of a united people. I heard the Prime Minister speaking to France the other day on the radio. Please congratulate him upon his splendid work and especially on his marvelous oratory." (In the broadcast to the French, Churchill had said: "Remember we shall never stop, never weary, and never give in, and that our whole people and Empire have vowed themselves to the task of cleansing Europe from the Nazi pestilence and saving the world from the new Dark Ages.")

Meyer was right that Americans were impressed with British courage, but an October 1940 poll found that 83 percent did not think "the United States should enter the war against Germany and Italy at once."

———

ON ELECTION NIGHT Roosevelt set up headquarters in the dining room at Hyde Park. There was a news ticker in the adjoining smoking room; the smoking room was small, dominated by bookcases and a huge pair of antlers over a fireplace. This evening was, Secret Serviceman Mike Reilly recalled, the one time he saw "FDR's nerves give him a real rough time." The early returns were not encouraging.

"Mike, I don't want to see anybody in here," Roosevelt said to Reilly.

"Including your family, Mr. President?"

Roosevelt replied, "I said 'anybody.'"

In the end, the news brightened, the room filled, and Franklin Roosevelt won, 54.7 percent to 44.8 percent.

ON THE DAY after the election, Churchill sent Roosevelt the following cable.

> I did not think it right for me as a Foreigner to express my opinion upon American politics while the Election was on, but now I feel you will not mind my saying that I prayed for your success and that I am truly thankful for it. This does not mean that I seek or wish for anything more than the full, fair and free play of your mind upon the world issues now at stake in which our

two nations have to discharge their respective duties. We are entering upon a sombre phase of what must evidently be a protracted and broadening war, and I look forward to being able to interchange my thoughts with you in all that confidence and goodwill which has grown up between us since I went to the Admiralty at the outbreak. Things are afoot which will be remembered as long as the English language is spoken in any quarter of the globe, and in expressing the comfort I feel that the people of the United States have once again cast these great burdens upon you, I must avow my sure faith that the lights by which we steer will bring us all safely to anchor.

A brilliant, generous, eloquent note—and Roosevelt chose not to answer it. Churchill was fretting. At the conclusion of another cable ten days later, Churchill wrote: "I hope you got my personal telegram of congratulation." Roosevelt did not reply.

Calculated or inadvertent, the oversight bothered Churchill for years. Anyone who has ever had a carefully composed, heartfelt letter go unacknowledged knows the feeling: The writer wants the satisfaction of knowing his words hit the mark. In this case, Churchill never got that.

He attended to the wound by explaining it away. In the volume of his memoirs published in 1949, Churchill wrote: "Curiously enough, I never received any answer to this telegram. It may well have been engulfed in the vast mass of congratulatory messages which were swept aside by urgent work." One thing is clear. Winston Churchill was still very much the suitor in the courtship of Franklin Roosevelt.

AS NOVEMBER FADED into December, Churchill was writing a letter he believed to be "one of the most important" of his life. Churchill's courage in the spring and summer had staved off the immediate threat of destruction, but Britain was now settling down into a drawn-out conflict. The cable went through numerous revisions, and Lord Lothian was a key adviser—an example of how Churchill shared Roosevelt's ability to profit from the ideas of those around him. The president was better at distilling the work and thinking of others; as a leader, he was in many ways more a conductor of an orchestra than a composer of music. The prime minister was more self-sufficient (and virtually always wrote his own speeches, cables, and minutes) but he liked to consult experts, and in this case Lothian, among others, helped him as he prepared the cable to Roosevelt. The result was classic Churchill—long, well argued, and passionate yet practical.

"Even if the United States were our Ally, instead of our friend and indispensable partner, we should not ask for a large American expeditionary army," Churchill wrote to Roosevelt; this was not the time to ask for soldiers. Congress had passed the Selective Service Act in September, but with the proviso that draftees could serve only in the Western Hemisphere or American territories like the Philippines. "Shipping, not men, is the limiting factor. . . . The danger of Great Britain being destroyed by a swift, overwhelming blow, has for the time being very greatly receded. In its place, there is a long, gradually-maturing danger, less sudden and less spectacular, but equally deadly. This mortal danger is the steady and increasing diminution of sea tonnage." To Roosevelt he argued: "The decision for 1941 lies upon the seas. Unless we can establish our ability to feed this Island, to import the munitions of all kinds which we need, unless we can move our armies to the various theatres where Hitler and his confederate, Mussolini, must be met, and maintain them there, and do all this with the assurance of being able to carry it on till the spirit of the Continental Dictators is broken, we may fall by the way, and the time needed by the United

States to complete her defensive preparations may not be forthcoming." Britain was running out of money, Germany had her essentially surrounded, and Churchill, who believed in taking the fight to fronts far from home, needed help.

Roosevelt and Hopkins had left for a cruise in the Caribbean aboard the *Tuscaloosa* in early December. "He had only his own intimates around him," Churchill recalled. "Harry Hopkins, then unknown to me, told me later that Mr. Roosevelt read and re-read this letter as he sat alone in his deck-chair, and that for two days he did not seem to have reached any clear conclusion. He was plunged in intense thought, and brooded silently." The result of the brooding: Lend-Lease, which would provide supplies and cash to Britain. Churchill's long letter had done its work.

In a fireside chat on December 29, Roosevelt spoke in a less ornate way than Churchill would have, but there was strength in the simplicity of his imagery.

> Tonight, in the presence of a world crisis, my mind goes back eight years to a night in the midst of a domestic crisis. It was a time when the wheels of American industry were grinding to a full stop, when the whole banking system of our country had ceased to function.

I well remember that while I sat in my study in the White House, preparing to talk with the people of the United States, I had before my eyes the picture of all those Americans with whom I was talking. I saw the workmen in the mills, the mines, the factories; the girl behind the counter; the small shopkeeper; the farmer doing his spring plowing; the widows and the old men wondering about their life's savings. I tried to convey to the great mass of American people what the banking crisis meant to them in their daily lives.

Tonight, I want to do the same thing, with the same people, in this new crisis which faces America.

We met the issue of 1933 with courage and realism.

We face this new crisis—this new threat to the security of our nation—with the same courage and realism.

Never before since Jamestown and Plymouth Rock has our American civilization been in such danger as now.

For on September 27, 1940, this year, by an agreement signed in Berlin, three powerful nations, two in Europe and one in Asia, joined themselves together in the threat that if the United States of America interfered with or blocked the expansion program of these three nations—a program aimed at world control—they would unite in ultimate action against the United States.

The Nazi masters of Germany have made it clear that they intend not only to dominate all life and thought in their own country, but also to enslave the whole of Europe, and then to use the resources of Europe to dominate the rest of the world. . . .

The history of recent years proves that the shootings and the chains and the concentration camps are not simply the transient tools but the very altars of modern dictatorships. They may talk of a "new order" in the world, but what they have in mind is only a revival of the oldest and the worst tyranny. In that there is no liberty, no religion, no hope.

Saluting Churchill's people, Roosevelt said, "In a military sense Great Britain and the British Empire are today the spearhead of resistance to world conquest. And they are putting up a fight which will live forever in the story of human gallantry." Though Roosevelt did not say so explicitly, the author of that story was Winston Churchill. The time had come, Roosevelt concluded, for America to be "the great arsenal of democracy."

IN MUCH THE way Churchill's rhetoric had defined the debate and shaped perceptions of the war since May 1940, the reelected Roosevelt's major speeches in late December and early January were designed to deepen his country's understanding of the conflict and its stakes. After his "arsenal of democracy" performance, the president went to work on his State of the Union message. Sitting in his study with Rosenman and Hopkins one night, Roosevelt dictated:

> We must look forward to a world based on four essential human freedoms.
>
> The first is freedom of speech and expression—everywhere in the world.
>
> The second is freedom of every person to worship God in his own way—everywhere in the world.
>
> The third is freedom from want—which, translated into world terms, means economic understandings which will secure to every nation everywhere a healthy peacetime life for its inhabitants.
>
> The fourth is freedom from fear—which, translated into international terms, means a world-wide reduction of armaments to such a point and in such a thorough fashion

that no nation anywhere will be in a position to commit an act of physical aggression against any neighbor.

Listening as Rosenman wrote the president's words on a yellow pad, Hopkins took issue with Roosevelt's term "everywhere in the world."

"That covers an awful lot of territory, Mr. President," Rosenman recalled Hopkins saying. "I don't know how interested Americans are going to be in the people of Java."

"I'm afraid they'll have to be someday, Harry," Roosevelt replied. "The world is getting so small that even the people in Java are getting to be our neighbors now."

Roosevelt was as much—if not more—a student of people as he was a man of ideas, and while he was enunciating the principles of a newly democratic world, he was increasingly interested in seeing Churchill.

At Christmastime, Roosevelt was talking with Hopkins, who had moved into the White House on May 10 and never left. "You know— a lot of this could be settled if Churchill and I could just sit down together for a while," Roosevelt said to Hopkins. Though ill—much of his stomach had been removed because of cancer in 1937, and he suffered from terrible digestive troubles—Hopkins, deeply loyal to Roosevelt, drove himself forward. "Harry had the capacity to be a relaxing friend," recalled Frances Perkins. "You could stand going on with a conversation at ten o'clock at night if you'd had a good laugh at nine."

"How about me going over, Mr. President?" Hopkins asked.

The idea made sense. "Harry is the perfect Ambassador for my purposes," Roosevelt often said. "He doesn't even know the meaning of the word 'protocol.' When he sees a piece of red tape, he just pulls out those old garden shears of his and snips it. And when he's talking to some foreign dignitary, he knows how to slump back in his chair and put his feet up on the conference table and say, 'Oh, *yeah*?' "

THERE WAS MUCH to discuss. As 1940 closed, Churchill was concerned about American plans to take some British gold reserves in South Africa as payment for supplies, about the condition of the destroyers that were finally making their way into English hands, and about the details of Lend-Lease. To load the gold aboard a U.S. warship in Cape Town, Churchill told Roosevelt, "will disturb public opinion here and throughout the Dominions and encourage the enemy, who will proclaim that you are sending for our last reserves." The destroyers were not, to say the least, in the best repair. "Please do not suppose we are making any complaints about the condition of these vessels," Churchill told the president. "It may however be an advantage to your yards to know the kind of things that happen when ships that have been laid up so long are put into the hardest service in the Atlantic." And Lend-Lease pleased but somewhat puzzled Churchill, who frankly admitted to Roosevelt that he felt "anxiety" about the details as they struggled to defend their homeland and take the fight to the Axis in other theaters. "Remember, Mr President," Churchill wrote on New Year's Eve 1940, "we do not know what you have in mind, or exactly what the United States is going to do, and we are fighting for our lives."

Jan 20 1941

THE WHITE HOUSE
WASHINGTON

Dear Churchill

Wendell Willkie will give you
this — He is truly helping to keep
politics out over here.

I think this verse applies to your
people as it does to us:

"Sail on, Oh Ship of State!
Sail on, Oh Union strong and great.
Humanity with all its fears,
With all the hopes of future years,
Is hanging breathless on thy fate"

As ever yours
Franklin D Roosevelt

"I think this verse applies to your people as it does to us"

The Longfellow quotation Roosevelt
wrote out from memory and sent to
Churchill, January 1941

JESUS CHRIST! WHAT A MAN!

A Mission to London–Churchill Courts Hopkins–
"Sail On, O Ship of State"

THE PRIME MINISTER did not understand who was coming to see him. "Churchill had no idea who my father was," said Robert Hopkins. "He thought he was some social worker and could not see why the President was sending him over." Harry Hopkins, John Martin recalled, was "not a person who had appeared on the world stage. The Foreign Office didn't realize he was as important as he was." Mary Soames remembered that Churchill's circle was "all geared up" before Hopkins—"a mystery man," she called him— arrived. Hopkins had concerns of his own. Jean Monnet, a Frenchman who was working with the British Purchasing Commission in Washington, told him "to waste no time with the Minister of This or That in the British Cabinet, for Churchill *is* the British War Cabinet, and no one else matters." According to Robert Sherwood, Hopkins "became a bit fed up with hearing so much about the almighty Churchill, and exclaimed, 'I suppose Churchill is convinced that he's the greatest man in the world!' "

Hopkins's insecurity is interesting. When he later went to Moscow to meet with Stalin, he said to himself, as he once recalled to Marquis Childs, "Here I am, the son of a harness maker from Grinnell, Iowa . . . walking down the hall of the Kremlin to meet the man who rules all these people, and I am going to talk to him, in a sense, as an equal, about the conduct of this war. Just think of it!" The remark struck Childs. "It seemed to me a rather tragic and in a sense poignant commentary on the man, and in a sense on America," Childs said. "In a sense it was a commentary on this fantastic role of responsibility and leadership into which we were precipitated, and our unreadiness for it, because at that moment you should not have been thinking about how you were the son of a harness maker."

Hopkins wanted to be respected, and he wanted his country and his chief to be respected. And Roosevelt, for all his self-confidence, was not immune to worrying about whether someone—in this case Churchill—

liked him. Joseph Lash related this anecdote of Felix Frankfurter: The justice had adopted two English children for the duration, and their nanny brought them by to meet Roosevelt. "Later the justice called Roosevelt to thank him and to report that although the president had made a conquest of the girl, her younger brother was holding out," Lash wrote. "That bothered Roosevelt. 'Send him over and give me half an hour with him alone,' Roosevelt demanded. The idea that anyone, male or female, could resist him really disturbed him." All of us want to be liked: Roosevelt was no exception. There was a rumor—Churchill believed it originated with Joseph Kennedy—that Churchill disliked both Roosevelt and the United States. (This despite the pleading, personally pleasant tone of most of Churchill's messages.) Hopkins's task, then, was not only diplomatic, it was human as well: to gauge whether Churchill and Roosevelt, who already thought of Churchill as a "stinker" from the Gray's Inn evening, could get along.

AS HOPKINS HEADED over in January 1941, Churchill was learning who his guest was, and, Robert Sherwood said, "ordered the unrolling of any red carpets that might have survived the Blitz." Within minutes of Hopkins's arrival in London, the Luftwaffe struck. The chargé d'affaires at the American embassy, Herschel V. Johnson, took Hopkins to Claridge's. They talked amid blasts of antiaircraft fire. Long a faraway drama, the war was now quite real.

Protective of Roosevelt, driven in part by the insecurities that he confessed to Childs, Hopkins was on edge as the mission began. Cannily, Churchill had struck a preemptive blow the afternoon of Hopkins's arrival. "Churchill had been informed of Hopkins' devotion to Roosevelt," Sherwood wrote, "and of his possible suspicion of anyone who might presume to challenge Roosevelt's position of pre-eminence among world statesmen."

So informed, Churchill said in a speech the day Hopkins landed in England: "I have always taken the view that the fortunes of mankind in its tremendous journey are principally decided for good or ill—but mainly for good, for the path is upward—by its greatest men and its greatest episodes. I therefore hail it as a most fortunate occurrence that at this awe-striking climax in world affairs there should stand at the head of the American Republic a famous statesman, long versed and experienced in the work of government and administration, in whose heart there burns the fire of resistance to aggression and oppression, and whose sympathies and nature make him the sincere and undoubted champion of justice and of freedom, and of the victims of wrongdoing wherever they may dwell."

Flattery worked. Johnson told Hopkins about the remarks, and there was a kind of thaw. Face is important: People like to think the people they are dealing with respect and like them; that tends to keep the waters smooth and tempers cool. Hopkins then asked Edward R. Murrow of CBS to come see him. Murrow's broadcasts of the Blitz had shaped America's sense of the war, and Hopkins wanted to get the journalist's take on the British political scene and the nation's morale. "I suppose you could say that I've come here to try to find a way to be a catalytic agent between two prima donnas," Hopkins said when Murrow asked him what he was in London to do. "I want to try to get an understanding of Churchill and of the men he sees after midnight."

The next day, Hopkins reported to Roosevelt, in notes written on Claridge's stationery, he found No. 10 Downing Street "a bit down at the heels because the Treasury next door has been bombed more than a bit." Looking around, he discovered that "most of the windows are out—workmen over the place repairing the damage."

In a small dining room in the basement, Brendan Bracken fixed Hopkins a sherry and excused himself. Suddenly, "a rotund—smiling—red faced gentleman appeared—extended a fat but none the less convincing hand and wished me welcome to England. A short black coat—striped trousers—a clear eye and a mushy voice was the impression of En-gland's leader as he showed me with obvious pride the photograph of his beautiful daughter-in-law and grandchild." (Pamela and young Winston, who had been born in October 1940.) Churchill and Hopkins took their seats.

CHURCHILL KNEW THE stakes of the lunch. He had to make the case that though Britain would fight on, she had to have more American aid. "Thus I met Harry Hopkins," Churchill wrote later, "that extraordinary man, who played, and was to play, a sometimes decisive part in the whole movement of the war. . . . This was the height of the London bombing, and many local worries imposed themselves upon us. But it was evident to me that here was an envoy from the President of supreme importance to our life." While Churchill's cook and housekeeper, Mrs. Landemare, brought lunch, the two men talked, Hopkins told Roosevelt, of "the difficulty of communication with the President at long range—there is no question but that he wants to meet the President—the sooner the better." As soup gave way to cold beef ("I didn't take enough jelly to suit the P.M.," Hopkins wrote Roosevelt, "and he gave me some more"), Hopkins was blunt. "I told him there was a feeling in some quarters that he, Churchill, did not like America, Americans or Roosevelt. This set him off on a bitter tho' fairly constrained attack on Ambassador Kennedy who he believes is responsible for this impression. He denied it vigorously—sent for a Secretary to show me a telegram which he had sent to the President immediately after his election in which he expressed his warm delight at the President's re-election"—the telegram Roosevelt had failed to acknowledge.

Churchill shifted from defense to solicitude. "I told of my mission," Hopkins said. "He seemed pleased—and several times assured me that he would make every detail of information and opinion available to me." Churchill (who "took snuff from a little silver box") "hoped that I would not leave England until I was fully satisfied of the exact state of England's need and the urgent necessity of the exact material assistance Britain requires to win the war."

Then Churchill took the offensive, alluding to 1940 and promising to hang on no matter what

Hitler might throw at him even yet. "He reviewed with obvious pride his own part in the war to date—he didn't *know* that England could withstand the onslaught after France fell—but he felt sure that it could—it did—and it will withstand the next one."

The meal had gone splendidly. Churchill and Hopkins "were so impressed with each other," Jock Colville wrote, "that their tête-à-tête did not break up till nearly 4." Churchill's luncheon performance, mixing praise of Roosevelt, a detailed grasp of the war, and reminders in a city under fire that it was Britain, not the United States, doing the fighting, made an impact. "I have never had such an enjoyable time," Hopkins said afterward. ". . . God, what a force that man has."

THE INITIAL CONNECTION between Roosevelt and Churchill was by proxy. The relationship was being shaped by not two but three men—the pragmatic Hopkins, the sentimental Churchill, and the wary Roosevelt. Churchill was charming Hopkins; Hopkins was assessing Churchill with a cold eye; Roosevelt was aloof, protected by distance as his emissary surveyed the landscape.

That Friday evening, Churchill, Clementine, and a handful of aides left for Ditchley, an eighteenth-century house near Blenheim; Hopkins would join them the next day. "Week-ends were anything but restful, because of the incessant concern of Churchill with everything that was going on everywhere (Roosevelt could get away from it all now and then, but Churchill never even wanted to try)," Sherwood wrote. Hopkins noted differences between Churchill's style and Roosevelt's. "Although hell might be popping all about Roosevelt, it was rarely audible in his immediate presence, where tranquillity prevailed," Sherwood wrote. "Churchill, on the other hand, always seemed to be at his Command Post on the precarious beachhead and the guns were continually blazing in his conversation; wherever he was, there was the battlefront—and he was involved in the battles not only of the current war but of the whole past, from Cannae to Gallipoli."

On the drive out of London, Bracken told Colville that "Hopkins, the confidant of Roosevelt, was the most important American visitor to this country we had ever had. He had come to tell the President what we needed and to form an opinion of the country's morale. He could influence the President more than any living man." Hopkins did know Roosevelt as well as anyone could. He had the best possible grasp of how Roosevelt's heart and mind worked; he had, in fact, developed the same way of thinking. Roosevelt and Hopkins were practical idealists. They believed the world could be made better and that it was their duty to do all they could to that end, but liberal rhetoric and utopian schemes sometimes made them uncomfortable. So they talked tough, charting a course between left and right.

As the weekend began, Churchill seemed pleased with his first encounter with Hopkins. "Before dinner," Colville recalled, "we drank and thawed." The meal was "exquisite," and "afterwards Winston smoked the biggest cigar in history and became very mellow." At bedtime, Churchill took his leave "with a very full box and in an excellent temper." In Washington, meanwhile, the White House released the text of the Lend-Lease legislation. Churchill woke early on Saturday, read the language of the law, and was "delighted by the new American bill which allows British warships the use of American ports and contains wide powers for the President in every sphere of assistance to us. He says this is tantamount to a declaration of war by the United States. At any rate it is an open challenge to Germany to declare war if she dares."

That evening, the party gathered in Ditchley's dining room. "The table," Colville noted, was "not over-decorated: four gilt candle sticks with tall yellow tapers and a single gilt cup in the centre." When the ladies withdrew, Hopkins "paid a graceful tribute to the P.M.'s speeches which had, he said, produced the most stirring and revolutionary effect on all classes and districts in America." Roosevelt, Hopkins said, had arranged to have a radio brought into a cabinet meeting so that they could listen to Churchill.

Churchill, Colville wrote, was "touched and gratified" and added that "he hardly knew what he said in his speeches last summer; he had just been imbued with the feeling that 'it would be better for us to be destroyed than to see the triumph of such an imposter.' When, at the time of Dunkirk, he had addressed a meeting of Ministers 'below the line' he had realised that there was only one thing they wanted to hear him say: that whatever happened to our army we should still go on. He had said it." This history was being recast for Hopkins's ears. Churchill was already reimagining the events of May 1940, editing out the push for possible negotiations with the enemy. This was no time to even hint that there was anything but steel in the British soul.

Then, as the candles flickered, Churchill struck conciliatory notes about his opponents on the left. "After the war he could never lead a party Government against the Opposition leaders who had co-operated so loyally," Colville noted. "He hoped a national Government would continue for two or three years after the war so that the country might be undivided in its efforts to put into effect certain principles— or rather measures—of reconstruction. He then proceeded to give—after saying that the text of the American Bill that morning had made him feel that a new world was coming into being— a graphic description of the future, as he visualised it, from an international point of view. He began by saying that there must be a United States of Europe and he believed it should be built by the English; if the Russians built it, there would be communism and squalor; if the Germans built it, there would be tyranny and brute force."

Speaking in the "unhesitating manner which means he has really warmed to his subject," Churchill continued, as Lord Chandos, who was present, later recalled:

We seek no treasure, we seek no territorial gains, we seek only the right of man to be free; we seek his rights to worship his God, to lead his life in his own way, secure from persecution. As the humble laborer returns from his work when the day is done, and sees the smoke curling upwards from his cottage home in the serene evening sky, we wish him to know that no rat-a-tat-tat—here he rapped on the table—of the secret police upon his door will disturb his leisure or interrupt his rest. We seek government with the consent of the people, man's freedom to say what he will, and when he thinks himself injured, to find himself equal in the eyes of the law. But war aims other than these we have none.

"What," Churchill asked Hopkins, "will the President say to all this?"

Hopkins was silent, Chandos remembered, for "the best part of a minute," and then replied, "Well, Mr Prime Minister, I don't think the President will give a dam' for all that." Listening, Chandos was terrified. "Heavens alive," he thought, "it's gone wrong." Then, after another pause, Hopkins added: "You see, we're only interested in seeing that that Goddam sonofabitch, Hitler, gets licked."

Amid laughter, the tension melted. "Winston hastily explained," Colville wrote, "that he had been speaking very freely and was just anxious to let Hopkins realise that we were not all devoid of thoughts of the future: he would be the first to agree that the destruction of 'those foul swine' was the primary and over-riding objective." "At that moment," Chandos

"The most important visitor to this country we had ever had"

Churchill, Brendan Bracken, and Harry Hopkins in London, January 10, 1941

recalled, "a friendship was cemented which no convulsion ever undermined."

The conversation masked a complex psychological and political dynamic. Here was Churchill, a soldier of empire, stepping back from the dire question of the moment—how to survive the Third Reich and liberate the conquered states on the Continent—to speak in sweeping terms about the philosophy behind the Allied effort. Churchill's remarks were calculated to reassure the old WPA administrator—and, through Hopkins, the president, who had given America the New Deal and often spoke about exporting democracy and social justice to other nations.

Hopkins's wry, streetwise reply suggests he was trying to impress his British hosts that the Americans were as unflinching as they were. It was not easy to land in a country that had taken the brunt of war for more than a year. For them, Hitler was not the unseen force behind Murrow's broadcasts. He was an all-too-real enemy. Hopkins found himself in a house with men and women who were dealing with death and destruction face-to-face, so he put on a brave act, pretending that Roosevelt—who cared deeply about the shape the world would take—was concerned only with the present, not the future. Churchill and Hopkins, each trying to win the other's trust, had reversed roles.

"The people here," Hopkins told Roosevelt in a handwritten letter after the weekend, "are amazing from Churchill down and if courage alone can win—the result will be inevitable." Churchill and Hopkins shared a love of action. At dinner, in a "slow, deliberate, halting" tone that "was a remarkable contrast to the ceaseless flow of eloquence to which we had listened"as Churchill spoke, Hopkins "said that there were two kinds of men: those who talked and those who acted. The President, like the Prime Minister, was one of the latter." Hopkins now sensed that "the almighty Churchill" he had scorned from afar might be just that.

ON SUNDAY, January 12, 1941, in the middle of the film *Night Train to Munich,* Colville was called away to the telephone: The HMS *Southampton* had been destroyed by German dive-bombers in the Mediterranean, and the aircraft carrier *Illustrious* was damaged. For Hopkins, the report, and how the British leaders reacted to it, was another important, first-hand lesson. Churchill was pained but tough. He had been this way from the beginning of the war. C. P. Snow recalled a small episode from the previous autumn: "I was sitting in an air raid shelter that September with a senior civil servant: we were discussing the theoretical plans for evacuating governmental departments. . . . 'It will not, however, happen,' he said, in a precise, old-fashioned, mandarin tone. 'The Prime Minister has determined that we shall die in the last ditch: and there is no one inclined to say him nay.' " Now the same flinty courage was evident as Hopkins watched Churchill. "Having had no direct experience of the realities of warfare," Sherwood wrote, Hopkins "was shocked by the stark immediacy of the information that ships had been sunk and that British sailors had been killed and maimed. But he had to learn that those who make the great decisions in this brutal business can take no time out for mourning or for penitence; and Winston Churchill, no respector of his own safety, was a good man from whom to learn it."

In all their hours together, Churchill did not tell Hopkins that by late October 1940 Britain's Enigma decrypts had suggested a German invasion was no longer an immediate danger, nor did he reveal another piece of signals intelligence confirming the point on January 12. It was, after all, in Churchill's interest to convince the United States that the danger was great—as it was, though a full-scale invasion of England was off for the moment. The sharing of intelligence would soon improve, with Americans visiting Bletchley and the British receiving American work on cracking Japanese codes.

———

THOUGH HOPKINS CUT an odd figure, the British enjoyed him. Mary Soames thought him a "most curious, fascinating character" whose "clothes always looked too big for him." Hopkins never quite acclimated himself to English weather. "I think he suffered desperately from the cold at Chequers," Mary said. "It's a great big Elizabethan house and we all found it fairly cold. But I think Harry Hopkins must have thought it was the North Pole and, poor man, we discovered in the end he used to take refuge in the downstairs bathroom where all the hot pipes ran through. He found it very convenient to sit in there in his overcoat reading all the official papers." His health was an issue, but one he seemed to pay little attention to. "Hopkins never seemed to eat anything," Pamela Churchill recalled. "He would have a Scotch." He seemed, Pamela said, "small, shrunken, sick. . . . This large overcoat over this small man and always kind of a dead cigarette out of the side of his mouth, looking sort of like a very sad dog." But duty drove him. "Then his face would light up and he would start talking about the war, and his purposes for being there and FDR and the whole man would change," Pamela said. "He became very determined, very strong. He was an extraordinary contrast. If you just came into a room and saw him sitting there, you would feel sorry for him. But if you heard him talk, you would listen with great respect."

Another side of his character—the shrewd observer—was evident as he composed a letter to Roosevelt.

Dear Mr. President—

   . . . *Churchill* is the gov't in every sense of the word—he controls the grand strategy and often the details—labor trusts him— the army, navy, air force are behind him to a man. The politicians and upper crust pretend to like him. I cannot emphasize too strongly that he is the one and only person over here with whom you need to have a full meeting of minds.

   Churchill wants to see you—the sooner the better—but I have told him of your problem until the bill is passed. I am convinced this meeting between you and Churchill is essential—and soon—for the battering continues and Hitler does not wait for Congress.

   I was with Churchill at 2 A.M. Sunday night when he got word of the loss of the

Southampton—the serious damage to the new aircraft carrier [*Illustrious*]—a second cruiser knocked about—but he never falters or displays the least despondence—till four o'clock he paced the floor telling me of his offensive and defensive plans.

I cannot believe that it is true that Churchill dislikes either you or America—it just doesn't make sense.

Churchill is prepared for a set back in Greece—the African campaign will proceed favorably—German bombers in the Mediterranean make the fleet's operation more difficult—convoys must all go around the Cape. An invasion they feel sure can be repelled—Churchill thinks it will not come soon but Beaverbrook and others think it will come and soon.

This island needs our help now Mr. President with everything we can give them.

There is no time to be out of London so I am staying here—the bombs aren't nice and seem to be quite impersonal. I have been offered a so called bomb proof apartment by Churchill—a tin hat and gas mask have been delivered—the best I can say for the hat is that it looks worse than my own and doesn't fit—the gas mask I can't get on—so I am alright.

There is much to tell but it will have to wait—for I must be off to Charing Cross.

                   Harry

Hopkins would always be wary of British political and economic imperialism, but on the question of the war, Churchill had won his man.

Roosevelt was pleased with the mission, in no small part because he believed that, across the fog of battle, he had picked the right envoy for the job. Churchill, Beaverbrook once said, "was not a sinner but he liked the company of sinners." Hopkins loved being around the rich and the glamorous. "One of the things he always did with those people was say this kind of thing: 'Oh, you blankety-blank rich!'" recalled Marquis Childs. "Still, he liked the champagne and he liked the diamonds." Hopkins very much liked Clementine, whom he found "the most charming and entertaining of all the people that he met." The feeling was mutual. "My mother, who was quite a critical person, and wasn't at all prone to naturally take to people at first sight, was captivated by him," Mary said. Clementine's innate sense of hospitality was part of the reason. "She realized how frail he was and took pains when he came to

visit to make sure he had what he needed,"
Mary recalled. But Hopkins and Clementine
also shared an appreciation of candor that probably provided common ground: Hopkins's
bluntness led Churchill to refer to him as "Lord
Root of the Matter."

CHURCHILL AND HOPKINS took a train
trip north through Scotland to Scapa Flow to
see Lord Halifax off to Washington. As the train
moved through the country, Churchill would
introduce Hopkins as "the personal representative of the President of the United States of
America."

At a dinner one evening, Hopkins stood and
said: "I suppose you wish to know what I am
going to say to President Roosevelt on my
return. Well, I'm going to quote you one verse
from that Book of Books . . . : 'Whither thou
goest, I will go; and where thou lodgest, I will
lodge: thy people shall be my people, and thy
God my God.' " Then, quietly: "Even to the
end."

Churchill wept. "He knew what it meant,"
Lord Moran, his doctor, wrote. "Even to us the
words seemed like a rope thrown to a drowning
man." Churchill long remembered Hopkins's
kindness. "His was a soul that flamed out of a

frail and failing body," Churchill wrote later. "He was a crumbling lighthouse from which shone the beams that led great fleets to harbour."

Hopkins returned the sentiment. After a long night with Churchill, Hopkins sat by a fire, so entranced by his host that he could only say, "Jesus Christ! What a man!"

IT WAS SNOWING when Churchill and Hopkins went to Chequers on Saturday, January 18. In a letter home, Eric Seal, Churchill's principal private secretary, wrote that Hopkins "is really a very charming and interesting man. Winston has taken to him enormously. Tonight . . . we rang up the President—and the Prime Minister spoke to him. He started off 'Mr President—it's me—Winston speaking'!!"

On January 19, Wendell Willkie, who was to leave for England the next day, stopped by the White House. As he chatted with Willkie, Roosevelt wrote out a verse from memory of Henry Wadsworth Longfellow's "The Building of the Ship" to take to Churchill:

Dear Churchill,

Wendell Willkie will give you this. He is truly helping to keep politics out over here.

I think this verse applies to your people as it does to us.

Sail on, O Ship of State!
Sail on, O Union, strong and great!
Humanity with all its fears,
With all the hopes of future years,
Is hanging breathless on thy fate!

As ever yours,
Franklin D. Roosevelt

In Washington, Charles Lindbergh was testifying against Lend-Lease. When it came to Hitler's Europe, Lindbergh said, he did not think it "possible for either America or Europe to invade the other successfully by air, or even by a combination of air, land, and sea, unless an internal collapse precedes invasion." For his part, he preferred "to see neither side win" and "would like to see a negotiated peace." Two days later, on Friday, Churchill and Hopkins went to Dover, where Hopkins told Churchill he had overheard a workman say to another as Churchill went by: "There goes the bloody British Empire." That pleased Churchill. "Winston's face wreathed itself in smiles and, turning to me, he lisped, '*Very* nice,'" wrote Colville. "I don't think anything has given him such pleasure for a long time." (Churchill's grandson Winston related a similar story. Three months later, Averell Harriman and Churchill were touring a bomb-ravaged area of Bristol. As cheering locals surrounded them, Harriman, having been told that Churchill was hard of hearing, remarked to Lord Ismay, "Isn't it wonderful how all the old ladies love the P.M.?" Overhearing, Churchill growled: "It isn't just the old ones.")

At midnight at Chequers on January 24, Churchill and Hopkins adjourned to Colville's office to talk. One topic: Churchill's opposition to cutting a deal with the Third Reich. "Never give in," Churchill said, "and you will never regret it." A negotiated peace "would be a German victory and leave open the way for another and final 'spring of the Tiger' in a few years' time. Hopkins agreed and said that Lindbergh, and others in America who favor a negotiated peace, really desired a German victory. The P.M. wound up by saying that after the last war he had been asked to provide an inscription for a French war memorial. His suggestion, which was rejected, had been: 'In war fury, in defeat defiance, in victory magnanimity, in peace good will.' "

Churchill's conquest of Hopkins was important but not conclusive. He knew Roosevelt was his real quarry—and that Roosevelt would come along only as American opinion warmed to Churchill and the British.

———

SPEAKING ON THE radio the next day, Churchill had a complex task: reassure Americans that the British were strong but not so strong that they could overcome Hitler without aid.

> We must all of us have been asking ourselves: What has that wicked man whose crime-stained regime and system are at bay and in the toils—what has he been preparing during these winter months? What new devilry is he planning? What new small country will he overrun or strike down? What fresh form of assault will he make upon our Island home and fortress; which—let there be no mistake about it—is all that stands between him and the dominion of the world?

He told the audience about Roosevelt's Longfellow quotation and read it out. Then:

> What is the answer that I shall give, in your name, to this great man, the thrice-chosen head of a nation of a hundred and thirty millions? Here is the answer which I will give to President Roosevelt: Put your confidence in us. Give us your faith and your blessing, and, under Providence, all will be well.

We shall not fail or falter; we shall not weaken or tire. Neither the sudden shock of battle, nor the long-drawn trials of vigilance and exertion will wear us down. Give us the tools, and we will finish the job.

HOPKINS'S CAPTIVATION WITH Churchill was clear, and it soon infected Roosevelt. Over a lunch of corned beef hash, poached eggs, and chocolate pudding in the Cabinet Room after Hopkins returned, Roosevelt was working on a speech for the White House Correspondents Association dinner. According to Sherwood, Hopkins "suggested that, since Churchill had made so many respectful references to Roosevelt in his speeches, perhaps the President might care to mention him. So Roosevelt dictated, 'In this historic crisis, Britain is blessed with a brilliant leader in Winston Churchill.' He thought that over for a moment, then added, 'Make that "a brilliant and a *great* leader." ' "

They were suddenly a long way from the grudging remark, made less than a year before in that very room, that Roosevelt "supposed" Churchill was "the best man" England had.

In these months—from January to March—American military planners were also meeting secretly with the British and produced strategic recommendations in line with previous American thought: that in the event of U.S. entry into the conflict, the defeat of Germany and Italy, along with control of the Atlantic, would be the primary goal; the Allies would fight a more defensive war in the Pacific.

Roosevelt won the Lend-Lease vote on February 8, 1941. Hopkins tried to reach Churchill on the telephone, but Churchill was asleep. Hopkins left a message and wrote Churchill: "I find my thoughts constantly with you in the desperate struggle which I am sure is going to result, in the last analysis, in your victory." Churchill was grateful, replying: "Thank God for your news. Strain is serious." To Roosevelt, Churchill cabled: "Our blessings from the whole of the British Empire go out to you and the American nation for this very present help in time of trouble." In his heart, however, Churchill knew this was not enough. "Far more was needed," he said later, "but we did our best."

Churchill and Roosevelt now shared something personal: faith in Hopkins and his judgment. "The President knew his man and sent the right man to the right place at the right time," Pamela Churchill said. "Hopkins had that extraordinary ability to make WSC feel Hopkins was working for him at the same time he was working for FDR" and could translate "Roosevelt into language that Churchill would understand." By fits and starts, Roosevelt and Churchill were moving ever closer. Because of Hopkins, Pamela recalled, when Roosevelt and Churchill got together, they were "able to meet as old friends."

"We are Christian soldiers, and we will go on, with God's help"

Roosevelt and Churchill at a church service aboard HMS Prince of Wales, August 10, 1941

CHAPTER 4

LUNCHING ALONE BROKE THE ICE

A Secret Meeting at Sea–Churchill and Roosevelt
Hit It Off–America Enters the War

A T A NO. 10 Downing Street lunch in March 1941 with James B. Conant, the president of Harvard, and Clementine, Churchill sat and listened as Conant said, "it was unfortunate that so many people in America were anxious to keep America out of the War at any cost because they took the view that 'nothing is worse than war.' " Hearing this, recalled Charles Eade, a fellow guest, "Mr. Churchill snapped in his best radio manner, 'Slavery is worse than war. Dishonour is worse than war.' "

Eloquent as always, but the prime minister's message was still failing to bring the United States fully into the conflict, and the Germans were having a fine time in the field in the spring of 1941. Churchill may have stymied Hitler, at least for the time being, in the skies over Britain, but Berlin continued to seize territory, capturing or cutting deals with Yugoslavia, Hungary, Bulgaria, and Greece. In North Africa, German General Erwin Rommel was scoring victories in Libya. Americans were producing three times as many combat munitions as they had been in 1940, but the total was still less than Germany's and Britain's. In Washington, Roosevelt decided it was time to sit down with Churchill.

"I was faced with a practical problem of extreme difficulty," Roosevelt later wrote in a private memorandum. He wanted to effect a clandestine session with Churchill off Newfoundland in August 1941 to, as Roosevelt put it, "talk over the problem of the defeat of Germany." Confidentiality was key for both security and politics. "It was constantly emphasized, both in London and Washington, that the utmost secrecy before and during the trip was essential," Roosevelt recalled. "This was, of course, obvious because the Prime Minister would traverse, both going and returning from Newfoundland, long distances in dangerous waters—the danger being from bombing planes, heavy raiders and submarines." Roosevelt also wanted to keep his critics quiet until the meeting was over. The United States was still neutral, and after Lend-Lease, the last thing he needed was to hand the isolationists something else to use against him.

Roosevelt took matters into his own hands, telling reporters he might take a cruise on the USS *Potomac* in Maine "to get some cool nights" that summer. "This," Roosevelt recalled with a touch of boys' adventure novel prose, "became the basis for the plan of escape."

Hopkins was the conduit to Churchill. Roosevelt dispatched his aide to England, where he landed with ham, cheese, and cigars for the Churchills. "Harry Hopkins came into the garden of Downing Street and we sat together in the sunshine," Churchill recalled. "Presently he said that the President would like very much to have a meeting with me in some lonely bay or other." Churchill jumped at the chance. That night, he and Hopkins spoke to Roosevelt on the telephone, and, Churchill said, "thus all was soon arranged." Churchill was eager to get on with it.

Roosevelt kept Eleanor in the dark, to the extent that his main communication with his wife in the run-up to the meeting was a "Memorandum for Mrs. Roosevelt" from Grace Tully that read: "The President asked me to check on your operator's license for New York State and on his also. . . . I have been in touch with the Bureau of Motor Vehicles and have been informed that both you and the President renewed yours at the beginning of this year."

Roosevelt did, however, tell his cousin Margaret "Daisy" Suckley, writing her: "Even at my ripe old age, I feel a thrill in making a getaway—especially from the American press." That he took Daisy into his confidence is revealing. Suckley is an intriguing figure in the Roosevelt world, one whose full significance became clear only after the biographer Geoffrey Ward edited and published excerpts from her diary and letters in 1995. A remote cousin of Roosevelt's, Suckley, a spinster obsessed with dogs, health, and Franklin Roosevelt—not necessarily in that order—was part of the genteel Hudson Valley squirearchy. Roosevelt enjoyed Daisy's quiet company, and there was apparently no romantic connection between the two. He liked having her around as an audience and a caretaker, and Daisy adored the man she often referred to in her diary as "the P." or "F."

"We always thought of him as a friend of our aunt's; we never talked about it," recalled Margaret Hendrick, Daisy's niece. "We did not want my aunt's friendship with him broadcast around. That just wasn't done. We underplayed everything. There was no great romance between them or anything; they both came from the Hudson River and liked spending time together, that's all."

Suckley's documents were found under her bed at Wilderstein, her Dutchess County house, after she died in 1991, and Ward prepared them for publication. Daisy thought of Roosevelt as the savior of the world—a view he did not vigorously reject—and worried about his health. "I don't want to harp *on* one string always," she wrote him in July 1941, "but *please* remember that you are going to be needed *more & more* with every passing month. *And still* more when the period of reconstruction comes!"

ON SUNDAY, JUNE 22, 1941, Germany invaded the Soviet Union. Having abandoned SEA LION for the time being, Hitler, who despised Bolsheviks—he blamed them, as well as the Jews, for Germany's defeat in World War I—believed that he could conquer the Soviet Union. Churchill rushed to make an alliance with his former foes. "No one has been a more consistent opponent of Communism than I have for the last twenty-five years," he said that Sunday evening. "I will unsay no word that I have spoken about it. But all this fades away before the spectacle which is now unfolding. The past, with its crimes, its follies, and its tragedies, flashes away."

Roosevelt said little about the invasion, puzzling over what to do. It was conceivable, he thought, that Stalin's stand against Germany might mean the United States could afford to stay out—a decision that would further frustrate Churchill. Nancy Astor wrote Agnes Meyer: "I pray America won't let the Huns wipe out Russia and so make our job five times as bad."

With Stalin as an unexpected ally, Hopkins flew from Britain to Moscow to size up the Soviet dictator. Churchill arranged for transportation. Weary, Hopkins arrived in Moscow on a sunny, warm day. "He looked very frail, weak, pale," recalled Valentin Berezhkov, a Stalin interpreter. Hopkins found Stalin steely but cooperative, which made sense: Russia needed its own version of Lend-Lease and, ultimately, a Second Front. A onetime seminary student who had become a brutal ruler, Stalin had gambled on Germany and lost. Betrayed by one ally, Stalin would be a wary figure in the trinity of leaders. "No man could forget the picture of the dictator of Russia," said Hopkins, "an austere, rugged, determined figure in boots that shone like mirrors, stout baggy trousers, and snug-fitting blouse. He wore no ornament, military or civilian. He's built close to the ground, like a football coach's dream of a tackle. He's about five feet six, about a hundred and ninety pounds. His hands are huge, as hard as his mind. His voice is harsh but ever under control."

Stalin's demands during the war—for Lend-Lease supplies and delivery, for a Second Front to help him in his blood-soaked battles against the Germans, for present and future concessions of territory and influence—affected the Roosevelt–Churchill alliance throughout the conflict. Stalin often seemed to believe he was doing most if not all of the real fighting (the Soviets would lose about 12,000,000 soldiers, compared to about 400,000 for Great Britain and about 300,000 for the United States). And there was the fear in London and in Washington that Stalin might fold, by either losing to Hitler or, under pressure, striking another separate peace. He was a man who had to be heeded—or, at the very least, handled with extreme care.

IN A SPEECH to the House of Commons on July 29, 1941, Churchill said the United States "is giving us aid on a gigantic scale and is advancing in rising wrath and conviction to the very verge of war." In a session with reporters in Washington the same day, Roosevelt was asked: "What do you think of Mr. Churchill's statement that the United States is on the verge of war?"

"Haven't read it."

"If you *had* read it?"

"If I had read it?" Roosevelt laughed.

"What was your answer, Mr. President?"

"That I hadn't read it."

"That's what he said, Mr. President."

"What?"

"That's what he did say."

". . . Try another one. I am afraid—I am afraid this heat's got you people here in Washington. It's bad. . . . Up in Hyde Park we had a grand time—lots of news and nice cool weather. Haven't any of you got any questions for me? Did you say 'Thank you, Mr. President,' Earl?" Roosevelt concluded with a laugh, teasing the reporter Earl Godwin, who traditionally closed conferences with those words.

Grace Tully, who had also been kept out of the loop about Newfoundland, thought Roosevelt was looking forward to "a nice quiet cruise . . . while catching 'the first fish,' 'the biggest fish,' and 'the most fish,' which was the way the betting ran aboard the Presidential yacht." The trip began at eleven in the morning on Sunday, August 3, when Roosevelt rode by train from Union Station to New London, Connecticut, where he boarded the *Potomac*. It was still light out when he transferred to the yacht, and, Roosevelt said, "many persons saw me and we stood out of the harbor into the Sound in full view of thousands, my Presidential flag flying from the main top." He told reporters that he would be spending the next few days fishing.

LET THE PROUD author of the plot explain
what happened next: "Strange thing happened
this morning—suddenly found ourselves transferred with all our baggage & mess crew from
the little 'Potomac' to the Great Big Cruiser
'Augusta'!" Roosevelt wrote Daisy. "And then,
the Island of Martha's Vineyard disappeared in
the distance, and as we head out into the
Atlantic all we can see is our protecting escort, a
heavy cruiser and four destroyers. Curiously
enough the Potomac still flies my flag & tonight
will be seen by thousands as she passes quietly
through the Cape Cod Canal, guarded on shore
by Secret Service and State Troopers while in
fact the Pres. will be about 250 miles away." Its
master safely—and secretly—in the hands of the
navy, the *Potomac* returned to the coast to
resume the previously announced cruise. In
what Roosevelt thought was a "delightful
story," the yacht's crewmen dressed up as the
president and his party and sat on deck.

To his wife, who was at Hyde Park, he maintained the fiction that he was fishing, routing a
message through Press Secretary Steve Early:
"The President sends word all well on boat and
getting real rest. Weather excellent." And he
left a bulletin to be released to the press in a few

days: "From USS Potomac," it read. "All members of party showing effects of sunning. Fishing luck good. No destination announced. President being kept in close touch international situation by navy radio. All on board well."

HOPKINS ARRIVED FROM Moscow to sail with Churchill, who cabled Roosevelt:

Harry returned dead beat from Russia but is lively again now. We shall get him in fine trim on the voyage. We are just off. It is 27 years ago today that the Huns began their last war. We all must make a good job of it this time. Twice ought to be enough. Look forward so much to our meeting. Kindest regards.

Churchill was thinking constantly of the encounter with Roosevelt, "planning all the details of the entertainment of the other fellow," John Martin noted, "ordering grouse, ordering turtle and ordering a band." This was his chance to shine. "I hope we shall have an interesting and enjoyable voyage," Churchill said to H. V. Morton, a writer whom Brendan Bracken had sent to record the events.

Then, Morton remembered, "with the slight hesitation and change of voice which are so effective on the radio," Churchill added, "And one not entirely without profit."

ONE NIGHT, CHURCHILL watched *Lady Hamilton,* a Vivien Leigh–Laurence Olivier movie about Lord Nelson and his affair with a diplomat's wife set during Britain's struggle to survive the Napoleonic wars. "Winston Churchill was completely absorbed in the story," Morton wrote. The tale of romance and war was a perfect diversion—and, Mary Soames recalled, Churchill found Vivien Leigh "ravishing."

"I have, my lords, in different countries, seen much of the miseries of war," Olivier-as-Nelson says in a scene in the House of Lords. "I am, therefore, in my inmost soul, a man of peace. Yet I would not for the sake of any peace, however fortunate, consent to sacrifice one chance of England's honor." Cut to Trafalgar, on October 21, 1805. Nelson issues the order Churchill had heard about at Harrow—"England expects that every man will do his duty"—and as the signals spell out the message, the camera stirringly captures the faces of ordinary sailors getting the word. When a French sniper wounds Nelson— fatally, as it turns out—he orders his officers to "cover my face, the decorations—no time for the men to see me like this." He is carried below, and as the end nears, he is told that he has won.

"Sir, sir . . . a great victory!" an officer tells him. "Thank God," Olivier whispers hoarsely. "I have done my duty." The admiral then dies. At that moment, Morton wrote, "the man who was watching so intently took a handkerchief from his pocket and wiped his eyes without shame." Cadogan thought the movie "quite good" and noted: "P.M., seeing it for 5th time, moved to tears." His imagination burning bright and eager to woo Roosevelt face-to-face, Churchill told the group: "Gentlemen, I thought this film would interest you, showing great events similar to those in which you have been taking part." He ended the night playing backgammon with Hopkins, who later told friends: "You'd have thought Winston was being carried up into the heavens to meet God!"

JUST AFTER DAWN on Saturday, August 9, Churchill appeared in his siren suit on the admiral's bridge of the *Prince of Wales*. "Can you see any sign of them yet?" Churchill asked Morton, who was already up and on the bridge. Churchill could not wait for the action to begin. "It was an interesting glimpse of him, and if in the future an historian wishes to describe him at that moment, he must picture the grey ship stained with the seas, striped with camouflage, her guns pointing forward in the stillness of the morning; no one about but a few sailors at their stations, and no sound but the hiss of water against her plates as she steamed through the quiet sea," Morton wrote. "High on the Admiral's Bridge, not in the steel and plate-glass bridge itself, but on the outside plat-form, stood Churchill on the eve of his mission. Just out of bed, his sandy hair still ruffled from the pillow, he stood watching the sea that stretched to the New World."

Churchill returned below, emerging in a dark blue uniform, which he liked to wear on naval occasions, a white handkerchief in his breast pocket. Aboard the *Augusta,* Roosevelt was being dressed in a suit. Two of his sons, Elliott and Franklin Jr., happened to be in that part of the Atlantic, and Roosevelt summoned them to the *Augusta.* At eleven A.M., Churchill crossed the bay to the *Augusta.* After the national anthems were played, Churchill approached Roosevelt, who stood leaning on Elliott's arm.

Getting there had not been easy. "The Boss insisted upon returning to the painful prison of his braces," recalled Mike Reilly. "He hated and mistrusted those braces, but it was a historic occasion and he meant to play his part as much as his limbs would permit. Even the slight pitch of the *Augusta* meant pain and the possibility of a humiliating fall." But Roosevelt would stand to greet his guest, and that was that.

With what Morton called "a slight bow," Churchill presented Roosevelt with a letter from George VI. Roosevelt charmed Churchill with what the prime minister called "the warmest of welcomes." As their hands met, Roosevelt said: "At last—we've gotten together." With a nod, Churchill replied: "We have."

Patrick Kinna, the Churchill stenographer who had brought the king's letter from London, watched the two men together. "There was a warmth there, on the deck, from the start," Kinna recalled.

ROOSEVELT AND CHURCHILL lunched together with Hopkins. The principals did not mirror each other exactly, but they understood each other. Bloodied by political wars, they had been shaped by the same events, though in different ways. Both had been influenced by progressive social-reform movements. Both had run, or helped to run, their nations' navies. Both had surpassed the men who had made their names great.

Hopkins saw why his boss and his new friend were getting along. "They were two men in the same line of business—politico-military leadership on a global scale—and theirs was a very limited field and the few who achieve it seldom have opportunities for getting together with fellow craftsmen in the same trade to compare notes and talk shop," Sherwood wrote. "They appraised each other through the practiced eyes of professionals and from this appraisal resulted a degree of admiration and sympathetic understanding of each other's professional problems that lesser craftsmen could not have achieved. . . . They had a large and wonderful capacity to stimulate and refresh each other."

In his memoirs, Churchill hinted at his professional admiration for Roosevelt. "I formed a very strong affection, which grew with our years of comradeship, for this formidable politician who had imposed his will for nearly ten years upon the American scene," wrote Churchill, "and whose heart seemed to respond to many of the impulses that stirred my own." They would compete with each other, but their jealousies were often—though not always—put to the side. The mission was the most important thing. They might not have felt that way if ultimate power had come to them in younger years. Certainly they did not click in 1918. Age and circumstance made connection easier.

There was one rough spot. Churchill said how delighted he was to meet Roosevelt for the first time, and Roosevelt corrected him, recalling the evening at Gray's Inn. "Papa completely forgot they had met before," Mary said. "He hadn't been warned or reminded, and it had just slipped his mind." Churchill's lapse annoyed Roosevelt, and in his memoirs, Churchill went out of his way to cover up the fact that he had not remembered the 1918 encounter, writing: "I had met him only once in the previous war. It was at a dinner at Gray's Inn, and I had been struck by his magnificent presence in all his youth and strength." He knew Roosevelt's kind. "Most Americans," Churchill wrote in his biography of his father, were "proud as the devil." It was important that both Churchill and Roosevelt learn to let hard words pass by. "Many men with so many grave and at times conflicting problems to settle would get their backs up about something and thereafter find it difficult to work together," recalled Roosevelt naval aide Wilson Brown, "but fortunately for us all, both Roosevelt and Churchill were adept at give and take."

ALL IN ALL, they fell in together very quickly. In those first hours, Elliott Roosevelt, who wrote a 1946 book about the wartime conferences that had a pro-Russian, anti-British tone but still offers a window on those sessions, observed that "it didn't take them long, talking about their correspondence, their transatlantic phone conversations, their health, their jobs and their worries, to be calling each other 'Franklin' and 'Winston.' "

Eager to find out how he had done with Roosevelt, Churchill later asked Averell Harriman, who had gone to London as an envoy after Hopkins's initial visit: "Does he like me?" The prime minister's first audition with the demanding Roosevelt had in fact gone well. "He is a tremendously vital person & in many ways is an English Mayor La Guardia!" Roosevelt confided to Daisy. "Don't say I said so! I like him—& lunching alone broke the ice both ways." And Roosevelt wanted to make sure he had charmed his visitor, asking aides: "What did *he* think of me?"

CHURCHILL RETURNED TO the *Prince of Wales* after lunch. Hopkins had sent over a note: "I have just talked to the President and he is very anxious, after dinner tonight, to invite in the balance of the staff and wants to ask you to talk very informally to them about your general appreciation of the war, and indeed to say anything that you would be disposed to say." That day, Inspector Thompson noticed a red leather bookmark Churchill had been using that bore the inscription "Ask and it shall be given you. Seek and you shall find." Picking it up, Thompson said, "That might be a good omen for the conference you are going to start, sir."

"I hope it will be," Churchill said, "for I have much to ask."

Whatever combination of factors drove Churchill—to find the means to win the war, the urge to please his father, to play his part as a hero like Marlborough, to make history—he was in the crucible, and the rest of us now know that he was succeeding at a level and to a degree beyond anything his venerated forebears accomplished. But he could not have grasped this as he dressed for dinner. He was only at the start, not even at the middle, let alone the end of the journey to the bittersweet glory of May 1945.

THERE WERE FAMILY frets. As Mary remembered it, 1941 had been a difficult year in the Churchills' private lives. Duncan Sandys, Diana's husband, was injured in an automobile accident; Sarah's marriage to the actor Vic Oliver collapsed; Goonie Churchill, the wife of Churchill's brother Jack, died of cancer, which shook Clementine. "Goonie had been her loyal and almost only confidante in the dark and troubled days of the Dardanelles crisis," Mary wrote.

Then Mary herself complicated the picture, if

only briefly. Writing in a charming way about it years later, she recalled: "I managed to cause a diversion on the domestic front, when I somewhat precipitately became engaged in May to an intelligent, charming, and entirely suitable young man whom, however, I knew very slightly. From the very first my mother was convinced that I was not really in love at all. . . . My mother not unnaturally did not relish bearing the whole responsibility for intervening in this delicate matter, and running the risk of being thereafter accused of 'wrecking my whole life.' But my father was totally preoccupied with events of national importance, and so my mother had to grapple with this emotional situation herself."

The family worries, the war work, and a bout of bronchitis were wearing Clementine down. "Since the beginning of the war she had had no holiday, merely an odd weekend here or there and occasionally a day or afternoon spent at Chartwell," Mary wrote. "It was not easy, however, for her to find a suitable moment to 'ease up,' and she hated the idea of leaving Winston, even for a week, in these hard and anxious days." The meeting with Roosevelt provided the perfect opportunity: Clementine slipped away for a rest cure while Churchill went to Newfoundland. "I have massage, osteopathy hot & cold showers etc. etc.—but nothing to eat so far but tomato juice & pineapple juice," she wrote her husband. "This is the fourth day & I am beginning to feel rested so that when you come home you should find a completely renovated (if not rejuvenated) cat."

Across the bay, Roosevelt may also have been thinking of home. An urgent item was Sara Roosevelt's health. She was eighty-six and spending what would be her last summer at Campobello. Confirming Trude Lash's observation that Eleanor spent more time with Sara than Roosevelt did, Eleanor had driven her mother-in-law up from Hyde Park herself, "worried about her because she did not seem very strong."

Time was running out that August, and the family knew Roosevelt would suffer when the inevitable happened. There was, James Roosevelt recalled, "a timeless permanence about her that made it even more of a shock when she died. Though Father often chafed and bridled under her efforts to treat him as if he were still the little boy she had raised with such fierce, almost consuming adoration, Father loved her dearly and sincerely."

SARA WOULD HAVE been proud—if not surprised, for she expected great things from her boy—that her Franklin was dining that evening with the prime minister of Great Britain. At a quarter to seven, Churchill and his party returned to the *Augusta* as Roosevelt's guests. "I had never met a person of the President's distinction who showed such apparently real interest in one's own replies to his questions," said Commander C. R. "Tommy" Thompson, Churchill's naval aide-de-camp—a sign that Roosevelt, who was a genius at charming others when he put his mind to it, was thoroughly engaged in the moment.

During the meal, the talk ranged from Roosevelt's chitchat about Hyde Park—he told his guests he hoped to raise Christmas trees for market—to Japan. Roosevelt also indicated, Cadogan said, that he "might be prepared to make a joint Anglo-American Declaration of Principles."

When dessert was cleared and Churchill prepared to speak, Elliott Roosevelt noticed something different about his father. "At dinner, and afterwards, too, as the evening wore on toward midnight, I saw Father in a new role," he wrote. "My experience of him in the past had been that he dominated every gathering he was part of; not because he insisted on it so much as that it always seemed his natural due." But for once Roosevelt ceded center stage to someone else. "Tonight," Elliott said, "Father listened."

Churchill was worth listening to. "His conversation was like that of Macaulay or Lord Curzon: it erred no doubt on the side of copious monologue," Lord Chandos recalled. "When the sails started to draw, the great ship, with every stitch of canvas set, heeled over to the wind and ploughed through the waves: the rigging sang and the spray broke unheeded over the prow. The listener had the vivid impression that he was living at a time of great human struggle or, to change the image, stood upon some battlefield at a turning point in history." On Churchill sailed, telling the tale of the war he had first spun for Hopkins in the winter. Cadogan was arch about Churchill's monologue—"not his best," was the verdict—but even lukewarm, Churchill was powerful.

"Churchill told us, in effect, that this was a mechanized war, not a war of 1917–18 where doughboys in the mud and trenches fought it out to a conclusion," recalled U.S. Army Air Forces General H. H. "Hap" Arnold. "This was a mobile war, in the air, on the land, and at sea. It was a scientific war where mechanized equipment was used to an extent never dreamed of before."

As Churchill spoke, he was articulating a strategy that held political appeal for Roosevelt, who was still struggling at home with the idea of sending another army across the sea. If the Americans could protect the lines of supply in the North Atlantic and, Arnold recalled, "give Britain material aid in personnel, ships, tanks, and antiaircraft," Churchill had a sense of what he would do to take the war to the Axis. "He said the British needed bombers to bring home to the Germans the horrors of war, just as the Germans had brought it home to the British," Arnold recalled. Churchill would go on the offensive. "He pointed out that British policies from now on would be to attack the Germans at all points; that in the areas where the Germans had long-extended lines of communication the British would meet them on even terms. By constant hammering, it was possible to prevent the German army from spreading out any further, and the British attacks should ultimately aid in breaking Germany's morale."

Roosevelt was impressed, telling Daisy the evening was "very grand. . . . A very good party & the 'opposite numbers' are getting to know each other."

Roosevelt and Churchill parted until morning.

"WE HAVE A grand day for a church parade, and I have chosen some grand hymns," Churchill said to H. V. Morton early the next day.

"The PM had given much thought to the

preparations for this Service (which he said should be fully choral and fully photographic), choosing the hymns . . . and vetting the prayers (which I had to read to him while he dried after his bath)," recalled John Martin. Roosevelt and Churchill would sit; their top officers and advisers, including Hopkins, would stand behind them. From a lectern decorated with the Union Jack and the Stars and Stripes, the chaplains would read the prayers. Nervously awaiting Roosevelt, "Mr. Churchill walked about inspecting every detail," Morton wrote, "often taking a hand by moving a chair an inch one way or another and by pulling out the folds of the Union Jack."

Roosevelt was thinking of his own performance. A memorandum written for Commander Thompson by John Beardall, Roosevelt's naval aide, reveals the care with which the presidential staff anticipated Roosevelt's every move. Every modern White House is fussy about "advance," but Roosevelt's paralysis added a poignant element of urgency to the planning. A tumble would not be fatal (unless, bizarrely, Roosevelt were to fall into the sea, where his braces might pull him under too quickly to be rescued), but one would be gravely embarrassing, particularly on an occasion of state like this one. "The President will embark in U.S.S. McDOUGAL at 1030," Beardall wrote.

"McDOUGAL will proceed alongside H.M.S. PRINCE OF WALES, bow to stern, McDOUGAL starboard side to starboard side with PRINCE OF WALES. Using PRINCE OF WALES crane, brow will be swung from McDOUGAL to PRINCE OF WALES, and the President will proceed on board."

Thinking past the service, Beardall wrote: "After the pictures have been taken, the President will inspect the top side in his wheelchair, and I understand ramps will be provided to facilitate this." Then a point put briefly but unmistakably: "For your information, the President is never photographed when walking, or in his wheelchair. However, it is perfectly all right to take pictures when he is standing still or sitting in a large chair." Appearances were important, and the actor in Roosevelt knew how to manage his audience.

ROOSEVELT'S SHIP CAME alongside. Roosevelt clutched Elliott's arm and, with his other hand on the rail of the gangway, walked painful step by painful step toward a waiting Churchill. He was determined not to use his chair as he called on Churchill and the men of the *Prince of Wales*. As soon as he reached the deck, the Royal Marines played the national anthem, and Roosevelt caught his breath. He tried, as always, to conceal the effort walking took, and it worked. Tommy Thompson noticed that "only the tenseness of his grip on the rail betrayed the strain he was undergoing." Morton thought he saw a "calm, carved face, the face of a St. George who has trampled the dragon under him."

Roosevelt then turned to the next steps of his journey—from the rail to his designated seat on the quarterdeck. Summoning his strength, Roosevelt, Churchill by his side, forced himself toward his chair near the lectern. There would have been a slight thud against the deck as Roosevelt, still balanced by Elliott, willed his paralyzed legs forward, his cane in his other hand. Sensitive to his guest's affliction, Churchill realized that "every step" was "causing him pain." "I shall always remember the look on his face," recalled Howard Spring, another of Brendan Bracken's writers. "Every muscle seemed to express his determination to complete that short walk on his own, and when he reached his chair he beamed with triumph." Roosevelt would tell Daisy with pride that he had been "received with 'honors,' inspected the guard & walked aft to the quarter deck." *Walked* was an important word to him. He trusted Daisy so much that, in more deprecating and darker moments, he referred to his efforts at moving without a wheelchair as "stumping." But not today: Today, he thought he had walked, and that pleased him. He had risen to the occasion.

TOGETHER, ROOSEVELT AND Churchill sat down, and the company sang the first hymn.

> O God, our help in ages past,
> Our hope for years to come,
> Our shelter from the stormy blast,
> And our eternal home. . . .

As Churchill had hoped, the Americans and the British were, as he later wrote, "completely intermingled" as they sang. "Every word seemed to stir the heart."

The service—a moved Roosevelt called it the "keynote" of his meeting with Churchill—was working a kind of magic, which is one of the points of liturgy and theater: to use the dramatic to convince people of a reality they cannot see. "In the long, frightful panorama of this war, a panorama full of guns and tanks crushing the life out of men, of women and children weeping and of homes blasted into rubble by bombs," Morton wrote, "there had been no scene like this, a scene, it seemed, from another world, conceived on lines different from anything known to the pageant-masters of the Axis, a scene rooted in the first principles of

European civilization which go back to the figure of Charlemagne kneeling before the Pope
on Christmas morning."

The chaplains led the reading of the General
Confession and of the Lord's Prayer, words that
in believers often trigger memories of where
they first learned them and have most frequently repeated them. Churchill could have
thought of Harrow. Roosevelt's mind may have
roamed back to St. James's in Hyde Park or to
the chapel at Groton where Dr. Peabody read
the rite—images of a world, Roosevelt's world,
that he would most want to protect from harm.

The second hymn began.

> Onward, Christian soldiers,
> Marching as to war,
> With the cross of Jesus
> Going on before!
> Christ, the Royal Master,
> Leads against the foe;
> Forward into battle,
> See, his banners go. . . .

Churchill was weeping and took a handkerchief
from his pocket. There was a reading from the
Book of Joshua. A few of the verses that rang
out across the deck: ". . . as I was with Moses, so
I will be with thee: I will not fail thee, nor for-
sake thee. Be strong and of good courage: for

unto this people shalt thou divide for an inheritance the land, which I swore unto their fathers to give them. . . . Have I not commanded thee? Be strong and of a good courage; be not afraid: for the Lord thy God is with thee whithersoever thou goest." More prayers followed, including this one: "Stablish our hearts, O God, in the day of battle, and strengthen our resolve, that we fight, not in enmity against men, but against the powers of darkness enslaving the souls of men; till all enmity and oppression be done away, and the peoples of the world be set free from fear to serve one another; as children of our Father, who above all and through all and in all, our God for ever and ever. Amen." A final hymn closed the service.

> Eternal Father, strong to save,
> Whose arm hath bound the restless wave,
> Who bidd'st the mighty ocean deep
> Its own appointed limits keep:
> O hear us when we cry to Thee
> For those in peril on the sea. . . .

"It was," Churchill said, "a great hour to live." To Elliott, the president said afterward: "If nothing else had happened while we were here, that would have cemented us. 'Onward, Christian Soldiers.' We *are,* and we *will* go on, with God's help." It had been worth the walk.

———

AS CAMERAS CLICKED, Roosevelt and Churchill smoked and indulged the ships' companies in posing for snapshots. "We were all photographed," Roosevelt told Daisy, "front, sides & rear!" Churchill was thrilled with the service. "When I looked upon that densely-packed congregation of fighting men of the same language, of the same faith, of the same fundamental laws and the same ideals, and now to a large extent of the same interests, and certainly in different degrees facing the same dangers," he said, "it swept across me that here was the only hope, but also the sure hope, of saving the world from measureless degradation."

Having proved his mettle before the service, Roosevelt shifted to his wheelchair for a tour of the ship; afterward they lunched, and Churchill made sure the menu included grouse, a treat for the game-loving Roosevelt. It was, Roosevelt told Daisy, a "beautiful" luncheon. Churchill had done well.

Roosevelt continued to impress the British. Cadogan found Roosevelt's informal conversational style "awfully good—just like his fireside chats."

As Churchill saw Roosevelt off, the ship's cat, Blackie, tried to follow the Americans back to the *Augusta*. Churchill scooped the cat up and

*"There seemed to be real friendship
& understanding between F.D.R.
and Churchill"*

Roosevelt with his distant cousin
Margaret "Daisy" Suckley, who was
frequently at the president's side
during the war years

saluted the departing Roosevelt. One of the officers who had enjoyed the grouse and good talk thanked Churchill.

"It's an honor for us all," Churchill replied. "And great things may come of it in the future. You have seen a great man this day." Yet he appeared to be churning inside as he tried to reconcile the goodwill of the time he was spending with Roosevelt with his feeling that the Americans might not take the plunge into war. "On this lovely day, the sun shining as it is on this beautiful harbor, surrounded as we are by American men of war," Churchill said to the officers, "it is difficult for you and me to realize that we are fighting for our very lives."

Then he was gone.

CHURCHILL FOUND HIMSELF restless. Trying to put his anxiety out of his mind, he went ashore in a whaler. "P.M. like a schoolboy and insisted on rolling boulders down a cliff," said Cadogan. The adventure was diverting, and Churchill snapped out of his worried humor. "A great load seemed to have been lifted off his mind," Inspector Thompson said.

That evening, Roosevelt told Daisy, was set aside for "dining Winston Churchill, his civilian aides & mine." There was a shift in tone from the previous night, probably the result of the fact that the two leaders were growing more comfortable with each other as they passed their fourth meal together. "You sensed that two men accustomed to leadership had sparred, had felt each other out, and were now readying themselves for outright challenge, each of the other," Elliott remembered. The future of the British empire came up.

The two disagreed, and would for the rest of the war, about colonialism. Roosevelt was a Wilsonian on the issue, believing, as had the president he had once served, in self-determination. Moreover, the progressive in Roosevelt wanted to ameliorate the conditions under which many colonial peoples lived. Churchill, of course, was to promise not to preside "over the liquidation of the British Empire," setting the stage for a long-running source of tension between the two men.

After dinner, Churchill introduced Inspector Thompson to Roosevelt. "Look after the Prime Minister," Roosevelt told Thompson. "He is one of the greatest men in the world."

Franklin Jr. accompanied Churchill back to the *Prince of Wales.* "Your father is a great man," Churchill said. "He has accomplished much. I am glad that our meeting has resulted in such understanding."

"My father," said FDR Jr., "is a very religious man, and has risen to great heights by his strength of character and determination."

"Your father is one of the greatest men of our day," Churchill said.

"Father was talking to me of you, and he said that Churchill—"

"No, no—Winston," Churchill interjected.

"—is the greatest statesman the world has ever known. I told my father, 'No, you and Mr. Churchill are the greatest men of the age, and together you can bring peace to the world.'" Even allowing for a son's affection and Churchill's hyperbole, the conversation is revealing in that it captures the warmth of the conversations at sea.

HOW DID CHURCHILL and Roosevelt see the possibilities for friendship? Churchill's vision was predictably grand. "I think of it in this way," Churchill had written of the idea of alliance in *Savrola*. "When the human race was emerging from the darkness of its origin and half-animal, half-human creatures trod the earth, there was no idea of justice, honesty, or virtue, only the motive power which we may call the 'will to live.' Then perhaps it was a minor peculiarity of some of these early ancestors of man to combine in twos and threes for their mutual protection. The first alliance was made; the combinations prospered where the isolated individuals failed. . . . Thus man became a social animal. Gradually the little societies became larger ones. From families to tribes, and from tribes to nations the species advanced, always finding that the better they combined, the better they succeeded. Now on what did this system of alliance depend? It depended on the members keeping faith with each other, on the practice of honesty, justice, and the rest of the virtues. Only those beings in whom such faculties were present were able to combine, and thus only the relatively honest men were preserved. The process repeated itself countless times during untold ages. At every step the race advanced, and at every step the realisation of the cause increased." Making friends now, at sea, with this American, would do something similar.

"Friendship among nations, as among individuals, calls for constructive efforts to muster the forces of humanity in order that an atmosphere of close understanding and cooperation may be cultivated," Roosevelt once said. Sizing up Churchill, Roosevelt saw him as a friend in this light: He too wanted close understanding for public purposes.

———

THE AMERICANS AGREED to join the British in warning the Japanese against further aggression. In July, Tokyo had moved on French Indochina—the next generation would know part of the region as Vietnam—continuing its imperial push in the Pacific; Roosevelt had struck back by freezing Japan's assets in America. British holdings in the Pacific were in danger, but few could have guessed how far east—and against whom—Tokyo would strike in a few months' time.

Churchill also won approval of "Western Hemisphere Defence Plan No. 4." The language of Churchill's report to the war cabinet was dry, but the meaning important. "At an early date (it is hoped by the 1st September) the United States Navy will take over the responsibility of our North Atlantic Convoys to the West of 26 West"—Iceland, which meant America was projecting power farther east to secure Britain and her supply lines. "They are sending us immediately 130,000 more rifles," Churchill informed London, "and I look for improved allocations of heavy bombers and tanks." Roosevelt told Churchill he would ask for another $5 billion in Lend-Lease aid, and together they sent Stalin a message that fore-shadowed years of debates over financial and military aid to the Soviets. "The war goes on upon many fronts, and before it is over there may be yet further fighting fronts that will be developed," Roosevelt and Churchill wrote Stalin on August 12. "Our resources, though immense, are limited, and it must become question as to where and when those resources can best be used to further to the greatest extent our common effort."

The most enduring piece of official conference business was the Atlantic Charter, a document of war and peace aims that included calls for self-determination and free trade. The British were more interested in a declaration of war and were nervous about the charter's possible implications for the empire and its system of protected trade, but Churchill thought it wise at this point to bow to Roosevelt's wishes. "I fear the President will be very much upset if no Joint Statement can be issued," Churchill told London, "and grave and vital interests might be affected." In other words, give the man what he wants now in hopes that we will get what we want later.

Roosevelt told Daisy he thought their final evening "delightful. . . . We talked about everything except the war! & Churchill said it was the nicest evening he had had! . . . How easy it is really to do big things if you can get an hour off!" The pleasure of being together was intoxicating for both. On a human level, it is easier to accede and more difficult to disagree when people are in one another's company. "The various officers came after dinner & we are satisfied that they understand each other & that any future needs or conversations will meet with less crossed wires," Roosevelt wrote Daisy.

They left Newfoundland with the kind of mutual fondness that often springs up in fox-holes or among travelers or colleagues who share common goals and face the same stresses. Many friendships are precisely that—formed on the fly, pitched and fulfilling for a time, some to be sustained in the face of passing years and changed circumstances, some not. Such relationships can be transitory, but few people who are in the midst of one feel less intensely or less genuinely fond of another even if the friendship fades in the future.

Roosevelt and Churchill were now at the beginning of this emotional journey. The leave-taking, Roosevelt told Daisy, was "a very moving scene" as Churchill and his officers "received full honors going over the side."

IN A BROADCAST to his people on August 24, 1941, Churchill invested the session with Roosevelt at Newfoundland with rhetorical splendor. "It symbolizes in a form and manner which everyone can understand in every land and every clime, the deep underlying unities which stir and at decisive moments rule the English-speaking peoples throughout the world," the prime minister said. "Would it be presumptuous of me to say that it symbolizes something even more majestic—namely: the marshaling of the good forces of the world against the evil forces which are now so formidable and triumphant and which have cast their cruel spell over the whole of Europe and a large part of Asia?"

The way Roosevelt was acting, Churchill could indeed be seen as "presumptuous," or at least overly optimistic. America was not at war. John Martin told Jock Colville that he had heard Roosevelt say, "I do not intend to declare war; I intend to wage it"—heartening words in the dramatic setting at Newfoundland, but ones that gave Roosevelt maximum flexibility, leaving Churchill to wonder what they meant in practice. In a letter to his son, Randolph, Churchill was honest about the meeting's mixed results. "The President for all his warm heart and good intentions, is thought by many of his admirers to move with public opinion rather than to lead and form it," he wrote.

Beginning what would become a pattern, at least one of the principals—this time Churchill, who came down with a bad cold—got sick in the aftermath of a meeting. Roosevelt, too, had difficulty decompressing. "All well & a bit of a let-down!" he wrote Daisy as the *Augusta* passed Nova Scotia en route home. "But the after-thoughts are good & we hope the country will approve." Tired, Roosevelt took advantage of smooth seas and slept twelve hours at a stretch.

ROOSEVELT'S "AFTERTHOUGHTS" may have been good, but while the two had been at sea, only a single vote in the House of Repre-sentatives had guaranteed an extension of the American military draft. In his first press con-ference back aboard the *Potomac* just after three in the afternoon of August 16 at Rockland, Maine, Roosevelt sent conflicting signals about the significance of the meeting.

"I think the first thing in the minds of all of us was a very remarkable religious service on the quarter deck of the *Prince of Wales* last Sunday morning," Roosevelt told "the boys" who had gathered on the yacht. "I think everybody there, officers and enlisted men, felt that it was one of the great historic services. I know I did." He and Churchill, Roosevelt added, had spo-ken of "what is happening to the world under the Nazi regime, as applied to other nations. The more that is discussed and looked into, the more terrible the thought becomes of having the world as a whole dominated by the kind of influences which have been at work in the occupied or affiliated nations. It's a thing that needs to be brought home to all of the Democracies, more and more."

Music to Churchill's ears—but then Roosevelt shifted to a different note. Had the two leaders, a reporter asked, discussed how to actually implement the provisions of the Atlantic Charter?

"Interchange of views, that's all. Nothing else."

Was America closer to war?

"I should say, no," Roosevelt replied.

Back in Washington, however, he gave his cabinet a bullish fill on the meeting. "When Roosevelt returned, he liked Churchill very much and was enthusiastic about him," Frances Perkins recalled. Roosevelt had apparently decided that the pre–Battle of Britain view of Churchill was outdated. "His mind is better than it was," Roosevelt said of Churchill. "His mind is improving. I'm sure that he's got a greater mind than he had twenty years ago. He's got a more developed mind."

Perkins, a longtime student of both men, was interested to hear this. "I realized that Churchill's spell was still good," she later said. "When he was a young man, Churchill could cast a spell over people. You've no idea what a persuasive person he is, or how polite, how very cordial and considerate he can be when he wants to. He has a most winning way of winning people's affection and confidence. . . . I remember being very, very glad that the President had liked Churchill and feeling that it was much safer for this country, as well as for the world, if President Roosevelt liked and was able to make rapprochement with Churchill, able to believe him, able to take some leadership from him."

But Perkins knew Roosevelt did not like following anyone, except for the broad American public. "That seems a queer thing to say and to feel," she admitted of her view that Roosevelt could learn from Churchill, "but actually Churchill had much more life experience of war, rumors of war, making war, making peace, keeping the world on an even keel than anybody in the USA did, including Franklin D. Roosevelt. . . . Churchill is the kind of man that people can be off of. Franklin Roosevelt had elements within his own nature that made it possible for him to get off, entirely off, the hooks with certain people, no matter how good they were . . . ," Perkins said. "Anyhow, I thought that the whole relationship with Churchill was very, very lucky."

Churchill's confidence had charmed Roosevelt. "You talked with Churchill and you understood the stubborn fight they were putting up and would continue to put up," Roosevelt

told the cabinet. On August 19, in a late afternoon chat with reporters, Roosevelt reiterated
this note. One asked: Will there be more
"punch" in American efforts against Hitler?

"Help for the Democracies of the world, yes,"
Roosevelt replied.

"As a result of this conference, sir?"

"Yes. In other words, it clarified many, many
things. It discussed operations. As I said the
other day, in practically every sector of the
whole world . . . it has brought a . . . better
meeting of the minds on needs, and the fight
that the Democracies are putting up against
Nazism."

THEN, MADDENINGLY TO Churchill, Roosevelt tacked away from warlike rhetoric once
more, reassuring the capital that he, and no one
else, was in charge. Churchill would not push
him around. At the cabinet meeting, someone
said, "You want to look out, Mr. President.
Churchill may be pulling your leg by letting you
win the first round." Roosevelt admitted,
Perkins recalled, "that he recognized some of
the qualities of a trader in Churchill." Then, out
of the pride that had driven the destroyer deal,
Roosevelt said: "But, of course, you know
Grandpa's pretty good at trading, too."

A writer named Alice Deane sent Eleanor a

letter tinged with isolationist criticism in the aftermath of the conference, saying that although America had gotten the wrong end of the deal on the destroyers-for-bases arrangement, she was pleased about Roosevelt's ability to "refuse to be duped" into intervening in the war during his meeting with Churchill. Roosevelt dictated a sharp memo in reply.

"I should say Alice Deane must be an ass. The destroyer deal was a 'deal'—and very successful from our trading point of view," Roosevelt wrote Eleanor. "In regard to the Atlantic conference, there was no pressure put on me at any time either by 'the overpowering Winston Churchill' or any of his five or six aides. Neither did 'our own aggregation of Army and Navy chiefs press for further steps toward war. . . .' How do people like she get that way anyway? . . . (You can send her a copy of this if you long to!)" Eleanor apparently did not.

Churchill watched Roosevelt's act with alarm. In what Robert Sherwood called "one of the gloomiest messages that ever came to the White House from the normally confident, ebullient Prime Minister," Churchill complained to Hopkins that Roosevelt's spin that America was no closer to war was sending a "wave of depression through Cabinet and other informed circles here. . . ." Touchingly, Churchill wrote: "If 1942 opens with Russia knocked out and

Britain left again alone, all kinds of dangers may arise. I do not think Hitler will help in any way." Hopkins, Churchill went on, "will know best whether anything more can be done. Should be grateful if you could give me any sort of hope."

The prime minister had to content himself with a kind of stoic optimism. "Talking of the war in general," Charles Eade said of the early years, "Mr. Churchill likened himself to a dead cat floating on the sea, but would be eventually washed up on the shores of victory."

CHURCHILL AND ROOSEVELT had personal concerns as well. Fortunately for Churchill, Clementine had recovered. "Your mother is much better now," Churchill wrote Randolph. "She was very tired, but retired for treatment to a home hard by, which has done her no end of good."

Roosevelt's news was not as reassuring. On Sunday, September 7, her son with her, Sara Delano Roosevelt died. It was a wrenching time. Sara had been difficult but devoted, and Roosevelt enjoyed being the object of devotion. "Those who were closest to Franklin Roosevelt could not presume to guess at the quality of sorrow caused him by his mother's death," Sherwood wrote. "One needed only a small realization of the tenacity with which he

clung to every surviving link with the lovely
world of his childhood—a world fantastically
different from the one in which he now lived
and fought—to know that his sorrow was very
deep indeed." Eleanor was a source of warmth.
"Mother went to father and consoled him"
after Sara's death, James Roosevelt recalled.
"She stayed with him and was by his side at the
funeral and through the difficult days immediately afterward. She showed him more affection
during those days than at any other time I can
recall. She was the kind you could count on in a
crisis, and father knew that." Sara had, of
course, left explicit instructions about her
funeral. "Franklin's mother had always wanted
to die in her own room at Hyde Park and be
buried simply in the churchyard, with the men
who had worked for her on the place for many
years carrying the casket," Eleanor recalled.
"Her wishes were carefully observed."

There was more grief to come. Hall Roosevelt, Eleanor's beloved brother, died a few
weeks later. Hall had been an alcoholic like her
father and her uncles, and he had been both a
joy and a disappointment to Eleanor. Roosevelt
repaid Eleanor's kindness at Sara's death; he
"did not fail her," James said. ". . . I remember
clearly the day she went to father and said simply, 'Hall has died.' Father struggled to her side

and put his arm around her. 'Sit down,' he said, so tenderly I can still hear it. And he sank down beside her and hugged her and kissed her and held her head on his chest.'"

HEARING OF SARA'S DEATH, Churchill sent a telegram to Roosevelt. "Pray accept my deep sympathy in your most grievous loss," he wrote. "Thank you for your kind and friendly message," Roosevelt replied. The next day, Churchill gave the House of Commons his report on Newfoundland, closing with an allusion to William Ernest Henley's poem "Invictus," which was also a Roosevelt favorite: "We still are master of our fate. We still are captain of our souls." Words like these buoyed Churchill as he tried to assess Roosevelt's true state of mind.

On a visit to London that September, Eugene Meyer of *The Washington Post* was in the Distinguished Visitors' Gallery as Churchill spoke in the House. "The P.M.'s address was in his usual admirable En-glish . . . ," Meyer wrote in a diary of the trip. "Churchill seemed in fine condition, physically and mentally and previous to his speech answered some questions of administration with snap and good-humour."

Meyer noticed the stresses beneath the surface

of wartime London. Lunching alone at Claridge's, he was struck by the faces of uniformed men in the hotel. "The young men are really fine looking, but behind the eyes of their mothers and the sweethearts with whom they lunch," Meyer wrote, "one reads many things which contradict the outer appearances of lightheartedness and enjoyment of the moment." At a lunch at Downing Street with Churchill and Clementine, Meyer found himself one of a number at the table, including Virginia Cowles, an American journalist, author, and friend of the Churchill family. "As we sat down to the mixed gathering, the situation naturally developed as to whether or not Virginia, who had written a book about her experiences on the Continent, or I, on the other side of the table, was going to have the Prime Minister's attention," Meyer wrote. "I am ashamed to say I was rather ruthless and as I had come quite a way to have this talk I got most of the attention that I needed." Churchill made sure he impressed his distinguished American guest. "Churchill was in fine form, the picture of health, vigour and of all the men I have ever seen grow in relation to power and responsibility, he has made the greatest jump," Meyer wrote. "His discussion of any subject is on the highest level, his ideas are clear and direct."

In these weeks, Churchill thought events were

about to push Roosevelt into full-blown hostilities. In the Atlantic, there had been a skirmish between a German U-boat and the *Greer,* an American destroyer. Could this be, Churchill wondered, the precipitating incident to bring Roosevelt into war? Churchill hoped so, taking comfort from the president's promise, made the night before Roosevelt was summoned to Hyde Park to watch his mother die, that "for your private and very confidential information I am planning to make a radio address Monday night relative to the attack on our destroyer and to make perfectly clear the action we intend to take in the Atlantic."

The fireside chat had been postponed until September 11, 1941, when Roosevelt put Berlin on notice. "We have sought no shooting war with Hitler," he told the nation. "We do not seek it now. . . . But when you see a rattlesnake poised to strike, you do not wait until he has struck before you crush him. . . . From now on, if German or Italian vessels of war enter the waters, the protection of which is necessary for American defense, they do so at their own peril. . . . I have no illusions about the gravity of this step. I have not taken it hurriedly or lightly. It is the result of months and months of constant thought and anxiety and prayer."

———

AT A LUNCHEON with British editors in London, Eugene Meyer was asked to talk about Roosevelt's thinking. "By way of starting discussion I brought up particularly the question of the apparent general eagerness to have us formally declare war and why we don't, which is being asked over here rather widely," Meyer recalled. "I pointed out that Mr. Roosevelt is carrying on undeclared war and doing most of the things we would be doing if war were declared, and doing them more quickly than could be done through action by Congress." A week earlier in Des Moines, Charles Lindbergh had asserted that "the three most important groups which have been pressing this country toward war are the British, the Jewish and the Roosevelt Administration." Referring to this isolationist rant, Meyer said: "Mr. Lindbergh's speech in Iowa showing that he practically adopted the Hitler programme appeared to me, I said, in very much the same way as Hitler's submarine attacks on our shipping, to have been forced by Roosevelt's continuous forward steps."

Listening to Roosevelt's *Greer* speech in London, Churchill was pleased. "Roosevelt this morning excellent," he wrote a friend. "As we used to sing at Sandhurst 'Now we *shan't* be long!' "

―――

IN THE END, of course, it would be Japan, not Germany, that proved Churchill right. Busy with diplomatic maneuverings with Tokyo's representatives in Washington, Roosevelt delayed his usual Thanksgiving trip to Warm Springs, where he traditionally hosted a feast with his fellow patients in the Georgia hills. Reaching his retreat on the Saturday after Thanksgiving, Roosevelt received a call from Secretary of State Cordell Hull: The crisis with Japan was getting worse.

He could not unwind after Hull's call. That night in the dining hall, Grace Tully noticed "a quiet chill in the great room." Roosevelt had listened to the Army-Navy football game off and on that afternoon and delivered a serious speech after the meal. "It may be that next Thanksgiving these boys of the Military Academy and of the Naval Academy will be actually fighting for the defense of these American institutions of ours," he said. Hull telephoned again; Roosevelt decided to leave the next morning. On the way to the station, he said his good-byes.

"This may be the last time I talk to you for a long time," Roosevelt told his Warm Springs neighbors, then disappeared north.

ON THE WEEKEND of December 7, Churchill was at Chequers, pacing outside the main entrance at midday Sunday when John G. "Gil" Winant, the current American ambassador, arrived for lunch.

Did Winant think there would be war with Japan? Churchill asked.

"Yes," Winant said.

"If they declare war on you, we shall declare war on them within the hour."

"I understand, Prime Minister. You have stated that publicly."

Then came the rub. "If they declare war on us," Churchill asked, "will you declare war on them?"

"I can't answer that, Prime Minister," Winant said, falling back on a civics lesson. "Only the Congress has the right to declare war under the United States Constitution." (From Roosevelt on down, Americans were always lecturing Churchill about the separation of powers.)

Winant guessed what was worrying Churchill. "He must have realized," Winant later wrote, "that if Japan attacked Siam or British territory it would force Great Britain into an Asiatic war and leave us out of the war."

Shaking off that cataclysmic prospect, Churchill said to Winant, "We're late, you know. You get washed and we will go in to lunch together."

SUNDAYS WERE RELAXING days at the White House. Roosevelt did not go to church regularly in Washington. "I can do almost everything in the 'Goldfish Bowl' of the President's life," he told Frances Perkins, "but I'll be hanged if I can say my prayers in it."

On Sunday, December 7, Hopkins and Roosevelt were lunching at Roosevelt's desk in the study, talking, Hopkins recalled, "about things far removed from war," when the secretary of the navy telephoned Roosevelt. The Japanese had surprised the fleet just after 7:30 that morning. About 2,400 people would die; 1,200 were wounded.

AS ROOSEVELT DIRECTED the American war effort's opening moves from the White House, the news had still not reached Chequers. Clementine did not feel well and had not come down for dinner. Churchill sat with Averell Harriman, his daughter Kathleen, Pamela Churchill, Gil Winant, John Martin, Tommy Thompson, and Lord Ismay. It was not an uncommon gathering for Churchill: a mix of family, close aides, and American envoys. Harriman usually got a lot of work done with the prime minister on such weekends. "Churchill had discovered that Averell could play bezique, which not many people could do, so they had a way to spend time together," Kathleen recalled, "and the conversation while shuffling the several decks at the end of a game took time and helped them resolve all kinds of issues."

There were no games tonight. "The Prime Minister seemed tired and depressed," Averell Harriman remembered. "He didn't have much to say throughout dinner and was immersed in his thoughts, with his head in his hands part of the time." The only thing worse than what Britain had endured since the spring of 1940 might be in the offing: a lonely two-front war. Shortly before the nine o'clock news, Sawyers, Churchill's valet, carried in a portable radio. Churchill was, Harriman recalled, "a bit slow" turning it on and missed the top headline. The first item the dinner party heard was about a tank battle in Libya.

Then the announcer returned to the top story. "The news has just been given that Japanese aircraft have raided Pearl Harbor, the American naval base in Hawaii. The announcement of the attack was made in a brief statement by President Roosevelt. Naval and military targets on the principal Hawaiian island of Oahu have also been attacked. No further details are yet available."

The report did not register with Churchill. "I did not personally sustain any direct impression," he later said. Harriman repeated the words he had heard: "The Japanese have raided Pearl Harbor." In the confusion of the moment, Commander Thompson interrupted, saying, "No, no, he said 'Pearl River.'" While Harriman and Thompson argued, Churchill, suddenly energized, "slammed the top of the radio down" and rose as Sawyers entered the dining room.

"It's quite true," Sawyers said. "We heard it ourselves outside. The Japanese have attacked the Americans." Martin, who had bolted from the table, returned with word that the Admiralty was on the line, confirming the news. There was, Churchill remembered, "a silence." The prime minister headed for the door, saying, "We shall declare war on Japan." Winant chased after him: "Good God, you can't declare war on a radio announcement."

Churchill paused. "What shall I do?" he asked.

"I will call up the President by telephone and ask him what the facts are," Winant said.

"And I shall talk with him, too," Churchill replied.

Reaching Washington, Winant listened as Roosevelt told him what he knew thus far.

Winant told Roosevelt he had a friend nearby who wanted to speak to him. "You will know who it is as soon as you hear his voice," Winant said.

Churchill took the phone. "Mr. President," he said, "what's this about Japan?"

"It's quite true," Roosevelt replied. "They have attacked us at Pearl Harbor. We are all in the same boat now."

Winant had another word with Roosevelt, and then Churchill took the telephone again. He could not hide his own feelings about the turn events had taken.

"This certainly simplifies things," Churchill told Roosevelt. Then he added: "God be with you."

THOUGH SHE WAS in the White House that Sunday, Eleanor felt shut out in the swarm of war. She remembered saying good-bye to her thirty luncheon guests—even before word of the attack, Roosevelt had sent his regrets, though some Delano cousins of his were staying with the Roosevelts—and she then "waited till Franklin was alone to slip into his study, but I realized he was concentrating on what had to be done and would not talk about what had happened until this first strain was over." Quietly his wife withdrew, closing the door and

leaving the president of the United States, surrounded by his nautical prints and model ships,
with his thoughts of the very real naval devastation that had now drawn America into war.
Eleanor sought what had been her refuge since
the summer of Lucy Mercer twenty-three years
before. "I went back to work," she recalled.

Roosevelt and Churchill were in character—
and in many ways at their best—on this December Sunday. Handling the telephone himself,
wearing an old sweater of his son James's he had
saved for years, Roosevelt was masterful, directing troop movements with General George
Marshall and planning diplomatic calls with
Cordell Hull. He was personally at the helm.
On the phone with an official in Honolulu at
one point, he turned to those gathered in the
room and said, "My God, there's another wave
of Jap planes over Hawaii right this minute."

It was a day during which Roosevelt's highly
personal leadership worked. "Many of the
moves required the President to sign an executive order," wrote Robert Sherwood. "The
President instructed the person to whom he
talked to go ahead and execute the order and he
would sign it later." At about five in the afternoon, Roosevelt summoned Grace Tully. "He
was alone, seated before his desk on which were
two or three neat piles of notes containing the
information of the past two hours," Tully said.

"The telephone was close by his hand. He was wearing a gray sack jacket and was lighting a cigarette as I entered the room. He took a deep drag and addressed me calmly: 'Sit down, Grace. I'm going before Congress tomorrow. I'd like to dictate my message. It will be short.' "

Roosevelt began, Tully recalled, with "the same calm tone in which he dictated his mail. Only his diction was a little different as he spoke each word incisively and slowly, carefully specifying each punctuation mark and paragraph. 'Yesterday comma December 7 comma 1941 dash a day which will live in world history dash the United States of America was suddenly and deliberately attacked by naval and air forces of the Empire of Japan period paragraph.' " The speech was brief. "I ask," Roosevelt concluded, "that the Congress declare that since the unprovoked and dastardly attack by Japan on Sunday comma December 7 comma a state of war has existed between the United States and the Japanese Empire period end." Hopkins came in and added one line: "With confidence in our armed forces—with the unbounded determination of our people—we will gain the inevitable triumph—so help us God." There was another edit, this one from Roosevelt: "world history" became "infamy."

Eleanor returned to the center of action and noted that her husband was "more serene than he had appeared in a long time." It was the same grace under pressure she had seen at Campobello two decades before. "I think it was steadying to know finally that the die was cast," Eleanor said of December 7. "One could no longer do anything but face the fact that this country was in a war; from here on, difficult and dangerous as the future looked, it presented a clearer challenge than the long uncertainty of the past." The president was calm as he faced the storm.

WHILE ROOSEVELT DEMONSTRATED his capacity to manage a crisis firsthand, Churchill hurled himself into action. "No American will think it wrong of me," he wrote after the war, "if I proclaim that to have the United States at our side was to me the greatest joy. I could not foretell the course of events. I do not pretend to have measured accurately the martial might of Japan, but now at this very moment I knew the United States was in the war, up to the neck and in to the death. So we had won after all! Yes, after Dunkirk; after the fall of France; after the horrible episode of Oran; after the threat of invasion, when, apart from the Air and the Navy, we were an almost unarmed people; after the deadly struggle of the U-boat war—the first Battle of the Atlantic, gained by a hand's-

breadth; after seventeen months of lonely fighting and nineteen months of my responsibility in
dire stress, we had won the war. England would
live; Britain would live; the Commonwealth of
Nations and the Empire would live."

He felt his obligations as host to Winant and
Harriman keenly and remembered that, after
the call to Roosevelt, "we then went back into
the hall and tried to adjust our thoughts to the
supreme world event which had occurred,
which was of so startling a nature as to make even
those who were near the centre gasp. My two
American friends took the shock with admirable
fortitude. We had no idea that any serious losses
had been inflicted on the United States Navy.
They did not wail or lament that their country
was at war. They wasted no words in reproach or
sorrow. In fact, one might almost have thought
they had been delivered from a long pain."

He wrote telegrams after midnight. One was
to Hopkins, cosigned with Harriman: "Thinking of you much at this historic moment—
Winston, Averell."

Foreign Secretary Anthony Eden, then en
route to the Soviet Union, reached Churchill
that night. "He was quite naturally in a high
state of excitement," Eden recalled. He found
Churchill was already full of plans to go to
Washington. Eden, however, "was not sure that
the Americans would want him so soon."

Eden was right. When Roosevelt dictated his speech to Grace Tully, it concerned one nation—Japan. He did not mention Germany. Eden seemed to understand this distinction; Churchill did not. "The United States and Britain were now allies," Eden said, "in the war against Japan."

Against Japan—not yet against Germany. Typically, Churchill had suppressed nuance in his delight over the events of the day. Thus began a fraught week as Roosevelt put off Churchill's excited talk of a quick trip to Washington.

Would Hitler take America on? There was no word. On Monday, Roosevelt put on his navy cape, went to Capitol Hill, and declared war. On the night of December 8, Robert Sherwood and Sam Rosenman left the White House after dark. "There had been wild rumors about a German air attack to be launched from submarines, and many cities in the United States had already instituted blackouts," Rosenman recalled. The bright lamp that usually lit the White House on the Pennsylvania Avenue side, Rosenman noticed, had been shut off. "I wonder how long it will be before that light gets turned on again," Rosenman recalled saying to Sherwood. "I don't know," Sherwood replied, "but until it does, the lights will stay turned off all over the world. That light has been the only ray of hope to millions of people, and those millions will still look to this house and to that man inside it as their only hope of deliverance."

On Tuesday, in a fireside chat, Roosevelt tied Germany, master of Europe for nearly a year and a half, to the emerging conflict. It was a brilliant strategic talk, one that connected seemingly disparate continents and players in a coherent whole for Americans still trying to make sense of the news. "We must realize for example that Japanese successes against the United States in the Pacific are helpful to German operations in Libya; that any German success against the Caucasus is inevitably an assistance to Japan in her operations against the Dutch East Indies; that a German attack against Algiers or Morocco opens the way to a German attack against South America and the Canal," Roosevelt said. ". . . We are now in the midst of a war, not for conquest, not for vengeance, but for a world in which this nation, and all that this nation represents, will be safe for our children. We expect to eliminate the danger from Japan, but it would serve us ill if we accomplished that and found that the rest of the world was dominated by Hitler and Mussolini."

Stirring words, but Roosevelt did not want Churchill descending on him until he had a better idea of what Hitler was going to do. Playing for time, Roosevelt drafted, but did not send, two letters suggesting he and Churchill wait to confer. "Delay of even a couple of weeks might be advantageous," one of them said.

The Americans apparently did raise questions about the dangers Churchill would face crossing the Atlantic, but the prime minister would not be thwarted. In a note to Churchill written after his speech declaring war, Roosevelt repeated a phrase from the call on Sunday. "Today all of us are in the same boat with you and the people of the Empire and it is a ship which will not and cannot be sunk." Churchill seized on the words and began quoting them back to Roosevelt. "Now that we are as you say 'in the same boat,'" he told Roosevelt on Tuesday, "would it not be wise for us to have another conference. . . . It would also be a very great pleasure to me to meet you again, and the sooner the better."

HITLER SETTLED THE question on Thursday, December 11, 1941, when he declared war on the United States. "I understand only too well that a world-wide distance separates Roosevelt's ideas and my ideas," Hitler said. "Roosevelt comes from a rich family and belongs to the class whose path is smoothed in the democracies. I was the only child of a small, poor family and had to fight my way by work and industry. When the Great War came Roosevelt occupied a position where he got to know only its pleasant consequences, enjoyed by those who do business while others bleed. . . . As for the German nation, it needs charity neither from Mr. Roosevelt nor from Mr. Churchill. . . . It wants only its rights! It will secure for itself this right to live even if thousands of Churchills and Roosevelts conspire against it."

Why did Hitler do it? Partly because he misjudged Roosevelt and America. "I don't see much future for the Americans," Hitler said in January 1942. "It's a decayed country. And they have their racial problem, and the problem of social inequalities. . . . My feelings against Americanism are feelings of hatred and deep repugnance. . . . Everything about the behavior of American society reveals that it's half Judaized, and the other half Negrified. How can one expect a State like that to hold together—a country where everything is built on the dollar." He had not counted on Churchill's stalwart defense of Britain in 1940; now, as 1941 drew to a close, he did not count on Roosevelt's strength and determination. It was one of Hitler's many mistakes, and one from which he could never recover.

"The Great Republic" was at war at last. Through the ensuing decades of what Henry

Luce, founder of the Time-Life magazine empire, would call "the American Century," a national myth took shape about World War II: that we fought to defeat Hitler and to preserve democracy. And America did—ultimately. Yet the United States hit back only when it was, as Roosevelt said on December 8, "suddenly and deliberately attacked by . . . the Empire of Japan"—and entered the war against Germany only when it was clear that Hitler would join Tokyo's fight. From Churchill's perspective, perhaps the better night to have celebrated was December 11, after Hitler's declaration, rather than December 7.

WITH CHRISTMAS COMING, Roosevelt and Churchill were united. "Delighted to have you here at White House," Roosevelt cabled Churchill. A new phase of their friendship was beginning. "At one of our meetings after the USA had come into the war, someone was still adopting the careful attitude that had been necessary before the entry of the USA . . . ," said General Sir Alan Brooke, chief of the imperial general staff. "Winston turned to him, and with a wicked leer in his eye, said, 'Oh! That is the way we talked to her while we were wooing her, now that she is in the harem we talk to her quite differently!' "

PART II

GETTING ON FAMOUSLY

Winter 1941 to Late Summer 1943

*"Let the children have their night
of fun and laughter"*

Roosevelt and Churchill light
the NationalChristmas Tree,
December 24, 1941

A COUPLE OF EMPERORS

A White House Holiday–Churchill's Heart Scare–
An Embarrassing Telephone Call

"I HAVE READ TWO BOOKS," Churchill wrote Clementine from his Atlantic crossing aboard the *Duke of York, "Brown on Resolution* and *Forty Centuries Look Down."* The novels may have fanned his romantic vision of his mission. The second is about Napoleon and Josephine; the first, a 1929 story by C. S. Forester, tells the tale of a bastard English boy, Albert Brown, who grows up to serve in the Royal Navy during World War I and, armed with only a rifle, single-handedly holds up a German crew on Resolution, a stony spit in the Galápagos Islands. It was the kind of story Churchill loved. Early in Brown's life, his mother decides he will go into the navy, and she lovingly tries to advance his career. What Churchill could have chosen to take from the tale was the image of a devoted mother doing her best for her boy, a boy who would grow to do great things. It was how he liked to remember Jennie and how he liked to think of himself, the warrior fighting against all odds.

"He is a different man since America came into the war," Lord Moran said of Churchill. "The Winston I knew in London frightened me. I used to watch him as he went to his room with swift paces, the head thrust forward, scowling at the ground, the sombre countenance clouded, the features set and resolute. . . . I could see that he was carrying the weight of the world, and wondered how long he could go on like that and what could be done about it. And now—in a night, it seems—a younger man has taken his place." Churchill, who flew from Hampton Roads, Virginia, to Washington, cabled Roosevelt to "on no account come out to meet me," but Roosevelt drove to the airfield on December 22 to greet the flight in the dusk.

Roosevelt's charm was in full force. "He made me feel that I had known him for a long time," Moran recalled of their first few minutes of conversation. "It was very sweet of him to think of shaking my hand," said Patrick Kinna, the Churchill assistant who had met Roosevelt at Newfoundland. Inspector Thompson was "honoured and touched" to find that Roosevelt remembered him from the Atlantic rendezvous. "Come along, Thompson, I am very pleased to see you again," Roosevelt said.

Churchill, *Time* noted, "swept in like a breath of fresh air, giving Washington new vigor, for he came as a new hero." Gone was Roosevelt's skepticism about Churchill's staying power; gone, too, was Churchill's frustration with Roosevelt's failure to fully engage the enemy.

They now shared largely identical interests and would treat the world, and themselves, to a pageant of personal diplomacy. Mutual admiration can be seductive—if you are one of the people being admired. These weeks at the White House belong to a vanished age, but the human forces shaping the time Roosevelt and Churchill spent together—affection, shared drama, and hints of tension—almost always play some role in high politics.

THERE WAS A vocal school in the United States that thought America's central focus should be Japan, not Germany. That Japan would consume Roosevelt worried Churchill as he wandered the White House. As Roosevelt and his generals saw it, however, Hitler represented the most significant long-term threat. "The principle of Germany first was based on strictly military reasoning," Sherwood wrote. "It was assumed—and, it would seem from the results, correctly—that Germany had far greater potential than Japan in productive power and scientific genius and, if given time to develop this during years of stalemate in Europe, would prove all the more difficult if not impossible to defeat." It would be Hitler first, Tojo after.

Churchill's main task on the *Duke of York*—the novels had been a diversion—were three long papers laying out his vision of the conflict's coming years. North Africa and the Middle East would be secured in 1942; the Allies must build naval strength in the Pacific; Germany would be bombed; and, in 1943, there would be Anglo-American landings in "three or four" of the countries from a pool of Norway, Denmark, Holland, Belgium, France, Italy, and the Balkans. Churchill believed, too, that bombings of the Reich's homeland and attacks on the German periphery could possibly do much of the Allies' work for them. "It must be remembered," he told Roosevelt, "that we place great hopes of affecting German production and German morale by ever more severe and more accurate bombing of their cities and harbours and that this, combined with their Russian defeats, may produce important effects upon the will to fight of the German people, with consequential internal reactions upon the German Government." Though the question of landings would become a critical point of political and personal contention, at this juncture Roosevelt largely agreed, and their decisions were made in an intimate setting. "As we both, by need or habit, were forced to do much of our work in bed, he visited me in my room whenever he felt inclined, and encouraged me to do the same to him," Churchill recalled. The prime minister's hours kept Roosevelt up later than he was accustomed to. "Churchill would wander into the President's bedroom at any hour if he had something to talk over," said George Elsey, a young naval reservist who went to work in the White House map room.

The late-night conversations were fueled by war and drink. "We had to remember to have imported brandy after dinner," Eleanor recalled. "This was something Franklin himself did not have as a rule." But the rules were all being broken. "Never had the staid butlers, ushers, maids, and other Executive Mansion workers seen anything like Winston before," said Mike Reilly. "He ate, and thoroughly enjoyed, more food than any two men or three diplomats; and he consumed brandy and scotch with a grace and enthusiasm that left us all openmouthed in awe."

Churchill's traveling map room caught Roosevelt's fancy. "FDR was fascinated and told his naval aide to set up the same kind of operation," recalled Elsey. "They found a small room downstairs next to the oval Diplomatic Reception Room on the ground floor and installed standard gray gunmetal desks and put cork on the walls, where they attached maps of the Atlantic and Pacific theaters." Once Roosevelt had his own version, "Churchill would come to the Map Room any time, day or night," said Elsey. "Once my Army counterpart had taken off his uniform and hung it up so that it would be fresh in the morning, and all of a sudden the Prime Minister came barging in and found the poor guy in his underwear."

ON CHURCHILL'S FIRST full day in the White House, Grace Tully looked out a French window next to the Oval Office and saw "a chubby, florid, bald-headed gentleman dressed in one-piece, blue denim coveralls and with a big cigar in his mouth shambling toward my office." In the White House for the first time, Churchill was exploring the house and grounds alone before lunching with Roosevelt.

They ate at the president's trinket-strewn desk, a Roosevelt tradition. (Lord Chandos once had cold lobster and mayonnaise sauce with Roosevelt in the Oval Office. "Soon there were lobster shells all over the desk," Chandos recalled, "and not a little mayonnaise had found its way on to the papers, the commissions, the

reprieves and the reports which littered it.")
The Roosevelt-Churchill lunch seems to have
gone swimmingly, for Churchill was twinkling
when, after changing from his siren suit into a
black coat and blue-and-white polka-dot bow
tie, he came back to the Oval Office at four P.M.
for a presidential press conference. Sitting to
Roosevelt's right behind the crowded desk, a
cigar in his mouth, a wire basket of papers and
a silver thermos of water just before him,
Churchill was in his element. His face, noted
one correspondent, had "a healthy pink tinge."
Watching the huge numbers of reporters file in,
Steve Early remarked, "I would like to get the
gate receipts today."

Introducing Churchill, Roosevelt, wearing
gray pinstripes and smoking a cigarette in an
ivory holder, said, "He is quite willing to take
on a conference, because we have one characteristic in common. We like new experiences in
life." The *Washington Star* noted the stagecraft:
"Two great statesmen-showmen, sharing the
star parts in a world drama that will be read and
studied for centuries to come, played a sparkling
and unique scene at the White House yesterday.
They were President Roosevelt, debonair and
facile as usual, and Britain's Prime Minister
Churchill, jaunty and ruddy." The atmosphere
in the office, the *Star* wrote, was "electric."

The room was full. "I wish you would just

stand up for one minute and let them see you," Roosevelt said to Churchill. "They can't see you." Churchill mounted his chair and waved his cigar. "It was terribly exciting," said Alistair Cooke, the British journalist. Accustomed to commanding this room and this audience, Roosevelt sat back and delightedly—even proudly—watched Churchill cast his spell.

"Go ahead and shoot," Roosevelt said to the reporters.

"Mr. Prime Minister, isn't Singapore the key to the whole situation out there?"

"The key to the whole situation is the resolute manner in which the British and American Democracies are going to throw themselves into the conflict."

"Mr. Minister, could you tell us what you think of conditions within Germany—the morale?"

"Well, I have always been feeling that one of these days we might get a windfall coming from that quarter, but I don't think we ought to count on it. Just go on as if they were keeping on as bad as they are, or as good as they are. And then one of these days, as we did in the last war, we may wake up and find we ran short of Huns." [Laughter]

"Do you think the war is turning in our favor in the last month or so?"

"I can't describe the feelings of relief with which I find Russia victorious, the United

States and Great Britain standing side by side. It is incredible to anyone who has lived through the lonely months of 1940. It is incredible. Thank God."

"Mr. Minister, can you tell us when you think we may lick these boys?"

For the first time, Churchill looked puzzled. To that point, *The Washington Post* reported, he had been "flinging back answers that almost caught the questions in mid-air." But he did not understand what "lick" meant; Early went over and translated for him.

"If we manage it well," Churchill answered with a smile, "it will only take half as long as if we manage it badly." [Loud laughter]

"Mr. Prime Minister, in one of your speeches you mentioned three or four of the great climacterics. Would you now add our entry into the war as one of those, sir?"

"I think I may almost say, 'I sure do.' " [Loud laughter]

"Mr. Prime Minister, during your talks here, will you take up economic, and diplomatic, and post-war problems?"

"I hope not too much on them. Well, really, we have to concentrate on the grim emergencies, and we—when we have solved them, we shall be in a position to deal with the future of the world in a manner to give the best results, and the most lasting results, for the common peoples of all the lands. But one has only a certain amount of life and strength, and only so many hours in the day, and other emergencies press upon us too much to be drawn into those very, very complicated, tangled and not in all cases attractive jungles."

"Mr. Minister, have you any doubt of the ultimate victory?"

"I have no doubt whatever."

Roosevelt took pride in his guest's triumphant turn. "The smiling President looked like an old trouper who, on turning impresario, had produced a smash hit," *Newsweek* wrote. "And some thought they detected in his face admiration for a man who had at least equaled him in the part in which he himself was a star."

The press conference was an example of how Roosevelt and Churchill helped transform how the story of politics was told in the middle of the twentieth century. They both understood the significance of mass media—of newspapers, radio, magazines, and newsreels—and always had. Roosevelt had been the top editor on the *Harvard Crimson,* and Churchill had made himself famous as a war reporter. Later both exploited radio. In America, Roosevelt's persona and habits—the cigarette and its holder, his dog—were part of the popular consciousness; in Britain, Churchill's oft photographed courageous countenance was a powerful symbol of defiance. On afternoons like this one in Washington, or on the deck of the *Prince of Wales* the previous August, these two political actors were, in a way, designing the stage set of modern politics.

THAT EVENING, the household assembled for cocktails in the Red Room before dinner. Making drinks was one of the few physical activities Roosevelt—who sometimes called it "children's hour"—could easily handle in public. "At cocktail time everything was beautifully stage-managed so that he could be in control, despite his disability," said Mary Soames. "He would be wheeled in and then spin around to be at the drinks table, where he could reach everything. There were the bottles, there was the shaker, there was the ice. It was all beautifully done. There was never an effort or scurry. He loved the ceremony of making the drinks; it was rather like, 'Look, I can do it.' It was formidable. And you knew you were supposed to just hand him your glass, and not reach for anything else. It was a lovely performance."

Roosevelt was fond of what he called martinis, but there was not a consistent recipe for his mixed drinks. "To my unpracticed eye he seemed to experiment on each occasion with a different percentage of vermouth, gin and fruit juice," recalled Sam Rosenman. "At times he varied it with rum—especially rum from the Virgin Islands." Roosevelt preferred gin.

Churchill was not a fan of Roosevelt's drinks. "Churchill could not abide cocktails of any kind," said Alistair Cooke of Churchill's experience as a presidential guest, "and so he was always handed this martini and . . . he got to the sort of routine that five minutes after, everybody was joking and so on, he would say, 'Mr. President, excuse me,' and he would go to the bathroom and he would immediately take the olive out and pour the thing down and then put water in it." (After leaving the White House, Churchill joked: "The problem in this country is the drinks are too hard and the toilet paper's too soft.")

Churchill was a purist of a drinker, preferring Johnnie Walker Scotch with soda, brandy, Pol Roger champagne, and good wines. "It was not the amount that impressed us, although that was quite impressive," Mike Reilly recalled, "but the complete sobriety that went hand in hand with his drinking." Remarkably few people ever saw Churchill intoxicated. There can be little question, however, that the cumulative effect of years of drinking was at least one factor among many in Churchill's personality. Alcohol raised his sense of drama, removed inhibitions, and invested the ordinary with a dimension of the extraordinary. His highs seemed higher, his lows lower.

Roosevelt did not attempt to match Churchill's pace, but he did consider cocktail hour sacred. It was one of the few moments in his day when the world's troubles seemed to recede. Roosevelt spent much of the hour, as Mary Soames noted, making drinks for others ("How about another sippy?" he would ask, or, "How about a little dividend?") and telling (and retelling) stories.

There was another reason for his fondness for gathering people around him: his paralysis. "He needed an audience; he had to have people around," said George Elsey. "He was trapped in that chair and could not go out and mix and mingle." His confinement was not to be talked about, but it was the central fact of his life, and the cocktail hour made a rough passage smooth.

As with so much else in the Roosevelt household, though, cocktail hour was complicated. Eleanor could never forget her family's history with alcoholism, and she worried about her sons indulging too much. "Mrs. Roosevelt was very afraid of excessive drinking, very bothered by it," Trude Lash said. "She couldn't stand it if she thought you'd had too many drinks." At times, Roosevelt conducted one party in the Oval Study and left Eleanor with lesser-known guests in the West Hall, where he would greet them on the way to the dining room on the first floor. "Drinking to excess is a type of emotional instability only one step short of what happens to people who actually go out of their minds," Eleanor once wrote. Occasionally she tried to make a go of it. "Mrs. Roosevelt was most abstemious, but she loved an Old Fashioned with lots of fruits and vegetables," Mrs. Lash recalled. " 'Warm it up a little,' she would say, which meant add more fruit, not more liquor."

ON THE EVENING of Churchill's afternoon session with reporters, whiskey sours were on offer. Churchill was delayed and so could skip the mixed drink without worrying about choking it down or beating a retreat to the bathroom. Percy Chubb, the husband of a grandniece of Theodore Roosevelt's, described the dinner party in detail to Martin Gilbert. "Churchill was subdued and looked tired" when he finally came in, Chubb recalled, noting that "after all, he had just arrived across the Atlantic and had faced a press conference on his arrival that day." The next morning, Churchill would write Clementine: "I have not had a minute since I got here to tell you about it. All is vy good indeed. . . . The Americans are magnificent in their breadth of view."

At dinner, Roosevelt and Churchill debated the Boer War, the conflict in which the Boers in South Africa rose up against their British masters. Roosevelt, who had supported the Boers when he was at Harvard, and Churchill, a veteran of those very battles, sparred for a time. Chubb thought "the President was in a buoyant mood and kept needling Churchill. . . . When he felt crowded too far, Churchill would take a puff of his cigar and counter attack with a verbal sally and then settle back again into his chair."

As Chubb recalled it, Roosevelt volunteered that he had been disappointed at Harvard—that he had not been as popular or as successful as he would have liked to have been, culminating in the snub by Porcellian. For Roosevelt this was an extraordinarily honest admission. "Churchill took a puff at his cigar and growled: 'When I hear a man say that his childhood was the happiest time of his life, I think (puff) my friend, you have had a pretty poor life.' "

A remarkable exchange: Roosevelt confiding, in mixed company, in Churchill; Churchill, who had long been forced to reimagine his childhood, striking a pugnacious pose in the face of an emotional confession. That Roosevelt was able to reveal something of his true feelings signaled his comfort with Churchill, and Churchill's bullish response was at heart affectionate. Life, Churchill was saying, was what happened when you grew up, not when you were growing up. That conviction was how he had coped, surviving his father's displeasure and his mother's occasional neglect, and now he passed the counsel along to his friend.

THE NEXT DAY was Christmas Eve, and the two men lit the Christmas tree on the South Lawn. The year before, Roosevelt had made a dark joke in the gloom of approaching war, saying with more than a little bitterness that the crowd was welcome to return in 1941 "if we are all still here." Now they were back—in no small measure because of Roosevelt's guest. "Our strongest weapon in this war is that conviction of the dignity and brotherhood of man which Christmas Day signifies—more than any other day or any other symbol," Roosevelt said. Such ceremonies can be routine, or flat, or overdone. Like the church service aboard the *Prince of Wales,* however, this one was apparently perfect. "There was a vast crowd, the voices drifted across the keen night air, the carols—old and yet for ever new—were sung in an atmosphere mellowed by the lights and the shadows," Inspector Thompson recalled. "The voices of the President and the Prime Minister rang out with a message of hope and courage to all who strove for freedom." Shivering, Churchill—whom Roosevelt introduced as "my associate, my old and good friend"—came to the microphones.

"I spend this anniversary and festival far from my country, far from my family, yet I cannot truthfully say that I feel far from home . . . ," Churchill said. "Here, in the midst of war, raging and roaring over all the lands and seas, creeping nearer to our hearts and homes, here, amid all the tumult, we have tonight the peace of the spirit in each cottage home and in every generous heart. Therefore we may cast aside for this night at least the cares and dangers which beset us, and make for the children an evening of happiness in a world of storm. Here, then, for one night only, each home throughout the English-speaking world should be a brightly-lighted island of happiness and peace."

Churchill evoked the hopes of a country, and a world, now living in fear. "Let the children have their night of fun and laughter," he continued. "Let the gifts of Father Christmas delight their play. Let us grown-ups share to the full in their unstinted pleasures before we turn again to the stern task and the formidable years that lie before us, resolved that, by our sacrifice and daring, these same children shall not be robbed of their inheritance or denied their right to live in a free and decent world." With Roosevelt taking in his moving words, Churchill concluded: "And so, in God's mercy, a happy Christmas to you all."

Struck by the solemnity of the task before her

husband and her guest—and perhaps thinking, too, of her absent sons in the line of fire—Mrs. Roosevelt recalled "there was little joy in our hearts. The cold gripped us all so intensely that we were glad of a cup of tea on our return to the house."

Churchill probably declined the tea; his heart was racing. As he returned inside, he told Moran he "had had palpitations during the ceremony."

ELEANOR HAD BEEN worried about how Roosevelt would cope with the holiday, and Churchill's visit rescued it. "This was to be the first Christmas without my mother-in-law and I had dreaded it for my husband's sake," Eleanor recalled, "but the sudden influx of guests and the increasing work made it practically impossible for him to think too much about any personal sorrow." On the family front, the Churchills were unhappy about being apart. "Tender love to you and all—my thoughts will be with you this strange Christmas eve," Churchill wrote Clementine. "I miss you dreadfully," Clementine replied. "Time seems to stand still."

DESPITE HIS GENERAL aversion to going to church in the capital, Roosevelt liked spending Christmas mornings in Washington at the

Foundry Methodist Church. Defending his decision to forgo an Episcopal service to mark the Nativity, Roosevelt once said, "What's the matter? I like to sing hymns with the Methodys." As they set off this year, he declared: "It is good for Winston to sing hymns with the Methodys." There were lilies on the altar in memory of Roosevelt's mother, *The Washington Post* reported, and the two men sat in the fourth pew from the front as the minister prayed for "those who are dying on land and sea this Christmas morning." "Certainly there was much to fortify the faith of all who believe in the moral governance of the universe," Churchill recalled.

The services and ceremonies were inspiring, but the business at hand was tangled and difficult. "In these first talks which my husband and the prime minister had," Eleanor recalled, "they faced the fact that there was a long-drawn-out war ahead during which there would be many setbacks, and that both of them, as leaders of their nations, would have to be prepared to bolster the morale of their people."

ROOSEVELT AND CHURCHILL were both intimately involved in strategic decisions and took a strong hand in running the military—Churchill more so in London than Roosevelt in Washington, but Roosevelt was an active commander in chief. After a conversation once with Lord Ismay, *The Washington Post*'s Eugene Meyer observed, "I got the impression, of course, that the particular shaping up of the organization is closely related to the personality of the Prime Minister, and the fact that the present P.M. is himself a strategist in military affairs and in naval affairs he is a very strong influence in present forms and procedures."

At Christmas, there were the inevitably complicated questions of command and resource allocation, and the Americans favored the creation of a Combined Chiefs of Staff Committee, in Washington, to coordinate Allied strategy. (To sweeten the deal for the British, the Americans offered them a theater command in the Western Pacific, but events there were moving so quickly—and so badly—that the arrangement did not last.) After much maneuvering, Churchill agreed. His basic view of the practicalities of the alliance remained what it had been in theory all these months: that he and the president could work together even if they did not reach complete agreement at once. "For the first time," Moran recalled, "I have seen Winston content to listen. You could almost feel the importance he attaches to bringing the President along with him, and in that good cause he has become a very model of restraint and self-discipline." Surrounded by a vast array of issues—of strategy, of tactics, of supply, of command, of production—Churchill believed that, with Roosevelt, all would be well. When it came to munitions, for example, an Anglo-American committee was established with this concluding note: "Any differences arising, which it is expected will be rare, will be resolved by the President and the Prime Minister in agreement."

Both men were familiar with power. Governing was what Churchills and Roosevelts did. "I am a child of the House of Commons," Churchill dictated on Christmas Day, preparing for a speech to Congress. He remembered meeting the elite of his father's day in his youth. "It seemed a very great world in which these men lived," he once wrote, "a world where high rules reigned and every trifle in public conduct counted: a dueling-ground where although the business might be ruthless, and the weapons loaded with ball, there was ceremonious personal courtesy and mutual respect." Churchill carried a walking stick that had been a wedding gift from Edward VII. Through his filial devotion to Lord Randolph and his connection to the duke of Marlborough, Churchill took to exercising authority and guiding the life of his nation with grace. "Most of Churchill's ancestors had been politicians of one kind or another," recalled Maurice Ashley, his research assistant. "Political history was to him an absorbing interest if only because it was in part the story of his own family."

Roosevelt heard the same music. He had now been president of the United States longer than any man ever had, and his personal history was intertwined with the evolution of American power. Franklin Roosevelt had first visited the White House with his father in Grover Cleveland's day. Cleveland received father and son in his study one night after a long day. They found him, Sara later said, looking "more careworn than ever." Cleveland patted the five-year-old Roosevelt on the head and said, "My little man, I am making a strange wish for you. It is that you may never be President of the United States." Few presidential prayers have gone as unanswered as that casual one.

Roosevelt would boast that his great-great-grandfather Isaac Roosevelt, an early New York state senator and one of the ratifiers of the Constitution, had led Washington's horse in the first inaugural parade. On election night in Hyde Park in 1940, he claimed he remembered the torchlight parade marking Cleveland's victory in 1884.

On Christmas Day 1941, a Roosevelt had ruled for sixteen of the forty years since the turn of the twentieth century, and Franklin Roosevelt had spent another seven years as part

"We like new experiences in life"

Meeting the press in the Oval Office,
December 23, 1941

of President Wilson's extended official circle. He had come to Alice Roosevelt's wedding to Nicholas Longworth here; his grandchildren played in the Oval Office. When Roosevelt was elected in 1932, the head usher remembered the new First Lady from her days as "Miss Eleanor," a favorite niece of TR's visiting in the first years of the new century.

Eleanor was struck, too, by how comfortable her husband felt in the White House on the night of his first inaugural in March 1933. "My husband did not go to the inaugural ball because he found it too difficult to go in and out of crowded places of that kind," Eleanor recalled. When she and the children returned from showing the flag, Eleanor wondered how Roosevelt was getting along. "I was interested because I felt that with my husband's sense of history, the first night in the White House would be a tremendously historic, impressive thing to him," she said. "But on this occasion, to my surprise, he behaved exactly as though he had always been there and never anywhere else."

CHRISTMAS DINNER 1941 WAS a large affair, with the British guests mingling with a pack of Roosevelt cousins. Churchill had been working on his congressional address and was thinking of putting a passage from the 112th Psalm into the text when it came time to join the party. He wondered whether Roosevelt would approve of the passage, and Lord Moran carried the Bible along to cocktail hour. "The P.M. took the Bible from me and read his quotation to the President, who liked it," Moran recalled. The verse: "He shall not be afraid of evil tidings: his heart is fixed, trusting in the Lord." At dinner, Roosevelt reminded his guests that the king and queen had dined in this room on their 1939 visit, an event that had marked "a beginning of the coming together of the two English-speaking races"—borrowing one of Churchill's favorite phrases—"which would go on after the war." Everyone except Churchill sipped champagne; he was drinking whiskey. Churchill, Moran recalled, was "silent and preoccupied. Perhaps he was turning over in his mind tomorrow's speech to Congress."

While Churchill crafted his address into the night, Harry Hopkins was concerned that the recently isolationist Congress might not make a warm audience. Roosevelt wished Churchill luck as the prime minister set out for the trip up Pennsylvania Avenue on December 26. The mystery about how Churchill would find the crowd was quickly cleared up. A roar greeted the prime minister as he was escorted down the aisle to the Senate rostrum. In the White

House, Roosevelt listened to the speech over the radio.

"The fact that my American forebears have for so many generations played their part in the life of the United States, and that here I am, an Englishman, welcomed in your midst, makes this experience one of the most moving and thrilling in my life, which is already long and has not been entirely uneventful," Churchill told the Congress. "I wish indeed that my mother, whose memory I cherish across the vale of years, could be here to see. By the way, I cannot help reflecting that if my father had been American and my mother British, instead of the other way round, I might have got here on my own."

THEY LOVED IT; he had them from the first. The opening of this speech is among the best-known passages in the Churchill canon, particularly in America, but even more interesting is his next point, which is quoted less often: "In that case, this would not have been the first time you would have heard my voice," he said. "In that case I should not have needed any invitation, but if I had, it is hardly likely it would have been unanimous. So perhaps things are better as they are."

Those three sentences reveal a striking self-awareness on Churchill's part. He knew he was a complex man, someone who could be hard to get along with. But he then proceeded to show why his peacetime fault of bullheadedness was a wartime gift. He had found in Washington, he said, "an Olympian fortitude which . . . is only the mask of an inflexible purpose and the proof of a sure and well-grounded confidence in the final outcome. We in Britain had the same feeling in our darkest days."

He spoke of battles to come. "Some people may be startled or momentarily depressed when, like your President, I speak of a long and hard war. But our peoples would rather know the truth, sombre though it may be. And after all, when we are doing the noblest work in the world, not only defending our hearths and homes but the cause of freedom in other lands, the question of whether deliverance comes in 1942, 1943, or 1944 falls into its proper place in the grand proportions of human history." Churchill questioned the sanity of the Japanese. "What kind of a people do they think we are?" he asked. "Is it possible they do not realize that we shall never cease to persevere against them until they have been taught a lesson which they and the world will never forget?"

Churchill spoke for thirty-five minutes, but

the performance was so fluid that one correspondent said it had seemed like just five minutes in the galleries. It had flown by for the
speaker, too. "Inside, the scene was impressive
and formidable, and the great semicircular hall,
visible to me through a grille of microphones,
was thronged," Churchill recalled, the orator
savoring his success. "What I said was received
with the utmost kindness and attention. I got
my laughter and applause just where I expected
them. . . . The sense of the might and will-
power of the American nation streamed up to
me from the august assembly. Who could doubt
that all would be well?"

As he left the floor, Churchill turned and
flashed his "V for Victory" sign. "The effect
was instantaneous, electric," *The Washington
Post* reported. "The cheers swelled into a roar.
Usually restrained Harlan Fiske Stone, Chief
Justice of the United States, raised his arm in
a return salute . . . and fingers spread in the
victory sign were raised in scores of places
throughout the chamber." Senator Millard
Tydings of Maryland was glowing with admiration. "That fellow's really got it," Tydings said.
"You can follow that fellow anywhere." Senator Burton Wheeler, an isolationist, allowed:
"It was a clever speech and one that generally
will appeal to the American people." Churchill
greeted the senator at lunch afterward and told

his companions, with typical magnanimity, that he had discouraged criticism of the men of Munich in Britain because "if the present criticizes the past, there is not much hope for the future."

Leaving the Capitol, Churchill felt as he had the night he became prime minister: that he was walking with destiny and fulfilling a mystical role. "It was with heart-stirrings that I fulfilled the invitation to address the Congress of the United States," Churchill recalled. "The occasion was important for what I was sure was the all-conquering alliance of the English-speaking peoples. I had never addressed a foreign Parliament before. Yet to me, who could trace unbroken male descent on my mother's side through five generations from a lieutenant who served in George Washington's army, it was possible to feel a blood-right to speak to the representatives of the great Republic in our common cause. It certainly was odd that it should all work out this way; and once again I had the feeling, for mentioning which I may be pardoned, of being used, however unworthy, in some appointed plan." When Churchill got back to the White House, he went to see Roosevelt, who "told me I had done quite well." Not exactly effusive praise, but Churchill was pleased by the compliment—he remembered it for years and included the detail in his memoirs.

———

THAT NIGHT, after Churchill went to bed, he rose to open a window. "It was very stiff," he told Moran the next day. "I had to use considerable force and I noticed all at once that I was short of breath. I had a dull pain over my heart. It went down my left arm. It didn't last very long, but it has never happened before. What is it? Is my heart all right?" After listening to Churchill's heart, Moran realized Churchill might have suffered an episode of angina pectoris. "The textbook treatment for this is at least six weeks in bed," the doctor calculated. "That would mean publishing to the world—and the American newspapers would see to this—that the P.M. was an invalid with a crippled heart and a doubtful future. And this at a moment when America has just come into the war, and there is no one but Winston to take her by the hand." Even telling Churchill the full truth, Moran believed, would be risky. "I knew, too, the consequences to one of his imaginative temperament of the feeling that his heart was affected. His work would suffer. . . . Right or wrong it seemed plain that I must sit tight on what had happened, whatever the consequences."

"Well," Churchill said, "is my heart all right?"

"There is nothing serious," Moran said. "You have been overdoing things."

"Now, Charles, you're not going to tell me to rest. I can't. I won't. Nobody else can do this job. I must. What actually happened when I opened the window?" Churchill asked. "My idea is that I strained one of my chest muscles. I used great force. I don't believe it was my heart at all."

Moran stuck to his plan. "Your circulation was a bit sluggish. It is nothing serious. You needn't rest in the sense of lying up, but you mustn't do more than you can help in the way of exertion for a little while."

In 1950 Churchill wrote that "in trying to open the window I strained my heart slightly, causing unpleasant sensations which continued for some days." Reflecting on the incident years later, a doctor told Martin Gilbert: "In fact the course adopted by Moran on this occasion was quite correct. To have ordered bed rest for six weeks would not have been good therapy as there is no evidence that this does the patient any good and only tends to make them neurotic." Churchill's acknowledgment of the episode in his memoirs was oblique. "These great occasions imposed heavy demands on my life and strength, and were additional to all the daily consultations and mass of current business," Churchill wrote of the Washington visit. "In fact, I do not know how I got through it all." Clementine worried he was working at a

desperate pace. "I have been thinking constantly of you & trying to picture & realize the
drama in which you are playing the principal—
or rather it seems—the only part," she wrote
him. "I pray that when you leave, that the fer-
vour you have aroused may not die down but
will consolidate into practical & far-reaching
action." It was her husband's prayer, too—one
he held so fervently that his blood was running
high.

ON NEW YEAR'S MORNING 1942, Roosevelt and Churchill sat together in George
Washington's pew at Christ Church in Alexandria and sang "The Battle Hymn of the Republic." The rector, Reverend Edward Randolph
Welles, read Washington's Prayer for the United
States and preached that "the spirit of Christ
alone stands in the way of successful Nazi world
domination, for it alone can inspire a successful
will to resist and provide sufficient power to
achieve victory." Eleanor had to slip her husband cash for the collection plate, since he
rarely carried money. "When these little things
are taken care of by others as a rule, it is easy
always to expect them to be arranged," Eleanor
recalled. The hymns echoing in their heads,
Roosevelt and Churchill drove on to Mount
Vernon, where Roosevelt watched as Churchill

laid a wreath of chrysanthemums and irises at the first president's tomb.

Back at the White House later that day, Joseph Lash was seated next to Churchill. "I was too awe-struck to open my mouth," Lash recalled. "Hitler had sounded awfully anxious in his New Year's Day message, Churchill observed, even invoking Almighty God," Lash recalled. " 'But we have a presumption on the Deity,' he added, looking at the president, who was known to be pressing the Russians hard to permit religious freedom." Roosevelt had been wrestling with the Soviets over adding a reference to the defense of religious freedom in an Allied declaration to be signed that evening. Ambassador Maxim Litvinov had resisted its inclusion, preferring the phrase *freedom of conscience.* Churchill remembered that Roosevelt had "had a long talk" with Litvinov alone "about his soul and the dangers of hell-fire," but what worked was a deft Rooseveltian formulation in which the president assured Litvinov that "conscience" and "religion" were synonymous. Roosevelt, Robert Sherwood recalled, said, "The traditional Jeffersonian principle of religious freedom was so broadly democratic that it included the right to have no religion at all—it gave to the individual the right to worship any God he chose or no god." Churchill was so amused by Roosevelt's theological maneuvering that he told Roosevelt he would make him archbishop of Canterbury if Roosevelt lost the next campaign. ("I did not however make any official recommendation to the Cabinet or the Crown upon this point," Churchill noted, "and as he won the election in 1944 it did not arise.")

Roosevelt was Churchill's sole concern. "He was always full of stories, but at meals, no matter how far apart the two were sitting or who was next to him, Churchill tried to talk with FDR—the whole flow of Churchill's conversation was directed at the President," said Trude Lash, who was at lunch that day and would marry Joe in 1944. "You couldn't have a big ego if you were sitting next to him, because you might be hurt that he didn't seem to take an interest in you."

THEY HAD WORK to do that night. Roosevelt and Churchill were to adopt "A Declaration by the United Nations," a kind of successor document to the Atlantic Charter, affirming that the Allies were fighting because they were "convinced that complete victory over their enemies is essential to defend life, liberty, independence, and religious freedom."

The guests came back together for dinner

before the signing. Roosevelt mentioned his "stab in the back" speech at Charlottesville—the address that had so excited and yet so disappointed Churchill about America's readiness for war. Not surprisingly, Roosevelt was the hero of Roosevelt's story, though Eleanor got a cameo. "Although il Duce had just brought Italy into the war," Joseph Lash recalled, "the State Department had made the president take the cutting ['stab in the back'] phrase out of the prepared text. On the way to the university, however, Roosevelt had decided to restore it. He asked Mrs. Roosevelt what she thought. If he felt he should, he ought to use it had been her advice."

Churchill was sympathetic. According to Lash, Churchill said "he knew that feeling. . . . He was always having to take things out of his speeches." It was a moment of commiseration for men at the top who could be prone—often understandably—to self-pity.

There was chat about Hitler and about Stalin. "The best thing to do with Hitler, the president . . . said, would be to put him on a ship from which he would disappear," Lash noted. Churchill reminisced about his own battle in Russia after the revolution there. "Churchill recalled that in 1918–1919 he had . . . gotten as far as Tula, just south of Moscow, in his effort to overthrow the Bolsheviks," Lash said. "Now, however, he forgave 'the Russians in proportion to the number of Huns they killed.'

" 'Do they forgive you?' Hopkins asked.

" 'In proportion to the number of tanks I send,' Churchill replied."

ROOSEVELT AND CHURCHILL adjourned to the Oval Study, where Roosevelt signed the declaration first, then Churchill. Then came the Soviet and Chinese envoys. For Churchill, long the only bulwark against the Axis, it was thrilling. "Four fifths of the human race," Churchill said. He liked this phrase, and as with many phrases he liked, this was not the first time he had used it. Three weeks before, declaring war on Japan, he had told the House of Commons: "We have at least four-fifths of the population of the globe upon our side."

Churchill's pride in what Britain had done alone under his leadership was never far from his mind, and he would later indulge it in debates with Roosevelt and Stalin. But tonight, twenty-eight months to the day since the invasion of Poland, Churchill, Joseph Lash wrote, "stalked around the study with a look of great satisfaction on his face."

———

THE MEN AROUND Roosevelt were worried that their guest's rhetorical triumph on Capitol Hill would overshadow their boss as the State of the Union message drew near. Steve Early, "fiercely loyal and jealous of his Chief's prestige," Sherwood recalled, "kept charts showing the fluctuations of the size of the President's radio audiences and he did not welcome the appearance of a new star attraction in a field which Roosevelt had so long monopolized." Roosevelt was as competitive as any man who ever lived, but in this flush season of friendship, Sherwood said, he "was not troubled; he was greatly amused by his friends' concern." Churchill may have sensed something of the behind-the-scenes drama, for when Roosevelt read a draft to him, Churchill was flattering. "It went over big," Roosevelt told his advisers later. Perhaps one reason Roosevelt was able to laugh off his aides' anxiety about his rank in the rhetorical arena was that the politician in him understood that whatever the style of the speech, its substance would guarantee his preeminence in the emerging firm of Roosevelt & Churchill.

American strength would carry the day, and power would follow the money, the men, the ships, the planes, the tanks—the lion's share of which would come from the United States, not Britain. Beaverbrook had arrived and urged more, more, more, with an energy that appealed to Roosevelt. "We cannot wage this war in a defensive spirit," Roosevelt told Congress on January 6, 1942. "As our power and our resources are fully mobilized, we shall carry the attack against the enemy—we shall hit him and hit him again wherever and whenever we can reach him."

Roosevelt, meanwhile, was praising his guest behind his back—a sign of genuine admiration. Sam Rosenman dined at the White House on a January evening when Churchill was out and recalled that "the conversation was mostly about Churchill—Roosevelt was most enthusiastic about him and praised his rugged, bold approach to the problems of the war."

It had been a long few weeks. "My American friends thought that I was looking tired and ought to have a rest," Churchill recalled, so he took off for five days at the shore in Florida, relaxing at Lend-Lease administrator Edward Stettinius's place near Palm Beach. Clementine was cheered by the thought that her husband would be getting a rest. "I am happy that you are slipping away to the South for . . . rest & sunshine," she wrote him. Churchill's hours were also weighing on Roosevelt. "This routine was beginning to get Roosevelt down," Rosenman said, "and he laughingly remarked that he was looking forward to the Prime Minister's departure in order to get some sleep."

TIRED, CHURCHILL TOOK his exhaustion out on his party at the beach. "Nothing seems to be right," recalled Lord Moran, noting that Churchill was "in a belligerent mood. . . . He was just hitting out blindly, like a child in a temper." The storm passed as Churchill splashed naked in the surf ("half-submerged in the water like a hippopotamus in a swamp," Moran said). Inspector Thompson had tried to get Churchill into a pair of swimming trunks but failed. "Nobody knows I am staying in this place, and I have only to step out of the back door into the sea," Churchill said.

"You could be seen through glasses, sir," Thompson said.

"If they are that much interested, it is their own fault what they see," Churchill replied. As he was swimming, there was word of a shark sighting. "They said it was only a 'ground shark'; but I was not wholly reassured," Churchill remembered. "It is as bad to be eaten by a ground shark as by any other. So I stayed in the shallows from then on." He told Thompson to stand watch against the shark as he lolled at the edge of the water, but, Thompson said, "we saw no more of it."

When Churchill rose to return to the villa, he merrily took credit for the shark's disappearance. "My bulk must have frightened him away!"

There was one uncomfortable moment for Churchill, an episode that suggests for all the warm words and cheery meals, he remained insecure about his place in Roosevelt's affections. Churchill described the incident as "amusing, though at the moment disconcerting." Wendell Willkie wanted to see Churchill while the prime minister was in the United States, but, Churchill recalled, "Roosevelt had not seemed at all keen about my meeting prominent members of the Opposition, and I had consequently so far not done so." Despite Roosevelt's tacit embargo on contacts with Republicans, Churchill asked his staff to get Willkie on the phone. This is Churchill's account of the ensuing debacle: "After some delay I was told, 'Your call is through.'

"I said in effect, 'I am so glad to speak to you. I hope we may meet. . . . Can you not join the train at some point and travel with me for a few hours? Where will you be on Saturday next?'

"A voice came back: 'Why, just where I am now, at my desk.'

"To this I replied, 'I do not understand.'

" 'Whom do you think you are speaking to?'

"I replied, 'To Mr. Wendell Willkie, am I not?'

" 'No,' was the answer, 'you are speaking to the President.'

"I did not hear this very well, and asked, 'Who?'

" 'You are speaking to me,' came the answer, 'Franklin Roosevelt.'

"I said, 'I did not mean to trouble you at this moment. I was trying to speak to Wendell Willkie, but your telephone exchange seems to have made a mistake.' "

Roosevelt ignored this. " 'I hope you are getting on all right down there and enjoying yourself,' said the President. Some pleasant conversation followed about personal movements and plans, at the end of which I asked, 'I presume you do not mind my having wished to speak to Wendell Willkie?'

"To this Roosevelt said, 'No.' And this was the end of our talk."

And this was the end of our talk: a distant and correct "No." Churchill was mortified. This was a serious gaffe, the fact of his going behind Roosevelt's back compounded by his failing to recognize Roosevelt's voice even after Roosevelt identified himself. That alone probably annoyed Roosevelt, who did have one of the most recognizable voices in the world in January 1942. Churchill must have been churning with anxiety, so he did what suitors and friends the world over do when they make a mistake:

He enlisted an envoy to see what the damage was. "It must be remembered that this was in the early days of our friendship," Churchill said, "and when I got back to Washington I thought it right to find out from Harry Hopkins whether any offence had been given." To Hopkins, Churchill wrote: "I rely on you to let me know if this action of mine in wishing to speak to the person named"—Churchill is so embarrassed now that he does not even use Willkie's name—"is in any way considered inappropriate, because I certainly thought I was acting in accordance with my duty to be civil to a public personage of importance." Hopkins was brief but reassuring. This was at worst a small bump in an ever wider road of friendship. "Hopkins said that no harm had been done," Churchill recalled.

Preparing to return, he had telephoned Roosevelt, and this time he knew whom he was talking to. Churchill tried charm—and it worked. "I mustn't tell you on the open line how we shall be travelling," he said, "but we shall be coming by puff puff."

THE AUTHOR LOUIS ADAMIC and his wife, Stella, were ushered into the White House for dinner with Roosevelt and Churchill on the evening of January 13, 1942. Thus began one of the odder and least-known episodes in the annals of the Roosevelt-Churchill friendship. Adamic was a Slovenian-born writer who had published a book, *Two-Way Passage,* which argued that Americans who had come from the devastated countries of Europe should return after the war to help build democratic institutions. Predictably, the idea attracted Mrs. Roosevelt's attention, and she invited the author and his wife to meet Roosevelt.

The tone of *Two-Way Passage*—and of the book Adamic would write about this single night, *Dinner at the White House*—was hostile to the British empire and to Churchill. Moreover, Adamic added a footnote to the 1946 book about the evening quoting a Washington columnist who alleged that Churchill had shaped British policy toward Greece because the country's chief English creditor, the Hambros Bank of London, had "bailed Winston Churchill out of bankruptcy in 1912." Churchill sued Adamic for libel in England and won. Yet even taking his ideological bias against Churchill into account, Adamic's description of the evening offers a window on the subtleties of the blossoming friendship.

AS THE ADAMICS entered the Oval Study for drinks, Roosevelt looked well. The last time Adamic had seen Roosevelt up close, in July

1940, had not been encouraging. Talking then about America's lack of preparedness for war, "His hands, gesturing for emphasis, lighting one cigarette after another, and flicking the ashes off his wrinkled seersucker coat, shook rather badly," Adamic wrote. "The rings under his eyes were very dark and deep." But now "there was no trace of ill-health, weariness or doubt. F.D.R. looked extraordinarily fit, self-possessed, relaxed—on top of the world."

Adamic was watching Roosevelt, taking everything in. "He was giving the last few flips to the silver cocktail shaker. His face was ruddy and his close-set gray eyes flashed with an infectious zest . . . ," Adamic wrote. "A servant placed a bowl of popcorn before F.D.R., who said, 'Ah—thank you,' and took a handful and began to toss it dexterously into his mouth. . . . Maybe an evening like this, I thought, is his way of keeping sane while in the dead center of an overwhelming insanity."

Churchill appeared. He struck Adamic at first as shorter than expected, "a rotund, dumpy figure. . . . Yet, as he advanced into the room, a semi-scowl on his big, chubby, pink-and-white face with its light-blue eyes, the knowledge of his performance since Dunkerque and something about his person gave him a massive stature. He moved as though he were without joints, all of a piece: solidly, unhurriedly, impervious to obstacles, like a tank or a bulldozer."

"Hello, Winston," Roosevelt said.

"Evening, Mr. President," Churchill said, calling him by his title in mixed company. It was a mark of deference not unlike Churchill's habit of wheeling Roosevelt around the house, a custom Churchill, in his active historical imagination, linked to Raleigh's spreading his cloak before Queen Elizabeth. Watching the two men, Adamic observed that "they were obviously friends, but—perhaps less obviously— friends of a special kind, in whose relations the personal and the supra-personal were turbulently mingled."

Roosevelt asked, "Had a good nap, Winston?"

"Churchill scowled . . . or perhaps 'pouted' is the more accurate word," Adamic wrote, "and sticking his cigar in his mouth, mumbled something neither Stella nor I understood, although the room was very still."

"Will you have one of these, Winston?" Roosevelt called out from the drinks tray.

"What are they?"

"Orange Blossoms."

"Churchill made a face," Adamic recalled, "but he accepted the cocktail and drank it dutifully."

They went downstairs for dinner. Churchill rode the elevator with Roosevelt, and when everyone reached the ground floor, Eleanor stopped the guests and discussed the portraits on the walls while Roosevelt went ahead to the dining room. "On the train going home that night it occurred to Stella and me," Adamic wrote, "that Mrs. Roosevelt had held Churchill and the ladies in the hall . . . to give the President, whom an attendant had wheeled from the elevator into the dining room, a chance to switch from the wheelchair to his seat at the table"—another example of Roosevelt's masterly stagecraft. "It's strange to say now," George Elsey said after the war, "but you did not really notice he could not walk. He was a sort of Mount Rushmore being wheeled around, and all you noticed after a while was the Mount Rushmore part."

Margaret "Rollie" Hambley (later Margaret Hendrick) was there, too, and wrote Daisy Suckley an observant letter about the dinner. "The Prime Minister is about 5' 7" and quite fat about the waist. . . . He has a very pink face, whitish-red thin hair, and very piercing pale blue eyes," Hambley wrote. "He looks just like his pictures and his nose has a very strange shape—it looks as if it were chiseled. . . . He has a very keen mind much more so than the Pres. but of course he has not all that wonderful charm and personality." Hambley also noticed that despite Churchill's public oratory, in person "he has a very poor voice. One can hardly understand him it is so indistinct and stammering, but he uses the most wonderful language imaginable. He speaks very often in similes and metaphors, comparing the Germans to hawks, and Von Ribbentrop to a clown." Twinkling, Churchill began to talk about how terrible Hitler was to "bomb all the beautiful scotch whiskey and cigar warehouses," Hambley wrote. "He said he didn't know what would happen to a country when its supplies of whiskey and cigars ran out."

Roosevelt was enjoying this, and he and Churchill then told a story about a Christmas gift gone bad. A box of cigars had arrived at the White House from Cuba, but, Hambley wrote, the box "was filled with worms." Groaning, Hambley "refused to eat any more food, but he seemed to delight in my illness and went into more & more detail of how they crept through each cigar."

Amid the ebb and flow of the conversation—which, Hambley wrote, touched on "cigars, the 30 points, German religion, Von Ribbentrop, Carol of Rumania . . . whiskey, college reunions"—a guest asked about King Zog of Albania.

As Adamic recalled it, Roosevelt cried out: " 'Zog!'

"The upper part of his body leapt up so that

he almost seemed to rise," Adamic wrote. "We all looked at him. He leaned over the table and pointed a finger at Churchill:

" 'Winston, we forgot Zog!'

"Churchill puckered his lips as if to say: So what, or, as he probably would have put it: Well? . . .

" 'Albania is a belligerent on our side,' said the President. He scratched his head. 'I believe there's an Albanian Minister or representative here—we must get him to sign our little document.' " Roosevelt and Churchill had neglected to get Albania, one of their allies, to affix an official signature to the declaration they had promulgated on New Year's Day. There was laughter, but Adamic was troubled by the tone of the gathering. "A couple of emperors!" he said to himself. ". . . Says one emperor to the other across the dinner table: 'Oh say, we forgot Zog.' It's funny as hell. But too damned personal, haphazard, high-handed, casual. What else have they overlooked?"

When the Adamics left for a concert with Eleanor, Roosevelt and Churchill stayed behind, chatting and joking. Hambley and Anne Curzon-Howe, a school friend of Hambley's, rose to leave Roosevelt and Churchill alone, but the president stopped them, saying, "Where do you think you're off to? Sit down."

He was relieved to have an undemanding audience. "Mrs. Roosevelt invited these people she got interested in," Hambley said of the Adamics, "and I don't think FDR was happy that they were there when Churchill was. FDR and Churchill relaxed after they left."

Churchill tried to be charming. He and young Miss Curzon-Howe shared a distant ancestral bond in England, and Churchill said to her, "Call me Cousin Winston because of our Curzon connection."

The subject of growing old came up. "The P.M. said that a woman was as old as she looked; a man was as old as he felt; and a boy was as old as he was treated," Hambley noted. Churchill appeared downcast. "You know I must be the oldest man ever to have been in the White House." No, no, Roosevelt interjected. "The Pres. said there had been someone 95 there, so he cheered up."

They were in their element. "Brandy and the usual cigars were going strong," Anne Curzon-Howe recalled, "and W. and FDR seemed to be getting on famously and capping each other's stories."

THE NEXT NIGHT was Churchill's last in Washington, and he dined alone with Roosevelt and Hopkins. There were documents to initial, and the three friends lingered an hour beyond the prime minister's scheduled departure time. It seems to have been a sentimental farewell. Hopkins tried a light touch in a letter he gave Churchill to take to Clementine, writing: "You would have been quite proud of your husband on this trip. First because he was ever so good-natured. I didn't see him take anybody's head off and he eats and drinks with his customary vigor, and still dislikes the same people. If he had half as good a time here as the President did in having him about the White House he surely will carry pleasant memories of the past three weeks."

Yet the friendly words were also tinged with the certain knowledge that victory would not be theirs overnight. Roosevelt and Churchill knew war was not a game; it was by their order that men would die. When Churchill signed a copy of the first volume of his book *The River War* for Roosevelt during his stay, his salutation captured the melancholy burden of ultimate command: "Inscribed for President Franklin D. Roosevelt by Winston S. Churchill," the prime minister wrote. "In rough times January 1942." Roosevelt's parting words to Churchill struck the same note. "Trust me," the president said, "to the bitter end." They would see the "rough times" through—side by side.

"There is no worse mistake in public leadership than to hold out false hopes soon to be swept away"

———

Clementine, Mary, and Winston Churchill
at Westminster Abbey on the National
Day of Prayer, March 19, 1942

CHAPTER 6

I THINK OF YOU OFTEN

Churchill Faces a Storm at Home–Family Dramas–
Roosevelt Comforts Churchill–A Sunday Morning
in the Oval Study

I T WAS TO NO sunlit prospect that I must
return," Churchill said of mid-January 1942.
Robert Sherwood called this season the "winter
of disaster." It had begun, really, more than a
month before, when the Japanese sank the *Prince
of Wales* and the *Repulse*. Many of the sailors who
had prayed with Churchill and Roosevelt were
killed. ("Nearly half those who sang," Churchill
wrote in his recollection of the church parade,
"were soon to die.") Pearl Harbor had been
another dark chapter. January and February
brought more horror. "The underrated Japanese
forces shattered all previous Allied appraisals and
calculations, and did so with such bewildering
speed that the pins on the walls of the map
rooms in Washington and London were usually

far out of date," Sherwood wrote. The war in North Africa was troubling, too. The German commander, Erwin Rommel, was successfully driving east toward Tobruk. This was the world Roosevelt and Churchill were confronting, and Roosevelt was drawing on his mysterious supply of confidence and courage to face it.

He had lit the fires of American production. The generals were building the army. The man who had overcome polio and restored faith during the Depression believed he would win this war, too. Late one night after the true extent of the damage at Pearl Harbor had become clear, Sam Rosenman stopped by the White House following a presidential broadcast and discovered Roosevelt in his study with his stamp collection. "There was no excitement here now, no hectic atmosphere of false rumors; there was no fear—not even disquietude," Rosenman recalled. Over ginger ale (for Rosenman) and a beer (for FDR), the speechwriter was impressed by the president's equanimity. "There was a man at a big desk, smoking a cigarette, poring over his stamps. There was concern, yes, deep concern; but it was a calm concern. He was worried, deeply worried; but there was no trace of panic. His face was resolute, even grim; but it was confident and composed." Hopkins sensed the same thing after Churchill's return to England. "The President is amazingly calm about the war," Hopkins noted after seeing Roosevelt on January 24.

CHURCHILL WAS FEELING queasier, at least politically. He faced a no-confidence vote in the House. "Home again with the Prime Minister who is now the daring young man on the flying trapeze," Lord Beaverbrook cabled Averell Harriman on January 18. "Clementine hated to see Winston so beset on all sides," wrote Mary Soames. Churchill was out of sorts. "One of the characteristics of this great man was his incapacity for dwelling anywhere but on the peaks, or in the abyss," recalled Beaverbrook. "Gloom or glory, near-despair or complete triumph—these were the opposed climates of his being." A cold made things worse. "In spite of the shocks and stresses which each day brought," Churchill said of the effort it took him to prepare a long speech defending himself to the House of Commons at this time, "I did not grudge the twelve or fourteen hours of concentrated thought which ten thousand words of original composition on a vast, many-sided subject demanded"—language that suggests he did "grudge" the task—"and while the flames of adverse war . . . licked my feet, I succeeded in preparing my statement and appreciation of our case." He then recalled—perhaps unconsciously, for he does not cite her—a point in Clementine's 1940 letter urging him to be gentler with his subordinates. "I also remembered that wise French saying, *'On ne règne sur les âmes que par le calme.'*" He was trying to do as Clementine had suggested—steady himself in public and keep the snarling in private to a minimum.

Churchill believed people reacted to the world in the way he did, and his understanding of leadership flowed from that premise. In Churchill's cosmos there was joy in the journey; without darkness there could be no light. This was one reason he often spoke of "our long story" or "our island story"—stories require conflict and challenges, victories and defeats. He wanted a part in the battles of his time so that he would live in the legend of the ages, and he assumed others did, too. It was no coincidence that in his "Finest Hour" broadcast he tied the trials of the present to the collective consciousness of the world to come. *Men will still say* was a call to arms reminiscent of Shakespeare's Henry V bracing his men to fight at Agincourt with the image of how the tale would be told from generation to generation: "This story shall the good man teach his son. . . ." Be brave now, and the future will cherish your memory and praise your name—an impressive, if risky, means of leadership, for under stress not all of us are like Bedford and Exeter.

For Churchill there was a fundamental democratic instinct at work, too. His definition of
heroism offered the possibility of glory for
everyone, not just great men like Marlborough
and Nelson and Wellington (or Churchill and
Roosevelt). "Trust the people," Lord Randolph
used to say. Because Churchill was leading a
nation that had been threatened by invasion
(and might yet be again) and in which people
faced attack from the air, he was talking about
war not as a distant phenomenon, but rather as
one in which all of his listeners were both targets and potential soldiers. They deserved the
truth. "There is no worse mistake in public
leadership than to hold out false hopes soon to
be swept away," Churchill wrote. "The British
people can face peril or misfortune with fortitude and buoyancy, but they bitterly resent
being deceived or finding that those responsible
for their affairs are themselves dwelling in a
fool's paradise."

At his best, Roosevelt held essentially the
same view as Churchill. "The news is going to
get worse and worse before it begins to get better," Roosevelt said in the winter of 1942.
"The American people must be prepared for it
and they must get it straight from the shoulder."
People respect candor if they are confident their
leaders have a plan for moving forward. They
do not like being talked down to or misled. It is

the covenant of modern democracies: Tell it to us straight, and we will do what it takes. In a Washington's Birthday broadcast from the White House while Churchill was confronting his problems on the home front, Roosevelt said: "For eight years General Washington and his Continental Army were faced continually with formidable odds and recurring defeats. Supplies and equipment were lacking. In a sense, every winter was a Valley Forge. Throughout the Thirteen States there existed . . . selfish men, jealous men, fearful men, who proclaimed that Washington's cause was hopeless, that he should ask for a negotiated peace." Roosevelt quoted Thomas Paine: "Tyranny, like hell, is not easily conquered." Churchill was grateful, calling the speech "heartening."

Rising above his cold, Churchill's ten thousand words answered his own critics with force. Before the vote on January 29, Churchill made a final point. "In no way have I mitigated the sense of danger and impending misfortunes—of a minor character and of a severe character—which still hang over us. But at the same time I avow my confidence, never stronger than at this moment, that we shall bring this conflict to an end in a manner agreeable to the interests of our country, and in a manner agreeable to the future of the world." He won 464 to 1. Behind the scenes, Churchill was still seething. "The naggers in the press were not however without resource," he snapped, lashing out, as many politicians do, at journalists. "They spun round with the alacrity of squirrels. How unnecessary it had been to ask for a Vote of Confidence! Who had ever dreamed of challenging the National Government?"

Roosevelt congratulated him by likening Churchill's parliamentary test to the American declaration of war on Japan. "We also had one vote in opposition," Roosevelt remarked on January 30, alluding to one pacifist dissent on Pearl Harbor. It was no small comparison, and Churchill understood that. Roosevelt was saying they were in this together.

Still, the critics were not going away. "There is very little to cheer us these days because the news is so dreadful," Nancy Astor wrote Eugene Meyer. "However, I am certain it will be better." But, in an apparent reference to Churchill's domestic woes, Lady Astor added: "These shake-ups are good, and there is no good following a man—you have got to follow a principle. I have never met a man I could follow always—I've only read of them."

SINGAPORE, BRITAIN'S PRIZE in the Pacific, soon fell, further complicating Churchill's life. "I speak to you all under the shadow of a heavy and far-reaching military defeat," Churchill said in a broadcast on February 15, 1942, admitting the scope of the disaster. "It is a British and Imperial defeat." It was a time, like 1940, for courage. "This, therefore, is one of those moments when the British race and nation can show their quality and their genius. This is one of those moments when it can draw from the heart of misfortune the vital impulses of victory. Here is the moment to display that calm and poise combined with grim determination which not so long ago brought us out of the very jaws of death"—another echo of Clementine's personal counsel, now being applied to the whole nation. "Here is another occasion to show—as so often in our long story—that we can meet reverses with dignity and with renewed accessions of strength."

Churchill pointed out that American sea power had been "dashed to the ground" at Pearl Harbor. "There were numerous expressions of irritation at this statement in Washington, as though Churchill were attempting to escape censure by blaming it all on the U.S. Navy," wrote Sherwood, "but it did not bother Roosevelt at all." The president waved away the talk. As a fellow politician, he understood what Churchill was going through. "Winston had to say *something*," Roosevelt said.

Privately, Churchill remained disconsolate. "I

realize how the fall of Singapore has affected you and the British people," Roosevelt wrote Churchill on February 18, dismissing attacks from those who did not know what it was like to be in their jobs. "It gives the well-known back seat drivers a field day but no matter how serious our setbacks have been, and I do not for a moment underrate them, we must constantly look forward to the next moves that need to be made to hit the enemy," he told Churchill. "I hope you will be of good heart in these trying weeks because I am very sure that you have the great confidence of the masses of the British people. I want you to know that I think of you often and I know you will not hesitate to ask me if there is anything you think I can do."

Roosevelt's words were a mark of the new Roosevelt-Churchill connection. Another mark was Churchill's reciprocal candor in confiding his troubles to Roosevelt. Two years before, Churchill had tried to conceal his anxiety from Roosevelt, but now he was more direct. "I do not like these days of personal stress and I have found it difficult to keep my eye on the ball," he wrote to Roosevelt on February 20.

Two weeks later, Churchill added: "When I reflect how I have longed and prayed for the entry of the United States into the war, I find it difficult to realize how gravely our British affairs have deteriorated by what has happened since December seven. We have suffered the greatest disaster in our history at Singapore, and other misfortunes will come thick and fast upon us. Your great power will only become effective gradually because of the vast distances and the shortage of ships."

"This may be a critical period," Roosevelt wrote back, still trying to cheer Churchill up, "but remember always it is not as bad as some you have so well survived before."

LIKE ROOSEVELT, Clementine wanted to find a way to help Churchill. "Clementine was of course deeply concerned for Winston: she saw every day the toll the weight of the war exacted from him, and he confided to her all his worries and tribulations," Mary wrote. "With her brave and stoical outlook"—a feature Clementine shared with Eleanor—"she accepted that the strain and burden of the work could scarcely be otherwise. But however and whenever she saw a chance to ease his burden or to spare him extra worry, she did so, and she could be fiercely protective if she thought unnecessary anxieties or problems were added to those it was inevitable he had to bear." By her own account, though, Clementine some-times made things worse (another parallel with

Eleanor). She and Churchill tangled over Beaverbrook's role—Churchill's old friend was causing friction in the government, and Clementine thought he should go. The force of the Churchills' quarrel can be inferred from a note Clementine wrote her husband: "I am ashamed that by my violent attitude I should just now have added to your agonizing anxieties—Please forgive me."

In the spring of 1942, their son, Randolph, who had been working as a staff officer in Cairo, decided to become part of a paratroop squad. It was a courageous, glamorous, impetuous thing to do—the kind of thing his father would have done. When Churchill told Clementine of Randolph's plan, she apparently turned to stone, later writing: "Please don't think I am indifferent because I was silent when you told me of Randolph's cable to Pamela saying he was joining a parachute unit . . . but I grieve he has done this because I know this will cause you harrowing anxiety, indeed even agony of mind. . . . Surely there is a halfway house between being a Staff Officer and a Parachute Jumper? . . . considering he has a very young wife with a baby to say nothing of a Father who is bearing not only the burden of his own country but for the moment that of an unprepared America, it would in my view have been his dignified & reasonable duty."

Mary called Clementine's view "a most uncharacteristic reflex, for she greatly admired spontaneous and brave actions." Randolph Churchill is often seen as a pale imitation of his father, with an outsize appetite for ambition (and drink). But he was fierce in war, felicitous in journalism, and his father's first official biographer. "In the event Clementine took no action, and Randolph pursued his intention of joining the Special Air Service," Mary wrote of his decision. Mary saw the likely truth: "One cannot help feeling that in this matter her judgment went a little astray; but at this time of intense strain her first thought was for Winston"—as it always had been and would be.

There was another source of tension in the Churchills' private universe this year. Randolph had learned that his wife, Pamela, had carried on an affair with Averell Harriman, who was also married. Pamela and Harriman had met when Harriman came to London at Roosevelt's behest in 1941. Randolph believed that his parents had known about the liaison and done nothing to stop it. Churchill, however, does not appear to have been a particularly good student of such things, and a letter of Clementine's from the period suggests she was unaware of the affair. Still, an anguished son lashed out at his parents. "When Randolph levelled this accusation against his father, a battle royal erupted at

Downing Street, following which his mother—fearful that Winston might have a seizure—banned Randolph from their home for the rest of the war," wrote Winston S. Churchill, the son of Randolph and Pamela. According to young Winston, Mary "was outraged that her father should be abused in this way. Though loyal to Randolph and, like her sisters, scandalized at what had befallen him, Mary . . . told him that the best thing he could do was to rejoin his unit and go to the Front. Mary poignantly records in her wartime diary: 'I think the greatest misfortune in R's life is that he is Papa's son—Papa has spoilt and indulged him & is very responsible.' "

ROOSEVELT PRESIDED OVER a spirited and sometimes tense household, too. "I think there was always a tendency on Franklin's part to try and draw his family into discussions of public affairs, and there was as a result a great deal of sometimes argument between us, on ideas and policies, and practical politics," recalled Eleanor. "But I think it was something that my husband enjoyed in an intellectual way." There was never any doubt where the true power lay. One evening on the presidential train, the Roosevelt children were at dinner with their parents and some members of the cabinet. The guests, Eleanor said, "looked so horrified when they heard the boys arguing violently with Franklin on a number of points that I finally felt impelled to explain that in our family the boys had always been encouraged to express their opinions." Then Eleanor concluded: "I did not add what was soon evident: that their father always waited while they expressed themselves loudly and forcefully and until each one had had his say, and then demolished them with a few well chosen arguments of his own." *Demolished* is a pretty strong word, one that suggests the president often liked having the last word.

The Roosevelts had to fight two overwhelming forces for their father's attention: polio and politics. But James, the eldest, insisted that "we five Roosevelt children never wholly lost our Pa—our affectionate, witty, loyal, and even overloyal Pa. He could find time, even while nations shook and the world burned, to write each of us debonair little notes about our personal affairs. He also could and did take infinite pains to bring us into his orbit, to give us front-row seats from which we might witness the shaping of the momentous events in which he was involved. But we did lose a good part of that personal Pa of ours—and not even he was strong enough to prevent it—when we had to begin sharing him with the world."

The Roosevelts had four sons and a daughter, the Churchills three daughters and a son. (Both families lost a child early on.) Every family—or nearly every family—has its private dramas and peculiar rhythms of affection and disappointment. Families at the top of political life are not really different: We just know more about them. Even in the middle of political and military storms, their broods—Roosevelt called his "the chicks"; Churchill referred to his as "the kittens"—were in their heads and hearts. Roosevelt and Churchill left the discipline to their wives, relishing their children unaffectedly. "His letters show a touching interest and concern for his nursery," Mary wrote of her father. "His children, and later his grandchildren, were always conscious that he loved to have them around. 'Come to luncheon,' he would say to someone, extending an invitation to Chartwell, adding with obvious relish: 'You'll find us all bunged up with brats.' " Anna Roosevelt was a great comfort to her father, and Mary was a source of enormous pride to both her parents.

Some of the children, though, were more difficult than others. In both families there were problems of unhappy marriages, serial divorces, drinking, and next-generation political and business failures. "One day in Washington I had a very delightful chat with the President about two weeks before he died," the war correspondent William Walton wrote Pamela Churchill after seeing Roosevelt in 1945. "He asked me all kinds of things about D-Day, parachuting, Paris, Germany and London." Pamela kept a portrait of Roosevelt next to one of Churchill in her house. "Eventually I told him the most beautiful woman in London had his picture in her drawing room," Walton wrote. "He was pleased to hear it was you and said he hoped to meet you someday because he'd heard so much about you. Then with a great roar of laughter he said, 'But that R[andolph] what a handful he is! What a handful!' I think for the PM to have such a problem child rather delighted him since he had so many of his own. . . ."

THERE IS NO question that the long shadow Churchill and Roosevelt threw had an impact on their children. "Nothing grows under the shadow of a great tree," Randolph said of his father. "It was a shock to the boys to discover that in the White House, if they wanted to really talk to their father beyond a casual conversation with other people around, they had to ask for an appointment," Eleanor recalled, "and even when they got the appointment, sometimes affairs of state would be so important that they didn't get the full attention of their father." Mary made a similar observation. "As children, we soon became aware that our parents' main interest and time were consumed by immensely important tasks, besides which our own demands and concerns were trivial," she wrote. "We never expected either of our parents to attend our school plays, prize-givings, or sports' days." But they made the best of it. "We knew they were both more urgently occupied, and any feelings of self-pity were overborne by a sense of gratification that their presence was so much required elsewhere."

A love of grandchildren linked Churchill and Roosevelt. Churchill wept at young Winston's baptism in 1940 ("Poor infant," Churchill said amid tears, "to be born into a world such as this"). Roosevelt insisted on having his grandchildren in the White House for his fourth inaugural in 1945.

Randolph and Pamela's divorce in December 1945 troubled Churchill, and he wrote a touching letter about it to Pamela's mother—a note of grace and magnanimity. "I grieve vy much for what has happened wh put an end to so many of my hopes for the future of Randolph & Pamela," Churchill said. "The war strode in havoc through the lives of millions. We must make the best of what is left among the ruins. Everything must be centred upon the well-being & happiness of the Boy. Pamela has brought him up splendidly. There must be friendship to shield him from the defects of a broken home. . . . It is a comfort that the relations between our families remain indestructible."

One of the things the Roosevelts and the Churchills shared with many of the people they led in the war was anxiety about their children in uniform. Concern for the children—their own and the other men's—became a running theme for Roosevelt, Churchill, Hopkins, and Beaverbrook. "I hope you have good news of your boys," Beaverbrook wrote Roosevelt in the summer of 1944. "It must be a constant preoccupation with you." It was. "I think my husband would have been very much upset if the boys had not wanted to go into the war immediately, but he did not have to worry very much because they either were already in before the war began, or they went in immediately," Eleanor recalled. "After that, actually, we had one advantage, I suppose, and that was that we always did know what was happening in the war picture, and therefore we knew more quickly where our own children were involved, and what was going on, but I think this made us more conscious of the difficulties of parents, whose children were scattered all over, and who couldn't know as quickly as we could know—perhaps had weeks of anxiety before they got news of any kind." James,

Elliott, John, and Franklin Jr. saw action. Randolph would be under fire in different theaters and sustained injuries; and his sisters, Diana, Sarah, and Mary, were in uniform, Mary manning an antiaircraft battery in London and later in northwest Europe. Hopkins's sons, Robert and Stephen, served (Stephen would die in the Pacific); Beaverbrook's son Max won fame as a fighter pilot.

This human dimension of Roosevelt's and Churchill's wartime lives has been largely forgotten, but the safety of their children was always on their minds, and they often asked after each other's broods. "Seeing their sons go off to war was hard on both my husband and Harry Hopkins," Eleanor recalled. "Both of them would have liked to take their sons' places. They wanted their sons to do what they could for the country, but humanly they wished they could be side by side with them. I think one of the secrets of Harry's eagerness to take any trips Franklin might suggest, and Franklin's insistence on himself taking trips which he felt might be of service lay in the strong subconscious desire to share the dangers their sons were going through." Those pins in the map rooms, from London to Washington, had faces attached to them—and some of those faces were their own children's.

———

THERE   WERE   FORTY-FIVE   months
between Pearl Harbor and V-J Day, and the
debate over where to establish a front other than
the one in the east, where the Germans and the
Soviets were slaughtering each other—a debate
carried out between Roosevelt and Churchill,
face-to-face and pen-to-pen—would consume
twenty-four of those months. Churchill himself
best expressed the cultural background of the
argument. "In the military as in the commercial
or production spheres the American mind runs
naturally to broad, sweeping, logical conclusions on the largest scale," he wrote. "It is on
these that they build their practical thought and
action. They feel that once the foundation has
been planned on true and comprehensive lines
all other stages will follow naturally and almost
inevitably. The British mind does not work
quite in this way. We do not think that logic and
clear-cut principles are necessarily the sole keys
to what ought to be done in swiftly changing
and indefinable situations. In war particularly
we assign a larger importance to opportunism
and improvisation, seeking rather to live and
conquer in accordance with the unfolding
event than to aspire to dominate it often by fundamental decisions. There is room for much

argument about both views. The difference is one of emphasis, but it is deep-seated."

Many American officials, led by George Marshall, believed the path to victory lay in going straight at Hitler's Fortress Europe. Churchill, however, worried that the Allies did not yet have the power to reconquer Europe and would continue to advance other operations, many in the Mediterranean, until he believed there was sufficient force to carry the day in France. The scale and scope of attacking a fortified French coast and establishing a bridgehead worried the prime minister, who was haunted by memories of past failures. "When I think of the beaches of Normandy choked with the flower of American and British youth, and when, in my mind's eye, I see the tides running red with their blood," Churchill would say to Dwight Eisenhower, "I have my doubts . . . I have my doubts." One day, the combined strength of Roosevelt and Stalin would force him to act. But until then, Churchill pushed with vigor and eloquence for action in other theaters in the hope of winning the war without a dangerous landing on the coast.

Roosevelt was thinking along different lines in early 1942 and dispatched Hopkins and Marshall to London. "What Harry and Geo. Marshall will tell you all about has my heart and *mind* in it," Roosevelt wrote Churchill on April 3. "Your people and mine demand the establishment of a front to draw pressure off the Russians, and these peoples are wise enough to see that the Russians are today killing more Germans and destroying more equipment than you and I put together." The idea: to prepare for an April 1, 1943, invasion across the Channel, with a plan, as a memorandum approved by Roosevelt put it, "for immediate action by such forces as may be available from time to time." A 1942 landing, in other words, might come either to "(*a*) take advantage of a sudden German disintegration or (*b*) 'as a sacrifice' to avert an imminent collapse of Russian resistance."

While saying that Roosevelt's strike, if successful, would be "one of the grand events in all the history of war," Churchill was anxious. The majority of troops would be British; there were enormous issues about landing craft and logistics; and, as Churchill recalled, "neither we nor our professional advisers could devise any practical plan for crossing the Channel with a large Anglo-American army before the late summer of 1943." Churchill had other concerns as well, including using troops to defend India from Japan. There had to be additional options for action against Germany while the Allies built up force to crack Fortress Europe. What about North Africa, a possibility that had first been

*"The war strode in havoc through
the lives of millions"*

Pamela Digby and Randolph Churchill
on their wedding day, October 4, 1939

broached by Roosevelt and Churchill at Washington? The conversations would go on.

THE FATE OF India was another area of disagreement between Roosevelt and Churchill. Roosevelt thought it past time to grant the Indians self-rule, and he had brought up the subject at Christmas 1941. "The President had first discussed the Indian problem with me, on the usual American lines during my visit to Washington in December, 1941," Churchill recalled. "I reacted so strongly and at such length"—translation: I went on and on and on—"that he never raised it verbally again." In the middle of the Second Front negotiations in April, Roosevelt had written Churchill urging that the British allow India to govern itself. The telegram arrived at three o'clock one morning at Chequers. Churchill rejected Roosevelt's advice in a late-night conversation with Harry Hopkins. The prime minister could not shut up about it. "Churchill said that he personally was quite ready to retire to private life if that would do any good in assuaging American public opinion," Sherwood wrote after reviewing Hopkins's notes, "but he felt certain that, regardless of whether or not he continued as Prime Minister, the Cabinet and Parliament would continue to assert the policy as he had stated it."

As he listened to Churchill rage on at this late hour, Hopkins became convinced that, as Sherwood put it, "India was one area where the minds of Roosevelt and Churchill would never meet." Roosevelt thought Churchill sentimental about the subcontinent; Churchill thought Roosevelt idealistic.

The next day, Churchill had calmed down. "I used to see a lot of Churchill in the two and a half years I was in England," Averell Harriman recalled, "and things would come up, and I would tell him, 'Don't send that telegram to the President, it's the wrong thing to say,' and he would growl and say he was going to send it. And the next morning it would be about 7:30. He'd call me into his room, while dictating, [and say,] 'What do you think of this?' He'd have an entirely new telegram. He'd never admit he was wrong. Then I'd say, 'Your idea about this is exactly right.' "

Hopkins now saw what Harriman had seen. After ranting at Hopkins in the wee hours, Churchill framed his actual answer to Roosevelt in as friendly a way as he could. "You know the weight which I attach to everything you say to me, but I did not feel I could take responsibility for the defence of India if everything has again to be thrown into the melting pot at this critical juncture . . . ," Churchill cabled Roosevelt on April 12, 1942. "Anything like a serious difference between you and me would break my heart and surely deeply injure both our countries at the height of this terrible struggle." Roosevelt dropped the subject—for the time being.

BY MID-JUNE 1942, the war news was better, at least in the Pacific. In the first week of June, the navy had won the critical battle at Midway, a victory that avenged Pearl Harbor. Churchill was coming to America to see Roosevelt about the conflicting strategic ideas. Would there be a landing, however small, in France in 1942, or would the Allies focus on North Africa?

Roosevelt was at Hyde Park when Churchill arrived in Washington. The old place had become even more important to him since Sara's funeral. Daisy Suckley noticed that the "big house without his mother seems awfully big & bare—she gave him that personal affection which his friends & secretaries cannot do, in the same way." To Sara, Daisy said, Roosevelt "was always 'my boy,' and he seemed to me often rather pathetic, and hungry for just that kind of thing." In front of the fireplace in the library one evening that winter with Roosevelt, Daisy noted that "Mrs. Roosevelt's chair [was] so very strikingly empty—I was conscious of it all the time, and feel he is, too."

In reaction to Sara's death, Roosevelt had become even more obsessed with continuity and control in his private universe. Eleanor had taken time in the spring to clear out the two East 65th Street homes. "We had lived in those houses since 1908 and one can imagine the accumulation of the years," Eleanor recalled. "My mother-in-law never threw anything away. It was a tremendous job. My husband had not been in either house since 1932, yet he could tell me exactly what he wanted and where it would be. That spring he spent about two hours in the houses and noticed everything that had been moved . . . the crates and boxes and barrels were marked so the things could be stored at Hyde Park and my husband could unpack gradually." Dips into these boxes—which were really dips into his past—sustained him. Sitting at Hyde Park, the pieces of his life around him, enabled Roosevelt to channel his grief into nostalgia. Eleanor was understandably ambivalent about Roosevelt's immersion in memory; he had apparently failed to say thank you for all she had done to move the belongings up the Hudson. "It did not all go as smoothly as we had hoped," she remembered, "and one or two things he later wanted especially could not be located until I had time myself to delve into the crates and boxes stored in the cellar of the house." A striking scene: Eleanor Roosevelt rooting around in the basement of a house in which she never felt entirely at home, seeking what her husband wanted.

ON THE MORNING of Friday, June 19, Churchill flew into New Hackensack airport near Hyde Park to "the roughest bump landing I have experienced." Roosevelt met him in his blue Ford, which he could drive by himself with hand-controlled levers, and whizzed his guest around the estate. Churchill was impressed with Roosevelt's driving but was a bit uneasy when the president would roar up to "the grass verges of the precipices over the Hudson." The prime minister offered a silent prayer: "I hoped," Churchill recalled, "the mechanical devices and brakes would show no defects."

It was a profitable ride. Driving along, Churchill said, "all the time we talked business, and . . . we made more progress than we might have done in formal conference." The tone of the strategic conversations between the two principals can be inferred from a note Churchill gave Roosevelt during the stay. It was impassioned, practical—and effective: "No responsible British military authority has so far been able to make a plan for September 1942 which had any chance of success unless the Germans become utterly demoralized, of which there is no likelihood," Churchill wrote. "Have the American staffs a plan? If so, what is it? What forces would be employed? At what points would they strike? What landing-craft and shipping are available? Who is the officer prepared to command the enterprise? What British forces and assistance are required?" Compelling words, and they would hit their mark.

Churchill was fascinated by his friend's home, which must have pleased Roosevelt. While the president got ready for lunch on this June Friday, Churchill was shown to his room upstairs. Known as the Pink Room, the small suite was filled with huge English prints and faced west, toward the Hudson. Coming down, Churchill found Daisy Suckley alone in the front hall. He became shy; where Roosevelt would have turned on the charm, tossing his head back and smiling broadly, Churchill hesitated. "Seeing a strange woman, he stopped on the lower stair landing & examined a painting," Daisy wrote. "I started to gaze at something, too—it may have been the trees! He turned & came down the last two steps—he smiled—I smiled. We shook hands—I introduced myself—We wandered down the hall to the Library." It was the kind of house familiar to Churchill, a mix of paintings, family portraits, books, photographs in silver frames, broad views of green, the scent of tobacco smoke.

"There seemed to be real friendship & understanding between F.D.R. & Churchill," Daisy noted as she watched them together for the first time. "F.D.R.'s manner was easy and intimate— His face humorous, or very serious, according to the subject of conversation, and entirely *natural*. Not a trace of having to guard his words or expressions, just the opposite of his manner at a press conference, when he is an actor on a stage—and a player on an instrument, at the same time."

EACH MAN WAS a good student of the other. Roosevelt asked Daisy a favor: Would she arrange for a tea at Top Cottage the next day? Scotch and ice were to be on offer—"in case Mr. C. might like some," Daisy noted. She innocently added in her diary: "He evidently takes it quite regularly." Meanwhile, Churchill used Harry Hopkins as a conduit for business, the prime minister recalled, "so that the ground was prepared and the President's mind armed upon each subject."

One afternoon, they all lunched in the minty green dining room. Afterward Roosevelt was wheeled into his little study on the ground floor, a secluded room facing east, where he could sit and look out across the front porch. Originally built in a 1915 addition to the house as a classroom for the Roosevelt children, the study had become a hideaway for Roosevelt, who liked to work there surrounded by nautical prints, a New York Democratic National Convention delegation sign, and glass-fronted bookcases.

Roosevelt invited Churchill and Hopkins in for a chat. "The room was dark and shaded from the sun," Churchill recalled. A globe sat on the floor; Churchill remembered the desk nearly filled the office. They had gathered to discuss what the British called "Tube Alloys"— the effort to build an atomic bomb.

In August 1939, Churchill had been briefed by Lindemann, his friend and scientific adviser, about the possibilities of splitting the atom, and Roosevelt had learned of the potential for such a weapon in October of that year, when Alexander Sachs, an occasional Roosevelt economics adviser who had served in the National Recovery Administration, brought the president a letter from Albert Einstein. In June 1940, Roosevelt approved pushing ahead on research. In Britain, Churchill had had the same reaction as the president: Push ahead. The British were making progress, Churchill now reported to Roosevelt in the small room, and the time had come for a research plant. Churchill suggested he and Roosevelt join forces. The Germans were in the race, too, and there was not a moment to lose. "What if the enemy should get an atomic bomb before we did!" Churchill said. "However skeptical one might feel about the assertions of scientists, much disputed among themselves and expressed in jargon incomprehensible to laymen, we could not run the mortal risk of being outstripped in this awful sphere." Amid the familiar—his books, his papers, his cigarettes—the sun shining outside, so focused on the momentous subject at hand that he did not appear to notice the heat, Roosevelt agreed. "I strongly urged that we should at once pool all our information, work together on equal terms, and share the results, if any, equally between us," Churchill recalled. And so it was. Soon the Manhattan Project would be under way.

It had been, Churchill said, a "grave and fateful decision." They then drove up to Top Cottage for "tea," where Daisy made sure Churchill got his Scotch while Roosevelt ate egg sandwiches with mustard greens. "Conversation was a little slow," Daisy noted. "Everyone sits around waiting for the P. & Mr. C. to speak—It must be quite a strain on them both—" It was, and therein lies one of the conundrums of a great leader's life. Being constantly, or nearly constantly, expected to perform is tiring, but perhaps the only thing worse would be to *not* be constantly, or nearly constantly, expected to perform.

ROOSEVELT AND CHURCHILL took the overnight train to Washington, where it was a warm Sunday with brief thundershowers expected in the afternoon and evening. At the White House, Churchill "glanced at the newspapers, read telegrams for an hour, had my breakfast, looked up Harry across the passage, and then went to see the President in his study." Lord Ismay—it was his birthday—was with him. A telegram on pink paper was brought in and handed to Roosevelt. "Tobruk has surrendered," the note read, "with twenty-five thousand men taken prisoners."

The Germans had humiliated the British. In the desert, Erwin Rommel had taken the garrison that could be key to the Middle East and its treasures. The notion of surrender was anathema to Churchill, who had sworn—to his people, to his enemies, to Franklin Roosevelt—never to give in. "Defeat is one thing; disgrace is another," Churchill thought. "Not only were its military effects grievous, but it had affected the reputation of the British armies. At Singapore 85,000 men had surrendered to inferior numbers of Japanese. Now in Tobruk . . . seasoned soldiers had laid down their arms to perhaps one-half of their number." Churchill believed Tobruk's fall to be "one of the heaviest blows I can recall during the war." It was, he said, "a bitter moment." Two summers before, he would not have let his true feelings show. Today he did. "I did not attempt to hide from the President the shock I had received," Churchill recalled. The meaning was immediately apparent to those in the White House. "This was a body blow for Churchill," wrote Sherwood. "It was another Singapore. It might well be far worse even than that catastrophe in its total effect—for, with Tobruk gone, there was little left with which to stop Rommel from pushing on to Alexandria, Cairo—and beyond. The prospect of a German-Japanese junction now loomed larger than ever as a possibility or even probability, and remained so for weeks thereafter."

ROOSEVELT SPOKE UP and, Ismay recalled, "in six monosyllables he epitomized his sympathy with Churchill, his determination to do his utmost to sustain him, and his recognition that we were all in the same boat."

"What can we do to help?" Roosevelt asked, reaching out to his anguished comrade. "I remember vividly being impressed by the tact and real heartfelt sympathy that lay behind these words," recalled General Brooke, who was there. "There was not one word too much or too little." In this same room in December, Roosevelt had received the news of Pearl Harbor. He knew what it was like to be in charge and yet feel powerless. His hard-earned powers of empathy were now deployed in the service of his friend, who himself had earned Roosevelt's trust by proving his courage and steadfastness in 1940 and 1941. "Roosevelt's heart warmed to his beleaguered friend and his sympathetic actions in support were the tonic which did as much as anything to restore Churchill," recalled Jock Colville.

"Give us as many Sherman tanks as you can spare, and ship them to the Middle East as quickly as possible," Churchill said, trying to think—and look—ahead.

After calling for George Marshall, Roosevelt put the problem to him. "Mr. President," Marshall replied, "the Shermans are only just coming into production. The first few hundred have been issued to our own armoured divisions, who have hitherto had to be content with obsolete equipment. It is a terrible thing to take the weapons out of a soldier's hands." But like Roosevelt, he was instinctively kind toward Churchill. "Nevertheless," Marshall continued, "if the British need is so great they must have them; and we could let them have a hundred 105-mm. self-propelled guns in addition." It was a critical gesture, for, as Ismay recalled, "they arrived in time to play a big part in the victory of Alamein."

THE DECISION WAS made quickly. "It is interesting to consider what might have happened if the business which they put through in a matter of minutes in the White House had been handled through normal official channels," Ismay recalled. "A desperate appeal for tanks might have come from General Auchinleck to the CIGS. The General Staff would have said to themselves: 'There are none available here, but there is just a chance that Washington might be able to help.' A telegram would have gone to the Pentagon, and the probable reaction would have been, 'We are sorry that we cannot do anything at the moment. The only available Shermans have just been issued to our own troops, and it would be impossible to take them away . . .' [and] the chances of this vital equipment arriving in time would have been remote."

They adjourned for lunch, and as they ate, Eleanor was amazed by the fortitude of her husband and his friend. "To neither of those men was there such a thing as not being able to meet a new situation," she noted. "I never heard either of them say that ultimately we would not win the war. This attitude was contagious, and no one around either of them would ever have dared to say, 'I'm afraid.' " Churchill was outwardly brave but inwardly crushed.

"What matters is that it should happen when I am here," he said to Moran later that day. "I am ashamed. I cannot understand why Tobruk gave in. More than 30,000 of our men put their hands up. If they won't fight—" Churchill, Moran recalled, stopped. "It was the President who told me," Churchill mused. "He was very kind." Writing long afterward about how Roosevelt and Hopkins reacted to Tobruk, Churchill noted: "Nothing could exceed the sympathy and chivalry of my two friends. There were no reproaches; not an unkind word was spoken." At that moment, Churchill recalled, he felt like the unhappiest Englishman in North America since General Burgoyne—the officer who surrendered at Saratoga.

IF ROOSEVELT HAD been distant or cross or even just ambivalent when the telegram arrived—not unthinkable prospects—Churchill might have had a harder time regaining his footing after the news came. Churchill quoted an aphorism to describe Roosevelt's reaction to Tobruk: "A friend in need is a friend indeed." On this Sunday morning, Roosevelt fulfilled a definition of friendship Churchill had written about in his novel, *Savrola:* "A man loves his friend," Churchill had noted, because "he has stood by him perhaps at doubtful moments."

Believing himself secure in Roosevelt's affections and esteem, Churchill was able to channel his uneasiness into action. "Winston's buoyant temperament is a tremendous asset," Moran noted in his diary. "The fall of Tobruk, like the loss of the *Prince of Wales* and the *Repulse,* has been a blow between the eyes. Not only Cairo and Alexandria, but the Suez Canal and all the oilfields of the Near East seem to be at the mercy of Rommel. And yet, before I left his bedroom on Sunday, Winston had refused to take the count; he got up a little dazed, but full of fight."

Though the prime minister and the president were determined to keep the mask of command on, there was much to worry about. Roosevelt rang Daisy that week and said, "The Germans are better trained, better generaled—'You can never *discipline* an Englishman or an American as you can a German'— . . . I asked where the blame lies for the present situation in Egypt. He said partly Churchill, mostly the bad generals— F. was depressed over the situation. If Egypt is taken, it means Arabia, Syria, Afghanistan, etc., i.e. the Japs & Germans control everything across from the Atlantic to the Pacific—that means all the oil wells, etc. of those regions—a bleak prospect for the United Nations."

On his way to his plane—he was taking off from Baltimore—Churchill had a brush with a potential assassin. "The narrow, closed-in gangway which led to the water was heavily guarded by armed American police," Churchill recalled. "There seemed to be an air of excitement, and the officers looked serious. Before we took off I was told that one of the plainclothes men on duty had been caught fingering a pistol and heard muttering that he would 'do me in,' with some other expressions of an unappreciative character. He had been pounced upon and arrested. Afterwards he turned out to be a lunatic. Crackpates are a special danger to public men, as they do not have to worry about the 'getaway.' " Roosevelt had the same stoic view of assassination. After the shooting in Miami in 1933, Roosevelt had called Eleanor, who was giving a speech in Ithaca, New York. Calmly, Eleanor recalled, Roosevelt had said, "Of course, if someone did not care whether they were caught or not, they could always attack anybody no matter how much care the Secret Service took, no matter what was done." He felt particularly vulnerable—touchingly—on his crutches, on which he said he was "slow, of necessity, in getting out of the car." Going forward, Roosevelt told Eleanor, "You can't live with that on your mind all the time—you've got to forget it. We will just have to force ourselves never to think of these possibilities, otherwise life will be impossible."

AS HE HEADED home in June 1942, "this seemed to me to be a bad time," Churchill recalled. He beat back a vote of censure, and in the House he let the mask slip just enough to show his humanity. "Some people assume too readily that, because a Government keeps cool and has steady nerves under reverses, its members do not feel the public misfortunes as keenly as do independent critics," he said. "On the contrary, I doubt whether anyone feels greater sorrow or pain than those who are responsible for the general conduct of our affairs."

"Good for you," Roosevelt wrote Churchill after the vote on July 2, 1942. Roosevelt got away for the Fourth of July, paying his first visit to Shangri-la, a camp built by the Civilian Conservation Corps that the president had taken over as a retreat near Washington. To unwind, Roosevelt browsed through a copy of *Jane's Fighting Ships*.

IN JULY, both Roosevelt and Churchill went on record about reports from Europe on the horrors facing the Jewish people. In his 1935 essay about Hitler, Churchill had been eloquent on the question. "The Jews, supposed to have contributed, by a disloyal and pacifist influence, to the collapse of Germany at the end of the Great War, were also deemed to be the main prop of communism and the authors of defeatist doctrines in every form," Churchill wrote. "Therefore, the Jews of Germany, a community numbered by many hundreds of thousands, were to be stripped of all power, driven from every position in public and social life, expelled from the professions, silenced in the Press, and declared a foul and odious race. The twentieth century has witnessed with surprise, not merely the promulgation of these ferocious doctrines, but their enforcement with brutal vigour by the Government and by the populace." In a speech to the Reichstag on January 30, 1939—Roosevelt's birthday—Hitler had pledged to destroy the Jewish race. At a secret conference in Wannsee, a suburb of Berlin, on January 20, 1942, a handful of top German officials laid out the mechanics of the Final Solution, which was already unfolding in parts of Europe.

On July 21, twenty thousand people attended an event in Madison Square Garden organized by American Jewish groups. Roosevelt and Churchill sent statements. "Citizens, regardless of religious allegiance, will share in the sorrow of our Jewish fellow-citizens over the savagery of the Nazis against their helpless victims," Roosevelt said. Churchill noted that "the Jews were Hitler's first victims" and said "retribution for these crimes" was "among the major purposes of this war."

It marked the first time they spoke out together against Hitler's crimes against the Jews. The debate over the Allied response to the Holocaust touches on anti-Semitism, prewar and wartime refugee policy, proposals for ransom and rescue, Arab sensitivities in the Middle East, and possible military strikes directed at rail lines or at the death camps. Churchill and Roosevelt spent little time on the issue together, however, and both men have been criticized since the war for failing to do more to save European Jewry from Hitler. Given the enormity of the crimes committed against the Jewish people and the central place the Holocaust has rightly come to occupy in our communal memory, some scholars now assign a measure of blame to the Allies for, in David S. Wyman's phrase, "the abandonment of the Jews." Critics say Roosevelt and Churchill were indifferent or even callous, refusing to take political or military risks for Jews; defenders argue that the two men were understandably focused on the complete military defeat of the Third Reich as the best way to save the Jews—and everyone else—from Nazism. In truth, neither man could have kept the Holocaust from happening, and the Allied military campaigns may have kept the Final Solution from being applied in the Middle East in the short term and unquestionably defeated Nazism entirely in the long term.

Churchill and Roosevelt had long grasped the threat Hitler posed to the Jews. In 1932, Churchill was researching his biography of Marlborough and went to Munich after touring the battlefield at Blenheim. Randolph and Clementine were with him. Hitler, who would come to power in January 1933, was also in Munich. A member of Hitler's entourage, the half-German, half-American Ernst Hanfstaengl (a Harvard alumnus who had become friendly with Franklin Roosevelt in the early years of the century) tried to arrange a meeting between Churchill and Hitler, but Hitler put Hanfstaengl off. "Hitler produced a thousand excuses, as he always did when he was afraid of meeting someone," recalled Hanfstaengl. "With a figure whom he knew to be his equal in political ability, the uncertain bourgeois re-emerged again, the man who would not go to a dancing-class for fear of making a fool of himself, the man who only acquired confidence in his manipulation of a yelling audience." That night, Hanfstaengl and the Churchill party dined without Hitler at the Hotel Continental. "Why is your chief so violent about the Jews?" Churchill, a longtime Zionist, said to Hanfstaengl. "I can quite understand being angry with Jews who have done wrong or are against the country, and I understand resisting them if they try to monopolise power in any walk of life; but what is the sense of being against a man simply because of his birth? How can any man help how he is born?" Hanfstaengl mounted a defense, but Churchill closed the subject with this remark: "Tell your boss from me that anti-Semitism may be a good starter, but it is a bad sticker." The next morning, Hitler—who had not been told about Churchill's remarks about the Jews—continued to duck the British visitors, saying: "In any case, what part does Churchill play? He is in opposition and no one pays any attention to him."

Roosevelt was also often seen as pro-Jewish (the "Jew Deal" was among the slurs his anti-Semitic foes used against him) in an era in which many Americans considered Jews suspect. As president he appointed many Jews to office, and when a sanitized translation of *Mein Kampf* was published in the West in 1933—one which censored some of Hitler's fiercer anti-Semitic observations—Roosevelt noted: "This translation is so expurgated as to give a wholly false view of what Hitler is and says—the German original would make a different story." After Kristallnacht, Roosevelt said that he "could scarcely believe that such things could occur in a twentieth century civilization" and summoned his ambassador home from Berlin. And after a 1942 White House meeting, Rabbi Stephen Wise, a prominent American Zionist, wrote: "Thank God for Roosevelt. We ought to distribute cards throughout the country bearing just four letters, TGFR, and as the Psalmist would have said, thank Him every day and every hour."

Yet immigration quotas and anti-Semitism were political realities in both nations before and during the war, and though Roosevelt and Churchill were the most courageous of politicians, they were still politicians. Both countries allowed refugees in after Hitler's rise to power (for instance, 120,000 Germans and Austrians, 90 percent of whom were Jewish, came to the United States; 70,000 went to Britain). But there were dark chapters. In May 1939, the ship *St. Louis* brought more than 900 Jewish refugees to Cuba in the hope that they would be allowed into the United States; the passengers were instead returned to pre-Holocaust Europe, where many nonetheless later died in the camps. Meanwhile, in 1939, London, worried about Arab reaction, limited immigration into Palestine, which was a British mandate. Immigration into Britain was also restricted.

Early in the war, the bureaucracies in London and Washington (Churchill and Roosevelt largely delegated the issue to the Foreign Office and the State Department) moved painfully slowly, if at all, in helping those Jews who could elude the grasp of the Third Reich to emigrate to safe havens. It is clear that Roosevelt and Churchill could have paid more attention to the question during the war and tried to take more action to move Jews out of harm's way, both by attempting to open their nations' doors wider to fleeing Jews and by more aggressively encouraging neutral countries to do the same. There were such efforts before 1944, but not many.

This is not just historical second-guessing: Some of Churchill's and Roosevelt's contemporaries believed the Allies should have been bolder. "In other days I would have come to you in sackcloth and ashes to plead for my people; it is in that spirit I write," Lady Reading of the World Jewish Congress wrote Churchill in January 1943. "Some can still be saved, if the iron fetters of the red-tape can be burst asunder." An aide to Treasury Secretary Henry

Morgenthau spent Christmas Day 1943—two years after America entered the war—writing a report entitled "Report to the Secretary on the Acquiescence of This Government in the Murder of the Jews."

A few weeks later, in January 1944, Morgenthau, believing that anti-Semites in the State Department were not doing enough for Europe's Jews, helped convince Roosevelt to establish a War Refugee Board. The board managed to rescue thousands of Jews in the last year and a half of the conflict—a sign that earlier attention and action could have made a difference, even if undertaken at a moment when the Allies were not as strong militarily as they were by 1944–45 and even if the number of the rescued was small.

Retribution, not rescue, was a central feature in Churchill's and Roosevelt's remarks on the Final Solution. "Assuredly in the day of victory the Jew's suffering and his part in the struggle will not be forgotten," Churchill wrote *The Jewish Chronicle* in November 1941. "Once again, at the appointed time, he will see vindicated those principles of righteousness which it was the glory of his fathers to proclaim to the world. Once again it will be shown that, though the mills of God grind slowly, they grind exceedingly small."

A little over a year later, in December 1942, a

Jewish delegation visited the White House to petition Roosevelt about the plight of their European brethren. "The mills of the gods grind slowly," the president said, "but they grind exceedingly small." Richard Breitman, a leading scholar of the Allied response to the Holocaust, pinpointed Churchill's and Roosevelt's parallel language, and noted: "Their renditions were slightly different—for example, Roosevelt had the 'mills of the gods' (not God)—but the reappearance of this phrase indicated that Chur-chill and Roosevelt were handling Jewish requests in virtually the same way. They both wanted to concentrate on winning the war as quickly as possible. The threat of postwar retribution was the only diversion they would consider."

On December 17, 1942, the United States, Great Britain, nine other nations, and the French National Committee issued the Allied Declaration, which condemned Germany for "now carrying into effect Hitler's oft-repeated intention to exterminate the Jewish people in Europe. From all the occupied countries, Jews are being transported, in conditions of appalling horror and brutality, to Eastern Europe. In Poland, which has been made the principal slaughterhouse, the ghettos established by the German invaders are being systematically emptied of all Jews except a few highly skilled workers required for war industries. None of those taken away are ever heard from again." The declaration proclaimed that "this policy of cold-blooded extermination . . . can only strengthen the resolve of all freedom-loving peoples to overthrow the barbarious Hitlerite tyranny" and resolved that "those responsible for these crimes shall not escape retribution." At the time, total military victory was widely seen as the fastest route to rescue. "The most tragic aspect of the situation is the world's helplessness to stop the horror while the war is going on," *The New York Times* editorialized the day after the Allied Declaration was issued. "The most it can do is to denounce the perpetrators and promise them individual and separate retribution. But at least this we know: that there can be no compromise with this evil force. It must be driven from the face of the earth." The day of victory over Hitler would come. It was far too late for millions of innocents. But the day did come.

"I FEEL DAMN depressed," Harry Hopkins scribbled across a piece of Downing Street stationery in the third week of July 1942. Churchill was like a cannon: wonderful and grand when he was at your side, blasting away at a common foe; terrible and defeating when he was across the field, blasting away at you. Hopkins was back in London, still haggling with the British over where the next major Allied operation would take place. While holding out hopes for an operation in Norway and suggesting planning for France should keep going, Churchill told Roosevelt he favored North Africa "as soon as possible." North Africa fit in with Roosevelt's main goal of the moment, which was, as Robert Sherwood characterized it, "U.S. ground forces must be put into position to fight German ground forces somewhere in 1942." Roosevelt had his reasons. "In this, Roosevelt was thinking not only of the effect on the Russians if eight autumn and winter months were to pass with no substantial action by Anglo-American forces; he was thinking also of the effect of inaction on the spirit of the American and British people, who might well begin to feel bogged down in the deadly lethargy of another period of 'Phony War,'" wrote Sherwood. That sealed it. Planning for an ultimate invasion in France would go forward, but the emphasis would be in the Mediterranean for now.

Delaying a major cross-Channel operation in 1942 was almost certainly the right call, and Churchill deserves credit for arguing that an attack on the periphery made more sense at this point. The Allies did not yet have the men, equipment, and experience they would need to break Hitler along the coast and inland, and a defeat would have been costly in lives and morale.

Roosevelt was pleased with the decision. "I cannot help feeling that the past week represented a turning point in the whole war and that now we are on our way shoulder to shoulder," he wrote Churchill on July 27. They were—though they were marching in a different direction from the one Roosevelt's own generals wanted. But Roosevelt and Churchill were in charge, and Operation TORCH was about to begin.

CHURCHILL SOON FOUND himself on his way to Moscow to explain to Stalin why there would be no Second Front in Europe that year. Before the August 1942 meeting, Roosevelt wrote Churchill about how best to handle "Uncle Joe" on a human level. "We have got always to bear in mind the personality of our ally and of the very difficult and dangerous situation that confronts him," Roosevelt told Churchill, who knew plenty about the fear of invasion. "No one can be expected to approach the war from a world point of view whose country has been invaded. I think we should try to put ourselves in his place." Churchill's skepticism about Stalin ran deep. A conversation among Churchill, Charles Eade, and Clementine shed light on Churchill's sense of the Soviets. "Mr. Churchill remarked on the difficulty of dealing with the Russians . . . ," noted Eade. "I suggested that they were suspicious of us. He said yes, that was probably true, but at any rate, we had never signed a pact with Germany. . . . He then said he wished to tell a story, but stressed that if we ever retold it we must not attribute it to him. He said that a British representative went to Russia and was shown around the sights. He was taken round by a guide who said at one point: 'This is Winston Churchill Square, late Adolf Hitler Square.' A little further the guide said: 'This is the Eden Hotel, late Marshal Goering Hotel,' and proceeding on their way a little further the guide said, 'This is Beaverbrook Street, late Himmler Street.' At this point the guide offered his English visitor a cigarette and the Englishman taking it said, 'Thank you comrade, late bastard.' "

INTERESTINGLY—IF NOT entirely surprisingly—Churchill enjoyed himself around Stalin in August 1942. ". . . I was sure it was my duty to tell them the facts personally and have it all out face to face with Stalin, rather than trust to telegrams and intermediaries," Churchill recalled. "At least it showed that one cared for their fortunes and understood what their struggle meant to the general war." This was part of Churchill's code. He respected men who fought bravely, either on the battlefields or in conferences or in legislatures, and believed such warriors should honor and be known to one another. A perpetual enthusiast, Churchill chose to think his time with Stalin all went well. He made the case for North Africa—all the while promising a more direct attack in France in 1943—with a visual aid. "To illustrate my point I had meanwhile drawn a picture of a crocodile, and explained to Stalin with the help of this picture how it was our intention to attack the soft belly of the crocodile as we attacked his hard snout. And Stalin, whose interest was now at high pitch, said: 'May God prosper this undertaking.' "

Back in London, Churchill told Charles Eade about his final evening with Stalin. "After their last official meeting, Stalin was quite worried at the thought of Mr. Churchill leaving Moscow without a further party, and the interpreter had asked whether the Prime Minister was 'preoccupied' that evening," Eade recalled. "As he was not, Churchill and Stalin had a drinking bout together which lasted through the night and caused Mr. Churchill to breakfast off aspirins in his plane high above Russia on his return journey."

———

WATCHING FROM AMERICA, Roosevelt
had been worried about Stalin's reaction and
about the approaching prospect of American
ground troops facing German fire for the first
time. "The P. has heavy worries about the
world just now, & when in repose, his face is
over serious & drawn," Daisy noted during a
visit to Hyde Park with Roosevelt during
Churchill's sojourn in Moscow. "His moments
of relaxation are few."

Slightly cheerier—but only slightly—word
about Roosevelt was reaching Churchill's circle. "The President is astonishingly well, in
spite of the fact that the war, I know, bears very
heavily on him," Hopkins wrote Beaverbrook
in the autumn of 1942, "and he never ceases to
think of ways and means of getting at the
enemy and is ever impatient with the progress
of the war."

At a lunch with Churchill around this time,
Daniel J. Tobin, the American Teamsters leader,
asked Churchill about how the Big Three—
Roosevelt, Churchill, and Stalin—would operate together. "The substance of Churchill's
reply to this was that he felt that Stalin was a
man with whom he could work," recalled
Charles Eade. "In any event he was quite sure
that he and Roosevelt would not allow Stalin to

exercise a predominating part in any post-war world, even if Stalin himself attempted to do so. At the same time he made it clear that his own view of Stalin was a high one." Then Churchill shifted his comments to Roosevelt. "His admiration for Roosevelt, however, was clearly of much greater quality. He spoke of Roosevelt's tremendous triumph over his physical disability and Mr. Churchill felt that here perhaps we had an example of the Almighty taking away with one hand the physical strength of a man, but, at the same time, giving with the other a great character which has played such a tremendous part in world affairs in the past few years." What Churchill intuited from afar in his 1934 article on Roosevelt—the connection between Roosevelt's paralysis and his courage and political passion—had been confirmed and strengthened by intimate experience and observation. Churchill knew bravery when he saw it, and he had seen it, up close, in Roosevelt.

*"The spirit of the English people
is something to bow down to"*

———

Eleanor in England, October 26, 1942

CHAPTER 7

YOU MAY KISS MY HAND

Eleanor Roosevelt Calls on the Churchills—
Rendezvous at Casablanca—A Sunset at the Pinnacle

I LIKE MR. CHURCHILL, he's loveable &
emotional & very human," Eleanor wrote her
daughter, Anna, in 1942, "but I don't want him
to write the peace or carry it out." Though
Churchill had a distinguished progressive record
from the early years of the century, Eleanor
could think of him only as a Tory imperialist.
The Churchill circle sensed Mrs. Roosevelt's
skepticism about the prime minister. "I do not
think Mrs. Roosevelt ever really got my father,"
said Mary Soames. "She was very suspicious of
him. He loved jokes and stories and was never
earnest—not her sort at all." Yet, for a moment
in the autumn of 1942, on a visit to England,
Eleanor and Churchill's differences were largely
submerged as Mrs. Roosevelt moved among

those who had been fighting Hitler far longer than America had.

She was rather arch about Churchill as she arrived. "Every time Mr. Churchill came to the White House, he spoke of the time when my husband would visit Great Britain, but one felt that he had in mind a visit to celebrate a victory either in sight or actually achieved," Eleanor recalled. "I do not think it ever occurred to him that there was any good reason why I should go to Great Britain during the war. He assumed, I think, that I would go in my proper capacity as a wife when my husband went. However, it evidently occurred to Queen Elizabeth, for Franklin received some tentative inquiries about whether I would be interested in going over and seeing the role that the British women were playing in the war." Eleanor was happy to accept. "I know our better halves will hit it off beautifully," Roosevelt wrote Churchill in a letter Eleanor carried with her. Several days later, the president cabled the prime minister: "I would appreciate it if you would let me know occasionally how things are going with her." Roosevelt also dispatched honey and a Virginia ham as bread-and-butter gifts for the Churchills. "I so *love* Virginia hams," Clementine wrote Roosevelt.

———

ON OCTOBER 23, 1942, at Buckingham Palace, Eleanor, the Churchills, and the Royal family watched In Which We Serve, a Noël Coward–David Lean movie telling the story of Lord Mountbatten's action under fire on the destroyer Kelly, which was sunk at the Battle of Crete. The film cuts back and forth between the men under fire and the lives and families they left behind at home. Mountbatten was there during the screening. "It was a novel experience to watch a movie about a man who was himself present," Eleanor recalled, "and a very moving experience to see it in the company of people who must have been deeply stirred by it." It was the kind of admiring reaction Harry Hopkins had had on his first visit. The evidence of the bombings in London also touched her, and the woman who had learned the art of close observation from her husband after he was stricken felt a sympathetic connection with the man who had led the country through its dark time.

People she met reminded her of characters in her own life and underscored the close ties between the world she was visiting and the one she inhabited at home. She spent a night with Queen Mary, George VI's mother. "This was something that Franklin had particularly wanted me to do because King George V and Queen Mary had been kind to his mother when she visited England," recalled Eleanor. "I think he thought of Queen Mary as in some ways rather like his mother, and therefore made a point of my seeing her." (Roosevelt had spent time with George V on the day in 1918 he had first met Churchill.) Eleanor's schedule was packed, her pace fast, and one day Clementine had to break off and rest while Eleanor went relentlessly on. In a personal letter to Roosevelt, Clementine tactfully neglected to mention how Eleanor was taxing her own energies. Like Churchill, Clementine was a gifted correspondent and knew the Roosevelts were to be handled carefully. "I have been fortunate in accompanying Mrs. Roosevelt on several occasions, & I wish I could describe the effect she has on our women & girls," Clementine wrote. "When she appears their faces light up with gladness & welcome. . . . Winston and I are both concerned that presently Mrs. Roosevelt may become very tired. . . ."

Churchill tried to intervene but was waved off. "I did my best to advise a reduction of her programme and also interspersing it with blank days, but I have not met with success," Churchill told Roosevelt on November 1, "and Mrs. Roosevelt proceeds indefatigably."

Clementine soldiered on. "On another day, when she was staying with us at Chequers, I took Mrs. Roosevelt to see a Maternity Hospital for the wives of officers in the three Fighting Services—She talked to each of the young mothers . . . ," Clementine wrote Roosevelt. "Then last Friday I accompanied Mrs. Roosevelt to Canterbury, & on to Dover—our front door step. We could just see the French coast line; it was a calm soft afternoon, & there was no enemy activity. Yet the very next day, Canterbury was viciously bombed by daylight & it may well be that among the casualties were some of the smiling excited women & children who pressed round her. It is indeed fortunate that her visit was twenty-four hours before the raid."

THEIR TIME TOGETHER was lit by the larger drama of the war—the near miss of the bombing of Canterbury, the sight of women in uniform as the whole population mobilized for the conflict—and both families could not help but see their lives intertwined with the struggle. The lines between the personal and the political were blurred, if not erased. "On each occasion that Winston has been to America he has told me of your great goodness and hospitality to him," Clementine told Roosevelt, "& I only wish that I could do something adequate to show you how I feel about this. I hope one day to meet you in person & tell you."

Churchill joined his wife in praising their guest to her husband. "Mrs. Roosevelt has been winning golden opinions here from all for her kindness and her unfailing interest in everything we are doing," Churchill wrote Roosevelt. "I think she has been impressed herself." She was, as were her liberal compatriots. "I remember my English friends saying, when the war broke out, 'Churchill belongs to another era,'" recalled Trude Lash, who had a left-leaning circle of acquaintances. "Then, to their credit, they later said, 'Churchill belongs to any era when England needs defending.'"

Asked at a London press conference about the possibility of closer ties between Britain and America after the war, Eleanor said, "I should say that there was such a prospect." Sounding much like her husband, she added: "It depends, of course, on knowing people; on how close your real feeling to them is." Later in her visit, she expanded on the theme. "I feel that the growing understanding between us will perhaps mean more in the future, not only to us but to the world, than we can now know."

Her words flowed partly out of her contact with the Churchills. "The spirit of the English people is something to bow down to," Eleanor wrote her husband. At one point, Eleanor and her hosts measured the dimensions and doorways of a Curzon Street apartment to make sure it could accommodate a wheelchair for Roosevelt's eventual visit to England.

There was one discordant note. At a small dinner in London, Eleanor and Churchill exchanged words over Loyalist Spain. "I remarked that I could not see why the Loyalist government could not have been helped, and the prime minister replied that he and I would have been the first to lose our heads if the Loyalists had won—the feeling against people like us would have spread," Mrs. Roosevelt recalled. "I said that losing my head was unimportant, whereupon he said: 'I don't want you to lose your head and neither do I want to lose mine.' Then Mrs. Churchill leaned across the table and said: 'I think perhaps Mrs. Roosevelt is right.' The prime minister was quite annoyed by this time and said: 'I have held certain beliefs for sixty years and I'm not going to change now.' "

Clementine, Eleanor recalled, "then got up as a signal that dinner was over." Eleanor's circle, of course, thought Churchill hopeless. "It annoyed Mrs. R. that Churchill would not let women argue with him," recalled Trude Lash. Actually he did let women argue with him: Violet Bonham Carter was one, and Clementine was a vocal interlocutor at the table and a frequent adviser on political questions; his letters to her are full of talk of his work, and she had always been a public help to him.

What he did not love was being interrupted. For a long time Clementine had dealt with her husband's storms by masking her true feelings (often later writing him about what had upset her). "One feels that, being in public life, she has had to assume a role and that the role is now a part of her," Eleanor recalled, "but one wonders what she is like underneath."

THE INVASION OF North Africa was at hand, and the two chiefs exchanged excited messages as the plans were approved in the first week of September.

"Hurrah!" Roosevelt cabled Churchill.

"Okay full blast," Churchill replied.

The news had been better of late. On the eve of El Alamein, a crucial battle, Churchill told Roosevelt: "All the Shermans and self-propelled guns which you gave me on that dark Tobruk morning will play their part." The ensuing victory over Rommel secured the Middle East and marked a key turning point in the war—one made possible, in part, because of Roosevelt and Churchill's Sunday together after Tobruk.

NOW THE ANGLO-AMERICAN landings in northwest Africa loomed. "For weeks, the P. has had something exciting up his sleeve—Only a handful knew about it . . . ," Daisy noted in early November. "He spoke of an egg that was about to be laid." The weekend of November 7–8, Roosevelt retreated to Shangri-la. "Quite cold—large fires in all fireplaces," Daisy noted. "There was a general feeling of excitement." The telephone would ring, "but the P. keeps conversation light—teases everyone." In the cabin on November 7, Suckley recalled, "There was a feeling of suspense through dinner though the Pres. as always was joking & teasing." A radio—shades of Pearl Harbor at Chequers, but this time the host knew what was coming—brought the news at nine P.M.: Allied troops had hit North Africa. "By now what happened is History, & in the papers—But it *was* thrilling," Daisy said, probably reflecting Roosevelt's excitement as well.

But the pressures of command tired the president. On Sunday, November 8, Suckley and Rollie Hambley rode back to the White House with Roosevelt, who, Daisy said, "paid us the great compliment of going to sleep for about a half-hour. I had to wake him as we approached the city: It wouldn't look well for the P. of the U.S. to be seen driving through the streets with his eyes closed & his head nodding!"

Churchill was relieved at the success in North Africa. "Once he began to bark," one of his secretaries recalled of these weeks, "then quickly stopped himself and said 'No, no; quite all right, *quite* all right. Tonight you may rejoice. Tonight there is sugar on the cake.' " A couple of days later, he went to the Lord Mayor's Luncheon at Mansion House. "I have never promised anything but blood, tears, toil and sweat," he said. "Now, however, we have a new experience. We have victory—a remarkable and definite victory. The bright gleam has caught the helmets of our soldiers, and warmed and cheered all our hearts." With American and British men fighting side by side, where did the war stand? "Now this is not the end," Churchill said. "It is not even the beginning of the end. But it is, perhaps, the end of the beginning." The combination of the victories at Midway, Stalin's stand against the Germans in the East, and progress in North Africa signaled a possible shift toward triumph. In eleven months, Churchill would sit at a lunch table, lean back, and say of 1943: "What a year it has been! What a magnificent year!"

THE LAST WEEKEND of November 1942 is telling about the range and play of Roosevelt's mind and emotions at this point in the war. There was success in North Africa but still no set plan for what George Marshall believed was the essential step: the invasion of occupied

France. Churchill would soon argue to capital-
ize on the Mediterranean victories by pushing
for more operations in that zone, and Stalin was
awaiting a Second Front in Western Europe.

But Roosevelt, at home in Hyde Park, was
thinking ahead to the shape of the world after
the conflict. One afternoon over Thanksgiving,
Roosevelt asked Daisy to go with him to Top
Cottage for a picnic. "Our conversation was
momentous," Daisy noted. He told her he was
hoping for another high-level meeting soon in
part because "there is a growing demand for a
definite statement about our intentions after the
war." Churchill's imperialism worried him—so
much so that Roosevelt predicted the Soviets
would be easier to deal with in the coming
years. "He thinks Stalin will understand his plan
better than Churchill," Suckley wrote. "In general it consists of an international police force
run by the four countries [the United States,
Britain, the Soviet Union, and China]. . . . Self
determination to be worked out for colonies
over a period of years, in the way it was done
for the Philippines. I wondered how the
Empire owners will take to it."

As Roosevelt pondered the idea of what
would become the United Nations, he and
Daisy went to his cousin Polly Delano's. "She
met us at the door, looking well. . . . We had a
lovely time at 'tea' with a crackling fire & Tom

Collinses," Daisy said. "Polly is so sweet with him & he is devoted to her. . . . F. was happy & full of stories." Warmed by the fire and the cocktails in the cool Hudson Valley dusk, cheered by his thoughts on building a new global order, Roosevelt had a bit too much to drink. "F. drove me home from Polly's," Suckley said. "He confessed on the way that he felt 'ivre' [drunk]—Polly must have made his [Tom Collins] very strong." But he had reason to indulge himself: The world was looking brighter.

On November 29, Churchill, who was turning sixty-eight the next day, told Britain that 1943 "must be a stern and terrible year," but it would, as always, be confronted "with a strong will, a bold heart and a good conscience." He did not want the good news from North Africa to lull his listeners into thinking the hard work was over. "I promise nothing," Churchill said. "I predict nothing." Winning battles did not mean winning the war, and just as the British had borne early defeats with equanimity, so now they must resist overreacting to success. He quoted Kipling, whose verses both he and Roosevelt carried in their heads.

> If you can dream—and not make dreams
>   your master;

If you can think—and not make thoughts
   your aim;
If you can meet with Triumph and Disaster
And treat those two impostors just the
   same . . .

This was insightful psychological leadership on a grand scale: The natural reaction of a war-weary people to the glory of El Alamein—it had indeed been a long time since London could celebrate a victory—was to exhale and begin to think that perhaps the worst was over. Churchill knew better and told the nation so. "I know of nothing that has happened yet which justifies the hope that the war will not be long, or that bitter and bloody years do not lie ahead," he said in his broadcast. "Certainly the most painful experiences would lie before us if we allowed ourselves to relax our exertions, to weaken the discipline, unity and order of our array, if we fell to quarrelling about what we should do with our victory before that victory had been won. We must not build on hopes or fears, but only on the continued faithful discharge of our duty, wherein alone will be found safety and peace of mind." Their duty would take them to Berlin. "Remember that Hitler with his armies and his secret police holds nearly all Europe in his grip. Remember that he has millions of slaves to toil for him, a vast mass of munitions, many mighty arsenals, many fertile fields."

CHURCHILL WAS CONDUCTING business but taking short breaks for personal occasions. Clementine gave him a lovely birthday party—Mary remembered that the rooms in the Annexe "looked particularly pretty with so many 'birthday' flowers." Despite his warnings about the road ahead, the outlook for the war was much more encouraging on Churchill's sixty-eighth birthday than it had been on either his sixty-sixth or sixty-seventh, and his intimates sensed the changing calculus. This year, Mary wrote, "the bright gleam of victory added luster and joy to these family rejoicings."

ROOSEVELT AND CHURCHILL were to meet in Casablanca in January 1943. Clementine was thinking fondly of her husband as he left. "My darling," she wrote him, "The 'Annexe' and 'No 10' are dead & empty without you—Smoky [the Annexe cat] wanders about disconsolate—I invite him into my room & he relieves his feelings by clawing my brocade bed-cover & when gently rebuked, biting my toe through it." The Roosevelts' pre-Casablanca exchanges

"Of course, I have seen the President constantly"

Churchill carries the strategic day at Casablanca, January 1943

seem to have centered less on how much they might miss each other and more on how much Roosevelt hated flying and the physical dangers he might face—hardly cheering thoughts. "It was his first long trip by air across the water and I had hoped he would be won over to flying, but instead he disliked it more than ever," Eleanor recalled. "I tried to tell him that the clouds could be as interesting as waves, but he always said: 'You can have your clouds. They bore me after a certain length of time.' " Daisy sensed Roosevelt's ambivalence about the flight across the sea. "I think F. has mixed feelings about this trip," she said. "He is somewhat excited about it—The adventure of it—seeing all he will see, etc. On the other hand it is a long trip, with definite risks—But one *can't* and *mustn't* think of that."

IN CASABLANCA, Churchill was in his element. "The weather is bright with occasional showers and like a nice day in May for temperature . . . ," Churchill wrote Clementine. "The countryside is verdant with lush grass in the meadows and many fine trees, some of which are palms. Around the whole circle of villas is drawn a circle of barbed wire, ceaselessly patrolled by American sentries, and around that again is a circle of anti-aircraft guns." Cabling

Clementine about Roosevelt, Churchill said: "I think he was delighted to see me, and I have a very strong sense of the friendship which prevails between us."

Casablanca was full of the principals' kith and kin: Elliott, FDR Jr., Randolph, and Robert Hopkins were within the compound. "These meetings meant a great deal to Franklin and also to the boys, and Franklin always came home full of stories of what they had said and done," Eleanor recalled. "For my part, I was always grateful when these meetings were possible, for it meant that I got firsthand news of my sons." Churchill loved spending time with Randolph; apparently life was less contentious away from home. "I was very glad to see him and have had long talks with him, and also quite a lot of Bezique," Churchill told Clementine. "He is very well, and the President, who has both his sons here, invited him to come to several of the Conferences." Harry Hopkins noted: "Much good talk of war—and families—and the French. I went to bed at 12 but I understand that the Pres. and Churchill stayed up till two."

There was debate about French politics, Allied strategy, and the tension between Western Europe, the Mediterranean, and the Pacific. Anfa, the Casablanca suburb where the conference unfolded, was comfortable, and Roosevelt and Churchill got along easily. "We had a very agreeable and successful evening, showing him our Map Room . . . ," Churchill told Clementine after dinner one night. "And then Harry Hopkins produced five negro soldiers who sang most melodiously to us." While the principals relaxed, the subordinates charged with their safety were jumpy—which amused Roosevelt and Churchill. Mike Reilly was on patrol one evening when he glimpsed someone walking in the darkness near Roosevelt's villa. "The old bloodhound in me took charge and I stalked the intruder," Reilly recalled. "I stepped from behind a bush, directly in his path, only to have Winston Churchill look up and inquire blandly, 'What's the matter, Mike, did you think I was some person of evil design?' "

Churchill had reason to be in good humor. The British were winning the strategic skirmishes. Their vision: Press ahead in the Mediterranean. Why not strike Sicily now and continue planning for an eventual cross-Channel operation? Churchill "was a man of extraordinarily strong convictions and a master in argument and debate," recalled Dwight Eisenhower, who watched Churchill at work in operational planning. "Completely devoted to winning the war and discharging his responsibility as Prime Minister of Great Britain, he was difficult indeed to combat when conviction compelled disagreement with his views. . . . He could become intensely oratorical, even in discussion with a single person, but at the same time his intensity of purpose made his delivery seem natural and appropriate. He used humor and pathos with equal facility, and drew on everything from the Greek classics to Donald Duck for quotation, cliché and forceful slang to support his position."

In conference, Churchill was often at his best in these January days. Despite the difficulties of preparing for a 1943 landing and bridgehead— difficulties that might not have been overcome in time—General Marshall continued to urge the direct approach over the British one. "Roosevelt seemed to hold a position midway between Marshall and Churchill, midway between wanting to thrust at the underbelly and thrust across the Channel," wrote James Mac-Gregor Burns, the Roosevelt biographer. The president knew the Western European operation was the "main effort," Burns noted, but "his fancy was taken by immediate, opportunistic ventures, especially when Churchill was there to suggest them."

At Casablanca, Churchill carried the point: The invasion of France would be delayed. Still, striking France in 1943 was not ruled out: Churchill and Roosevelt approved a buildup of troops in England for a possible landing in France in 1943 and also signed off on the strategic bombing of Germany.

———

"IT IS IN every respect as I wished & proposed," Churchill wrote his wife. "Of course I have seen the President constantly and we have had nearly all our meals together."

One day, Churchill was strolling on the beach near the compound and came across a group of American sailors. "One of them had a guitar, and they were playing and singing," said an army photographer who recorded the story in the private Secret Service log of the conference. "The Prime Minister got in his car and started to drive off, but after a moment told his driver to stop and back up. When he got back to where the sailors were, Mr. Churchill stuck his head out of the window and said, 'How about playing me a tune?' Of course the sailors agreed, and they gathered around Mr. Churchill's car and sang him two songs, one of them being, 'You Are My Sunshine.'" Churchill—a fan of popular songs, the worse the better—loved it. Later, before a session with photographers, "Churchill asked his man Sawyers for his false teeth [really a few teeth in a removable plate] and said he wished the pictures were going to be taken later in the day, because he didn't look his best at twelve o'clock, but he liked the idea of pictures because he loved publicity," recalled Harry Hopkins. "He told me he could put on a very warlike look whenever he wanted to."

Victorious on strategy, Churchill could afford to worry about other things. The king of Morocco was to dine with the president and the prime minister, and since Muslim tradition forbade serving alcohol, Churchill told Hopkins, the meal was to be "Dry, alas!; with the Sultan. After dinner, recovery from the effects of the above."

THE MEETING, which had been conducted in secrecy, was made public on Sunday, January 24, 1943. The first item of business in the press conference held on the lawn outside Roosevelt's villa was a handshake between Charles de Gaulle and Henri Giraud. The rivalry between the leaders of the French consumed a great deal of Roosevelt and Churchill's time and energy in Casablanca and throughout the war. Roughly put, de Gaulle, whose defiant Free French spirit impressed Churchill and resonated with Churchill's own worldview, was in exile in London and considered himself the representative of the one true France. Roosevelt was, to say the least, less enthralled with the tall, haughty de Gaulle. After the successful invasion of North Africa, the Roosevelt administration recognized Admiral Jean Darlan, a Vichyite, as the governor of the French colonies in North Africa—until Darlan was shot to death on Christmas Eve 1942. Then Roosevelt—again passing over de Gaulle—turned to General Giraud, a de Gaulle rival. By the time Roosevelt and Churchill reached Casablanca, it had become clear that the two factions needed to unite. When de Gaulle finally arrived at Anfa— he had come only under pressure from Churchill, who wanted to please Roosevelt— he was underwhelmed by the president. "Behind his patrician mask of courtesy, Roosevelt regarded me without benevolence . . . ," de Gaulle wrote. "He meant the peace to be an American peace, convinced that he must be the one to dictate its structure . . . and that France in particular should recognize him as its savior and arbiter." In any event, Roosevelt and Churchill wanted a de Gaulle–Giraud photo and got it during the press conference. France was a consistent irritant, one more problem for Churchill to have to manage in order to keep Roosevelt cheerful and in good humor. (To Clementine, Churchill referred to "the squalid tangles of French North African politics.")

ROOSEVELT AND CHURCHILL were the picture of unity in the sunlight that Sunday. Reporters, *Time* noted, "found a well-pleased

Franklin Roosevelt in the garden of the villa where he had stayed: he was comfortable in a light grey suit, the angle of his long cigarette holder was even jauntier than usual." Churchill seemed at home, too. "Somehow it all seemed the most natural thing in the world," *Newsweek* wrote of the image of the two of them.

After the photograph of the Frenchmen was taken, Roosevelt announced: "The elimination of German, Japanese and Italian war power means the unconditional surrender by Germany, Italy, or Japan. That means a reasonable assurance of future world peace. It does not mean the destruction of the population of Germany, Italy or Japan, but it does mean the destruction of the philosophies in those countries which are based on conquest and the subjugation of other people."

The conference had its headline. "Unconditional surrender" has provoked much historical debate—did such an inflexible Allied position discourage anti-Hitler Germans from rising up? Did the ultimatum make our enemies fight even more viciously?—but it became fixed policy. One important aspect of Roosevelt's proclamation is what it says about his ability to pursue seemingly contradictory courses at once, a gift that made him a remarkable leader. Picnicking with Daisy at Hyde Park, he had laid out his view of an order in which countries would move into an era of multilateralism in an international organization; sitting with Churchill in the garden at Anfa, he made the most extreme kind of unilateral statement. But the ideas were linked: Crush the dictators in order to make a new world. It was a complicated political and diplomatic maneuver to execute, but Roosevelt, who could operate on different intellectual and emotional levels, was suited to the task in a way a less nimble politician would not have been.

WHILE THE WORLD took in the spectacle of the conference—PRESIDENT'S DARING AIR TRIP, FIRST EVER BY U.S. EXECUTIVE, GIVES WHOLE ALLIED WORLD A THRILL; SEVERE BLOW TO AXIS MORALE SEEN, reported *The Washington Post*— Roosevelt and Churchill drove to Marrakech. Along the way, they had a picnic lunch. "Many thousand American troops were posted along the road to protect us from any danger," Churchill recalled, "and aeroplanes circled ceaselessly overhead."

They were to stay at a villa called La Saadia (variously known as the Villa Taylor and Flower Villa), then occupied by Kenneth Pendar, the American vice-consul in Marrakech. As Roosevelt and Churchill arrived in an olive-drab

Daimler limousine, Pendar's servant Louis produced a tea service that, Pendar recalled, "looked like an Oriental potentate's." Churchill asked Pendar to show him the villa's tower. "As we climbed up, I saw his shrewd eyes taking in everything," Pendar wrote. "From the open terrace he told me how much he loved Marrakech and how much he had enjoyed sketching here before the war, during his last visit."

"Don't you believe, Pendar," Churchill said, "that it can be arranged for the President to be brought up here? I am so fond of this superb view that it has been my dream to see it with him. All during the Conference I have looked forward to coming down here to this beautiful spot."

Churchill counted the steps—there were sixty of them—on the way back down. "Mr. President, both Mr. Pendar and I are most anxious for you to see the view from the tower," Churchill said to Roosevelt when they returned to the terrace. "It is unique. Do you think you could be persuaded to make the trip?"

"I have every intention of going up there if these good men can take me," Roosevelt said, gesturing to his aides. "Two men carried the President up with his arms around their shoulders, while another went ahead to open doors, and the rest of the entire party followed," Pendar recalled. Roosevelt kept up a stream of cheerful chatter. Churchill followed, singing, "Oh, there ain't no war, there ain't no war."

It was sunset. Pendar described the scene in nearly mystical terms. "Never have I seen the sun set on those snow-capped peaks with such magnificence," he wrote of the view Roosevelt and Churchill took in together. "There had evidently been snow storms recently in the mountains, for they were white almost to their base, and looked more wild and rugged than ever, their sheer walls rising some 12,000 feet before us. The range runs more or less from east to west, and the setting sun over the palm oasis to our right shed a pink light on the snowy flank of the mountains. With the clear air, and the snow on the range, it looked near enough for us to reach out and touch its magnificence."

As the temperature dropped, Churchill sent for Roosevelt's coat, which he then put around the president's shoulders—shades, again, of Sir Walter Raleigh and Elizabeth. "It's the most lovely spot in the whole world," Churchill said to Roosevelt. "Just as the sun set (we were all silent) the electric light on the top of every mosque tower in Marrakech flashed on to indicate to the faithful the hour of prayer," Pendar wrote. There is a photograph of this moment at the pinnacle, with a seated Roosevelt gazing out and a gentle Churchill looking at Roosevelt with tenderness in his eyes.

A little while later, Churchill donned a siren suit and monogrammed black velvet slippers for dinner. Roosevelt was lying on a couch in the salon. As Pendar approached him, Roosevelt smiled and said, "I am the Pasha, you may kiss my hand."

AT THE DINNER TABLE, Pendar sat between Roosevelt and Churchill. In a sign both of the holiday spirit of the occasion and of the eternal truth that when presidents crack jokes, their audiences laugh—however unfunny the jokes may be—the Secret Service log of the evening records this: "Mr. Pendar was telling the President of a Sultan who, of all things, had a steamboat in one of the large pools located in the extensive garden surrounding his palace. It seemed that the boat capsized with the Sultan in it and that the Sultan was drowned. A round of laughter greeted the President's remark that perhaps the Sultan had never been in water before."

There was lobster and filet mignon, and Louis, Pendar's servant, appeared with a massive dessert, a profiterole about three feet high. "I see the pastry cooks have been busy for days and

days, preparing for our secret visit," Churchill
said to Pendar. Lord Moran noted that the president and the prime minister "made little affectionate speeches to each other, and Winston
sang." Pendar raised the subject of de Gaulle,
but Churchill shut him down, saying: "Oh, let's
don't speak of him. We call him Jeanne d'Arc
and we're looking for some bishops to burn
him."

There was, Harry Hopkins recalled, "much
banter." Pendar was "struck by the fact that,
though Mr. Churchill spoke much more amus-
ingly than the President, it was Mr. Roosevelt
who dominated any room they were in, not
merely because he was President of the United
States, but because he had more spiritual quality
than Mr. Churchill, and, I could not help but
feel, a more profound understanding of human
beings. I was very much surprised by this
because, having seen Mr. Churchill often in the
pre-war days, I had felt sure that no one could
eclipse his personality."

The party adjourned to a salon to work on a
message to Stalin. At a makeshift writing
table—as Pendar put it, "The *salon* at La Saadia
was not meant for work"—Roosevelt and
Churchill stayed at it until three-thirty in the
morning, telling Stalin about the decisions they
had made—decisions that, with their emphasis
on the Mediterranean rather than Western

Europe, were not going to please Stalin, who continued to feel he was doing most of the fighting against the Germans.

"Both men had a catching quality of optimism, but with the President I kept feeling that it was tinged with a deep realization of far distant and over-all problems," Pendar recalled. "The Prime Minister seemed much more in the present and more of an extrovert. The President, on the other hand, often sat gazing into space as he worked. That night he had a look that was not exactly sad, yet it was the look of someone who comprehended sadness." Over a nightcap, Roosevelt said to Churchill: "Now, Winston, don't you get up in the morning to see me off. I'll be wheeled into your room to kiss you goodbye."

"Not at all, Mr. President," Churchill said. "I can get into my rompers in two twos, and I'll be on hand to see you off." But Churchill was still in bed when Roosevelt arrived in Churchill's room four hours later to say farewell. Churchill leapt from his pillows—"we heard his bedroom slippers flopping on the stone floor" with the force of his exertions, Moran recalled—and put on what Pendar called "the weirdest outfit I have ever seen"—rompers, slippers, an air marshal's cap, and a flowing dressing gown with black velvet collar and cuffs. (Hopkins, who was also seeing his son Robert off to the front on another flight, referred to it as Churchill's "ever flaming bathrobe.") The president and the prime minister went to the airport together, and Churchill hurried into the plane to get Roosevelt settled, "greatly admiring his courage under all his physical disabilities and feeling very anxious about the hazards he had to undertake." As Roosevelt made himself comfortable on board, Churchill and Harry Hopkins chatted for a moment. "Churchill and I took one last walk together," Hopkins recalled. "He is pleased by the conference—expressed great confidence of victory—but warned of the hard road ahead."

CHURCHILL SAID, "Come, Pendar, let's go home. I don't like to see them take off." From the limousine, Pendar looked back and watched the president's plane climb into the Moroccan morning. "Don't tell me when they take off," Churchill said. "It makes me far too nervous. If anything happened to that man, I couldn't stand it. He is the truest friend; he has the farthest vision; he is the greatest man I've ever known."

Back at La Saadia, Churchill told Moran that he could say one thing for rising so early—"You can get in an extra cigar." Cabling Clementine, Churchill was warm about Roosevelt and proud that Marrakech had been such a hit. "My friend has gone," he wrote. "They all admit I had not over-stated the beauty of this place." After returning to bed for an hour, Churchill, Pendar recalled, was "storming around the blue-green-and-silver bed like a furious cherub." Irrepressible, he was ready for the next thing. "Sawyers, my painting things," Churchill said to his valet. "Please put them out on the tower." He mounted the steps again and, his friend in his thoughts, painted the view for Roosevelt. Churchill was full of Anglo-American visions as he later lunched on the terrace. He talked of a future common currency, striking the same note he had long before with James Roosevelt at Chartwell. "This is as I see it—the money of the future, the dollar sterling." Relaxed, he said, "Now, Pendar, why don't you give us Morocco, and we shall give you India. We shall even give you Gandhi, and he's awfully cheap to keep, now that he's on a hunger strike." Staying on India, Churchill added, "There are always earnest spinsters in Pennsylvania, Utah, Edinburgh, or Dublin, persistently writing letters and signing petitions and ardently giving their advice to the British Government, urging that India be given back to the Indians and South Africa back to the Zulus or Boers, but as long as I am called by His Majesty the King to be his First Minister, I shall not assist at the dismemberment of the British Empire."

Clementine was eager to see Churchill, whose code name was "Mr. Bullfinch" and who went on to meetings in Cairo and Turkey after Casablanca. Writing him, she said: "I am following your movements with intense interest. The cage is swept and garnished fresh water and hemp seed are temptingly displayed, the door is open and it is hoped that soon Mr Bullfinch will fly home." Charmed, Churchill replied: "Keep cage open for Saturday or Sunday. Much love." In Washington, Eleanor was also waiting "anxiously," she recalled, "for news of my husband and the rest of the party."

IN THE WEEKS after Churchill and Roosevelt parted, Churchill came down with pneumonia, and Roosevelt found himself with a slight temperature and sinus problems on the trip home, which included a stop in Gambia. Roosevelt wrote Churchill a double-edged get-well note. "I think I picked up sleeping sickness or Gambia fever or some kindred bug in that hell-hole of yours called Bathurst," he told the prime minister. Then he was all kindness: "Please, please, for the sake of the world, don't overdo these days. You must remember that it takes about a month of occasional let-ups to get back your full strength. . . ."

January 30, 1943, was Roosevelt's sixty-first birthday. Never one to miss marking such an occasion with Roosevelt, Churchill wrote: "Many happy and glorious returns of the day from your friend. Winston." "Gone are the days when the democracies shivered in their boots while two scrubby dictators put their heads together at the top of the Brenner Pass," *The New York Times* wrote on January 30. "It is for the dictators to speculate and shiver now."

"Churchill will understand. I will take care of that."

Churchill and Roosevelt at Shangri-la,
May 1943

I KNOW HE MEANS TO MEET STALIN

*A Letter from Lucy Rutherfurd–Roosevelt's Secret Over-
ture to Moscow–Fishing at Shangri-la–A Moonlit Drive*

I N   W A S H I N G T O N   A G A I N in May 1943,
Churchill was nostalgic, reciting limericks about
sex and savoring the drama of 1940. Roosevelt
asked him whether the Belgian refugees now in
England were "behaving any better this time than
they did in World War I." Yes, Churchill replied.
"He said in War No. I unfortunately there were a
large number of 'tarts' from Ostend," Henry
Wallace recalled. "He spoke of a very Victorian
lady friend of his who had taken in a couple of
these tarts as her patriotic duty. They proceeded
to stay in bed until along about 10 o'clock in the
morning and doing no work about the house.
The lady suggested that they might make themselves useful which they proceeded to do by
bringing in some gentleman friends, quite horri-

fying the Victorian lady." Breaking into "some rather ribald verse," Churchill added: "Put on your bustle and get out and hustle."

One night, Roosevelt showed a new Signal Corps film called *The Battle of Britain*. "It is excellent, so much so that the P.M. wept," recalled Anna Roosevelt.

But Churchill did not tarry long in reliving World War I and the heady first summer of his premiership. This was, Averell Harriman recalled, a "bitter season." George Elsey was alone in the map room one May night when Roosevelt and Churchill came down to debate the Second Front. "Of course, once Churchill got us in the Mediterranean and North Africa, he didn't want to let go—it was always more, more, more," Elsey recalled. "Stalin had been pushing, basically saying, 'When the hell are you guys going to get on with your invasion?'" George Marshall and Sir John Dill, the British military representative in Washington, joined Roosevelt and Churchill. The argument went back and forth. "It was Marshall versus Dill, with the Prime Minister chiming in," Elsey said. "The President sat back and listened very carefully; Churchill never sat back. Roosevelt would let others duke it out, but not Churchill." Tonight it was a draw. The message to Moscow would be inconclusive. Elsey made a note to himself: "Americans overwhelmed by British oratory." Decades later, Elsey recalled:

"Churchill was pressing for his 'soft underbelly of Europe' strategy, whereas Marshall—speaking for the U.S. Chiefs of Staff—was adamant that preparations for a cross-Channel attack must be made. The reply had to be evasive because there was still no agreement between the U.S. and U.K. leaders—and the Americans just could not match the torrent of the voluble Brits, especially Churchill."

In Washington, the British agreed to a target date of May 1, 1944, for the cross-Channel invasion. But would Churchill—*could* Churchill—stick to it? His seeming reluctance to cross the Channel inspired jokes. Henry Wallace recorded this one in his diary: "Someone called No. 10 Downing Street and insisted on speaking with the Prime Minister without giving his name. Churchill was finally put on and said, 'Look here, this is most irregular. This is Churchill speaking at this end.' The reply came back, 'Well, this is Joe at this end.' Churchill replied, 'Joe who?' The other voice said, 'Joe Stalin.' Churchill said, 'Hello Joe. Where are you?' Joe Stalin replied, 'Oh, I am at Calais.' "

To Roosevelt, Churchill was becoming less of a separate power with whom he had to deal and more a part of the Roosevelt circle in the way so many others were—someone who was cherished but would be told what Roosevelt wanted to tell them, on Roosevelt's terms. When Roosevelt and Churchill had first gotten together at sea and then at Washington, said George Elsey, "Here was Winston Churchill, ten times larger than life to Americans at that point, the shining knight who had kept Hitler at bay." Trude Lash remembered him as "the big man in the war, especially that first Christmas." In the spring and summer of 1943, though, Churchill's claim on Roosevelt's attention and energy in the circle of world leaders was loosening.

THEIR FAMILY LIVES were typically stressful this season. Clementine had had a tough spring. "Once again the pace and strain of her life and work were telling on her and the anxiety she had felt over my father's illness was now taking its forfeit," wrote Mary Soames. "She developed a painful boil, and had to undergo a series of inoculations and X-ray treatment, which were most exhausting, and for a short period she was virtually laid up. Although the treatments soon resulted in her improvement, Clementine was so obviously in an exhausted and rundown state that her doctor advised her to go away to the seaside." Meanwhile, John Boettiger, Anna Roosevelt's husband, was going into the service, which meant the Roosevelts had someone else close to them to worry about. "I imagine every mother felt as I did when I said good-bye to the children during the war," Eleanor recalled. "I had a feeling that I might be saying good-bye for the last time. It was a sort of precursor of what it would be like if your children were killed and never to come back. Life had to go on and you had to do what was required of you, but something inside of you quietly died."

With her husband in Washington, Clementine kept Churchill up-to-date on family and political news from London. She told him about an attempted "rapprochement" between Pamela and Randolph and baby Winston's service as a page in the wedding of a daughter of the duke of Marlborough ("Winston decided it was a bore standing," Clementine wrote on May 15, "so he lugged a hassock out of a pew into the aisle & sat on it"). Replying, Churchill alluded to the puzzling Roosevelt domestic scene. Eleanor, Churchill said, "was away practically all the time, and I think she was offended at the President not telling her until a few hours before I arrived of what was pouring down on her. He does not tell her the secrets because she is always making speeches and writing articles and he is afraid she might forget what was secret and what was not." Still, Churchill allowed, "no-one could have been more friendly than she was during the two or three nights she turned up."

ROOSEVELT WAS INDEED keeping secrets from his wife. The most explosive subject in the Roosevelt marriage—Lucy Mercer, who had married the wealthy Winthrop Rutherfurd in early 1920—was on his mind. FDR and Lucy had stayed in touch through the years, and their feelings for each other evidently remained strong. Eleanor was unaware of the enduring link between Franklin and Lucy, but the Rutherfurd circle was not unknown to the president. According to Joseph Alsop, when Lucy's husband became sick in 1941, Lucy "brought him to Washington for treatment," and Roosevelt was kind during his illness; family members recall that the president helped Mr. Rutherfurd get the best of care in the capital with a particularly good doctor at Walter Reed Hospital. Roosevelt received one of Lucy's stepsons, Winthrop, in the White House on occasion, as well as her daughter Barbara. The president also helped smooth out the details of one of the stepsons' military service, and once asked Anna, who was living in Seattle at the time, to "be nice" to a Rutherfurd stepson when he was briefly stationed there while in uniform. When

Churchill addressed Congress again on this May trip, the president gave two tickets to Mr. and Mrs. John Rutherfurd, another Lucy stepson.

The Lucy-Roosevelt connection, however, was deeper and more complex than that of one old family friend to another. Tucked away in the Roosevelt archives in Hyde Park is part of a letter, almost certainly written in 1941, from Lucy to the president, whom she calls "poor darling." Long and handwritten, alternately practical, emotional, encouraging, sentimental, chatty, and sad, the note reveals much about the nature and extent of their relationship: her grasp of his need to be reassured and bolstered and praised; her eagerness (like Eleanor's) to give him counsel on politics and the mood of the country, even mentioning Churchill; her dependence on his judgment about the affairs of her own family; and, most poignantly, a hint of her regret that his sense of duty had, along with the coming of World War II, foreclosed the possibilities of a quiet life, perhaps a quiet life spent together. The letter indicates a striking level of engagement with the nuances of each other's worlds. Lucy jokes about catching a cold when he has one because they talk on the telephone, has a dead-on understanding of Harry Hopkins's role in the White House, knows about Roosevelt's travel plans, and refers to Barbara Rutherfurd as the "smallest"—signs that Lucy and FDR were in very close contact as the president prepared the nation for war.

The note was written from Aiken, South Carolina, where the Rutherfurds had a house, on the eve of a trip an ill Roosevelt was planning to take. Lucy begins by offering kind words about his plight in facing isolationist sentiment—and recommending potential allies in the business community.

> Day by day the news becomes increasingly ominous and complex and one feels that the responsible heads of the Democracies must indeed be super-men—or at least a dozen super-men to each nation—clothed with the power of life and death. Living—as we do here—in a community of pleasure-seekers—who cannot see farther than the gloves in their hands—one is terrified by the lack of vision—or understanding of what is going on in the world and so close to us—but T[hank] G[od] there seems to be more sympathy with the administration and a backing up of its foreign policy. . . .
>
> The most able man in these parts is George Mead of the Mead Corporation—who served on the Business Men's Council for a number of years—I always feel he might be a help to

you—in some capacity—as an ironer-outer of sorts—though I may have the wrong slant on him—I think you might get Harry Hopkins to bring him to lunch with you sometime when you are alone. . . .

Then Lucy turns to family matters.

This kind of letter is best unwritten and unmailed—and poor darling—to give you one more thing to read or think about is practically criminal—though some day I should like to ask your advice about my youngest step-son who is studying law at the University of Virginia and has one more year—He wonders if it would be more interesting and better training for him to take a job in Washington—perhaps with a political slant to it. . . . It seems to me life in Washington where he could have a house and a garden would be better than life in N.Y. where they say most of the lawyers work themselves to death.

I hope my other s. son wrote you to thank you about his company—He was to have done so—but the letter may not have reached you.

Of course the war may change everything for these boys—and making plans ahead these days makes very little sense.

I am so thankful that you are getting away

soon—the only thing is that all your anxieties go away with you—even your bad throat.

The 'smallest' sends you her love—Bless you—

As ever

L.

In an almost dreamy postscript, Lucy talks of things as she would like them to be—and, possibly, how she would have liked them to have been if affairs of the heart had turned out differently in the last years of the last world war.

<u>P.S.</u>

Time is closing in on going-away time and I hesitate to send this without last-minute instructions—Have been housed with a bad cold (caught over the telephone?) and not allowed out! Never the less worried— Newspapers arrive a day late here—which is trying, and radio reception the worst in the world—which is even more trying. I suppose now more than ever one must live each day as it comes. . . . If only it will be a friendly world—a *small* house would be a joy—and one could grow vegetables as well as flowers—or instead of—oh dear—there is so much I should like to know—how much hope you have—and the thousand questions one does not like to ask—The old gentle-

man here [someone in Aiken] says you have
a close agreement with Churchill as to what
will happen after the war—

I know one should be proud—very very
proud of your Greatness—instead of wishing
for the soft life—of joy—and . . . the world
shut out. One is proud—and thankful for
what you have given to the world—and realizes how much more must still be given—
this greedy world—which never asks in
vain—You have breathed new life into its
spirit—and the fate of all that is good is in
your dear blessed & Capable hands———. . . .

As always
L.

NOW, IN THE SPRING of 1943, Lucy commissioned Elizabeth Shoumatoff, a Russian-
born artist, to paint Roosevelt's portrait in the
White House.

Shoumatoff's description of Lucy helps
explain Mrs. Rutherfurd's enduring appeal to
Roosevelt. "Very tall . . . exquisitely lovely and
gracious, she impressed you not so much by her
striking appearance as by the shining quality in
her features, particularly in her smile . . . ,"
Shoumatoff wrote. The painter had also done a
portrait of Winthrop Rutherfurd. "He looked
like an English peer with his chiseled features,

sharp eyes, and a sarcastic expression around his mouth; yet there was something about his face that vaguely resembled FDR," Shoumatoff said of Mr. Rutherfurd. "Lucy, at one time, admitted this herself." Lucy asked Shoumatoff if she would like to paint Roosevelt. "He has such a remarkable face," Lucy said. "There is no painting of him that gives his true expression." As Shoumatoff walked into the Oval Office, Roosevelt asked, "How is Mrs. Rutherfurd? And how is Barbara?"

Lucy had nearly ruined his career—a divorced man could never have had a future in politics in those days, and for all the complexities of their marriage, Roosevelt loved Eleanor, and she him—but down the years, amid global war, Roosevelt was willing to risk a row with his wife to maintain a link with a woman who had captured his imagination when he was young. Roosevelt's gift for secrecy was one of his most fundamental characteristics. A man who could juggle so many conflicting emotions in his relationships with women could do the same in his relationships with men—a lesson Churchill was about to learn.

THE PRESIDENT AND the prime minister had spent enough time together by May 1943 that they were accustomed to each other's man-

ners and moods, for better and for worse. On
the one hand, they were comfortable with each
other through long hours, and from Churchill's
everlastingly enthusiastic point of view, they
remained the chummy comrades-in-arms they
had been since Newfoundland. When the subject of the 1944 presidential election came up,
Churchill told Roosevelt, "I simply can't go on
without you."

Churchill was so taken by the atmosphere of
friendship and goodwill that an old fear was new
again: What if Roosevelt were to leave the
White House? "In my long talks with the President I naturally discussed American politics,"
Churchill wrote Clementine from Washington
on this trip. "Although after 12 arduous years he
would gladly be quit of it"—though given
Roosevelt's love of office and sense of duty, that
was debatable—"it would be painful to leave
with the war unfinished and break the theme of
his action. To me this would be a disaster of the
first magnitude. There is no-one to replace him,
and all my hopes for the Anglo-American future
would be withered for the lifetime of the present
generation—probably for the present century."
Churchill's bet for British power was centered
on America and on Roosevelt. The United
States and England, Churchill said in Washington, "could pull out of any mess together."

Riding with Roosevelt, Eleanor, and Hopkins

to Shangri-la for the weekend of May 15, Churchill saw a sign for a candy named for Barbara Frietchie, the Civil War character who had defied Confederate troops. Roosevelt could recall only a few lines of John Greenleaf Whittier's poem about her:

> Shoot, if you must, this old gray head,
> But spare your country's flag, she said.

Churchill jumped in and "sailed steadily on," reciting the rest of the verses. "I got full marks for this from my highly select American audience, none of whom corrected my many misquotations."

Noticing a sign for Gettysburg, he asked how far away the battlefield was. About forty miles, he was told. "Why, this may have been the very road by which Longstreet moved up," Churchill said. He was transported back eighty years and told the tale of the battle. As he remembered this phase of the conversation in the car, he "was encouraged to discuss at some length the characters of Stonewall Jackson and Robert E. Lee, two of the noblest men ever born on the American continent." Military history was a shared passion between Roosevelt and Churchill, a perennial source of "animated conversation," as Grace Tully put it. But was he really *encouraged* to lecture his fellow passengers? There was more monologue than discussion this afternoon: Churchill appears to have held forth at such length, and in such detail, that he put his listeners to sleep. "After a while silence and slumber descended upon the company as we climbed with many a twist and turn up the spurs of the Alleghenies," Churchill recalled. On the grounds at Shangri-la, Churchill was excited to see a pool of trout, "newly caught in the neighbouring stream and awaiting the consummation of their existence."

IN HIS CABIN, Roosevelt worked on his stamps. Churchill painted an evocative portrait of the afternoon in his memoirs: "I watched him with much interest and in silence for perhaps half an hour as he stuck them in, each in its proper place, and so forgot the cares of State," Churchill wrote. That Roosevelt felt familiar enough with Churchill to have Churchill with him in this most private of moments—it was with his stamps that he unwound and refreshed himself for formidable guests like Churchill—suggests a level of comfort. "My friendship with the President was vastly stimulated," Churchill told Clementine. In Roosevelt's mind, however, Churchill was now less a force to contend with than he was a permanent part of Roosevelt's universe—a universe in which Roosevelt was in charge.

Lord Beaverbrook was also at Shangri-la, and he left an account at odds with Churchill's more sentimental version. "Roosevelt sat in a big chair, his wheelchair placed in a corner between two windows so that he got the bright light," Beaverbrook recalled after the war. "Churchill, at his side, was pressing for tanks, oil, and every conceivable article of war. And Roosevelt was dodging all the while—he would have to consult George Marshall, he said, or one or another person. Roosevelt would bring their conversations to an end by taking out his stamp book. 'Isn't this a beauty from Newfoundland?' he would say. And Churchill would stump off into another room, fretting at the delay." If Beaverbrook's memory is sound, Churchill was interpreting his time with Roosevelt as he would have liked it to go rather than as it went—which was in keeping with Churchill's character.

"IT'S A BEAUTIFUL spot and dinner was fun . . . ," Anna Roosevelt wrote her husband of that night at Shangri-la. "This evening I also discovered for the first time that the P.M. picks his teeth all through dinner and uses snuff liberally. The sneezes which follow the latter practically rock the foundations of the house and he then blows his nose about three times like a foghorn. I admired his snuff box and found it was one that had once belonged to Lord Nelson—and then, like the idiot I am, I allowed him to badger me into trying some of the snuff. No sneezes came to relieve the tickle in my snozzle and I wept copious tears for at least five minutes! The P.M. teased me unmercifully for not taking enough . . . !" Churchill found the family setting congenial. "We could not have been on easier terms," he wrote Clementine.

Yet Roosevelt was not being entirely open with Churchill. "The President had great charm," Mary Soames recalled, "but it was rather like a searchlight beam that moves." While Roosevelt was tinkering with his stamps and Churchill was taking snuff with Anna, a Roosevelt envoy, former American Ambassador Joseph E. Davies, was en route to Stalin with a private letter from Roosevelt, asking to see Stalin—without Churchill. Davies had left for the Soviet Union on May 6; Churchill arrived at the White House on May 11. It was classic Roosevelt: Be seemingly open and friendly with Churchill, keep him close at Shangri-la, but also try to win over Stalin.

The president had not told Churchill he was suggesting a private session with Stalin. And in fact, Roosevelt's message went out of its way to emphasize that Churchill should be excluded from an initial meeting. Roosevelt's secret letter to Stalin worked through the options for a summer rendezvous. He ruled out Africa ("too hot"), Khartoum ("in British territory"), and Iceland ("too difficult a flight"). Then Roosevelt, saying he was speaking "quite frankly," revealed his true thinking about why they should avoid the Atlantic: "That would make it difficult not to invite Churchill." But they had to find a solution. "Discussions were always simpler and less apt to be prolonged as between two than three," Roosevelt said. Why not the other side of the world? Either the American or Soviet side of the Bering Strait, Roosevelt said, "would be convenient." It would be a long haul from Washington, but the president thought it worth the journey. "F. said he will be taking another trip in about two months. I know he means to meet Stalin somewhere," Daisy wrote. "He feels it will do a great deal of good toward mutual understanding & working out a better system for after the war."

ROOSEVELT THOUGHT OF the maneuver in personal terms. "Three is a crowd and we can arrange for the Big Three to get together thereafter," Roosevelt told Davies. "Churchill will understand. I will take care of that."

He took care of it by lying. Averell Harriman, not Roosevelt, initially broke the news to Churchill after the prime minister returned to London. (Harry Hopkins, Sherwood recalled, "laughed as he wished Harriman the best of luck in his mission.") As Hopkins suspected (and Roosevelt, too, or he would not have kept the feeler secret from a friend with whom he was in constant company), Churchill was disturbed by the prospect of being sidelined.

"My father was a very limpid character in some ways," Mary said. "I don't say naïve; he was not naïve. He was limpid." His daughter used the word *limpid* in the sense of being transparent, not weak, and he expected others to be transparent, too. Churchill's anguish at the overture to Stalin is evident in a cable he wrote Roosevelt. "Averell told me last night of your wish for a meeting with U.J. in Alaska a deux," Churchill said, pleading to be included in any meeting.

Confronted by evidence of his craftiness, Roosevelt falsely protested his innocence. "I did not suggest to UJ that we meet alone," Roosevelt replied, "but he told Davies that he assumed (a) that we would meet alone and (b) that he agreed that we should not bring staffs to what would be a preliminary meeting." Now that the idea was on the table, however, Roosevelt said, he saw a lot of merit in it. Stalin, he told Churchill, might "be more frank" if Churchill was not there. Roosevelt was looking ahead. "I want to explore his thinking as fully as possible concerning Russia's post-war hopes and ambitions," he told Churchill. Roosevelt proposed a compromise. He would have his session with "UJ," and then Churchill could pop over to North America— say, the Citadel in Quebec—and they would catch up then. In midcentury American courtship terms, Roosevelt was saying: "Let me go to the movies with the other girl, and we'll have a hamburger afterward."

Still playing fast and loose with the truth, Roosevelt added, "Of course, you and I are completely frank in matters of this kind. . . ."

Stalin soon took the issue off the table. His fury at the decisions Roosevelt and Churchill made at Washington—chiefly to schedule the cross-Channel attack for May 1, 1944, ruling out 1943—brought Roosevelt and Churchill back together. There would be no Roosevelt-Stalin meeting.

TWO DAYS AFTER Roosevelt's letter denying his unilateral gesture to Stalin, the president and the prime minister corresponded about Jewish refugees. In April 1943, American and British officials had held a meeting at Bermuda to discuss what could be done and suggested the

Allies establish a camp in North Africa to house refugees who were fleeing Europe through Spain. Roosevelt and Churchill discussed the subject at Washington in May—one of their few known exchanges on the subject of the Holocaust—but apparently reached no final decision. "Our immediate facilities for helping the victims of Hitler's Anti Jewish drive are so limited at present that the opening of the small camp proposed for the purpose of removing some of them to safety seems all the more incumbent on us," Churchill wrote to Roosevelt on June 30, 1943, "and I should be grateful if you could let me know whether it has been found possible to bring the scheme into operation." After fighting objections from within the American bureaucracy, Roosevelt said yes, and plans for the camp went forward, though in the end the number rescued was tiny compared to Hitler's ruthless killing machines.

STUNG BY STALIN'S rejection of his invitation to confer, Roosevelt paid particular attention to Churchill that spring and summer. Roosevelt sent along photographs of the two of them fishing at Shangri-la (Churchill thought them "a charming souvenir") and shared shop talk, writing him: "My Congress has retired for the night and I am still going strong." Roosevelt and Churchill were to meet at Quebec in August. Stalin refused to join them. When Churchill cabled Roosevelt about the arrangements, using the code name "Warden" and announcing that "Mrs. Warden" (Clementine) and "Lt. Mary Warden" (Mary Churchill) were coming with him, Roosevelt replied: "I am perfectly delighted." "Isn't he a wonderful old Tory to have on our side?" Roosevelt once asked Eisenhower.

Churchill rarely bore a grudge. "Not against a single person," said Anthony Montague Browne, who spent long years with Churchill after the war. "Not against a single soul." It was an extraordinary personal grace. "He seldom carries forward from the ledger of today into tomorrow's account," wrote Lord Chandos. "It has befallen me more than once to have a sharp and almost bitter argument with him of an evening, when hard blows were exchanged, and to find him the next morning benign and smiling and affectionate." Almost anything could be forgiven— and was.

ANOTHER CRUCIAL SUBJECT had been in the air at Washington—the structure of the peace, when peace came. Roosevelt was predictably gauzy on what he had in mind for what would become known as the United Nations.

Early in the war—even before America was in the war, in fact—he and Churchill had alluded to a "wider and permanent system of general security" in the Atlantic Charter. On March 27, 1942, in a session with Anthony Eden in Washington, Roosevelt, according to Hopkins's notes, had said such a body "should be world-wide in scope" but that "there would be under this body regional councils." Then came the most interesting point: ". . . but, finally, that the real decisions should be made by the United States, Great Britain, Russia and China, who would be the powers for many years to come that would have to police the world." Much to Churchill's and Stalin's annoyance, Roosevelt's notion of the "Four Policemen" included China, which was America's hope for a demo-cratic force in the Pacific amid competing British, French, Soviet, and Japanese interests. More than a year later, at a May 22, 1943, meet-ing at the British embassy in Washington, Churchill explained his own views to Vice Pres-ident Wallace, Secretary of War Henry Stimson, and others, suggesting that three regional coun-cils (for Europe, the Americas, and the Pacific) be set up under a "World Council." According to the notes of the session prepared by the British, Churchill "attached great importance to the regional principle." Influenced by Secre-tary of State Cordell Hull over the next several years, Roosevelt would subtly shift his thinking from a regional division of the world to a more encompassing global organization—but the shift would be slow and not unmarked by mixed signals from the president. A significant point about the Roosevelt-Churchill negotiations (and later, at Teheran and Yalta, the Roosevelt-Churchill-Stalin negotiations) over some kind of postwar structure was that they were trying to find some better way to manage conflicting interests and, if not eliminate, at least contain the threat of military and humanitarian disasters. They would not always agree about the means, but Roosevelt and Churchill shared the goal.

OVER THE FOURTH of July 1943, Roosevelt and Eleanor were together at Hyde Park. Roald Dahl, a fighter pilot, British secret service agent, and later the author of books such as *Charlie and the Chocolate Factory,* was visiting; in wartime Washington, Dahl was a friend of Vice President Henry Wallace's. Exaggerating a bit as he sat with Dahl, Roosevelt said, "I have had four dispatches from Winston today, one only a few minutes ago, and I have replied to each one of them. That is equivalent to writing four full pages of newspaper articles."

Later, over drinks at Polly Delano's—

Roosevelt's tongue may have been loosened by the three jiggers of gin Polly poured into his Tom Collins—the president was asked: "Sir, what do you think of Churchill as a post-war Premier?"

"Well, I don't know," Roosevelt replied. "I think I would give him two years after the war has finished." Roosevelt understood that nothing was forever in politics. For his part, he said the American people have "seen so much of me and had me for so long that they will now do anything for a change. They are restless because they have nothing against me, but they have, as I said, seen so much of me that they want someone else. They just want a change. But, mark my words, after two years they will be shouting and yelling to go back to what they had before."

Sipping the stiff drink and talking of dogs—Fala was "engaged" to a dog of Daisy's, and Polly had a houseful of Irish setters—Roosevelt recalled one of his earliest transactions with Churchill: the destroyers-for-bases deal. As the president remembered it, "Winston said, 'Now how in the heck am I going to explain all this to the British people? They will say the Americans are taking our territory.' I said, 'Listen, Winston, those places are nothing but a headache to you—you know that.'" According to Dahl, Roosevelt said that he had told Churchill the British possessions in the Caribbean and the

"His humorous twinkle is infectious"

Churchill in a ten-gallon Stetson at a
Val-Kill picnic, August 1943

Atlantic were too costly and a "headache" for another reason. "Furthermore, these places are inhabited by some eight million dark-skinned gentlemen and I don't want them coming to this country and adding to the problem which we already have with our thirteen million black men," Roosevelt said. "I tell you, Winston, it is just a headache and you can keep it."

The anecdote is secondhand—Dahl reported it to Henry Wallace—and may well have been embellished in the retelling. But assuming Roosevelt had such a conversation with Churchill—it could have taken place by telephone or at Newfoundland—it is interesting that he used racism to reassure Churchill. By casting the issue in such terms, Roosevelt may have been playing to the prime minister's colonial prejudices.

THE NEXT FEW weeks were to be the Roosevelt–Churchill friendship's last great summer holiday, with fishing and Anglo-American fanfare. Their wives were both acting out familiar dramas, with Clementine under the weather and Eleanor flying off at a critical moment.

Clementine, who had not yet met the man so central to her husband's life and work, was finally traveling to a conference but was exhausted and had to stay in Quebec while Churchill and Mary, who had come along as her father's aide-de-camp, visited Hyde Park.

Eleanor played hostess along the Hudson, but she was thinking of an imminent trip to the Pacific. She would be on hand for the Churchills for the first few days, then disappear west, leaving her husband to handle Churchill's party as it divided its time for the next few weeks among Quebec, Washington, and then again at Hyde Park. Left on his own amid important business and the potential collapse of Italy—it would surrender on September 3—Roosevelt turned to Daisy. "The P. asked me to lunch with them at Mrs. R's cottage, today, and to 'take care of Mary Churchill. . . .' "

It was now a twenty-five-year-old Roosevelt ritual. Roosevelt and Eleanor operated in their own worlds, which sometimes intersected and sometimes did not. Eleanor's delight in her quasi independence was evident in the relish she took in retelling the story of the impression her Pacific travel plans made on Churchill. "It was decided that my visit should be kept secret, so I went on about my daily business as usual," Eleanor wrote after the war. "Prime Minister Churchill, who was staying with us, still speaks occasionally of how surprised he was when I casually mentioned at dinner one night that I was leaving the next day for the Southwest Pacific. He looked aghast." Churchill, himself a man of adventure, admired her adventurous spirit. "Mr. Churchill insisted on cabling to all his people in the Pacific," Eleanor recalled, "and they were most kind wherever I met them."

THERE WAS A swim and picnic at Val-Kill that weekend. Very much at home, surrounded by family and friends, the two men chatted for about half an hour before getting into the president's car for the short trip to the picnic ground. Eleanor was coming out of the water when Roosevelt and Churchill pulled up to the cottage. "Mrs. R. had a couple of card tables set up; a broiler on wheels, for the hot dogs, and all supplies laid out for a large picnic lunch," Daisy noted. There was watermelon, which flummoxed the twenty-one-year-old Mary. "I didn't know how to manage at all," she said, prompting Roosevelt to warn her not to swallow any seeds "lest they grow watermelons in her stomach." Churchill, who wore a "ten-gallon" Stetson, sipped Scotch (he had what Daisy called a "special little ice-pail" on hand to cool his drink). As he downed a hot dog and a half, Churchill slipped a bite to Fala, whom he then patted and sent off to the edge of the pond, where the dog spent much of the picnic chasing an elusive muskrat. Sitting in the sun, the prime minister made a fascinating subject of study.

"He is a strange looking little man," Daisy noted. "Fat & round, his clothes bunched up on him. Practically no hair on his head . . . He talks as though he had terrible adenoids—sometimes says very little, then talks quite a lot—His humorous twinkle is infectious. Mary & he are evidently very close; now & then they would joke together."

Watching Roosevelt and Churchill this weekend, Suckley "took away the impression that Churchill *adores* the P., loves him, as a man, looks up to him, defers to him, leans on him." In Churchill's company, meanwhile, Roosevelt was "relaxed and seemingly cheerful in the midst of the deepest problems."

That stifling weekend, they decided that an American would command OVERLORD, the major cross-Channel operation, given the larger number of Americans in the field, and—together this time—the two invited Stalin to meet with them, proposing Alaska in the fall. Following up on their June 1942 conversation about the atomic bomb, they also took another step forward, preparing a memorandum—the final version would be typewritten on Citadel stationery and signed by both men—promising to share the results of the Manhattan Project, keep it secret, and not to use the weapon against each other, or against anyone else, without mutual consent. Churchill had been worried that the Americans were cutting the British out of the loop, a violation of the deal he and Roosevelt had first struck on that hot afternoon the year before in the president's little study. Now, again at the pinnacle, Churchill reassured himself that all would be well.

WHEN CHURCHILL ARRIVED at Quebec from Hyde Park on Sunday morning, August 15, Clementine met the train. Mary found her "looking better," but Mrs. Churchill had not greatly improved. Even without having to make public appearances, Mary wrote, " 'Quiet little lunches' and long sight-seeing drives with kindly strangers are not restful and relaxing to someone like Clementine, whose strict sense of obligation always meant she would appear at her best, and be at her best, however tired she might feel."

Mrs. Churchill was underwhelmed by her husband's comrade-in-arms. After such a buildup over the years, Clementine found Roosevelt a bit much. "My mother could be very critical and, at the same time, admire somebody very much," Mary said. "That's how she was with the President. She respected him enormously, but she was also a sharp spotter of clay feet, and she thought he could be very vain." Roosevelt's early sin: assuming too much familiarity. "He took the liberty of calling her 'Clemmie,' " Mary said. " 'Cheek!' she said. I howled with laughter; I thought it was very funny."

ONE DAY AT the conference, Princess Alice, a granddaughter of Queen Victoria's and wife of Canada's governor-general, asked one of her husband's assistants if Roosevelt and Churchill would sign her autograph album, a book that had been bound and rebound through the decades as her collection grew. The man went to the traveling map room and asked George Elsey if he would get Roosevelt's signature. "I took it, and it had everybody in it you could think of: the Kaiser, the Czar, countless royal names that didn't mean anything to me," recalled Elsey. "When the President came in, I handed the Princess's collection to him, and Roosevelt sat there in wonder. As he took my Waterman in hand to sign, he said, 'How my mother would have loved this!' "

Churchill came in, signed his name without a second thought, and turned back to business. He may have been thinking of many other things. As Admiral Wilson Brown, Roosevelt's naval aide, saw it, "there was always a good deal of chaffing between the two leaders. Both seemed to enjoy the give and take of friendly sparring to reach a compromise." By the time they reached Quebec, Brown said, "we had driven the Germans out of Africa and Sicily; we had landed in Italy, and Mussolini's fall was expected at any moment." As Brown and others set up the traveling map room for Roosevelt, though, the major issue was the cross-Channel attack. "The Prime Minister's lively imagination was working at full blast," Brown recalled.

Churchill brought his feverish planning instincts to Quebec. "The problems facing the conference were . . . for the Normandy landing—how much steel could be spared to build landing craft, landing piers and temporary harbors without interfering with the shipbuilding schedule already underway to maintain our steady flow of troops to England with necessary supplies and equipment," said Brown. Churchill and Roosevelt were so absorbed by the details, so "excited and enthusiastic," that Brown had to be clever about intervening to keep the "Winston hours" from exhausting Roosevelt. "To break up a night session I several times invented a fictitious telephone call from Washington when I could tell by [Roosevelt's] expression that he had had enough," said Brown. "He was always pleased by the subterfuge."

THE CONFERENCE WAS also full of bad jokes and fishing outings. One afternoon,

Churchill took a sip of iced water and said, "This water tastes very funny."

"Of course it does," Harry Hopkins replied. "It's got no whisky in it. Fancy you a judge of water!"

Churchill cut closer to the bone with his wit. A U.S. operation in the Aleutians, two American possessions occupied by the Japanese in the Pacific, had not gone as planned. "Churchill was tickled at the American chagrin when we launched this enormous attack and the Japanese had evacuated before we could get there," recalled George Elsey. "Our force had been met by barking dogs, and for days Churchill would come into the traveling Map Room and say, 'How are we today—*woof, woof, woof!*' This annoyed FDR intensely—it was funny the first time, but it began to grate."

Roosevelt and Churchill took off one Friday for a fishing and picnic excursion. Roosevelt struck out completely, and Churchill caught a single fish, prompting the two to dub the fishing hole "One Lake." As Warren Kimball, the editor of the Churchill-Roosevelt correspondence, noted wryly, "The fifty small trout caught by others in the party apparently did not count."

As always, there were tangled military and political problems to settle—or, in many cases, to try to settle. Angry because he thought he was being shut out of the negotiations over the

Italian surrender, Stalin dispatched a furious cable. The Soviet Union, he said, was tired of being the third wheel in the alliance: "I have to tell you," Stalin wrote, "that it is impossible to tolerate such situation any longer."

Stalin's rebuke was not received well. "We are both mad," Roosevelt told his aides after he and Churchill read it on August 24. Roosevelt's anger, Harriman recalled, made him "gayer than usual" at dinner that night, while Churchill "arrived with a scowl and never really got out of his ill humor all evening."

After the president went to bed, Churchill struck a dark note. "Stalin is an unnatural man," he mused. "There will be grave troubles."

"I HOPE LADY WARDEN is getting a real rest and that you are also. Also I hope you have gone to One Lake. Be sure to have big ones weighed and verified," Roosevelt, unable to let the inside joke drop, cabled Churchill, who had slipped away for a break after the meetings at Quebec. Both men were tired and trying to regain their energy. The Churchill party decamped to a lodge in the Laurentian Mountains. "We lived in comfortable log houses," John Martin recalled, "complete with electric light, sanitation, hot baths and a blazing log fire to sit round at night." There was a bath for Churchill, and the prime minister relaxed in the same way he had done two years before on holiday in Florida during the first meeting in Washington.

"W.S.C. in terrific form, singing Dan Leno's songs and other favourites of the Halls of forty years ago, together with the latest Noel Coward," recalled Alexander Cadogan; after a nap, there was "more singing at dinner." It was perfect for Churchill. "The President had wanted to come himself," Churchill recalled, "but other duties claimed him."

Roosevelt was probably just being polite. He needed to catch his breath, and more long nights with the prime minister was not the way to do that. When the president arrived back at Hyde Park after Quebec, Daisy thought he was "looking well, but tired. He said he would try to get rested before Churchill comes to Wash. next Wednesday. . . ."

Eleanor was still in the Pacific. Confiding in his cousin, Roosevelt told Daisy that "the Quebec Conference was a success but Russia is a worry. . . . The P. believes he can do more by consistent politeness, but they fear Stalin may be building up a case—The Allies not opening a second front, etc.—and make a separate peace with Germany."

In Washington, Harry Hopkins had collapsed again, though he refused to stay in bed when Roosevelt and Churchill regathered at the White

House on September 1. The years of strain were showing. "Mr. [Churchill] didn't feel well; he had a cold . . . ," Daisy noted, and Roosevelt "looked rather tired, with dark rings under his eyes." Hopkins's doctors were prescribing three months of rest, but he waved them off, saying, "All those boys at the front are fighting & getting hurt & dying. I have a job to do here, & I'm going to do it." Cadogan spent a day "running between the P.M. in bed and the President in his study. The P.M.'s sleeping arrangements have now become quite promiscuous. He talks with the President till 2 a.m. and consequently spends a large part of the day hurling himself violently in and out of bed, bathing at unsuitable moments and rushing up and down corridors in his dressing-gown."

Still fighting to regain her equilibrium, Clementine toured Washington with Daisy. With Mary along, Suckley showed them the Lincoln Memorial ("very moving," Mary said), and Mrs. Churchill's perfectionist instincts were engaged at the Jefferson Memorial. "Mrs. C. & I were bothered with the dirty water which two dirty mops were flopping around the floor," noted Daisy. "We decided a hose would be much better." Clementine later took a tumble. "On our last day in Washington," Mary wrote, "while in a bookshop, Clementine missed her footing and fell down some steps, cracking her elbow; it was not serious, but very painful and hampering, as she had to carry her arm in a sling." Her host was not helping matters. One night, the names of Sarah Churchill and Elliott Roosevelt came up, and, Mary said, "the President leaned over to my mother and said, 'Wouldn't it be wonderful if something happened between those two?' Whereupon my mother drew herself up and said, 'Mr. President, I have to point out to you that they are both married to other people!' He met his match all right."

By this time Roosevelt was tired, using movies in the evenings, as Daisy put it, "to think, & to *not* have to talk to his guests." Churchill was still keeping him up too late.

"I'm nearly dead," Roosevelt told Frances Perkins. "I have to talk to the P.M. all night, and he gets bright ideas in the middle of the night and comes pattering down the hall to my bedroom in his bare feet." They were probably good ideas, Roosevelt allowed, but "I have to have my sleep." At two-thirty one afternoon, finishing a lunch with Daisy, Roosevelt "said he was so sleepy his brain wouldn't work, and he would take a nap at 3. . . . Just at this moment, in breezed the P.M., full of all sorts of things. . . . So vanishes the nap!"

CHURCHILL SPENT MONDAY, September 6, 1943, in Massachusetts receiving an honorary degree from Harvard. Roosevelt "wants the ceremony at his old University to be up to English standards in pomp and colour," wrote Lord Moran. "I think he has been sticking pins into Conant, the President of Harvard."

"Twice in my lifetime," Churchill said at the Harvard convocation, "the long arm of destiny has searched across the oceans and involved the entire life and manhood of the United States in a deadly struggle." He put the challenge directly to his young listeners, many of whom wore military uniforms.

> There was no use in saying "We don't want it; we won't have it; our forebears left Europe to avoid these quarrels; we have founded a new world which has no contact with the old." There was no use in that. The long arm reaches out remorselessly, and everyone's existence, everyone's environment, and outlook undergo a swift and irresistible change.

Why, Churchill asked, had this fate fallen to America? In words that echoed Roosevelt's own arguments against isolation and self-absorption, he went on:

> I will offer you one explanation—there are others, but one will suffice. The price of greatness is responsibility. If the people of the

United States had continued in a mediocre station, struggling with the wilderness, absorbed in their own affairs, and a factor of no consequence in the movement of the world, they might have remained forgotten and undisturbed beyond their protecting oceans: but one cannot rise to be in many ways the leading community in the civilized world without being involved in its problems, without being convulsed by its agonies and inspired by its causes.

If this has been proved in the past, as it has been, it will become indisputable in the future. The people of the United States cannot escape world responsibility.

The people of Britain and America, Churchill said, must stand together.

There is no halting-place at this point. We have now reached a stage in the journey where there can be no pause. We must go on. It must be world anarchy or world order. Throughout all this ordeal and struggle which is characteristic of our age, you will find in the British Commonwealth and Empire good comrades to whom you are united by other ties besides those of State policy and public need. To a large extent, they are the ties of blood and history. Naturally, I, a child of both worlds, am conscious of these.

ON THE TRAIN trip back to Washington, "Winston enjoyed himself hugely, making V-signs from the train window at all the engine drivers on the line and at all the passers-by," Cadogan said. "He quite unnecessarily rushes out on to the rear platform of the car, in a flowered silk dressing-gown, to attract and chat with anyone he can find on the platform at stopping-places. Makes Clemmie and Mary do the same—only they are conventionally dressed!"

The Harvard speech was the capstone of a longtime Churchill obsession, and it raised questions about a controversial idea: Anglo-Saxon superiority. After an earlier lunch in Washington with Roosevelt and Henry Wallace, Churchill had spoken "on his favorite theme, joint citizenship for certain purposes for the citizens of the British Empire and the United States—freedom to travel in any part of the United States or the British Empire for citizens of both countries," Wallace wrote in his diary. Churchill "expected England and the United States to run the world," Wallace noted. "I said bluntly that I thought the notion of Anglo-Saxon superiority inherent in Churchill's approach would be offensive to many of the nations of the world as

well as to a number of people in the United
States," Wallace recalled. "Churchill had had
quite a bit of whisky which, however, did not
affect the clarity of his thinking process but did
perhaps increase his frankness. He said why be
apologetic about Anglo-Saxon superiority, that
we were superior, that we had the common heritage which had been worked out over the centuries in England and had been perfected by our
constitution." The prime minister believed this
deeply. "He himself was half American," Wallace recorded, and "he felt that he was called on
as a result to serve the function of uniting the
two great Anglo-Saxon civilizations in order to
confer the benefit of freedom on the rest of the
world."

Wallace pursued a more progressive line of
argument. "I suggested it might be a good plan
to bring in the Latin American nations so that
the citizens of the New World and the British
Empire could all travel freely without pass-
ports," the vice president recalled. "Churchill
did not like this. He said that if we took all the
colors on the painter's palette and mix them up
together, we get just a smudgy gray brown."
Wallace pushed back. "And so you believe in
the pure Anglo-Saxon race or Anglo-Saxon-
dom-ueber alles." Churchill replied that "his
concept was not a race concept but a concept of
common ideals and common history."

At its best, Churchill's vision of an Anglo-Saxon world order emphasized unique democratic virtues, and without his defense of freedom in the 1940s, the advances in civil rights and liberties that took place in the second half of the twentieth century might not have happened at all. Churchill and Roosevelt were both largely creatures of their time on questions of race and ethnicity, but fortunately their overriding concern was the preservation of those forces and institutions—the American and British understandings of justice and fair play—that would ultimately move us to higher ground.

ON SEPTEMBER 10, Roosevelt left for Hyde Park. "He asked me to use the White House not only as a residence but for any conference I might wish to hold," Churchill recalled. "I availed myself fully of these generous facilities." He called a meeting to review the military situation in Italy and in the Pacific; events certainly warranted the session, but one suspects it would not have taken much for Churchill, so fresh from his Harvard address, to bring American and British officials together in the White House. Looking back, Churchill thought the gathering "an event in Anglo-American history."

But the transatlantic balance of power was shifting even as Churchill called the meeting to order. "All I want is compliance with my wishes, after reasonable discussion," Churchill once half joked, and since Pearl Harbor he had largely won Roosevelt's compliance. Now, though, an American, not a Brit, would lead the great invasion of Europe, and America's combat munitions production had moved from less than Britain's in 1940 to nearly four times as much. The New World was outpacing the Old.

It was time for Churchill to go home, and he accepted Roosevelt's invitation to stop in Hyde Park before the Atlantic crossing. Roosevelt apparently agreed to come to England around the time of the invasion, a prospect that elated Churchill. The day at Hyde Park, Mary wrote, "passed very happily." The Churchills celebrated their thirty-fifth wedding anniversary, and Winston told Clementine that "he loved her more and more every year."

Roosevelt organized a small supper. There were cocktails and sherry by the fireplace; Daisy gave Mary a "signed" copy of *The True Story of Fala,* a book Suckley coauthored on the president's Scottie.

"The P.M. remarked on how well the P. looked—we all agreed that it was extraordinary—It seems as though the trials & difficulties of the office of President, in these days, act as a stimulant to the P.," Daisy noted. "They may take the place of the exercise which he can't have like other people."

Roosevelt toasted the Churchills. At about ten-twenty, Roosevelt drove Churchill down the hill to the special railroad siding.

"It was," Daisy noted, "a beautiful moonlit night," and Churchill's train was waiting. Passing beneath the trees, the chug of the blue Ford's motor echoing in the quiet woods, Roosevelt and Churchill knew the most difficult battles and issues lay ahead: the cross-Channel operation, the ongoing war against Japan, the atomic bomb, the structure of the United Nations. Churchill still thought he might be able to carry the day—perhaps control the timing of OVERLORD to pursue the war in the Mediterranean and, in the long run, preserve Britain's central role in world affairs. He hoped all this was possible because of the man driving him through the Dutchess County night. They were friends; was not anything possible if the American president and the British prime minister were together, which they seemed to be?

They came to a stop along the Hudson.

Just before boarding, Churchill leaned into Roosevelt's car. "God bless you," Churchill said.

Looking into Churchill's face now, in the darkness, Roosevelt may have sensed the rising emotion in his guest. So many years together by now; so many decisions; so many young men sent into battle. And it was really only beginning. Roosevelt's own heart was stirred.

"I'll be over with you, next spring," Roosevelt said. Churchill boarded the special.

"My dear Franklin," Churchill wrote from the train, ". . . We have all greatly enjoyed this trip, and I cannot tell you what a pleasure it has been to me, to Clemmie and to Mary to receive your charming hospitality at the White House and at Hyde Park. You know how I treasure the friendship with which you have honoured me and how profoundly I feel that we might together do something really fine and lasting for our two countries and, through them, for the future of all. Yours ever, W."

Roosevelt's reply was generous. "Delighted you are all safely home, and I hope you had a smooth run. All is quiet here. Congress has been here for a week and it is still quiet. My best to all three of you."

But Daisy had noticed something else at that last supper. There was, she told her diary, "a first very definite chill of autumn."

PART III

THE CHILL OF AUTUMN

Fall 1943 to the End

*"Winston, I hope you won't be sore
at me for what I am going to do"*

The Big Three at Teheran,
November 1943

CHAPTER 9

I HAD TO DO SOMETHING DESPERATE

*A Makeshift Thanksgiving–Tough Times in Teheran–
Roosevelt Turns on Churchill*

THE CHILL BETWEEN Roosevelt and Churchill came from the east, and it settled in slowly. "No lover," Churchill said after the war, "ever studied the whims of his mistress as I did those of President Roosevelt." In Teheran, the bill for Churchill's seduction of Roosevelt came due. From the destroyer deal to Lend-Lease, from the shipment of Shermans after Tobruk to cooperation on the atomic bomb, Roosevelt's intimate style of governing had long worked to Churchill's benefit. Now, at a meeting of the Big Three in Teheran, Roosevelt would turn on his old friend.

"By the time we got to the Teheran conference, one noticed that things were changing," recalled Sir Ian Jacob, military assistant secretary to the war cabinet. "The American power was building up. Up to that point there were just as many British forces involved in all these things as there were American, but not so in the future. And it was becoming clear also to Roosevelt that at the end of the war there would be only two great powers in existence—Russia and America. . . . So from that moment on, we were nothing like so close as we had been."

Churchill was ill with a cold and sore throat as he began his trip on November 12, 1943—his health would soon get worse—and Roosevelt added an affectionate note to an official cable: ". . . it will be grand to see you again. I hope your cold is better."

Before Teheran the two were to get together at Cairo for sessions with Chiang Kai-shek. There were, however, worries about security: Roosevelt cabled Churchill that their "meeting place is known to enemy" and suggested moving to Khartoum. Perhaps a bit too glibly, Churchill, who thought Cairo well protected by British forces, dismissed the anxieties: "See St. John, chapter 14, verses 1 to 4," he cabled back. The passage from the King James Version reads in part: "Let not your heart be troubled: ye believe in God, believe also in me. . . . I go to prepare a place for you."

The message was on its way when Churchill began to second-guess himself. Had he been too grandiose in comparing himself to Jesus? Had he been too quick, he worried, in "taking too much upon myself and thus giving offence"? What would Roosevelt think of him? To Churchill's relief, the news from that quarter was good. The president, he recalled, "brushed all objections aside and our plans continued unchanged."

Clementine gently warned Churchill to handle himself with care around the president in the coming days. Knowing Churchill was upset that the Americans would not support a British operation involving the island of Leros in the eastern Mediterranean, she wrote Winston: "I'm afraid that so far your journey has not been pleasant or refreshing—Your cold must have made you miserable & uncomfortable & then I know Leros must cause you deep unhappiness— But never forget that when History looks back upon your vision & your piercing energy coupled with your patience & magnanimity will all be part of your greatness. So don't allow yourself to be made angry—I often think of your saying, that the only worse thing than Allies is <u>not</u> having Allies! . . ."

Sarah Churchill, the actress, now an officer in the Women's Auxiliary Air Force, joined her father on this journey. She had never met Roosevelt and was soon charmed. "One knew, of course, of his physical handicap, but after two

minutes one never thought of it again"—a tribute to Roosevelt's mastery of her professional
craft. One day in Cairo, Churchill said to Sarah:
"Arrange a car. I want to go and have a look at
the Sphinx and the Pyramids. I want to see how
close you can get in a car, because if it is possible
I want to take the President, but I don't want to
raise his hopes if we can't get close enough."
After a brief survey, they discovered it could be
done. The prime minister hurried back to the
compound, found Roosevelt, and said, "Mr.
President, you simply must come and see the
Sphinx and Pyramids. I've arranged it all."
Churchill's enthusiasm was so infectious that,
Sarah recalled, Roosevelt "leaned forward on
the arms of his chair and seemed about to rise,
when he remembered that he could not and
sank back again. It was a painful moment."
Turning from Roosevelt, Churchill said, "We'll
wait for you in the car." Sarah went with her
father. "Outside in the shining sun," she
remembered, "I saw that his eyes were bright
with tears." Churchill's affections were engaged.
"I love that man," he said.

THANKSGIVING FELL DURING the stay at
Cairo, and Roosevelt had brought along a supply
of turkeys. "Let us make it a family affair," Roosevelt said to Churchill, and the two men dined

with Sarah, Elliott Roosevelt, John Boettiger, and Harry and Robert Hopkins. "Harry had arranged an army band to play in the balcony of the drawing room," Boettiger wrote Anna Roosevelt. "We had several cocktails before dinner, then went in and there was champagne." Churchill threw himself into the party with his usual vigor. "We had a pleasant and peaceful feast," he recalled. "Two enormous turkeys were brought in with all ceremony. The President, propped up high in his chair, carved for all with masterly, indefatigable skill. As we were above twenty, this took a long time, and those who were helped first had finished before the President had cut anything for himself."

Churchill was sweet to worry but soon saw that Roosevelt "had calculated to a nicety, and I was relieved, when at last the two skeletons were removed, to see him set about his own share." In a toast to Churchill, Roosevelt explained the history of the day and "how our American soldiers are now spreading that custom all over the world" and that he "was delighted to share this one with the Prime Minister." Churchill answered in the spirit "of warm and intimate friendship," saying he wished to give thanks that "in these crucial times, you, Sir, are President of the United States, and a great defender of the right." Churchill had spoken, Boettiger recalled, with "deep feeling."

It felt like old times. "Upon this happy note, we all retired to the drawing room for more music: 'Carry Me Back to Old Virginny,' 'Marching Through Georgia' and similar tunes," said Boettiger. Sarah had a full card, so Churchill—much to Roosevelt's amusement—asked Pa Watson, the president's beloved appointments secretary, to dance with him. "It is an enormous satisfaction to have my mess crew from the Potomac & Shangri-La, Music by an army band, & later W.S.C. cake-walked with Pa Watson," Roosevelt wrote in a diary of the trip. "For a couple of hours we cast care aside," Churchill recalled.

TEHERAN WAS NEXT. Roosevelt flew into the Iranian capital about forty-five minutes ahead of the British and was swept away. Sarah Churchill said the trip into the city was "spine-chilling" for her and her father. Their car moved slowly—too slowly—through cavalry-lined streets crowded with people. "Anyone could have shot my father at point blank range or just dropped a nice little grenade in our laps," Sarah recalled. "The crowd pressed around the car. I put my hand on his knee lightly and as lightly he covered my hand with his." Churchill engaged the enemy. "I grinned at the crowd, and on the whole they grinned at me," he recalled. When they finally arrived at the British legation,

Churchill ordered Inspector Thompson to ratchet up security.

It was not to be Churchill's last uncomfortable moment in the capital. A young Russian-speaking American diplomat, Chip Bohlen, was along to translate for Roosevelt. Bohlen remembered November 28 as "a beautiful Iranian Sunday afternoon, gold and blue, mild and sunny." Churchill, however, was still feeling bad. "By an unfortunate coincidence my voice has left me through a damn cold on this somewhat unusual occasion," he cabled Clementine. Churchill had wanted Roosevelt to stay with him at the British legation. Roosevelt wanted his own headquarters at the American embassy. Amid rumors of assassination plots, though, Roosevelt wound up under Stalin's roof.

Churchill requested time with Roosevelt before the first three-way meeting, Harriman recalled, to "settle beforehand on the military matters they would discuss with Stalin." Roosevelt said no. "He wanted to see Stalin first and to see him alone," Harriman wrote. "Roosevelt believed that he would get along better with Stalin in Churchill's absence." Roosevelt, Harriman said, "did not want to be pinned down" by Churchill, did not want to sit and listen to speeches about this operation or that campaign. "The President had reason to suspect that Churchill would press him to support a British plan to capture Rhodes and open the Dardanelles," Harriman recalled, "even if this meant a delay of one or two months in the cross-Channel invasion." Word reached Harriman that "storm signals were flying" in the British camp because of Churchill's exclusion from the Roosevelt-Stalin get-together.

And so Harriman—who always seemed to get stuck with Churchill at tough moments—went over. "PM has bad throat and has practically lost his voice," General Brooke told his diary. "He is not fit and consequently not in the best of moods." "Grumbling but whimsical," Churchill gave Harriman a short speech. "He said that he was glad to obey orders; that he had a right to be chairman of the meeting, because of his age, because his name began with C and because of the historic importance of the British Empire which he represented," Harriman recalled. "He waived all these claims but he would insist on one thing, which was that he should be allowed to give a dinner party on the 30th, which was his 69th birthday." He would, he said, "get thoroughly drunk and be prepared to leave the following day." Nursing his cold and his hurt feelings, Churchill recalled: "I continued to be far from well, and my cold and sore throat were so vicious that for a time I could hardly speak. However, Lord Moran with sprays and ceaseless care enabled me to say what I had to say—which was a lot." But he would have to wait until four o'clock.

AT THREE A short distance away, Stalin arrived to call on Roosevelt. In a khaki tunic with the star of the Order of Lenin on his chest, Stalin smiled as he walked toward Roosevelt, who was in his wheelchair. Mike Reilly, who was trying to stare down the NKVD guards who accompanied Stalin, thought the Soviet dictator "was a very small man, indeed, but there was something about him that made him look awfully big."

"I am glad to see you," Roosevelt said to Stalin. "I have tried for a long time to bring this about." Stalin said he was pleased to meet Roosevelt and, Bohlen recalled, noted that the long delay "had been entirely due to his preoccupation with military matters"—a not very subtle allusion to the Soviet battle against the Germans, a phase of the war in its thirtieth month.

Roosevelt and Stalin knew to keep their points short in order to maintain a comprehensible flow of conversation—something the voluble Churchill sometimes forgot to do with the Russians. "Churchill was his charming best when he started talking, but that does not work quite as well when you're dealing through an interpreter," recalled Kathleen Harriman. "Long speeches like the ones the Prime Minister gave, even in close company, took too long to translate, and he would lose his audience."

Roosevelt was not going to let that happen to him as he and Stalin surveyed the world situation in bursts. "This being primarily a get-to-know-you meeting, the conversation jumped quickly from subject to subject," Bohlen recalled. The first was the most important. According to Bohlen's minutes, Roosevelt asked how things stood on the Soviet lines, and Stalin replied that they were "not too good"; Roosevelt said "he wished that it were within his power to bring about the removal of 30 or 40 German divisions from the Eastern Front and that the question, of course, was one of the things he desired to discuss here in Teheran."

When France came up, Roosevelt wasted no time in signaling that he and Churchill did not always agree. Roosevelt and Stalin were critical of de Gaulle, and Bohlen noted that Stalin's anti–de Gaulle attitude was partly "the reaction of one who felt that any country that collapsed as quickly as France did was not deserving of respect or consideration." Bohlen sensed something else, too: "I could not help feeling suspicious, as I listened to Stalin, that he was also thinking a little bit along other lines. He foresaw in the revival of a strong and healthy France an obstacle to Soviet ambitions in Europe."

Roosevelt mentioned India, warning Stalin against bringing up independence for the subcontinent with Churchill. Yes, Stalin said, that was a "sore spot" for Churchill.

As they parted, Roosevelt told Stalin he was happy to be staying in the Soviet compound since it would give him "the opportunity of meeting" his host "more frequently in completely informal . . . circumstances."

In the British camp, Churchill was stewing, his circle as worried as he was about the Roosevelt–Stalin session. Eager for intelligence as the talk ended, the British got wind of the colonial part of the conversation, including Roosevelt's advice that it was not worth discussing India with Churchill. As Harry Hopkins described all this to Moran, Moran noted, "Stalin's slits of eyes do not miss much; he must have taken it all in. As I listened to Harry, I felt that the President's attitude will encourage Stalin to take a stiff line in the conference."

ROOSEVELT, CHURCHILL, AND Stalin soon took their places for the initial plenary session in the Soviet embassy. "The setting was rather heavy for the warm climate," Bohlen recalled. "The room, which was fairly big, was furnished with large chairs and a round table with a green baize cover. There were curtains on the windows and tapestries on the walls." Roosevelt was the presiding officer, and this was to be the kind of proceeding he liked—free-flowing, even chatty.

In their opening words, the Big Three were each in character. Roosevelt tried charm. "As the youngest of the three," Bohlen recalled, "he welcomed his elders." Alluding to Stalin, Roosevelt said he was delighted to have the Russians as "new members of the family circle." Churchill struck historical notes: "This meeting, I said, probably represented the greatest concentration of worldly power that had ever been seen in the history of mankind." Stalin was to the point. "Now let us get down to business."

Roosevelt started out with the Pacific, and Stalin replied that the Soviets "much appreciated what we were doing in that theatre, and that it was only the fact that the Germans fully engaged him that prevented him cooperating with us!" General Brooke wrote. "This was cheering news and implied Russian help as soon as Germany was defeated." The conversation inevitably turned to OVERLORD. Roosevelt said they must stand by the Quebec decision for a May invasion, but doing anything earlier in 1944 was out of the question because the Channel was such "a disagreeable body of water."

Churchill weighed in, noting pointedly that the British "had every reason to be thankful that the English Channel was such a disagreeable body of water"—a reference to 1940 and the first half of 1941, when the other two men at the table with Churchill were not in the fight, but he was.

Hopkins was watching the interplay of the three men with fascination, and his eyes fell on the one man with the power to break up the Roosevelt-Churchill friendship. "Hopkins noted that Stalin was grayer than when he had seen him last in the summer of 1941 and also much dressier, now wearing a uniform with gold epaulettes each bearing a large, white star fastened with a red pin," Sherwood wrote. "Stalin doodled and smoked during the meetings. His voice was quiet—barely audible."

He may have felt that he did not need to speak loudly to make his case. He knew what he wanted. Roosevelt asked Stalin his thoughts about operations in the Mediterranean—operations that, if undertaken, might mean delaying the cross-Channel attack. "Stalin replied that it seemed to him unwise to scatter the Allied effort," Harriman recalled. "He argued for treating Overlord as the main operation." France was the place to strike.

Churchill seemed game and delivered a determined speech about the preeminence of OVER-LORD. "The enterprise was absorbing most of our preparations and resources," he recalled telling Roosevelt and Stalin. "The British and American Governments had now set themselves the task of carrying out a cross-Channel invasion in the late spring or summer of 1944. The forces which could be accumulated by that time amounted to about sixteen British and nineteen United States divisions—a total of thirty-five divisions."

After conjuring the power of OVERLORD, Churchill made a different case to his colleagues at the table; as Bohlen put it, his "real feelings then began to emerge."

"THE EARLY SPRING and summer of 1944," Churchill recalled saying, "were still six months away however, and the President and I had been asking ourselves what could be done during these six months with the resources available in the Mediterranean that would best take the weight off Russia, without postponing Overlord for more than perhaps a month or two." Might it be worth having the staffs look into what could be possible in the Mediterranean? Roosevelt said he "personally felt that nothing should be done to delay the carrying out of Overlord"—and a delay, he went on, "might be necessary if any operations in the eastern Mediterranean were undertaken." Churchill, however, would not give up on the other fronts.

"I earnestly hoped that I should not be asked to agree to any such rigid timing of operations as the President had suggested," Churchill recalled. To the contrary, Bohlen noted, Churchill "said that he personally favored some flexibility in the exact date of Overlord, and proposed that the staffs examine the various possibilities in the morning. Stalin, for the first time a little grumpy, complained that he had not expected to discuss technical military questions and had no military staff, but Marshal Voroshilov would do his best."

Churchill tried to put the best face on the disagreement, saying "although we were all great friends, it would be idle for us to delude ourselves that we saw eye to eye on all matters. Time and patience were necessary." There was, Churchill seemed to think, some hope. Perhaps, in the end, at the highest level, he could rescue British strategy from Roosevelt and Stalin.

FRESH FROM ROASTING turkeys and baking pumpkin pies in Cairo, Roosevelt's *Potomac* mess crew grilled steaks for dinner. After making martinis, Roosevelt gave one to Stalin and waited for a reaction. Stalin said nothing. Roosevelt finally asked him what he thought of the drink, and Stalin replied, "Well, all right, but it is cold on the stomach." The two of them were already playing to each other and excluding

Churchill. "When I first got to Teheran, Stalin came to call on me," Roosevelt later told Daisy. "Of course I did not get up when he came into the room. We shook hands, & he sat down, and I caught him looking curiously at my legs and ankles. Later, I entertained him at dinner, and was sitting at the table when he & the others came in. When Stalin was seated, on my right, he turned to the interpreter & said: 'Tell the President that I now understand what it has meant for him to make the effort to come on such a long journey—Tell him that the next time I will go to him.' " Across culture, ideology, and temperament, they were trying to form a connection. (As it turned out, though, the "next time," at Yalta in 1945, Roosevelt would have to travel even farther.)

The dinner conversation took a turn that Churchill did not like. Picking up on his earlier remarks to Roosevelt, Stalin denounced the French. "The entire French ruling class, he said, was rotten to the core," Harriman recalled. "Having handed their country over to Hitler, the French now were actively helping the common enemy, and, in Stalin's view, they deserved no consideration from the Allies. It would be unjust and positively dangerous to leave them in possession of their former empire, Stalin insisted."

Churchill nobly rose to the defense of his

downtrodden ally across the Channel. "When Churchill protested that he could not conceive of the civilized world without a flourishing France," Harriman recalled, Stalin brushed Churchill aside. Stalin knew from his meeting with the president, of course, that this tracked with Roosevelt's view (in fact, Roosevelt said at the table that he "in part agreed" with Stalin), leaving Churchill—not for the first time, or the last—as the odd man out.

Turning to Germany, Stalin "seemed to favor dismemberment and the harshest possible treatment to prevent the recrudescence of German militarism," Bohlen noted. Stalin claimed he did not think the country could be trusted to remain peaceful, and, Harriman recalled, "told of visiting Leipzig in 1907 when some two hundred German workers failed to appear at an important rally because, Stalin said, there was no controller on the railway platform to punch their tickets on arrival. Without properly punched tickets, these stalwart representatives of the German working class were too timid to leave the station. There was, as he saw it, no hope of changing a popular mentality so totally obedient to authority." No one in the room appears to have been bold enough, or impolite enough, to point out the irony of a Soviet dictator making this argument about another nation. The president thought the whole evening "very jolly" until, for him, it came to an abrupt end.

"ROOSEVELT WAS ABOUT to say something else when suddenly, in the flick of an eye, he turned green and great drops of sweat began to bead off his face; he put a shaky hand to his forehead," Bohlen recalled. "We were all caught by surprise. The President had made no complaint, and none of us had detected any sign of discomfort." It was about half-past ten in the evening. Mike Reilly, John Boettiger, and Vice Admiral Ross McIntire, the president's physician, were dining outside the embassy when word came of the collapse.

"I tried to ask questions but they practically pushed me into the car and Mike said, 'We've got to hurry, the Boss is sick,' " Boettiger later told Anna. "My heart sunk at that and we dashed off to the Soviet embassy. . . . We rushed up to the house and to FDR's room. . . . Ross went in immediately to see what was what. The P. had been feeling fine all day but after dinner was over got to feeling faint. Ross said he had a lot of gas on his stomach, but he made him quite comfortable and we were all greatly relieved." Chatting with his son-in-law for ten minutes, Roosevelt appeared pleased with how the day had gone—a day on which Churchill

*"I might have added, but did not, that
we had been the longest in the war"*

Churchill's sixty-ninth-birthday dinner
at Teheran, November 30, 1943

had felt at least occasionally overlooked and contradicted. "He was greatly set up over the day's events," Boettiger wrote Anna, "felt a great deal had been accomplished and he was thoroughly satisfied in every way."

Back in the conference room, where the guests had gone after Roosevelt was wheeled away, Churchill, perhaps hoping to keep the Big Three from becoming the Big Two, had his own chance to talk with Stalin without Roosevelt. Sitting on a sofa, they engaged in a substantive exchange about Germany and Poland. The gossipy American take on the scene, however, had an anti-Churchill flavor. "I learned later that the P.M. had done most of the talking," wrote Boettiger.

ANXIOUS TO RECONNECT with his friend to compare notes, Churchill reached out to Roosevelt the next morning. "As I knew that Stalin and Roosevelt had already had a private conversation, and were of course staying in the same building, I suggested that the President and I might lunch together before the second plenary meeting that afternoon," Churchill recalled. "Roosevelt however declined, and sent Harriman to me to explain that he did not want Stalin to know that he and I were meeting privately. I was surprised at this," Churchill added, "for I thought we all three should treat each other with equal confidence."

This second rebuff stung, too. "It is not like him," Churchill said to Moran. Roosevelt was refusing to break bread with someone whom he had just toasted at Thanksgiving in the warmest possible terms. Suddenly uncertain of his place in Roosevelt's world—typically, Churchill seems to have suppressed Roosevelt's springtime subterfuge with Stalin, which had foreshadowed this autumnal drama—Churchill was keeping count, noting: "The President after luncheon had a further interview with Stalin and Molotov, at which many important matters were discussed, including particularly Mr. Roosevelt's plan for the government of the post-war world."

In his quarters with Stalin at three forty-five P.M. on November 29, Roosevelt spun out his vision of the Four Policemen and a United Nations organization with an executive committee to settle disputes and enforce order. Stalin appeared interested but noncommittal, wondering whether such a body's decisions would be "binding." Roosevelt's reply: "Yes and no"—a sign that there was still much work to be done. But the conversations were continuing. (On the final day of the meeting, Stalin would weigh in for "a world-wide and not regional" organization.)

The two then went next door, where

Churchill had a presentation to make. In a gesture to its unlikely ally, Britain had commissioned a ceremonial saber, the Sword of Stalingrad, to honor the Soviet resistance to Hitler. Despite his likely curiosity about what had transpired between Roosevelt and Stalin moments before, Churchill, as always, drew reassurance from ceremony.

"When, after a few sentences of explanation, I handed the splendid weapon to Marshal Stalin, he raised it in a most impressive gesture to his lips and kissed the blade," Churchill recalled. "It was carried from the room in great solemnity, escorted by a Russian guard of honour. As this procession moved away, I saw the President sitting at the side of the room, obviously stirred by the ceremony." The moment of unity dissipated fast as the three sat down to business.

THE CONFERENCE, Chip Bohlen believed, "was approaching a crisis; there was a real question whether it was to be a success. At a meeting of military chiefs a few hours earlier, the British, at first hesitant, were raising additional objections to fixing the date for Overlord."

Stalin, as Moran had suggested on Sunday, missed little. "Stalin would have made a fine poker player," Ismay wrote. "His expression was inscrutable as the Sphinx and it was impossible to know what he was thinking about. He did not speak much, but his interventions, made in a quiet voice and without any gestures, were direct and decided. Sometimes they were so abrupt as to be rude. He left no doubt in anyone's mind that he was master in his own house." He spoke that way now. More than two years of Allied debate, changing minds, tactical feints, and evasive cables were coming to a head around the green-covered table.

"Who will command Overlord?" Stalin asked. Roosevelt admitted that this was not settled: The president was trying to choose between Marshall and Eisenhower.

Watching the uncomfortable exchange between Roosevelt and Stalin, Churchill could not have missed the tension. "Stalin said bluntly," Churchill recalled, "that the operation would come to nought unless one man was placed in charge of all the preparation for it." Stalin waved off the news that a British officer, Lieutenant General Frederick Morgan, was to be the chief staff officer to the still unnamed supreme commander. "Stalin made it plain that until the supreme commander was appointed he could not take seriously the promise of a cross-Channel invasion," noted Harriman. "For him the appointment was a specific assurance that the invasion would take place." Roosevelt, who prided himself on being practical and hardheaded, may have been embarrassed by the challenge from Stalin, fearing that the lack of a definitive answer could make him look as soft as Churchill on the larger question of the invasion. Reading the conference documents later, Robert Sherwood, a gifted observer, wrote that Roosevelt must have been "sorely tempted" to name one of the generals then and there and move on, but another part of the Roosevelt character—the instinct to wait and see—won out. Roosevelt could guess the conference was going to end with OVERLORD as the next great commitment, so he absorbed the blow and let the conversation roll on. Sherwood sensed the currents at work: "Churchill employed all the debater's arts, the brilliant locutions and circumlocutions, of which he was a master, and Stalin wielded his bludgeon with relentless indifference to all the dodges and feints of his practiced adversary; while Roosevelt sat in the middle, by common consent the moderator, arbitrator and final authority."

Stalin pushed for a firm date in May—no later. "I don't care if it is the 1st, 15th, or 20th, but a definite date is important," Stalin told Roosevelt and Churchill in what Bohlen thought was "an almost matter-of-fact tone."

CHURCHILL'S LAST CHANCE was at hand. Stalin, with Roosevelt's tacit and sometimes explicit help, was leading the Allied cause from the east to the west, to a dangerous operation that evoked memories of the debacles of a generation before. After relighting his cigar, Churchill plunged ahead. "He talked of keeping the enemy busy by capturing Rhodes, then starving out the other Greek islands and reopening the Dardanelles," Harriman recalled. "If Turkey agreed to enter the war . . . these operations could be carried out with comparatively few troops. But it would be necessary to keep in the Mediterranean some sixty-eight landing craft needed for the cross-Channel invasion, which could force a delay of a month or two in that operation. He was, therefore, reluctant to give Stalin his unalterable commitment that Overlord would be scheduled for May."

There was much back-and-forth, but in the end Roosevelt came down closer to Stalin's position than to Churchill's. OVERLORD would be the "dominating operation." That was that. Churchill had lost. Roosevelt had chosen Stalin over him.

"I wish to pose a very direct question to the Prime Minister about 'Overlord,' " Stalin said, eyeing Churchill. "Do the Prime Minister and the British Staff really believe in 'Overlord'?"

Even when he was under stress, Churchill's eloquence did not desert him. "Provided the conditions previously stated for 'Overlord' are established when the time comes," Churchill replied, "it will be our stern duty to hurl across the Channel against the Germans every sinew of our strength."

The meeting broke up. "Churchill was irked, to put it mildly, by Stalin's pointed question," Bohlen noted. Moran found a gloomy Churchill getting ready for dinner. "Winston was pacing the room, mumbling to himself: 'Nothing more can be done here,' he muttered." It was going to be a long night: Stalin was the host for the evening. "You are late, Sir," his valet told Churchill.

"Bloody," Churchill said, then left for the banquet.

STALIN GAVE A classic Russian dinner, with rivers of vodka and wine. The prime minister also seemed to be on the menu. Stalin "overlooked no opportunity to needle Churchill," Bohlen said. And Harriman noted needling "without mercy," with Stalin implying that Churchill—who had made the case against Hitler earlier, and better, than anyone—was "nursing some secret affection for the Germans" and "wanted a soft peace." Hard words to take from a man who had cut a deal with Hitler four years before. With a worsening cold, about to turn sixty-nine, and tired from the day, Churchill could not find the right key in which to respond. "Instead of getting honestly indignant or passing the teasing off as a joke, Churchill adopted a plaintive tone that conveyed a sense of guilt," Bohlen recalled. "The performance was certainly not one of Churchill's best."

Stalin's dinner-table strategy seemed designed to cast Churchill's reservations about a direct assault on France as part of a broader pattern of weakness. "Stalin's remarks at the dinner included one to the effect that he and FDR saw eye to eye on things," noted John Boettiger, "but that Churchill had softened up between wars."

Watching Churchill's distress at dinner, Roosevelt apparently offered no help, no reassuring gesture, no kind word. "I did not like the attitude of the President, who not only backed Stalin but seemed to enjoy the Churchill-Stalin exchanges," Bohlen recalled. "Roosevelt should have come to the defense of a close friend and ally, who was really being put upon by Stalin." Harriman noticed the same unattractive streak in Roosevelt's character: "He always enjoyed other people's discomfort. I think it is fair to say that it never bothered him very much when other people were unhappy." As long as Roosevelt was cheerful and getting his way—and the two were connected—he could live with the fact that others might be off balance, which was the case tonight. "I have gathered that we and the Russians are in practically complete agreement," Boettiger wrote Anna, "and that the British are not too happy about it."

The Stalin-Churchill conversation was, Bohlen noted, "acrid." Facing Stalin and feeling removed from Roosevelt's orbit—he had still not met alone with the president in Teheran—Churchill divined a larger political truth in his personal dilemma. "I realized at Teheran for the first time what a small nation we are," he said later. "There I sat with the great Russian bear on one side of me, with paws outstretched, and on the other side sat the great American buffalo, and between the two sat the poor little English donkey who was the only one, the only one of the three, who knew the right way home."

Throughout the edgy exchanges, Roosevelt was either silent or sided with Stalin, leaving Churchill on his own. Roosevelt had his plan: Under no circumstances should he be seen joining forces with Churchill against Stalin, even at the dinner table. Churchill was taking it all well, but then Stalin began to joke about "a serious and even deadly aspect of the punishment to be inflicted upon the Germans," Churchill recalled. "The German General Staff, he said, must be liquidated." Fifty thousand, Stalin said, should be "rounded up and shot."

Churchill was appalled. Stalin, others in the room believed, was speaking in what was, for him, a jocular vein. He made the remark about the fifty thousand Germans, Bohlen said, "with a sardonic smile and wave of the hand."

Churchill, however, believed Stalin was proposing a serious plan for retribution. And Churchill had had enough.

"The British Parliament and public will never tolerate mass executions," Churchill told the room. "Even if in war passion they allowed them to begin, they would turn violently against those responsible after the first butchery had taken place. The Soviets must be under no delusion on this point."

Stalin did not budge. "Fifty thousand," he said, "must be shot."

By his own account, Churchill was now "deeply angered" and said: "I would rather be taken out into the garden here and now and be shot myself than sully my own and my country's honour by such infamy."

It was all going wrong, and Roosevelt, who, Boettiger recalled, "had seen the twinkle in Stalin's eye," sailed into the conversation. Signaling his own opinion of his role as arbiter of the Allied fate, he adopted Stalin's tone. "As usual, it seems to be my function to mediate this dispute," Roosevelt said. So he would offer a compromise—only forty-nine thousand German officers should be shot. "By this he hoped, no doubt, to reduce the whole matter to ridicule," Churchill recalled, and the prime minister noticed that "Eden also made signs and gestures intended to reassure me that it was all a joke." The crisis was beginning to pass when Elliott Roosevelt, of all people, made matters worse. Roosevelt's son had not been asked to the occasion but had been spotted lurking by the door and invited in. Just after his father spoke, Elliott, who had been deep into the champagne, in his own recollection rose "somewhat uncertainly" and, Churchill recalled, "made a speech, saying how cordially he agreed with Marshal Stalin's plan and how sure he was that the United States Army would support it."

This "intrusion," as Churchill called it, sent the prime minister into a fury, and he stormed from the table. Churchill could not afford to be honest about his frustration with the president, so he may have over-reacted to Roosevelt's son: After all, Churchill had no other way of expressing his mounting resentment about how he was being treated by the man he had thought was his friend.

With no plan or destination in mind, Churchill marched into another room, which, he recalled, "was in semi-darkness. I had not been there a minute before hands were clapped upon my shoulders from behind, and there was Stalin, with Molotov at his side, both grinning broadly, and eagerly declaring that they were only playing, and that nothing of a serious character had entered their heads." Churchill was touched. "Stalin has a very captivating manner when he chooses to use it, and I never saw him do so to such an extent as at this moment."

Churchill agreed to rejoin Stalin and Roosevelt but never conceded he was wrong. "Although I was not then, and am not now, fully convinced that all was chaff and there was no serious intent lurking behind," he reflected in 1951, "I consented to return, and the rest of the evening passed pleasantly."

STILL, IT HAD been a tempestuous day. That Churchill was so upset he bolted from the company of his allies suggests the scope of the emotional storm raging at Teheran and the degree to which Roosevelt had successfully distanced himself from Churchill. If Roosevelt sympathized with Churchill's feelings, he did not show it. He rather enjoyed the spectacle. "Joe teased the P.M. like a boy," Roosevelt reported to his cabinet, "and it was very amusing."

IN THE MORNING, Churchill regrouped. Two could play this game. "The fact that the President was in private contact with Marshal Stalin and dwelling at the Soviet Embassy, and that he had avoided ever seeing me alone since we left Cairo, in spite of our hitherto intimate relations and the way in which our vital affairs were interwoven, led me to seek a direct personal interview with Stalin," Churchill recalled of November 30.

Alone with Stalin, Churchill professed devotion to the United States and then suggested Roosevelt was also a stumbling block to the Second Front. "I began by reminding the Marshal that I was half American and had a great affection for the American people," Churchill recalled. "What I was going to say was not to be understood as disparaging to the Americans and I would be perfectly loyal towards them, but there were things which it was better to say outright, between two persons."

The possible OVERLORD delay, he suggested to Stalin, was more their fault than his. The Americans were pressing an amphibious operation against Japan in the Bay of Bengal, and "I was not keen about it," Churchill told Stalin. If not

I Had to Do Something Desperate

for that, there would be enough resources to carry on in the Mediterranean and launch OVERLORD as scheduled. Then, playing to Stalin's point about a supreme commander for OVERLORD, Churchill said "it was vital to get an early decision on the appointment of the Commander-in-Chief." Churchill solemnly assured Stalin that he "had urged" Roosevelt "to decide before we all left Teheran." Stalin, Churchill reported, "said that was good."

With Churchill, Stalin was blunt about why he was so insistent on OVERLORD at the soonest possible date. "If there were no operations in May 1944, then the Red Army would think that there would be no operations at all that year," Stalin said. "The weather would be bad and there would be transport difficulties. . . . If there was no big change in the European war in 1944, it would be very difficult for the Russians to carry on. They were war-weary. He feared that a feeling of isolation might develop in the Red Army"—a veiled threat, but still a threat, of a separate peace with Hitler.

The Big Three lunched together, and Roosevelt read the Allied recommendations aloud: "We will launch Overlord during May, in conjunction with a supporting operation against the South of France on the largest scale that is permitted by the landing craft available at that time." In his diary, Roosevelt wrote: "The conferences have been going well—tho' I found I had to go along with the Russians on Military plans. This morning the British came along too, to my great relief."

IT WAS CHURCHILL'S sixty-ninth birthday, and his joy at being in the arena—he called it a "crowded and memorable day" on which he transacted "some of the most important business with which I have ever been concerned"— was mixed with flashes of pride. In his memoirs, he tried to be lighthearted about the preparations for the dinner that night, but he could not keep from betraying a note of resentment about his declining role in the alliance, and his remarks echoed his words with Harriman on Sunday. "Hitherto we had assembled for our conferences or meals in the Soviet Embassy," Churchill recalled. "I had claimed however that I should be the host at the third dinner, which should be held in the British Legation. This could not well be disputed. Great Britain and myself both came first alphabetically, and in seniority I was four or five years older than Roosevelt or Stalin. We were by centuries the longest established of the three Governments; I might have added, but did not, that we had been the longest in the war; and finally, November 30 was my birthday." Note the not very well suppressed anger: "*I might have added, but did not*"—except for posterity in his memoirs— "*that we had been the longest in the war.*"

It was, Sarah Churchill said, "a never-to-be-forgotten party." Chip Bohlen admired the scene. "The table was set with British elegance," he wrote. "The crystal and silver sparkled in the candlelight." Roosevelt sat on Churchill's right, Stalin on his left. "Together we controlled practically all the naval and three-quarters of all the air forces in the world, and could direct armies of nearly twenty millions of men, engaged in the most terrible of wars that had yet occurred in human history," Churchill recalled. "I could not help rejoicing at the long way we had come on the road to victory since the summer of 1940, when we had been alone, and, apart from the Navy and the Air, practically unarmed, against the triumphant and unbroken might of Germany and Italy, with almost all Europe and its resources in their grasp."

Churchill and Roosevelt wore black tie, Stalin a uniform. "Glasses were never permitted to stand empty and the champagne consumed would float a battleship!" John Boettiger wrote home. To Sarah, Stalin was "a frightening figure with his slit, bear eyes," yet tonight he seemed jovial. "Specks of light danced in his eyes like cold sunshine on dark waters," she noted. "He pounced on every remark with a dry and often sly humour." Usually, the target was Churchill. "When the President spoke, Stalin listened closely with deference," recalled Averell Harriman, "whereas he did not hesitate to interrupt or stick a knife into Churchill whenever he had the chance."

Aware of the drama of the occasion, the "little English donkey" rose to toast Roosevelt and Stalin. Roosevelt, Churchill said, "had devoted his entire life to the cause of defending the weak and the helpless." His Soviet guest, Churchill said, had earned the title "Stalin the Great." Roosevelt then spoke of his "long admiration for Winston Churchill and his joy in the friendship which had developed between them in the midst of their common efforts in this war."

AFTER CHURCHILL DELIVERED what he, as host, had planned to be the last toast of the evening, Stalin asked if he might have the floor. And thus the focus of the party moved from the guest of honor and his nation's sacrifices to Roosevelt and America.

"I want to tell you, from the Russian point of view, what the President and the United States have done to win the war," Stalin said. "The most important things in this war are machines. The United States has proven that it can turn out from 8,000 to 10,000 airplanes per month.

Russia can only turn out, at most, 3,000 airplanes a month. England turns out 3,000 to 3,500, which are principally heavy bombers. The United States, therefore, is a country of machines. Without the use of those machines, through Lend Lease, we would lose this war." True enough, but without Churchill, much of Europe might have been lost to Hitler before Roosevelt and Stalin were in the fight at all.

ROOSEVELT APPARENTLY WENT to bed that night still worried he had not truly broken through to Stalin. He needed to feel he had charmed Stalin and thought he had failed so far. When he got back to Washington, he told the story of the attempt to Frances Perkins—an account that mixed pride and evident hunger for control.

"You know, the Russians are interesting people," Roosevelt said to Perkins. "For the first three days I made absolutely no progress. I couldn't get any personal connection with Stalin, although I had done everything he asked me to do. I had stayed at his Embassy, gone to his dinners, been introduced to his ministers and generals. He was correct, stiff, solemn, not smiling, nothing human to get hold of. I felt pretty discouraged. If it was all going to be official paper work, there was no sense in my having made this long journey which the Russians had wanted. They couldn't come to America or any place in Europe for it. I had come there to accommodate Stalin. I felt pretty discouraged because I thought I was making no personal headway. What we were doing could have been done by the foreign ministers."

Roosevelt had fretted about his next move. "I thought it over all night and made up my mind I had to do something desperate," he said. "I couldn't stay in Teheran forever. I had to cut through this icy surface so that later I could talk by telephone or letter in a personal way. I had scarcely seen Churchill alone during the conference. I had a feeling that the Russians did not feel right about seeing us conferring together in a language which we understood and they didn't."

Roosevelt decided on his course. It was, he knew, a maneuver for political gain executed on an emotional battlefield. "On my way to the conference room that morning we caught up with Winston," the president recalled, and he put Churchill on warning.

"Winston, I hope you won't be sore at me for what I am going to do," the president said to him. Churchill, Roosevelt recalled, "shifted his cigar and grunted."

"I began almost as soon as we got into the conference room," Roosevelt said. "I talked privately with Stalin. I didn't say anything that I hadn't said before, but it appeared quite chummy and confidential, enough so that the other Russians joined us to listen. Still no smile."

By now, Churchill must have seen what was coming.

"Then I said," Roosevelt recalled to Perkins, "lifting my hand up to cover a whisper (which of course had to be interpreted), 'Winston is cranky this morning, he got up on the wrong side of the bed.'

"A vague smile passed over Stalin's eyes, and I decided I was on the right track."

Encouraged, Roosevelt picked away at Churchill. "As soon as I sat down at the conference table, I began to tease Churchill about his Britishness, about John Bull, about his cigars, about his habits. It began to register with Stalin. Winston got red and scowled, and the more he did so, the more Stalin smiled. Finally Stalin broke out into a deep, hearty guffaw, and for the first time in three days I saw light."

Roosevelt pushed even more. "I kept it up until Stalin was laughing with me, and it was then that I called him 'Uncle Joe.' He would have thought me fresh the day before, but that day he laughed and came over and shook my hand. . . . From that time on our relations were personal, and Stalin himself indulged in an occasional witticism. The ice was broken and we talked like men and brothers."

Roosevelt may have exaggerated in his retelling of the tale to Perkins, but there is other evidence such a scene occurred. "I asked someone who was present if this episode actually had taken place as frequently described," wrote John Gunther. "You bet it did," Gunther's source said, "and it wasn't funny, either!"

Churchill himself, Roosevelt said, "behaved very decently afterward," but Churchill's stoicism was a brave front. "My father was awfully wounded at Teheran," said Mary Soames. "For reasons of state, it seems to me President Roosevelt was out to charm Stalin, and my father was the odd man out. He felt that very keenly." After a further moment's reflection, she added: "My father was very hurt, I think."

AFTER THE TWO had left Teheran, they returned to Cairo; on his way home to Washington from there, Roosevelt told Eisenhower he would command OVERLORD. Meanwhile Churchill was suffering from pneumonia and ended up convalescing in Marrakech, in the villa where he and Roosevelt had spent the evening at the beginning of the year. It was a scary time for the Churchills. The prime minister could not remember ever feeling so tired. He did not have the strength to paint. "Even tottering from the motor-car to a picnic luncheon in lovely weather amid the foothills of the Atlas was limited to eighty or a hundred yards," Churchill recalled. "I passed eighteen hours out of the twenty four supine." Churchill still found himself drawn to the war—"events," he said, "continued to offer irresistible distraction." Clementine accepted his failure as a patient with good grace. "This is his day: He works in bed all the morning and gets up just in time to go for an expedition or for lunch in the garden, after which he goes for a drive," she told Mary. "Then he goes back again to bed till dinner. We try to prevent him sitting up late, but I am afraid he does." During his illness, Clementine told a friend: "I never think of after the war. You see, I think Winston will die when it's over."

AT THREE O'CLOCK on Christmas Eve afternoon, Roosevelt was wheeled into his presidential library at Hyde Park to deliver a fireside chat on Teheran. "The room was a mess, with microphones on his desk, Klieg lights facing him from every direction," Daisy noted. There were cables on the floor, and Eleanor, Anna, and Trude Lash tried to make themselves comfortable on the floor behind FDR's desk in the crowded room. Sitting with his family and friends on this fair but cold day in Dutchess County, Roosevelt explained the strange hour of the address to his listeners with a conceit that once again told Americans they were now a global force, whether they liked it or not. "That this is truly a world war was demonstrated to me when arrangements were being made with our overseas broadcasting agencies for the time for me to speak today to our soldiers and sailors and marines and merchant seamen in every part of the world," the president said into the microphones. "In fixing the time for this broadcast, we took into consideration that at this moment here in the United States, and in the Caribbean, and on the northeast coast of South America, it is afternoon. In Alaska and in Hawaii and the mid-Pacific, it is still morning. In Iceland, in Great Britain, in North Africa, in Italy and the Middle East, it is now evening. In the Southwest Pacific, in Australia, in China and Burma and India, it is already Christmas Day. So we can correctly say that at this moment, in those Far Eastern parts where Americans are fighting, today is tomorrow."

In a generous gesture to the ailing Churchill, Roosevelt said: "Of course, as you all know, Mr. Churchill and I have happily met many times before, and we know and understand each other very well." Perhaps still trying to soothe any lingering wounds, the president added: "Indeed, Mr. Churchill has become known and beloved by many millions of Americans, and the heartfelt prayers of all of us have been with this great citizen of the world in his recent illness." Kind thoughts, expressed in the most public of forums.

Then Roosevelt turned to the conversations at Teheran, glossing over the give-and-take around the green table. "Within three days of intense and consistently amicable discussions"—they were not, of course, consistently amicable from Churchill's point of view, or even from Roosevelt's, but this was no time to reveal any tensions within the alliance—"we agreed on every point concerned with the launching of a gigantic attack upon Germany."

As Churchill had done so often with the British, Roosevelt tried to prepare his people for hard work ahead. "The war is now reaching the stage where we shall all have to look forward to large casualty lists—dead, wounded, and missing," FDR said. "War entails just that. There is no easy road to victory. And the end is not yet in sight."

The paragraphs of the speech rolling on, the president got to a notable passage, one that conveyed the sense of what Roosevelt had boasted about to Frances Perkins without going into the details of his personal maneuvering at the meeting. With no mention of Churchill—or of his teasing the prime minister "about his Britishness, about John Bull, about his cigars, about his habits"—the president said: "To use an American and somewhat ungrammatical colloquialism, I may say that I 'got along fine' with Marshal Stalin. He is a man who combines a tremendous, relentless determination with a stalwart good humor. I believe he is truly representative of the heart and soul of Russia; and I believe that we are going to get along very well with him and the Russian people—very well indeed." It was, after all, Christmas—a time for wishes.

"There are wonderful sights to see with all these thousands of vessels"

Allied troops strike the Normandy coast on June 6, 1944

CHAPTER 10

THE HOUR WAS NOW STRIKING

*Both Men Battle Their Mortality–Tension and Triumph
on D-Day–A Fight over the Next Front*

I T's BEEN A wonderful year in many ways: a complete change in the war situation," Alexander Cadogan wrote in his diary on New Year's Eve 1943. "Germany is beat—but when? That cowed herd of people can do nothing to help themselves, except fight like caged rats. And if they continue to do that, it will take us a long time to wipe them out. They *may* break at any moment, but I don't expect it. Meanwhile, I suppose we must, in the spring, embark on the most hazardous enterprise ever undertaken. If it goes wrong, it will set us back 2 years. I don't mean to be pessimistic, but it will be an awful gamble."

It was to be a twilight year for Roosevelt and Churchill, a time when light and dark were intermingled—a period of victories and casualties, of sentimental moments together and sour personal exchanges. The most significant act of the war was still to come, and, as Cadogan saw, a debacle in France would exact a high price. Churchill's government could be on the line: Remember the ferocity of questions about Singapore and Tobruk. Roosevelt faced a November election, and a defeat in northern France might tilt the race to New York Governor Thomas E. Dewey, the Republican nominee.

The tone of the friendship between Roosevelt and Churchill grew autumnal in 1944. They joked and argued, then consoled and comforted each other. For both men, what was once charming or not worth mentioning could now grate, and after Teheran they were sometimes waspish about each other in private. "Winston has developed a tendency to make long speeches which are repetitious of long speeches which he has made before," Roosevelt told Sam Rosenman—"rather tartly," Rosenman remembered. One evening during the 1943–1944 holidays, Churchill and Beaverbrook were musing about World War I and the conflict still raging—familiar topics around Churchill's table. At one point Churchill turned to his aide Commander C. R. "Tommy" Thompson and said, "But, Tommy, you will bear witness that I do not repeat my stories so often as my dear friend, the President of the United States."

For all the tensions, and there were many, each could still be warm to the other when together and speak fondly of the other when apart—a sign that, aside from the politics of the alliance, there was a personal bond at work that, though often tested, held them together.

AFTER A FAMILY Christmas at Hyde Park, Roosevelt was, Daisy said, "feeling a *little* miserably." By December 30, Anna and Daisy found he had a temperature and seemed "hectic & flushed. He felt 'at loose ends.'" At eleven-thirty on New Year's Eve, Roosevelt forced himself out of bed, put on a white bathrobe, and joined guests in his study. A fire was burning, and butlers arrived with eggnog, a drinks tray, and cakes. "Mrs. R. . . . looked pale & tired," Daisy said, "but has a lovely expression—With her & Anna I kept seeing in their faces the constant thought of their men overseas—What a pall hangs over them all—"

"Auld Lang Syne" was playing on the radio. Then Roosevelt said, "Our first toast will be the U.S. of A." Henry Morgenthau added: "The President of the U.S., God bless him." Mrs. Roosevelt then raised her glass: "Our boys overseas."

The Churchills were having their own complicated holiday in Marrakech. Clementine called the villa "a mixture of Arabian Nights and Hollywood," but Churchill was not bouncing back as quickly as he would like. "He is gaining strength every day, but very slowly indeed," Clementine wrote the family back home. "He is disappointed that his recovery is slow; but when in the end he is quite well, the slowness of his convalescence may be a blessing in disguise, as it may make him a little more careful when he has to travel." Like many families in close quarters, the Churchills got on one another's nerves. The day after New Year's was, Clementine said, "bad temper day! Everyone was cross—me especially. Sarah was very sensible and said 'Let's have a bad day, and make a fresh start tomorrow.' So that is what we are doing."

Churchill returned to England in mid-January 1944. "I have now got home again safely," he told Roosevelt on January 18, confiding that he was "all right except for being rather shaky on my pins." Pamela kept Averell and Kathleen Harriman in the loop, too, writing: "The P.M. is back today—It's always a relief to know he's safe home." Churchill was out of the woods: "Now thanked we all our God," Mary wrote.

IT WAS THE blackest of times for Harry Hopkins. He had married Louise Macy, a former fashion editor, in the president's study on July 30, 1942. (Hopkins had three sons by a first marriage that had ended in divorce, and a daughter, Diana, by his second wife, Barbara. Barbara had died of cancer in 1937.) Roosevelt wanted Harry and Louise and Diana to stay on and live in the White House, as Harry and Diana had since May 1940. "It seemed to me very hard on them to be obliged to start their married life in someone else's house, even though that house happened to be the White House," wrote Eleanor, who knew something about starting a marriage under another person's control. "Franklin finally said that the most important thing in the world at that time was the conduct of the war and it was absolutely necessary that Harry be in the house. That settled that."

The fit among Harry, Louise, Eleanor, and the White House had not turned out to be a good one. Daisy Suckley's diaries chronicled Louise's struggle to become part of the surpassingly strange Roosevelt domestic sphere: "She is pretty, and I think has all good intentions, but she's 'not very bright,' as the P. put it one day, and her conversation is never illuminating, at least when I have heard it."

In late 1943, the Hopkinses were about to leave the White House. "For obvious reasons, Hopkins and his wife had cherished the natural desire to have a home of their own where they could live and entertain their friends as they pleased," Sherwood wrote, "free from the circumscriptions which were inevitable in the Executive Mansion." (One night at dinner in the White House, Mrs. Hopkins had changed Eleanor's seating plan at the table—"and that," Trude Lash said, "you did not do." It is a small but telling glimpse of daily life, and daily tensions, inside the Roosevelt White House.)

Louise and Diana moved to Georgetown while Roosevelt and Hopkins were in Teheran. "Harry went there after this trip," Eleanor wrote. "Franklin had known before he left of their decision to move, and had not felt he could oppose it: it was natural that Harry and Louise should want their own home, and the end of the war was now in sight. Harry's health was very poor, and this move, plus his illness, really began to make it difficult for him to work as closely with Franklin as he had done when living in the White House." Shortly after the move, Hopkins became so sick that he could not work, and as a result, he lost much of his influence with Roosevelt. "You must know I am not what I was," Hopkins would say to Churchill in the summer of 1944.

Nothing was worse than what happened in early February: Private First Class Stephen Hopkins, Harry's eighteen-year-old son, died in combat in the Marshall Islands. The news reached Hopkins while he was heading to

Florida to recuperate. "I am terribly distressed to have to tell you that Stephen was killed in action at Kwajalein," Roosevelt cabled Hopkins. "We have no details as yet other than that he was buried at sea. His mother has been notified. I am confident that when we get details we will all be even prouder of him than ever. I am thinking of you much. FDR."

Churchill took his friend's loss hard. "Dear Harry," Churchill wrote to Hopkins, "Please accept our most profound sympathy with you in your honour and grief. Winston and Clementine Churchill."

There followed a lettered scroll of lines from *Macbeth*.

Stephen Peter Hopkins
Age 18

"Your son, my lord, has paid a soldier's debt:
He only liv'd but till he was a man;
The which no sooner had his prowess confirm'd
In the unshrinking station where he fought,
But like a man he died."
Shakespeare.

To Harry Hopkins from Winston S. Churchill
13 February, 1944.

To Averell Harriman, Pamela wrote: "Wasn't it sad about Harry's youngest son being killed on the Marshall Islands. Poor Harry, I'm afraid he is very ill himself too. He wrote Papa & said he was going to a sunny place for several weeks or months. It didn't sound too good."

IN EARLY 1944, Anna Roosevelt moved into the White House and became an essential part of her father's circle. Anna had known his moods from her earliest moments. Roosevelt was the heroic father, so active and vibrant before his bout with polio in 1921, but so weak after it. She had seen the mask fall. In the spring of 1922, Roosevelt and Anna, then sixteen, were alone in the library at Hyde Park. "I was on a ladder moving some of the books to make room for others," she recalled. "Father was in his wheelchair giving me directions. Suddenly an armful of books slipped from my grasp and crashed to the floor. I saw Father start, and an expression of pain passed swiftly over his face. My apologies were interrupted by his voice, very sternly accusing me of being too careless for words and no help at all."

On that long-ago afternoon, Eleanor had reassured Anna, reminding her of the battles her father faced in his illness. "Back I went to the library where, of course, I not only found forgiveness but also a sincere and smilingly given invitation to resume my place on the library ladder."

Now, twenty-two years later, Roosevelt again needed her help. Eleanor, her friend Joseph Lash wrote, "was too independent, too strong, ethically too unrelenting to provide him with the kind of relaxed, unjudging company he wanted." Anna, Daisy, Polly Delano, and a few others could, and did.

IN THE OPENING months of 1944, Roosevelt battled both ill health and growing political worries. A Roper poll in *Fortune* in November 1943 found that while 70 percent favored Roosevelt's "conduct of the war and foreign policy," the number fell to 56 percent when they were asked about his handling of problems at home. Churchill knew what it was like to return to domestic storms and challenges. In a February election for Parliament, the Government candidate—that is, Churchill's candidate—was defeated by a Labourite. "This caused a pall of the blackest gloom to fall on the P.M.," wrote Jock Colville.

A reminder of the battles still to fight—as though any reminder were needed in London—arrived in the form of German bombs, which again fell on the capital from January to

April 1944. The British called it the "Little Blitz." Two days after the dark political news reached him in the Annexe, Churchill got word that German bombers had struck Whitehall and the Horse Guards Parade—the approximate equivalent of hitting the Old Executive Office Building and Lafayette Park. "We have just had a stick of bombs around 10, Downing Street and there are no more windows," Churchill wrote Roosevelt on February 21. "Clemmie and I were at Chequers and luckily all the servants were in the shelter. Four persons killed outside."

Worse terror still awaited London.

AT A ONE-ON-ONE dinner with General Brooke on February 25, after a long day of strategic wranglings, Churchill was "quite charming, as if he meant to make up for some of the rough passages of the day. He has astonishing sides to his character. We discussed Randolph and his difficulties of controlling him. . . . His daughters, my daughters. The President's unpleasant attitude lately."

A series of irritating disagreements between Britain and the United States would produce enormous cable traffic between Roosevelt and Churchill for the next fourteen months. From the Italian monarchy to Argentine beef to civil aviation rights to Middle Eastern oil and from France to Poland to the Balkans to Greece, the two would jockey over short- and long-term questions about the end of the war and the structure of the peace. The fights were both polite and fierce, with Churchill concerned about Britain's place in the postwar universe and Roosevelt pressing American interests. They would argue their positions, but they always kept the mission—and their relation-ship—in mind, understanding that statecraft is an intrinsically imperfect and often frustrating endeavor.

ROOSEVELT WAS SICK—sicker than he would let on, to Churchill or almost anyone else. Yet it was becoming clear to Roosevelt's intimates that something more than the usual "grippe" was troubling him. "Raining in Wash-ington, on top of some snow," Daisy noted on March 20, 1944. "Found the P. in bed again, with a slight fever coming & going. He needs a complete rest, and a complete cleaning out of his whole system, *I* think!"

Even he could not charm his way past age and disease. Eleanor chose not to try to intervene even as the presidential campaign approached. "I think all of us knew that Franklin was far from well, but none of us ever said anything about it—I suppose because we felt that if he believed it was his duty to continue in office, there was nothing for us to do but make it as easy as possible for him," Eleanor recalled. Anna, however, prevailed on Admiral McIntire to set up an appointment at the naval hospital in Bethesda for Tuesday, March 28.

Roosevelt left for Hyde Park the weekend before the examination. Eleanor was in Guatemala while her husband spent a springtime Sunday in Dutchess County—with Lucy.

Winthrop Rutherfurd had died six days earlier, at the age of eighty-two, and his death opened the way for ambitious visits like this one on March 26. By that evening, Roosevelt would tell Daisy he "felt fever coming on," but in the daylight hours, he and Lucy lunched together, visited the new library, and drove to Top Cottage. She did not leave until about six-thirty.

He was in the middle of war, he felt miserable, he had a world to run, and he could be lonely. After dinner in the White House one night a few weeks earlier, he left his guests and asked Daisy to join him in his study. "He got on the sofa . . . and said he was exhausted—He looked it," she wrote. "He said: 'I'm either Exhibit A, or left completely alone.' It made me feel terrible—I've never heard a word of complaint from him, but it seemed to slip out, unintentionally, & spoke volumes."

To cheer himself, Roosevelt kept Daisy and Anna around; now he added Lucy. Roosevelt's circle was very discreet. When the president was with Lucy, Joseph Lash wrote, there was probably "the magic of remembered love to cast its glow over their present encounters. There were always other people around—Anna, Daisy Suckley, Laura Delano, the Secret Service, White House secretaries like Pa Watson, Steve Early, and Bill Hassett. It was all aboveboard, except that Eleanor was not told. They said to themselves that they were protecting her, and they wanted to do so, for she was a woman of commanding dignity and of an almost saintly selflessness, whom all admired and some even loved. Within the limits of their loyalty to Franklin, they were eager to do everything possible to protect her from hurt and humiliation."

ROOSEVELT'S MEDICAL APPOINTMENT at Bethesda that week was with Dr. Howard Bruenn, a thirty-nine-year-old cardiologist. "At the end of the examination," wrote the historian Robert H. Ferrell, "Bruenn diagnosed hypertension, hypertensive heart disease, cardiac failure (left ventricular) and . . . acute bronchitis." Roosevelt's condition, Bruenn later told Ferrell, was "God-awful."

Churchill sensed his friend was ebbing and

feared he was, too. One night nearly four years after he first came to power, Churchill was at No. 10 with General Brooke. "He looked very old and very tired," Brooke noted. "He said Roosevelt was not well and that he was no longer the man he had been; this, he said, also applied to himself (Winston). He said he could still always sleep well, eat well and especially drink well! but that he no longer jumped out of bed the way he used to, and felt as if he would be quite content to spend the whole day in bed. I have never yet heard him admit that he was beginning to fail." Even before Teheran, Charles Eade thought Churchill, "although looking fit and happy, was, in my view, looking rather older. . . ." Yet, like Roosevelt, Churchill kept going, bouncing back from illness and exhaustion that might have killed other men their age or driven them into retirement.

Of course Roosevelt and Churchill looked tired. Of course they looked old. One of the most interesting features of Roosevelt's management of his illness is what his maneuvering says about how he lived his life: He was comfortable with secrets. Reports about Churchill's condition tell us that a man who worked hard and lived hard had his physical and emotional ups and downs—good days and bad days. His gloomy remarks were those of a complicated

Stephen Peter Hopkins
Age 18

"Your son, my lord, has paid a soldier's debt:
He only liv'd but till he was a man;
The which no sooner had his prowess confirm'd
In the unshrinking station where he fought,
But like a man he died."
Shakespeare.

To Harry Hopkins from Winston S. Churchill
13 February, 1944.

The scroll the Churchills sent to Harry
Hopkins after the death of Stephen
Hopkins in combat in the Marshall
Islands, February 1944

human being who voiced much of what came
into his head around diarists.

While Roosevelt rested at Bernard Baruch's
place in South Carolina that spring—Lucy
came to visit from Aiken, though not on the
day Eleanor breezed down to say hello—Churchill thrived on action. It was therapeutic. He
plunged into the planning for OVERLORD. He
once held a meeting after midnight at Downing
Street with Ismay, Eisenhower, and others, trying to determine the best precise time for the
Channel crossing. "They were arguing back and
forth, back and forth, what should be done,"
recalled Admiral Alan Kirk, the senior U.S.
naval commander during the Normandy landings. "Finally Mr. Churchill lost patience, and
he smote the table and said, 'Well, what I would
like to know is, when did William cross?' The
accused stood mute. No one could remember.
He was obviously talking about William the
Conqueror. Finally Pug Ismay, standing behind
Mr. Churchill, coughed into his hand and said,
'Sir, I think it was 1066.' "

Churchill smashed his fist down on the table
again and said, "Dammit, everybody knows it
was 1066. I want to know what month and what
day." None of the officers could tell him. "Class
dismissed," Churchill said. In the end, they discovered William had come in the autumn, but

neither Stalin nor Roosevelt would stand for any further delay, and neither would Churchill, who believed this was the moment.

CHURCHILL "WOULD BE among the first on the bridgehead in France if he possibly could," noted Jock Colville. Now the plan seemed right to him, the technology in the Allies' favor, the timing propitious. "I do not agree with the loose talk which has been going on on both sides of the Atlantic about the undue heavy casualties which we shall sustain," Churchill wrote Roosevelt on April 12, 1944. "In my view it is the Germans who will suffer very heavy casualties when our band of brothers gets among them."

What had long been theoretical was about to become reality. The invasion of Europe, a topic of conversation, cajoling, maneuvering, and planning, from the White House holidays of 1941–1942 to Teheran, would now move from the tables where presidents and prime ministers sat to the coasts of the Channel. Rome fell on June 5, but neither Roosevelt nor Churchill could celebrate much. "We have just heard of the fall of Rome and I am about to drink a mint julep to your very good health," Roosevelt cabled Churchill. It would be a quick drink: OVERLORD was at hand.

———

CLEMENTINE AND ELEANOR captured the tension of the first week of June. "I feel so much for you at this agonising moment," Clementine wrote her husband, "so full of suspense . . . !" Eleanor remembered that "when the time came . . . our hearts were with the men on the beaches."

D-Day was set for dawn, Monday, June 5, 1944. Churchill was shifting from confidence to concern, and back again. Once he had converted to a creed, there could be no stopping him: He was insisting that he go along on the invasion. Eisenhower hated the idea. "As Supreme Commander he could not bear the responsibility," Churchill recalled. Churchill dismissed the worries. After the king wrote him two frank letters asking him not to go, Churchill finally gave in.

Seven years later, Churchill still regretted missing the spectacle. "A man who has to play an effective part in taking, with the highest responsibility, grave and terrible decisions of war may need the refreshment of adventure," he wrote in his memoirs. "He may need also the comfort that when sending so many others to their death he may share in a small way their risks." Churchill had to content himself with a trip to the supreme commander's headquarters in the south of England.

In a train near Eisenhower's command post, Churchill tried to work, but, Ismay recalled, there was just one telephone line. "The Prime Minister wanted to talk to all and sundry at one and the same moment—to the President in the White House, to Eden at the Foreign Office, and to the Chiefs of Staff in Whitehall," Ismay noted. "When the inevitable delays occurred, he was full of complaints. When I suggested in desperation that it might be better to get back to civilization, my head was bitten off. Were we not next-door to Eisenhower at the very centre of affairs?"

ROOSEVELT SPENT THE weekend in Charlottesville, at Kenwood, Pa Watson's estate. A charming southerner, Watson was a comforting figure in Roosevelt's world, guarding access to the Oval Office and providing a strong arm and a ready joke for Roosevelt when the president needed to stand or "walk." Amiable, there to serve, undemanding, Watson was part of the wallpaper of Roosevelt's life.

On the porch on Sunday night, under what Daisy called "a moonlit mackerel sky," Roosevelt talked of Churchill and Stalin, the past

and the future. According to Daisy, John Boettiger and Watson said that "without the P."
Teheran "would have been a tragic failure"
because "Stalin loves & trusts the P. The P. is the
'solvent,' the 'Moderator,' between Churchill,
Stalin, etc." Not really: Stalin loved and trusted
few people, and Franklin Roosevelt was not
one of them. Roosevelt's conception of himself
as the referee of the Big Three, though, was
largely accurate. He would like, he appeared to
be thinking, to keep playing the role of global
arbiter. "The P. used the word 'Moderator' as
the possible title for the [head of the] future
League of Nations," Daisy said. "It would be a
good one. The P. would like to be that person if
he could. Who can see that far ahead—even he
cannot."

ON THE EVENING of June 3–4, while Roosevelt was in the Virginia countryside, Churchill
went to bed on his train near Eisenhower's
headquarters; overnight, the supreme commander decided to postpone for a day because of the
weather.

A letter arrived from Roosevelt. It was charming, thanking Churchill for a portrait the prime
minister had sent the president and regretting
they were not together. "Dear Winston," he
began,

That picture of you I particularly like. So much so that it too becomes an inhabitant of my bedroom wall. I am awfully glad to have it.

I am safely back in Washington trying to catch up and I am really practically all right again though I am still having some tests made on my plumbing and am keeping regular hours with much allocation to sleep. The old bronchial pneumonia has completely disappeared. The real triumph is that I have lost nearly ten pounds in the last couple of months and now I have begun the struggle to maintain the loss.

I do not believe I can get away for over a month. Of course, I am greatly disappointed that I could not be in England just at this moment, but perhaps having missed the boat it will be best not to make the trip until the events of the near future are more clear.

I got awfully good reports of you from Averell and Winant. Remember what I told old Moran to make you do—obey his orders. Thus the Commander-in-Chief in one country orders around a mere Minister of Defense in another country. . . . With my affectionate regards.

Touched, Churchill long remembered Roosevelt's letter for how it "expressed in most kindly terms his feelings about our joint work and comradeship, and his hopes and longings for our success." Replying from Portsmouth, Churchill wrote, "Our friendship is my greatest stand-by amid the ever-increasing complications of this exacting war. . . . I am here near Ike's headquarters in my train. His main preoccupation is with the weather. There are wondering sights to see with all these thousands of vessels."

THERE WAS NOTHING to do but wait. Roosevelt and Churchill had done what they could. "The hour was now striking," Churchill said. The moments passed slowly. "We returned to London in an agony of uncertainty," Ismay recalled.

When word of the weather delay reached Roosevelt, he drew on personal experience to keep his equanimity. He had, Eleanor noted, "learned from polio that when there was nothing you could do about a situation, then you'd better try to put it out of your mind and go on with your work at hand."

Churchill and Clementine dined alone at No. 10 on Monday, June 5. It was, Mary wrote, one of only four such occasions for the couple in the months between January and September; every other meal required official entertaining or work. Afterward Churchill went to the map room. Clementine came in to say good night. "Do you realise," Churchill said to her, "that by the time you wake up in the morning twenty thousand men may have been killed?"

Back in the White House, Roosevelt gathered his household in the study for drinks. "Fala had not been taken to the Watsons," Daisy said, "so he rushed in, full of excitement at having his master home again." There was dinner in the West Hall (Roosevelt and Eleanor talked about de Gaulle), and at eight-thirty Roosevelt delivered his broadcast on the fall of Rome.

Heading for bed, Roosevelt briefed Eleanor on what was happening in the Channel. Despite the psychological wear and tear of the years, in times of stress the bond of marriage tended to reassert itself for both the Churchills and the Roosevelts. Churchill could be demanding, Clementine difficult, Franklin deceptive, and Eleanor wearying, but what Mary Soames once called "the golden thread of love" bound each couple together.

ELEANOR BROUGHT WORD of H-Hour to her husband. "On D-Day, about three o'clock in the morning, I was called by the White House switchboard and told to awaken the President, that the War Department wanted him on the telephone—General Marshall was speaking himself," Mrs. Roosevelt recalled. "I went in and wakened my husband. He sat up in bed and put on his sweater, and from then on was on the telephone."

She thought Franklin "was tense waiting for news." Calm on the surface, Roosevelt was thinking of the men under fire. "Even then," Eleanor remembered of her apparently serene husband, "the only thing he said was: 'I wonder how Linaka will come out.' Mr. Linaka, a retired naval veteran of the First World War, had worked for my husband on his tree plantations and was now back in the navy. He commanded one of the landing craft on D-Day." (And made it through.)

In London, Churchill worked in the map room. In the White House, Roosevelt spent the hours getting reports. They knew their men were facing death—in the end, there were about 10,300 American, British, and Canadian casualties—and they knew history would hold them to account. Until the issue of dropping an atomic weapon was more than theoretical, OVERLORD was arguably the most difficult decision a president or a prime minister of the twentieth century had had to make. And Roosevelt and Churchill had made it. "All that weekend," Pamela Churchill wrote Averell

Harriman, who was in Moscow, "the drone of airplanes was more intense & continuous than ever before."

AT NOON LONDON time, Churchill went to the House and spent ten minutes talking about Italy. "After thus keeping them on tenterhooks for a little," Churchill recalled, he came to the point: "I have also to announce to the House that during the night and the early hours of this morning the first of the series of landings in force upon the European continent has taken place." Churchill listed the specifics, then said: "The battle that has now begun will grow constantly in scale and in intensity for many weeks to come, and I shall not attempt to speculate upon its course. This I may say however. Complete unity prevails throughout the Allied armies. There is a brotherhood in arms between us and our friends of the United States."

The operation appeared to be succeeding. "Thank God!" Roosevelt said of lighter-than-expected early casualties.

"Except for the planes overhead it was all so quiet," Pamela Churchill told Harriman. She ran into Martha Gellhorn, the writer, who, Pamela said, "was having difficulty in making her cab driver believe it was D-Day. He was quite certain that as a member of the Home Guard, the invasion could not possibly have started without him. Rather touching."

AT LAST, THE Second Front was open, a bridgehead soon established, the journey to Berlin set to begin. Decades later, there is still debate over whether such an operation could have taken place in 1943, but the preponderance of the evidence—and the resulting victory—suggests that Churchill and Roosevelt, whatever their differing motivations through the months from the first Washington conference to Teheran, followed a sound course. With the luxury of retrospection, we can see that the events of 1943 and early 1944 (the combat experience gained in North Africa, Sicily, and Italy, and the achievement of air superiority over northwest France by April of 1944), the extraordinary buildup of forces and matériel, and the Allied triumph in the Battle of the Atlantic, which kept supplies coming to the liberating armies, all took time. (And the landings were just the beginning; it was a long and bloody slog to V-E Day.)

Churchill and Roosevelt dealt with a staggering number of substantive issues during the war, from huge economic questions to colonialism to China to postwar political arrangements in countries large and small. All important, all of moment. In the sweep of what Churchill might have called the long story of the great democracies, however, the liberation of Europe and, in time, the defeat of Japan made a new world possible—a world that was, for many, a better one than existed before. World War II was marked by incalculable bloodshed, immeasurable suffering, and the horrifying and unforgivable sacrifice of the innocent. Faced with a world at war, however, Churchill and Roosevelt did their best, together, to find the means to guide a coalition of nations through one of the defining storms of human history. Sometimes one was right, sometimes the other. But they always stayed in the arena, grappling with each other and with Stalin to find a way to win. Had they failed, or truly fallen out with each other, we could be living in a different world.

STRANGELY, ROOSEVELT TOOK a moment on D-Day to dispatch two typewriters to Churchill. Warren Kimball later explained the background: "After returning from a visit with British military officials in England, General Joseph T. McNarney had written to thank the Prime Minister for his hospitality," Kimball wrote. "Churchill indicated that he would like two typewriters which had the typeface used in

McNarney's letter (a modified 'square serif')."
Roosevelt's jocular accompanying note read:
"My dear Winston: I am informed that you
liked the type script of a letter recently sent you
by General McNarney, U.S. Army Deputy
Chief of Staff. Two electric typewriters that
produce this type script are being shipped without delay which I hope you will accept as a gift
from me and as a symbol of the strong bond
between the people of America and Great
Britain."

AS THE DAY wore on, Churchill and Roosevelt
played roles each found comfortable. Churchill
would again brief the House, "obviously enjoying," *The New York Times* said, "his old role of war
reporter [and] painting a glowing picture of the
initial Allied successes, which he said were
accomplished with 'extremely little loss.' " The
president assumed the part of national pastor.
That night, Roosevelt broadcast a D-Day prayer;
the White House had distributed the text beforehand so that the audience—an estimated one
hundred million Americans—could recite the
words with Roosevelt.

Almighty God: Our sons, pride of our
Nation, this day have set upon a mighty
endeavor, a struggle to preserve our

Republic, our religion and our civilization, and to set free a suffering humanity.

Lead them straight and true; give strength to their arms, stoutness to their hearts, steadfastness in their faith.

They will need Thy blessings. Their road will be long and hard. For the enemy is strong. He may hurl back our forces. Success may not come with rushing speed, but we shall return again and again; and we know that by Thy grace, and by the righteousness of our cause, our sons will triumph. . . .

Thy will be done, Almighty God.

Amen.

Roosevelt had the prayer bound in leather and sent a copy to Churchill.

In Moscow, the Russians were delighted with the news from Western Europe—the Soviets, Averell Harriman said, were "awash in boozy good feeling."

"THE FIRST WAVE of excitement over D-Day is passing—& people are reverting to normal again . . . ," Pamela wrote Harriman by the end of that first week. As Churchill played bezique at Chequers with his daughter-in-law the weekend after the landings, the story of the conflict between the Mediterranean and France was about to get a new chapter. The latest controversy: an operation code-named ANVIL, a follow-up landing in southern France. Churchill wanted to use the resources to push ahead in Italy and possibly on into Austria.

Churchill sent a long memo to make the case. "I am shocked to think of the length of the message that I shall be sending you tonight," Churchill told Roosevelt on June 28. "It is a purely personal communication between you and me in our capacity as heads of the two western democracies."

Roosevelt rejected Churchill's pleas.

"At Teheran," Roosevelt wrote back, "we agreed upon a definite plan of attack. That plan has gone well so far. Nothing has occurred to require any change. Now that we are fully involved in our major blow, history will never forgive us if we lose precious time and lives in indecision and debate. My dear friend, I beg you let us go ahead with our plan."

Reading Roosevelt's cable, Churchill called for General Brooke, who told his diary: "I thought at first we might have trouble with him, he looked like he wanted to fight the President. However in the end we got him to agree to our outlook which is: 'All right, if you insist on being damned fools, sooner than falling out with you, which would be fatal, we shall be damned fools with you, and we shall see that we perform the role of damned fools damned well!' "

Churchill, who had been pushing for a trip to Washington to make his case personally, composed a reply to Roosevelt. It must have been a difficult night, one not unlike the evenings at Teheran, when Churchill felt his influence with Roosevelt waning. His disappointment leapt off the page. "We are deeply grieved by your telegram," he wrote Roosevelt. This was, he said, "the first major strategic and political error for which we two have to be responsible. . . . It is with the greatest sorrow that I write to you in this sense. But I am sure that if we could have met, as I so frequently proposed, we should have reached a happy agreement. I send you every personal good wish. However we may differ on the conduct of the war, my personal gratitude to you for your kindness to me and for all you have done for the cause of freedom will never be diminished."

Tough words, but saying them lifted his spirits. Having made his case, he was ready to move on. Brooke found Churchill "in a good mood" the next day. Going over the cable at Hyde Park, a "tired & listless" Roosevelt tried to soothe Churchill. "I appreciate deeply your clear exposition of your feelings and views on this decision we are making," Roosevelt wrote. "I honestly believe that God will be with us as he has in Overlord and in Italy and in North Africa. I always think of my early geometry 'A straight line is the shortest distance between two points.' "

The future with the Soviets was also an issue. Over the Fourth, Roosevelt and Daisy talked of Russia. Stalin, Daisy said, had been quoted saying that "the President is my friend, we will always understand each other." His dealings with Stalin, Daisy told Roosevelt, "are one of the great triumphs of his career, and only the future can tell how *much* that relationship is going to count in rebuilding our shattered world—Before they met, there was doubt & suspicion on Stalin's part, & also, probably, on the P.'s. Now, there is the basis for talking, for working things out together—but the P. smiled & said he keeps his fingers crossed!"

CHURCHILL WAS ALSO confronting a new threat at home: Hitler's "flying bombs"—V–1 and later V–2 rockets—were terrorizing London. Mary had to deal with the missiles first-hand in her antiaircraft battery. For Clementine, it was one more worry to add to all the others.

Randolph was in a plane crash in July 1944, prompting a kind note to Churchill from Roosevelt. "I am very happy that Randolph has come through all right," Roosevelt wrote. "Thank you so much," Churchill replied. "Ten died and nine survived."

Family, war, and politics were interwoven for both men. One night early in 1944, Franklin Jr. and John Boettiger got into a heated dinner debate about the war. Franklin Jr. raised his voice; Boettiger countered him point by point. Looking "rather wan," Daisy said, Roosevelt listened as young Franklin made an interesting point. "To a man," the president's son said, "from the highest to the lowest, every individual in the armed forces would consider the P. was a 'quitter' if he did *not* run again this year." Afterward, Roosevelt "did a little work," Daisy said, but "didn't feel up to much."

"London is as black as ever, one notices no difference"

Winston and Mary Churchill survey an antiaircraft battery directing fire at a V-1 rocket overhead, summer 1944

LIFE IS NOT VERY EASY

Churchill Worries About Roosevelt's Reelection–
Stalin and Churchill in Moscow–Roosevelt's Global
Vision–"It's in the Bag"

As the rockets struck London, the Allies fought through the Norman hedgerows, and the Japanese dug in for years of war to come, Churchill mused aloud about the press of business to Roosevelt. "We have immense tasks before us," he wrote Roosevelt in the weeks after D-Day. "Indeed, I cannot think of any moment when the burden of the war has laid more heavily upon me or when I have felt so unequal to its ever-more entangled problems. I greatly admire the strength and courage with which you face your difficulties, especially in a year when you have, what I may venture to call, other preoccupations." The central "preoccupation" was the 1944 presidential race, and the old campaigners understood each other.

"Over here new political situations crop up every day but so far, by constant attention, I am keeping my head above water," Roosevelt had written Churchill a few days before OVERLORD. Roosevelt had a few health scares—a collapse in his train in California and an angina attack during a speech aboard a warship among them— but only a handful of people knew the specifics. "Nothing," wrote John Gunther, "was going to budge him from the driver's seat except death."

Churchill's circle monitored FDR's fortunes on the home front with care. A year earlier, in mid-1943, Beaverbrook had come to the United States to take political soundings about the upcoming race. What Beaverbrook heard from Roosevelt's foes suggested that a Roosevelt loss—MacArthur, Dewey, and Willkie were the most likely Republican nominees— would make Churchill's job harder. According to Beaverbrook's notes, a bitter Joseph Kennedy believed that "Roosevelt will be defeated. The Republican candidate will be Dewey. . . . Roosevelt's chances, Kennedy declared, are declining steadily. . . . Kennedy makes attacks on the President for yielding to Churchill's strategy [on Africa in 1942 and '43]. . . . This is bad business for the Americans, and damaging to the President." The next day, with Willkie: "Willkie is moving in the direction of hostility to Great Britain's public men," Beaverbrook noted. ". . . And he speaks with admiration of Stalin." The day after that, with Dewey himself: "Dewey's conversation is given up altogether to domestic issues. He is too far removed from the war front to give close study to Europe, and he is of the opinion anyway that the war is nearly over." Beaverbrook's summation as he returned to London: "Danger of hurting Roosevelt by coming up too strongly in his favor." All Churchill could do was watch. "I saw a lot of Richard Pim, who ran the Prime Minister's map room, and he made it very clear that they were praying for FDR to win," recalled George Elsey. They would have to be quiet prayers, said in the shadows.

DEWEY WAS GOING to make Roosevelt's age part of the campaign. Anna knew it was coming. "One must not minimize his evident strategy," Daisy noted after talking with Anna, "which will include harping on the subject of the *age* of the members of the cabinet, F.D.R.'s health, etc."

Anna had another issue concerning her father to deal with. "Father asked me one day . . . whether I would mind if he invited a very close friend to dinner," she recalled. His daughter guessed who it was before he could tell her: "He said Mrs. Rutherfurd." Anna agreed. "It was a terrible decision to have to make in a hurry, because I realized that Mother wasn't going to be there, and I was sure she didn't know about it, but my quick decision was that the private lives of these people were not my business," Anna said. "After all, it was their business. And who was I to say you can or cannot?" Eleanor would not be told. "I didn't feel guilty or anything else," Anna said. "I never said anything to Mother just because I thought you don't want to hurt somebody else's feelings, that was all. . . . I just felt, while they were my parents, nevertheless they had reached an age where they certainly were entitled to lead their own private lives without having me, of all people, or any of their children, say, 'You shouldn't do this' or 'You shouldn't see this person or the other person.' "

Roosevelt's ability to operate on different levels simultaneously was remarkable. Concealing his contacts with Lucy from Eleanor, he could also be an amiable husband, father, and grandfather. Eleanor related this story: their son John Roosevelt, a naval officer, was dropping his wife, Anne, and children, including a new baby, off for a White House stay while he went to sea. "Johnny called me one evening just before Anne and the children were to come," Eleanor wrote. "I was out, so he talked to his father who was already in bed. . . . Finally he said: 'Be sure to order the diaper service.' Franklin, who had never heard of the diaper service, said, 'What did you say?' Johnny replied, 'The diaper service,' and explained what it was and said the order should be for two hundred. This bewildered his father who asked: 'Is there anything wrong with the baby? We always boiled ours.' Johnny said: 'Oh, father, people don't do things like that any more. . . . This is just a supply to have on hand.' Franklin dutifully made a mental note. . . . He thought to himself, 'I will call Hacky (Miss Hackmeister, the head telephone operator) and say: 'Hacky get me the diaper service immediately' and Hacky will say 'What did you say, Mr. President' and then I will answer: 'The diaper service, Hacky, I do not know what it is but please get it.' After Hacky completes the call I will say: 'This is the President of the United States and I want to order two hundred diapers sent to me at the White House.' All of this having been carefully decided in his mind, he put out his light and went to sleep." Roosevelt enjoyed retelling the tale, which suggests a fond engagement with the life of his family. He could regulate his emotions, balancing secrets with the life he had built with Eleanor.

ROOSEVELT WAS ALSO running cold and then hot about Churchill. At tea in late June with the

Chinese ambassador, Roosevelt joked about Churchill's stubbornness. To Chiang Kai-shek through the envoy, Daisy noted, "The P. sent word, confidentially, & by word of mouth, that later this year, he hopes for a meeting of the *four* powers: Churchill, Stalin, Chiang & himself— probably in Scotland, or North England—with a laugh he said: 'I think that Stalin, Chiang, & I can bring Brother Churchill around.' "

At the same time, he was giving Churchill a number of souvenirs tied to Churchill's love of history. First went a batch of naval papers bearing the signatures of a number of British officers who died at Jutland in World War I and, in Roosevelt's words, "various items which relate to some early Churchills. I thought you would like to have them for your family papers." They thrilled Churchill, evoking a moment of reminiscence about Lord Randolph. One of the papers, Churchill said in a note of thanks, was a "visiting card signed by my Father in 1886 when, as you know, he was Chancellor of the Exchequer." *As you know.* Just the sight of his father's handwriting pulled him back in his imagination to the legend of Lord Randolph; it is touching that Churchill believed in the myth of his father so strongly that he would assume everyone could chart the milestones of his long-ago career. Roosevelt also sent Churchill a framed copy of the Declaration of the United

Nations, a reminder of their happy New Year's Day two and a half years before.

IN MIDSUMMER 1944, there was talk in London and in Washington about military action against the deadly machinery of the Holocaust. The potential target: Auschwitz. Telling Churchill on July 7, 1944, of a request by the Jewish Agency of Palestine to bomb railway lines leading to the death camp, Anthony Eden suggested looking into striking the killing complex as well. "Get anything out of the Air Force you can," Churchill replied, "and invoke me if necessary." Citing technical military reasons, the British secretary of state for air, Sir Archibald Sinclair, thought the operation beyond their capabilities but said they should propose it to the Americans "to see if they are prepared to try it." Washington, however, was resisting the idea. Bombing the rail lines would probably have done little: The Germans were always quick to repair infrastructure. Attacking Auschwitz itself was also problematic, for the mission would have killed some of those it was intended to save. Advocates of the proposal, however, argue that the symbolic value of the strike would have outweighed these other considerations. In any event, from the available evidence, Roosevelt and Churchill did not discuss the bombing of the rail lines or the camps, and nothing came of the proposed mission.

CHURCHILL PROPOSED A summer summit—anywhere. Roosevelt, who was managing his nomination for a fourth term, traveling to the West Coast and heading to Hawaii to ponder Pacific strategy, thought it best to wait a bit on seeing Churchill. "I wholly agree that we three should meet but it would be a lot easier for me if we could make it the tenth or fifteenth of September," Roosevelt wrote on July 17. "This would get me back in plenty of time for the election, although that is in the lap of the Gods."

Roosevelt was trying to have everything his way this season, including who was to be his running mate. Henry Wallace was out—the party regulars thought him too ethereal and too liberal.

Senator Harry Truman of Missouri, who had led a panel investigating war production, fit the moment. Roosevelt did not know Truman well, but, as Democratic boss Ed Flynn noted, "his record as head of the Senate Committee . . . was excellent, his labor votes in the Senate were good; on the other hand he seemed to represent to some degree the conservatives in the party, he came from a border state, and he had never made any 'racial' remarks. He just dropped into the slot."

CHURCHILL WAS CONSUMED with the crush of government, military strategy, the German rocket attacks, and some family strife.

There was more trouble with Randolph and Pamela. Writing to Harriman on July 1 after speaking with her estranged husband, Pamela reported: "It is difficult for me to describe my conversation with R. I think it would take too long & it could not all be put on paper. Roughly, the idea behind it all was this—R had such a row with his father that they were not going to see each other again. . . . The major part of the row I believe to have been over me & the child being at C[hequers], which R resents very much." Trying to negotiate these complex currents—currents that were consuming at least a part of Winston Churchill's time and emotional energy in the middle of the war—Pamela and Randolph lunched. "As R was leaving the country at 4 o'clock there was no time to mince words—So I told him that I had heard many 2nd and 3rd hand talks of what he had said—& that if he had any grievances I'd like to hear them direct from him. Well we had the most amiable lunch—He saw my point of view & I saw his. The outcome being that we parted better friends than we've been for years."

She and Randolph apparently struck a deal. "Me, having agreed to remove the baby from C. & to find a place of *my own* in the country for the baby, & that during this last year until our divorce is through & complete that I will not see too much of his parents. Now, I consider that quite reasonable, & one thing I know now, is that R is just as keen as I am to get free—and that if I stick to this bargain, which I will do, I think everything will go forward smoothly & there should be no more rows over me. . . ."

What may have been driving Randolph to take such a hard line about Pamela enjoying the glamour of his parents' company was not any desire to separate young Winston from his grandparents—far from it—but the simmering suspicion in Randolph's heart that his father did nothing to stop (and, in Randolph's view, may have abetted) Pamela's affair with Harriman.

It was a suspicion so deep-seated that it managed to disrupt a cruise aboard Aristotle Onassis's yacht in 1963, less than two years before Churchill's death. Onassis often hosted the former prime minister aboard the *Christina* in those last years, and this time Randolph joined the party. One night Randolph began spewing what Anthony Montague Browne, who was there, politely called in his memoirs "violent reproaches relating to his wartime marriage." It was a difficult moment. "Short of hitting him on the head with a bottle, nothing could have stopped him," Montague Browne recalled. "It was one of the most painful scenes I have ever witnessed." If the destruction of the Randolph-Pamela marriage could evoke such rage on a pleasant evening two decades later, then the wartime "rows" over Pamela between Churchill and Randolph must have indeed been painful for both father and son at a time when Churchill was leading the nation.

CHURCHILL AND ROOSEVELT would see each other again at Quebec in September. "This visit of mine to the President is the most necessary one that I have ever made since the very beginning as it is there that various differences that exist between the Staffs, and also between me and the American Chiefs of Staff, must be brought to a decision," Churchill wrote Clementine on August 17. "We have three armies in the field. The first is fighting under American Command in France, the second under General Alexander is relegated to a secondary and frustrated situation by the United States' insistence on this landing on the Riviera. The third on the Burmese frontier is fighting in the most unhealthy country in the world under the worst possible conditions to guard the American line over the Himalayas into their very over-rated China. Thus two-thirds of our forces are being mis-employed for American convenience, and the other third is under American command." He was feeling the loss of control but tried to be cheerful. "These are delicate and serious matters to be handled between friends in careful and patient personal discussion," Churchill added. "I have no doubt we shall reach a good conclusion, but you will see that life is not very easy."

Churchill was sick again. On September 1—the fifth anniversary of Hitler's invasion of Poland—Churchill landed back in England after a journey to Italy. He had a temperature of 103. Clementine found him "crumpled & feverish," she told Mary. "I was sick with fright." A touch of pneumonia was back, but all was soon well. "I was on a 24-hour leave pass, and I bolted up to London," Mary wrote. "On my arrival at the Annexe I found my parents having dinner together in my father's room—he was sitting up in bed attired in his glorious many-hued bedjacket, with my mother by his side in one of her lovely housecoats: It was a most reassuring sight, and I enjoyed the loving welcome they gave me." Still, Churchill was nearly seventy, under the greatest imaginable stress and fending off pneumonia. Life was indeed far from easy.

CHURCHILL WAS ALSO increasingly worried about Soviet influence in the east. "Good God," he stormed to Lord Moran, "can't you see that the Russians are spreading across Europe like a tide; they have invaded Poland, and there is nothing to prevent them marching into Turkey and Greece!" A crisis in the Polish capital was a particularly tragic case. What Churchill called "the martyrdom of Warsaw" was under way. Closing in on the city, the Soviets broadcast an appeal for the Poles to rise up against their German occupiers, which the underground heroically did—while the Russians sat outside the capital. The Germans and the Poles, whom Stalin wanted to dominate after the war, were destroying each other at close quarters.

Churchill and Roosevelt asked Stalin to intervene—or at least let Anglo-American forces intervene, by dropping supplies to the Polish fighters. "We believe that all three of us should do the utmost to save as many of the patriots there as possible," Roosevelt wrote in a message Churchill cosigned on August 19. Moscow balked, saying the Americans and the British could go ahead but could not use landing grounds in Soviet territory to refuel. Stymied— they needed those bases; two British attempts to fly from Italy were, Churchill said, "forlorn and inadequate"—Roosevelt and Churchill were losing the point to the Soviets as the Germans killed innocent Poles. Calling the Warsaw situation "a dirty business" in a letter written the week of August 19, Averell Harriman said of the Soviets: "I realize it is essential that we make every effort to find a way to work with them and, in spite of disagreements, I am still hopeful. But one thing is certain, that when they depart from common decency we have got to make them realize it."

Churchill was outraged by accounts of the violence in the city and forwarded an eyewitness report to Roosevelt and Stalin. "The dead," it said, "are buried in backyards and squares." The Poles needed help, and Churchill, his heart stirred, proposed a radical solution to Roosevelt: If Stalin failed to reply to a renewed request from both of them, then they should proceed without him, send the flights over, use the bases behind Soviet lines, and take their chances. It was a dramatic, bold, brave idea, but Roosevelt said no. He had business to do with Stalin— the Americans wanted rights to Soviet bases in Siberia for assaults on Japan—and was not willing to risk a fight with him over Warsaw.

Churchill was long anguished over the episode, one that would come to seem typical of disputes with the Soviets as the war drew to a close. "When the Russians entered the city three months later they found little but shattered streets and the unburied dead," Churchill wrote in 1953. "Such was their liberation of Poland, where they now rule. But this cannot be the end of the story." And, of course, it would not be.

By now, both Churchill and Roosevelt seemed to be accustomed to the cycle of their friendship. They would disagree about some large matter (about Warsaw, Greece, Italy, the Balkans), but the policy question would seem to be soothed with personal words and, often, affectionate companionship. A ritual—and, like most rituals, reassuring in its familiarity. The consistent elements were Churchill's optimism and magnanimity ("I have no doubt we shall reach a good conclusion," as he had told Clementine) and Roosevelt's capacity to do what he wanted to do while trying to make Churchill feel loved and valued. ("Where is your landing spot?" Roosevelt asked the America-bound Churchill in the middle of the uprising. "If New York you and I could go to [Quebec] together on my train.")

———

THEIR PRIVATE WORLDS in the days before meeting in Quebec in September 1944 reflected their personalities and explain their approaches to each other. Aboard the *Queen Mary*, Churchill, still sick, was by turns expansive, indulgent, hilarious, gloomy, verbose, and hardworking. In Washington and Hyde Park, Roosevelt, also sick and complaining that he felt "like a boiled owl," was secretive, ebullient, and able to shift from one universe to another with ease.

Surrounded by the people he was most comfortable with—Clementine, Colville, Lindemann, and Ismay—Churchill was thinking about British politics. Mulling over a more liberal postwar era, he suspected there would be "inevitable disillusionment at the non-appearance of an immediate millennium" after the victory over the Axis, something that would make "the glamour fade from a Government which had won the war." But the prime minister claimed to be resigned to any fate that came his way. If a left-wing majority was inevitable, "what is good enough for the English people, is good enough for me." He was generous minded, musing that he would not "beat up" on the Americans again about the ANVIL argument. "He will suggest that the controversy be left to history and add that he intends to be one of the historians," Colville wrote. Churchill played bezique and tucked into two Trollope novels—*Phineas Finn* and *The Duke's Children*.

His mood grew more melancholy. Toward the end of the voyage, he plunged into his work, once losing his temper over a proposal from the war cabinet. "He dictated a violent reply (which was never sent) full of dire threats," Colville said.

AS CHURCHILL HELD forth, played cards, and escaped the crush of work for a few hours in the fictional milieu of Victorian politics, Roosevelt hid his emotional life in plain sight. Roosevelt was aboard his train bearing north from Washington to Hyde Park and then on to Quebec. Instead of heading straight to the Hudson, however, the train stopped in north-western New Jersey, near Allamuchy, to see Lucy at her late husband's estate.

The Rutherfurds' English-style manor house was set amid fields and woods; the weather was pleasantly breezy. Daisy, who accompanied FDR, and Lucy had seen to it that everything was arranged for Roosevelt's comfort. "Mrs. Rutherfurd had a lovely room all ready for the P. to take his rest," Daisy wrote, "even to turn-ing down the best linen sheets—but he wasn't going to miss any of his visit & did not rest until we got back on the train." Lucy knew her man, letting him play expert in chief on all matters rural. (He liked to call himself a "tree grower.") "The Pres. is going to look over the whole 1,300 acres—farms, woods, etc. & advise them what to do," Daisy noted. "It is the usual problem of diminished incomes & how to keep a large place going with fewer servants than one needs."

After Roosevelt's tour of the grounds, there was discussion of where he should be seated for lunch. "I finally went to the Pres.," said Daisy, "& he settled it: he sat at Mrs. Rutherfurd's right!" Daisy was struck by the tableau before her: Guests included Lucy's stepchildren and Prince and Princess Alexandre Chimay. "The whole thing was out of a book—a complete setting for a novel, with all the characters at that lunch table, if one counts"—she knowingly added—"the absent husbands and wives etc." It was a remarkable scene: a wartime president of the United States, en route to a conference with the prime minister of Great Britain, stealing a few hours to lunch with a long-ago love, surrounded by titled guests and extended relatives, all discreet enough to know that the whereabouts of this most public of men were to be guarded with tact.

Back on the train, Roosevelt took a nap. The claims of real life asserted themselves. Earlier in the day, Churchill had written him to announce he was bringing Mrs. Churchill to Quebec. When Roosevelt awoke from his rest, he cabled Churchill: "Perfectly delighted that Clemmie will be with you. Eleanor will go with me." Eleanor was on the platform at Hyde Park's Highland Station, and she drove Daisy and Roosevelt to Val-Kill for supper. There were lobsters, and Trude Lash served applekuchen. No one talked about what Roosevelt had had for lunch—or where. As Daisy wrote in her diary that day: "How little one knows of the inner life of others."

THE ROOSEVELTS ARRIVED at Quebec a few minutes ahead of the Churchills. As the prime minister and the president greeted each other, a reporter noted the "look of affection on the faces of the two men as they clasped hands."

"Hello, Winston!"

"Hello, Franklin!"

While the men talked of war, their wives' contrasting styles created some friction. "Clementine was less 'public relations' conscious than Mrs. Roosevelt, and was somewhat put about when the latter announced her intention of broadcasting to the Canadian people, and told Clementine that she had been invited to do so too," wrote Mary. "I was staggered and reluctant," Mrs. Churchill recalled. "First of all I said I could not possibly do it at such short notice and thought that I had nothing to say. But finally I was hounded into doing it." The prodigious pace Mrs. Roosevelt set for herself was not Mrs. Churchill's, who was a more deliberate and more easily tired woman. "Clementine's struggles with the preparation of the broadcast had been severely interrupted by the necessity for her to attend, with Mrs. Roosevelt, a luncheon party given by the wife of the Lieutenant-Governor of Quebec," wrote Mary. It did not go well. She was working on the radio speech—part of which was to be in French—when an official luncheon intervened, with seven courses, four wines, several liqueurs, and sixty-five guests to greet. "I am sorry to confess that I was in a filthy temper," Clementine wrote her children.

After lunch, the lieutenant-governor's wife, Lady Fiset, announced that Eleanor had a few words to say to the group. "I tried to hide behind a palm tree because I saw what was coming next," Clementine wrote home in the third person. "But it was no use. When Mrs. Roosevelt had ceased, Lady Fiset said Mrs. Churchill would now like to reply to Mrs. Roosevelt. Mrs. Churchill was fished from behind the palm tree—and I won't repeat to you what I said because I have forgotten, being under the influence of the luncheon."

As harried as she was, Clementine apparently did not show it, and Eleanor seemed not to notice.

ROOSEVELT AND CHURCHILL were in their usual pattern, discussing weighty subjects, dining, and unwinding with an evening movie before another late-night session. Dr. McIntire had sent word to Admiral Brown, the naval aide, that Roosevelt should not stay up late. It was a losing battle until Brown thought to enlist Churchill's help in keeping something approaching reasonable hours. "The party broke up that night immediately after the movies, about ten thirty," recalled Brown. "As we all moved off together toward our quarters, Mr. Churchill, his arm firmly held by Mrs. Churchill, muttered to me, 'Aren't I a good boy?' "

Much to Churchill's satisfaction, Roosevelt offered Churchill generous economic aid. "While going to bed the P.M. told me some of the financial advantages the Americans had promised us," Colville wrote on September 14. " 'Beyond the dreams of avarice,' I said. 'Beyond the dreams of justice,' he replied." Churchill offered, and Roosevelt accepted, the use of the Royal Navy in the closing conflict against Japan—a means, in part, of maintaining Britain's role as America's partner. And there

*"I am sorry to confess that I was
in a filthy temper"*

Eleanor and Clementine delivering
a joint radio address at Quebec,
September 1944

was the inevitable talk of European strategy. Churchill quoted Milton's *Lycidas* (after the Germans left Italy, Churchill said, "We should have to look 'for fresh fields and pastures anew' ") as he raised the possibility of a thrust out of Italy toward Vienna, saying that "an added reason for this right-handed movement was the rapid encroachment of the Russians into the Balkans and the consequent dangerous spread of Russian influence in this area."

Then there was the curious episode of the "Morgenthau Plan." The idea: Return Germany to a preindustrial, pastoral state by taking away its industrial capacity. Though the concept got as far as a paper signed by both Roosevelt and Churchill, it died after the conference.

Before leaving Quebec, the two men, wearing academic regalia, received honorary degrees from McGill University in the sunshine on the roof of the Citadel. Then they met the press, with Churchill the more eloquent; Roosevelt spoke in a whisper that Colville thought could barely be heard above the click of the cameras.

IT WAS A touching scene. In private at Quebec, Churchill had told Colville he believed Roosevelt was "very frail," and now, on the sun-splashed roof of the old fort, the St. Lawrence River far below, Churchill talked about the importance of personal contact in political affairs—in particular, of the importance of his personal contact with the president sitting to his side.

"Our affairs are so intermingled, our troops fighting in the line together, and our plans for the future are so interwoven that it is not possible to conduct these great affairs . . . without frequent meetings between the principals," Churchill said. When, he continued, he had "the rare and fortunate chance to meet the President of the United States, we are not limited in our discussions by any sphere. We talk over the whole position in every aspect—the military, economic, diplomatic, financial. All—all is examined. And obviously that should be so. And the fact that we have worked so long together, and the fact that we have got to know each other so well under the hard stresses of war, makes the solution of problems so much simpler, so swift and so easy it is."

In a passage that suggests he understood how much easier it was for leaders to turn each other down when they were exchanging wires instead of glances across a table, Churchill added: "What an ineffectual method of conveying human thought correspondence is [laughter]—telegraphed with all its rapidity, all the facilities of our—of modern intercommunication. They are simply dead, blank walls compared to personal—personal contacts. And that applies not only to the President and the Prime Minister of Great Britain, it applies to our principal officers who at every stage enter in the closest association, and have established friendships which have greatly aided the tasks and toil of our fighting troops."

Chieftains, Churchill was saying, must meet in camp together. It was the same point Roosevelt had tried to make on that lost night at Gray's Inn more than a quarter century before. Now Churchill saw that even the most passionate words—and Lord knows he wrote millions of them, in cables and books and speeches—did not have the same power to convince as many fewer words spoken within a room of human beings trained in the arts of manners and devoted to the same ends. Meetings often produce a kind of magic, but magic can fade. Such is the power and peril of personal diplomacy.

The hours were wearying. Roosevelt phoned Daisy when he arrived in Hyde Park on September 17 and told her "it was a *good* conference; much was accomplished," but "he wanted to *sleep* all the time."

HARRY HOPKINS WAS at Hyde Park, too. "He was obviously invited to please me," recalled Churchill, and Hopkins tried to explain his fall from grace. "He had declined in the favour of the President," Churchill said, and Roosevelt once even failed to speak to Hopkins when he was a little late for a meal. But soon the old three-way chemistry kicked in, and "it was remarkable how definitely my contacts with the President improved," Churchill recalled, "and our affairs moved quicker as Hopkins appeared to regain his influence." Roosevelt and Churchill were back in their old, good form, friends united against the world, with the loyal Hopkins just a step behind, there to serve.

Even by Roosevelt standards, it was an eclectic gathering. The Churchills and the duke of Windsor were there, along with Roosevelt's Hudson Valley circle. Eleanor, Clementine told her daughters, "loves her meals out of doors and so life at Hyde Park is a succession of picnics. It is rather fun really, and clever, because, when you have a lot of foreign guests whom you do not know planked down on top of you, it all fills in the time. I went for two terrific walks with Mrs. Roosevelt, who has very long legs and out-walks me easily."

Clementine also worried about Roosevelt's apparently waning powers. She had not seen him for a year and, like her husband, thought the president weaker than he had seemed in August–September 1943. Roosevelt, she wrote home to Mary, "with all his genius does not—indeed cannot (partly because of his health and partly because of his make-up)—function round the clock, like your Father. I should not think that his mind was pinpointed on the war for more than four hours a day, which is not really enough when one is a supreme war lord."

Roosevelt and Churchill also talked about Tube Alloys. (They always seemed to be discussing the bomb at Hyde Park.) A group of scientists in the know had been arguing that the United States and Britain should tell the international community what was in the offing; Churchill and Roosevelt said no. "The suggestion that the world should be informed regarding Tube Alloys, with a view to international agreement regarding its control and use, is not accepted," read a secret memorandum approved by Churchill and Roosevelt. "The matter should continue to be regarded as of the utmost secrecy; but when a 'bomb' is finally available, it might perhaps, after mature consideration, be used against the Japanese, who should be warned that this bombardment will be repeated until they surrender."

Churchill had his money, his role in the Pacific, and his way on the atomic project. He was refreshed by his time with Roosevelt. On the way to Quebec, Moran and Colville had had a chat about Churchill's condition. "The P.M. had slight temperature again and was highly irascible," Colville wrote. "Lord Moran . . . told me he does not give him a long life and he thinks that when he goes it will be either a stroke or the heart trouble which first showed itself last winter at Carthage." Meeting Churchill in New York after the prime minister's stay in Hyde Park, Colville thought he was "looking far, far better. . . ."

Roosevelt, however, was looking worse and worse. After Churchill left Hyde Park, Roosevelt spent some time there with Anna and Daisy. "The Pres. roused himself & went off to get washed up for dinner," Suckley said. He did not like the look of the political scene. "The Pres. says he feels there is an excellent chance of his being defeated in the election—that Dewey is making a very good campaign," Daisy wrote. "The Pres. is planning his life after he leaves the W.H. It will be so different, without the many 'services' supplied to him by the govt. He will 'write' and can make a lot of money that way— Also, his corr. will be tremendous—he feels he won't be able to afford Miss Tully & that *she* would not be happy in Hyde Park, away from her family—More problems!" In the first week of October, George Elsey accompanied Roosevelt on another trip to Hyde Park. "The President thought it was conceivable that Dewey could beat him," Elsey recalled, "and he wanted me to inspect the library and recommend what security measures would be necessary to protect his classified papers."

CHURCHILL AND CLEMENTINE had a luncheon table dustup when they got home. The subject is unknown, but it can be inferred that Churchill spoke roughly, contradicting Clementine. At one-thirty in the morning on October 8, Churchill wrote his wife: "My darling One, I have been fretting over our interchange at luncheon yesterday. I am sure that no one thought of it as more than my making my own position clear, and that it all passed in the ripple of a most successful party. Anyhow forgive me for anything that seemed disrespectful to you, & let yr morning thoughts dwell kindly on yr penitent apologetic & ever loving W."

Churchill had adventure on his mind in October and decided to try his luck a second time with a three-way meeting. "I feel sure that personal contact is most necessary," he cabled Roosevelt on September 29, 1944, urging him to join a session with Stalin. With the election at hand, Roosevelt said no, but Churchill went ahead. "As the Soviet armies moved into Eastern Europe, Churchill became concerned about the political structure Moscow would set up with its military power," Chip Bohlen recalled. "The Soviets were making military moves with obvious post-war implications. Instead of keeping full pressure on the central target, Germany, Stalin was diverting troops to Bulgaria and Hungary, two secondary targets. Churchill made up his mind to go to Moscow without Roosevelt, and notified the President accordingly."

Churchill thought he could do business with Stalin. For all his skepticism about Stalin's motives and designs, Churchill—like Roosevelt—believed in personal diplomacy. "All might yet be well if he could win Stalin's friendship," Moran noted. "After all, it was stupid of the President to suppose that he was the only person who could manage Stalin." Churchill would go to Moscow while Roosevelt campaigned. "In the afternoon the P.M., while signing photographs (including one for Stalin) and books, began reading Vol. I of Marlborough aloud to me and continued about Sir Winston Churchill's home life and passion for heraldry for nearly an hour," wrote Colville. "At the end he said that as I had been subjected to this ordeal he would give me a copy for Christmas."

In the first week of October, Roosevelt drafted a cable wishing Churchill "every success" on his trip. Bohlen was at the State Department when Hopkins, who had come across the message to Churchill in the map room, called him. "Chip, get the hell over here in a hurry," Hopkins said. Bohlen recalled, "I found Hopkins sitting in his White House office, one leg draped over the arm of a chair." He handed Bohlen Roosevelt's cable—Hopkins had stopped it from being sent; in the map room, Robert Sherwood wrote, "the officers had no way of knowing that there had been any change in Hopkins' position in the White House and they complied with his order"—and asked what Bohlen thought. "I said that . . . it was dangerous to allow Churchill to speak for us in dealing with Stalin," Bohlen recalled. "In effect, that was what Roosevelt was doing."

Hopkins agreed and asked Bohlen to work on a replacement, as well as a cable to Stalin. "While I was drafting the telegrams, Hopkins found the President shaving," Bohlen said. "Hopkins pointed out the danger we had seen in the 'good luck' message. Realizing his mistake, Roosevelt became somewhat agitated and instructed Hopkins to stop the message. He was relieved when Hopkins told him that he had taken the liberty of holding it." Bohlen's new cable to Churchill asked that Averell Harriman be allowed to observe the sessions, and, more important, the note to Stalin read:

> You, naturally, understand that in this global war there is literally no question, political or military, in which the United

States is not interested. I am firmly convinced that the three of us, and only the
three of us, can find the solution to the still
unresolved questions. In this sense, while
appreciating the Prime Minister's desire for
a meeting, I prefer to regard your forthcoming talks with Churchill as preliminary
to a meeting of all three of us. . . .

Stalin's reply was dry and revealing: "I supposed
that Mr. Churchill was going to Moscow in
accordance with the agreement reached with
you at Quebec. It happened, however, that this
supposition of mine does not seem to correspond to reality." The team in the White House
was relieved. "It was apparent that Churchill
had told Stalin that he was in a position to speak
for Roosevelt, since he knew, from a recent
meeting with the President in Quebec, the
President's thoughts," Bohlen recalled. "Our
wire certainly put Stalin on his guard."

LATE ON HIS first evening in Moscow in
October 1944, after struggling to get enough
hot water for his bath, Churchill sat down with
Stalin in the Kremlin.

"The moment was apt for business," Churchill recalled, and the two spent hours talking
diplomacy and politics, from the Balkans to

Poland to Germany. In personal terms for the prime minister, the problems of the past (of Stalin's pact with Hitler, the angry cables, the harsh hours at Teheran, Warsaw, among so many other things) and fears about the future (which Churchill occasionally worried would be marked by conflicts with Moscow) were largely put to the side as they worked.

"Churchill had high regard for all very powerful, top men," recalled Anthony Montague Browne. From Moscow, Churchill wrote Clementine: "I have had vy nice talks with the Old Bear. I like him the more I see him." He was anxious about whether he had fully recovered in his wife's affections after his note of apology, adding: "Darling you can write anything but war secrets & it reaches me in a few hours. So do send me a letter from yr dear hand." (He was out of the marital woods: Clementine replied with "Tender love. I hope to see you soon.")

Churchill, who briefly ran a fever and worried that his pneumonia was back yet again, was attentive to Roosevelt, writing him frequently. "I have to keep the President in constant touch & this is the delicate side," Churchill told Clementine. He spoke of the presidential campaign. "Although I hear the most encouraging accounts from various quarters about United States politics," Churchill cabled Roosevelt on

October 18, "I feel the suspense probably far more than you do or more than I should if my own affairs were concerned in this zone. My kindest regards and warmest good wishes." Roosevelt appreciated the sentiments. When reviewing the draft of a reply, he changed the awkward "I do hope your health has not been undermined" to a warmer "I do hope you are free of the temperature and really feeling all right again."

SATURDAY, OCTOBER 21, 1944, was, Sam Rosenman remembered, "a cold, rainy, bone-chilling day" in New York City. Scheduled to tour the city's five boroughs, Roosevelt refused to cancel and hurled himself into the task, riding fifty-one miles through the city's streets in an open car—"letting the elements have their way," *The New York Times* wrote, "while he had his." It was a tactical masterstroke: Pictures of his resilience in the rain, printed around the country so late in the campaign, helped undercut the argument that he was too old and too sick for another term. "After this, the rumors about Roosevelt's bad health became less audible," recalled Rosenman. While Roosevelt kept moving, Mayor Fiorello La Guardia was worn out. "I think I am tough," the mayor said after riding through the rain, "but he took it better than I did."

After a change of clothes and a drink of bourbon at Eleanor's Washington Square apartment—she had taken it as a Manhattan pied-à-terre—Roosevelt went to the Waldorf to sketch a vision of America's new role in the world. There could be no more isolation; the United States had paid too high a price for the Lindbergh view. In October, a *Life* editorial entitled "Republicans in Congress: Their Record Is 'Isolationist' and So Are a Few of Them. But Isolationism Is Dead" argued that isolationism was no longer an issue, a point that annoyed Roosevelt, who had invested so much in trying to educate the nation about its inescapable ties to the rest of the world. "Anybody who thinks that isolationism is dead in this country is crazy," Roosevelt told Sherwood. "As soon as this war is over, it may well be stronger than ever." Roosevelt balked when Sherwood suggested using a quotation from a recent Churchill address in which Churchill declared, "The United States was now at the highest pinnacle of her power and fame." Sherwood was surprised at Roosevelt's reaction. "What Winston says may be true at the moment, but I'd hate to say it," Roosevelt said. "Because we may be heading before very long for the pinnacle of our weakness." The lure of Fortress America might reassert itself. Reflecting on Roosevelt's remark, Sherwood noted: "I've always assumed that he was looking forward to the approaching moment when the reaction might set in, and isolationism again be rampant, and the American people might again tell the rest of the world to stew in its own juice."

Roosevelt saw how the nation could address itself to the outside world, keep the peace, and spread democracy. His speech in Manhattan on this rainy night was the testament of a practical idealist. "The power which this nation has attained—the political, the economic, the military, and above all the moral power—has brought to us the responsibility, and with it the opportunity, for leadership in the community of nations," the president said. "In our own best interest, in the name of peace and humanity, this nation cannot, must not, and will not shirk that responsibility."

But we should not swagger. "The kind of world order which we, the peace-loving nations must achieve, must depend essentially on friendly human relations, on acquaintance, on tolerance, on unassailable sincerity and goodwill and good faith. We have achieved that relationship to a very remarkable degree in our dealings with our Allies in this war—as I think the events of the war have proved." Humility was essential. "We are not fighting for, and we shall not attain a Utopia," Roosevelt said. "Indeed, in our own land, the work to be done is never finished. We have yet to realize the full and equal enjoyment of our freedom. So, in embarking on the building of a world fellowship, we have set ourselves a long and arduous task, a task which will challenge our patience, our intelligence, our imagination, as well as our faith."

CHURCHILL HAD SEEN the gray images of the day and wrote a note of concern and congratulation. "I was delighted to see the proofs of your robust vigour in New York," Churchill told Roosevelt on October 23. "Nevertheless I cannot believe that four hours in an open car and pouring rain with a temperature of 40 and clothes wet through conform to those limits of prudence which you would be so ready to prescribe if it were my case. I earnestly hope you are none the worse and should be grateful for reassurance. I cannot think about anything except this . . . election."

Roosevelt's reply was charming. "My journey to New York was useful and rain does not hurt an old sailor," he wrote back. "Thank you for your advice nevertheless. I am in top form." He could always do two things at once and was now enjoying the fight. In Hartford, Connecticut, one day, Alistair Cooke watched as Roosevelt gave a flat whistle-stop speech to a crowd of insurance workers. Smiling his big, toothy smile, waving broadly at the audience, he whispered to a Secret Service man out of the side of his mouth: "Let's get the hell out of here." Cooke remembered being "shocked" at the deftness of the performance: Roosevelt was "so tough and yet could keep this smile."

He and Churchill debated a new Big Three meeting. "The Pres. was full of pep—'exalte'—as he put it," Daisy noted the Sunday before the election. "Two more days & then preparations for his meeting with Churchill & Stalin." The dangers Churchill had faced informed Roosevelt's election eve broadcast. "When we think of the speed and long-distance possibilities of air travel of all kinds to the remotest corners of the earth, we must consider the devastation wrought on the people of England, for example, by the new long-range bombs," Roosevelt said. "Another war would be bound to bring even more devilish and powerful instruments of destruction to wipe out civilian populations. No coastal defenses, however strong, could prevent these silent missiles of death, fired perhaps from planes or ships at sea, from crashing deep within the United States itself. This time, this time, we must be certain that the peace-loving nations of the world band together in determination to outlaw and to prevent war."

On election day, Hopkins kept Churchill up-to-date. "The voting is very heavy in industrial centers," he cabled Churchill. "We are not likely to know definitely before 10:00 p.m. our time which will make it pretty late even for you." Still, Churchill kept watch, receiving the verdict from Hopkins deep in the London night: "It's in the bag," Hopkins told him.

Roosevelt spent the evening as he always did, in the dining room at Hyde Park, with three telephones and tabulation sheets. Anna, Trude Lash, John Roosevelt, and William Hassett, a White House secretary, brought reports back and forth from the ticker machine in the smoking room. He won, 53.5 percent to 46 percent. Late in the evening, Roosevelt went out to speak to the torchlight parade; in the flush of history—a third term had been unprecedented, a fourth beyond imagination—he did not appear to notice the cold. "It was chilly out there, but F.D.R. only, with cape open, seemed unconscious of it," said Daisy. He was, she added, "full of 'fight'!"

Warm words arrived from London the next afternoon. "I always said that a great people could be trusted to stand by the pilot who weathered the storm," Churchill wrote Roosevelt. "It is an indescribable relief to me that our comradeship will continue and will help to bring the world out of misery." Then, smarting still from the snub when Roosevelt failed to acknowledge his 1940 telegram of congratulations, Churchill enclosed it once more. He never gave up.

"THE ELECTION WAS a great triumph for the President," Hopkins wrote Beaverbrook on November 15. "Even in the middle west, where we thought isolationism was rampant, we found that not to be the case and President got a very large vote even in the states he failed to carry. . . . The election was all the more amazing in view of the fact that there was indication of great prejudice against the Fourth Term and toward our past domestic policies. A great many people who would not normally have voted for the President, voted for him, I think largely because of the war and the feeling that Dewey was not quite grown up enough to handle the peace."

Hopkins knew his chief and the prime minister had heavy work ahead. "The President is, naturally, pleased," he told Beaverbrook, "but I am sure realizes fully the many headaches that are before him."

"THE WAR UNFORTUNATELY seems to have stagnated a bit doesn't it," Pamela Churchill wrote Averell Harriman in the autumn of 1944, "the foolish optimism of a few weeks ago seems to have died down, & people are resigned to the fact that they will have to grind their way through another long winter of war. . . . London is as black as ever, one notices no difference."

Remembering that November 30 was Churchill's seventieth birthday—Roosevelt did not always commemorate the occasion, but he did this year—Roosevelt wrote: "Ever so many happy returns of the day. I shall never forget the party with you and UJ a year ago and we must have more of them that are even better. Affectionate regards." Roosevelt chose to forget—or chose to act as though he had forgotten—his chilliness toward Churchill in those busy days.

The Churchills were happy to have Winston at home for his birthday. "There was a glorious dinner party at the Annexe," Mary wrote: flowers, a cake with seventy candles, bundles of presents. Beaverbrook toasted Churchill, who answered with words that brought tears to Mary's eyes. "He said we were 'the dearest there are'—he said he had been comforted and supported by our love." It was not an entirely serene family season. The Churchills had apparently asked Pamela and young Winston to join them for Christmas, but there were the old worries about Randolph's reaction to his estranged wife's being included in his own family's celebrations. Churchill found himself writing a delicate note to his daughter-in-law. "I find that our Christmas plans may cause friction as some of the family are worried about the effect on Randolph when he hears the news," he told her. "Clemmie & I therefore with great regret suggest to you that we fix another date for you to come and bring Winston. She & I were looking forward so much to seeing you & him around the Christmas tree. But I am sure that another weekend later on will be better for all. I do hope this will not cause you inconvenience."

Then it was back to the war. Roosevelt had a quotation from Lincoln framed and dispatched to England with a note: "For Winston on his Birthday—I would go even to Teheran to be with him again." The greetings gave Churchill "the greatest pleasure . . . I cannot tell you how much I value your friendship or how much I hope upon it for the future of the world, should we both be spared," Churchill wrote Roosevelt. A touching—and appropriate—prayer: *Should we both be spared.*

"I hope to do in one hour what Winston did in two"

———

Roosevelt addresses Congress after Yalta,
March 1, 1945

I SAW WSC TO SAY GOODBYE

The Meeting at Yalta–Roosevelt and Churchill Part–
A "Lovers' Quarrel"–The President Goes
to Warm Springs

THEIR LAST TIME together would be far from home. "We could not have found a worse place for a meeting if we had spent ten years on research," Churchill grumbled to Hopkins as the Big Three prepared to meet at Yalta. He would get through it, he said, "by bringing an adequate supply of whiskey" to fend off typhus and lice. "The P.M. remained in bed," Jock Colville wrote of one morning in early January 1945. "He is disgusted that the President should want to spend only five or six days at the coming meeting between 'the Big Three' and says that even the Almighty required seven to settle the world. (An inaccuracy which was quickly pointed out to him. Viz. Genesis I.)"

Churchill wanted a preconference session with Roosevelt. Arguing for a meeting at Malta before they traveled to Russia, Churchill ignored the scriptural hairsplitters around him and told Roosevelt, "I do not see any other way of realising our hopes about World Organisation in five or six days. Even the Almighty took seven." Roosevelt finally agreed, pleasing Churchill. "I shall be waiting on the quay," he had cabled Roosevelt on January 1. "No more let us falter! From Malta to Yalta! Let nobody alter!"

The days of companionship and brinksmanship were warmer then than they seem from afar. Yalta is now seen as the opening diplomatic act of the cold war, the point at which Stalin began to stitch what Churchill called the "Iron Curtain." To the players in the Crimea, though, the meeting was hard but hopeful work—and it was the true twilight of Roosevelt and Churchill's friendship.

FOR ROOSEVELT, IT had been a quiet fourth Inauguration Day. With difficulty he stood in his braces. ("All the sentimental ladies who love him were ready for tears!" noted Daisy.) He did not go to the Capitol but took the oath on the South Portico of the White House. His address to a small crowd of five thousand was brief, about five minutes long, an encapsulation of his creed that politics is not clinical but human, America an unfinished experiment, the world a neighborhood and nations families within it. "Our Constitution of 1787 was not a perfect instrument; it is not perfect yet," he said. "But it provided a firm base upon which all manner of men, of all races and colors and creeds, could build our solid structure of democracy."

Engagement, not isolation, was the right road ahead. "And so today in this year of war, 1945, we have learned lessons—at a fearful cost—and we shall profit by them," he said. "We have learned that we cannot live alone, at peace; that our own well-being is dependent upon the well-being of other nations, far away. We have learned that we must live as men and not as ostriches, nor as dogs in the manger. We have learned to be citizens of the world, members of the human community. We have learned the simple truth, as Emerson said, that 'the only way to have a friend is to be one.' "

He was fighting to preserve his strength— "after the inauguration it was clearer every day that Franklin was far from well," Eleanor recalled—and he decided that Anna should go with him. "Anna was very, very good at looking after her father—having the right people talk to him at the right time, protecting him," said Kathleen Harriman, who would be at Yalta, as would Sarah Churchill.

———

AROUND THE SHIP en route to the conference, Roosevelt joked about Churchill's determination to rendezvous beforehand. "There
was a lot of sort of amusing talk about the fact
that Churchill insisted on meeting us when we
docked at Malta," Anna remembered. "The
joke was that a cable came through from Stalin
saying, 'I said Yalta, not Malta.' " Not especially
witty, but the chatter shows the Roosevelt party
poking fun at Churchill's eagerness to stay close
to Roosevelt.

Churchill, meanwhile, was flying through the
winter night. "I had a serious alarm coming
over lest I was going to have another attack, for
my temperature went to 102½ in the night,"
Churchill wrote Clementine on February 1.
"But it all passed off agreeably. . . . The President arrives at the first light of dawn and I shall
go to see him as soon as he desires it."

Roosevelt and Churchill met in the Grand
Harbor at Valletta, Malta. Churchill and Sarah
went over to lunch with Roosevelt aboard the
Quincy. "We found him sitting in the sun with
his daughter," recalled Sarah. Roosevelt was
"very friendly," Churchill told Moran. "He must
have noticed the candle by my bed when we
were at the White House, because there was a

small lighted candle on the luncheon table by my place to light my cigar."

The small attentions meant much to Churchill. "If you talk to him about books and let him quote to you from his marvelous memory everything on earth from Barbara Frietchie to the Nonsense Rhymes and Greek tragedy, you will find him easier to deal with on political subjects," Eleanor advised Harry Truman after Roosevelt's death. "He is a gentleman to whom the personal element means a great deal." The personal had to suffice at Malta. Roosevelt declined to talk about substance, preferring to wait for the sessions with Stalin. The two flew to the Crimea. Upon landing at Saki, Bohlen recalled, they were offered vodka, champagne, caviar, smoked sturgeon, and black bread.

They needed the sustenance. They had a difficult ride ahead of them. "The eighty-mile drive over the mountains to Yalta was made under lowering clouds that spat rain and a little wet snow," Bohlen wrote. Roosevelt tried to rest en route. He rode with Anna, and the prime minister was in a separate car with Sarah. "How the President endured that endless and tiring drive I cannot imagine," Sarah recalled. One way was by not riding with Churchill, who would have talked during the trip. "I put the clamps on," Anna wrote John Boettiger, and they pressed on to Yalta with the prime minister safely out of the way for a few restful hours.

THE SLEEP IN the car had done Roosevelt good. When he reached Livadia Palace, he was greeted by Kathleen Harriman. "The Pres. arrived in great form & is very pleased with his suite," Kathleen wrote Pamela Churchill. "Harry arrived not very well & went straight to bed with dia (can't spell it) anyway. . . . The doctors ordered him to eat nothing but cereal & the fool had 2 huge helpings of caviar, cabbage soup with sour cream & then his cereal," Kathleen told Pamela. "He really is a fool. That brought his pains back & since then he's eaten in bed, but been at all the meetings." Churchill was in the Vorontsov villa, and Stalin came to see him, arriving five minutes early. "W was only just rushed to the door in time," Charles Portal wrote to Pamela.

Roosevelt repeated his Teheran play and asked to see Stalin alone the first day. (He would not meet privately with Churchill until the fifth day.) "The two leaders greeted each other as old friends . . . ," noted Bohlen. "Smiling broadly, the President grasped Stalin by the hand and shook it warmly."

Talking with Roosevelt, Stalin broke into a rare ("if slight," Bohlen recalled) smile. Roosevelt told his host that the scenes of destruction on the drive to Yalta—the Germans had fought here—had made him even "more bloodthirsty than a year ago," and he said he hoped Stalin would again offer his Teheran toast about executing fifty thousand German officers—a reminder of the moments when they froze Churchill out, and a signal to Stalin, Bohlen wrote, "that the United States was not joining Britain in any united negotiating position." Playing to Stalin's distrust of the English, Roosevelt added that he would now "tell the Marshal something indiscreet, since he would not wish to say it in front of Prime Minister Churchill, namely that the British for two years have had the idea of artificially building up France into a strong power. . . ."

As always, Churchill had much on his mind as Roosevelt and Stalin spoke. A plane carrying part of the British delegation crashed en route, killing thirteen people. "Ave went over & saw the P.M. last night late—He's apparently in a discouraged state of mind," Kathleen wrote Pamela. "It must be sort of dampening too to the spirits of their party—having that accident. At this point everyone's crossing their fingers & hoping for the best."

At dinner after the first session on Sunday, February 4, Churchill seemed defensive at times. According to Bohlen's minutes, Stalin had made some dismissive remarks about the rights of small nations to play a role on the global stage, and there was talk about "the rights of people to govern themselves in relation to their leaders." Then Churchill "said that although he was constantly being 'beaten up' as a reactionary, he was the only representative present who could be thrown out at any time by the universal suffrage of his own people"—and that "personally he gloried in that danger."

Roosevelt hung back as Stalin said that "the Prime Minister seemed to fear these elections." Churchill was quick to reply, Bohlen noted, that "he not only did not fear them but that he was proud of the right of the British people to change their government at any time they saw fit."

Stalin was once again Roosevelt's main focus. The Pacific was high on Roosevelt's agenda. The conflict was expected to take another two years—at their lunch aboard the *Quincy* at Malta, Roosevelt and Churchill talked about 1947 as the likely year for victory over Japan—so the Soviet role loomed large before anyone knew whether the Manhattan Project would produce a usable weapon. In that light, Stalin's agreement to join the fight against Japan—first discussed in Teheran—was critical. "When the Russians said at Yalta that they would fight Japan, Admiral King came out and said, 'We've just saved two million Americans,'" recalled Kathleen Harriman. The casualty estimate would vary, but whatever the number, the stakes were enormous.

CHURCHILL EXPERIENCED A wide range of emotions at Yalta. "I do not suppose that at any moment in history has the agony of the world been so great or widespread," he told Sarah one day. "Tonight the sun goes down on more suffering than ever before in the world." Yet, one evening, Churchill would call for three cheers for Stalin.

"Winston is puzzled and distressed," Lord Moran said. "The President no longer seems to the P.M. to take an intelligent interest in the war; often he does not seem even to read the papers the P.M. gives him." Churchill was facing similar criticism. In January, his Labour colleague Clement Attlee had written Churchill a candid letter protesting, Jock Colville said, "the PM's lengthy disquisitions in Cabinet on papers which he has not read and on subjects which he has not taken the trouble to master."

ROOSEVELT WAS GROWING exasperated with Churchill along the same lines. "I suppose they became quite wearied with Papa banging on about things they didn't think were important," said Mary Soames.

In the Livadia Palace, as Churchill launched into a speech, a tired Roosevelt wrote a note to Ed Stettinius, the new secretary of state: "Now we're in for a half hour of it." According to John Gunther, Roosevelt once snapped: "Yes, I *am* tired! So would you be if you had spent the last five years pushing Winston uphill in a wheelbarrow." Roosevelt must have signaled some of this feeling to Churchill, Gunther reported, for Churchill looked "as if he were about to get hit" in these sessions at the end of the war.

In private, Roosevelt—who Kathleen noted was "getting a big kick out of presiding over the meetings (he's the youngest you know)"—was alternately kind and snappish about Churchill. "When they were apart, FDR could be very emotional about 'Winnie,' as he called him when Churchill wasn't around," said George Elsey, "but then seconds later he'd put him down." Almost certainly exaggerating at a small dinner one night with Anna and a handful of other Americans, Roosevelt claimed Churchill had been in poor fettle at the plenary that afternoon; the prime minister had not had his nap. "According to the President, the Prime Minister had sat at the table and drifted off into a sound sleep from which he would awake very suddenly making speeches about the Monroe Doctrine," one guest said. "The President said he had to tell him repeatedly that it was a very fine speech, but that it was not the subject under discussion."

Others also noticed Roosevelt's speaking ill of Churchill. "Towards the end of the war, when he was an ailing man," Lord Chandos wrote of Roosevelt, "he . . . could not help a derogatory and ironical tone from creeping in, even when talking to a devoted lieutenant like myself."

"Poor old Winston keeps on thinking . . . ," Roosevelt once said to Chandos, only to find that Churchill's colleague, as Chandos put it, "profoundly believed that poor old Winston was right."

TO CHURCHILL'S CREDIT, he was careful about how he talked about Roosevelt. At Yalta, Moran noted that "though we have moved a long way since Winston, speaking of Roosevelt, said to me in the garden at Marrakesh, 'I love that man,' he is still very reticent in criticism. It seems to be dragged out of him against his will. And with half a chance he will tell over dinner how many divisions the Americans had in a particular show against our handful, and how their casualties in that engagement dwarfed ours, and things of that kind." As Churchill lost point after point to Roosevelt and to Stalin— usually about Poland or the Balkans—he kept his tongue in check. "In all these arguments, the President's view carried the day," Mary said. "Yet I never heard my father, at any time during all the stress of war, say a vengeful or savage word about the President."

They knew each other so well. One day, Roosevelt complained to James Byrnes that Churchill's monologues were holding up business. "Yes, but they were good speeches," Byrnes said. Snapped out of his irritation, Roosevelt chuckled. "Winston doesn't make any other kind," he replied.

AFTER A RUSSIAN BANQUET, Charles Portal, Churchill's trusted air chief, wrote a blunt account to Pamela Churchill. Acknowledging that he was writing as he "let the vodka settle," Portal gave Roosevelt no quarter. "FD was very wet indeed and just blathered," he said. "U.J. in marvelous form & so was big W, but as usual he ran away from the interpreter & was untranslatable. . . . Honestly, FDR spoke more tripe to the minute than I have ever heard before, sentimental twaddle without a spark of real wit." Was Roosevelt too sick to be effective at the conference? Most observers thought him unwell but in basic control of the public business before him. "He was lethargic, but when important moments arose, he was mentally sharp," recalled Bohlen. "Our leader was ill at

Yalta, the most important of the wartime conferences, but he was effective."

Hours and hours were spent in the big white ballroom debating Poland. By the time the leaders sat down in the Crimea, the Red Army controlled the nation over whose sovereignty Britain had gone to war nearly six years before, and, as Stalin once remarked, "Whoever occupies a territory also imposes on it his own social system. Everyone imposes his own system as far as his army can reach. It cannot be otherwise." At Yalta there were disputes over borders and the postwar Polish government, and Stalin made vague promises about "free and unfettered elections," but in the end came the cold war, and a Soviet sphere. Looking back, Averell Harriman thought Roosevelt and Churchill made "an honest attempt to build an orderly relationship with the Russians and there was a certain amount of give and take on our part in the hope of achieving orderly settlements. The fact that we tried and failed left the main responsibility for the Cold War with Stalin, where it belongs."

Anna tried to keep Roosevelt rested, but it was not easy. "While they were away, Anna kept us posted about her father's health and what was happening on the trip," Eleanor recalled. "I am a bit exhausted but really all right," Roosevelt wrote his wife.

Churchill hosted dinner at the Vorontsov villa

on the last night, February 10. It was a convivial evening of shop talk, reminiscence, and promises of great things to come. Churchill was variously upset and sentimental; Stalin was both friendly and vicious; Roosevelt played referee.

Roosevelt had not spoken of Eleanor much, but tonight he invoked her, recalling the first summer of his presidency. "In 1933 my wife visited a school in our country," he said. "In one of the classrooms she saw a map with a large blank space on it. She asked what was the blank space, and was told they were not allowed to mention the place—it was the Soviet Union." That story of Eleanor's, Roosevelt said, was one of the reasons he had reached out to Moscow to open diplomatic relations. The personal was a consistent theme. "There was a time when the Marshal was not so kindly towards us, and I remember that I said a few rude things about him, but our common dangers and common loyalties have wiped all that out," Churchill said in a toast to Stalin. "The fire of war has burnt up the misunderstandings of the past. We feel we have a friend whom we can trust, and I hope he will continue to feel the same about us. I pray he may live to see his beloved Russia not only glorious in war, but also happy in peace."

Churchill took Roosevelt and Stalin into the traveling map room so that they could survey their joint progress. It was, Churchill said, "the zenith of the Map Room's career." For half an hour, the three men talked and contemplated what they had wrought. Cleves had fallen, prompting Churchill to regale Roosevelt and Stalin with the story of Anne of Cleves, one of Henry VIII's wives. Then he began to sing the World War I song "When We've Wound Up the Watch on the Rhine."

Perhaps weary of song and story, Stalin took a shot at Churchill. As Sir Richard Pim recalled it, Stalin "suggested that the British might wish to make an earlier armistice than the Russians." Taunted out of his happy mood, Churchill "looked hurt and in a corner of the Map Room, with his hands in his pockets, gave us a few lines of his favourite song 'Keep right on to the end of the road.' Stalin looked extremely puzzled." Roosevelt waded in with a grin, saying to the Soviet interpreter, "Tell your Chief that this singing by the Prime Minister is Britain's secret weapon." Roosevelt was doing what he liked best: keeping peace between his two allies. And, for a moment, it was working.

The issue of the United Nations organization played a central role at Yalta. After several years of imprecise talk—usually by Roosevelt—a plan thrashed out in the summer and fall of 1944 at Dumbarton Oaks in Washington proposed a Security Council (the United States, Britain, the Soviet Union, China, and ultimately France would be permanent members) and a General Assembly. The organization would have the ability, with its members, to exert force—militarily, by sanction, or by suasion—to try to keep order in what was inevitably a disorderly world. Gone were the debates about regional councils; a global body was to take shape—if it all could be worked out with Stalin, who wanted extra votes in the General Assembly for the Soviet Republics. (Eventually he got two.) There were other issues—questions of veto power, trusteeships for former colonies, and refugee matters among them—and a conference in San Francisco in late April would finalize things. Roosevelt died believing a global, not a regional, organization was the proper means for a new international order. The UN agreements at Yalta, Roosevelt would tell Congress on March 1, 1945, "ought to spell the end of the system of unilateral action, the exclusive alliances, the spheres of influence, the balances of power, and all the other expedients that have been tried for centuries—and have always failed," he said, sitting as he spoke for the first and only time in a congressional address in his twelve years as president. "We propose to substitute for all of these, a universal organization in which all peace-loving nations will finally have a chance to join."

Churchill long defended the regional approach,

with "men of the greatest eminence" from each sphere serving on a "Supreme Body." He was not particularly impressed by the UN's early days: "The summoning of all nations, great and small, powerful or powerless, on even terms to the central body may be compared with the organization of an army without any division between the High Command and the divisional and brigade commanders." Churchill, though, never ruled out the possibility of progress. "But," he added, "we must persevere."

Hope—with Churchill, as with Roosevelt, there was always hope. In these last years of the war, from establishing monetary policy at Bretton Woods to the United Nations, the two men were trying to build institutions to prevent the last half of the twentieth century from repeating the mistakes of the first half, which had given the world two wars. Ultimately, because of Soviet aggression, the Americans, the British, and much of Western Europe would add the Atlantic alliance to that equation, but Roosevelt's and Churchill's ability to see far ahead— or at least to attempt to see far ahead—was striking. They were not soft, but they were optimistic. "The purpose of the United Nations is to make sure that the force of right will, in the ultimate issue, be protected by the right of force," Churchill said in 1946. His words about the organization's other missions might surprise those who tend to think of him as a creature of the nineteenth, not the twentieth, much less the twenty-first, century. "Peace is no passive state, but calls for qualities of high adventure and endeavor," Churchill said in 1950. "Through the United Nations we must not only prevent war but feed the hungry, heal the sick, restore the ravages of former wars, and assist the peoples of Africa and Asia to achieve by peaceful means their hopes of a new and better life."

ON SUNDAY MORNING, February 11, 1945, the final editing session for the communiqué went smoothly. Churchill had the most changes. Among them, he wanted to eliminate the use of the word *joint,* arguing that to him the term meant "the Sunday family roast of mutton." In the czar's former billiards room, the Big Three signed the Declaration on Liberated Europe, pledging that "The establishment of order in Europe and the rebuilding of national economic life must be achieved by processes which will enable the liberated peoples to destroy the last vestiges of nazism and fascism and to create democratic institutions of their own choice. This is a principle of the Atlantic Charter—the right of all peoples to choose the form of Government under which they will live—the restoration of

"U.J. in marvelous form & so was big W,
but as usual he ran away from the
interpreter & was untranslatable"

Churchill at Livadia Palace,
February 8, 1945

sovereign rights and self-Government to those peoples who have been forcibly deprived of them by the aggressor nations." The Allies would continue to strive for peace in which "all the men in all the lands may live out their lives in freedom from fear and want."

"I hope you will like communique published tomorrow morning," Churchill wrote Clementine. "We have covered a great amount of ground and I am very pleased with the decisions we have gained." He was in a good humor. "P.M. seems well," Alexander Cadogan noted, "though drinking buckets of Caucasian champagne which would undermine the health of any ordinary man."

Churchill would live to see and fight the cold war. Roosevelt would be dead by then, but whatever compromises the president made at Yalta on issues relating to the postwar world, there is evidence that he would have taken a hard line against Soviet totalitarianism had he lived. "Yalta was only a step towards the ultimate solution Franklin had in mind," Eleanor recalled. "He knew it was not the final step. He knew there had to be more negotiation, other meetings. He hoped for an era of peace and understanding, but he knew that peace was not won in a day—that days upon days and years upon years lay before us in which we must keep the peace by constant effort."

Churchill is often depicted as the more perceptive of the two men on the question of the Soviets, and there is no doubt that during the war the prime minister predicted "grave troubles" from Stalin, to use his phrase from Quebec in 1943. Anti-Soviet testimony from Churchill is not hard to come by. But the fact of the matter is that Churchill, like Roosevelt, did not like to foreclose options; he, like Roosevelt, understood that politics is almost always a matter of nuance and shades of gray. In 1940 it had not been: Opposing Hitler was a moral imperative in which Churchill had, rightly, seen only black and white. Returning from Yalta, Churchill thought all might be well. "The impression I brought back from the Crimea, and from all my other contacts, is that Marshal Stalin and the Soviet leaders wish to live in honourable friendship and equality with the Western Democracies . . . ," he told the House of Commons. Privately, Churchill said: "Poor Neville Chamberlain believed he could trust Hitler. He was wrong. But I don't think I'm wrong about Stalin." When it turned out that the facts did not support these hopeful words, Churchill would be the first to take a strong stand against the spread of communism. He would have agreed with Eleanor's assessment of Roosevelt's view: that politics and diplomacy are stories without end, requiring constant attention, keen thinking, and an appreciation of complexity.

Leaving Livadia on that Sunday, Roosevelt was driven to Sevastopol to survey the battlefield where the Light Brigade had made its doomed charge nearly a century before. Stalin—"like some genie," Sarah recalled—disappeared. As Roosevelt departed, Churchill—who was to see Roosevelt once more on Thursday—tried to maintain his cheer but found it difficult. "The President's decrepitude has filled him with grief and dismay," Moran said. Sarah thought her father "suddenly felt lonely."

CHURCHILL DECIDED IT was time for an adventure. To him action was generally the answer to anything. Rather than following the plan to "easily, orderly, and quietly" leave Yalta the next morning, Sarah recalled, her father announced that they would leave *now*. "Why do we stay here?" Churchill asked. "Why don't we go tonight—I see no reason to stay here a minute longer—we're off!"

There was silence, then chaos. "Trunks and large mysterious paper parcels given to us by the Russians—caviar we hoped—filled the hall," Sarah wrote. "Laundry arrived back clean but damp. Naturally fifty minutes gave my father time to change our minds several more times." He nearly broke his valet's spirits. "Sawyers on his knees, tears in his eyes, surrounded by half-packed suitcases, literally beat his chest in truly classical style and said: 'They can't do this to me.'" Churchill, Sarah recalled, relished the rumpus. "My father, genial and sprightly like a boy out of school, his homework done, walked from room to room saying: 'Come on, come on!'" They were off to spend a few days aboard HMS *Franconia*. Later, when Sarah asked him whether he was tired, Churchill said: "Strangely enough, no. Yet I have felt the weight of responsibility more than ever before and in my heart there is anxiety."

BACK ON THE *Quincy,* moored in Great Bitter Lake in the Suez Canal, Roosevelt settled in for a few days of royal Middle Eastern callers. "We got away safely from the Crimea, flew to the Canal & saw King Farouk, then emperor Haile Selassie, & the next day, King Ibn Saud of Arabia with his whole court, slaves (black), taster, astrologer, & 8 live sheep," Roosevelt wrote Daisy. "Whole party was a scream!" He was enjoying the fact that Churchill was annoyed he was meeting alone with the three kings. Churchill had summoned all three to come to him after they had seen Roosevelt. "Mr. Churchill was rather suspicious of why was Father talking to these three heads of state and he was not invited," Anna recalled. "Father was thoroughly amused. . . . He was getting a great kick out of life."

ON THURSDAY, FEBRUARY 15, 1945, off Alexandria, Roosevelt and Churchill sat together aboard the *Quincy.* The world had turned over many times since their hands had first clasped at sea. "The President seemed placid and frail," Churchill said. With Hopkins they discussed Britain's role in developing atomic weapons after the war. Churchill and Lindemann (the "Prof") were eager "to do work here on a scale commensurate with our resources"—a bid to remain in the arena, vital and respected. Roosevelt, Churchill told Lindemann later, "made no objection of any kind" and said that the first real trials for the bomb would come in September. (As it happened, events at Los Alamos moved more quickly.)

They then had what Churchill called "an informal family luncheon" with Anna, Sarah and Randolph Churchill, Hopkins, and Gil Winant. "I saw WSC to say goodbye," Roosevelt told Daisy. Their visit lasted an hour and fifty-six minutes; just before four o'clock, Roosevelt gave Churchill an album of photographs from the 1944 Quebec meeting and they took their leave of each other. It was not to be for long: Roosevelt was due in England soon. "I felt that he had a slender contact with life," Churchill recalled. "I was not to see him again. We bade affectionate farewells."

AT HIS MEETING with Ibn Saud after the president's, Churchill and Muslim custom collided, but Churchill won. "I had been told that neither smoking nor alcoholic beverages were allowed in the Royal Presence," Churchill recalled. "As I was the host at luncheon I raised the matter at once, and said to the interpreter that if it was the religion of His Majesty to deprive himself of smoking and alcohol I must point out that my rule of life prescribed as an absolutely sacred rite smoking cigars and also the drinking of alcohol before, after, and if need be during all meals and in the intervals between them," Churchill told the Saudi potentate. "The King graciously accepted the position."

EVEN FROM WASHINGTON, Eleanor could tell that there were "dark clouds" hovering over the *Quincy* on its voyage home. Pa Watson was stricken. Roosevelt had been counting on Hopkins to help him prepare his speech to Congress about Yalta, but Hopkins was too sick to go on. He would recuperate at Marrakech, staying at La Saadia. Roosevelt's good-bye,

Robert Sherwood wrote, "was not a very amiable one." Roosevelt asked Sam Rosenman, who was on a mission to London, to cross the Atlantic with him. "I had never seen him look so tired," Rosenman said once he saw the president. "He had lost a great deal more weight; he was listless and apparently uninterested in conversation—he was all burnt out."

Then Watson died at sea. From afar Daisy knew what it meant: "Franklin feels his death very much, & will miss him dreadfully—He always leaned on him, both figuratively and physically—'Pa' was a Rock, the only one of the aides who gave a feeling of security to F.D.R. when he stood with his braces—Always cheerful, ready with a joke, and completely & unselfishly devoted to F.D.R." Roosevelt rarely showed sadness, but it was different this time. His aides worried, Sherwood recalled, that "the very extent to which he talked about his sadness" could mean "he himself was failing."

In his grief, Roosevelt gave rein to his tarter feelings about Churchill. Deeply competitive, he was possibly reacting to the world with some bitterness as he sensed his own powers dimming. "Roosevelt was prone to jealousy of competitors in his field," Rosenman wrote. "He liked flattery, especially as he grew older, and seemed frequently to be jealous of compliments paid to others for political sagacity, eloquence, statesmanship or accomplishments in public life. He liked so much to excel that he took almost as much pleasure in being told he was a better poker player than someone else as he did in being told that Willkie was not as good an orator as he was, or that he, Roosevelt, was a better politician than Farley." On the voyage, Roosevelt told Rosenman that " 'dear old Winston' was quite loquacious in these conferences; that he liked to make long speeches—sometimes getting into irrelevancies; that he quite obviously irritated Stalin by these long discourses; and that at times he, Roosevelt, had to get Churchill back to the subject at hand. Now that victory seemed pretty close and the time was drawing near for carrying out some of the tough principles contained in the Atlantic Charter, the President was beginning to feel that the traditions of British imperialism were playing too heavy a part in Churchill's thinking."

Roosevelt called the reporters on board into his cabin and took the same superior tone about Churchill when the conversation turned to colonial possessions in the Pacific.

Question: Is that Churchill's idea on all territory out there, he wants them all back just the way they were?

The President: Yes, he is mid-Victorian on all things like that.

Question: You would think some of that would be knocked out of him by now.

The President: I read something Queen Wilhelmina said about the Dutch East Indies. She's got a very interesting point of view. I think it was a public statement concerning the plans about her islands; they differ so from the British plans. The Javanese are not quite ready for self-government, but very nearly. Java, with a little help by other nations, can probably be ready for independence in a few years. The Javanese are good people—pretty civilized country. The Dutch marry the Javanese, and the Javanese are permitted to join the clubs. The British would not permit the Malayans to join their clubs. . . .

Question: This idea of Churchill's seems inconsistent with the policy of self-determination?

The President: Yes, that is true.

Question: He seems to undercut the Atlantic Charter. He made a statement the other day that it was not a rule, just a guide.

The President: The Atlantic Charter is a beautiful idea. When it was drawn up, the situation was that England was about to lose the war. They needed hope, and it gave it to them. We have improved the military situation since then at every chance, so that really you might say we have a much better chance of winning the war now than ever before. . . .

Question: Do you remember the speech the Prime Minister made about the fact that he was not made Prime Minister of Great Britain to see the empire fall apart?

The President: Dear old Winston will never learn on that point. He has made his specialty on that point. This is, of course, off the record.

The Roosevelt who said all of this—from the condescending "dear old Winston" to the insensitive "England was about to lose the war" (a war Roosevelt had not joined at that point)— was falling back on an old, unattractive trait: self-importance, the unfortunate flip side of his wonderful confidence.

He was tired, and sick, and, as Rosenman saw, jealous of rivals. Anthony Trollope once wrote that a blind giant—a creature who has lost great strength but is doomed to remember what it was like to wield power even in his weakened state—is the essential tragic figure. There was a trace of Trollopian tragedy about Roosevelt's view of Churchill in these days after Yalta as the failing president lashed out, reminding the world that he was the true power.

———

CHURCHILL, WHO KNEW Roosevelt's circle well, sensed what Roosevelt was feeling about Watson, Churchill's Thanksgiving dance partner in Cairo. "Accept my deep sympathy in your personal loss . . . ," he cabled Roosevelt. "I know how much this will grieve you. . . . I do hope you have benefited by the voyage and will return refreshed." Daisy found Roosevelt both optimistic and worn out on his return on February 27. "He says the conference turned out better than he dared hoped for; he is happy about it," she noted. But he was having "an exhausting time seeing people—'fixing' things which have gotten out of hand during his absence. Everyone waits around for him to 'lead' & guide."

At sea, he had worked with Rosenman on a speech to deliver to Congress. He knew what Churchill had reported to the House of Commons. In 1940 and 1941, Churchill told his colleagues, Britain's course "seemed plain and simple. If a man is coming across the sea to kill you, you do everything in your power to make sure he dies before finishing his journey. This may be difficult, it may be painful, but at least it is simple." Now, however:

We are now entering a world of imponderables, and at every stage occasions for self-questioning arise. It is a mistake to look too far ahead. Only one link in the chain of destiny can be handled at a time. . . .

No one can guarantee the future of the world. There are some who fear it will tear itself to pieces and that an awful lapse in human history may occur. I do not believe it. There must be hope. The alternative is despair, which is madness. The British race has never yielded to counsels of despair.

Just before entering the House of Representatives to deliver his own report on March 1, Roosevelt remarked, "I hope to do in one hour what Winston did in two."

WRITING MARY ABOUT Churchill's homecoming to England after Yalta, Clementine said that she found Churchill "imbibing whisky and soda. He is marvellously well—much, much better than when he went off for this most trying and difficult of Conferences." At this late hour in the war, the Churchills seemed to be drawing closer to each other while the Roosevelts continued their long minuet of affection and annoyance. Clementine was to travel to Russia for the Red Cross, a long and dangerous journey even in the best of times, and the war was still going on. She turned sixty en route, and Churchill made sure the British ambassador in Cairo gave her his birthday note. "Your lovely Birthday telegram was handed to me in Church this morning . . . ," Clementine wrote Churchill. "I was so pleased."

Eleanor and Roosevelt were not having as smooth a time. "For the first time I was beginning to realize that he could no longer bear to have a real discussion, such as we had always had," Eleanor recalled of the post-Yalta period. Eleanor drew her own strength—her own identity—from constant action and work and may have assumed everyone else did, too, even her ailing husband. Roosevelt's faltering condition, she recalled, "was impressed on me one night" in a three-way discussion with Harry Hooker, a New York lawyer who was close to the Roosevelts. The subject, Eleanor wrote, was "the question of compulsory military service for all young men as a peacetime measure." Hooker was for it; Eleanor "argued against it heatedly." The debate went too far. "In the end, I evidently made Franklin feel I was really arguing against him and I suddenly realized he was upset," Eleanor recalled. "I had forgotten that Franklin was no longer the calm and imperturbable person who, in the past, had always goaded me on to vehement arguments when questions of policy came up. It was just another indication of the change which we were all so unwilling to acknowledge."

As their fortieth wedding anniversary came in March, Eleanor had spent nearly twenty-seven years since learning of her husband's love affair taking refuge in public affairs. Now, sadly, Roosevelt was losing his ability to meet her on that common ground.

STALIN WAS ALREADY breaking his Yalta promises, strengthening the communist hand in Poland and other parts of Eastern Europe. Churchill began inundating Roosevelt with cables—thirteen in the thirty days since they parted. "I feel that this is a test case between us and the Russians of the meaning which is to be attached to such terms as Democracy, Sovereignty, Independence, representative Government and free and unfettered elections," Churchill wrote Roosevelt of Poland. In the middle of March, however, Roosevelt was willing to see how events turned out as Allied diplomats in Moscow wrangled over Poland, telling Churchill: "I feel that our personal intervention would best be withheld until every other possibility of bringing the Soviet Government into line has been exhausted." Churchill was stymied again.

Stymied, but thinking warmly of the president. "I hope that the rather numerous telegrams I have to send you on so many of our difficult and intertwined affairs are not becoming a bore to you . . . ," Churchill wrote on March 17.

> I always think of those tremendous days when you devised Lend-Lease, when we met at Argentia, when you decided with my heartfelt agreement to launch the invasion of Africa, and when you comforted me for the loss of Tobruk by giving me the 300 Shermans of subsequent Alamein fame. . . .
>
> I am sending to Washington and San Francisco most of my ministerial colleagues on one mission or another, and I shall on this occasion stay at home to mind the shop. All the time I shall be looking forward to your long-promised visit. Clemmie is off to Russia next week for a Red Cross tour as far as the Urals to which she has been invited by Uncle Joe (if we may venture to describe him thus), but she will be back in time to welcome you and Eleanor.
>
> Peace with Germany and Japan on our terms will not bring much rest to you and me (if I am still responsible). As I observed

last time, when the war of the giants is over, the wars of the pygmies will begin. There will be a torn, ragged and hungry world to help to its feet: and what will Uncle Joe or his successor say to the way we should both like to do it? . . . The advantage of this telegram is that it has nothing to do with shop. . . . All good wishes.

Winston.

Roosevelt did not answer, which worried Churchill the way Roosevelt's silence in 1940 about the reelection telegram did. Thirteen days later, Churchill added this line to another cable: "By the way, did you ever receive a telegram from me of a purely private character . . . ? It required no answer. But I should like to know that you received it."

In the end, it was as it had been in the beginning—an anxious Churchill, a colder Roosevelt. The next day, from Warm Springs, Roosevelt finally replied, saying, "I did receive your very pleasing message. . . . We hope that Clemmie's long flying tour in Russia will first be safe and next be productive of good which I am sure it will be. The war business today seems to be going very well from our point of view and we may now hope for the collapse of Hitlerism at an earlier date than had heretofore been anticipated."

Roosevelt seemed to be moving closer to Churchill's vantage point on Russia. "I cannot conceal from you the concern with which I view the development of events of mutual interest since our fruitful meeting at Yalta," Roosevelt wrote Stalin.

Churchill had another case to press with Roosevelt: the race to Berlin. Eisenhower was pursuing a strategy that might allow the Soviets to reach the German capital first. Calling themselves "the truest friends and comrades that ever fought side by side," Churchill urged Roosevelt to overrule Eisenhower. "I say quite frankly that Berlin remains of high strategic importance . . . ," Churchill told Roosevelt. "The Russian armies will no doubt overrun all Austria and enter Vienna. If they also take Berlin, will not their impression that they have been the overwhelming contributor to our common victory be unduly imprinted in their minds, and may this not lead them into a mood which will raise grave and formidable difficulties in the future?" Told a change in course might cost one hundred thousand casualties, Roosevelt turned down Churchill's impassioned request. On April 5, throwing in his hand, Churchill wrote, "I regard the matter as closed and to prove my sincerity I will use one of my very few Latin quotations, 'Amantium irae amoris integratio est.' "

The map room's translation: "Lovers' quarrels always go with true love."

THE DAY BEFORE he left for a rest in Warm Springs at the end of March, Roosevelt had a word with Frances Perkins. Perkins asked if she could bring by some guests for a quick meeting in the middle of May. "I can't do that," Roosevelt told her. "I am going out to San Francisco to open the meeting, make my speech, and receive the delegates in a social and personal way." After that it was on to England with Eleanor. "I have long wanted to do it," Roosevelt said. "I want to see the British people myself. Eleanor's visit in wartime was a great success. I mean a success for her and for me so that we understood more about their problems. I think they liked her too. But I want to go. We owe it as a return visit, and this seems to be the best time to go. It is going to be all right. I told Eleanor to order her clothes and get some fine ones so that she will make a really handsome appearance."

"But the war!" Perkins said. "I don't think you ought to go. It is dangerous. The Germans will get after you."

"The war in Europe," Roosevelt said, "will be over by the end of May."

Churchill was also thinking of Roosevelt's pending visit to England. As he ate breakfast in bed at Chequers one morning, he talked about Roosevelt with Sam Rosenman, who was back in England. "The look which came into Churchill's eyes as he talked showed the strong bond of affection that had grown between these two great leaders," Rosenman recalled.

"There are two things which I wish you would convey for me to your great President—both matters of personal interest to me," Churchill said. "First, as you know, the President and Mrs. Roosevelt have accepted the invitations of their Majesties to make a visit to England during the month of May. Will you tell him for me that he is going to get from the British people the greatest reception ever accorded to any human being since Lord Nelson made his triumphant return to London? I want you to tell him that when he sees the reception he is going to get, he should realize that it is not an artificial or stimulated one. It will come genuinely and spontaneously from the hearts of the British people; they all love him for what he has done to save them from destruction by the Huns; they love him also for what he has done for the cause of peace in the world, for what he has done to relieve their fear that the horrors they have been through for five years might come upon them again in increased fury.

"Here is the second thing I want you to tell

him," Churchill continued, Rosenman noted, "a bit sheepishly."

"Do you remember when I came over to your country in the summer of 1944 when your election campaigning was beginning? Do you remember that when I arrived, I said something favorable to the election of the President, and immediately the associates of the President sent word to me in no uncertain terms to 'lay off' discussing the American election? Do you remember I was told that if I wanted to help the President get re-elected, the best thing I could do was to keep my mouth shut; that the American people would resent any interference or suggestion by a foreigner about how they should vote?"

With what Rosenman called "one of his most engaging laughs," Churchill said, "Now what I want you to tell the President is this. When he comes over here in May I shall be in the midst of a political campaign myself; we shall be holding our own elections about that time. I want you to tell him that I impose no such inhibitions upon him as he imposed upon me. The British people would not resent—and of course I would particularly welcome—any word that he might want to say in favor of my candidacy." Rosenman was impressed with his host. "I felt anew the glow of his warm personality—frank, blunt and direct."

Rosenman would never have a chance to deliver Churchill's message.

"We have fifteen minutes more to work"

Roosevelt and Lucy Mercer Rutherfurd
at Warm Springs, April 1945

YOU KNOW HOW THIS WILL HIT ME

*The Last Letters—"I Had a True Affection
for Franklin"—Churchill in Winter*

IN THE MIDDLE of March 1945, Isador
Lubin, the White House statistician, brought
Roosevelt a new supply of gin from London.
Roosevelt wrote to thank him in code, referring to the liquor as "it." " 'It' is going to Warm
Springs and I am made very happy by 'it,' "
Roosevelt wrote Lubin. " 'It' will be doled out
with extreme care." The president had a bad
cold. "All I need is some early spring sun and
I'll be all fine," he said to Chester Bowles, the
administrator of the Office of Price Administration. Anna could not come along to Georgia—
her little boy Johnny was sick—but Roosevelt
arranged for Daisy and Polly Delano to join
him. "I kissed him goodbye and wished him a
restful holiday," recalled Eleanor.

In the Little White House, Roosevelt relaxed, dipping into a new paperback mystery, *The Punch and Judy Murders,* an installment in the Sir Henry Merrivale series. A highlight of the stay was to be a big barbecue hosted by the mayor on Thursday, April 12; Roosevelt was then due in San Francisco for the founding meeting of the United Nations, where Anthony Eden would represent Britain. And, after that, at last, to London.

IN WARM SPRINGS, Churchill and war were in the foreground. "Another beautiful, warm day," Daisy noted on April 10. "F had his usual morning, with me reading the paper by his window, while he had his breakfast [and] read all the war dispatches in 2 or 3 papers— He has the whole western front in Europe in his head, knows exactly where each army is at any one moment. He says he *has* to, for sometimes he has to make decisions about operations. I was surprised at this, thinking that Eisenhower would have the final say about such things, but F explained it this way: Some time ago, Eisenhower made a forward movement in the southern part of the line. Winston Churchill promptly cabled F a protest. . . . F, knowing what the plans were, sent an explanation to W.S.C. backing up Eisenhower."

Roosevelt now shared Churchill's belief that Yalta was in tatters. "We've taken a great risk here, an enormous risk, and it involves the Russian intentions," Roosevelt had said to his aide Chester Bowles before leaving Washington. "I'm worried. I still think Stalin will be out of his mind if he doesn't cooperate, but maybe he's not going to; in which case, we're going to have to take a different view"—in essence, Churchill's view, which was, Bowles recalled, "Let's shake hands with the Russians as far east as possible."

Stalin was furious over reports that the Americans and the British were having conversations with an SS commander about the potential surrender of German forces in Italy. The Soviets, Churchill recalled, "might be suspicious of a separate military surrender in the South, which would enable our armies to advance against reduced opposition as far as Vienna and beyond, or indeed towards the Elbe or Berlin." The Kremlin was indeed suspicious, and Stalin dispatched scorching telegrams protesting the fact that the Soviets had not been included in the talks, which had taken place in Bern, Switzerland. In a blunt message of his own, Roosevelt told Stalin that "it would be one of the great tragedies of history if at the very moment of victory, now within our grasp, such distrust, such lack of faith should prejudice the entire undertaking after the collossal [*sic*] losses of life, materiel and treasure involved." Roosevelt sent a copy of the note to Churchill.

Churchill read it with satisfaction. This was more like it—Churchill and Roosevelt versus Stalin, not Roosevelt and Stalin versus Churchill. "If they are ever convinced that we are afraid of them and can be bullied into submission, then indeed I should despair of our future relations with them and much else," Churchill told Roosevelt on Thursday, April 5. Roosevelt agreed. "We must not permit anybody to entertain a false impression that we are afraid," he replied to Churchill the next day from Warm Springs. "Our Armies will in a very few days be in a position that will permit us to become 'tougher' than has heretofore appeared advantageous to the war effort."

BULLISH TALK, but Churchill could tell Roosevelt was feeling low. In a letter to Clementine, who was in Russia, Churchill said that "my poor friend is very much alone and, according to all accounts I receive, is bereft of much of his vigor."

In his weariness, Roosevelt was weighing drastic steps. He told Daisy and Polly that he was thinking of retiring in 1946, "after he gets the peace organization well started," Suckley said. "I don't believe he thinks he will be *able* to carry on. . . . On thinking further, one realizes that if he cannot, physically, carry on, he will *have* to resign. There is no possible sense in his killing himself by slow degrees, the while not filling his job—Far better to hand it over, and avoid the period of his possible illness, when he wouldn't be *able* to function."

It was a scenario he would mention again as he smoked a last cigarette on the night of Saturday, April 7. "He talked seriously about the S. Francisco Conference, & his part in World Peace, etc.," Daisy wrote. "He says again that he can probably resign some time next year, when the peace organization—The United Nations—is well started." It is difficult to imagine he would ever have followed through with these most intimate of musings. He thought he was, as Daisy said elsewhere, "the hope of the world." And like Churchill, he had never surrendered.

AT CHEQUERS ON Friday, April 6, Churchill spoke of Roosevelt's nation with admiration and envy. "Talk was of the Americans, the P.M. saying that there was no greater exhibition of power in history than that of the American army fighting the battle of the Ardennes with its left hand and advancing from island to island towards Japan with its right," Jock Colville wrote. Churchill hated that the empire was no longer the great force in the world. He felt the loss. "The only times I ever quarrel with the Americans are when they fail to give us a fair share of opportunity to win glory," he wrote Clementine that same day. "Undoubtedly I feel much pain when I see our armies so much smaller than theirs. It has always been my wish to keep equal, but how can you do that against so mighty a nation and a population nearly three times your own?"

The architect of the American achievement was wavering between strength and weakness in his little house. Sitting by the fire, working on his stamps, Roosevelt sketched one to mark the San Francisco UN meeting. "What do you think of this?" he asked Daisy and Polly, who were on the sofa. "A simple new stamp without engraving: '3 cents 3' on the top line, 'United States Postage' on the bottom line, and in the middle, 'April 25, 1945; Towards United Nations.' " Excited, Roosevelt asked for Frank Walker, the postmaster general. Told Walker was at the theater but could call back, Roosevelt sat up until the call came through. The design, Walker told Roosevelt, would be approved by midweek. "So can people in high places sometimes get things done in a few minutes!" Daisy said.

As he was tucked into bed, Roosevelt indulged in a touching ritual he had begun to play with his cousins. Under orders to take gruel to help regain weight, Roosevelt liked to pretend he was a child who had to be fed, with his cousins playing the role of mother. "I get the gruel & Polly & I take it to him," Daisy said. "I sit on the edge of the bed & he 'puts on an act': he is too weak to raise his head, his hands are weak, he must be fed! So I proceed to feed him with a tea spoon & he loves it! Just to be able to turn from his world problems & behave like a complete nut for a few moments, with an appreciative audience laughing with him & at him, both!" Daisy sensed the absurdity of the scene. "On paper it sounds too silly for words, and it *is* silly—but he's *very* funny and laughs at himself with us." When the gruel is gone, he is "left . . . relaxed & laughing—"

LUCY RUTHERFURD AND Elizabeth Shoumatoff arrived on Monday, April 9—they had come through Macon—and were shown their quarters in the cottage up the driveway from the main house. When they appeared in the big room at the Little White House, they found Roosevelt at his card table with cocktail supplies. Surrounded by four women, the war going well, Roosevelt was relaxed. When

Shoumatoff asked about the distance between Aiken and Macon, Roosevelt was reminded of Churchill's recent joke about the Crimea and happily repeated it for the company: "Let's not falter twixt Malta and Yalta!"

This led him to another Churchill story. If Shoumatoff's account is accurate, Roosevelt conflated events at Casablanca and Yalta, but the tale, both affectionate and condescending, is typical of Roosevelt's late view of Churchill. "I was giving a banquet for the King of Saudi Arabia, and you cannot drink or smoke in his presence, according to Eastern etiquette," Roosevelt said. (He may have meant the dinner for the sultan of Morocco at Casablanca.) "So I called up Winnie to remind him to have his drinks before, which he promptly forgot. At the dinner table, realizing this, he proceeded to sulk through the whole evening, just like this," and Roosevelt, Shoumatoff recalled, "made an amusing imitation of Churchill's expression." Carrying on with the story, Roosevelt said: "The idea of the banquet was to exchange friendly bows with the sultan, who controlled great quantities of oil, and surely Churchill's attitude was of no help. At ten o'clock the sultan started to bid farewell. He had hardly left with his entourage when Winnie was already pouring Scotch into a glass!"

———

FOR PEOPLE—INCLUDING Churchill—who thought they ever understood Roosevelt, or that what they saw was what they got, there was one last reminder for his daughter that Roosevelt was a man of shadows. He kept Lucy's visit secret from his daughter. "He used to call me every night on the phone to find out how Johnny was," Anna recalled. "He called me the night before [he died], and he was just fine. He told me all about the barbecue that they were going to have the next day, and everything else. But there was a funny little thing there, just to show that he never discussed his real personal life with anyone. . . . Lucy Mercer was at Warm Springs. . . . In other words, his private life was his private life. And there was no doubt about it. Which I admire him for, I think it's fine. So I didn't know Lucy was there. No idea."

And he avoided confrontation to the very end. On April 11, Roosevelt, drafting a cable to Churchill at midday in the Little White House, suggested a middle course with Stalin. "I would minimize the general Soviet problem as much as possible because these problems, in one form or another, seem to arise every day and most of them straighten out as in the case of the Bern meeting," Roosevelt said. "We must be firm, however, and our course thus far is correct."

In the afternoon he took a ride with Lucy and Daisy. "Lucy is so sweet with F—No wonder he loves to have her around," Daisy noted of that Wednesday. "Toward the end of the drive, it began to be chilly and she put her sweater over his knees—I can imagine just how she took care of her husband—She would think of little things which make so much difference to a semi-invalid, or even a person who is just tired, like F."

Henry Morgenthau joined the party for supper on the night of April 11. They had a bowl of caviar from Stalin, but once that was gone there was only uninspiring fare—meatballs and waffles with chocolate sauce for dessert. The evening improved, Shoumatoff recalled, "as Roosevelt and Morgenthau began recalling different amusing and entertaining incidents about Churchill."

IN LONDON THAT WEEK, Churchill was writing Clementine, promising her that he would "let you know about the President's moves." Attending an April 9 war cabinet meeting, Churchill "said that he hoped the day of the celebrations would be known as VE-day," according to the minutes. From the Soviet

Union, Clementine cabled Churchill: "I miss my quiet evenings with you"—as rare as they were. Churchill had added this note in his own hand to a long letter to her: "My darling one I think always of you & am so proud of you." Roosevelt and Eleanor were in touch, if in a more restrained way. "I carried on my usual round of duties," Eleanor said of that week, "hearing by telephone daily from Warm Springs. All the news was good."

As Wednesday, April 11, drew to a close, Roosevelt was listening to ghost stories around the fire. Shoumatoff had the floor with a spooky saga about the black pearl necklace of Catherine the Great. "Upon finishing my story, another was about to be told when Dr. Bruenn and his assistant arrived," she recalled. "The President, like a little boy, asked to stay up longer, but finally consented to retire, telling me he would be ready for my painting in the morning."

It had been a good day. Roosevelt took his gruel and, settling into bed, said: "Now I'm all relaxed again!"

EARLY ON THURSDAY, April 12, Roosevelt read old newspapers while he waited for the new editions to arrive from Atlanta. In London, Churchill would take Bernard Baruch, the

American financier, to dinner at the Savoy with the Other Club that evening. "Churchill talked with admiration about the President," Baruch recalled, "and about Harry Hopkins, of whom he was also very fond."

Roosevelt was dressed and brought into the living room. "His colour was good & he looked smiling & happy & ready for anything," wrote Daisy. He was looking out at the sunlight as Bill Hassett arrived with the mail. His feet up on a wicker stool, his card table before him, Roosevelt set to work.

At about twelve-forty, the tray with midday gruel was brought in. "He interrupted his reading for a moment & took some gruel," Daisy noted, "continued his reading, took more gruel." Roosevelt told the women: "We have fifteen minutes more to work." Daisy was crocheting; Shoumatoff was painting; Lucy sat nearby; Polly was putting water in a bowl of roses in her room.

Daisy shifted her gaze from her sewing to Roosevelt. "F seemed to be looking for something: his head forward, his hands fumbling—I went forward & looked into his face."

"Have you dropped your cigarette?" she asked him.

"I have a terrific pain in the back of my head," Roosevelt said.

"I told him to [put] his head back on his chair," Daisy recalled, but he could no longer control what he did. It was one-fifteen, and the president of the United States was suffering a cerebral hemorrhage.

Daisy reached for Roosevelt's telephone—it sat next to his chair, connecting him to the world he had governed until that moment—to call for Dr. Bruenn as the president was carried to bed.

Daisy opened his collar and clutched his right hand. "Two or three times he rolled his head from side to side, opened his eyes," Suckley recalled. "Polly thinks he looked at us all in turn. He may have, I could see no signs of real recognition in those eyes—twice he drew up the left side of his face, as if in pain." Lucy tried to help, waving camphor beneath his nose. Nothing worked. Soon Bruenn rushed in.

"We must pack and go," Lucy said to Shoumatoff. Franklin Roosevelt's secrets would be kept.

They went across the yard. By two-thirty, Lucy and Shoumatoff were off.

ELEANOR WAS IN the White House discussing the United Nations conference with an adviser to the American delegation when Polly

Delano rang Washington. "We are worried about Franklin, he has had a fainting spell," she told Eleanor. Eleanor talked to Dr. McIntire, who was in contact with Bruenn and suggested Eleanor keep an engagement at a benefit at the Sulgrave Club. They would fly together to Warm Springs that night. McIntire, Eleanor said, "was not alarmed." At three thirty-five, Roosevelt stopped breathing.

Churchill and Baruch, who knew nothing of this, were still at the Savoy. Lucy wiped tears away as her car moved toward Aiken.

At the Sulgrave, Eleanor was called to the telephone. It was Steve Early, asking her to return to the White House. Ever dutiful, Eleanor said her good-byes at the party and then sat, she recalled, "with clenched hands" as she was driven home. "I knew down in my heart that something dreadful had happened."

In a soft southern spring, he slipped away. Just sixty-three years old, Franklin Roosevelt was dead.

STEVE EARLY BROKE the news to Eleanor at the White House. She sent a telegram to her sons, all of whom were overseas. "Father slept away. He would expect you to carry on and finish your jobs."

The Other Club had adjourned. Churchill was in the Annexe. "I am very glad your visit to Leningrad was so pleasant and interesting," he was writing to Clementine. "Here everything is quiet except politics. Love."

Then came a call from Washington with the news from Warm Springs. "I felt as if I had been struck a physical blow," Churchill recalled. The long courtship, with its joys and frustrations, had come to an end. "I have just heard the grievous news of President Roosevelt's death," he added to the cable to Clementine. He had been writing Mary, too, who had just been decorated for her service in antiaircraft batteries in northwest Europe. Telling her the news in a postscript, Churchill noted: "You know how this will hit me."

It was late, too late to do much, but Churchill discharged his duties. "Get me the palace," he said to an aide, and Churchill briefed the king's private secretary, who told George VI. In the night, Churchill cabled Lord Halifax in Washington to ask if he might come to the funeral. Halifax put in calls to Harry Hopkins and Ed Stettinius.

AT FIVE FORTY-FIVE P.M. in New York, in Studio 28 at CBS, an episode of *Wilderness*

Road, a serial about the adventures of Daniel Boone, was beginning. Four minutes later, armed with only a two-word news bulletin from Warm Springs—"F.D.R. DEAD"—broadcaster John Charles Daly announced: "We interrupt this program to bring you a special news bulletin from CBS World News. . . . President Roosevelt is dead."

In his Washington office, Richard Strout of *The New Republic* was reminded of Edwin M. Stanton's words at the death of Lincoln: "Now he belongs to the ages."

CBS cut to Douglas Edwards in London. "London and the British nation are deeply shocked at the news," Edwards reported. "I was in a Red Cross canteen filled with American soldiers getting a late night snack. They were stunned. . . . Everyone wondered if there couldn't be some mistake. . . . Both King George and Prime Minister Churchill were informed immediately and were deeply shocked and grieved. . . . Britain will always remember President Roosevelt as one of the first men who saw the danger, even before America entered the War. He was the man who sent to these islands the implements with which to fight after the dark days of Dunkirk."

From the State Department, Chip Bohlen called to give the news to Harry Hopkins, who was at the Mayo Clinic. "I guess I better be going to Washington," was all Hopkins could say.

Clementine was aboard a train in Moscow, waiting to pull out for Stalingrad, when she heard. "We come with bad news," Molotov told her. "President Roosevelt is dead." Clementine, Mary wrote, "was stunned by this grievous news: She at once understood its import to the course of events, and knew also what a deep and personal loss the President's death would be to Winston." At Clementine's suggestion, the party paused in respectful silence, and then she made her way to the British embassy to call her husband.

After flying from Washington, Eleanor entered the Little White House in Georgia. "At Warm Springs, everybody was scared to tell her Lucy had been there," recalled Trude Lash. "They were right to be scared." But in a sudden outburst, Polly Delano revealed that Lucy had been there; Anna had often been the go-between. "The one thing that hurt again, when he died, was finding out he saw Lucy again, which he had promised not to do," said Mrs. Lash. "Mrs. R. was estranged from Anna over this for quite a while. My feeling was, and I told Mrs. R. this, 'How could Anna not do what her sick and ailing father asked her to do?' Anna said, 'I could not do much for my father but I could do that.'"

Whatever anguish the news of Lucy caused—and it must have been severe—Eleanor once again coped by following form and fulfilling a public role. "E.R. sent us off to bed, for some rest," noted Daisy, "even if we don't sleep." Eleanor prepared to see her husband home.

"Poor E.R.—I believe she loved him more deeply than she knows herself, and his feeling for her was deep & lasting," Daisy noted. "The fact that they could not relax together, or play together, is the tragedy of their joint lives, for I believe, from everything that I have seen of them, that they had everything else in common. It was probably a matter of personalities, of a certain lack of humor on her part—I can not blame either of them. They are both remarkable people."

"JESUS IT WAS a shock," Kathleen Harriman wrote Pamela Churchill of Roosevelt's death. "Red flags with black borders hung from all houses today throughout Moscow—something I'd have not guessed would happen." Of Truman, Kathleen noted: "The best that can be said is that he's 'safe.' What a time to have a leader replaced by a safe man!"

Readers of the *London News Chronicle* were told this as they rose in the morning after Roosevelt's death: "FDR had won the affection of the world. It is not only the Americans but all the United Nations who have lost a great leader. Franklin D. Roosevelt was the 20th century's man of destiny. He became democracy's champion when many other statesmen much closer to the threat of danger were slumbering or appeasing. As for Britain, Franklin D. Roosevelt must always hold a place in its affections so long as this nation lasts, a place that few if any foreigners have ever held in Britain." At midnight in New York, as dawn approached in London, CBS broadcast a hymn: "Now the Day Is Over." A few of its verses:

> Now the day is over,
> Night is drawing nigh,
> Shadows of the evening
> Steal across the sky.
>
> Jesus, give the weary
> Calm and sweet repose;
> With thy tenderest blessing
> May our eyelids close.
>
> Grant to little children
> Visions bright of thee;
> Guard the sailors tossing
> On the deep, blue sea.
>
> Comfort every sufferer
> Watching late in pain

*"I feel a very painful personal loss,
quite apart from the ties of public action
which bound us so closely together"*

———

Clementine, Eleanor, and Churchill at
Roosevelt's grave, March 12, 1946

Those who plan some evil
From their sin restrain.

EARLY THE NEXT morning, Friday, April 13,
Churchill received Halifax's answer to his
overnight cable. "Have spoken to Harry Hopkins
and Stettinius, who are both much moved by
your thought of possibly coming over and who
both warmly agree with my judgment of the
immense effect for good that would be produced," Halifax wrote. "Nor do I overlook the
value if you came of your seeing Truman." Churchill ordered that a plane be ready to fly to Washington that night. During the day he did what
he did so well: compose compassionate cables. A
world seemed to be ending—the very personal
one of car rides at Hyde Park, Christmas at the
White House, and fishing at Shangri-la.

He dictated a message to Eleanor. "Accept my
most profound sympathy in your grievous loss,
which is also the loss of the British nation and
of the cause of freedom in every land. I feel so
deeply for you all. As for myself, I have lost a
dear and cherished friendship which was forged
in the fire of war. I trust you may find consola-
tion in the magnitude of his work and the glory
of his name."

To Hopkins, who, as Churchill knew, understood Roosevelt's shifting affections, he cabled:

"I understand how deep your feelings of grief must be. I feel with you that we have lost one of our greatest friends and one of the most valiant champions of the causes for which we fight. I feel a very painful personal loss, quite apart from the ties of public action which bound us so closely together. I had a true affection for Franklin."

Writing Truman, whom he had never met, Churchill said: "Pray accept from me the expression of my personal sympathy in the loss which you and the American nation have sustained in the death of our illustrious friend. I hope that I may be privileged to renew with you the intimate comradeship in the great cause we all serve that I enjoyed through these terrible years with him. I offer you my respectful good wishes as you step into the breach in the victorious lines of the United Nations."

He went to the House of Commons and, in a hushed voice, said, "The House will have learned with deepest sorrow the grievous news which has come to us from across the Atlantic and which conveys to us the loss of a famous President of the United States, whose friendship for the cause of freedom and for the causes of the weak and poor have won him immortal renown. It is not fitting that we should continue our work this day. I feel that the House will wish to render its token of respect to the memory of this great departed statesman and war leader by adjourning immediately."

George VI sent Churchill a handwritten note. "I cannot tell you how sad I am at the sudden death of President Roosevelt. The news came as a great shock to me. I have lost a friend, but to you who have known him for so long & so intimately during this war, the sudden loss to yourself personally of a colleague & helpmate in the framing of far reaching decisions both for the prosecution of the war & for the future peace of the world must be overwhelming. I send you all my sympathy at this moment."

All the trumpets were sounding. Churchill was at his eloquent, emotional best. As the hours passed by, however, he wavered on going to Washington. The flight was scheduled for eight-thirty that evening, but by seven forty-five, with "no decision reached—P.M. said he would decide at aerodrome," Alexander Cadogan noted. The tide of emotion and reminiscence and mourning running high, he nevertheless chose not to go.

EVERYTHING IN HIM would have pressed him to make the trip. It was a dramatic occasion— the death of a great man—and he knew he should see Truman, who was unknown to him. "It would have been a solace to me to be present at Franklin's funeral," Churchill told Hopkins, "but everyone here thought my duty next week lay at home, at a time when so many Ministers are out of the country." But the logistics of a weekend in Washington and Hyde Park could have been managed, even with the travel time involved in 1945, even with Germany on the verge of collapse. Churchill, meanwhile, often decided to do what he wanted to do despite what "everyone here" thought. The king was an exception to that (there had been the D-Day contretemps), but the prime minister's letter to George VI does not suggest that the king had taken a stand either way.

Here is what Churchill told George VI: "I am touched by the kindness of Your Majesty's letter. The sudden loss of this great friend and comrade in all our affairs is very hard for me. Ties have been shorn asunder which years had woven. We have to begin again in many ways. I was tempted during the day to go over for the funeral and begin relations with the new man. However so many of Your Majesty's Ministers are out of the country, and the Foreign Secretary had arranged to go anyhow, and I felt the business next week in Parliament and also the ceremonies connected with the death of Mr Roosevelt are so important that I should be failing in my duty if I left the House of Commons without my close personal attention. I had to consider the tribute which should be paid to the late President, which clearly it is my business to deliver. The press of work is also very heavy. Therefore I thought it better that I should remain here in charge at this juncture."

Some have argued that his failure to go to Washington and Hyde Park suggests the relationship between Roosevelt and Churchill was professional, not personal. There is, however, a more complicated possibility: that the decision was partly political and partly emotional, the product of a prideful moment in which Churchill, after playing the suitor to Roosevelt, wanted to himself be courted. If raw politics had been the sole force in their friendship, there would have been no question about Churchill's going. He needed to get on good terms with Truman. This was the optimum time for Churchill to shape a new president's worldview. He could unleash his eloquence about the dangers of Stalin on a new audience, one not yet tired of being lectured. Truman was eager. "At no time in our respective histories, has it been more important that the intimate, solid relations which you and the late President had forged between our countries be preserved and developed," Truman cabled Churchill on April 13. "It is my earnest hope that before too long, in the furtherance of this, we can arrange a personal meeting. . . . You can count on me to continue the loyal and close collaboration which to the benefit of the entire world existed between you and our great President."

Still, Churchill stayed home. Was Churchill, tired of dancing to another man's tune, relieved Roosevelt was dead? Had it all been an act? No—like so many human relationships, Roosevelt and Churchill's was a mix of the selfish and the unselfish, of artifice and affection. Churchill could be put out with Roosevelt. Who, having spent five years in such an exhausting and exhilarating dance, would not have been—much earlier and much more so than Churchill was? From Churchill's perspective, Roosevelt withheld some essential part of himself to the end. What Churchill may not have realized is that Franklin Roosevelt did that with everyone in his life—it was how he lived. Even Roosevelt's widow was coming to terms with her husband's emotional deceptions in these hours.

A possible answer to the funeral riddle may lie in this paragraph from Churchill's letter to George VI:

Moreover I think that it would be a good thing that President Truman should come over here at about the same time as was proposed by his predecessor. He could visit his Armies in Germany, and he could be

Your Majesty's guest. The actual ceremonial would have to be reconsidered but I am sure it would be a great advantage if he could come during the month of May, even if the clouds of May were likely to dissolve in rain. I am making this proposal to him and to Stettinius very strongly through Anthony.

He wanted Truman to come to him. Perhaps Churchill was making a bid to take Roosevelt's place as the senior partner in the alliance, to become, in the last hours of the war he had fought longer and harder than anyone, the quarry rather than the suitor. Years of slights may have welled up in those hours, exacerbated by the glowing tributes flowing to Roosevelt. Yes, Roosevelt had seen the dangers of the dictators, but Churchill had, too. Yes, Roosevelt had saved the world, but Churchill had, too.

Remaining in London was a close call. No one could be more forgiving than Churchill, but for a moment, a passing moment, he seems to have indulged in a fit of pride, for himself and for Britain. Roosevelt had never traveled far to see only Churchill, instead forcing Churchill to come to him—or to him and Stalin. The question of a state visit was important in those days. "England has lost a great friend and a hero," CBS's Larry LeSueur had broadcast from London on April 12. "Above all, they had one day dreamed of seeing Roosevelt in the British capital." If he could get Truman to come to him, Churchill may have thought in those feverish hours on April 13, then perhaps the world would see that he, and Britain, were still forces to be reckoned with. It was the kind of maneuver Roosevelt would have appreciated. The word of his decision went out. "Prime Minister Churchill wanted to come but was too busy," reported the Associated Press. The gamble failed. Truman had too much to do, too much to learn, to travel in those crowded first weeks. Thus a Churchill dream died a little, largely unremarked death. "In the after-light I regret that I did not adopt the new President's suggestion," Churchill recalled. He had taken a leap—and fallen short. He got back up and moved forward.

THE RITES FOR ROOSEVELT IN the East Room were brief. Angus Dun, the Episcopal bishop of Washington, presided over the twenty-three-minute service. "In his first inaugural the President bore this testimony to his own deep faith: 'So first of all let me assert my firm belief that the only thing we have to fear is fear itself—nameless, unreasoning, unjustified terror which paralyzes needed efforts to convert retreat into advance,' " Bishop Dun said. "As that was his first word to us, I am sure he would wish it to be his last; that as we go forward to the tasks in which he has led us, we shall go forward without fear, without fear of the future, without fear of our allies or of our friends, and without fear of our own insufficiency."

Roosevelt was taken north by train to Hyde Park. There was the clop-clop-clop of the horses drawing Roosevelt's caisson up the hill from the railway siding, along the same road he and Churchill had traveled together, talking of war. In the rose garden, the rector of St. James's, George Anthony, read the burial office for his senior warden.

"I WAS SO terribly sad about FDR—he is deeply and genuinely mourned here," Pamela Churchill wrote Kathleen Harriman. In London, Roosevelt was remembered at St. Paul's. "We who represent the two great English-speaking peoples," said the cathedral's dean, "are specially bound to pray that through our cooperation one with another the great causes for which Franklin Delano Roosevelt laboured may be brought to fruition for the lasting benefit of all the nations of the world." The congregation sang "The Battle Hymn of the Republic"—"to its great tune," *The Times* of London observed, "known familiarly enough to British people though less familiar, as it appeared, in their mouths." Afterward, Ambassador Gil Winant, who had read the lesson from Revelation, walked Churchill, who was crying, to the door. Churchill lunched at the Annexe, "feverishly composing," recalled Jock Colville, the tribute he was to pay Roosevelt in the House that afternoon.

"MY FRIENDSHIP WITH the great man to whose work and fame we pay our tribute today began and ripened during this war," Churchill told the House of Commons. "I had met him, but only for a few minutes, after the close of the last war, and as soon as I went to the Admiralty in September 1939, he telegraphed inviting me to correspond with him direct on naval or other matters if at any time I felt inclined. Having obtained the permission of the Prime Minister, I did so. . . . When I became Prime Minister, and the war broke out in all its hideous fury, when our own life and survival hung in the balance, I was already in a position to telegraph to the President on terms of an association which had become most intimate and, to me, most agreeable. This continued through all the ups and downs of the world struggle until Thursday last, when I received my last messages from him."

He ran through an accounting of their contacts, from the number of messages to days spent together.

"I conceived an admiration for him as a statesman, a man of affairs, and a war leader. I felt the utmost confidence in his upright, inspiring character and outlook, and a personal regard—affection I must say—for him beyond my power to express today. His love of his own country, his respect for its constitution, his power of gauging the tides and currents of mobile public opinion, were always evident, but added to these were the beatings of that generous heart which was always stirred to anger and to action by spectacles of aggression and oppression by the strong against the weak. It is, indeed, a loss, a bitter loss to humanity that those heartbeats are stilled forever."

Growing more emotional, Churchill turned to the central fact about Roosevelt that shaped his life: his paralysis. Churchill was candid and caring. He had watched Roosevelt force himself across the deck of the *Prince of Wales;* he had wheeled Roosevelt through White House corridors, bargaining for his nation's survival; he had mounted the steps of Marrakech as the president of the United States was carried to the top of the tall tower, vulnerable yet dominant.

"President Roosevelt's physical affliction lay heavily upon him. It was a marvel that he bore up against it through all the many years of tumult and storm. Not one man in ten millions, stricken and crippled as he was, would have attempted to plunge into a life of physical and mental exertion and of hard, ceaseless political controversy. Not one in ten millions would have tried, not one in a generation would have succeeded, not only in entering this sphere, not only in acting vehemently in it, but in becoming indisputable master of the scene. In this extraordinary effort of the spirit over the flesh, of will-power over physical infirmity, he was inspired and sustained by that noble woman his devoted wife, whose high ideals marched with his own, and to whom the deep and respectful sympathy of the House of Commons flows out today in all fullness."

He saluted Roosevelt's clarity in the isolationist fog, his leadership in drafting the Atlantic Charter, and his role in the "great operations" in all theaters. But at Yalta, Churchill said, he noticed that Roosevelt was ailing.

"His captivating smile, his gay and charming manner, had not deserted him, but his face had a transparency, an air of purification, and often there was a faraway look in his eyes. When I took my leave of him in Alexandria harbor, I must confess that I had an indefinable sense of fear that his health and his strength were on the ebb. But nothing altered his inflexible sense of duty. To the end he faced his innumerable tasks unflinching. One of the tasks of the President is to sign maybe a hundred or two State papers with his own hand every day, commissions and so forth. All this he continued to carry out with the utmost strictness. When death came suddenly upon him 'he had finished his mail.' That portion of his day's work was done. As the saying goes, he died in harness, and we may well say battle harness, like his soldiers, sailors, and airmen, who side by side with ours are carrying on their task to the end all over the world. What an enviable death was his! He had brought his country through the worst of its perils and the heaviest of its toils. Victory had cast its sure and steady beam upon him."

An admirer of the glorious, Churchill bowed to what the birthplace of his mother had become under Roosevelt.

"In the days of peace he had broadened and stabilized the foundations of American life and union. In war he had raised the strength, might and glory of the great Republic to a height never attained by any nation in history. With her left hand she was leading the advance of the conquering Allied armies into the heart of Germany, and with her right, on the other side of the globe, she was irresistibly and swiftly breaking up the power of Japan. And all the time ships, munitions, supplies, and food of every kind were aiding on a gigantic scale her allies, great and small, in the course of the long struggle. But all this was no more than worldly power and grandeur, had it not been that the causes of human freedom and of social justice, to which so much of his life had been given, added a luster to this power and pomp and warlike might, a luster which will long be discernible among men. He has left behind him a band of resolute and able men handling the numerous interrelated parts of the vast American war machine. He has left a successor who comes forward with firm step and sure conviction to carry on the task to its appointed end. For us, it remains only to say that in Franklin Roosevelt there died the greatest American friend we have ever known, and the greatest champion of freedom who has ever brought help and comfort from the new world to the old."

MOVING WORDS. "Winston rose and spoke about Roosevelt," Harold Nicolson, the author and Labour MP, wrote his son. "I did not think him very good—nothing like as good as when he made the funeral oration on Neville Chamberlain, which was truly Periclean." But, Nicolson added, "Which all shows that when one really does mind deeply about a thing, it is more difficult to write or speak about it than when one is just faintly moved by pity or terror."

THE MAGNITUDE OF the evil Roosevelt and Churchill had been fighting against was becoming ever more widely known. On April 12, Eisenhower visited a Nazi concentration camp at Ohrdruf, near Buchenwald. The general was so horrified, Martin Gilbert wrote, that he "at once telephoned Churchill to describe what he had seen, and then sent photographs of the dead prisoners to Churchill, who circulated them to each member of the British Cabinet." "There is no doubt that this is probably the greatest and most horrible crime ever committed in the whole history of the world, and it has been done by scientific machinery by nominally civilised men in the name of a great State and one of the leading races of Europe," Churchill told Anthony Eden in the last year of the war.

The day Roosevelt died, Ed Murrow of CBS walked through Buchenwald. The prisoners he saw were too weak to rise from their cots; he watched a man fall over dead. Inmates showed Murrow the numbers tattooed on their arms. He walked into a room with a concrete floor. "There were two rows of bodies stacked up like cordwood," Murrow told his listeners. "They were thin and very white. Some of the bodies were terribly bruised, though there seemed to be little flesh to bruise. Some had been shot through the head, but they bled but little."

It was a painful report. "If I've offended you by this rather mild account of Buchenwald, I'm not in the least sorry," Murrow said of the scenes he saw on April 12. "I was there on Thursday, and many men in many tongues blessed the name of Roosevelt. For long years his name had meant the full measure of their hope. These men who had kept close company with death for many years did not know that Mr. Roosevelt would, within hours, join their comrades who had laid their lives on the scales of freedom."

In the early days of the war, Murrow said, Churchill had said to him: "One day the world and history will recognize and acknowledge what it owes to your President." There had been tears in Churchill's eyes.

"I saw and heard the first installment of that at Buchenwald on Thursday," Murrow said. "It came from men from all over Europe. Their faces, with more flesh on them, might have been found anywhere at home. To them the name 'Roosevelt' was a symbol, a code word for a lot of guys named 'Joe' who are somewhere out in the blue with the armor heading east." Churchill had promised to never surrender; with the

might of America, Roosevelt had made Churchill's vows reality.

HITLER SHOT HIMSELF in his Berlin bunker
on April 30. Clementine was still in the Soviet
Union when the news arrived of the German
surrender on May 8. "All my thoughts are with
you on this supreme day my darling," she
cabled Winston. "It could not have happened
without you. All my love."

Churchill had won. Thinking of the masses in
London, "during the morning, following
enquiries which he had made," wrote Martin
Gilbert, "he received assurances from Scotland
Yard and the Ministry of Food that there was
no shortage of beer in the capital." Addressing
the nation, Churchill reviewed the war and
reminded his people of the magnitude of their
achievement. "After gallant France had been
struck down we, from this Island and from our
united Empire, maintained the struggle single-
handed for a whole year until we were joined
by the military might of Soviet Russia, and later
by the overwhelming power and resources of
the United States of America," Churchill said.
"Finally almost the whole world was combined
against the evil-doers, who are now prostrate
before us." The day was theirs.

Late that evening, after Churchill dined with Sarah and Diana, thousands surged through London, crying for Churchill. From a balcony overlooking Whitehall, Churchill stood at the summit of his long life. "My dear friends, this is your hour," he said. "This is not victory of a party or of any class. It's a victory of the great British nation as a whole. We were the first, in this ancient island, to draw the sword against tyranny. After a while we were left all alone against the most tremendous military power that has been seen. We were all alone for a whole year."

He had them as he had before, appealing to their courage, giving them faith, lifting them to heights they did not know they could reach until he pointed the way. "The lights went out and the bombs came down," Churchill said. "But every man, woman and child in the country had no thought of quitting the struggle. London can take it. So we came back after long months from the jaws of death, out of the mouth of hell, while all the world wondered. When shall the reputation and faith of this generation of English men and women fail? I say that in the long years to come not only will the people of this island but of the world, wherever the bird of freedom chirps in human hearts, look back to what we've done and they will say

'Do not despair, do not yield to violence and tyranny, march straight forward and die if need be—unconquered.' "

VERY SHORTLY AFTER the president's death, Eleanor apparently gave Daisy a Shoumatoff picture of Roosevelt to pass on to Lucy Rutherfurd. Given the turmoil Lucy had caused her not once, in 1918, but again now, with the revelation of her continuing role in Roosevelt's life, Eleanor's gesture is intriguing. It was exquisitely gracious, the act of a noble, sensitive woman who had hated sharing her husband with Lucy during his lifetime yet was able to rise above the jealousies and pain of such a moment to share something of him now. (To argue that Eleanor was banishing any trace of Lucy or Shoumatoff would be wrong: A copy of the artist's 1943 portrait of Roosevelt hung in Eleanor's living room at Val-Kill.) The present also accomplished something else, whether Eleanor consciously calculated this or not. As she had after 1918, she remained Mrs. Roosevelt, and the power to give gifts confers a certain authority and status on the giver. Sending Lucy the picture showed that Eleanor knew all and was in control. In Aiken on Wednesday, May 2, 1945, Lucy took up a pen to write Eleanor a note of thanks.

Dear Eleanor—

Margaret Suckley has written me that you gave her the little water color of Franklin by Mme. Shoumatoff to send me. Thank you so very much—you must know that it will be treasured always—

I have wanted to write you for a long time to tell you that I had seen Franklin and of his great kindness about my husband when he was desperately ill in Washington, & of how helpful he was too to his boys—and that I hoped so very much that I might see you again—

I can't tell you how deeply I feel for you and how constantly I think of your sorrow— You—whom I have always felt to be the most blessed and privileged of women— must now feel immeasurable grief and pain and they must be almost unbearable—

The whole universe finds it difficult to readjust itself to a world without Franklin— and to you and to his family—the emptiness must be appalling—

I send you—as I find it impossible not to—my love and my deep deep sympathy.

As always—
Affectionately
Lucy Rutherfurd

With these well-chosen words, which are now in Eleanor's papers at Hyde Park, Lucy made the best of the most awkward of situations. In the upper left-hand corner of the first page of the letter, there is a faint abbreviation in pencil: "ans," shorthand for "answered." Though there is no copy of Eleanor's reply, the notation means that she, too, followed well-mannered form and acknowledged Lucy's letter. The episode is an elegant epilogue to one of the most complicated personal stories in presidential history—a story that ends with two women who loved Franklin Roosevelt treating each other with civility and grace.

Lucy was much immersed in the past as the spring wore on. Daisy sent her some snapshots, including some taken at Top Cottage. "I have looked at them long—& with the magnifying glass—and they are good," Lucy wrote Daisy on May 9, 1945, and happily accepted Daisy's apparent offer to mail her pictures from the last days in Georgia—which then produced another thank-you letter from Lucy. "Your note with the enclosure was a v. great pleasure and joy," she wrote Daisy on May 20. "I love having the one from Warm Springs—though they make the pain in one's heart even sharper." Suckley, who was working on organizing the Roosevelt archives at Hyde Park, seems to have asked Lucy

about the possible whereabouts of a diary that
FDR had kept of his trip to Europe in 1918—
the trip that ended, of course, with Eleanor's
discovery of the love affair. The diary might be
in Eleanor's or Franklin's papers, Lucy told
Daisy, and then, from memory, she wrote out
the details of Roosevelt's tour with some preci-
sion: who he had been with, battlefields he had
visited, what he had seen at the front. Writing
inside a folded notecard imprinted AIKEN, SOUTH
CAROLINA, she then recounted what had happened on July 29, 1918. "He called on King
George V—met Churchill—spoke—I think—
at a Gray's Inn dinner?—where there was
much oratory—from elder statesmen." Perhaps
engrossed in thoughts of that difficult time
when she had fallen in love with a married man,
Lucy hurriedly concluded: "Let me know if you
do not find it—the diary—Thank you *so* much
for the snapshots—I must run—as they are calling me—With love Lucy."

There is other evidence that her memories of
Roosevelt were sometimes painful; she seems to
have missed him deeply. Anna arranged for
Lucy and a friend to visit Hyde Park on Saturday, June 9, a time when the home and the
grave were not yet open to the public—and a
day that Eleanor spent in New York City. It was
fair, mild, and partly cloudy; Roosevelt had
been lying in the rose garden for not quite

two months. "The memory will be with me always," Lucy later wrote Daisy of that summer Saturday. But the reminders of the president appear to have been rather too much for Lucy, for when Suckley invited her to return to Dutchess County for a holiday at Wilderstein, she declined. "And now about your very great thoughtfulness in asking me to stay—You know how much I should like to—and someday perhaps I may be able to ask you if you will have me," Lucy wrote Daisy from Allamuchy on June 19. "But you—who know all of the facts—will understand that just now I do not feel I should go."

According to Suckley's unpublished account of Lucy and her friend's stop in Hyde Park, there was "much excitement a half hour after they left: The lieutenant in charge of the guard was handed their card of admis[sion] given them in Wash. by Anna. It appears that the cards have to be signed by either Mrs. R. or Mr. Palmer the new superintendent—*and* they have to be given up at the main entrance, where the visitor has to register! Much ado about very little! The ladies had got safely away however!" Though the library was open to the public, the 1235 Military Police Battalion kept watch over the gravesite and the house in those early days after Roosevelt's death. Presumably hearing of the bureaucratic flap later in a letter from Daisy, Lucy wrote:

"It distresses me that you were given so much trouble by my descent upon you. I had been led to believe that I could slide in and out again without being a burden to anyone—but evidently this was not to be—and I am sorry that you were held up all down the line—in your work and by the guards—I loved seeing you however and thank you for making it all as easy as possible—in difficult circumstances for all."

MARY, WHO WENT with Churchill to Potsdam for a meeting of the new Big Three near Berlin in July 1945, was relieved when her father emerged happy from his first conversation with Truman. "He told me he liked the President immensely—they talk the same language," Mary wrote Clementine. "I nearly wept for joy and thankfulness, it seemed like divine providence. Perhaps it is FDR's legacy."

For Averell Harriman, there was evidence at Potsdam that Churchill's fears about Stalin were on the mark. "Marshal," Harriman remarked to Stalin at the conference, "this must be a great satisfaction to you to be in Berlin." Stalin paused before answering. "Czar Alexander," he replied, "got to Paris."

———

IN THE NEW MEXICO desert, the first atomic test was successful. "The atomic bomb is a reality," Henry Stimson told Churchill on July 17. The prime minister and Mary returned to England on July 25 for the general election— the one Churchill had hoped Roosevelt might help him with. The map room was on watch to monitor the returns, and Churchill went to bed thinking he would win. "However, just before dawn I woke suddenly with a sharp stab of almost physical pain," Churchill recalled. "A hitherto subconscious conviction that we were beaten broke forth and dominated my mind. All the pressure of great events, on and against which I had mentally so long maintained my 'flying speed,' would cease and I should fall."

The man who had spent his life hurling himself forward found one of his worst night-mares—the loss of altitude, a crash to earth—coming true. He was turned out of office. "What is there to say—nothing but that there has been a landslide to the left in British politics," Pamela wrote Averell and Kathleen Harriman. "The leader in the Times today summed it up best when they said, 'Gratitude belongs to history & not to politics.' . . . On the personal angle, the P.M. has taken it wonderfully—but it's hard all the same. . . . Poor Clemmie I feel very deeply for her—and I know you both will feel as I do for we all three feel very deeply towards W. don't we."

In August, Japan gave in under the blow of two products of Tube Alloys, weapons Churchill had helped make possible on distant afternoons at Hyde Park. But the voters had made their choice.

Patrick Kinna saw Churchill at No. 10 after the electoral defeat was clear. "Come to the Cabinet Room with me," Churchill said. Then, Kinna recalled, "the Prime Minister started reminiscing about the war, back to the days when he first met Roosevelt and met Stalin." Visibly upset, Churchill said: "And now the British people do not want me anymore."

Eleanor tried to put a good face on things, writing Churchill: "I know that you and Mrs. Churchill both are probably very happy and look forward to a few years of less strenuous life, and yet to those who lay down the burdens of great responsibility, there must come for a while a sense of being rudderless." Her last point was closer to the truth than her first. Churchill could think of little worse than a "less strenuous life."

ROOSEVELT HAD BEEN dead nearly a year when Churchill's motorcade drove up the tree-lined drive to the main house at Hyde Park. It was March 12, 1946. Churchill was in America to speak at a college in Truman's home state—Westminster in Fulton, Missouri—to warn the world about Stalin's expanding sphere. Playing poker on the train to Missouri, Churchill had turned sentimental about his mother's country. "If I were to be born again, there is one country in which I would want to be a citizen. There is one country where a man knows he has an unbounded future." Where? he was asked. "The USA, even though I deplore some of your customs." Which ones? "You stop drinking with your meals."

Now, along the Hudson, Eleanor met Churchill and Clementine, and they walked to the garden. The former prime minister stood, hatless, staring at his friend's grave. Watching Churchill, Eleanor "felt sure that he was thinking of the years when he and my husband had worked in such close cooperation to win the war." Only the clicks of newsmen's cameras capturing the scene broke the silence as Churchill contemplated the white tombstone and the flowers before it. "I think it was a day of great emotion for Mr. Churchill," Eleanor wrote. "Besides the respect he had for my husband as a statesman, which made it possible for them to work together even when they differed, he also had a real affection for him as a human being, just as my husband had for him."

For three minutes Churchill said nothing, his hands in his overcoat pockets. Franklin Roosevelt had been perhaps the most complex human being he had ever known—difficult and demanding and frustrating, but compelling and warm and sparkling. Dark and light, mixed up together.

CHURCHILL LIVED ANOTHER two decades. He became philosophical about his defeat at the polls in 1945. Walter Annenberg, the American publishing magnate and future ambassador to the Court of St. James's, sat next to Churchill at a dinner hosted by Bernard Baruch in the early autumn of 1949. "During the course of our conversation I happened to mention my great disappointment in the British voters in their summary rejection of him so soon after the war, the point being one of ingratitude," Annenberg recalled in a letter to Kay Halle. With a chuckle, Churchill had replied: "Neither look for nor expect gratitude but rather get whatever comfort you can out of the belief that your effort is constructive in purpose."

He returned to Downing Street as prime minister from 1951 to 1955, won the Nobel Prize for Literature, accepted the Order of the Garter, became an honorary citizen of the United States, and in the eyes of much of the world he was considered, as Isaiah Berlin put it, "the largest human being of our time." A letter from America addressed only to "The greatest man in the World, England" was quickly delivered to his house. At seventy-five, Churchill said: "I am prepared to meet my Maker. But whether my Maker is prepared for the great ordeal of meeting me is another matter." He was stoic and charming about his mortality. "I look forward to dying," he once said. "Sleep, endless, wonderful sleep—on a purple, velvety cushion. Every so often I will wake up, turn over, and go to sleep again."

When he died in 1965—on the same date his father had died in 1895, January 24—Churchill was borne through London on the gun carriage that had carried the coffin of Queen Victoria. "He, with Franklin Roosevelt, gave us our finest hour," remarked Adlai Stevenson, the American ambassador and twice the Democratic nominee for president. "He was not afraid of blood or sweat—or anything else, for that matter." In a heavy black veil, walking on Randolph's arm, Clementine followed the coffin in and out of St. Paul's, with Mary and Sarah just behind. Churchill would have loved the voices of the mourners along the route—the people whose supply of beer he had worried about on the day Hitler was defeated. A reporter for *The New York Times* heard a Cockney dismiss the cold winter wind. "Little enough to do for him," the man said. "Think what he did for us. I'm Labor, mind, but we wouldn't have got through if it weren't for the old gentleman. What was I doing? The P.B.I.—Poor Bloody Infantry—France, Africa, Italy, the lot. I tell you, we wouldn't have got through if it hadn't been for him."

In St. Paul's, the congregation sang "The Battle Hymn of the Republic" and, as the coffin was carried from the church, "O God Our Help in Ages Past." Churchill was taken to St. Martin's Churchyard at Bladon, just outside the walls of the park at Blenheim Palace. He was buried next to his parents.

*"My husband had looked forward
to the joy of sharing with Mr. Churchill
the gratitude of the people of England"*

Eleanor Roosevelt visits Winston
Churchill in London, April 1948

THEM'S MY SENTIMENTS EXACTLY

ON THE DAY Churchill celebrated his sixty-ninth birthday at Teheran, Roosevelt dispatched Averell Harriman to find a present before the evening's dinner. Harriman went to see an old friend, Joseph M. Upton, a curator at New York's Metropolitan Museum of Art who was then stationed in the Iranian capital. Upton sold Harriman a twelfth-century Kashan bowl from his personal collection. "Mr. Roosevelt gave me for a birthday present a beautiful Persian porcelain vase," Churchill wrote after the war, "which, although it was broken into fragments on the homeward journey, has been marvelously reconstructed and is one of my treasures."

In his memory, Churchill put many things back together, including his friendship with

Roosevelt, which in Churchill's mind also became one of his treasures. He had done the same with his relationship with his father, and with his mother, and with so many other things in his life. As the years went by, he remembered the high moments with Roosevelt more than he did the low.

Politics was part of the reason. During the war and afterward, Churchill believed Anglo-American unity was essential to maintaining Britain's role in the world. He went out of his way to play down his differences with Roosevelt, preferring to look back on the war as a time of warm Allied camaraderie. In the late 1940s, John Kenneth Galbraith dined with the Churchills at London's Connaught Hotel during an international conference. "He invited three or four of us for a long evening of talk—overwhelmingly by him," Galbraith recalled. "We covered the whole range of problems during the war, with a favorable view taken of all decisions in London and in Washington." As Churchill surveyed the scene, recalling his time with Roosevelt with unnuanced pleasure, Clementine would occasionally reach out to restrain him from drinking too much of the Connaught's good wine.

Churchill's English-speaking union never quite came to official reality, but the Anglo-American alliance has been a bedrock of the global order for decades. However turbulent, however tinged with sentimentality, however much resented by others in the world, in fact the deep connection between the two nations has been a force for democracy and liberty through what Churchill might have called the "storm and strife" of battles against tyrants and terrorists. When an American president and a British prime minister walk through the woods of Camp David or confer on a transatlantic telephone, they are working in the style and in the shadow of Roosevelt and Churchill.

Churchill's personal grace was another reason for his reimagination of reality. "Churchill has never turned his back on a friend, never shown rancour," said Lord Beaverbrook. "From all small things he had a grand immunity," Violet Bonham Carter recalled. "He seemed to have been endowed by fortune with a double charge of life and with a double dose of human nature, for transcending all was his warm and wide humanity." Very late in Churchill's life, Clementine invited James Roosevelt to call on her husband in retirement. "He'd like that, and maybe it'd perk him up a bit," she said. "He's been a bit down." Churchill seemed feeble, but when he saw Roosevelt his face lit up. Holding his guest's hand, he asked him to sit and talk. "From time to time he'd ask me if I remembered someone I'd never met, and he spoke about a message he'd sent me, when he'd never sent me a message in his life," James recalled. "At first I was puzzled. Then I realized he thought I was my father." Seeing his mistake, Churchill was "terribly disappointed and his expression and posture seemed to sag." For a fleeting instant, Winston Churchill and Franklin Roosevelt had been at the pinnacle again, if only in an old man's mind, and the thought had been pleasing. "Churchill's attitude toward Roosevelt was one of profound affection and regard," recalled Anthony Montague Browne, "and it never changed."

ON THE FIRST day of March 1955, Churchill made his final major address in the House of Commons. The topic was the hydrogen bomb and arms control, a remarkable subject for a man who had galloped in the cavalry charge at Omdurman so long before. "What ought we to do?" Churchill asked rhetorically. "Which way shall we turn to save our lives and the future of the world? It does not matter so much to old people; they are going soon anyway; but I find it poignant to look at youth in all its activity and ardour and, most of all, to watch little children playing their merry games, and wonder what would lie before them if God wearied of mankind." But he had endured too much, won too many improbable victories, to give in.

"To conclude: mercifully, there is time and hope if we combine patience and courage . . . ," Churchill continued. "The day may dawn when fair play, love for one's fellow men, respect for justice and freedom, will enable tormented generations to march forth serene and triumphant from the hideous epoch in which we have to dwell. Meanwhile, never flinch, never weary, never despair." No matter how bleak the forecast, courage would carry us forward. For courage, Churchill once said, was the essential virtue because "it guaranteed all the others."

His friend, long dead, had been working on a Jefferson Day speech on the porch at Warm Springs the day before the end, a decade before. "Today, science has brought all the different quarters of the globe so close together that it is impossible to isolate them one from another," Franklin Roosevelt wrote. "Today we are faced with the pre-eminent fact that, if civilization is to survive, we must cultivate the science of human relationships—the ability of all peoples, of all kinds, to live together and work together in the same world, at peace." And finally, this: "The only limit to our realization of tomorrow will be our doubts of today. Let us move forward with strong and active faith."

It was Franklin Roosevelt's last testament. Winston Churchill had the better of the contest. The Englishman's cadences trumped the

American's. But in the end, their hearts were together.

LIKE MOST FRIENDS, Churchill and Roosevelt were sometimes affectionate, sometimes cross, alternately ready to die for or murder the other. But each helped make what the other did possible. Churchill's unflinching countenance in the chaos of 1940 gave the British the strength to endure in the face of the seemingly unendurable. The conviction that someday, somehow, Roosevelt would come to his side was the engine of Churchill's heroic resistance.

Roosevelt's reluctance to fully enter the war before December 1941 was not about opposing totalitarianism—which he did—but about leading an unready and divided nation into combat. Perhaps the only thing worse than America's aloofness from September 1, 1939, to December 11, 1941, would have been a president who pushed an ill-equipped country into political and military battles that, if lost—and they may well have been—might have sent the United States back behind its own walls for good. But for the American president's caution in those early years, we could be living in the grim shadow of an isolationist Age of Lindbergh, not in the light of the Age of Roosevelt.

Roosevelt saw that what happened far from our shores—in Europe, in distant Asia, in caves and camps—mattered. The world was connected, one nation and one people to another, and he understood that we could not—cannot—escape history, no matter how much we might like to. "Wishful thinking," Eleanor Roosevelt once said, "is one of our besetting sins."

In the spring of 1963, Randolph Churchill came to Washington to accept his father's honorary American citizenship from President Kennedy in the Rose Garden. Over late-night drinks at Kay Halle's Georgetown house, Arthur Schlesinger Jr. asked Randolph about Roosevelt. Randolph told Schlesinger that he had found Roosevelt "rather a 'feminine' figure with visible prima-donna traits of jealousy"—the analysis of a loyal son. Yet, being his father's son (a phrase young Winston used as the title of his biography of Randolph), Randolph generously added: "But his voice—a great voice—instinct with courage. Even more so than my father's." A graceful point.

IN THE MIDDLE of the war, Harry Hopkins noticed a "Notes and Comment" piece of E. B. White's in *The New Yorker* and passed it on to Roosevelt. White had received a letter from the

Writers' War Board asking for a statement on "The Meaning of Democracy." The request got White thinking.

"Surely the Board knows what democracy is," he wrote in the magazine. "It is the line that forms on the right. It is the don't in don't shove. It is the hole in the stuffed shirt through which the sawdust slowly trickles; it is the dent in the high hat. Democracy is the recurrent suspicion that more than half the people are right more than half of the time. It is the feeling of privacy in the voting booths, the feeling of communion in the libraries, the feeling of vitality everywhere. Democracy is a letter to the editor. Democracy is the score at the beginning of the ninth. It is an idea which hasn't been disproved yet, a song the words of which have not gone bad. It's the mustard on the hot dog and the cream in the rationed coffee."

"I *love* it!" Roosevelt said when he read the piece, which he would later quote, adding happily: "Them's my sentiments exactly."

They were Churchill's, too, though he would have phrased the point in a more ornate way. The Americans and the British, he said at Fulton in 1946, "must never cease to proclaim in fearless tones the great principles of freedom and the rights of man which are the joint inheritance of the English-speaking world and which through Magna Carta, the Bill of Rights, the Habeas Corpus, trial by jury, and the English common law find their most famous expression in the American Declaration of Independence." These were the pillars of free societies. "Here are the title deeds of freedom which should lie in every cottage home," Churchill said. "Here is the message of the British and American peoples to mankind. Let us preach what we practise—let us practise what we preach."

ELEANOR ROOSEVELT RETURNED to London in the spring of 1948 for the unveiling of a statue of her husband in Grosvenor Square. No longer prime minister but still in Parliament, Churchill was there, and during the ceremony Eleanor's thoughts returned to the war. "My husband had looked forward to the joy of sharing with Mr. Churchill the gratitude of the people of England," she recalled. Her musings turned bittersweet. "But just as Moses was shown the promised land and could not enter, I imagine there are many men who see their hopes and plans developing but who are never actually allowed to have on this earth the recognition they might well have enjoyed. One can only hope that, if they have labored with the love of God in their hearts, they will have a more perfect satisfaction than we can ever experience here."

THERE ARE MEMORIALS to Roosevelt and Churchill just inside the West Door of Westminster Abbey. The first, a gray tablet that hangs far below a window depicting Abraham, Isaac, Jacob, and the twelve tribes of Israel, reads: TO THE HONORED MEMORY OF FRANKLIN DELANO ROOSEVELT, A FAITHFUL FRIEND OF FREEDOM AND OF BRITAIN. Nearby, a large, dark green marble slab lies on the floor of the great nave, its inscription simple but profound: REMEMBER WINSTON CHURCHILL. On sunny days in London, light slips in the gloom of the ancient church, both through the stained glass and from the open doors—light from a world Roosevelt and Churchill together delivered from evil.

Their Days and Nights: A Summary of the Roosevelt-Churchill Meetings, 1941–1945

1941

Placentia Bay, Newfoundland: Code Name RIVERIA

Saturday, August 9–Tuesday, August 12: Aboard the USS *Augusta* and HMS *Prince of Wales*

Roosevelt agrees to extend escorts to protect shipping in the Atlantic to Iceland, an important step in the Battle of the Atlantic against German U-boats; a message to Japan warning against continued aggression in the Pacific is considered (but ultimately much weakened); a mission is planned to the Soviet Union to determine Lend-Lease needs for Stalin; the Atlantic Charter, a declaration of war and peace aims, is debated, drafted, and issued.

Washington, D.C.: Code Name ARCADIA

Monday, December 22–Sunday, December 28, 1941: The White House

Monday, December 29, 1941–Wednesday, December 31, 1941: Churchill visits Ottawa, Canada

1942

Thursday, January 1, 1942–Monday, January 5: The White House

Tuesday, January 6–Saturday, January 10: Churchill visits Pompano, Florida

Sunday, January 11–Wednesday, January 14: The White House

The strategic principle of Germany First is affirmed; the Combined Chiefs of Staff Committee is formed and based in Washington; the American-British-Dutch-Australia Command is briefly constituted to cover the Southwest Pacific; a Combined Raw Materials Board to direct munitions production is established, as is an Anglo-American Shipping Adjustment Board to coordinate needs at sea; Roosevelt and Churchill move to alleviate Singapore's military plight as the Japanese close in; Roosevelt sends troops to Ireland and Iceland; American production goals are set; the Declaration of the United Nations is signed; debate begins over Mediterranean vs. Western European operations.

Washington, D.C.: Code Name ARGONAUT (1942)

Friday, June 19–Saturday, June 20: Hyde Park, New York

Sunday, June 21–Thursday, June 24: The White House

Thursday, June 24: Churchill visits Fort Jackson, South Carolina, for the day

Thursday, June 24–Friday, June 25: The White House

Roosevelt agrees to supply the British with an emergency shipment of Sherman tanks and other weapons after the fall of Tobruk in North Africa; Churchill argues against American plans for a 1942 cross-Channel operation, instead pushing for landings in North Africa or Norway; Roosevelt and Churchill agree to work together on the secret project to produce an atomic weapon.

1943

Casablanca, Morocco: Code Name SYMBOL

Thursday, January 14–Sunday, January 24: Anfa, Casablanca

Sunday, January 24–Monday, January 25: Marrakech

The Allied doctrine of "unconditional surrender" is proclaimed; Roosevelt agrees to Churchill's plan for further operations in the Mediterranean, including an invasion of Sicily, essentially ruling out a cross-Channel attack in 1943; the Allies debate the allocation of resources between the Pacific and the Mediterranean; Churchill and Roosevelt consent to pursue the strategic bombing of Germany in the Combined Bomber Offensive, code-named POINT-BLANK, which would prove essential for the success of OVERLORD in early 1944; Roosevelt and Churchill struggle to bring differing French factions together, a step toward the French National Committee for Liberation, which ultimately (and after much controversy) provided a provisional government for liberated France in 1944.

Washington, D.C.: Code Name TRIDENT

Tuesday, May 11–Friday, May 14: The White House

Friday, May 14–Monday, May 17: Shangri-la

Monday, May 17–Tuesday, May 26: The White House

Churchill argues for pushing Italy out of the war "by whatever means might be the best"; Roosevelt and Churchill receive word of triumph in Tunisia, which gives the Allies control of North Africa; Churchill addresses Congress a second time; the British begin behind-the-lines operations in Yugoslavia to increase pressure on the Axis; the prime minister consents to setting a target of May 1944 for the cross-Channel operation; Churchill and Roosevelt resolve tensions over sharing information over the making of the atomic bomb, and it becomes a truly joint project; the Allies approach Portugal for air and sea rights in the Azores.

Quebec, Canada: Code Name QUADRANT

Thursday, August 12–Saturday, August 14: Hyde Park, New York

Tuesday, August 17–Tuesday, August 24: The Citadel, Quebec

Wednesday, September 1–Monday, September 6: The White House

Monday, September 6: Churchill visits Cambridge, Massachusetts, to receive an honorary degree at Harvard University

Tuesday, September 7–Friday, September 10: The White House

Saturday, September 11–Sunday, September 12: Hyde Park, New York

Plans go forward for OVERLORD, *still slated for May 1944; Roosevelt and Churchill agree that an American officer, not a British one, should lead the invasion; the South-East Asia Command is formed under Lord Mountbatten; Churchill and Roosevelt deal with details arising from the collapse of Italy; they affirm Anglo-American cooperation on the atomic bomb; they again invite Stalin to meet with them, this time in the autumn.*

Cairo and Teheran: Code Names SEXTANT and EUREKA

Tuesday, November 23–Saturday, November 27: Cairo

Sunday, November 28–Wednesday, December 1: Teheran

Thursday, December 2–Tuesday, December 7: Cairo

At Cairo, Roosevelt, Churchill, and Chiang Kai-shek plan Pacific strategy, particularly concerning BUCCANEER, *amphibious landings against Japanese-held islands in the Bay of Bengal (Roosevelt, who was always trying to build China into a great power, would ultimately have to tell Chiang* BUCCANEER *could not happen—*OVERLORD *and its supporting European operations would foreclose any other options); at Teheran, under pressure from Roosevelt and Stalin, Churchill agrees to a cross-Channel invasion in May 1944; Stalin signals that he will join the fight against Japan once Germany is defeated; Stalin also suggested the Soviets would participate in a postwar world* *organization; there are discussions about the fate of postwar Germany; back in Cairo, the Allies try to talk the long-neutral Turkey into the war; and Roosevelt tells Churchill that Eisenhower, not Marshall, would be* OVERLORD*'s supreme commander.*

1944

Quebec, Canada: Code Name OCTAGON

Monday, September 11–Saturday, September 16: The Citadel, Quebec

Sunday, September 17–Tuesday, September 19: Hyde Park, New York

America consents to extend Lend-Lease and indicates that Britain will receive postwar economic aid; Roosevelt agrees to use British sea power in the Pacific; the Morgenthau Plan to pastoralize postwar Germany is signed (but later killed); there is discussion of occupation zones in a conquered Germany; Roosevelt and Churchill agree to keep the atomic project secret and to continue "full collaboration" on what the British call "Tube Alloys" and the Americans the "Manhattan Project"; they also handle details about postsurrender Italy, including economic assistance as the nation is rebuilt.

1945

Malta-Yalta: Code Name ARGONAUT

Friday, February 2–Saturday, February 3: Malta and Saki

Sunday, February 4–Sunday, February 11: Yalta

Thursday, February 15: USS *Quincy*, Great Bitter Lake, Alexandria, Egypt

Plans for the Allied treatment of Germany after the war are set, giving each power an occupation zone, including a possible one for France; the Soviets affirm their intention to join in the final stages of the war against Japan in exchange for territorial concessions in the Far East; in a debate over the future of Poland, the nation's borders are shifted west and postwar government arrangements appear to favor Stalin, who wants the nation to be a satellite of the Soviet Union, not a truly independent state; Stalin agrees to participate in the new United Nations organization partly in exchange for Roosevelt's conceding extra votes in the General Assembly for several Russian republics.

Sources: The dates and summaries of key events have been closely drawn from *FDR: Day by Day—The Pare Lorentz Chronology*, FDRL; Dear, ed., *The Oxford Companion to World War II*; Gilbert, *Road to Victory* and *Never Despair*; Kimball, *Forged in War*; Kimball, ed., *Churchill and Roosevelt: The Complete Correspondence; Foreign Relations of the United States*; Churchill, *The Second World War*, vols. III–VI; Polmar and Allen, *World War II: America at War, 1941–1945*, and *World War II: An Encyclopedia of the War Years, 1941–1945*.

AUTHOR'S NOTE AND ACKNOWLEDGMENTS

Composing a tribute to her friend Winston Churchill on his eightieth birthday in 1954, Violet Bonham Carter noted that "though he may be the best Great Man to know, he is the most difficult man to write about—because he has written better of himself than anyone can ever write about him." In reconstructing the Roosevelt-Churchill relationship, I have relied both on Churchill's own brilliant written legacy and on the work of many people.

This book is not intended to be read as a scholarly work. Some readers will wonder how I could fail to address this issue or that controversy. I believe, however, that my rendering of the tale, which draws on new archival research in the United States and in Britain, original interviews, and oral histories, casts fresh light on an old friendship and its relevance in a new century at a time when Americans are rediscovering the importance of war leadership and the art of alliance.

I was fortunate to be able to draw on several previously unavailable or largely untapped sources along the way. Among them: Several unpublished letters of Lucy Mercer Rutherfurd, including one to President Roosevelt in 1941, which reveal more detail about her place in Roosevelt's affections and her role in his larger circle than I believe has been previously known. The 1941 letter is riveting (see Chapter 8), and from her correspondence with Margaret "Daisy" Suckley after FDR's death, I discovered that she remembered Roosevelt's 1918 meeting with Churchill (the evening at Gray's Inn that the prime minister failed to recall), even though the summer concluded with the searing event of Eleanor's learning of the Lucy-FDR affair. From Mrs. Rutherfurd's letters I was also able to confirm that she came to Hyde Park after the president's burial and could therefore tell the story of that quiet, poignant episode. The late prime minister's grandson Winston S. Churchill kindly granted me access to the World War II papers of his mother, Pamela Churchill Harriman, who as Mrs. Randolph Churchill was close to Clementine and Winston Churchill during the war. The papers of *Washington Post* owner Eugene Meyer and of his wife, Agnes, offer insights both on the prewar view of Churchill in America and on how the British attempted to influence American opinion makers in Roosevelt's Washington. The diary of *Sunday Dispatch* editor Charles Eade, who also edited volumes of Churchill's speeches, gives us a window on Churchill's thoughts and state of mind at several points from his return to the Admiralty in 1939 through the war years. The biographer Geoffrey Ward's edition of Suckley's diaries, *Closest Companion,* was essential, as was the Wilderstein Collection, where I found several letters of Lucy Rutherfurd's. A distant Roosevelt cousin, Suckley kept Roosevelt's letters to her, and her wartime diaries give us fuller detail about Roosevelt and Churchill up close than we have had before. I also interviewed many of those people still alive who spent time in the men's joint company—conversations that shed light on the social interplay between the two leaders.

The literature on Churchill and Roosevelt is vast, and this book bears the cumulative mark of what has come before. The notes and bibliography list the sources I consulted in whole or in part; a few merit special mention here. Sir Martin Gilbert's landmark Churchill biography—his six narrative volumes and his eleven books of documents on Churchill's life and work—is a treasure, as is his memoir, *In Search of Churchill: A Historian's Journey.* John Kenneth Galbraith once called Gilbert's Churchill document volumes "the best kept secret in publishing history"; Sir Martin's books are essential reading, and he also gave me wise and generous counsel on many points. Readers and scholars who contemplate Churchill and Roosevelt together owe a great debt to Warren F. Kimball, Robert Treat Professor of History at Rutgers University, who edited the Churchill-Roosevelt correspondence and has written numerous insightful books and essays about their alliance. Professor Kimball was gracious to me in discussing the subject and in reading and commenting on a draft of this book.

Michael Beschloss's *Kennedy and Roosevelt* is an excellent dual biography, and his book on Roosevelt, Churchill, and Truman, *The Conquerors,* tells an important story with grace and skill. Arthur Schlesinger Jr.'s three-volume *The Age of Roosevelt* is a masterful portrait of Roosevelt's New Deal White House. James MacGregor Burns's two-volume Roosevelt biography remains a wonder: deep, far-reaching, and knowing. Geoffrey Ward's two books on Roosevelt, *Before the Trumpet* and *A First-Class Temperament,* are powerful and a joy to read; and his edition of the Suckley diaries, *Closest Companion,* is indispensable to those interested in Roosevelt during the pivotal years of the war. Joseph P. Lash's *Eleanor and Franklin* is invaluable, as are so many of his books. I learned much from his *Roosevelt and Churchill, 1939–1941: The Partnership That Saved the West,* and I treasured my interviews with his widow, Trude. And like so many readers, I cherish the sparkling volumes of William Manchester's *The Last Lion.*

I owe many thanks to all the people who took the time to be interviewed for this book. For me, these conversations were at once illuminating and fun. My largest debt is to Mary Soames, a loving but not uncritical student of her parents' lives and times. An accomplished biographer, she answered numerous questions over the past three years with candor and grace. I showed her a draft of this book in order to guard against my making any factual errors, and she kindly read the manuscript with care, writing me a thoughtful letter about several of the issues raised in the book and allowing me to reprint a touching photograph of her parents from her personal collection. Though Lady Soames does not agree with all of my conclusions, she has been unfailingly kind to me, and I am grateful. Winston S. Churchill—author, former member of Parliament, and grandson of the late prime minister—was gracious, talking with me about his grandfather and his family and replying to inquiries with great courtesy. As noted above, he also granted me access to—and permission to quote from—his mother's World War II papers, even taking the trouble to help me fix an elusive date on one of the letters. I am thankful for his help and his hospitality.

The presidential historian Michael Beschloss has been a faithful adviser and reader from the beginning. Scrupulous, selfless, and wise, Michael helped me think through difficult issues and read the manuscript with care and concern. I am indebted to his scholarship and grateful for his friendship.

Several other distinguished historians and writers went out of their way to read drafts and set me right where I was wrong: John Morton Blum, Richard Breitman, Harold Evans, David Reynolds, Arthur Schlesinger Jr., Richard Somerset-Ward, William vanden Heuvel, and Geoffrey Ward. Professor Schlesinger was particularly kind in advising me over several years. Richard Holbrooke kindly offered the perspective of a historian who has been in the arena. Henry Kissinger, diplomat, strategist, and historian, shed light on the connection between the personal and the political for me. Verne Newton, a former director of the Franklin D. Roosevelt Library, directed me to a trove of videotaped interviews he conducted for a Harry Hopkins documentary and took the trouble to read and comment on my manuscript. Charles Peters, the founder of *The Washington Monthly,* brought me to Washington, nurtured my interest in Roosevelt, and read the manuscript with his characteristic vigor and wit. Jonathan Alter, Tom Brokaw, Tina Brown, Blanche Weisen Cook, Robert Cowley, Alex Danchev, Ellen Feldman, John Hyde, Walter Isaacson, Daniel Klaidman, William Manchester, Williamson Murray, Peter Osnos, Sally Bedell Smith, Russell F. Weigley, Fareed Zakaria, and the late Roy Jenkins were kind enough to share insights with me about different aspects of the project.

I must add that in the end any mistakes are my own and that the wonderful people who helped me along the way bear no responsibility for anything I may have gotten wrong or for interpretations with which they disagree.

The indefatigable Mike Hill did heroic research for this book. Unflappable, enthusiastic, and kind, Mike is one of the world's great souls, and I will always be grateful for the energy and intelligence he brought to discovering new archival ground. A warm word of thanks to Jack Bales, master of bibliographical detail. Dan Blumenthal and Charles Wilson were tireless fact checkers and a great help in the closing phase of the project, as was David Olivenbaum.

Many terrific people in libraries and archives on both sides of the Atlantic were helpful. At the Franklin D. Roosevelt Library at Hyde Park, Bob Clark was resourceful, thoughtful, and cheerful. Thanks as well to Raymond Teichman, Alycia Vivona, and Mark Renovitch. Dr. John Haynes and Jeffrey Flannery of the Library of Congress in Washington provided invaluable guidance. The entire staff of the Churchill Archives, Churchill College, Cambridge, was unfailingly helpful; a special word of gratitude to Rachel Lloyd and Jude Brimmer. Thanks to Ms. K. V. Bligh of the House of Lords Record Office, House of Lords, London, and to Brian Sullivan of the Harvard Archives. Duane and Linda Watson of Wilderstein, the home of Daisy Suckley, were generous and thoughtful. I am grateful to Evelyn Small, who led me to the Meyer Papers and helped in several other ways. Thanks, too, to Bryson Clevinger Jr., Roy Strohl of Mary Washington College Library, Louisa Thomas, and Ken Moody.

I am grateful to Winston S. Churchill for permission to quote from works within his copyright; to Kathleen Harriman Mortimer for permission to quote from her wartime letters found in the Pamela Harriman Papers; to Matthew Walton for permission to quote from a letter of his father's; to Nancy Roosevelt Ireland, literary executor for Anna Eleanor Roosevelt's estate, for permission to quote from the writings of the late First Lady; to Her Majesty's Stationery Office for permission to quote from wartime documents under Crown copyright; to the Clerk of the Records of the House of Lords Record Office, acting on behalf of the Beaverbrook Foundation Trust, for permission to quote from the Lord Beaverbrook Papers; to the Oral History Collection of Columbia University for permission to quote from the Reminiscences of Sir Norman Angell, Chester Bowles, Marquis Childs, Anna Roosevelt Halsted, W. Averell Harriman, Alan Kirk, Walter Lippmann, Frances Perkins, and Henry A. Wallace; to Christine Eade for permission to quote from her father's papers; to Duane Watson for permission to quote from the Suckley diary and letters, which are part of the Wilderstein Collection at Rhinebeck, New York; and to the Rutherfurd family for permission to quote from the letters of Lucy Mercer Rutherfurd.

One of the most delightful things about this project was seeing the places where Roosevelt and Churchill lived and worked. Many thanks to those who went out of their way to help me, including Anne Jordan and Tara McGill of the National Park Service, who made it possible for me to inspect several rooms at Hyde Park that are ordinarily closed to the public; to Phil Reed of the Cabinet War Rooms, who personally showed me that London warren; to Lady Soames for arranging a before-hours tour of Chartwell in Kent; and to Major General David Jenkins, undertreasurer of the Honourable Society of

Gray's Inn, who allowed me to tour the hall where Roosevelt and Churchill first met.

Lally Weymouth generously helped in her own matchless way, often asking me to move from 1945 into the present. Sofia and Herbert Wentz were unfailing sources of intelligence and good sense, slogging through a particularly long draft early on. For counsel and kindnesses large and small I am also grateful to Richard Abate, Kenneth Auchincloss, Louis Auchincloss, Deborah Baker, Sylvia Baldwin, Robert Batscha, Joe Bingham, Douglas Brinkley, Ginanne Brownell, Douglas Brown, Peter Canby, Geoff Chester, Robert Coles, Catherine and Grant Collins, Michael Elliott, Howard Fineman, John Ghazvinian, Doris Kearns Goodwin, Ralph Gradilone, David Halberstam, Robert Harling, Dorothy Kalins, Addison Klein, Richard Langworth, Nicholas Lapham, Stryker McGuire, Pamela Macfie, Ted Marmor, Kati Marton, Alice Mayhew, Anthea Morton-Saner, Andrew Nagorski, Holly Peterson, Julia Reed, Dale Richardson, Douglas Robbe, Roger Sherman, Lynn Staley, Sarah Stapleton, Julie Tate, William Underhill, Franceska Macsali Urbin, Manny Vella, Dr. Steve Waddell of West Point, and the staff of the *Newsweek* research center. Barbara DiVittorio and Deborah Millan were cheerful mainstays, as was Becca Pratt, who straightened out more than a few of my self-created computer tangles.

At Random House, I am grateful to Jonathan Jao, Dennis Ambrose, and Sona Vogel for their patience and wonderful work.

My editor, Jonathan Karp, was astute, witty, and perceptive. He is an extraordinary man. Thanks, too, to Ann Godoff, who said yes to this idea. Amanda Urban is, of course, one of a kind: generous, candid, and fun. She is a formidable ally in life's wars.

At *Newsweek,* I am, as always, grateful to Rick Smith and Mark Whitaker for their kindness, generosity, and friendship. They endured several years of increasingly obscure Roosevelt-Churchill anecdotes with good cheer. They are terrific bosses, and I am lucky to have the chance to work for them, and for Donald Graham, who was enthusiastic about the project.

For almost a decade, Evan Thomas and Ann McDaniel have put up with more of my mumbling than I suspect they would like to recall, but I cannot imagine life without being able to mutter in their charming and reassuring company. Evan and Ann read various drafts with discernment, giving unselfishly of their time and gifts. As great as they are at the craft of editing, however, they are even better at the art of friendship.

My wife, Keith, makes all things possible; I owe her the most, and I always will. Our son was born in the middle of this project, and I knew it was time to wrap things up when he began trying to gnaw on a copy of the third volume of *The Churchill War Papers.* This book is dedicated to his mother, but both his parents know that everything is now really for Sam.

Abbreviations Used

C & R   Churchill & Roosevelt: The Complete Correspondence, edited with commentary by Warren F. Kimball

Volume I. *Alliance Emerging, October 1933–November 1942*

Volume II. *Alliance Forged, November 1942–February 1944*

Volume III. *Alliance Declining, February 1944–April 1945*

CC   Geoffrey C. Ward, ed., *Closest Companion: The Unknown Story of the Intimate Friendship Between Franklin Roosevelt and Margaret Suckley*

CCTBOM   Mary Soames, *Clementine Churchill: The Biography of a Marriage*

CEP   The Charles Eade Papers

COH   Oral History Collection of Columbia University

CWP *The Churchill War Papers,* compiled by Martin Gilbert

Volume I. *At the Admiralty, September 1939–May 1940*

Volume II. *Never Surrender, May 1940–December 1940*

Volume III. *The Ever-Widening War, 1941*

EROH Eleanor Roosevelt Oral History, Graff Collection, FDRL

FDRL Franklin Delano Roosevelt Library

FRUS Foreign Relations of the United States

LBP Lord Beaverbrook Papers

MEL Winston S. Churchill, *My Early Life*

MP The Agnes and Eugene Meyer Papers

PHP The Pamela Harriman Papers

RAH Robert E. Sherwood, *Roosevelt and Hopkins: An Intimate History*

TFOP John Colville, *The Fringes of Power: 10 Downing Street Diaries, 1939–1955*

TIR Eleanor Roosevelt, *This I Remember*

TSFS The Struggle for Survival: The Diaries of Lord Moran

WAC Mary Soames, ed., *Winston and Clementine: The Personal Letters of the Churchills*

WSC   Winston S. Churchill

Volume I. *Youth, 1874–1900,* by Randolph S. Churchill

Volume I. Companion (in two parts)

Volume II. *Young Statesman, 1901–1914,* by Randolph S. Churchill

Volume II. Companion (in three parts)

Volume III. *The Challenge of War, 1914–1916,* by Martin Gilbert

Volume III. Companion (in two parts)

Volume IV. *The Stricken World, 1916–1922,* by Martin Gilbert

Volume IV. Companion (in three parts)

Volume V. *The Prophet of Truth: 1922–1939,* by Martin Gilbert

Volume V. Companion (in three parts)

Volume VI. *Finest Hour, 1939–1941,* by Martin Gilbert

Volume VII. *Road to Victory, 1941–1945,* by Martin Gilbert

Volume VIII. *"Never Despair," 1945–1965,* by Martin Gilbert

INTRODUCTION: A FORTUNATE FRIENDSHIP

ix Epigraph "The future is unknowable" Winston S. Churchill, *A History of the English-Speaking Peoples,* IV, 387.

xv The light was fading The sun set in Yalta by 4:56 P.M. that day. (U.S. Naval Observatory Astronomical Applications Department, "Sun and Moon Data for One Day" for February 4, 1945, Yalta, Crimea.) The first plenary session began at 5 P.M. (*FRUS, Conferences at Malta and Yalta,* 573.)

xv the Grand Ballroom Charles E. Bohlen, *Witness to History, 1929–1969* (New York, 1973), 180.

xv "He is very thin & his face is drawn" Air Chief Marshal Charles Portal to Pamela Churchill, January/February 1945, PHP.

xvi suffering from congestive heart failure *Clinical Notes on the Illness and Death of President Franklin D. Roosevelt,* Howard G. Bruenn, M.D., FDRL.

xvi "Our friendship" *C & R,* III, 574.

xvi "He's really absolutely sweet" Kathleen Harriman to Pamela Churchill, January 20–February 4, 1945, PHP. Kathleen Harriman would become Kathleen Harriman Mortimer. Her father, Averell Harriman, conducted a love affair with Pamela Churchill, then married to the prime minister's son, Randolph, and the mother of Churchill's eldest grandchild, Winston S. Churchill. Pamela and Averell Harriman would marry in 1971.

xvi "I am sure" Portal to Pamela Churchill, PHP.

xvii "I remember the part" *C & R,* III, 574.

xvii "My thoughts are always with you" Ibid.

xvii To meet Roosevelt the president Kay Halle Papers, Box 10.

xvii "forged" *WSC,* VII, 1292.

xvii Between September 11, 1939, and April 11, 1945 *C & R,* I, 3.

xviii one hundred and thirteen days Churchill put the figure at 120 days in his tribute to Roosevelt after Roosevelt's death. For the eulogy, see Winston S. Churchill, ed., *The Great Republic: A History of America by Sir Winston Churchill* (New York, 1999), 365. See appendix for my accounting of their time together, which fixes the number at one hundred and thirteen.

xviii the only picture Churchill produced Author interview with the Lady Soames, DBE (Mary Churchill).

xviii The spring that Roosevelt died Frances Perkins, *The Roosevelt I Knew* (New York, 1946), 396.

xviii "In love, there is always" Author interview with Lady Soames.

xviii Their friendship mirrored To be sure, national interests were an essential force in their dealings with each other, but by and large I believe my characterization accurately captures their discernible personal dynamics.

xix more than a few about the two of them together See, for example, Warren F. Kimball, *Forged in War: Roosevelt, Churchill, and the Second World War* (New

York, 1997);Joseph P. Lash, *Roosevelt and Churchill, 1939–1941: The Partnership That Saved the West* (New York, 1976); Keith Alldritt, *The Greatest of Friends: Franklin D. Roosevelt and Winston Churchill, 1941–1945* (London, 1995); Keith Sainsbury, *Churchill and Roosevelt at War: The War They Fought and the Peace They Hoped to Make* (New York, 1994); David Stafford, *Roosevelt and Churchill: Men of Secrets* (London, 1999). The relationship is also a running subtheme in many other biographies. See James MacGregor Burns, *Franklin D. Roosevelt: The Soldier of Freedom, 1940–1945* (New York, 1970); Doris Kearns Goodwin, *No Ordinary Time: Franklin and Eleanor Roosevelt: The Home Front in World War II* (New York, 1994); Roy Jenkins, *Churchill: A Biography* (New York, 2001); Robert E. Sherwood, *Roosevelt and Hopkins: An Intimate History* (New York, 1948).

xix Told of a new effort to write about his life and work Virginia Cowles, *Winston Churchill: The Era and the Man* (New York, 1953). In the foreword to her biography, Cowles tells the story of her informing Churchill about her impending book at the French embassy in London in 1950— and recalled that Churchill "growled good-naturedly" as he reflected on the well-chronicled nature of his own life.

xx more than fifty-five million people Richard Holmes, ed., *The Oxford Companion to Military History* (Oxford, 2001), 1004.

xx there was talk of exploring a settlement *WSC,*

VI, 411–413; 417–421. Also see, for instance, John Lukacs, *Five Days in London: May 1940* (New Haven, 1999), and Andrew Roberts, *"The Holy Fox": The Life of Lord Halifax*(London, 1991), for detailed discussions of these fascinating days.

xx And so, on July 16, 1940 William L. Shirer, *The Rise and Fall of the Third Reich: A History of Nazi Germany* (New York, 1960), 753.

xxi was in Berlin when Britain's reply Ibid., 755.

xxii Some historians have argued David K. Adams called the relationship "a marriage of convenience" (see "Churchill and Franklin D. Roosevelt: A Marriage of Convenience," in *FDR and His Contemporaries: Foreign Perceptions of an American President* [New York, 1992], eds. Cornelis A. van Minnen and John F. Sears). Warren Kimball wrote of his own "nagging suspicion that, had it been Neville Chamberlain and Wendell Willkie— a plausible prospect—wartime relations between the two nations would not have been fundamentally different. Churchill and Roosevelt did their job well, even magnificently at times, and they are great fun to study. . . . But the basic relationship was that of Britain and the United States, allied in war in large part because of intersected histories, the forces of geography and economics, and a broad range of shared values. Those shared values found expression in the Churchill-Roosevelt relationship, with its massive correspondence, its personal touches, its role in smoothing over the rough edges. But it would have found expression, albeit in a different way, in a Willkie-Chamberlain, or Halifax-Hull relationship. There would have been differences, particularly in the arena of post-war planning and relations with the Soviet Union, but Hitler's Germany and Japan would have been defeated, the Red Army would have liberated eastern and central Europe, the atomic bomb would have obliterated part of Japan, and the United States would have assembled its system of monetary, military, mercantile, and moral leadership in the post-war world. Moreover, forces outside the grasp of Roosevelt and Churchill—forces of nationalism, revolution, change, and resistance to change—would have acted as much as they did to shape that post-war world." (See Warren Kimball, "Wheel Within a Wheel: Churchill, Roosevelt, and the Special Relationship," in *Churchill* [New York, 1993], eds. Robert Blake and William Roger Louis, 306–307.)

xxiii "A man in high public office" *TIR*, 349.

xxiii "It would, however, be wrong" John Colville in *Action This Day: Working with Churchill*, ed. Sir John Wheeler-Bennett (London, 1968), 60. Colville pointed out that Churchill's affection for Truman and Eisenhower was also "entirely sincere."

xxiii "My father's friendship and love" Author interview with Lady Soames.

xxiv "He was the coldest man" Robert H. Ferrell, *The Dying President: Franklin D. Roosevelt, 1944–1945* (Columbia, Mo., 1998), 168.

xxiv "Mrs. R. used to say"   Author interview with Trude Lash.

xxv calling himself the "President's lieutenant"   Sir Ian Jacob in *Action This Day,* ed. Wheeler-Bennett, 207.

xxv "It's up to the Boss"   Frances Perkins, COH, 644.

xxv "You must remember"   Author interview with Trude Lash.

xxv thought Churchill too conservative   *TIR,* 253.

xxv "I shall never cease"   Ibid., 255.

xxv Churchill, fresh from his bath   Author interview with Patrick Kinna.

xxvi "You see, Mr. President"   Ibid. This story is among the most famous in the Roosevelt-Churchill canon. My telling is drawn from my interview with Kinna.

xxvi "Chuckling like a small boy"   Grace Tully, *FDR: My Boss* (New York, 1949), 305.

xxvi "It is fun to be"   *C & R,* I, 337.

xxvi "The friendship and affection"   *TIR,* 251.

xxvi a handwritten letter to Roosevelt   Clementine Churchill to FDR, September 16, 1943, FDR Papers, microfilm edition, Diplomatic Correspondence, Part 2, Reel 15.

xxvi Robert E. Sherwood, the playwright   *RAH,* 363.

xxvii Quoting Ralph Waldo Emerson in an essay   C. S. Lewis, *The Four Loves* (New York, 1960), 97.

xxvii "each appeared to the other"   Isaiah Berlin,

Mr. Churchill in 1940 (Boston, 1964), 37–38. Originally a review of Churchill's war memoirs in the *Atlantic Monthly,* Berlin's essay is an excellent examination of the Churchill-Roosevelt connection, and I am indebted to his analysis of both men and their relationship.

xxviii They were men before they were monuments I am grateful to the distinguished Martin Luther King Jr. biographer Taylor Branch for this general point, which arose out of a conversation we once had about why it is important to recall the faults of heroic figures and put those failings in context in order to remind future generations that those who did great things were not perfect—which holds open the possibility of greatness for the most flawed among us.

xxviii "To do justice to a great man" Sir Charles Webster, "The Chronicler," in *Winston Spencer Churchill: Servant of Crown and Commonwealth,* ed. Sir James Marchant (London, 1954), 116. The quotation is from the second volume of Churchill's *The River War* (London, 1899), 375.

xxix "a fortunate friendship" *TIR,* 255. In his thoughtful book *Churchill and Roosevelt at War,* Keith Sainsbury also quotes this observation of Mrs. Roosevelt's, and, in an interesting elaboration, writes: "But perhaps in the end the old adage 'there is no friendship at the top,' must be held to apply to the Roosevelt-Churchill partnership: or maybe the truth lies somewhere between this bleak judgment and Mrs Roosevelt's 'it was a fortunate friendship.' " I believe that if the truth does lie in between, it lies much closer to Mrs. Roosevelt's part of the field than to any other. The Roosevelt-Churchill connection, as I hope to show, was certainly political—but it was also inescapably personal.

CHAPTER 1: TWO LIONS ROARING AT THE SAME TIME

3 a typewritten "Memorandum For Assistant Secretary" Memorandum for Assistant Secretary, July 24, 1918. Papers of the Assistant Secretary of Navy, 1913–1920, FDR Papers, FDRL.

3 a clear evening National Meteorological Library and Archives, Berkshire, England.

4 portrait of Elizabeth I Author observation. It is a formidable room, and one can see how the young Roosevelt may have been intimidated by both the company and the setting on that summer evening.

4 She first encountered Roosevelt Perkins, *The Roosevelt I Knew*, 9.

4 "There was nothing particularly interesting" Ibid.

4 They spoke briefly of Roosevelt's cousin Ibid.

4 "a second thought" until she ran Ibid., 10.

4 "tall and slender" Ibid., 11.

5 Later, the toss of the head Ibid.

5 "slightly supercilious" Ibid.

5 She once heard a fellow politician Ibid.

5 He was, she recalled, "a very" Perkins, COH, 18.

5 Churchill, she would tell President Roosevelt Ibid., 19.

5 "so sure of himself"   Ibid.

5 "He's pig-headed"   Ibid.

5 a glittering occasion   "Speeches At a Dinner Given to the Ministers Responsible for the Fighting Forces of the Crown in Gray's Inn Hall on Monday, the 29th of July, 1918," in *The War Book of Gray's Inn* (London, 1921), 32–60.

6 Hailing Roosevelt as "the member of"   Ibid., 37.

6 "No one will welcome"   Ibid., 38.

6 to his "horror"   Elliott Roosevelt, ed., *The Personal Letters of Franklin D. Roosevelt,* II (New York, 1948), 392.

6 "given to understand"   *The War Book of Gray's Inn,* 57.

6 Citing the need for an "intimate"   Ibid.

6 "We are with you"   Ibid., 58.

6 "I always disliked him"   Amanda Smith, ed., *Hostage to Fortune: The Letters of Joseph P. Kennedy* (New York, 2001), 411.

7 who won the Iron Cross, First Class   Alan Bullock, *Hitler: A Study in Tyranny* (New York, 1952), 46. Hitler was awarded the decoration on August 4.

7 They had been born eight years and an ocean apart Many writers—first contemporaries of the two men, and later historians and biographers—have undertaken to compare and contrast Churchill and Roosevelt and summarize the course of their alliance. See, for instance, *TIR,* 251–255; John Gunther, *Roosevelt in Retrospect* (New York, 1950),

13–19; Kimball, *Forged in War,* 1–23 and *C & R,* I, 3–20; Lash, *Roosevelt and Churchill,* 179–195; Sainsbury, *Churchill and Roosevelt at War,* 1–16; Stafford, *Roosevelt and Churchill: Men of Secrets,* xiii–xviii; Tully, *FDR: My Boss,* 299–305.

7 "Being with them was like sitting"   Author interview with Lady Soames.

7 "There was a good deal"   Mike Reilly as told to William J. Slocum, *Reilly of the White House* (New York, 1947), 124.

8 romanced by Winthrop Rutherfurd   Elizabeth Shoumatoff, *FDR's Unfinished Portrait* (Pittsburgh, Pa., 1990), 75. Rutherfurd even played a role in the annulment of the Marlborough marriage in 1926. "On Nov. 24, 1926, from Rome came the announcement of the annulment of the marriage of Consuelo Vanderbilt and the Duke of Marlborough, with the reason for the annulment granted by the Sacred Rota of the Roman Catholic Church revealed in the fact that Consuelo, then 17, and in love with 'an American named Rutherfurd,' had been forced by her mother, Mrs. O.H.P. Belmont, to give him up and marry the Duke," wrote *The New York Times* in Rutherfurd's obituary on March 21, 1944. "When asked in New York about his acquaintance with Consuelo in 1895, Mr. Rutherfurd said, 'Yes, some thirty years ago I knew Miss Vanderbilt and I was one of her great admirers.' "

8 stamps, birds, books, and naval prints   Rita S. Halle Kleeman, *Gracious Lady: The Life of Sara Delano Roosevelt* (New York, 1935), 176–177; 223.

8 toy soldiers and butterflies for Churchill   *MEL,* 10; 28.

8 Cousin Theodore's legend fired young Roosevelt's political imagination   James MacGregor Burns, *Roosevelt: The Lion and the Fox*(New York, 1956), 24–25.

8 Lord Randolph's career fascinated his son   *MEL,* 46–47, is just one example.

8 they read the same books   For Roosevelt's important "early books," see "Memorandum for Hon. Lowell Mellett," February 8, 1944, Mellett Papers, White House, 1944 File, Box 6, FDRL; for Churchill's, see *MEL,* xvi, 18, 111–112. Churchill's view of the Sermon on the Mount is in Anthony Montague Browne, *Long Sunset: Memoirs of Winston Churchill's Last Private Secretary* (London, 1995), 204.

9 "My husband always had a joy"   EROH, Session 5, 18. "Nobody ever knew more about American politics than FDR; his knowledge ranged from constitutional precedents on the highest level to exactly what was going on in the First Ward in Chicago or who was postmaster in Walla Walla, Washington," wrote John Gunther. "His ability to keep in mind the smallest political details was 'aldermanic,' the late Mayor La Guardia of New York once told me." Gunther, *Roosevelt in Retrospect,* 66.

9 "Westminster is his ambience"   Colin Coote, "Churchill the Politician," in *Servant of Crown and Commonwealth,* ed. Marchant, 35–36.

10 "There are only two ways" *WSC,* IV, 43–44.

10 "bold, persistent experimentation" May 22, 1932, *Public Papers and Addresses of Franklin D. Roosevelt,* I, 639–647.

10 liked to lecture Middle Eastern leaders Perkins, *The Roosevelt I Knew,* 88–89; FDR to His Imperial Majesty Mohammad Rez Pahlavi, September 2, 1944, FDR Papers, microfilm edition, Diplomatic Correspondence, Part 2, Reel 19.

10 Felix Frankfurter was visiting Cliveden Harlan B. Phillips, *Felix Frankfurter Reminisces* (New York, 1960), 185–186.

10 took time to confer about the music Papers of the White House Office of Social Entertainment, Box 108, FDRL.

11 dined together in the Pinafore Room Montague Browne, *Long Sunset,* 314. Also see *WSC,* III, 35.

11 Roosevelt "really had military genius" Walter Lippmann, COH, 219.

11 "I have seen war" Frank Freidel, *Franklin D. Roosevelt: The Apprenticeship* (Boston, 1952), 356. The remarks were made in 1936.

11 "War, which used to be cruel and magnificent" *MEL,* 65.

12 an assassin armed with a revolver Burns, *Roosevelt: The Lion and the Fox,* 147.

12 That evening, the president-elect Frank Freidel, *A Rendezvous with Destiny* (New York, 1990), 87–88.

12 Facing a ferocious storm Wilson Brown Memoir, 136, FDRL.

12 "as if all the devils"   Ibid.

12 "He was interested but not"   Ibid.

12 At Omdurman   *MEL,* 182–196.

12 preferred rooftops   *WSC,* VII, 697.

12 En route to Washington   W. Averell Harriman and Elie Abel, *Special Envoy to Churchill and Stalin, 1941–1946* (New York, 1975), 205.

13 Seated next to Violet Bonham Carter   Lady Violet Bonham Carter, "Winston Churchill—As I Know Him," in *Servant of Crown and Commonwealth,* ed. Marchant, 149.

13 first American lecture tour   Arthur Schlesinger Jr., "Randolph Churchill," in *The Grand Original: Portraits of Randolph Churchill by His Friends,* ed. Kay Halle (Boston, 1971), 281.

13 "Why don't you run"   Ibid.

13 Some of his critics, he wrote   *MEL,* 162.

14 In an editorial addressed   Freidel, *The Apprenticeship,* 52.

14 "Sometimes he'd have nightmares"   EROH, Session 1, 1–2.

14 "His parents' friends found him"   John Colville, *Winston Churchill and His Inner Circle* (New York, 1981), 11. There is also evidence that contemporaries saw evidence of greatness in Churchill. See, for instance, Martin Gilbert, *Churchill: A Life* (New York, 1991), 125, and Martin Gilbert, *In Search of Churchill: A Historian's Journey* (New York, 1994), 214–215.

14 blackballed from Porcellian   Burns, *The Lion and the Fox,* 18.

15 "He was the kind of boy" Joseph P. Lash, *Eleanor and Franklin* (New York, 1971), 103.

15 One December 8 Tully, *FDR: My Boss,* 12.

15 On January 24, 1945 *TFOP,* 555.

15 Later, in the 1950s Colville, *Inner Circle,* 30.

15 "His capacity to inspire" Perkins, *The Roosevelt I Knew,* 385.

16 Lord Bridges, secretary to the British cabinet Lord Bridges in *Action This Day,* ed. Wheeler-Bennett, 232.

17 "I can see now" Ibid., 240.

17 "It was not as a crusader" Violet Bonham Carter, *Winston Churchill: An Intimate Portrait* (New York, 1965), 76.

17 "All the members of the Brains Trust" Rexford Tugwell, *The Democratic Roosevelt* (Garden City, N.Y., 1957), 36.

18 Churchill "would sometimes listen to the news" Author interview with Kathleen Harriman Mortimer.

18 seen with tears in his eyes Geoffrey C. Ward, *A First-Class Temperament: The Emergence of FDR* (New York, 1989), 9.

18 "It is said that famous men" Winston S. Churchill, *Marlborough: His Life and Times,* ed. Henry Steele Commager (New York, 1968), 9.

19 "I did once ask a very old" Author interview with Lady Soames.

19 "My nurse was my confidante" *MEL,* 5.

19 "I have told you often" *WSC,* I, 190.

19 "Lord Randolph had less" Ibid., 191.

20 Lord Randolph suffered from "general paralysis" related to syphilis   Gilbert, *Churchill: A Life,* 48.

20 "I loved her dearly"   *MEL,* 5.

20 Even the worst parents   Author interview with Lady Soames.

20 "He put her on a pedestal"   Ibid.

20 "I do think Jennie"   Ibid.

21 "In fact to me he seemed"   *MEL,* 46.

21 "Her almost complete neglect of me"   *WSC,* I, 44.

21 Churchill tried to get close   *MEL,* 46.

21 "Now it is a good thing"   *WSC,* I, 189.

22 "a system of believing"   *MEL,* 117.

22 his daughter Sarah asked him   *WSC,* VIII, 364.

22 In November 1947, Churchill was   For *The Dream* setting and quotations, see *WSC,* VIII, 364–372. I am grateful to Winston S. Churchill, who, in a moving moment in our interview for this book, read parts of *The Dream* aloud to me as he reflected on his grandfather.

23 "Winston was often right"   William Manchester, *The Last Lion: Winston Spencer Churchill, Visions of Glory 1874–1932* (Boston, 1983), 20.

24 "Not any part"   L. S. Amery, "Two Great War Leaders," in *Servant of Crown and Commonwealth,* ed. Marchant, 70–71.

24 "I passed out of Sandhurst"   *MEL,* 59.

24 In 1945, Churchill was at dinner   David Schoenbrun to Theodore White, undated, Box 20, File 4, White Papers, Harvard Archives.

25 "You must not forget" Churchill to Beaverbrook, BBK C/87, January 7, 1941, LBP.

25 was with him one evening Charles Eade, Diary of Meeting, February 14, 1940, CEP.

25 One morning during his second premiership Author interview with Anthony Montague Browne.

25 When he visited the White House EROH, Session 14, 3.

26 James "often told me" Mrs. James Roosevelt as told to Isabel Leighton and Gabrielle Forbush, *My Boy Franklin* (New York, 1933), 5. For insightful analysis of Roosevelt's emotional development, also see Geoffrey C. Ward, *Before the Trumpet: Young Franklin Roosevelt, 1882–1905* (New York, 1995), and *A First-Class Temperament.*

26 he decided to play a practical joke EROH, Session 10, 5–6.

26 "Mummie," the young Franklin once said Mrs. James Roosevelt, *My Boy Franklin,* 26.

26 He spotted a winter wren Ibid., 15–16.

27 "Franklin, I don't think" Ibid., 34. Sara's language describing her own frustration is interesting, too. On this occasion, her son, she said, "seemed less interested in the sound of my voice than usual," which led her to "put down the book of stories." Mrs. Roosevelt was a woman who wanted to be heeded. (Ibid.)

27 In White House receiving lines Wilson Brown Memoir, 120, FDRL.

27 "The only thing we have to fear"   March 4, 1933, *Public Papers and Addresses of Franklin D. Roosevelt,* II, 11.

27 Robert Hopkins, the son of   Author interview with Robert Hopkins.

28 "Franklin would say to Eleanor"   Author interview with Trude Lash.

29 "People would go away thinking"   Author interview with Kathleen Harriman Mortimer.

29 At Harrow, Churchill was placed   *MEL,* 16.

30 The lecturer was a master named   Ibid., 42.

30 "The warrior heroes of the past"   *CWP,* I, 794–795.

30 "The other boys had already formed"   *TIR,* 43.

31 influenced by the preaching of   Frank D. Ashburn, *Peabody of Groton* (New York, 1944), 181.

31 he would cite Peabody   *The New York Times,* January 21, 1945.

32 The first time Churchill was introduced   *CCTBOM,* 43.

32 As they stood together   Ibid., 44.

32 "brief and unpropitious"   Ibid., 43.

32 Four years later   Ibid., 48.

32 would telephone Clementine   Colville, *Inner Circle,* 16.

32 "Her judgment, given after"   Ibid., 33.

32 "When her nerves were stretched"   Ibid., 34.

34 A child of a broken home   *CCTBOM,* 10.

34 "She had a most sensitive conscience"   Ibid., 8. My details of the marriage are drawn from

CCTBOM, WAC, and author interview with Lady Soames.

34 a worrier   WAC, xviii.

34 "It is a great fault in me"   Ibid.

34 Churchill's reply was full   Ibid., 11.

35 "I have been able to think"   Ibid., 13.

35 One of Roosevelt's most disturbing memories EROH, Session 10, 5. Other fires marred Roosevelt's childhood. The worst: A favorite aunt burned to death, and he watched the Groton stables razed. See Ward, *Before the Trumpet,* 117–119.

35 "I was stupid last night"   WAC, 69.

36 designing his siren suits   CCTBOM, 402.

36 "fell romantically in love"   Ibid., 351. The details of the Philip interlude are drawn from CCTBOM.

36 Clementine quoted a French saying   Ibid.

36 "The Prime Minister does not 'dominate'" Diary of Dinner at 10 Downing Street, July 24, 1941, CEP.

37 Clementine, Mary wrote, "was not"   WAC, xiv.

37 "Such discussions"   Ibid.

37 "Papa once said to the President"   Author interview with Lady Soames.

38 Anna Eleanor Roosevelt   Lash, *Eleanor and Franklin,* 3–20.

38 Eleanor's mother called her "Granny"   EROH, Session 3, 1.

39 On November 22, 1903   Lash, *Eleanor and Franklin,* 107.

39 "with your help"   Ibid.

39 "Why me?"   Ibid.

39 Sara was stunned   Ibid., 109.

40 "the matriarch of the family"   Anna Roosevelt Halsted, COH, 3–4.

40 "Mother had not"   Ibid., 4.

41 Before midnight, Eleanor excused   Joseph Alsop, *FDR: A Centenary Remembrance* (New York, 1982), 67.

42 "like 'dark velvet' "   Lash, *Eleanor and Franklin,* 221. The Lucy story is a familiar one in the Roosevelt annals. My version of its early days is based on Joseph Lash's *Eleanor and Franklin,* a sensitive but not sentimental portrait of the affair and its impact on Eleanor.

42 "She knew how to please"   Ibid.

42 The truth emerged   Ibid., 226.

42 "The bottom dropped out"   Ibid., 220.

42 "Eleanor gave him a choice"   Ibid., 226.

43 "There was a marked tendency"   Author interview with John Kenneth Galbraith.

43 "I was going up the staircase"   Author interview with Patrick Kinna.

43 "She shook everyone's hand"   Author interview with Carol R. Lubin.

44 Eleanor must never discover   Lash, *Eleanor and Franklin,* 700.

44 Churchill seems never to have carried on   There is another view of this. William Manchester cites "confidential information" in writing that Churchill "has committed but one act of infidelity, at

Golfe-Juan, on the Mediterranean, with a divorced, titled Englishwoman whose seductive skills and sexual experience far exceeded his." See Manchester, *The Last Lion: Alone,* 15. To my mind, as noted in the text, the most interesting issue is not sex but secrecy.

44 On the Churchills' fortieth anniversary   *WAC,* 549.

45 Gallipoli and polio changed their lives   Joseph Lash is interesting on this point, writing that the Dardenelles and its fallout for Churchill "began to teach him the lesson of biding his time, of curbing his ego, lessons that Roosevelt learned when polio brought him low." See Lash, *Roosevelt and Churchill,* 60.

45 Feeling he should not   Gilbert, *Churchill: A Life,* 328. I am grateful to Sir Martin Gilbert for this point.

45 Clementine tried to reassure him   *WAC,* 163.

45 A portrait of Churchill painted by Sir William Orpen   Author viewing of the portrait courtesy of—and in the company of—Winston S. Churchill.

45 "He is convinced his political career"   Author interview with Winston S. Churchill.

45 worked with Bernard Baruch   Gilbert, *Churchill: A Life,* 379.

46 "He took us on many weekends"   Anna Roosevelt Halsted, COH, 33.

46 "He grinned at us"   James Roosevelt and Sidney Shalett, *Affectionately, FDR* (New York, 1959), 143.

47 "He never said anything at all" EROH, Session 4, 3.

47 "He never, never gave up" Ibid.

47 "touch of triviality" Joseph Gides, *Franklin D. Roosevelt: Portrait of a President* (Garden City, N.Y., 1971), 214.

48 "Sometimes I wonder whether he would" Author interview with Mrs. Margaret Hendrick (Rollie Hambley).

48 thought Roosevelt had "the quality" Marquis Childs, COH, 109–110.

48 "He's standing with his head" Ibid., 110.

48 "That was the Garbo in me" Gunther, *Roosevelt in Retrospect,* 62.

48 "You know, Orson" Ibid.

49 Bohlen said that Roosevelt Bohlen, *Witness to History,* 210.

49 "a frustrated clergyman" James Roosevelt, *Affectionately, FDR,* 99.

49 the church's senior warden Gunther, *Roosevelt in Retrospect,* 79. Of St. James's, Gunther noted, "The joke was that 'This is Roosevelt's church, once God's.'" (Ibid.)

50 As James told the story James Roosevelt, *Affectionately, FDR,* 99–101.

50 On Easter Sunday 1934 Ibid., 100–101.

51 the Beatitudes and the thirteenth chapter Memorandum for Mellett, FDRL; TIR, 346.

52 "Once, in talking to him" TIR, 346.

52 "Hitherto I had dutifully accepted" For Chur-

chill's account of his early faith and later readings, see *MEL,* 113–116.

52 This began a brief "violent"   Ibid.

53 "I believe that man is"   Montague Browne, *Long Sunset,* 204.

53 "an optimistic agnostic"   Ibid.

53 "Whether you believe or disbelieve"   Ibid. Of Churchill's faith, Moran wrote: "King and country, in that order, that's about all the religion Winston has. But it means a lot to him." (*TSFS,* 207)

53 As he was retiring as prime minister   *WSC,* VIII, 1123. I am grateful to Sir Martin Gilbert for leading me specifically to this passage.

53 The three Americans closest to Roosevelt   Arthur M. Schlesinger Jr., *The Age of Roosevelt:The Coming of the New Deal* (Boston, 1958), 577.

54 Brendan Bracken . . . who was said—falsely—to be Churchill's illegitimate son   William Manchester, *The Last Lion: Winston Spencer Churchill: Alone, 1932–1940* (Boston, 1988), 14.

54 "He behaved in public"   Colville in *Action This Day,* ed. Wheeler-Bennett, 54.

54 What, Beaverbrook once asked himself   BBK G/11/4, LBP.

54 "He was intensely pugnacious"   Ibid.

55 "He enjoyed a conflict of ideas"   *WSC,* VIII, 1364.

55 "He was a warrior"   *The Times* (London), January 26, 1965.

55 something said or done was "malicious"   Author interview with Lady Soames.

55 "He never sought to trample" *The Times* (London), January 26, 1965.

55 "Anger is a waste" Diary of Meeting, Charles Eade, July 24, 1941, CEP.

56 "Opinions differ" Ibid.

56 After becoming prime minister Gilbert, *Churchill: A Life,* 663.

56 Albert Einstein, Lawrence of Arabia Mary Soames, ed., *A Churchill Family Album* (London, 1982).

56 Isaiah Berlin wrote weekly political reports *TFOP,* 471–472.

57 John Wheeler-Bennett, the future biographer of George VI Sir John Wheeler-Bennett, *Special Relationships: America in Peace and War* (London, 1975), 89–90.

57 Roosevelt's interests were varied Tully, *FDR: My Boss,* 7–12.

57 Roosevelt tried to make money EROH, Session 7, 1.

57 "Not very successful" Ibid., 7.

57 a "hurricane-proof" house *RAH,* 378.

57 "He was a man" Burns, *The Lion and the Fox,* 90. Joseph Lash was amusing on Roosevelt's literary work. "He embarked on several writing projects: a biography of John Paul Jones ('a little volume' that would show that much of the published material about Jones was 'romance') and a history of the United States. He wrote five pages of the first and fourteen of the second." See Lash, *Roosevelt and Churchill,* 189.

57 "Roosevelt close to was" Walter Lippmann, COH, 220.

58 "Judge Roosevelt" Michael Beschloss, *The Conquerors: Roosevelt, Truman and the Destruction of Hitler's Germany, 1941–1945* (New York, 2002), 187.

58 In 1930, Felix Frankfurter Max Freedman, ed., *Roosevelt and Frankfurter: Their Correspondence, 1928–1945* (Boston, 1967), 37–38.

58 Sir David Pitblado, a Churchill private secretary Manchester, *The Last Lion: Visions of Glory*, 35.

59 John Gunther picked out Gunther, *Roosevelt in Retrospect*, 69.

59 Musing about Churchill's flow of "brilliant ideas" Perkins, *The Roosevelt I Knew*, 383.

59 Roosevelt's interest in polling data Winston S. Churchill, *His Father's Son: The Life of Randolph Churchill* (London, 1996), 197.

59 "My father never wanted to switch off" Author interview with Lady Soames.

59 "Great fellow, that Churchill" Perkins, *The Roosevelt I Knew*, 383.

60 "The prime minister took a long nap" TIR, 242–243. Churchill had learned the virtues of the siesta on a trip to Cuba as a young soldier. "For every purpose of business or pleasure, mental or physical, we ought to break our days and our marches in two." (*MEL*, 81)

60 "the Winston hours" CC, 199.

60 "I went to bed" Winston S. Churchill, *The Hinge of Fate: The Second World War* (Boston, 1950),

390. Churchill claimed one of the few nights he could not sleep was in 1938, when Anthony Eden resigned from Neville Chamberlain's cabinet in the march to war. See *The Gathering Storm: The Second World War* (Boston, 1948), 257–258.

60 Churchill "made an effort" Author interview with Lady Soames.

61 "Winston was on his way" Robert Gathorne-Hardy, ed., *Memoirs of Lady Ottoline Morrell* (New York, 1964), 194–195.

61 TR found the young man a bit much Elting E. Morison, ed., *The Letters of Theodore Roosevelt,* III, 116–117.

61 "I have been over" Ibid., V, 408.

61 "I have refused to meet Winston Churchill" Ibid., VII, 87.

61 Arthur Schlesinger Jr. once asked Arthur Schlesinger Jr. letter to author, August 6, 2001.

62 "I'm willing to help them" Smith, ed., *Hostage to Fortune,* 411.

62 Churchill "found it easy" *MEL,* 362.

62 "Roosevelt was a wonderful finagler" Walter Lippmann, COH, 220.

64 "I was a child of the Victorian era" *MEL,* xxi.

64 "He has a very gloomy future" Sir Norman Angell, COH, 233.

64 Churchill referred to his bluer episodes Gilbert, *In Search of Churchill,* 210.

64 "He experienced a sensation of annoyance" Winston S. Churchill, *Savrola* (New York, 1956),

129. Joseph Lash, among other writers, has also noted the link between Savrola and his creator.

65 "When the notes of life" Ibid., 130.

65 Back in England, sitting with his researcher Maurice Ashley, *Churchill As Historian* (London, 1968), 8.

65 Perhaps because he intuitively understood Churchill indicated as much more than once. "If our country were defeated I hope we should find a champion as indomitable to restore our courage and lead us back to our place among the nations." See John Lukacs, *The Duel: The Eighty-Day Struggle Between Churchill and Hitler* (New Haven, Conn., 1990), 40.

66 "The story of the human race" Churchill, *Marlborough, His Life and Times,* ed. Commager, xxvii.

66 "Mr. Chamberlain" Virginia Cowles, *Winston Churchill: The Era and the Man* (New York, 1953), 9.

67 would bring Germany back "serene" Winston S. Churchill, *Great Contemporaries* (Chicago, 1973), 261.

67 "If . . . we look only at the past" Ibid., 267.

68 At a Chartwell dinner in 1933 Kay Halle, *Irrepressible Churchill* (Cleveland, 1966), 7.

68 Churchill wrote an article about Roosevelt Churchill, *Great Contemporaries,* 371–382.

69 Beginning in 1938 *TIR,* 182.

69 "Convinced that bad things" Ibid., 183.

69 As the train left Hyde Park Ibid., 198.

CHAPTER 2: THOSE BLOODY YANKEES

71 After a tough summer   *Newsweek,* July 31, 1939.

71 who liked the relaxing rhythms of life at sea "Down to the Sea with the 'Skipper,' " *The New York Times Magazine,* August 13, 1939.

71 After an equally tough summer   See, for instance, Martin Gilbert, *Churchill: A Life,* 617–618.

72 In a broadcast over NBC   *The New York Times,* August 9, 1939.

72 took off for his fishing trip   Ibid., August 13, 1939; *Time,* August 28, 1939.

72 Foggy weather   *The New York Times,* August 21, 1939.

72 Poland was in the crosshairs   Burns, *The Lion and the Fox,* 393.

72 spent a holiday near Dreux   *CCTBOM,* 369.

72 arrived in England on August 23   Gilbert, *Churchill: A Life,* 619.

72 the same day Roosevelt   *The New York Times,* August 24, 1939.

73 Churchill called for Clementine   Winston S. Churchill, *The Gathering Storm, The Second World War* (Boston, 1948), 401.

73 crossed the Channel   Ibid.

73 "Yes . . . it was called"   William Manchester, *The Glory and the Dream: A Narrative History of America, 1932–1972* (Boston, 1974), 31.

73 sending him a signed copy of the first volume   *C & R,* I, 23. Kimball also noted that Scribner's,

Churchill's publisher, attempted to interest Roosevelt in reviewing Churchill's history of the First World War, *The World Crisis,* but failed, and that Churchill tried unsuccessfully to meet with Roosevelt in October 1929. (Ibid.)

74 the duke of Windsor wrote him Montague Browne, *Long Sunset,* 225.

74 answering questions at a meeting *WSC,* V, Comp. Pt. 2, 726.

74 "The quarrel in which" Winston S. Churchill, *Step by Step* (New York, 1939), 166.

75 Chamberlain believed Churchill Joseph P. Kennedy to FDR, July 20, 1939, FDR Papers, Diplomatic Correspondence, FDRL.

75 spent time with Clementine Agnes E. Meyer Diary, February 13, 1932, MP.

75 When Churchill died, Evelyn Waugh Mark Amory, ed., *The Letters of Evelyn Waugh* (New Haven, Conn., 1980), 630.

75 For those who think the Churchill of legend See, for instance, Christopher Hitchens, "The Medals of His Defeats," *Atlantic Monthly,* April 2002, 118–137. The most serious revisionist view of Churchill can be found in the work of the British historian John Charmley. Particularly in *Churchill: The End of Glory, A Political Biography* (London, 1993) and in *Churchill's Grand Alliance: The Anglo-American Special Relationship, 1940–1957* (New York, 1995), Charmley argues that Churchill's determination to fight Germany and to cultivate America cost Britain and her empire a more

influential role in the world. By coming to an agreement with Hitler, Charmley's case implies, Britain would have been a powerful player on the global stage rather than watch as Roosevelt's America and Stalin's Soviet Union rose to dominance first in the alliance and then in the postwar world. Charmley's books are interesting and challenging, but to accept his argument means one must accept the idea of a German-dominated Continent as a fact of life—which, given what Hitler wrought in the few years he did dominate much of the Continent, is a deeply offensive proposition.

76 the new issue of Henry Luce's *Time*   *Time,* September 4, 1939.

77 churches were unusually full   *TFOP,* 19.

77 the first air-raid warning   W. H. Thompson, *I Was Churchill's Shadow* (London, 1951), 18–19.

77 The appointment alarmed the Germans   Albert Speer, *Inside the Third Reich* (New York, 1970), 165.

78 he heard ancient drumbeats   Churchill, *The Gathering Storm,* 410.

78 "It is easy for you and for me"   Russell D. Buhite and David W. Levy, eds., *FDR's Fireside Chats* (Norman, Okla., 1992), 149.

79 "When the President found out I was so anti-Hitler"   Author interview with Trude Lash.

79 "Franklin always said"   EROH, Session 14, 4.

80 Charles Eade left a snapshot   Diary of Meeting, Charles Eade, September 1939, CEP.

81 The president understood that it was Churchill

Roosevelt seems not to have had much trust in Chamberlain's leadership; the prime minister had spurned Roosevelt's diplomatic overtures in the late 1930s for a world conference to see if war could be averted. Churchill invested Chamberlain's failure to take Roosevelt up on the proposal with sweeping importance, writing that "we must regard its rejection—for such it was—as the loss of the last frail chance to save the world from tyranny otherwise than by war." (*The Gathering Storm,* 254–255) For a counterview, see Charmley, *Churchill: The End of Glory,* 332–333. In writing Churchill, Roosevelt, it seems likely, was looking for any promising channel he could find to assess and monitor the situation. Roosevelt also regularly corresponded with Chamberlain in Chamberlain's remaining months as prime minister.

81 Joseph Kennedy, who held the darkest of views Lash, *Roosevelt and Churchill,* 22.

82 Answering for Roosevelt Ibid., 23.

82 a clear Monday *The New York Times,* September 12, 1939.

82 between suspending limitations on sugar marketing *FDR: Day by Day—The Pare-Lorentz Chronology,* FDRL.

82 "My dear Churchill" *CWP,* I, 76.

83 "responded with alacrity" Churchill, *The Gathering Storm,* 441.

83 Their first telephone conversation Lord Fraser, "Churchill and the Navy," in *Servant of Crown and Commonwealth,* ed. Marchant, 80–81.

84 The Germans had sent word   *C & R,* I, 25; *WSC,* VI, 54–55. Also see *The New York Times,* October 6, 1939, for details about the *Iroquois,* which carried 566 passengers—"virtually all Americans"—and a crew of 210. A similar drama had unfolded with the British liner *Athenia* on September 3, which a German U-boat sank off Ireland, killing 28 Americans. Berlin blamed the British, particularly Churchill.

85 On the last day of October   Beaverbrook to FDR, October 31, 1939, BBK C/227, LBP.

85 "I think I ought to send something more"   David Reynolds, *The Creation of the Anglo-American Alliance 1937–41: A Study in Competitive Co-operation* (Chapel Hill, N.C., 1981), 87.

86 As Roosevelt had breakfast in bed   Smith, ed., *Hostage to Fortune,* 411.

86 "supposed Churchill was the best man"   Diary of Harold L. Ickes, May 12, 1940, Ickes Papers. *The Secret Diary of Harold L. Ickes: Volume III, The Lowering Clouds, 1939–1941,* 176, has the same scene, but the published version eliminates Roosevelt's qualifier "even if he was drunk half of his time," which is in the original cited here.

86 As Churchill went to bed   Churchill, *The Gathering Storm,* 667.

87 "blood, toil, tears and sweat"   *WSC,* VI, 333.

87 In early March 1940   Ickes, *The Secret Diary,* III, 146–147.

87 "Bill is not at all sure"   Ibid., 147.

87 Welles had seen Churchill up close   Benjamin

Welles, *Sumner Welles: FDR's Global Strategist* (New York, 1997), 253.

88 "was so uncertain" Perkins, *The Roosevelt I Knew,* 80.

88 "what kind of a fellow" Frances Perkins, COH, 20.

88 On Wednesday, May 15, 1940, Churchill, calling himself "Former Naval Person" *C & R,* I, 37.

88 "Although I have changed my office" *CWP,* II, 45–46.

90 "I have just received your message" Ibid., 69–70.

91 "I do not need to tell you" Ibid., 71.

91 "what went on inside FDR's head" Gunther, *Roosevelt in Retrospect,* 53.

91 On the evening of May 14 J.R.M. Butler, *Lord Lothian (Philip Kerr), 1882–1940* (New York, 1960), 283–284. Also see *CWP,* II, 33–34, for Jock Colville's version of the rather madcap scene at Admiralty House that night.

91 "Why, the Government will move" Butler, *Lord Lothian,* 284.

91 In a subsequent talk with Lord Lothian Ibid.

91 the president and Henry Morgenthau scrounged up David Reynolds, *From Munich to Pearl Harbor: Roosevelt's America and the Origins of the Second World War* (Chicago, 2001), 79.

92 In a Gallup poll *The Washington Post,* October 22, 1939; see also William L. Langer and S. Everett Gleason, *The Challenge to Isolation* (New York, 1952), 288.

92 in November the president signed   Reynolds, *From Munich to Pearl Harbor,* 66–67.

92 aid to the Allies might come at a steep cost Langer and Gleason, *The Challenge to Isolation,* 568–569.

92 Germany, which had outspent America   Eliot A. Cohen, "Churchill and Coalition Strategy in World War II," in *Grand Strategies in War and Peace,* ed. Paul Kennedy (New Haven, Conn., 1991), 51. Cohen's numbers are "Volume of Combat Munitions Production of the Major Belligerents in Terms of Annual Expenditure ($ Million 1944 U.S. Munitions Prices)."

93 "How the British people"   Winston S. Churchill, *The Second World War, Their Finest Hour* (Boston: Houghton Mifflin, 1949), ix.

93 Churchill's son, Randolph   *CWP,* II, 70.

94 "It was the only thing he would wear to sleep in" Author interview with Winston S. Churchill.

94 "Sit down, dear boy"   *WSC,* VI, 358.

95 Sumner Welles told Henry Morgenthau   Henry A. Wallace, COH, August 26, 1943, 2671.

95 "the fine true thing"   A. P. Herbert, "The Master of Words," in *Servant of Crown and Commonwealth,* ed. Marchant, 101.

95 "Those Greeks and Romans"   Bonham Carter in *Servant of Crown and Commonwealth,* ed. Marchant, 153.

95 to soak up some sun   *CWP,* II, 80.

95 "full of fight"   *TFOP,* 134.

96 "Our task is not only"   *CWP,* II, 88–90.

97 "were a tonic to us here"   *TIR,* 255.

97 "To explain to one's country"   Ibid., 246–247.

98 At Admiralty House   *TFOP,* 136.

98 "With regard to the closing part"   *CWP,* II, 93. On May 20, the date of this telegram, came a scandal: Tyler Kent, a clerk at the American embassy in London, had stolen documents, including pieces of the Churchill-Roosevelt correspondence. "Kent's intention," wrote Martin Gilbert, "had been to smuggle his documents back to the United States, to serve as ammunition for the isolationist organisations opposed to Roosevelt's pro-British policies." Kent was tried, convicted, and held in England until the end of the war. (Ibid.) Also see Beschloss, *Kennedy and Roosevelt,* 206–207.

99 "Considering the soothing words"   *TFOP,* 136.

100 "We need not fear"   *The New York Times,* May 20, 1940.

101 Roosevelt had been cruising   Ibid.

101 "Colonel Lindbergh has given"   Ibid.

101 "A Summons to Speak Out"   Langer and Gleason, *The Challenge to Isolation,* 507.

102 "indicated that only 7.7 percent"   Ibid., 495–496.

102 "Although President is our best friend"   *CWP,* II, 255.

102 about four hundred thousand men   Martin Gilbert, *The Second World War: A Complete History* (New York, 1989), 72.

103 "should prepare itself"   *CWP,* II, 179.

103 "Tonight there was no levity" Samuel I. Rosenman, *Working with Roosevelt* (New York, 1952) 195–196.

103 On May 27 came a disturbing cable Lash, *Roosevelt and Churchill*, 146.

104 Lord Halifax, then the foreign secretary, suggested *CWP,* II, 180.

104 "there are signs that Halifax is being defeatist" *TFOP,* 140–141.

104 Churchill resisted *CWP,* II, 180.

104 Halifax said that he did not see why Ibid., 181.

105 "too rambling and romantic" David Dilks, ed., *The Diaries of Sir Alexander Cadogan* (New York, 1972), 290. For more on this early period of Churchill's prime ministership, see Lukacs, *Five Days in London, May 1940.* Also see Andrew Roberts, *Eminent Churchillians* (New York, 1994) and *"The Holy Fox."*

105 Neville Chamberlain, who was now lord president *CWP,* II, 181.

105 "nations which went down fighting" Ibid.

105 "The Foreign Secretary said" Ibid.

105 "the chances of decent terms" Ibid.

106 "He was determined to prepare public opinion" Ibid., 183. Dalton's diary also recorded this version of Churchill's peroration: "If this long island story of ours is to end at last, let it end only when each one of us lies choking in his own blood upon the ground." (Ibid.)

107 "There was a murmur" Ibid., 184.

107 "They had not expressed alarm" Ibid., 185.

108 nearly 340,000   Norman Polmar and Thomas B. Allen, *World War II: America at War* (New York, 1991), 262.

108 "Even though large tracts of Europe"   *CWP,* II, 247.

110 "We understood the kind of courage"   *TIR,* 211.

110 at the Brenner Pass in March 1940   Shirer, *The Rise and Fall of the Third Reich,* 690–692.

111 "It was a curious trip"   *TIR,* 211.

111 The day was rainy   *The New York Times,* June 11, 1940.

111 "On this 10th day of June"   Ibid.

112 "In our American unity"   Ibid.

112 "We all listened to you last night"   *CWP,* II, 287–288.

113 "Of course I made it clear"   Ibid., 308.

113 "As I have already stated"   *C & R,* I, 45–46.

114 "Mr President," Churchill wrote   *CWP,* II, 324.

114 "I appreciate fully the significance"   *C & R,* I, 48.

114 "I understand all of your difficulties"   *CWP,* II, 337–338.

116 "the French will very quickly"   Ibid., 341.

116 Churchill seemed lost in his thoughts   Author interview with Winston S. Churchill.

117 "Upon this battle depends"   *CWP,* II, 368.

118 "was furious"   *TFOP,* 165.

118 "He was an alarming master"   Sir John Martin in *Action This Day,* ed. Wheeler-Bennett, 140.

119 "On one of those early nights" Ibid.

119 "the only person who was never" Colville in *Action This Day*, ed. Wheeler-Bennett, 65.

119 "My Darling" *WAC*, 454.

121 became lifelong Churchillians *CCTBOM*, 383–384.

121 "For forty years" C. P. Snow, *Variety of Men* (New York, 1967), 166.

121 a recommendation from the joint planners Langer and Gleason, *The Challenge to Isolation*, 568.

122 even the Dutch were stronger Reynolds, *From Munich to Pearl Harbor*, 78.

122 "There was no doubt" Langer and Gleason, *The Challenge to Isolation,* 569.

123 "The night he decided" BBK 480, LBP.

123 "served forcibly to underscore" *RAH*, 149.

123 were beginning to figure out how to decipher Gilbert, *Churchill: A Life,* 637.

124 In July Roosevelt dispatched David Stafford, *Roosevelt and Churchill: Men of Secrets* (London, 1999), 43–44.

124 "Are we going to throw all our secrets" *WSC,* VI, 672.

124 "If Hitler fails to invade" *CWP,* II, 384–386.

126 It would not much matter There was no constitutional limit on presidential terms until the ratification of the Twenty-second Amendment in 1951.

126 he had begun to build *CC,* 112.

126 a $75,000 annual deal with *Collier's* Frank

Freidel, *A Rendezvous with Destiny* (Boston, 1990), 328.

127 "I think my husband was torn"   EROH, Session 9, 10.

127 "In times like these"   FDR speech by radio to the Democratic convention, July 19, 1940. Rosenman, ed., *Public Papers and Addresses of Franklin Roosevelt,* IX, 296–297.

129 "I think the greatest drive"   EROH, Session 1, 15–16.

129 "feminine intuition"   Marquis Childs, COH, 109.

129 "I think they'll resist"   Lippmann, COH, 179.

129 "It is some time since"   *CWP,* II, 593–594.

131 "Well, that'll do it"   Lippmann, COH, 179.

131 "The President, having always"   Churchill, *Their Finest Hour,* 408.

132 "We intend to fight this out here"   *CWP,* II, 668.

132 "But in any use"   Ibid.

132 "Oddly enough"   Snow, *Variety of Men,* 150.

133 "You ask, Mr President"   *CWP,* II, 746–747.

134 "Thus all was happily settled"   Churchill, *Their Finest Hour,* 414.

134 "to place the transaction"   Ibid., 408.

134 "somewhat mixed up together"   *CWP,* II, 697.

134 "the Day of the Eagle"   Gilbert, *The Second World War,* 116.

135 went to the operations room   General the Lord Ismay, *The Memoirs of General Lord Ismay* (New York, 1960), 181–182.

135 On August 23, the Luftwaffe bombed London Gilbert, *The Second World War,* 118.

135 Then, on September 7 *WSC,* VI, 775.

135 "How I wish you could see" Nancy Astor to Eugene Meyer, May 27, 1941, 120–121.

136 Hitler postponed sea lion Norman Polmar and Thomas B. Allen, *World War II: The Encyclopedia of the War Years, 1941–1945* (New York, 1976), 721.

136 killing in all more than forty thousand people— at least five thousand of them children Ibid., 161.

136 The Battle of the Atlantic Ibid., 139–142.

137 oil-rich Middle East The military historian John Keegan has argued that Hitler could have won the war by focusing on driving through the Middle East rather than invading the Soviet Union, possibly linking up with the Japanese. See Keegan, "How Hitler Could Have Won the War," in *What If?* ed. Robert Cowley (New York, 1999), 295–305.

137 "Let me say to you" *The New York Times,* September 14, 1940.

137 "'Your boys are not going'" Rosenman, *Working with Roosevelt,* 242.

137 "except in case of attack" Ibid.

137 "Of course we'll fight if" *RAH,* 191.

138 "profound anxiety" Churchill, *Their Finest Hour,* 553.

138 "expressed himself as having" Henry A. Wallace Diary, August 7, 1942, 4–5.

139 "You cannot imagine" Brendan Bracken to Eugene Meyer, October 11, 1940, MP.

140 "America is profoundly impressed" Eugene Meyer to Brendan Bracken, October 25, 1940, MP.

140 In the broadcast to the French *CWP,* II, 982.

140 an October 1940 poll William L. Langer and S. Everett Gleason, *The Undeclared War, 1940–1941* (New York, 1953), 198.

141 There was a news ticker Author tour of Hyde Park. In an interview with Henry Morgenthau III, Eleanor remembered that her husband "would have a regular set-up in the dining room and in the little room off it, where machines would be put." See Ellen Paul Denker, *Historic Furnishings Report: Springwood, Home of Franklin D. Roosevelt,* I (Northeast Museum Services Center, Boston Support Office, National Park Service, 1998), 50.

141 "FDR's nerves" Reilly and Slocum, *Reilly of the White House,* 66.

141 "Mike, I don't want to see" Ibid.

141 "I did not think it right" *CWP,* II, 1053–1054.

142 "I hope you" Ibid., 1099.

143 "Curiously enough, I never received" Churchill, *Their Finest Hour,* 554. Joseph Lash speculates that Roosevelt may have been annoyed at Willkie's use of Churchill's old anti–New Deal rhetoric the Republican nominee quoted during the fall campaign. Lash quotes quite a few pieces of British diplomatic correspondence on the question of

whether Roosevelt received the letter and, after deciding that Roosevelt had, whether the Willkie issue had rankled Roosevelt. (See Lash, *Roosevelt and Churchill*, 245–247.) Whatever the reason, the fact that Roosevelt felt he could ignore the letter suggests he felt a strong sense of superiority.

143 "one of the most important"   Ibid., 558.

143 The cable went through numerous revisions *C & R*, I, 87–109; Lash, *Roosevelt and Churchill*, 256–259; Reynolds, *From Munich to Pearl Harbor*, 103–105. I am grateful to Professor Reynolds for focusing my attention on the point about Churchill's help from Lothian. "WSC didn't dream up every bright idea—like every good leader he was quick to see and develop the ideas of others." (David Reynolds letter to author, April 1, 2003.) As I note in the text, that was also certainly true of Roosevelt.

144 "Even if the United States"   *CWP*, II, 1190–1191.

145 Roosevelt and Hopkins had left   *RAH*, 223.

145 "He had only his own intimates around him" Churchill, *Their Finest Hour*, 567.

145 "Tonight, in the presence of a world crisis" Buhite and Levy, eds., *FDR's Fireside Chats*, 164–173.

148 Sitting in his study with Rosenman and Hopkins Rosenman, *Working with Roosevelt*, 263–264. I drew the scene and the "Four Freedoms" passage from Rosenman's account. Roosevelt delivered the speech to Congress on January 6, 1941.

149 "You know—a lot of this" *RAH,* 230.

149 much of his stomach Ibid., 92.

149 "Harry had the capacity" Frances Perkins, COH, 563.

150 "How about me going over" *RAH,* 230.

150 "Harry is the perfect Ambassador" Ibid., 4.

150 To load the gold aboard a U.S. warship *CWP,* II, 1309.

151 "Please do not suppose" Ibid., 1296–1297.

151 "anxiety" Ibid., 1309.

151 "Remember, Mr President" Ibid.

CHAPTER 3: JESUS CHRIST!
WHAT A MAN!

153 "Churchill had no idea" Author interview with Robert Hopkins.

153 was "not a person" Sir John Martin interview, Newton Collection, FDRL.

153 "all geared up" Lady Soames interview, Newton Collection, FDRL.

153 "a mystery man" Ibid.

153 Jean Monnet, a Frenchman *RAH,* 232.

154 Hopkins "became a bit fed up" Ibid.

154 "Here I am, the son of" Childs, COH, 55–56.

154 "It seemed to me" Ibid.

155 Joseph Lash related this anecdote Lash, *Roosevelt and Churchill,* 185.

155 There was a rumor *RAH,* 238.

155 was learning who his guest was Ibid., 234.

155 Within minutes of Hopkins's arrival Ibid., 235.

156 Herschel V. Johnson, took Hopkins   Ibid.

156 They talked amid blasts   Ibid.

156 "Churchill had been informed"   Ibid., 236. Also see Lash, *Roosevelt and Churchill*, 274–275, for correspondence related to Churchill's speech, which was delivered during a lunch marking Halifax's departure for Washington as ambassador after Lothian's death.

156 "I have always taken the view"   *CWP*, III, 51.

157 Johnson told Hopkins   *RAH*, 237.

157 Hopkins then asked Edward R. Murrow   Ibid., 236.

157 Hopkins wanted to get the journalist's take   Ibid.

157 "I suppose you could say"   Ibid.

157 notes written on Claridge's stationery   Ibid., 237.

157 he found No. 10 Downing Street   Ibid., 238.

157 "most of the windows are out"   Ibid.

158 In a small dining room   Ibid.

158 "a rotund—smiling—red faced"   Ibid.

158 "Thus I met Harry Hopkins"   Winston S. Churchill, *The Grand Alliance: The Second World War* (Boston, 1950), 23.

158 While Churchill's cook and housekeeper   I am grateful to Sir Martin Gilbert for this detail.

158 the two men talked   *RAH*, 238–240.

160 "were so impressed"   *TFOP*, 331.

160 "I have never had such an enjoyable"   Lash, *Roosevelt and Churchill*, 277.

160 Ditchley, an eighteenth-century house   *RAH,* 240.

161 "Week-ends were anything but restful"   Ibid.

161 Bracken told Colville   *TFOP,* 331.

162 As the weekend began, Churchill seemed pleased   Ibid.

162 In Washington   Ibid., 331–332.

162 That evening, the party gathered   Ibid., 332–333.

163 was "touched and gratified"   Ibid., 333.

164 Speaking in the "unhesitating"   Ibid.

164 "We seek no treasure"   Lyttleton, *Memoirs,* 165. Joseph Lash, an unabashed liberal, also rendered this scene at Ditchley and thought Churchill's sentences on this evening "limp," the result of political advice Churchill had received to tell Hopkins what Hopkins wanted to hear (see Lash, *Roosevelt and Churchill,* 277–281). They do not seem limp to me, and I am not so sure we should dismiss Churchill's postwar vision too easily; he was unquestionably focused on winning the war, but it is a dangerous thing to try to state categorically that Winston Churchill believed this or believed that. Though he was no New Dealer and no Labourite, he was defending democracy and keeping the possibility of progress alive.

165 "the best part of a minute"   Lyttleton, *Memoirs,* 165.

165 "Well, Mr Prime Minister, I don't think"   Ibid.

165 "Winston hastily explained"   *TFOP,* 334.

165 "At that moment," Lyttleton, *Memoirs,* 166.

168 "The people here . . . are amazing" *RAH,* 243.

168 "slow, deliberate, halting" *TFOP,* 333.

168 in the middle of the film Ibid., 334.

168 The HMS *Southampton* had been destroyed Ibid.

168 "I was sitting in an air raid shelter" Snow, *Variety of Men,* 151.

169 "Having had no direct experience" *RAH,* 240.

169 Churchill did not tell Hopkins Stafford, *Roosevelt and Churchill: Men of Secrets,* 51–54.

169 another piece of signals intelligence Gilbert, *Churchill: A Life,* 688.

169 The sharing of intelligence would soon improve Stafford, *Roosevelt and Churchill: Men of Secrets,* 56–57.

170 Mary Soames thought him Lady Soames interview, Newton Collection, FDRL.

170 "I think he suffered desperately" Ibid.

170 "Hopkins never seemed to eat anything" Pamela Churchill Harriman interview, Newton Collection, FDRL.

170 "small, shrunken, sick" Ibid.

170 "Then his face would light up" Ibid.

171 "Dear Mr. President—" *RAH,* 243–246. Also see *CWP,* III, 76–77.

173 "was not a sinner but" BBK G/11/4, LBP.

173 "One of the things he always did" Childs, COH, 115.

173 "the most charming and entertaining" *RAH,* 241.

173 "My mother, who was quite a critical person" Lady Soames interview, Newton Collection, FDRL.

174 "Lord Root of the Matter" Pamela Churchill Harriman interview, Newton Collection, FDRL.

174 took a train trip north *WSC,* VI, 990.

174 Churchill would introduce Hopkins *RAH,* 247.

174 Hopkins stood and said *TSFS,* 6. Sir Charles Wilson, Churchill's doctor, became Lord Moran in 1943. For simplicity, he is called only Lord Moran here.

174 Churchill wept Ibid.

174 "He knew what it meant" Ibid.

174 "His was a soul" Churchill, *The Grand Alliance,* 23.

175 After a long night with Churchill Lash, *Roosevelt and Churchill,* 282.

175 It was snowing *WSC,* VI, 992.

175 Hopkins "is really" *CWP,* III, 97.

175 Willkie, who was to leave for England *RAH,* 233.

175 "The Building of the Ship" Ibid., 234.

176 "Sail on, O Ship of State!" Ibid.

176 In Washington, Charles Lindbergh was testifying *The New York Times,* January 24, 1941; Warren F. Kimball, *The Most Unsordid Act: Lend-Lease, 1939–1941* (Baltimore, 1969), 189–190.

176 Churchill and Hopkins went to Dover *WSC,* VI, 992.

176 "There goes the bloody British Empire" *TFOP,* 341.

176 Churchill's grandson Winston related   Author interview with Winston S. Churchill.

177 At midnight at Chequers   *TFOP,* 342.

178 "We must all of us"   *CWP,* III, 196–200. Joseph Lash reported that the speech itself "was written with the assistance of Hopkins" and "had been urged by, among others, Walter Lippmann, who was afraid that 'Americans might still be frightened into thinking that their help was too late to be of use. . . . Colonel Lindbergh had cleverly and successfully touched this weak and cowardly spot in the American character by his testimony before the Foreign Affairs Committee last week.'" (Lash, *Roosevelt and Churchill,* 283–284)

179 Over a lunch of corned beef hash   *RAH,* 267.

179 According to Sherwood   Ibid.

179 American military planners   Reynolds, *From Munich to Pearl Harbor,* 116–119.

180 won the Lend-Lease vote   *The New York Times,* February 9, 1941.

180 Churchill was asleep   *RAH,* 265.

180 "I find my thoughts constantly with you"   Ibid.

180 "Thank God for your news"   Churchill, *The Grand Alliance,* 128.

180 "Our blessings from the whole of"   Ibid.

180 "Far more was needed"   Ibid.

180 "The President knew his man"   Pamela Chur-

chill Harriman interview, Newton Collection, FDRL.

CHAPTER 4: LUNCHING ALONE BROKE THE ICE

183 At a No. 10 Downing Street lunch   Diary of Meeting, Charles Eade, March 6, 1941, CEP.

184 Berlin continued to seize territory   I.C.B. Dear, ed., *The Oxford Companion to World War II* (New York, 1995), 422.

184 In North Africa   Ibid., 748.

184 Americans were producing three times as many   Cohen in *Grand Strategies in War and Peace,* ed. Kennedy, 51.

184 "I was faced with a practical problem"   Memorandum of Trip to Meet Winston Churchill, August 23, 1941, PSF, Safe, Atlantic Charter, FDRL. Roosevelt dictated the document after his return.

185 telling reporters   Ibid.

185 "This . . . became the basis"   Ibid.

185 ham, cheese, and cigars   *TFOP,* 415.

185 "Harry Hopkins came into the garden"   Churchill, *The Grand Alliance,* 427.

185 Roosevelt kept Eleanor in the dark   August 2, 1941, FDR Papers, microfilm edition, "Mrs. Roosevelt's Folder," Office Files, Subject Files, Part 4.

186 "Even at my ripe old age"   *CC,* 140.

186 an intriguing figure in the Roosevelt world Ibid., ix–xvii.

186 "We always thought of him" Author interview with Margaret Hendrick.

187 "I don't want to harp" *CC*, 138.

187 Churchill rushed *WSC*, VI, 1120.

187 Roosevelt said little Burns, *The Soldier of Freedom*, 103.

188 "I pray America won't let the Huns" Nancy Astor to Agnes Meyer, October 10, 1941, MP.

188 Churchill arranged *RAH*, 318–319.

188 a sunny, warm day Valentin Berezhkov interview, Newton Collection, FDRL.

188 "He looked very frail" Ibid.

188 "No man could forget the picture of" *RAH*, 343–344.

189 the Soviets would lose about 12,000,000 soldiers Polmar and Allen, eds., *World War II: The Encyclopedia of the War Years,* 836; the British and Americans figures are on 193. Statistics on battles losses (those killed or missing) are slippery, but whatever numbers one chooses to settle on, it is clear that the Soviet Union paid a vastly steeper price in blood than its allies did—which is not to minimize in any way the horrific casualties, military and civilian, sustained by those nations who took up arms against the Axis.

189 In a speech to the House *The New York Times,* July 30, 1941.

189 "What do you think of" *Complete Presidential Press Conferences,* July 29, 1941, XVIII, 63.

190 Grace Tully, who had also been   Tully, *FDR: My Boss,* 246.

190 rode by train from Union Station   Log of the President's Cruise, FDR Papers, microfilm edition, Office Files, Part 1, Safe and Confidential.

190 It was still light out   Memorandum of Trip to Meet Winston Churchill, August 23, 1941, FDRL.

190 "many persons saw me"   Ibid.

191 "Strange thing happened this morning"   *CC,* 140.

191 "delightful story"   Memorandum of Trip to Meet Winston Churchill, August 23, 1941, FDRL.

191 "The President sends word"   August 7, 1941, FDR Papers, microfilm edition, Office Files, Part 1, Safe and Confidential; *The Washington Post,* August 8, 1941.

192 "From USS Potomac"   August 7, 1941, FDR Papers, microfilm edition, Office Files, Part 1, Safe and Confidential; *The New York Times,* August 8, 1941.

192 Hopkins arrived from   *C & R,* I, 226.

192 Churchill was thinking constantly of   Sir John Martin, *Downing Street: The War Years* (New York, 1991), 57.

192 "I hope we shall have an interesting"   H. V. Morton, *Atlantic Meeting* (New York, 1943), 34–35.

193 "Winston Churchill was completely absorbed"   Ibid., 85–86.

193 found Vivien Leigh "ravishing"   Lady Soames note to author, January 12, 2003.

193 "I have, my lords, in different countries" Author viewing of Alexander Korda's *Lady Hamilton* (also known as *That Hamilton Woman*). Korda was friendly with Churchill and once asked him to write a treatment about the life of George V. Nothing ultimately came of Churchill's screenwriting career. See D. J. Wenden, "Churchill, Radio, and Cinema," in *Churchill,* eds. Blake and Louis, 232–233.

194 "the man who was watching"   Morton, *Atlantic Meeting,* 86.

194 Cadogan thought the movie   Dilks, ed., *The Diaries of Sir Alexander Cadogan,* 396–397.

194 "Gentlemen, I thought this film"   *CWP,* III, 1039.

194 "You'd have thought Winston"   *RAH,* 351.

194 Just after dawn   Morton, *Atlantic Meeting,* 90.

195 a dark blue uniform   Details drawn from photographs of the day, FDRL. See also Alsop, *FDR,* 180.

195 a suit   Ibid. See also Alsop, *FDR,* 180.

195 Two of his sons   Theodore A. Wilson, *The First Summit: Roosevelt & Churchill at Placentia Bay, 1941* (Lawrence, Kans., 1991), 65.

195 At eleven A.M., Churchill crossed the bay   The first Churchill-Roosevelt handshake has been well described by many writers. See, for example, Burns, *The Soldier of Freedom,* 126, and Wilson, *The First Summit,* 78–79. In addition, I also drew

on Burns, 125–131, and *WSC,* VI, 1154–1168, for my account of the gathering at Newfoundland. For the ensuing meetings between the two men, from this one at sea until the last lunch about the *Quincy,* readers seeking more detail can consult Burns, *The Soldier of Freedom,* Churchill's own war memoirs, and *WSC,* VI–VII, as well as all the other sources cited throughout the book.

195 "The Boss insisted"   Reilly and Slocum, *Reilly of the White House,* 120.

196 "a slight bow"   Morton, *Atlantic Meeting,* 98.

196 "the warmest of welcomes"   Churchill, *The Grand Alliance,* 431.

196 "At last—we've gotten together"   Reilly and Slocum, *Reilly of the White House,* 120.

196 "We have"   Ibid.

196 "There was a warmth there"   Author interview with Patrick Kinna.

196 "They were two men"   *RAH,* 363–364.

197 In his memoirs, Churchill hinted   Churchill, *The Grand Alliance,* 663.

197 "Papa completely forgot"   Author interview with Lady Soames.

198 Churchill's lapse annoyed Roosevelt   Kimball, "Wheel Within a Wheel: Churchill, Roosevelt, and the Special Relationship," in *Churchill,* eds. Blake and Louis, 297.

198 "I had met him"   Churchill, *The Gathering Storm,* 440.

198 "Most Americans"   Winston S. Churchill, *Lord Randolph Churchill* (London, 1907), 35.

198 "Many men with so many grave" Wilson Brown Memoir, 168, FDRL.

198 "it didn't take them long" Elliott Roosevelt, *As He Saw It* (New York, 1946), 25. In interviews, Lady Soames and George Elsey, both of whom spent time in private settings with Roosevelt and Churchill, confirmed to me that Churchill, who often referred to Roosevelt as "Mr. President" in larger gatherings, called Roosevelt "Franklin" when fewer people were present. Further evidence of this is Churchill's use of the salutation "My dear Franklin" on messages of a more personal nature later in the war.

199 "Does he like me?" Lash, *Roosevelt and Churchill,* 391.

199 "He is a tremendously vital person" *CC,* 141.

199 "What did *he* think of me?" Gunther, *Roosevelt in Retrospect,* 16.

199 "I have just talked" Note of Harry Hopkins to Winston Churchill, August 9, 1941, from on board the USS *Augusta,* Ship Harbor, Newfoundland, Hopkins Papers, FDRL.

199 Inspector Thompson noticed a red leather Thompson, *I Was Churchill's Shadow,* 72.

200 As Mary remembered it *CCTBOM,* 402–403.

201 "I managed to cause a diversion" Ibid., 403–404.

201 "Since the beginning of the war" Ibid., 404.

201 "I have massage, osteopathy" *WAC,* 457.

202 Eleanor had driven her mother-in-law *TIR,* 223.

202 "a timeless permanence" James Roosevelt, *Affectionately, FDR,* 316.

203 At a quarter to seven Dilks, ed., *The Diaries of Sir Alexander Cadogan,* 397.

203 "I had never met" Gerald Pawle, *The War and Colonel Warden* (New York, 1963), 117.

203 During the meal, the talk ranged Dilks, ed., *The Diaries of Sir Alexander Cadogan,* 398.

203 "might be prepared" Ibid.

203 When dessert was cleared Elliott Roosevelt, *As He Saw It,* 28.

203 "His conversation was" Lyttleton, *Memoirs,* 164.

204 "not his best" Dilks, ed., *The Diaries of Sir Alexander Cadogan,* 397.

204 "Churchill told us" H. H. Arnold, *Global Mission* (New York, 1949), 252.

205 "very grand" *CC,* 141.

205 "We have a grand day" Morton, *Atlantic Meeting,* 109–110. The Sunday morning service has been well chronicled. My version owes much to Morton, *Atlantic Meeting;* to Wilson, *The First Summit;* and to Churchill's own impressions. As the man behind the Sunday ceremony, Churchill left several moving accounts. See *The Grand Alliance,* 431–432, and *CWP,* III, 1099–1106. My order of the hymns and prayers, which differs in some accounts, is based on the original "Order of Service, August 10th, 1941," President's Official File 200-1-R: Trips of the President: Cruise on the USS AUGUSTA, Aug. 1941, FDRL. The hymns

were numbered 450, 643, and 540 in *The English Hymnal.*

205 "The PM had given much thought" Martin, *Downing Street: The War Years,* 58.

206 "Mr. Churchill walked about inspecting" Morton, *Atlantic Meeting,* 110.

206 "The President will embark" Memorandum for Commander C. R. Thompson, August 9, 1941, Prime Minister's Office Papers 1940–1945, Unit 10, PREM 4/71, Reel 247.

207 Roosevelt's ship came alongside Morton, *Atlantic Meeting,* 111.

208 "only the tenseness" Pawle, *The War and Colonel Warden,* 117.

208 "calm, carved face" Morton, *Atlantic Meeting,* 111.

208 Churchill by his side Ibid., 112.

208 "every step" *WSC,* VI, 1167.

208 "I shall always remember the look" Pawle, *The War and Colonel Warden,* 117.

208 Roosevelt would tell Daisy *CC,* 141.

208 "stumping" Ibid., 130.

209 "completely intermingled" Churchill, *The Grand Alliance,* 431.

209 "Every word seemed to stir the heart" Ibid., 432.

209 "In the long, frightful panorama" Morton, *Atlantic Meeting,* 113–114.

210 Churchill was weeping Ibid., 114.

211 "It was . . . a great hour to live" Churchill, *The Grand Alliance,* 432.

211 "If nothing else had happened" Elliott Roosevelt, *As He Saw It*, 33.

212 "We were all photographed" *CC*, 141.

212 "When I looked upon that densely-packed" *CWP*, III, 1105.

212 the menu included grouse Martin, *Downing Street: The War Years*, 59.

212 game-loving Gunther, *Roosevelt in Retrospect*, 92.

212 a "beautiful" luncheon *CC*, 141.

212 Cadogan found Roosevelt's informal conversational style Dilks, ed., *The Diaries of Sir Alexander Cadogan*, 398.

212 the ship's cat, Blackie Morton, *Atlantic Meeting*, 120.

214 thanked Churchill Ibid.

214 "It's an honor for us all" Ibid., 121.

214 went ashore Dilks, ed., *The Diaries of Sir Alexander Cadogan*, 398.

214 "A great load" Thompson, *I Was Churchill's Shadow*, 73.

214 "dining Winston Churchill" *CC*, 141.

215 "You sensed that two men" Elliott Roosevelt, *As He Saw It*, 35.

215 After dinner Thompson, *I Was Churchill's Shadow*, 73–74.

215 "Your father is a great man" Ibid., 74.

216 "I think of it in this way" Churchill, *Savrola*, 84–85.

217 "Friendship among nations" Rosenman, ed., *Public Papers and Addresses of Franklin D. Roosevelt*, II, 130.

218 The Americans agreed   *WSC,* VI, 1160.

218 In July, Tokyo had   Burns, *The Soldier of Freedom,* 108–110.

218 "Western Hemisphere Defence Plan No. 4"   *CWP,* III, 1047–1048.

218 "They are sending us"   Ibid., 1061.

218 would ask for another $5 billion   Ibid.

219 "The war goes on upon"   Ibid., 1065.

219 "I fear the President"   Churchill, *The Grand Alliance,* 442.

219 Roosevelt told Daisy   *CC,* 141–142.

220 "The various officers"   Ibid., 142.

220 The leave-taking   Ibid.

220 "It symbolizes"   *CWP,* III, 1100.

221 John Martin told Jock Colville   Colville, *Inner Circle,* 120.

221 In a letter to his son   *WSC,* VI, 1177.

222 "All well & a bit of a let-down!"   *CC,* 142.

222 smooth seas and slept twelve hours   Ibid.

222 only a single vote in the House   Burns, *The Soldier of Freedom,* 120.

222 In his first press conference   *Complete Presidential Press Conferences,* August 16, 1941, XVIII, 76–84.

223 "When Roosevelt returned"   Frances Perkins, COH, 21–25.

223 Perkins, a longtime student of both   Ibid.

225 On August 19   *Complete Presidential Press Conferences,* August 19, 1941, XVIII, 85–97.

225 At the cabinet meeting   Frances Perkins, COH, 25.

225 Alice Deane sent Eleanor   Eleanor Roosevelt

Papers, Part I, 1877 to April 12, 1945, Series 100, Personal Letters, 1941, Folder Da–Deg, Box 737.

226 "I should say Alice Deane"   Ibid.

226 In what Robert Sherwood called   *RAH,* 373.

226 a "wave of depression"   *WSC,* VI, 1176.

226 "If 1942 opens"   Ibid.

227 "Talking of the war in general"   Diary of Meeting, Charles Eade, November 19, 1941, CEP.

227 "Your mother is much better"   Ibid., 1177.

227 Sara Delano Roosevelt died   A finely detailed account of Mrs. Roosevelt's last days can be found in Ward, *A First-Class Temperament,* 1–9.

227 "Those who were closest"   *RAH,* 385.

228 "Mother went to father"   James Roosevelt, *My Parents: A Differing View,* (Chicago, 1976), 113.

228 "Franklin's mother had always wanted"   *TIR,* 227–228.

228 Hall Roosevelt, Eleanor's beloved brother   Ibid., 228–230.

228 he "did not fail her"   James Roosevelt, *My Parents: A Differing View,* 113.

229 "Pray accept my deep sympathy"   *CWP,* III, 1182.

229 "Thank you for your kind"   Ibid., 1182, footnote 1.

229 "Invictus"   Ibid., 1196. Though Henley wrote "soul," Churchill said "souls."

230 "The young men are really"   Eugene Meyer Diary of Trip to London, September 10, 1941, 4–5, 7, MP.

230 "As we sat down"   Ibid., 41–42.

231 there had been a skirmish   Burns, *The Soldier of Freedom*, 139.

231 "for your private and very confidential"   *C & R*, I, 237.

231 "We have sought"   Buhite and Levy, eds., *FDR's Fireside Chats*, 194–196.

232 At a luncheon with British editors   Eugene Meyer Diary of Trip to London, 20, MP.

232 Charles Lindbergh had asserted   *The New York Times*, September 12, 1941.

232 "Mr. Lindbergh's speech in Iowa"   Eugene Meyer Diary of Trip to London, 20, MP.

232 "Roosevelt this morning excellent"   *WSC*, VI, 1188.

233 Roosevelt delayed his usual Thanksgiving trip   Tully, *FDR: My Boss*, 248–249.

233 That night in the dining hall   Ibid., 250–251.

233 "This may be the last time"   Ibid., 251.

234 Churchill was at Chequers   *CWP*, III, 1574.

235 "I can do almost everything"   Perkins, *The Roosevelt I Knew*, 144–145. Geoffrey Ward speculated to me that the difficulty he faced in trying to kneel may also have played a role.

235 Hopkins and Roosevelt were lunching   *RAH*, 430–431.

235 About 2,400   Dear, ed., *The Oxford Companion to World War II*, 680.

235 Clementine did not feel well   Harriman and Abel, *Special Envoy*, 111.

236 "Churchill had discovered that"   Author interview with Kathleen Harriman Mortimer.

236 "The Prime Minister seemed" Harriman and Abel, *Special Envoy*, 111.

236 "a bit slow" Ibid.

236 The first item Ibid.

236 "The news has just been given" *CWP*, III, 1576.

237 "I did not personally sustain" Churchill, *The Grand Alliance*, 605.

237 Harriman repeated the words Harriman and Abel, *Special Envoy*, 112.

237 While Harriman and Thompson argued Ibid.

237 "slammed the top of the radio" Ibid.

237 as Sawyers entered the dining room Churchill, *The Grand Alliance*, 605.

237 Martin, who had bolted Harriman and Abel, *Special Envoy*, 112.

237 "a silence" Churchill, *The Grand Alliance*, 605.

237 The prime minister headed for the door Churchill, *The Grand Alliance*, 605.

237 "We shall declare war on Japan" *CWP*, III, 1577.

237 Winant chased after him Ibid.

237 Churchill paused Ibid.

238 "Mr. President, . . . what's this about Japan?" Churchill, *The Grand Alliance*, 605.

238 "This certainly simplifies things" Ibid.

238 She remembered saying good-bye *TIR*, 232–233.

238 "waited till Franklin was alone" Ibid., 233.

239 "I went back to work" Ibid.

239 Handling the telephone himself *RAH*, 431–432.

239 wearing an old sweater James Roosevelt, *Affectionately, FDR,* 327.

239 directing troop movements with General George Marshall *RAH,* 432.

239 "My God, there's another wave" Tully, *FDR: My Boss,* 255.

239 "Many of the moves required" *RAH,* 432.

239 At about five in the afternoon Tully, *FDR: My Boss,* 256.

240 There was another edit James Roosevelt, *Affectionately, FDR,* 328.

240 Eleanor returned to the center of action *TIR,* 233.

241 "No American will think it wrong" Churchill, *The Grand Alliance,* 606.

242 He felt his obligations Ibid., 605.

242 He wrote telegrams after midnight *CWP,* III, 1580.

242 "He was quite naturally" Ibid., 1579.

243 "The United States and Britain were now" Ibid.

243 navy cape Forrest Davis and Ernest K. Lindley, *How War Came* (New York, 1942), 319.

243 Robert Sherwood and Sam Rosenman left the White House after dark Rosenman, *Working with Roosevelt,* 309–310.

243 The bright lamp that usually lit the White House Ibid., 310.

243 "I wonder how long" Ibid.

243 "I don't know" Ibid.

244 On Tuesday, in a fireside chat Buhite and Levy, eds., *FDR's Fireside Chats*, 198–205.

244 Roosevelt drafted, but did not send *C & R*, I, 285.

245 did raise questions Ibid., 284.

245 "Today all of us" Ibid., 283.

245 "Now that we are as you say" Ibid., 283–284.

245 "I understand only too well" Shirer, *The Rise and Fall of the Third Reich*, 898.

246 "I don't see" Ibid., 895.

247 "the American Century" *Life*, February 17, 1941.

247 "Delighted to have you here" *C & R*, I, 286.

247 "At one of our meetings" Alex Danchev and Daniel Todman, eds., *War Diaries, 1939–1945: Field Marshal Lord Alanbrooke* (Berkeley, Calif., 2001), 209.

CHAPTER 5: A COUPLE OF EMPERORS

251 "I have read two books" *WAC*, 461.

251 The novels may have fanned Author readings of F. Britten Austin, *Forty Centuries Look Down*, and C. S. Forester, *Brown on Resolution*.

252 "He is a different man" *TSFS*, 9–10.

140 flew from Hampton Roads *WSC*, VII, 23. Burns, *The Soldier of Freedom*, 175–190, is also good on the Christmas visit.

252 cabled Roosevelt *C & R*, I, 292.

252 the dusk   *TSFS,* 11.

252 "It was very sweet of him"   Author interview with Patrick Kinna.

252 "honoured and touched"   Thompson, *I Was Churchill's Shadow,* 79.

253 "swept in like"   *Time,* January 5, 1942.

253 worried Churchill   *RAH,* 445. The British, Sherwood wrote, "suspected that extraordinary events in the Pacific might . . . be met with plans for all-out American effort against Japan, leaving the British and Russians to handle the German enemy in Europe."

253 "The principle of Germany first"   Ibid., 446.

254 three long papers laying out his vision   Churchill, *The Grand Alliance,* 645.

254 North Africa and the Middle East   Ibid., 651.

254 must build naval strength   Ibid., 653–654.

254 Germany would be bombed   Ibid., 649.

254 there would be Anglo-American landings   Ibid., 656.

254 "three or four"   Ibid., 657.

254 "It must be remembered"   Ibid., 649.

255 "As we both, by need"   Ibid., 663.

255 The prime minister's hours kept Roosevelt up   Author interview with George Elsey.

255 "We had to remember"   EROH, Session 16, 2.

255 "Never had the staid butlers"   Reilly and Slocum, *Reilly of the White House,* 125.

256 Grace Tully looked out   Tully, *FDR: My Boss,* 300.

256 Lord Chandos once had cold lobster Lyttleton, *Memoirs,* 308.

257 changing from his siren suit *The New York
Times,* December 24, 1941.

257 wire basket of papers and a silver thermos of
water Details of office and dress drawn from
photograph of press conference, FDRL, *The New
York Times,* and *The Washington Post.*

257 "a healthy pink tinge" *The New York Times,*
December 24, 1941.

257 "I would like to get" *Complete Presidential
Press Conferences,* December 23, 1941, XVIII, 382.

257 gray pinstripes and smoking a cigarette *The
New York Times,* December 24, 1941.

257 "He is quite willing to take on a conference"
Complete Presidential Press Conferences, December
23, 1941, XVIII, 383.

257 "Two great statesmen-showmen" *Washington
Star,* December 24, 1941.

257 "I wish you would just stand" *Complete Presidential Press Conferences,* December 23, 1941,
XVIII, 386.

258 Churchill mounted his chair *Washington Star,*
December 24, 1941.

258 "It was terribly exciting" Conversation
between Curtis Roosevelt and Alistair Cooke,
New York City, October 20, 1993, Acc#95-03,
FDRL.

258 "Go ahead and shoot" *Complete Presidential
Press Conferences,* December 23, 1941, XVIII,
386–392.

259 To that point   *The Washington Post,* December 24, 1941.

259 "If we manage it well"   *Complete Presidential Press Conferences,* December 23, 1941, XVIII, 388.

260 "The smiling President looked like" *Newsweek,* January 5, 1942; *The New York Times,* December 24, 1941.

260 They both understood the significance   For essays touching on Roosevelt's and Churchill's grasp of what a later generation would call "image making," see William E. Leuchtenburg, *The FDR Years: On Roosevelt and His Legacy* (New York, 1995), 1–34, and D. J. Wenden, "Churchill, Radio, and Cinema," in *Churchill,* eds. Blake and Louis, 215–239.

261 assembled for cocktails   *CWP,* III, 1675.

261 "children's hour"   Freidel, *Launching the New Deal,* 281.

261 "At cocktail time everything was"   Author interview with Lady Soames.

261 not a consistent recipe   Rosenman, *Working with Roosevelt,* 150. Grace Tully is also amusing on this topic. See Tully, *FDR: My Boss,* 22–25.

262 "Churchill could not abide"   Conversation between Curtis Roosevelt and Alistair Cooke, October 20, 1993, New York City, Acc# 95-03, 18, FDRL.

262 "The problem in this country"   Ibid.

262 "It was not the amount"   Reilly and Slocum, *Reilly of the White House,* 125.

263 one of the few moments   Gunther, *Roosevelt in Retrospect*, 95.

263 "How about another sippy?"   Tully, *FDR: My Boss*, 24.

263 "He needed an audience"   Author interview with George Elsey.

263 "Mrs. Roosevelt was very afraid"   Author interview with Trude Lash.

263 At times, Roosevelt conducted   Rosenman, *Working with Roosevelt*, 152–153.

264 "Drinking to excess is a type"   *TIR*, 312.

264 "Mrs. Roosevelt was most abstemious"   Author interview with Trude Lash.

264 whiskey sours were on offer   *CWP*, III, 1675.

264 Churchill was delayed   Ibid.

264 Percy Chubb, the husband of a grandniece   Ibid.

264 "I have not had a minute"   *WAC*, 461.

264 At dinner, Roosevelt and Churchill   *CWP*, III, 1675.

265 Roosevelt, who had supported the Boers   Ibid.

265 Chubb thought "the President"   Ibid.

265 Roosevelt volunteered that   Ibid., 1676.

266 Roosevelt had made a dark joke   *The Washington Post*, December 25, 1941.

266 "Our strongest weapon in this war"   Ibid.

266 "There was a vast crowd"   Thompson, *I Was Churchill's Shadow*, 80.

266 Shivering, Churchill   *The Washington Post*, December 25, 1941.

266 "my associate, my old and good friend" *The New York Times,* December 25, 1941.

267 "I spend this anniversary and festival" *CWP,* III, 1679.

268 "there was little joy" *TIR,* 243.

268 As he returned inside *TSFS,* 12–13.

268 Eleanor had been worried *TIR,* 243.

268 "Tender love" *WAC,* 461.

268 "I miss you" Ibid., 463.

269 Defending his decision Perkins, *The Roosevelt I Knew,* 146.

269 "It is good for Winston" Ibid.

269 lilies on the altar *The Washington Post,* December 26, 1941.

269 the fourth pew from the front Ibid.

269 for "those who are dying" Ibid.

269 "Certainly there was much to fortify" Churchill, *The Grand Alliance,* 670.

269 "In these first talks" *TIR,* 246.

270 "I got the impression" Diary of Trip to London, Eugene Meyer, 1942, 17, MP.

270 the Americans favored Burns, *The Soldier of Freedom,* 181–183; *C & R,* II, 292–293.

270 "For the first time" *WSC,* VII, 34–35.

271 When it came to munitions Ibid., 39–40.

271 "I am a child of the House of Commons" *CWP,* III, 1685.

271 "It seemed a very great world" *MEL,* 34.

271 Churchill carried a walking stick Manchester, *The Last Lion: Visions of Glory,* 398.

271 "Most of Churchill's ancestors" Ashley, *Churchill As Historian,* 12–13.

272 had first visited the White House Kleeman, *Gracious Lady,* 145–146.

272 Roosevelt would boast Tully, *FDR: My Boss,* 12.

272 an early New York State senator Freidel, *A Rendezvous with Destiny,* 4.

272 had led Washington's horse Tully, *FDR: My Boss,* 12.

272 On election night in Hyde Park Burns, *The Soldier of Freedom,* 4.

274 He had come to Alice Roosevelt's wedding Ward, *A First-Class Temperament,* 45–47.

274 his grandchildren played Tully, *FDR: My Boss,* 9.

274 head usher remembered EROH, Session 3, 2–3.

274 "My husband did not go" Ibid., Session 7, 7.

274 Christmas dinner 1941 was a large affair *TIR,* 244.

274 Churchill had been working *TSFS,* 14.

275 sipped champagne *CWP,* III, 1684.

275 "silent and preoccupied" *TSFS,* 15.

275 Hopkins was concerned *RAH,* 444.

275 Roosevelt wished Churchill luck Churchill, *The Grand Alliance,* 671.

275 A roar greeted the prime minister *The Washington Post,* December 27, 1941.

276 Roosevelt listened to the speech *Washington Star,* December 27, 1941.

276 "The fact that my American forebears" *CWP,* III, 1685.

277 He had found in Washington Ibid., 1686–1690.

278 it had seemed like just five *The Washington Post,* December 27, 1941.

278 "Inside, the scene was impressive" Churchill, *The Grand Alliance,* 671.

278 Churchill turned and flashed *The Washington Post,* December 27, 1941.

278 "V for Victory" sign Ibid.

278 "That fellow's really got it" Ibid.

278 "It was a clever speech" Ibid.

278 Churchill greeted the senator *The New York Times,* December 28, 1941.

279 "It was with heart-stirrings" Churchill, *The Grand Alliance,* 671.

279 "told me I had done" Ibid., 673.

280 after Churchill went to bed *TSFS,* 17–18.

281 "in trying to open the window" Churchill, *The Grand Alliance,* 691.

281 "In fact the course adopted by Moran" *WSC,* VII, 32.

281 "These great occasions imposed" Churchill, *The Grand Alliance,* 663.

282 "I have been thinking constantly" *WAC,* 462.

282 On New Year's morning *The Washington Post,* January 2, 1942.

282 Eleanor had to slip her husband *TIR,* 246.

283 a wreath of chrysanthemums *The Washington Post,* January 2, 1942.

283 Joseph Lash was seated   Lash, *Roosevelt and Churchill,* 15–16.

283 had been wrestling   *RAH,* 448.

283 Churchill remembered that Roosevelt   Churchill, *The Grand Alliance,* 682.

283 the president assured Litvinov   *RAH,* 448–449.

283 Churchill was so amused   Churchill, *The Grand Alliance,* 683.

284 "He was always full of stories"   Author interview with Trude Lash.

284 "A Declaration by the United Nations"   *The New York Times,* January 3, 1942.

285 mentioned his "stab in the back" speech   Lash, *Roosevelt and Churchill,* 16.

285 "Although il Duce"   Ibid.

285 "The best thing to do with Hitler"   Ibid., 19.

285 "Churchill recalled that in 1918–1919"   Ibid., 18.

186 "Four fifths"   Ibid., 20.

286 "We have at least four-fifths"   *CWP,* III, 1584.

286 "stalked around"   Lash, *Roosevelt and Churchill,* 20.

287 The men around Roosevelt   *RAH,* 444.

287 "It went over big"   Ibid.

287 Beaverbrook had arrived and urged   Churchill, *The Grand Alliance,* 688–689.

288 "We cannot wage this war"   *RAH,* 455.

288 Sam Rosenman dined   Rosenman, *Working with Roosevelt,* 319.

288 "My American friends thought that I"   Churchill, *The Grand Alliance,* 691.

288 "I am happy that you are" *WAC,* 463.

288 "This routine was beginning" Rosenman, *Working with Roosevelt,* 319.

289 "Nothing seems to be right" *TSFS,* 22.

289 Thompson had tried to get Churchill Thompson, *I Was Churchill's Shadow,* 83.

289 "They said it was only" Churchill, *The Grand Alliance,* 691.

289 "we saw no more of it" Thompson, *I Was Churchill's Shadow,* 84.

290 Churchill described the incident Churchill, *The Grand Alliance,* 696–697.

292 Preparing to return, he had telephoned *WSC,* VII, 38.

292 were ushered into the White House Louis Adamic, *Dinner at the White House* (New York, 1946), 9.

293 Adamic added a footnote *Newsweek,* January 27, 1947, 32.

293 The last time Adamic had seen Adamic, *Dinner at the White House,* 15.

294 "there was" Ibid.

294 "He was giving" Ibid., 15–16, 18, 19.

294 He struck Adamic at first Ibid., 25.

295 Raleigh's spreading his cloak Churchill, *The Grand Alliance,* 663.

295 Watching the two men, Adamic Adamic, *Dinner at the White House,* 26.

296 "It's strange to say now" Author interview with George Elsey.

296 "The Prime Minister is about" *CC,* 165–166.

297 Roosevelt cried out Adamic, *Dinner at the White House,* 60–62.

298 When the Adamics left Author interview with Margaret Hendrick.

1298 "Where do you think" Author interview with Anne Edwards (Anne Curzon-Howe).

299 "Mrs. Roosevelt invited these people" Author interview with Margaret Hendrick.

299 "Call me Cousin Winston" Author interview with Anne Edwards.

299 The subject of growing old *CC,* 166.

299 "Brandy and the usual cigars" Author interview with Anne Edwards.

299 dined alone with Roosevelt and Hopkins *RAH,* 477.

300 documents to initial Ibid.

300 lingered an hour Ibid., 478.

300 "You would have been quite proud" Ibid.

300 "Inscribed for President Franklin D. Roosevelt" *R & C,* I, 310.

300 "Trust me" *WSC,* VII, 43. According to the War Cabinet records, Churchill also told his colleagues that the "United States Administration were tackling war problems with the greatest vigour, and were clearly resolved not to be diverted from using all the resources of their country to the utmost to crush Hitler, our major enemy." Then, in an interesting sign of a lingering British sense of strategic superiority to their former colonies, Churchill said

he thought the Americans "were not above learning from us, provided that we did not set out to teach them." Ibid.

CHAPTER 6: I THINK OF YOU OFTEN

303 "It was to no sunlit prospect" Churchill, *The Grand Alliance,* 706.

303 "winter of disaster" *RAH,* 490.

303 "Nearly half those who sang" Churchill, *The Grand Alliance,* 432.

303 "The underrated Japanese forces" *RAH,* 490–491.

304 Rommel . . . driving east Polmar and Allen, *World War II: The Encyclopedia of the War Years,* 589.

304 "There was no excitement here now" Rosenman, *Working with Roosevelt,* 312.

304 "The President is amazingly calm" *RAH,* 492.

305 He faced a no-confidence vote Churchill, *The Hinge of Fate,* 61–62.

305 "Home again with the Prime Minister" Telegram from Beaverbrook to Averell Harriman, January 18, 1942, BBK D/463, LBP.

305 "Clementine hated to see" *CCTBOM,* 413.

305 "One of the characteristics" BBK G/11/4, LBP.

305 A cold made things worse *WSC,* VII, 49.

305 "In spite of the shocks" Churchill, *The Hinge of Fate,* 62.

306 "This story shall the good man" William Shakespeare, *Henry V,* act 4, scene 2, *The Complete*

Oxford Shakespeare, volume 1, Stanley Wells and Gary Taylor, eds., 356.

307 "Trust the people" *CWP,* III, 1685.

307 "There is no worse mistake" Churchill, *The Hinge of Fate,* 61.

307 "The news is going to get worse" Rosenman, *Working with Roosevelt,* 315.

308 In a Washington's Birthday broadcast *RAH,* 504.

308 "heartening" *C & R,* I, 370.

308 "In no way have I mitigated" *WSC,* VII, 51.

308 464 to 1 Churchill, *The Hinge of Fate,* 71.

308 "The naggers in the press" Ibid.

309 Roosevelt congratulated him *C & R,* I, 337. This was the message with the touching "It is fun to be in the same decade with you" remark of Roosevelt's.

309 "There is very little to cheer" Nancy Astor to Eugene Meyer, February 18, 1942, MP.

309 "I speak to you all" *WSC,* VII, 58–59.

310 "dashed to the ground" *RAH,* 501.

310 "There were numerous expressions" Ibid.

310 "Winston had to say *something"* Ibid.

310 "I realize how the fall" *C & R,* I, 362–363.

311 "I do not like these days" Ibid., 364.

311 "When I reflect how I have longed" Ibid., 381.

312 "This may be a critical period" Ibid., 393.

312 "Clementine was of course" *CCTBOM,* 415.

313 She and Churchill tangled over Beaverbrook's role Ibid., 413–414.

313 "I am ashamed that"   *WAC,* 463.

313 In the spring of 1942   *CCTBOM,* 415–416.

313 "Please don't think"   Ibid., 464.

314 "a most uncharacteristic reflex"   Ibid., 415.

314 "In the event Clementine"   Ibid., 416.

314 "One cannot help feeling"   Ibid.

314 Randolph had learned   Sally Bedell Smith, *Reflected Glory* (New York, 1996), 84.

314 Randolph believed   Churchill, *His Father's Son,* 202. "Randolph found it impossible ever to forgive his parents for, as he saw it, condoning what had happened and, worse still, seeming to take Pamela's side by telling Randolph to be kinder to his young wife, of whom they were both so deeply fond." (Ibid.)

314 a letter of Clementine's   *WAC,* 464. The note, written to Churchill about her anger over Randolph's parachute plan, says in part: "I think his action is selfish & unjust. . . . as regards Pamela one might imagine she had betrayed or left him—"

314 "When Randolph levelled this accusation"   Churchill, *His Father's Son,* 202–203.

315 Mary "was outraged"   Ibid., 203.

315 "I think there was always"   EROH, Session 15, 3.

315 One evening on the presidential train   *TIR,* 144.

316 "we five Roosevelt children"   James Roosevelt, *Affectionately, FDR,* 5.

317 Roosevelt called his "the chicks"   Ibid., 8.

317 Churchill referred to his as "the kittens" *WAC,* 153.

317 "His letters show" *CCTBOM,* 312.

317 "One day in Washington" William Walton to Pamela Churchill, April 23, 1945, PHP.

318 "Nothing grows under the shadow" Montague Browne, *Long Sunset,* 148.

318 "It was a shock" EROH, Session 5, 20.

318 "As children, we soon became aware" *CCTBOM,* 313.

319 Churchill wept at young Winston's baptism Churchill, *His Father's Son,* 181.

319 Roosevelt insisted on having EROH, Session 14, 2.

319 Randolph and Pamela's divorce in December 1945 Churchill, *His Father's Son,* 276.

320 "I hope you have good news" Beaverbrook to Roosevelt, June 21, 1944, BBK C/277, LBP.

320 "I think my husband" EROH, Session 11, 6–7.

321 "Seeing their sons go off" *TIR,* 240.

322 "In the military as in the commercial" Churchill, *The Grand Alliance,* 673.

323 "When I think of the beaches" Dwight D. Eisenhower, *At Ease: Stories I Tell to Friends* (Garden City, N.Y., 1967), 273.

323 "What Harry and Geo. Marshall" *C & R,* I, 441.

324 a memorandum approved by Roosevelt Churchill, *The Hinge of Fate,* 314–315.

324 "one of the grand events" Ibid., 317.

324 "neither we nor our professional advisers" Ibid., 316.

326 "The President had first discussed" Churchill, *The Hinge of Fate*, 209.

326 The telegram arrived *RAH*, 530.

326 "Churchill said that he personally" Ibid., 531.

327 As he listened to Churchill Ibid.

327 "I used to see a lot" Harriman COH, 89.

327 "You know the weight" *C & R*, I, 449.

328 The old place had become *CC*, 148.

328 In front of the fireplace Ibid.

329 Eleanor had taken time *TIR*, 251.

329 "It did not all go" *TIR*, 251.

330 On the morning of Friday, June 19 *CC*, 160–161.

330 Churchill flew into New Hackensack Churchill, *The Hinge of Fate*, 377. These June days, from Churchill's drive with Roosevelt to the events surrounding the fall of Tobruk, offer perhaps the most telling example of the link between the personal and the political for the prime minister and the president. My version draws heavily on Churchill's own account in his memoirs, which, like his later portrait of the conference at Teheran, is an unusually revealing and thorough sketch of his feelings, the political and military stakes, and—in this case more so than at Teheran—the affection he felt for (and from) Roosevelt. Churchill's own testimony about the effect of Roosevelt's generosity, buttressed by Brooke, Ismay, Moran, and Colville,

shows this to be a critical moment in the friendship—an instance, as I describe it in the narrative, of one of the men drawing strength from the other. See also *WSC*, VII, 126–129; *TIR*, 251–252; and Burns, *The Soldier of Freedom*, 235–236.

330 could drive by himself   Churchill, *The Hinge of Fate*, 377.

330 "the grass verges"   Ibid.

330 "I hoped"   Ibid.

330 "No responsible British military authority"   *C & R*, I, 515.

331 the small suite was filled   Author tour of Hyde Park.

331 Coming down, Churchill found Daisy   *CC*, 162.

332 "There seemed to be real friendship"   Ibid.

332 Roosevelt asked Daisy a favor   Ibid., 163.

332 Churchill used Harry Hopkins as a conduit   Churchill, *The Hinge of Fate*, 377.

332 his little study on the ground floor   Author tour of Hyde Park. For the history of the room and its features, see Denker, *Historic Furnishings Report: Springwood, Home of Franklin D. Roosevelt*, I, 54–55.

333 "The room was dark"   Churchill, *The Hinge of Fate*, 379.

333 Churchill had been briefed   Churchill, *The Gathering Storm*, 386.

333 Roosevelt had learned   Richard Rhodes, *The Making of the Atomic Bomb* (New York, 1986), 305, for description of Sachs; 313–314 for briefing.

333 In Britain, Churchill had   Ibid., 371–372.

334 "What if the enemy"   Churchill, *The Hinge of Fate*, 380–381.

334 drove up to Top Cottage   *CC*, 163.

335 a warm Sunday with brief thundershowers *The Washington Post*, June 21, 1942.

335 At the White House   Churchill, *The Hinge of Fate*, 382.

335 it was his birthday   Ismay, *Memoirs*, 254.

335 pink paper   Danchev and Todman, eds., *War Diaries: Alanbrooke*, 269.

335 was brought in   Churchill, *The Hinge of Fate*, 382. See also Ismay, *Memoirs*, 255.

335 "Tobruk has surrendered"   Churchill, *The Hinge of Fate*, 382.

335 "Defeat is one thing"   Ibid., 383.

335 "Not only"   Ibid.

336 "one of the heaviest"   Ibid.

336 "a bitter moment"   Ibid.

336 "I did not attempt"   Ibid.

336 The meaning was immediately apparent *RAH*, 591–592.

336 Roosevelt spoke up   Ismay, *Memoirs*, 255.

336 "What can we do to help?"   Ibid.

336 "I remember vividly being impressed" Danchev and Todman, eds., *War Diaries: Alanbrooke*, 269.

337 "Roosevelt's heart warmed"   Colville, *Inner Circle*, 122. Also see Alldritt, *The Greatest of Friends*, 94, and Jenkins, *Churchill*, 692–693.

337 "Give us as many Sherman tanks" Churchill, *The Hinge of Fate*, 383.

337 "Mr. President," Marshall replied Ibid.

338 "they arrived in time" Ismay, *Memoirs*, 255.

338 "It is interesting to consider" Ibid., 255–256.

338 Eleanor was amazed *TIR*, 252.

339 "What matters is that" *TSFS*, 40–41.

339 "Nothing could exceed" Churchill, *The Hinge of Fate*, 383.

340 "A friend in need is a friend" Ibid.

340 "A man loves his friend" Churchill, *Savrola*, 33.

340 "Winston's buoyant temperament" *TSFS*, 41–42.

340 Roosevelt rang Daisy that week *CC*, 167.

341 brush with a potential assassin Churchill, *The Hinge of Fate*, 389–390.

341 After the shooting in Miami EROH, Session 7, 4.

342 "this seemed to me to be" Churchill, *The Hinge of Fate*, 390.

342 "Some people assume too readily" Ibid., 402.

342 "Good for you" *C & R*, I, 517.

342 *Jane's Fighting Ships* *CC*, 168.

343 "The Jews, supposed to have" Churchill, *Great Contemporaries*, 267.

343 In a speech to the Reichstag Martin Gilbert, *The Holocaust* (New York, 1985), 76.

343 At a secret conference in Wannsee Ibid., 280–293; also see Richard Breitman, *Official*

Secrets: What the Nazis Planned, What the Americans and British Knew (New York, 1998), 86–87.

344 On July 21, twenty thousand people   *The New York Times,* July 22, 1942.

344 The debate over the Allied response   Breitman, *Official Secrets,* is an excellent guide to this issue, and I am grateful to Professor Breitman for discussing the subject with me.

344 both men have been criticized since the war For the most prominent critique, see David S. Wyman, *The Abandonment of the Jews: America and the Holocaust, 1941–1945* (New York, 1998). For a useful short guide to the shifting historical opinion on the subject, see Robert H. Abzug, ed., *America Views the Holocaust, 1933–1945: A Brief Documentary History* (New York, 1999), 207–213.

344 Critics say   As noted above, Wyman, *The Abandonment of the Jews,* is a clear articulation of this point of view.

345 defenders argue that the two men   Arthur M. Schlesinger Jr., "Did FDR Betray the Jews? Or Did He Do More Than Anyone Else to Save Them?" in *FDR and the Holocaust,* ed. Verne W. Newton (New York, 1996), 159–161; Schlesinger, *A Life in the 20th Century: Innocent Beginnings, 1917–1950* (New York, 2000), 306–312; William J. vanden Heuvel, "America and the Holocaust," *American Heritage,* July/August 1999, 34–52. Also see William D. Rubenstein, *The Myth of Rescue: Why the Democracies Could Not Have Saved More Jews from the Nazis* (New York, 1997), which argues just what its subtitle says.

345 Churchill was researching his biography of Marlborough Churchill, *The Gathering Storm,* 83–84; also see Ernst Hanstaengl, *Hitler: The Missing Years* (New York, 1994), 184–187.

345 a Harvard alumnus Hanfstaengl, *Hitler: The Missing Years,* 27.

345 "Hitler produced a thousand excuses" Ibid., 185.

346 "Why is your chief so violent about the Jews?" Churchill, *The Gathering Storm,* 83–84.

346 Hanfstaengl mounted a defense Hanfstaengl, *Hitler: The Missing Years,* 185.

346 "Tell your boss from me" Ibid.

346 The next morning, Hitler Ibid., 187.

346 the "Jew Deal" Schlesinger, *A Life in the 20th Century,* 311.

346 when a sanitized translation of *Mein Kampf* Breitman, *Official Secrets,* 24–25.

347 "could scarcely believe that such things" Freidel, *A Rendezvous with Destiny,* 314.

347 "Thank God for Roosevelt" Breitman, "Roosevelt and the Holocaust" in *FDR and the Holocaust,* ed. Newton, 117–118.

347 Both countries allowed refugees in after Hitler's rise to power Richard Breitman and Alan M. Kraut, *American Refugee Policy and American Jewry, 1933–1945* (Bloomington, Ind., 1987), 9.

347 In May 1939, the ship *St. Louis* Ibid., 70–73.

190 London, worried about Arab reaction Wyman, *The Abandonment of the Jews,* 157.

348 Immigration into Britain Bernard Wasser-

stein, *Britain and the Jews of Europe, 1939–1945* (New York, 1979), 81.

348 the bureaucracies in London and Washington See, for instance, Breitman, *Official Secrets,* 168–172; 177–187; 192–202; 225–233; Wyman, *The Abandonment of the Jews,* 311–317; Richard Breitman, "The Failure to Provide a Safe Haven for European Jewry" in *FDR and the Holocaust,* ed. Newton, 129–138; Beschloss, *The Conquerors,* 38–42; 51–55.

348 "In other days" Breitman, *Official Secrets,* 171.

348 An aide to Treasury Secretary Henry Morgenthau Ibid., 200.

349 Morgenthau, believing that anti-Semites Beschloss, *The Conquerors,* 56–57.

349 establish a War Refugee Board Gilbert, *Auschwitz and the Allies,* 172.

349 The board managed to rescue thousands Wyman, *The Abandonment of the Jews,* 285.

349 earlier attention and action could have made a difference The historian Gerhard L. Weinberg has written eloquently on this point, noting: "Every single life counts, and every individual saved counts. There cannot be the slightest doubt that more efforts could have been made by an earlier establishment of the War Refugee Board and by any number of other steps and actions. The general picture in terms of overall statistics would not have been very different; but the record of the Allies would have been brighter, and each person saved could have lived out a decent life. The exer-

tions of the Allies in World War II saved not only themselves but also the majority of the world's Jews. But the shadow of doubt whether enough was done will always remain, even if there really were not many things that could have been done." See Gerhard L. Weinberg, "The Allies and the Holocaust" in *The Holocaust and History: The Known, the Unknown, the Disputed, and the Reexamined,* eds. Michael Berenbaum and Abraham J. Peck (Bloomington, Ind., 1998), 490.

349 "Assuredly in the day of victory" Breitman, *Official Secrets,* 106.

350 "The mills of the gods" Ibid., 152.

350 "Their renditions were slightly different" Ibid.

350 the Allied Declaration *The Times* (London), December 18, 1942.

351 "The most tragic aspect" Wyman, *The Abandonment of the Jews,* 76, cites the first part of the editorial; see *The New York Times,* December 18, 1941, for the full quotation.

351 "I feel damn depressed" *RAH,* 609–612.

352 "U.S. ground forces" Ibid.

352 "In this, Roosevelt was thinking" Ibid.

352 almost certainly the right call For a useful summary of Churchill and the Second Front debates, see John Keegan, "Churchill's Strategy," in *Churchill,* eds. Blake and Louis, 327–352. Also see Alex Danchev, *On Specialness* (New York, 1998), 29–45. I am also grateful to Professor Danchev for talking with me about the subject.

352 arguing that an attack   *C & R,* I, 520.

353 "I cannot help feeling"   Ibid., 544.

353 "We have got always"   Ibid., 545.

354 "Mr. Churchill remarked on the difficulty" Diary of Meeting, Charles Eade, November 19, 1941, CEP.

354 ". . . I was sure it was"   Churchill, *The Hinge of Fate,* 475.

355 He made the case for North Africa   Ibid., 481.

355 "After their last official meeting"   Diary of Meeting, Charles Eade, September 30, 1942, CEP.

356 "The P. has heavy worries"   *CC,* 171.

356 "The President is astonishingly well"   Harry Hopkins to Beaverbrook, September 26, 1942, BBK C 175, LBP.

356 "The substance of Churchill's reply"   Diary of Meeting, Charles Eade, September 11, 1942, CEP.

CHAPTER 7: YOU MAY KISS MY HAND

359 "I like Mr. Churchill"   Bernard Asbell, ed., *Mother & Daughter: The Letters of Eleanor and Anna Roosevelt* (New York, 1982), 141.

359 Mrs. Roosevelt's skepticism   Lash, *Eleanor and Franklin,* 664, is one example.

359 "I do not think Mrs. Roosevelt"   Author interview with Lady Soames.

360 She was rather arch   *TIR,* 260.

360 "I know our better halves"   *C & R,* I, 633.

360 "I would appreciate"   Ibid., 639.

360 honey and a Virginia ham   Clementine Churchill to FDR, November 2, 1942, President's Secretary's Files, Diplomatic Correspondence, Great Britain, Churchill, Winston: 1940–1942, Box 37.

360 "I so *love*"   Ibid.

361 Mountbatten's action under fire   For a devastating revision of the Mountbatten legend, see Andrew Roberts, *Eminent Churchillians*, 55–136.

361 The film cuts back and forth   Author viewing of *In Which We Serve*.

361 "It was a novel experience"   *TIR*, 265.

361 The evidence of the bombings   Ibid., 267. Also see *The New York Times*, October 25, 1942.

361 "This was something that Franklin"   Ibid., 269.

362 one day Clementine had to break off   *CCT-BOM*, 420. Lady Soames's key line: "The First Lady's pace was too much for her—visibly—on one occasion, when . . . Clementine simply sat down on a marble staircase, and joined up with Mrs. Roosevelt later!" Kathleen Harriman, who was in England at the time, followed Eleanor on this trip as well and recalled: "I was exhausted. She would walk us all off our feet and then want to keep on going. She was tireless." (Author interview with Kathleen Harriman Mortimer)

362 "I have been fortunate"   Clementine Churchill to FDR, November 2, 1942.

362 "I did my best to advise"   *C & R,* I, 655.

362 "On another day, when she was"   Clementine Churchill to FDR, November 2, 1942.

363 "On each occasion"   Ibid.

364 Churchill joined his wife   *C & R,* I, 655.

364 "I remember my English friends"   Author interview with Trude Lash.

364 Asked at a London press conference   *The New York Times,* October 25, 1942.

364 "I feel that"   *The New York Times,* October 28, 1942.

364 "The spirit of the English people"   Lash, *Eleanor and Franklin,* 662.

364 measured the dimensions and doorways   November 20, 1942, FDR Papers, Diplomatic Correspondence, microfilm edition, Part 2, Reel 15.

365 Eleanor and Churchill exchanged words   *TIR,* 275.

365 "It annoyed Mrs. R."   Author interview with Trude Lash.

366 "One feels that, being in"   *TIR,* 267.

366 "Hurrah!"   *C & R,* I, 592.

366 "Okay full blast"   Ibid.

366 "All the Shermans"   Churchill, *The Hinge of Fate,* 589.

366 "For weeks, the P."   *CC,* 184.

367 "Quite cold"   Ibid., 184–186.

367 On Sunday, November 8   Ibid., 186.

367 "Once he began to bark"   *WSC,* VII, 252.

368 "I have never promised"   Ibid., 254.

368 lean back, and say of 1943   Diary of Meeting, Charles Eade, October 14, 1943, CEP.

369 One afternoon over Thanksgiving   CC, 187–188.

370 Churchill, who was turning sixty-eight   WSC, VII, 267.

370 "I predict nothing"   Robert Rhodes James, ed., *Complete Speeches of Winston Churchill*, VI (New York, 1974), 6714.

370 He quoted Kipling   Ibid.

371 "I know of nothing"   Ibid., 6714–6715.

372 Clementine gave him a lovely   CCTBOM, 421.

372 "My darling"   WAC, 471.

372 The Roosevelts' pre-Casablanca exchanges   TIR, 279.

374 "I think F. has mixed feelings"   CC, 194.

374 "The weather is bright"   WAC, 471–473.

374 Cabling Clementine about Roosevelt   Ibid., 473.

375 the principals' kith and kin   RAH, 674.

375 "These meetings meant a great deal"   TIR, 282.

375 "I was very glad to see him"   WAC, 475.

375 "Much good talk of war"   RAH, 674.

375 "We had a very agreeable"   WAC, 475.

376 Mike Reilly was on patrol   Reilly and Slocum, *Reilly of the White House*, 155.

376 Their vision   Burns, *The Soldier of Freedom*, 317–318.

376 "was a man of extraordinarily"   Dwight D. Eisenhower, "Churchill as an Ally in War," in

Churchill by His Contemporaries (New York, 1954), ed. Charles Eade, 159.

377 Marshall continued to urge the direct approach Burns, *The Soldier of Freedom,* 318.

377 striking France in 1943 was not ruled out *WSC,* VII, 311.

378 "It is in every respect" *WAC,* 475.

378 One day, Churchill was strolling "Trip to Casablanca, January 1943," U.S. Secret Service Records, Box 20, FDRL.

378 "Churchill asked his man Sawyers" Harry Hopkins Papers, Box 330, FDRL.

378 really a few teeth in a removable plate Lady Soames note to author, January 12, 2003.

379 The king of Morocco was to dine *RAH,* 685.

379 The rivalry between the leaders Claude Fohlen, "De Gaulle and Franklin D. Roosevelt," in *FDR and His Contemporaries,* eds. van Minnen and Sears, 34. I am indebted to Fohlen's essay for its succinct summary of this complicated story.

380 "Behind his patrician mask" Ibid., 36.

380 "the squalid tangles" *WAC,* 475.

380 Reporters, *Time* noted *Time,* February 1, 1943.

381 "Somehow it all seemed" *Newsweek,* February 1, 1943.

381 "The elimination of" Harriman and Abel, *Special Envoy,* 187–188.

381 Picnicking with Daisy at Hyde Park *CC,* 187.

382 "PRESIDENT'S DARING AIR TRIP" *The Washington Post,* January 27, 1943.

382 "Many thousand American troops" Churchill, *The Hinge of Fate,* 694.

382 olive-drab Daimler Kenneth Pendar, *Adventure in Diplomacy* (London, 1966), 144.

383 "looked like an Oriental potentate's" Ibid.

383 Churchill asked Pendar Ibid., 145.

383 Churchill counted the steps Ibid.

383 sixty of them Ibid.

383 "I have every intention" Ibid.

384 "Never have I seen" Ibid., 145–146.

384 Churchill sent for Ibid., 146.

384 "It's the most lovely spot" *TSFS,* 90.

384 "Just as the sun set" Pendar, *Adventure in Diplomacy,* 146.

385 donned a siren suit Ibid., 147.

2385 lying on a couch Ibid., 146.

385 "I am the Pasha" Ibid.

385 "Mr. Pendar was telling" "Trip to Casablanca, January 1943," U.S. Secret Service Records, Box 20, FDRL.

385 There was lobster and filet mignon Pendar, *Adventure in Diplomacy,* 147.

386 "made little affectionate speeches" *TSFS,* 90.

386 "Oh, let's don't" Pendar, *Adventure in Diplomacy,* 148.

386 "much banter" *RAH,* 694.

386 "struck by the fact" Pendar, *Adventure in Diplomacy,* 149.

387 were not going to please Burns, *The Soldier of Freedom,* 324–325.

387 "Both men had a catching"   Pendar, *Adventure in Diplomacy,* 150.

387 Over a nightcap   Ibid.

387 "we heard his bedroom slippers"   *TSFS,* 90.

387 "the weirdest outfit"   Pendar, *Adventure in Diplomacy,* 151.

387 Hopkins, who was also seeing   *RAH,* 694.

388 went to the airport together   Churchill, *The Hinge of Fate,* 695.

388 "Churchill and I took one last"   *RAH,* 694.

388 "Come, Pendar"   Pendar, *Adventure in Diplomacy,* 151–152.

388 "You can get in"   Ibid., 152.

388 Cabling Clementine, Churchill was warm   *WAC,* 476.

389 After returning to bed   Pendar, *Adventure in Diplomacy,* 152.

389 He talked of a future   Ibid., 153.

389 "Now, Pendar"   Ibid., 154.

390 code name was "Mr. Bullfinch"   *WAC,* 477.

390 "I am following your movements"   Ibid.

390 Eleanor was also waiting "anxiously"   *TIR,* 280.

390 Churchill came down with pneumonia   *WSC,* VII, 343.

390 Roosevelt found himself   Burns, *The Soldier of Freedom,* 324.

390 "I think I picked up"   *C & R,* II, 156–157.

391 "Many happy and glorious"   Ibid., 127.

391 "Gone are the days"   *The New York Times,* January 30, 1943.

CHAPTER 8: I KNOW HE MEANS TO MEET STALIN

393 Roosevelt asked him whether the Belgian refugees   Henry A. Wallace Diary, May 24, 1943.

394 a new Signal Corps film   Boettiger Papers, Box 5, FDRL.

394 "bitter season"   Harriman and Abel, *Special Envoy,* 199.

394 George Elsey was alone   Author interview with George Elsey.

395 the British agreed   Burns, *The Soldier of Freedom,* 370.

395 "Someone called No. 10"   Henry A. Wallace Diary, April 11, 1944.

396 "Here was Winston Churchill"   Author interview with George Elsey.

396 "the big man in the war"   Author interview with Trude Lash.

396 "Once again the pace and strain"   *CCTBOM,* 440.

396 John Boettiger . . . was going   *TIR,* 287.

397 "I imagine every mother felt"   Ibid., 292.

397 She told him about   *WAC,* 480.

397 Eleanor, Churchill said   Ibid., 483.

398 who had married the wealthy Winthrop Rutherfurd in early 1920   In a letter to Sara Roosevelt on February 14, 1920, Eleanor had written: "Did you know Lucy Mercer married Mr. Wintie Rutherfurd two days ago?" See Lash, *Eleanor and Franklin,* 227. To Eleanor, the event

may have seemed to close that terrible chapter in her marriage. It would take her a quarter of a century to find out that it had not.

398 Eleanor was unaware   Joseph Lash, Mrs. Roosevelt's friend and biographer, called her ultimate knowledge of the connection—which came on the day the president died in 1945—"a bitter discovery." Ibid., 722. Lash understood why so many in FDR's circle kept the news from her through the years, but added: "Yet for a woman who was intransigent about knowing the truth and facing up to it, such a deception, if and when she learned of it, would prove to be almost the final indignity. Franklin knew that even if no one else did." Ibid., 700.

398 Lucy "brought him to Washington"   Alsop, *FDR: A Centenary Remembrance,* 72.

398 family members recall   Confidential author interviews.

398 with a particularly good doctor at Walter Reed Hospital   Ibid. Also see Lucy Rutherfurd to Eleanor Roosevelt, May 2, 1945; File: Russey-Ruz; General Correspondence, 1945–1952; Eleanor Roosevelt Papers, Part II: April 12, 1945–1964, FDRL. In this letter, Lucy tells Eleanor of the president's "great kindness about my husband when he was desperately ill in Washington." The full text of this extraordinary letter is reprinted in my Chapter 13.

398 Roosevelt received one of Lucy's stepsons, Winthrop   Jonathan Daniels, *Washington Quadrille:*

The Dance Beside the Documents (Garden City, N.Y., 1968), 293.

398 as well as her daughter Barbara   Ibid.

398 helped smooth out the details of one of the stepsons' military service   Confidential author interviews.

398 once asked Anna, who was living in Seattle at the time, to "be nice"   Unpublished article by Anna Roosevelt, 4, Anna Roosevelt Halsted Papers, Box 70, FDRL.

399 the president gave two tickets to Mr. and Mrs. John Rutherfurd   Daniels, *Washington Quadrille*, 294.

399 Tucked away in the Roosevelt archives   Undated letter from Lucy Rutherfurd to FDR, Anna Roosevelt Halsted Papers, Box 70, File Ru, FDRL. The letter was unsealed at the Roosevelt library on October 18, 2001. It runs eight hand-written pages and is missing at least one and possibly more of its early pages, since there is no salutation or date on the letter. The eight surviving pages, however, do form a coherent whole.

399 almost certainly written in 1941   The allusion to "my youngest stepson" is to Guy Rutherfurd, who graduated from the University of Virginia law school in 1942, which, given Lucy's phrase about his finishing school "next year," places the letter in 1941. In the full text, she also mentions the specific law firm in New York the young man was considering, and the name of the cousin who had offered him the job, details I confirmed in confi-

dential interviews. The language and context also seem to place it before Pearl Harbor and Hitler's subsequent declaration of war on the United States.

399 "poor darling" Ibid.

400 The note was written from Aiken, South Carolina The evidence on this point is strong. Lucy writes of Mead being "the most able man in these parts"; Mead, like the Rutherfurds, owned a house in Aiken (See *Who's Who in America,* vol. 21, 1941–1942, Chicago, 1940). The later complaints about delayed newspaper delivery and poor radio reception also suggest Aiken as opposed to Allamuchy, New Jersey, where the Rutherfurds also had an estate.

400 "Day by day the news becomes increasingly ominous and complex" Undated letter from Lucy Rutherfurd to FDR, Anna Roosevelt Halsted Papers, Box 70, File Ru, FDRL.

401 "This kind of letter is best unwritten and unmailed" Ibid.

402 "*P.S.* Time is closing in on going-away time" Ibid.

403 in the spring of 1943, Lucy commissioned Elizabeth Shoumatoff, *FDR's Unfinished Portrait,* 80. Also see Goodwin, *No Ordinary Time,* 432–435; Asbell, *The F.D.R. Memoirs,* 410–416; Asbell, *Mother and Daughter: The Letters of Anna and Eleanor Roosevelt,* 186–189.

403 Shoumatoff's description of Lucy Ibid., 75.

404 Lucy asked Shoumatoff Ibid., 80.

404 As Shoumatoff walked into   Ibid., 81–82.

405 "I simply can't go on"   *CC*, 221.

405 "In my long talks"   *WAC*, 482.

405 The United States and England   Henry Wallace, COH, May 22, 1943, 2460.

405 Riding with Roosevelt   Churchill, *The Hinge of Fate*, 795–797.

406 Churchill saw a sign   *RAH*, 729.

406 Roosevelt could recall only   Ibid. Sherwood reports that Roosevelt quoted the lines; Churchill recalled that it was Hopkins. See Churchill, *The Hinge of Fate*, 795–796.

406 "animated conversation"   Tully, *FDR: My Boss*, 300–301.

407 "After a while silence and slumber"   Churchill, *The Hinge of Fate*, 797.

407 an evocative portrait   Ibid.

407 "My friendship with the President"   *WAC*, 483.

408 an account at odds   BBK-H/262, LBP.

408 "It's a beautiful spot"   Boettiger Papers, Box 5, FDRL.

409 "We could not have been"   *WAC*, 483.

409 "The President had great charm"   Author interview with Lady Soames.

409 Davies had left . . . on May 6   Elizabeth Kimball MacLean, *Joseph E. Davies: Envoy to the Soviets* (Westport, Conn., 1992), 101.

409 Churchill arrived   *WSC*, VII, 402.

409 Roosevelt's message went out of its way   "FDR's Last Instructions on Moscow," Diary of

Joseph E. Davies, May 5, 1943, Davies Papers. The quotations are from what Davies characterized as the "gist of the letter" to Stalin. Also see Burns, *The Soldier of Freedom,* 368; *C & R,* I, 13, and II, 283; and Elizabeth Kimball MacLean, "Joseph E. Davies and Soviet-American Relations, 1941–43," in *Diplomatic History* 4, no. 1 (Winter 1980): 73–93.

410 "F. said he will be taking"   *CC,* 221.

410 "Three is a crowd"   MacLean, *Joseph E. Davies,* 100.

410 "Churchill will understand"   Ibid.

411 Hopkins, Sherwood recalled   *RAH,* 737.

411 "My father was a very limpid"   Author interview with Lady Soames.

411 "Averell told me"   *C & R,* II, 278.

411 "I did not suggest"   Ibid., 283.

412 "Of course, you and I"   Ibid., 284.

412 His fury   "There was now an atmosphere alarmingly reminiscent of that which had preceded the Molotov-Ribbentrop Pact of August, 1939, and the fears of a separate Russo-German Armistice were revived," Sherwood wrote. "It was fortunate that Hitler did not know how bad the relations were between the Allies at that moment, how close they were to the disruption which was his only hope of survival." (*RAH,* 734) The ferocity of Stalin's cable prompted Churchill to tell Roosevelt to go ahead and meet alone with the Soviet leader if it could be arranged.

412 American and British officials . . . at Bermuda

Gilbert, *Auschwitz and the Allies,* 131–133; *C & R,* II, 293.

413 discussed the subject *FRUS, Conferences at Washington and Quebec, 1943,* 336.

413 "Our immediate facilities for helping the victims" *C & R,* II, 293.

413 After fighting objections Wyman, *The Abandonment of the Jews,* 117; Breitman, *Official Secrets,* 185.

413 Roosevelt said yes *C & R,* II, 315–316.

227 the number rescued was tiny Wyman, *The Abandonment of the Jews,* 117.

413 "a charming souvenir" Ibid., 322.

413 "My Congress has retired" Ibid., 323.

414 "I am perfectly delighted" Ibid., 348.

414 "Isn't he a wonderful old Tory" Gunther, *Roosevelt in Retrospect,* 16.

414 "Not against a single person" Author interview with Sir Anthony Montague Browne.

414 "He seldom carries forward" Lyttleton, *Memoirs,* 168.

415 "wider and permanent system of general security" Burns, *The Soldier of Freedom,* 130. Among others, the historian Robert Dallek points out that Roosevelt resisted Churchill's language mentioning an "effective international organization" because the president was afraid of "isolationist 'suspicions.' " See Dallek, *Franklin D. Roosevelt and American Foreign Policy* (New York, 1979), 283–284.

415 Roosevelt, according to Hopkins's notes *RAH,* 717–718.

415 at a May 22, 1943, meeting *FRUS, Conferences at Washington and Quebec,* 167–172. Also see Townsend Hoopes and Douglas Brinkley, *FDR and the Creation of the U.N.* (New Haven, Conn., 1997), 69–73.

415 Influenced by Secretary of State Cordell Hull Burns, *The Soldier of Freedom,* 429.

416 Roald Dahl, a fighter pilot, British secret service agent John C. Culver and John Hyde, *American Dreamer: The Life and Times of Henry A. Wallace* (New York, 2002), 342–343. Also see Mark I. West, *Roald Dahl* (New York, 1992), 10. I am grateful to John Morton Blum and John Hyde for their counsel on the Dahl-Wallace relationship.

416 "I have had four dispatches" Roald Dahl, "Visit to Hyde Park, July 2nd to 4th," dated July 6, 1943, Henry A. Wallace Diary, University of Iowa Library, Special Collections, Iowa City, Iowa, 4. The fact of Dahl's authorship is found in Henry A. Wallace, COH, 2558. The ensuing scenes and dialogue are drawn from the "Visit to Hyde Park, July 2nd to 4th" [1943], in the Wallace diary. Also see Henry A. Wallace, COH, 2558–2562.

417 the three jiggers of gin "Visit to Hyde Park, July 2nd to 4th" [1943], 9.

417 "Sir, what do you think of Churchill" Ibid.

417 Fala was "engaged" Ibid.

417 Roosevelt recalled one of his earliest transactions with Churchill Ibid., 10.

419 exhausted and had to stay *CCTBOM,* 446.

420 Roosevelt turned to Daisy   *CC,* 228.

420 "The P. asked me"   Ibid.

420 the relish she took in retelling   *TIR,* 296.

421 "Mr. Churchill insisted"   Ibid., 296–297.

421 a swim and picnic at Val-Kill   *CC,* 229.

421 "I didn't know how to manage"   Author interview with Lady Soames.

421 Churchill, who wore   *CC,* 229.

422 "He is a strange looking little man"   Ibid.

422 "took away the impression"   Ibid., 230.

422 they decided that   Kimball, *Forged in War,* 220–221; also see *WSC,* VII, 470–471.

422 typewritten on Citadel   *FRUS, Second Washington and First Quebec,* 1117.

422 Churchill had been worried   Kimball, *Forged in War,* 220.

423 Mary found her "looking better"   *CCTBOM,* 446.

423 "My mother could be"   Author interview with Lady Soames.

423 "He took the liberty"   Ibid.

424 if Roosevelt and Churchill would sign   Author interview with George Elsey.

424 "there was always a good deal"   Wilson Brown Memoir, 161, FDRL.

425 "The problems facing"   Ibid., 161–162.

426 Churchill took a sip of iced water   Dilks, ed., *The Diaries of Sir Alexander Cadogan,* 554–555.

426 A U.S. operation in the Aleutians   Author interview with George Elsey.

426 "One Lake"   Kimball, *Forged in War,* 221.

426 thought he was being shut out   Harriman and Abel, *Special Envoy*, 225.

427 "I hope Lady Warden"   *C & R*, II, 432.

427 The Churchill party decamped   *CCTBOM*, 447.

427 "We lived in comfortable log houses"   Martin, *Downing Street: The War Years*, 13.

428 "W.S.C. in terrific form"   Dilks, ed., *The Diaries of Sir Alexander Cadogan*, 556.

428 "The President had wanted"   Winston S. Churchill, *Closing the Ring: The Second World War* (Boston, 1951), 120.

428 "looking well, but tired"   *CC*, 231.

428 Hopkins had collapsed again   *RAH*, 750.

429 "Mr. [Churchill] didn't feel well"   *CC*, 232–233.

429 prescribing three months of rest   Ibid., 233.

429 Cadogan spent a day "running between"   Dilks, ed., *The Diaries of Sir Alexander Cadogan*, 559.

429 With Mary along, Suckley showed them   *CC*, 233.

429 Clementine later took a tumble   *CCTBOM*, 447–448.

430 One night, the names of   Author interview with Lady Soames.

430 using movies in the evenings   *CC*, 234.

430 "I'm nearly dead"   Frances Perkins, OH, 640 FDRL.

430 At two-thirty one afternoon   *CC*, 235.

431 Roosevelt "wants the ceremony"   *TSFS*, 124.

431 "Twice in my lifetime" James, ed., *Complete Speeches of Winston Churchill,* VII, 6823–6824.

433 "Winston enjoyed himself" Dilks, ed., *The Diaries of Sir Alexander Cadogan,* 559–560.

433 Churchill had spoken "on his favorite theme" Henry A. Wallace Diary, May 22, 1943, 31.

433 "I said bluntly" Ibid.

434 "Churchill had had quite a bit of whisky" Ibid.

434 "I suggested it might be a good plan" Ibid., 32.

434 "Churchill did not like this" Ibid.

435 "He asked me to use" Churchill, *Closing the Ring,* 137.

436 "All I want is compliance" Kay Halle Papers, Box 10, 24.

436 America's combat munitions Cohen in *Grand Strategies in War and Peace,* ed. Kennedy, 51.

436 The day at Hyde Park *CCTBOM,* 448.

436 "he loved her more and more" Ibid.

436 a small supper *CC,* 237–238.

437 Roosevelt toasted the Churchills *CCTBOM,* 448.

437 At about ten-twenty *CC,* 238–239.

437 "God bless you" Ibid.

438 "My dear Franklin" *C & R,* II, 447.

438 "Delighted you are all" Ibid., 454.

438 "a first very definite" *CC,* 238.

CHAPTER 9: I HAD TO DO
SOMETHING DESPERATE

441 "No lover"   David Dimbleby and David Rey-
nolds, *An Ocean Apart: The Relationship Between
Britain and America in the Twentieth Century* (New
York, 1988), 135.

441 "By the time we got to"   Sir Ian Jacob interview, Newton Collection, FDRL.

2442 ill with a cold and sore throat   *WAC,* 485;
WSC, VII, 552.

442 "it will be grand"   *C & R,* II, 603.

442 worries about security   Churchill, *Closing the
Ring,* 327.

442 "meeting place is known to enemy"   *C & R,*
II, 601.

442 "See St. John"   Ibid., 604.

443 "taking too much upon myself"   Churchill,
Closing the Ring, 327.

443 "brushed all objections aside"   Ibid.

443 Knowing Churchill was upset   *WAC,* 486.

443 She had never met Roosevelt   Sarah Churchill,
A Thread in the Tapestry (New York, 1966), 62.

444 One day in Cairo, Churchill said   Ibid., 62–63.

444 "Let us make it"   Churchill, *Closing the Ring,*
340.

445 "Harry had arranged"   John Boettiger Diary
of Cairo and Tehran, November 25, 1943, 89,
FDRL.

445 Churchill threw himself   Churchill, *Closing the
Ring,* 341.

445 "had calculated" Ibid.

445 In a toast to Churchill *FRUS, Conference at Cairo and Tehran,* 1943, 299.

445 Churchill answered Churchill, *Closing the Ring,* 341.

445 "in these crucial times" John Boettiger Diary of Cairo and Tehran, November 25, 1943, 89, FDRL.

445 "deep feeling" Ibid.

446 "Upon this happy note" Ibid.

446 Sarah had a full card Churchill, *Closing the Ring,* 341.

446 "It is an enormous satisfaction" Diary of FDR, November 26, 1943, Handwritten Notes of Cairo-Tehran, FDRL.

446 "For a couple of hours" Churchill, *Closing the Ring,* 341.

446 flew into the Iranian capital about forty-five minutes Sarah Churchill, *A Thread in the Tapestry,* 64.

446 "spine-chilling" Ibid. Also see Churchill, *Closing the Ring,* 342.

446 "Anyone could have shot" Sarah Churchill, *A Thread in the Tapestry,* 64.

446 "I grinned at the crowd" Churchill, *Closing the Ring,* 343.

248 ordered Inspector Thompson Thompson, *I Was Churchill's Shadow,* 122.

447 "a beautiful Iranian Sunday" Bohlen, *Witness to History,* 139.

447 "By an unfortunate coincidence" *WAC,* 489.

447 Churchill had wanted   *WSC,* VII, 568; Harriman and Abel, *Special Envoy,* 262–265.

447 Churchill requested time   Harriman and Abel, *Special Envoy,* 265.

447 "The President had reason to suspect"   Ibid.

448 Word reached Harriman   Ibid.

448 "PM has bad throat"   Danchev and Todman, eds., *War Diaries: Alanbrooke,* 482.

448 "Grumbling but whimsical"   Harriman and Abel, *Special Envoy,* 265.

448 "I continued"   Churchill, *Closing the Ring,* 344.

449 At three a short distance away   Bohlen, *Witness to History,* 139. There are different accounts of the shifting and fluid conversations among the principals at Cairo-Teheran. My account is distilled from Bohlen, *Witness to History,* 134–154; Burns, *The Soldier of Freedom,* 406–417; Churchill, *Closing the Ring,* 342–407; *FRUS, Cairo and Tehran,* 482–605; Freidel, *A Rendezvous with Destiny,* 477–493; Harriman and Abel, *Special Envoy,* 256–283; *RAH,* 775–799; Keith Sainsbury, *The Turning Point* (New York, 1985); *WSC,* VII, 556–593; and the other sources cited below.

449 In a khaki tunic   Bohlen, *Witness to History,* 139.

449 smiled as he walked   Reilly and Slocum, *Reilly of the White House,* 179.

449 in his wheelchair   Bohlen, *Witness to History,* 139.

449 trying to stare down the NKVD   Reilly and Slocum, *Reilly of the White House,* 180.

449 "was a very small man" Ibid.

449 "I am glad to see you" Bohlen, *Witness to History*, 139.

449 pleased to meet Roosevelt Ibid.

449 "had been entirely due" Ibid.

449 knew to keep their points short Ibid., 136–137.

449 "Churchill was his charming best" Author interview with Kathleen Harriman Mortimer.

450 "This being primarily" Bohlen, *Witness to History*, 139.

450 According to Bohlen's minutes *FRUS, Cairo and Tehran*, 483.

450 When France came up Bohlen, *Witness to History*, 139.

450 Stalin's anti–de Gaulle attitude Ibid.

450 "I could not help feeling" Ibid., 139–140.

451 that was a "sore spot" *FRUS, Cairo and Tehran*, 486.

451 As they parted Ibid.

451 he was happy Ibid.

451 the British got wind *TSFS*, 144.

451 "Stalin's slits of eyes" Ibid., 145.

451 "The setting was rather heavy" Bohlen, *Witness to History*, 141.

452 Roosevelt was the presiding officer Churchill, *Closing the Ring*, 347.

452 the kind of proceeding he liked Ibid., 347–348.

2452 Roosevelt tried charm Bohlen, *Witness to History*, 142.

452 "As the youngest of the three" Ibid.

452 "he welcomed his elders" Ibid.

452 "new members" *RAH*, 778.

452 "This meeting, I said" Churchill, *Closing the Ring*, 348.

452 "Now let us" Bohlen, *Witness to History*, 142.

452 Roosevelt started out Ibid.

452 "much appreciated" Danchev and Todman, eds., *War Diaries: Alanbrooke*, 483.

452 inevitably turned to overlord Bohlen, *Witness to History*, 142.

452 "a disagreeable body of water" Harriman and Abel, *Special Envoy*, 267.

452 "had every reason" *RAH*, 779.

453 Hopkins was watching the interplay Ibid., 781.

453 Roosevelt asked Stalin his thoughts *FRUS, Cairo and Tehran*, 489.

453 "Stalin replied" Harriman and Abel, *Special Envoy*, 267.

453 "The enterprise was absorbing" Churchill, *Closing the Ring*, 350–351.

454 his "real feelings" Bohlen, *Witness to History*, 142.

454 "The early spring" Churchill, *Closing the Ring*, 351.

454 Roosevelt said he "personally" *FRUS, Cairo and Tehran*, 495.

454 "might be necessary" Ibid.

455 "I earnestly hoped" Churchill, *Closing the Ring*, 357.

455 "said that he personally favored" Bohlen, *Witness to History*, 142.

455 "although we were" Churchill, *Closing the Ring*, 358.

455 grilled steaks Bohlen, *Witness to History*, 143.

455 After making martinis Ibid.

455 Roosevelt finally asked him Ibid.

456 "When I first got to Teheran" *CC*, 299.

456 Stalin denounced the French Harriman and Abel, *Special Envoy*, 268.

457 "When Churchill protested" Ibid.

457 brushed Churchill aside Ibid. Harriman called Stalin's reply "contemptuous."

457 he "in part agreed" *FRUS, Cairo and Tehran*, 509.

457 Turning to Germany, Stalin Bohlen, *Witness to History*, 143.

457 "told of visiting Leipzig" Harriman and Abel, *Special Envoy*, 268.

458 "very jolly" FDR Diary of Cairo and Tehran, November 29, 1943, Handwritten Notes, FDRL.

458 "Roosevelt was about" Bohlen, *Witness to History*, 143–144.

458 "I tried to ask" John Boettiger Diary of Cairo and Tehran, November 29, 1943, 100, FDRL.

460 "He was greatly set up" Ibid.

460 Sitting on a sofa Churchill, *Closing the Ring*, 359.

460 "I learned later" John Boettiger Diary of Cairo and Tehran, November 29, 1943, 101, FDRL.

460 Churchill reached out to Roosevelt   Churchill, *Closing the Ring,* 363.

461 "It is not like him"   *TSFS,* 146.

461 "The President after luncheon"   Churchill, *Closing the Ring,* 363.

461 In his quarters with Stalin   *RAH,* 784–786.

461 appeared interested but noncommittal   *FRUS, Cairo and Tehran,* 530.

461 "a world-wide"   Ibid., 596.

462 Churchill had a presentation to make   Churchill, *Closing the Ring,* 364.

462 The conference, Chip Bohlen believed   Bohlen, *Witness to History,* 145.

462 "Stalin would have made"   Ismay, *Memoirs,* 338.

463 "Who will command Overlord?"   Churchill, *Closing the Ring,* 365.

463 admitted this was not settled   Ibid.

463 could not have missed   Churchill later told Stalin that he "had urged" FDR to "decide before we all left Teheran." Ibid., 378.

463 "Stalin said bluntly"   Ibid., 365.

463 the news that   *FRUS,* Cairo and Tehran, 535. Morgan wrote an interesting book about his assignment. See Frederick Morgan, *Overture to Overlord* (Garden City, N.Y., 1950).

463 "Stalin made it plain"   Harriman and Abel, *Special Envoy,* 271.

464 Reading the conference documents   *RAH,* 787.

464 "Churchill employed"   Ibid., 789.

464 Stalin pushed for a firm date   Bohlen, *Witness to History,* 145.

465 After relighting his cigar   Ibid.

465 "He talked of keeping the enemy"   Harriman and Abel, *Special Envoy,* 273.

465 much back-and-forth   *FRUS, Cairo and Tehran,* 535–538.

465 "dominating operation"   Ibid., 539.

465 "I wish to pose"   Churchill, *Closing the Ring,* 373.

465 "Provided the conditions"   Ibid.

466 "Churchill was irked"   Bohlen, *Witness to History,* 146.

466 Moran found a gloomy Churchill   *TSFS,* 148.

466 a classic Russian dinner   Bohlen, *Witness to History,* 147.

466 "overlooked no opportunity"   Ibid., 146.

466 "without mercy"   Harriman and Abel, *Special Envoy,* 273.

466 "nursing some secret affection"   Ibid.

467 "Instead of getting"   Bohlen, *Witness to History,* 146.

467 "Stalin's remarks"   John Boettiger Diary of Cairo and Tehran, November 29, 1943, 109, FDRL.

467 "I did not like"   Bohlen, *Witness to History,* 146.

467 "He always enjoyed"   Harriman and Abel, *Special Envoy,* 191.

468 "I have gathered that"   John Boettiger Diary of Cairo and Tehran, November 29, 1943, 105, FDRL.

468 The Stalin-Churchill conversation Bohlen, *Witness to History,* 146.

468 "I realized at Teheran" Colville in *Action This Day,* ed. Wheeler-Bennett, 96. Later in the war, he would alter the image slightly. "In February 1945 Churchill said to President Benes of Czechoslovakia that a small lion was walking between a huge Russian bear and a great American elephant, but that perhaps it would turn out to be the lion that knew the way." (Ibid.)

468 Churchill was taking it all well Churchill, *Closing the Ring,* 373–374.

469 "with a sardonic smile" Bohlen, *Witness to History,* 147.

469 "The British Parliament and public" Churchill, *Closing the Ring,* 374.

469 "Fifty thousand" Ibid.

469 "deeply angered" Ibid.

469 "had seen the twinkle" John Boettiger Diary of Cairo and Teheran, November 30, 1943, 108, FDRL.

469 sailed into the conversation Churchill, *Closing the Ring,* 374.

470 "As usual, it seems" Elliott Roosevelt, *As He Saw It,* 189.

470 only forty-nine thousand German officers Churchill, *Closing the Ring,* 374.

470 "By this he hoped" Ibid.

470 "Eden also made signs" Ibid.

470 spotted lurking by the door Elliott Roosevelt,

As He Saw It, 186. "I had not been invited, but during the first course one of the Russian secret service men standing in back of Stalin noticed me at a side entrance, and he leaned over and whispered to Stalin . . . ," Elliott Roosevelt wrote. "With gestures, he made it quite clear that he wanted me to join the party; an interpreter doubled his invitation in English, explaining that the Marshal said graciously that he had not realized his secretary had not invited me." So Elliott may not have quite crashed the party, but he does seem to have mightily angled for his late-breaking invitation.

470 deep into the champagne   Ibid., 190.

470 "made a speech"   Churchill, *Closing the Ring,* 374.

470 "intrusion"   Ibid.

471 Churchill marched into another room   Ibid.

471 "I had not been there"   Ibid.

471 "Joe teased the P.M."   Freidel, *A Rendezvous with Destiny,* 485.

472 "The fact that"   Churchill, *Closing the Ring,* 375.

472 "I began by"   Ibid., 376–377.

472 were pressing an amphibious operation   Ibid., 377.

473 "it was vital"   Ibid.

473 "had urged"   Ibid., 378.

473 With Churchill, Stalin was blunt   Ibid., 379–380.

473 Roosevelt read the Allied recommendations aloud   Harriman and Abel, *Special Envoy,* 274.

473 "The conferences have been going well" Diary of FDR, December 1, 1943, Handwritten Notes of Cairo and Tehran, FDRL.

474 It was Churchill's sixty-ninth birthday Churchill, *Closing the Ring,* 375.

474 "Hitherto we had" Ibid., 384.

475 "a never-to-be-forgotten party" Sarah Churchill, *A Thread in the Tapestry,* 65.

475 "The table was set" Bohlen, *Witness to History,* 149.

475 "Together we controlled" Churchill, *Closing the Ring,* 384–385.

475 Churchill and Roosevelt wore black tie Detail drawn from photographs of the dinner, FDRL.

475 To Sarah, Stalin was Sarah Churchill, *A Thread in the Tapestry,* 65.

476 "When the President" Harriman and Abel, *Special Envoy,* 278.

476 "had devoted his entire life" *FRUS, Cairo and Tehran,* 583.

476 "Stalin the Great" Ibid.

476 Roosevelt then spoke of his "long admiration" Ibid.

476 Stalin asked if he might John Boettiger Diary of Cairo and Tehran, November 30, 1943, 111, FDRL.

476 "I want to tell you" Harriman and Abel, *Special Envoy,* 277.

477 worried he had not truly broken through Perkins, *The Roosevelt I Knew,* 83–85.

477 "You know, the Russians" Ibid., 83.

478 "I thought it over all night"   Ibid., 84.

478 "On my way"   Ibid.

478 "Winston, I hope you"   Ibid.

478 "shifted his cigar"   Ibid.

478 "I began almost as soon"   Ibid.

479 "Then I said"   Ibid.

479 "As soon as I"   Ibid.

479 "I kept it up"   Ibid. Also see Alldritt, *The Greatest of Friends,* 176.

480 "I asked someone"   Gunther, *Roosevelt in Retrospect,* 17.

480 "behaved very decently"   Perkins, *The Roosevelt I Knew,* 84.

480 "My father was awfully wounded"   Author interview with Lady Soames.

480 "My father was very hurt, I think"   Ibid.

480 Roosevelt told Eisenhower   Burns, *The Soldier of Freedom,* 416.

480 Churchill was suffering from pneumonia   *WSC,* VII, 604.

481 could not remember ever feeling   Churchill, *Closing the Ring,* 450.

481 Clementine accepted his failure   *CCTBOM,* 457.

481 "I never think of after the war"   *CCTBOM,* 461.

481 At three o'clock on Christmas Eve afternoon   *CC,* 263.

481 "The room was a mess"   Ibid.

481 Eleanor, Anna, and Trude Lash tried to make themselves comfortable   Ibid.

482 fair but cold day   *The New York Times,* December 24, 1943, and December 25, 1943.

482 "That this is truly a world war"   Buhite and Levy, eds. *FDR's Fireside Chats,* 273–274.

482 "Of course, as you all know"   Ibid., 275.

483 "Within three days"   Ibid., 276.

483 "The war is now reaching the stage"   Ibid., 280.

484 "To use an American and somewhat ungrammatical colloquialism"   Ibid., 277–278. Also see Burns, *The Soldier of Freedom,* 416–417.

CHAPTER 10: THE HOUR WAS NOW STRIKING

487 "It's been a wonderful year"   Dilks, ed., *The Diaries of Sir Alexander Cadogan,* 592.

488 a debacle in France would exact a high price   Stephen E. Ambrose, "D Day Fails" in *What If?* ed. Cowley, 346–347.

488 "Winston has developed a tendency"   Rosenman, *Working with Roosevelt,* 407.

488 One evening during the 1943–1944 holidays   *TFOP,* 461.

489 "feeling a *little* miserably"   *CC,* 264.

489 By December 30   Ibid., 266.

489 At eleven-thirty on New Year's Eve   Ibid., 267.

489 "Mrs. R. . . . ," Daisy said   Ibid.

489 "Auld Lang Syne"   Ibid.

489 Clementine called the villa   *CCTBOM,* 456.

490 "He is gaining strength"   Ibid., 457.

490 "bad temper day!"   Ibid.

490 "I have now got home"   *C & R,* II, 668.

490 "The P.M. is back"   Pamela Churchill to Averell and Kathleen Harriman, February 19, 1944, PHP.

490 "Now thanked we all"   *WAC,* 495.

490 He had married Louise Macy   *TIR,* 257. Also see *CC,* 170.

490 Hopkins had three sons by a first marriage   Henry H. Adams, *Harry Hopkins: A Biography* (New York, 1977), 36; 44–45.

491 "It seemed to me very hard"   *TIR,* 257.

491 "She is pretty"   *CC,* 224–225. Daisy did once acknowledge she was being "catty" about Louise. (Ibid., 224)

491 the Hopkinses were about   *RAH,* 752.

492 Mrs. Hopkins had changed Eleanor's seating plan   Author interview with Trude Lash.

492 Louise and Diana moved   *TIR,* 317.

492 so sick that he could not work   *RAH,* 804–809.

492 "You must know I am not"   Winston S. Churchill, *Triumph and Tragedy: The Second World War* (Boston, 1953), 161. There is a mystery here. Churchill repeats the exact paragraph about Hopkins's decline in two volumes of the war memoirs: first on 82 of *Closing the Ring,* about First Quebec, and second on 161 of *Triumph and Tragedy.* Given other evidence—including a 1944 letter from Clementine to Mary about Hopkins's apparent fall

from favor at Second Quebec—my guess is that Churchill meant to attach the sentiment and scene to 1944, not to 1943.

492 Nothing was worse   *RAH*, 805.

493 "I am terribly"   Ibid.

493 "Dear Harry"   *C & R*, II, 726.

493 a lettered scroll of lines   *RAH*, 806. Robert Hopkins graciously showed me the scroll dedicated to his brother's memory; the gift from Churchill now hangs in Mr. Hopkins's house in Washington.

494 "Wasn't it sad"   Pamela Churchill to Averell Harriman, February 15, 1944, PHP.

494 Anna Roosevelt moved into   *TIR*, 319. Doris Kearns Goodwin is interesting on the FDR-Anna relationship. See, for instance, Goodwin, *No Ordinary Time*, 488–491.

494 She had seen the mask fall   John Boettiger, *A Love in Shadow* (New York, 1978), 94–95.

495 Roosevelt again needed her help   Lash, *Eleanor and Franklin*, 699–700.

495 A Roper poll   Freidel, *A Rendezvous with Destiny*, 495.

495 In a February election   *TFOP*, 474. The candidate was Lord Hartington, who had married Joseph Kennedy's daughter Kathleen.

495 "This caused"   *TFOP*, 474.

496 the "Little Blitz"   *CCTBOM*, 462.

496 German bombers   *WSC*, VII, 689. See also *C & R*, II, 739.

496 "We have just had"   *C & R*, II, 740.

496 At a one-on-one dinner Danchev and Todman, eds., *War Diaries: Alanbrooke*, 525.

496 A series of irritating disagreements See especially Kimball, *Forged in War*, and *WSC*, VII and
VIII.

497 sicker than he would let on See Robert H.
Ferrell, *The Dying President: Franklin D. Roosevelt,
1944–1945* (Columbia, Mo., 1998), for a comprehensive account of Roosevelt's health in the
last year or so of his life—and Roosevelt's efforts
to conceal his condition.

497 "Raining in Washington" *CC*, 285–287.

497 "I think all of us" *TIR*, 329. See *CC* and Ferrell, *The Dying President*, for evidence that FDR
did talk about his health with Daisy.

498 Anna . . . prevailed on Admiral McIntire
Burns, *The Soldier of Freedom*, 447–448.

498 Eleanor was in Guatemala *The New York Times*,
March 28, 1944.

498 Winthrop Rutherfurd had died *CC*, 287.

498 "felt fever coming on" Ibid., 288.

498 lunched together Ibid.

498 did not leave until about six-thirty Ibid., 288.

498 "He got on the sofa" Ibid., 201–202.

499 Roosevelt's circle was Lash, *Eleanor and
Franklin*, 700.

499 Roosevelt's medical appointment in Washington Ferrell, *The Dying President*, 36–37.

499 "God-awful" Ibid., 37.

500 Churchill was at No. 10 Danchev and Todman,
eds., *War Diaries: Alanbrooke*, May 7, 1944, 544.

500 "although looking fit" Diary of Meeting, Charles Eade, October 14, 1943, CEP.

500 Of course Roosevelt and Churchill looked tired For a discussion of the question of their health and the conduct of the war, see Kimball, *Forged in War,* 339–341.

502 Lucy came to visit Asbell, *The FDR Memoirs,* 412.

502 a meeting after midnight Alan Kirk, COH, 297–298.

503 Churchill "would be" *TFOP,* 485.

503 "I do not agree" *C & R,* III, 87.

503 "We have just heard" Ibid., 167.

504 "I feel so much for you" *WAC,* 496.

504 Eleanor remembered that *TIR,* 328.

504 Eisenhower hated the idea Churchill, *Closing the Ring,* 619.

504 two frank letters Ibid., 620–621.

504 Churchill still regretted Ibid., 624.

594 had to content himself Ismay, *Memoirs,* 353.

505 In a train Ibid.

505 Roosevelt spent the weekend *CC,* 307.

505 On the porch Ibid., 308.

506 "The P. used" Ibid.

506 Churchill went to bed Ismay, *Memoirs,* 355.

506 A letter arrived from Roosevelt Churchill, *Closing the Ring,* 626.

506 "Dear Winston" *C & R,* III, 139.

507 Churchill long remembered Churchill, *Closing the Ring,* 626.

508 Replying from Portsmouth *C & R,* III, 162.

508 "The hour was now striking" Churchill, *Closing the Ring,* 631.

508 "We returned to London" Ismay, *Memoirs,* 357.

508 He had, Eleanor noted, "learned" EROH, Session 12, 2.

508 one of only four such occasions *CCTBOM,* 463.

509 Clementine came in to say good night Ibid., 468.

509 Back in the White House *CC,* 309.

509 Roosevelt briefed Eleanor Lash, *Eleanor and Franklin,* 701.

509 "the golden thread of love" *WAC,* xx. Lady Soames used the image in connection with her parents, but I believe the sense of her point applies to the Roosevelts as well.

509 "On D-Day" EROH, Session 12, 2.

510 She thought Franklin *TIR,* 252.

510 "Even then" Ibid.

510 made it through Russell W. Linaka survived, and there is correspondence at FDRL about his future assignments. PPF 7548: Linaka, Russell W., December 11, 1944.

510 there were about 10,300 American, British, and Canadian casualties Dear, ed., *The Oxford Companion to World War II,* 667.

510 "All that weekend" Pamela Churchill to Averell Harriman, June 11, 1944, PHP.

511 spent ten minutes talking about Italy Churchill, *Triumph and Tragedy,* 5–6.

511 "Thank God!" EROH, Session 12, 2.

511 "Except for the planes overhead" Pamela Churchill to Averell Harriman, June 11, 1944, PHP.

511 ran into Martha Gellhorn Ibid.

512 the preponderance of the evidence I am grateful to the military historian Williamson Murray for his insights on this subject.

513 Warren Kimball later explained *C & R*, III, 168.

514 "My dear Winston" Ibid., 168–169.

514 Churchill would again brief the House *The New York Times*, June 7, 1944.

514 had distributed the text beforehand Ibid.

514 one hundred million *Newsweek*, June 19, 1944. The prayer had been published in the afternoon editions of the nation's newspapers. See Stephen E. Ambrose, *D-Day: June 6, 1944* (New York, 1994), 491.

514 "Almighty God" *The New York Times*, June 7, 1944.

515 Roosevelt had the prayer bound *C & R*, III, 507.

515 the Soviets, Averell Harriman said Harriman and Abel, *Special Envoy*, 314.

515 "The first wave of excitement" Pamela Churchill to Averell Harriman, June 15, 1944, PHP.

515 played bezique at Chequers Ibid., June 11, 1944, PHP.

516 an operation code-named ANVIL Burns, *The Soldier of Freedom*, 478–479.

516 "I am shocked" *C & R,* III, 213.

516 Roosevelt rejected Ibid., 221–223.

516 called for General Brooke Danchev and Todman, eds., *War Diaries: Alanbrooke,* 565.

517 "We are deeply grieved" *C & R,* III, 227–229.

517 Brooke found Churchill Danchev and Todman, eds., *War Diaries: Alanbrooke,* 565.

517 "tired & listless" *CC,* 315.

517 "I appreciate deeply" *C & R,* III, 232.

518 Stalin, Daisy said, had been quoted *CC,* 316.

518 Mary had to deal *CCTBOM,* 468–469.

518 "I am very happy" *C & R,* III, 258.

519 "Thank you so much" Ibid., 259.

519 a heated dinner debate *CC,* 276.

CHAPTER 11: LIFE IS NOT VERY EASY

521 "We have immense tasks" *C & R,* III, 203.

522 "Over here" Ibid., 161.

522 had a few health scares Burns, *The Soldier of Freedom,* 507–508.

522 "Nothing," wrote John Gunther Gunther, *Roosevelt in Retrospect,* 345.

522 What Beaverbrook heard "Notes on Conversations," 1943, LBP.

523 "I saw a lot of Richard Pim" Author interview with George Elsey.

523 "Father asked me" Anna Roosevelt Halsted, COH, 48–49.

523 "It was a terrible decision" Ibid.

524 "Johnny called" *TIR,* 318.

525 At tea in late June with the Chinese ambassador *CC,* 314.

526 giving Churchill a number of *C & R,* III, 238–239.

526 "visiting card" Ibid., 271.

526 Roosevelt also sent Churchill Ibid., 266.

527 In midsummer 1944 Breitman, *Official Secrets,* 208.

527 Telling Churchill on July 7, 1944 Gilbert, *Auschwitz and the Allies,* 270.

527 Citing technical military reasons Ibid., 284–285. For more on this topic, see Breitman, *Official Secrets,* 207–211; Beschloss, *The Conquerors,* 63–67; and Michael J. Neufeld and Michael Berenbaum, eds., *The Bombing of Auschwitz: Should the Allies Have Attempted It?* (New York, 2000).

528 Churchill proposed a summer summit *C & R,* III, 249.

528 Roosevelt, who was Freidel, *A Rendezvous with Destiny,* 539–542.

528 "I wholly agree" *C & R,* III, 250.

528 Henry Wallace was out Freidel, *A Rendezvous with Destiny,* 529–530.

528 Senator Harry Truman of Missouri David McCullough, *Truman* (New York, 1992), 297.

529 Writing to Harriman on July 1 Pamela Churchill to Averell Harriman, July 1, 1944, PHP.

530 "violent reproaches" Montague Browne, *Long Sunset,* 299.

531 "Short of hitting him" Ibid.

531 "This visit of mine" *WAC*, 501.

532 a temperature of 103 *CCTBOM*, 470.

532 "I was on a 24-hour leave pass" Ibid., 479.

533 "Good God" *TSFS*, 173.

533 "the martyrdom of Warsaw" Churchill, *Triumph and Tragedy*, 128.

533 asked Stalin to intervene *C & R*, III, 283.

533 Moscow balked *WSC*, VII, 924–926. There was also a political reason: Stalin believed the Poles who started the fighting had failed to coordinate their attack with the Soviets and were allied not with his favored Lublin Committee, which was pro-Soviet, but with the London Poles, who were more democratic.

534 two British attempts to fly Harriman and Abel, *Special Envoy*, 338.

534 Calling the Warsaw situation "a dirty business" Ibid., 342.

534 "The dead" *C & R*, III, 293.

534 a radical solution Ibid., 295.

534 the Americans wanted rights *WSC*, VII, 927.

535 "When the Russians entered the city" Churchill, *Triumph and Tragedy*, 145.

535 would disagree about some large matter For the crises that complicated the rest of the war, from Greece to Italy, see, in part, Kimball, *Forged in War*, 241–337; *RAH*, 837–843; *WSC*, VII and VIII.

535 "Where is your landing spot?" *C & R*, III, 303.

536 "like a boiled owl" *CC*, 325.

536 Surrounded by the people   *TFOP,* 509–512.

537 Roosevelt was aboard his train   *CC,* 323.

537 to see Lucy at her late husband's estate   Ibid., 323–325.

538 "tree grower"   Gunther, *Roosevelt in Retrospect,* 80.

538 "The Pres. is going to look"   *CC,* 323–324.

538 Churchill had written him   *C & R,* III, 307.

539 "Perfectly delighted"   Ibid.

539 Eleanor was on the platform   *CC,* 325.

539 "How little one knows"   Ibid., 323.

539 The Roosevelts arrived   Richard L. Strout, *TRB: Views and Perspectives on the Presidency* (New York, 1979), 27.

539 "Clementine was less 'public relations' conscious"   *CCTBOM,* 472.

540 She was working   Ibid., 472–473.

541 McIntire had sent word to Admiral Brown   Wilson Brown Memoir, 163–164, FDRL.

541 generous economic aid   *WSC,* VII, 964.

541 "While going to bed"   *TFOP,* 515.

541 Churchill offered   Burns, *The Soldier of Freedom,* 519.

543 Churchill quoted Milton's *Lycidas*   *WSC,* VII, 959.

543 the possibility of a thrust out of Italy   Ibid.

543 the "Morgenthau Plan"   See Beschloss, *The Conquerors;* Warren F. Kimball, *Swords or Ploughshares?: The Morgenthau Plan for Defeated Nazi Germany, 1943–1946* (Philadelphia, 1976).

543 the two men, wearing academic regalia *TFOP,* 515.

543 Roosevelt spoke in a whisper Ibid., 516.

543 he believed Roosevelt was "very frail" Ibid., 513.

543 sun-splashed roof of the old fort Ibid., 515–516.

544 "Our affairs are so intermingled" *Complete Presidential Press Conferences,* XXIV, September 16, 1944, 111–116.

545 Meetings often produce a kind of magic See Jenkins, *Churchill,* 750–752, for an insightful passage on Churchill's hunger for personal meetings—a hunger that marked his behavior throughout the war.

545 "it was a *good* conference" *CC,* 326.

545 Harry Hopkins was at Hyde Park Churchill, *Triumph and Tragedy,* 161.

546 eclectic gathering *CC,* 327.

546 Eleanor, Clementine told her daughters *CCTBOM,* 474–475.

546 Clementine also worried *WSC,* VII, 969.

547 A group of scientists in the know Rhodes, *The Making of the Atomic Bomb,* 525–538.

547 "The suggestion that the world" Ibid., 538.

547 Moran and Colville had had *TFOP,* 511.

548 Colville thought he was Ibid., 517.

548 Roosevelt spent some time *CC,* 328.

548 George Elsey accompanied Roosevelt Author interview with George Elsey.

549 "My darling One" *WAC,* 505.

549 decided to try his luck *C & R,* III, 341.

549 Roosevelt said no Ibid., 344.

549 "As the Soviet armies" Bohlen, *Witness to History,* 161.

550 "In the afternoon the P.M." *TFOP,* 523.

550 Roosevelt drafted a cable *C & R,* III, 343.

550 Bohlen was at the State Department Bohlen, *Witness to History,* 162.

550 in the map room, Robert Sherwood *RAH,* 833.

551 "I said that" Bohlen, *Witness to History,* 162.

551 "While I was drafting" Ibid., 163.

551 "You, naturally" Ibid., 162.

552 "I supposed that Mr. Churchill" Ibid., 163.

552 "It was apparent" Ibid.

552 after struggling to get enough hot water *WSC,* VII, 989.

552 "The moment was apt for business" Churchill, *Triumph and Tragedy,* 227.

552 diplomacy and politics *WSC,* VII, 989–1033.

553 "Churchill had high regard" Author interview with Anthony Montague Browne.

553 "I have had vy nice talks" *WAC,* 506.

553 "Tender love" Ibid., 507.

553 briefly ran a fever *TSFS,* 216.

553 "I have to keep the President" *WAC,* 506.

553 "Although I hear" *C & R,* III, 359.

554 "I do hope your health" Ibid., 362–363.

554 Saturday, October 21, 1944 Rosenman, *Working with Roosevelt,* 480–483.

554 riding fifty-one miles   *The New York Times,* October 22, 1944.

554 helped undercut the argument   Rosenman, *Working with Roosevelt,* 483.

554 Mayor Fiorello La Guardia was worn out   *The New York Times,* October 22, 1944.

555 change of clothes and a drink of bourbon   Tully, *FDR: My Boss,* 281.

555 There could be no more isolation   *RAH,* 827.

555 "Republicans in Congress"   *Life,* October 30, 1944, 24.

555 "Anybody who thinks that"   *RAH,* 827.

556 His speech in Manhattan   *The New York Times,* October 22, 1944.

557 Churchill had seen the gray images   *C & R,* III, 368.

557 reply was charming   Ibid., 371.

558 In Hartford, Connecticut, one day   Conversation between Curtis Roosevelt and Alistair Cooke, New York City, October 20, 1993, Acc#95-03, FDRL.

558 debated a new Big Three meeting   *C & R,* III, 371.

558 "The Pres. was full of pep"   *CC,* 339.

558 "When we think"   Rosenman, *Working with Roosevelt,* 505.

559 Hopkins kept Churchill up-to-date   *RAH,* 830.

559 Roosevelt spent the evening   *CC,* 341.

559 53.5 percent to 46 percent   Freidel, *A Rendezvous with Destiny,* 567. According to *The Amer-*

ican Heritage Illustrated History of the Presidents (2000 edition), FDR received 25,612,610 votes to Dewey's 22,017,617 (388).

559 Warm words arrived   *C & R*, III, 383.

560 enclosed it once more   Ibid., 382–383.

560 "The election was a great triumph"   Harry Hopkins to Beaverbrook, November 15, 1944, BBK C 175, LBP.

561 "The war unfortunately seems"   Pamela Churchill to Averell Harriman, October 7, 1944, PHP.

561 "Ever so many happy returns"   *C & R,* III, 385. Roosevelt also said he had not forgotten Churchill's 1940 message, evidence that he had read it but had chosen not to reply in those far-off days, perhaps to keep Churchill somewhat off balance in the early phase of their relationship.

561 "There was a glorious dinner party"   *CCT-BOM,* 477.

562 a delicate note to his daughter-in-law   Winston Churchill to Pamela Churchill, December 12, 1944, PHP.

562 had a quotation from Lincoln   *C & R,* III, 400. Despite inquiries at the Roosevelt Library, the Churchill Archives, and of Winston S. Churchill, I have been unable to discover which Lincoln quotation Roosevelt sent Churchill.

562 "I cannot tell you"   Ibid., 429.

CHAPTER 12: I SAW WSC TO SAY
GOODBYE

565 "We could not have found" *RAH,* 847.

565 He would get through it Harriman and Abel,
Special Envoy, 390.

565 "The P.M. remained" *TFOP,* 551.

566 "I do not see" *C & R,* III, 505–506.

566 "I shall be waiting" Ibid., 488.

566 he stood in his braces *RAH,* 846.

566 "All the sentimental ladies" *CC,* 387.

566 did not go to the Capitol *The New York Times,*
January 21, 1945.

566 His address to a small crowd Ibid.

567 "after the inauguration" *TIR,* 339.

567 "Anna was very, very good" Author interview
with Kathleen Harriman Mortimer.

568 Around the ship en route Anna Roosevelt Halsted, COH, 42–48. For accounts of Malta and Yalta,
see, for instance, Churchill, *Triumph and Tragedy,*
329–402; Burns, *The Soldier of Freedom,* 564–580;
Freidel, *A Rendezvous with Destiny,* 577–592; and
Goodwin, *No Ordinary Time,* 573–585.

568 flying through the winter night *WSC,* VII,
1163.

568 "I had a serious alarm" *WAC,* 511–513.

568 met in the Grand Harbor Churchill, *Triumph
and Tragedy,* 343.

568 Churchill and Sarah went over Sarah Churchill, *A Thread in the Tapestry,* 75–76.

568 Roosevelt was "very friendly" *TSFS,* 234.

569 "If you talk to him about books"   Leonard C. Schlup and Donald W. Whisenhunt, eds. *"It Seems to Me": Selected Letters of Eleanor Roosevelt* (Lexington, Ky., 2001), 58.

569 Roosevelt declined to talk about substance   *WSC,* VII, 1168.

569 Upon landing at Saki   Bohlen, *Witness to History,* 173.

569 "The eighty-mile drive"   Ibid.

569 "How the President"   Sarah Churchill, *A Thread in the Tapestry,* 76.

569 "I put the clamps on"   Anna to John Boettiger, February 4, 1945, Boettiger Papers, Box 6, FDRL.

570 When he reached Livadia Palace   Kathleen Harriman to Pamela Churchill, January 20–February 4, 1945, PHP.

570 "Harry arrived"   Ibid., February 7, 1945, PHP.

570 Churchill was in the Vorontsov villa   *WSC,* VII, 1172.

570 five minutes early   Charles Portal to Pamela Churchill, PHP.

570 "W was only just rushed"   Ibid.

570 He would not meet   Harriman and Abel, *Special Envoy,* 390.

570 "The two leaders"   Bohlen, *Witness to History,* 180.

570 Stalin broke into a rare   Ibid.

571 had made him even "more bloodthirsty"   Harriman and Abel, *Special Envoy,* 391.

571 he said he hoped Stalin Bohlen, *Witness to History,* 180.

571 Roosevelt added that he would *FRUS, Conferences at Malta and Yalta,* 572.

571 "Ave went over" Kathleen Harriman to Pamela Churchill, February 7, 1945, PHP.

571 According to Bohlen's minutes *FRUS, Conferences at Malta and Yalta,* 590.

572 talked about 1947 Edward R. Stettinius Jr., *Roosevelt and the Russians* (Garden City, N.Y., 1949), 72.

572 "When the Russians said at Yalta" Author interview with Kathleen Harriman Mortimer.

573 experienced a wide range of emotions Sarah Churchill, *A Thread in the Tapestry,* 80.

573 Churchill would call for three cheers Churchill, *Triumph and Tragedy,* 393.

573 "Winston is puzzled" *TSFS,* 243.

573 In January, his Labour colleague *TFOP,* 554.

573 "I suppose they became quite wearied" Author interview with Lady Soames.

574 a tired Roosevelt wrote a note to Ed Stettinius Gunther, *Roosevelt in Retrospect,* 18.

574 once snapped Ibid.

574 Churchill looked "as if" Ibid.

574 who Kathleen noted was Kathleen Harriman to Pamela Churchill, February 7, 1945, PHP.

574 "When they were apart" Author interview with George Elsey.

574 Roosevelt claimed Churchill had been Freidel, *A Rendezvous with Destiny,* 584.

575 "Towards the end" Chandos, *Memoirs,* 310 (see 497).

575 "though we have moved" *TSFS,* 243.

575 "In all these arguments" Author interview with Lady Soames.

576 One day, Roosevelt complained Gunther, *Roosevelt in Retrospect,* 18.

576 a blunt account to Pamela Churchill Charles Portal to Pamela Churchill, PHP.

576 "He was lethargic" Bohlen, *Witness to History,* 172.

577 "While they were away" *TIR,* 340.

577 "I am a bit exhausted" Elliott Roosevelt, ed. *FDR Personal Letters,* IV, 1570.

578 recalling the first summer of his presidency Churchill, *Triumph and Tragedy,* 391.

578 "There was a time" Ibid., 392.

578 Churchill took Roosevelt and Stalin *WSC,* VII, 1208–1209.

579 at Dumbarton Oaks in Washington Dear, ed., *The Oxford Companion to World War II,* 242–243.

580 Roosevelt died believing Burns, *The Soldier of Freedom,* 582.

580 Churchill long defended the regional approach Churchill, *Triumph and Tragedy,* 610.

581 "The purpose of the United Nations" Kenneth W. Thompson, *Winston Churchill's World View: Statesmanship and Power* (Baton Rouge, La., 1983), 328.

582 "Peace is no passive state" Ibid., 330.

582 wanted to eliminate the use   Remarks of Hugh Lunghi, March 1, 1997, Churchill Archives.

582 "The establishment"   Harriman and Abel, *Special Envoy,* 413–414.

584 "I hope you will like"   *WAC,* 515.

584 "P.M. seems well"   Dilks, ed., *The Diaries of Sir Alexander Cadogan,* 707.

584 "Yalta was only a step"   *TIR,* 340–341.

585 "grave troubles"   Harriman and Abel, *Special Envoy,* 226.

585 "The impression I brought back from the Crimea"   Dilks, ed., *The Diaries of Sir Alexander Cadogan,* 716.

585 "Poor Neville Chamberlain"   Ibid.

586 Roosevelt was driven   *FRUS, Conferences at Malta and Yalta,* 560.

586 "like some genie"   Sarah Churchill, *A Thread in the Tapestry,* 82.

586 "The President's decrepitude"   *TSFS,* 250.

586 "suddenly felt lonely"   Sarah Churchill, *A Thread in the Tapestry,* 81.

586 Churchill decided it was time   Ibid., 81–83.

587 "Strangely enough, no"   Ibid., 83.

587 a few days of royal Middle Eastern   *CC,* 396.

587 "Mr. Churchill was rather suspicious"   Anna Roosevelt Halsted, COH, 46.

588 "The President seemed"   Churchill, *Triumph and Tragedy,* 397.

588 With Hopkins they discussed   *WSC,* VII, 1222–1223.

588 "an informal family luncheon" Churchill, *Triumph and Tragedy*, 397.

588 "I saw WSC" *CC*, 396.

588 lasted an hour and fifty-six minutes *FDR: Day by Day—The Pare Lorentz Chronology*, February 15, 1945.

588 an album of photographs Ibid.

588 they took their leave Churchill, *Triumph and Tragedy*, 397.

589 Churchill and Muslim custom collided Ibid., 397–398.

589 "dark clouds" *TIR*, 340.

589 Pa Watson was stricken Burns, *The Soldier of Freedom*, 579.

589 Roosevelt's good-bye *RAH*, 874.

590 Roosevelt asked Sam Rosenman Rosenman, *Working with Roosevelt*, 522.

590 "Franklin feels his death" *CC*, 397.

590 His aides worried *RAH*, 874.

590 "Roosevelt was prone" Rosenman, *Working with Roosevelt*, 526–527.

591 " 'dear old Winston' was quite loquacious" Ibid., 527.

591 called the reporters on board *Complete Presidential Press Conferences*, February 23, 1945, 70–73. I am indebted to Sam Rosenman, who highlighted this section of the conference in his *Working with Roosevelt* (525–526).

593 Anthony Trollope once wrote Anthony Trollope, *The Last Chronicle of Barset* (New York:

Oxford University Press, 1989 ed., chapter LXI), 676–677. The context is the anguish of the Reverend Josiah Crawley, who is thinking mostly of Samson, "eyeless in Gaza."

594 Churchill, who knew Roosevelt's circle *C & R,* III, 539.

594 Daisy found Roosevelt *CC,* 397.

594 In 1940 and 1941, Churchill told his colleagues *WSC,* VII, 1234.

595 Just before entering the House Freidel, *A Rendezvous with Destiny,* 597.

595 "imbibing whisky and soda" *CCTBOM,* 480–481.

595 was to travel to Russia Ibid., 482.

596 "Your lovely Birthday telegram" *WAC,* 520.

596 "For the first time I was beginning" *TIR,* 343.

597 Stalin was already breaking Bohlen, *Witness to History,* 207.

597 "I feel that this is a test case" *C & R,* III, 549.

597 "I feel that our personal intervention" Ibid., 562.

598 "I hope that the rather numerous" Ibid., 574.

599 Thirteen days later, Churchill Ibid., 597.

599 "I did receive" Ibid., 601.

600 "I cannot conceal" Ibid., 595.

600 the race to Berlin Kimball, *Forged in War,* 323–324.

600 "the truest friends" *C & R,* III, 604–605.

600 "The Russian armies" Ibid., 605.

600 one hundred thousand casualties Stephen E.

Ambrose, *The Supreme Commander: The War Years of General Dwight D. Eisenhower* (New York, 1970), 630.

600 "I regard"   *C & R*, III, 612.

601 Roosevelt had a word with   Perkins, *The Roosevelt I Knew*, 396.

602 he talked about Roosevelt with Sam Rosenman   Rosenman, *Working with Roosevelt*, 544–547.

CHAPTER 13: YOU KNOW HOW THIS WILL HIT ME

605 " 'It' is going to Warm Springs"   Roosevelt to Dr. Isador Lubin, March 16, 1945. I am grateful to Carol Lubin for sharing the original of this letter with me.

605 "All I need is some early spring sun"   Chester Bowles, COH, 174.

605 Anna could not come along   *TIR*, 343.

605 "I kissed him goodbye"   EROH, Session 16, 8.

606 *The Punch and Judy Murders*   Bernard Asbell, *When FDR Died*, 12.

606 a big barbecue   Ibid., 3.

606 "Another beautiful, warm day"   *CC*, 413–414.

607 Roosevelt now shared Churchill's belief   Chester Bowles, COH, 174–175.

607 "Let's shake hands"   Ibid., 179.

607 Stalin was furious   Kimball, *Forged in War*, 325–326; Burns, *The Soldier of Freedom*, 585–587.

607 The Soviets, Churchill recalled   Churchill, *Triumph and Tragedy,* 441.

607 Stalin dispatched scorching telegrams   Burns, *The Soldier of Freedom,* 585–587.

607 Roosevelt told Stalin that "it would be"   *C & R,* III, 612.

608 "If they are ever convinced"   Ibid., 613.

608 "We must not permit"   Ibid., 617.

608 "my poor friend is very much alone"   *WAC,* 522.

608 Roosevelt was weighing drastic steps   *CC,* 411.

609 he would mention again as   Ibid., 412.

609 "the hope of the world"   Ibid., 419.

609 "Talk was of the Americans"   *TFOP,* 583.

610 "The only times I ever"   *WAC,* 523.

610 Sitting by the fire   *CC,* 411.

611 Under orders to take gruel   Ibid., 408.

611 arrived on Monday, April 9   Shoumatoff, *FDR's Unfinished Portrait,* 102.

611 they found Roosevelt   Ibid.

612 "Let's not falter"   Ibid.

612 "I was giving a banquet"   Ibid., 103.

613 "He used to call me every night"   Anna Roosevelt Halsted, COH, 48.

613 "I would minimize"   *C & R,* III, 630.

614 "Lucy is so sweet"   *CC,* 416.

614 Henry Morgenthau joined the party   Shoumatoff, *FDR's Unfinished Portrait,* 111.

614 The evening improved   Ibid.

614 would "let you know"   *WSC,* VII, 1287.

614 Churchill "said that he hoped" Ibid.

615 "I miss my quiet evenings" *WAC*, 525.

615 added this note in his own hand Ibid., 524.

615 Roosevelt and Eleanor were in touch *TIR*, 343.

615 Roosevelt was listening to ghost stories Shoumatoff, *FDR's Unfinished Portrait*, 114.

615 took his gruel . . . "Now I'm all" *CC*, 416.

615 read old newspapers Ibid., 416–417.

615 would take Bernard Baruch *WSC*, VII, 1291.

616 "Churchill talked with admiration" Bernard M. Baruch, *Baruch: The Public Years* (New York, 1960), 346.

616 Roosevelt was dressed *CC*, 417.

616 "His colour was good" Ibid.

616 His feet up Ibid.

616 At about twelve-forty Ibid.

616 "We have fifteen minutes" Ibid., 418.

616 Daisy was crocheting Ibid. The ensuing scene is drawn from *CC*, 418–419.

617 "We must pack and go" Shoumatoff, *FDR's Unfinished Portrait*, 119.

617 Eleanor was in the White House Asbell, *When FDR Died*, 49–50.

618 "We are worried" *CC*, 419.

618 Eleanor talked to Dr. McIntire *TIR*, 343.

618 At three thirty-five *CC*, 419.

618 Lucy wiped tears away Shoumatoff, *FDR's Unfinished Portrait*, 119–120.

618 At the Sulgrave *TIR*, 344.

618 "Father slept away" Ibid.

619 Churchill was in the Annexe *WSC,* VII, 1291.

619 a call from Washington *The New York Times,* April 14, 1945.

619 "I felt as if" Churchill, *Triumph and Tragedy,* 471.

619 "I have just heard" *WSC,* VII, 1291.

619 added to the cable Ibid.

619 He had been writing Mary Author interview with Lady Soames.

619 "You know how this will" Ibid.

619 "Get me the palace" Asbell, *When FDR Died,* 95.

619 Churchill cabled Lord Halifax *WSC,* VII, 1291.

619 Halifax put in calls Ibid.

619 At five forty-five P.M. in New York Donald Porter Geddes, ed., *Franklin Delano Roosevelt: A Memorial* (New York, 1945), 1.

620 Richard Strout of *The New Republic* Strout, *TRB: Views and Perspectives on the Presidency,* 24.

620 CBS cut to Douglas Edwards Geddes, ed., *Franklin Delano Roosevelt: A Memorial,* 6.

620 From the State Department Bohlen, *Witness to History,* 209.

621 Clementine was aboard a train *CCTBOM,* 489.

621 "At Warm Springs" Author interview with Trude Lash.

621 in a sudden outburst, Polly Delano Lash, *Eleanor and Franklin,* 722.

621 "The one thing" Author interview with Trude Lash.

622 "E.R. sent us off to bed"   CC, 420.

622 "Poor E.R."   Ibid.

622 "Jesus it was a shock"   Kathleen Harriman to Pamela Churchill, April 12, 1945, PHP.

622 Of Truman, Kathleen noted   Kathleen Harriman to Pamela Churchill, April 12, 1945, PHP.

622 Readers of the *London News Chronicle*   Geddes, ed., *Franklin Delano Roosevelt: A Memorial*, 25.

623 At midnight in New York   Ibid., 39.

623 "Now the Day Is Over"   Ibid.

625 Churchill received Halifax's answer   *WSC*, VII, 1291.

625 Churchill ordered that a plane   Dilks, ed., *The Diaries of Sir Alexander Cadogan*, 727.

625 He dictated a message to Eleanor   Churchill, *Triumph and Tragedy*, 472.

626 "I understand how deep"   Ibid.

626 Writing Truman   *C & R*, III, 632.

626 in a hushed voice   Geddes, ed., *Franklin Delano Roosevelt: A Memorial*, 48.

626 "The House will have learned"   Ibid.

627 George VI sent Churchill   *WSC*, VII, 1293.

627 scheduled for eight-thirty   Dilks, ed., *The Diaries of Sir Alexander Cadogan*, 727.

627 Everything in him would have pressed him   Roy Jenkins, as noted below, is interesting in this question. See Jenkins, *Churchill*, 783.

627 "It would have been"   *WSC*, VII, 1294.

628 decided to do what he wanted   Ibid., 1155–1156, is an example of Churchill's independent-mindedness in these months.

628 "I am touched" Ibid., 1294.

629 Some have argued Jenkins's *Churchill,* 783–786, is an eloquent example of this view, and he was kind to discuss the subject with me. "It is more probable," Jenkins wrote, "that the emotional link between Churchill and Roosevelt was never as close as was commonly thought. It was more a partnership of circumstance and convenience than a friendship of individuals, each of whom, as was noted previously, was a star of brightness which needed its own unimpeded orbit" (785). Jenkins's argument about the funeral is thoughtful.

629 "At no time in our respective histories" *WSC,* VII, 1294–1295.

630 "Moreover I think that it would be" Ibid., 1294.

631 "England has lost" Geddes, ed., *Franklin Delano Roosevelt: A Memorial,* 25.

632 "Prime Minister Churchill" Ibid., 111.

632 "In the after-light" Churchill, *Triumph and Tragedy,* 479.

632 Angus Dun, the Episcopal bishop Geddes, ed., *Franklin Delano Roosevelt: A Memorial,* 111–112.

633 clop-clop-clop Author interview with Trude Lash.

633 In the rose garden *The New York Times,* April 15, 1945.

633 "I was so terribly sad" Pamela Churchill to Kathleen Harriman, April 20, 1945, PHP.

633 "We who represent" *The Times* (London), April 18, 1945.

634 walked Churchill, who was crying *WSC,* VII, 1301.

634 Churchill lunched at the Annexe *TFOP,* 589.

634 "My friendship with the great man" Winston S. Churchill, ed., *The Great Republic,* 364–368. The ensuing quotations are all from these pages of *The Great Republic.*

638 "Winston rose and spoke" Nigel Nicolson, ed., *Harold Nicolson: The War Years, 1939–1945* (New York, 1967), 449.

639 On April 12, Eisenhower visited a Gilbert, *The Holocaust,* 790. Also see Eric Joseph Epstein and Philip Rosen, eds., *Dictionary of the Holocaust* (Westport, Conn., 1997), 217.

639 "There is no doubt" Churchill, *Triumph and Tragedy,* 693.

639 Ed Murrow of CBS walked through Edward J. Bliss, ed., *In Search of Light: The Broadcasts of Edward R. Murrow* (New York, 1967), 94–95.

641 Hitler shot himself Shirer, *The Rise and Fall of the Third Reich,* 1133.

641 "All my thoughts" *WAC,* 531.

641 Thinking of the masses *WSC,* VII, 1341.

641 "After gallant France" Ibid., 1344.

642 Late that evening Ibid., 1347.

642 "My dear friends" Ibid., 1348.

642 "The lights went out" Ibid.

643 hung in Eleanor's living room at Val-Kill Author observation. That the print hung there

during Mrs. Roosevelt's lifetime is confirmed by photographs from the era and to the author by officials of the Eleanor Roosevelt Historic Site.

644 "Dear Eleanor" Lucy Rutherfurd to Eleanor Roosevelt, May 2, 1945; File: Russey-Ruz; General Correspondence, 1945–1952; Eleanor Roosevelt Papers, Part II: April 12, 1945–1964, FDRL. Arthur Schlesinger Jr. also reprints the letter in his *A Life in the 20th Century: Innocent Beginnings, 1917–1950,* 431, and I am grateful to him for drawing my attention to it.

645 "ans," shorthand for "answered" "It was an unbreakable rule that engagements must be kept, equally so that letters must be answered," Joseph Lash wrote of Mrs. Roosevelt. See Lash, *Eleanor: The Years Alone* (New York, 1972), 170.

645 there is no copy of Eleanor's reply At least there is no copy at FDRL, and if the original exists, it has never, to my knowledge, come to public light.

645 "I have looked at them long" Lucy Rutherfurd to Daisy Suckley, May 9, 1945, Margaret Suckley Papers, Wilderstein Collection.

645 "Your note with the enclosure was a v. great pleasure" Lucy Rutherfurd to Daisy Suckley, May 20, 1945, Margaret Suckley Papers, Wilderstein Collection.

646 a diary FDR had kept of his trip to Europe in 1918 The diary was indeed ultimately located. See Folder: Diary, 1918; Subject; Personal Files; Franklin D. Roosevelt Papers as Assistant Secretary of the Navy, Box 33, FDRL.

646 The diary might be in Eleanor's or Franklin's papers   Lucy Rutherfurd to Daisy Suckley, May 20, 1945, Margaret Suckley Papers, Wilderstein Collection.

646 from memory   Lucy was most likely drawing on both her recollections of Roosevelt's trip from those distant days and from his later reminiscences about it.

646 inside a folded notecard imprinted AIKEN, SOUTH CAROLINA   Ibid.

646 "He called on King George V"   Ibid.

646 "Let me know"   Ibid.

646 Anna arranged for Lucy and friend to visit Hyde Park   "Day Book 1945," Saturday, June 9, 1945, Margaret Suckley Papers, Wilderstein Collection. According to the "Day Book," Lucy traveled with a Mrs. Kittredge.

646 a time when the home and grave were not yet open to the public   James P. Horracks, "The Establishment of the Franklin D. Roosevelt Home as a National Historic Site" (Roosevelt-Vanderbilt National Historic Sites, Hyde Park, New York, December 20, 1962), 7. Also see Kristen Baker, "Cultural Landscape Report for the Home of Franklin D. Roosevelt," 2001, 179. "After FDR's death people could visit the library grounds," Baker wrote, "but the military police prohibited the public from the gravesite or the house grounds except for important officials, relatives, or business associates of thePresident."

646 a day that Eleanor spent in New York City

Eleanor's engagement book for June 9, 1945, shows she caught a 10:00 A.M. train to New York and had several appointments during the day; the 6:30 P.M. entry says "arrive home." Engagement Book, June 9, 1945, Eleanor Roosevelt Papers, Part II, Box 4719. It is unclear from the documents available to me whether Eleanor knew of Lucy's visit. Given that, as will be seen below, Anna had signed the papers she thought sufficient to allow Lucy into the largely closed grounds, and that Daisy appears to have taken care of things on the scene, it seems likely that Eleanor did not know beforehand and may or may not have learned about the visit afterward. Since Daisy and presumably Anna knew that Eleanor had had the Shoumatoff picture sent to Lucy, they may have felt somewhat secure in arranging a discreet visit for Lucy on a day when Eleanor was not in Hyde Park. (The day before, on June 8, 1945, Anna had left the East for Seattle with her family. See Asbell, *Mother and Daughter: The Letters of Eleanor and Anna Roosevelt,* 191.)

646 It was fair, mild, and partly cloudy   *The New York Times,* June 9, 1945, and June 10, 1945.

647 "The memory will be with me always"   Lucy Rutherfurd to Daisy Suckley, June 19, 1945, Margaret Suckley Papers, Wilderstein Collection.

647 "And now about your very great thoughtfulness in asking me to stay"   Ibid.

647 there was "much excitement a half hour after they left"   "Day Book 1945," Saturday, June 9,

1945, Margaret Suckley Papers, Wilderstein Collection.

647 the 1235 Military Police Battalion   Horracks, "The Establishment of the Franklin D. Roosevelt Home as a National Historic Site," 7. Also see Baker, "Cultural Landscape Report for the Home of Franklin D. Roosevelt," 179.

647 Presumably hearing of the bureaucratic flap later in a letter from Daisy   Lucy Rutherfurd to Daisy Suckley, June 19, 1945, Margaret Suckley Papers, Wilderstein Collection. The visit had been June 9, and Lucy's letter of June 19 thanks Daisy for sending her a letter, so there seems to have been a note from Daisy to Lucy in the intervening ten days. Given Daisy's use of the past tense in her "Day Book" for the day of the stop, it seems likely that Lucy did not know of the stir her visit had caused until Daisy told her about it afterward.

648 Mary, who went with Churchill   *WSC*, VIII, 61.

648 there was evidence at Potsdam   Averell Harriman COH, 257.

649 "The atomic bomb"   Churchill, *Triumph and Tragedy*, 637.

649 returned to England on July 25   Ibid., 674.

649 Churchill went to bed thinking   Ibid.

649 "What is there to say"   Pamela Churchill to Averell and Kathleen Harriman, July 27, 1945, PHP.

650 "Come to the Cabinet Room"   Author interview with Patrick Kinna.

650 "I know that you" Schlup and Whisenhut, eds., *"It Seems to Me,"* 62.

650 Churchill's motorcade drove up *New York Herald-Tribune,* March 13, 1946.

651 Playing poker on the train *WSC,* VIII, 196–197.

651 Eleanor met Churchill and Clementine *New York Herald-Tribune,* March 13, 1946.

651 Eleanor "felt sure" Eleanor Roosevelt, *My Day,* March 14, 1946, FDRL.

652 For three minutes Churchill said nothing *New York Herald-Tribune,* March 13, 1946.

652 Walter Annenberg, the American publishing magnate Kay Halle Papers, Folder 2, Box 5.

653 "the largest human being" Berlin, *Mr. Churchill in 1940,* 39.

653 A letter from America Montague Browne, *Long Sunset,* 318.

653 "I am prepared" *Newsweek,* February 1, 1965.

653 "I look forward to dying" Walter Graebner, *My Dear Mister Churchill* (London, 1965), 128.

653 gun carriage *Newsweek,* February 8, 1965.

653 "He, with Franklin Roosevelt" *The New York Times,* January 26, 1965.

653 In a heavy black veil *The New York Times,* January 31, 1965.

653 heard a Cockney dismiss Ibid.

654 He was buried next to his parents *WSC,* VIII, 1363. Sir Martin's moving account of Churchill's last days and his funeral can be found in ibid., 1356–1366. Sir Martin chose to conclude the

monumental official biography with a quotation from a note Lady Soames had written to her father in 1964: "In addition to all the feelings a daughter has for a loving, generous father, I owe you what every Englishman, woman & child does—Liberty itself." I am also grateful to Lady Soames for helping me sort out some details of her father's burial.

EPILOGUE: THEM'S MY SENTIMENTS EXACTLY

657 Roosevelt dispatched Averell Harriman   Harriman and Abel, *Special Envoy,* 276.

657 "Mr. Roosevelt gave"   Churchill, *Closing the Ring,* 385.

658 "He invited"   Author interview with John Kenneth Galbraith.

659 "Churchill has never"   BBK G/11/4, LBP.

659 "From all small things"   *The Times* (London), January 26, 1965.

659 "He'd like that"   James Roosevelt, *My Parents: A Differing View,* 204–205.

660 "Churchill's attitude toward Roosevelt"   Author interview with Anthony Montague Browne.

660 "What ought we to do?"   James, ed., *Complete Speeches,* VIII, 8627.

661 "To conclude"   Ibid., 8633.

661 courage, Churchill once said, was the essential virtue   *The Times* (London), January 26, 1965.

661 "Today, science has brought"   Geddes, ed., *Franklin Delano Roosevelt: A Memorial,* 217–218.

663 "Wishful thinking" *TIR*, 235.

663 Randolph Churchill came to Washington Arthur Schlesinger Jr., "Randolph Churchill," in *The Grand Original*, ed. Halle, 281.

663 Hopkins noticed a "Notes and Comment" piece *RAH*, 734.

664 "Surely the Board knows what democracy is" Ibid., 735.

664 "I *love* it!" Ibid.

664 "must never cease" James, ed., *Complete Speeches*, VII, 7288.

665 Eleanor Roosevelt returned to London Eleanor Roosevelt, *On My Own* (New York, 1958), 37.

665 "My husband had looked forward" Ibid.

BIBLIOGRAPHY

MANUSCRIPT COLLECTIONS

Lord Beaverbrook Papers, House of Lords Archives, London, England

John Boettiger Papers, Franklin D. Roosevelt Library, Hyde Park, New York

Wilson Brown Papers, Franklin D. Roosevelt Library, Hyde Park, New York

Howard Bruenn Papers, Franklin D. Roosevelt Library, Hyde Park, New York

Winston Churchill Papers, Churchill Archives Centre, Churchill College, Cambridge, England

Joseph E. Davies Papers, Library of Congress, Washington, D.C.

Charles Eade Papers, Churchill Archives Centre, Churchill College, Cambridge, England

Robert D. Graff Papers, Franklin D. Roosevelt Library, Hyde Park, New York

Kay Halle Papers, John F. Kennedy Presidential Library, Boston, Massachusetts

Anna Roosevelt Halsted Papers, Franklin D. Roosevelt Library, Hyde Park, New York

Pamela Harriman Papers, Library of Congress, Washington, D.C.

W. Averell Harriman Papers, Library of Congress, Washington, D.C.

Harry Hopkins Papers, Franklin D. Roosevelt Library, Hyde Park, New York

Harold L. Ickes Papers, Library of Congress, Washington, D.C.

Tyler Kent Papers, Franklin D. Roosevelt Presidential Library and Museum, Hyde Park, New York

Agnes and Eugene Meyer Papers, Library of Congress, Washington, D.C.

Edward R. Murrow Papers, Fletcher School of Law and Diplomacy, Tufts University, Boston, Massachusetts

Eleanor Roosevelt Papers, Franklin D. Roosevelt Presidential Library and Museum, Hyde Park, New York

Franklin D. Roosevelt Papers, Franklin D. Roosevelt Presidential Library and Museum, Hyde Park, New York

Margaret Suckley Papers, Wilderstein Collection, Rhinebeck, New York

United States Secret Service Records, Franklin D. Roosevelt Library, Hyde Park, New York

Henry A. Wallace Papers and Diaries, University of Iowa Library Special Collections, Iowa City, Iowa

Theodore White Papers, Harvard University, Cambridge, Massachusetts

AUTHOR INTERVIEWS

The date and location indicate my initial conversation with these sources; many of them subsequently and generously answered additional questions and shared other insights in person, by letter, and by telephone.

The Lady Soames, DBE (Mary Churchill), August 25, 2000, London

Winston S. Churchill, August 26, 2000, London

Mrs. Ian Edwards (Anne Curzon-Howe), October 15, 2002, by telephone, New York City–Southampton, England

George M. Elsey, June 5, 2000, Washington, D.C.

John Kenneth Galbraith, October 21, 2002, Cambridge, Massachusetts

Mrs. Margaret Hendrick (Rollie Hambley), June 26, 2002, by telephone, New York City–Annapolis, Maryland

Robert Hopkins, December 18, 2000, Washington, D.C.

Patrick Kinna, November 11, 2002, Brighton, England

Henry A. Kissinger, September 30, 2002, New York City

Trude Pratt Lash, November 27, 2000, New York City

Carol R. Lubin, September 30, 2002, New York City

Sir Anthony Montague Browne, November 11, 2002, London

Robert M. Morgenthau, February 27, 2002, New York City

Kathleen Harriman Mortimer, January 30, 2002, New York City

Curtis Roosevelt, December 9, 2002, by telephone, New York City–Saint-Bonnet- du-Gard, France

Elie Wiesel, August 27, 2002, by telephone, New York City

Rivington Winant, September 10, 2002, New York City

ORAL HISTORIES

Columbia University

Sir Norman Angell

Chester Bowles

Marquis Childs

Lucius Clay

Anna Roosevelt Halsted

W. Averell Harriman

Admiral H. Kent Hewitt

Alan Kirk

Arthur Krock

Walter Lippmann

Frances Perkins

Henry Wallace

Sir Robert Alexander Watson-Watt

Franklin D. Roosevelt Library

John Allison—Verne Newton Collection

Valentin Berezhkov—Verne Newton Collection

Alistair Cooke

Pamela Churchill Harriman—Verne Newton Collection

Sir Ian Jacob—Verne Newton Collection

Sir John Martin—Verne Newton Collection

Air Vice Marshal David McKinley—Verne Newton Collection

Frances Perkins

Eleanor Roosevelt—Robert D. Graff Papers Collection

The Lady Soames, DBE (Mary Churchill)—Verne Newton Collection

BOOKS AND ARTICLES CONSULTED

Adamic, Louis. *Dinner at the White House.* New York: Harper & Brothers, 1946.

Adams, Henry H. *Harry Hopkins: A Biography.* New York: G. P. Putnam's Sons, 1977.

Alexander, Bevin. *How Hitler Could Have Won World War II: The Fatal Errors That Led to Nazi Defeat.* New York: Crown, 2000.

Alldritt, Keith. *The Greatest of Friends: Franklin D. Roosevelt and Winston Churchill, 1941–1945.* London: Robert Hale, 1995.

Alphand, Hervé. *L'Etonnement d'être: Journal, 1939–1973.* Paris: Fayard, 1977.

Alsop, Joseph. *FDR, 1882–1945: A Centenary Remembrance.* New York: Viking Press, 1982.

Alsop, Joseph, and Robert Kintner. *American White Paper: The Story of American Diplomacy and the Second World War.* London: Michael Joseph, 1940.

———. *Men Around the President.* New York: Doubleday, Doran & Co., 1939.

Ambrose, Stephen E. *D-Day, June 6, 1944: The Climactic Battle of World War II.* New York: Simon & Schuster, 1994.

———. *The Supreme Commander: The War Years of General Dwight D. Eisenhower.* Garden City, N.Y.: Doubleday, 1970.

Amory, Mark, ed. *The Letters of Evelyn Waugh.* New Haven, Conn.: Ticknor and Fields, 1980.

Arnold, H. H. *Global Mission.* New York: Harper & Brothers, 1949.

Asbell, Bernard. *The F.D.R. Memoirs.* Garden City, N.Y.: Doubleday, 1973.

————. *When F.D.R. Died*. New York: Holt, Rinehart & Winston, 1961.

————, ed. *Mother and Daughter: The Letters of Eleanor and Anna Roosevelt*. New York: Coward, McCann & Geoghegan, 1982.

Ashley, Maurice. *Churchill As Historian*. New York: Charles Scribner's Sons, 1969.

Asquith, H. H. *Memories and Reflections, 1852–1927*. 2 vols. Boston: Little, Brown, 1928.

Atkinson, Rick. *An Army at Dawn: The War in North Africa, 1942–1943*. New York: Henry Holt, 2002.

Austin, F. Britten. *Forty Centuries Look Down: A Biographical Novel of Napoleon*. New York: Frederick A. Stokes Company, 1937.

Barone, Michael. *Our Country: The Shaping of America from Roosevelt to Reagan*. New York: Free Press, 1990.

Barton, D. Plunket, Charles Benham, and Francis Watt. *The Story of the Inns of Court*. Boston: Houghton Mifflin, 1928.

Baruch, Bernard M. *Baruch: The Public Years*. New York: Holt, Rinehart & Winston, 1960.

Beaverbrook, Max Aitken. *Men and Power, 1917–1918*. New York: Duell, Sloan and Pearce, 1956.

Belair, Felix. "Down to the Sea with the 'Skipper.'" *The New York Times Magazine*, August 13, 1939.

Bell, P.M.H. *A Certain Eventuality: Britain and the Fall of France*. Farnborough, Hants: Saxon House, 1974.

Berenbaum, Michael, and Abraham J. Peck, eds. *The Holocaust and History: The Known, the Unknown, the Disputed, and the Reexamined.* Bloomington: University of Indiana Press, 1998.

Berg, A. Scott. *Lindbergh.* New York: G. P. Putnam's Sons, 1998.

Berlin, Isaiah. *Mr. Churchill in 1940.* Boston: Houghton Mifflin, 1964.

Beschloss, Michael. *The Conquerors: Roosevelt, Truman and the Destruction of Hitler's Germany, 1941–1945.* New York: Simon & Schuster, 2002.

————. *Kennedy and Roosevelt: The Uneasy Alliance.* New York: W. W. Norton, 1980.

Best, Geoffrey. *Churchill: A Study in Greatness.* New York: Hambledon and London, 2001.

Biddle, George. "As I Remember Groton." *Harper's,* August 1939.

Bishop, Jim. *FDR's Last Year, April 1944–April 1945.* New York: Morrow, 1974.

Blake, Robert, and William Roger Louis, eds. *Churchill.* New York: W. W. Norton, 1993.

Bliss, Edward, Jr., ed. *In Search of Light: The Broadcasts of Edward R. Murrow, 1938–1961.* New York: Alfred A. Knopf, 1967.

Blum, John Morton, ed. *From the Morgenthau Diaries.* Boston: Houghton Mifflin, 1964–1967. Vol. 2: *Years of Urgency, 1938–1941,* 1964. Vol. 3: *Years of War, 1941–1945,* 1967.

————, ed. *The Price of Vision: The Diary of Henry A. Wallace, 1942–1946.* Boston: Houghton Mifflin, 1973.

Boettiger, John. *A Love in Shadow.* New York: W. W. Norton, 1978.

Bohlen, Charles E. *Witness to History, 1929–1969.* New York: W. W. Norton, 1973.

Bonham Carter, Violet. *Winston Churchill: An Intimate Portrait.* New York: Harcourt, Brace & World, 1965.

Boothby, Robert John Graham. *My Yesterday, Your Tomorrow.* London: Hutchinson, 1962.

Breitman, Richard. *Official Secrets: What the Nazis Planned, What the British and Americans Knew.* New York: Hill & Wang, 1998.

Breitman, Richard, and Alan M. Kraut. *American Refugee Policy and European Jewry, 1933–1945.* Bloomington: Indiana University Press, 1987.

Brinkley, Douglas, and David R. Facey-Crowther, eds. *The Atlantic Charter.* New York: St. Martin's Press, 1994.

Brown, Malcolm, ed. *T. E. Lawrence: The Selected Letters.* New York: W. W. Norton, 1989.

Browne, Anthony Montague. *Long Sunset: Memoirs of Winston Churchill's Last Private Secretary.* London: Cassell, 1995.

Buhite, Russell D., and David W. Levy, eds. *FDR's Fireside Chats.* Norman, Okla.: University of Oklahoma Press, 1992.

Bullock, Alan. *Hitler and Stalin: Parallel Lives.* London: Fontana Press, 1998.

———. *Hitler: A Study in Tyranny.* New York: Harper & Brothers, 1952.

Burns, James MacGregor. *Roosevelt: The Lion and the Fox.* New York: Harcourt, Brace, 1956.

———. *Roosevelt: The Soldier of Freedom.* New York: Harcourt Brace Jovanovich 1970.

Butler, J.R.M. *Lord Lothian, Philip Kerr, 1882–1940.* New York: St. Martin's Press, 1960.

Byrnes, James F. *Speaking Frankly.* New York: Harper & Brothers, 1947.

Cannadine, David. *In Churchill's Shadow: Confronting the Past in Modern Britain.* New York: Oxford University Press, 2002.

———, ed. *Blood, Toil, Tears and Sweat: The Speeches of Winston Churchill.* Boston: Houghton Mifflin, 1989.

Cannadine, David, and Roland Quinault. "Churchill in the Twenty-first Century: A Conference Held at the Institute of Historical Research, University of London, 11–13 January 2001." *Transactions of the Royal Historical Society,* 6th ser., 11 (December 2001).

Casey, Steven. *Cautious Crusade: Franklin D. Roosevelt, American Public Opinion, and the War Against Nazi Germany.* New York: Oxford University Press, 2001.

Cecil of Chelwood, Robert Gascoyne-Cecil. *All the Way.* London: Hodder and Stoughton, 1949.

Charmley, John. *Churchill's Grand Alliance: The Anglo-American Special Relationship, 1940–1957*. New York: Harcourt, Brace, 1995.

————. *Churchill: The End of Glory: A Political Biography*. New York: Harcourt Brace, 1994.

Chisholm, Anne, and Michael Davie. *Lord Beaverbrook: A Life*. New York: Alfred A. Knopf, 1993.

Churchill, Randolph S., and Martin Gilbert. *Winston S. Churchill*. 8 vols. and 5 companions. Boston: Houghton Mifflin, 1966–1988. Vols. 1–2 and companions 1–2 by Randolph S. Churchill; vols. 3–8 and companions 3–5 by Martin Gilbert. Vol. 1: *Youth, 1874–1900*, 1966. *Companion*, vol. 1. Part 1: *1874–1896*, 1967. Part 2: *1896–1900*, 1967. Vol. 2: *Young Statesman, 1901–1914*, 1967. *Companion*, vol. 2. Part 1: *1901–1907*, 1969. Part 2: *1907–1911*, 1969. Part 3: *1911–1914*, 1969. Vol. 3: *The Challenge of War, 1914–1916*, 1971. *Companion*, vol. 3. Part 1: *July 1914–April 1915*, 1973. Part 2: *May 1915–December 1916*, 1973. Vol. 4: *The Stricken World, 1916–1922*, 1975. *Companion*, vol. 4. Part 1: *January 1917–June 1919*, 1978. Part 2: *July 1919–March 1921*, 1978. Part 3: *April 1921–November 1922*, 1978. Vol. 5: *The Prophet of Truth: 1922–1939*, 1977. *Companion*, vol. 5. Part 1: *The Exchequer Years, 1922–1929*, 1981. Part 2: *The Wilderness Years, 1929–1935*, 1982. Part 3: *The Coming of War, 1936–1939*, 1983. Vol. 6: *Finest Hour, 1939–1941*, 1983. Vol. 7: *Road to Victory, 1941–1945*, 1986. Vol. 8: *"Never Despair," 1945–1965*, 1988.

Churchill, Sarah. *Keep On Dancing: An Autobiography*. London: Weidenfeld & Nicolson, 1981.

————. *A Thread in the Tapestry.* New York: Dodd, Mead, 1967.

Churchill, Winston S. *Great Contemporaries.* Chicago: University of Chicago Press, 1973.

————. *His Father's Son: The Life of Randolph Churchill.* London: Weidenfeld & Nicolson, 1996.

————. *A History of the English-Speaking Peoples.* 4 vols. New York: Dodd, Mead, 1956–1958.

————. "How We Carry Liquor." *Collier's,* August 25, 1934.

————. *Lord Randolph Churchill.* London: Macmillan, 1907.

————. *Marlborough: His Life and Times.* Abridged and with an introduction by Henry Steele Commager. New York: Scribner, 1968.

————. *My Early Life.* New York: Simon & Schuster, 1996.

————. *The River War,* Vol. 2. London: Longmans, Green, and Company, 1899.

————. *Savrola: A Tale of the Revolution in Laurania.* New York: Random House, 1956.

————. *The Second World War.* 6 vols. Boston: Houghton Mifflin, 1948–1953. Vol. 1: *The Gathering Storm,* 1948. Vol. 2: *Their Finest Hour,* 1949. Vol. 3: *The Grand Alliance,* 1950. Vol. 4: *The Hinge of Fate,* 1950. Vol. 5: *Closing the Ring,* 1951. Vol. 6: *Triumph and Tragedy,* 1953.

————. *Step by Step, 1936–1939.* New York: G. P. Putnam's Sons, 1939.

————. *The World Crisis, 1911–1918.* 2 vols. London: Odhams Press, 1938.

Churchill by His Contemporaries: An Observer Appreciation. London: Hodder and Stoughton, 1965.

Cockett, Richard, ed. *My Dear Max: The Letters of Brendan Bracken to Lord Beaverbrook, 1925–1958.* London: Historians' Press, 1990.

Cole, Wayne S. *Roosevelt and the Isolationists, 1932–45.* Lincoln: University of Nebraska Press, 1983.

Colville, John Rupert. *The Fringes of Power: 10 Downing Street Diaries, 1939–1955.* New York: W. W. Norton, 1985.

————. *Winston Churchill and His Inner Circle.* New York: Wyndham Books, 1981.

Complete Presidential Press Conferences of Franklin D. Roosevelt. 25 vols. New York: Da Capo Press, 1972.

Conant, James B. *My Several Lives.* New York: Harper & Row, 1970.

Cowles, Virginia. *Churchill: The Era and the Man.* New York: Harper & Brothers, 1953.

Cowley, Robert, ed. *What If?: The World's Foremost Military Historians Imagine What Might Have Been.* New York: G. P. Putnam's Sons, 1999.

Culver, John C., and John Hyde. *American Dreamer: The Life and Times of Henry A. Wallace.* New York: W. W. Norton, 2000.

Dallek, Robert. *Franklin D. Roosevelt and American Foreign Policy, 1932–1945.* New York: Oxford University Press, 1979.

Danchev, Alex. *On Specialness: Essays in Anglo-American Relations.* New York: St. Martin's Press, 1998.

Danchev, Alex, and Daniel Todman, eds. *War Diaries, 1939–1945: Field Marshal Lord Alanbrooke.* Berkeley: University of California Press, 2001.

Daniels, Jonathan. *The End of Innocence.* Philadelphia: J. B. Lippincott, 1954.

———. *Washington Quadrille: The Dance Beside the Documents.* Garden City, N.Y.: Doubleday, 1968.

———. *White House Witness, 1942–1945.* Garden City, N.Y.: Doubleday, 1975.

Davie, Michael, ed. *The Diaries of Evelyn Waugh.* London: Weidenfeld and Nicolson, 1976.

Davis, Forrest, and Ernest K. Lindley. *How War Came: An American White Paper: From the Fall of France to Pearl Harbor.* New York: Simon & Schuster, 1942.

Davis, Kenneth S. *FDR: Into the Storm, 1937–1940: A History.* New York: Random House, 1993.

———. *FDR: The Beckoning of Destiny, 1882–1928: A History.* New York: G. P. Putnam's Sons, 1972.

———. *FDR: The War President, 1940–1943: A History.* New York: Random House, 2000.

Dear, I.C.B., ed. *The Oxford Companion to World War II.* New York: Oxford University Press, 1995.

Dilks, David, ed. *The Diaries of Sir Alexander Cadogan, O.M., 1938–1945.* New York: G. P. Putnam's Sons, 1972.

Dimbleby, David, and David Reynolds. *An Ocean Apart: The Relationship Between Britain and America in the Twentieth Century.* New York: Vintage, 1989.

Dows, Olin. *Franklin Roosevelt at Hyde Park.* New York: American Artists Group, 1949.

Doyle, William. *Inside the Oval Office: The White House Tapes from FDR to Clinton.* New York: Kodansha International, 1999.

Dunn, Walter Scott Jr. *Second Front Now, 1943.* University: University of Alabama Press, 1980.

Eade, Charles, ed. *Churchill, by His Contemporaries.* New York: Simon & Schuster, 1954.

Eden, Anthony. *The Memoirs of Anthony Eden: The Reckoning.* London: Cassell, 1965.

Edmonds, Robin. *The Big Three: Churchill, Roosevelt & Stalin in Peace and War.* London: Hamish Hamilton, 1991.

Eisenhower, Dwight. *At Ease: Stories I Tell to Friends.* Blue Ridge Summit, Pa.: TAB Books, 1988.

Elsey, George. "Some White House Recollections, 1942–53." *Diplomatic History* 12 (Summer 1988): 357–364.

Emblidge, David, ed. *My Day: The Best of Eleanor Roosevelt's Acclaimed Newspaper Columns, 1936–1962.* New York: Da Capo Press, 2001.

Ferrell, Robert H. *The Dying President: Franklin D. Roosevelt, 1944–1945.* Columbia: University of Missouri Press, 1998.

————. *Harry S. Truman: A Life.* Columbia: University of Missouri Press, 1994.

Fields, Alonzo. *My 21 Years in the White House.* New York: Coward-McCann, 1961.

Forester, C. S. *Brown on Resolution.* Harmondsworth, Eng.: Penguin Books, 1956.

Freedman, Max, ed. *Roosevelt and Frankfurter: Their Correspondence, 1928–1945.* Boston: Little, Brown, 1968.

Freidel, Frank. *Franklin D. Roosevelt.* 4 vols. Boston: Little, Brown, 1952–1973. Vol. 1: *The Apprenticeship,* 1952. Vol. 2: *The Ordeal,* 1954. Vol. 3: *The Triumph,* 1956. Vol. 4: *Launching the New Deal,* 1973.

————. *Franklin D. Roosevelt: A Rendezvous with Destiny.* Boston: Little, Brown, 1990.

Fromkin, David. *In the Time of the Americans: The Generation That Changed America's Role in the World.* New York: Alfred A. Knopf, 1995.

Galbraith, John Kenneth. *Name-Dropping: From FDR On.* Boston: Houghton Mifflin, 1999.

Gallagher, Hugh Gregory. *FDR's Splendid Deception.* Arlington, Va.: Vandamere Press, 1994.

Gathorne-Hardy, Robert, ed. *Memoirs of Lady Ottoline Morrell: A Study in Friendship, 1873–1915.* New York: Alfred A. Knopf, 1964.

Geddes, Donald Porter, ed. *Franklin Delano Roosevelt: A Memorial.* New York: Dial Press, 1945.

Gilbert, Martin. *Auschwitz and the Allies: A Devastating Account of How the Allies Responded to the News of Hitler's Mass Murder.* New York: Henry Holt, 1981.

————. *Churchill: A Life.* New York: Henry Holt, 1991.

————. *The Churchill War Papers.* 3 vols. New York: W. W. Norton, 1993–2000. Vol. 1: *At the Admiralty, September 1939–May 1940,* 1993. Vol. 2: *Never Surrender, May 1940–December 1940,* 1995. Vol. 3: *The Ever-Widening War, 1941,* 2000.

————. *The Holocaust: A History of the Jews of Europe During the Second World War.* New York: Holt, Rinehart and Winston, 1986.

————. *In Search of Churchill: A Historian's Journey.* New York: John Wiley and Sons, 1994.

————. *The Second World War: A Complete History.* New York: Henry Holt, 1989.

————. *Winston Churchill: The Wilderness Years.* London: Macmillan, 1981.

Goodwin, Doris Kearns. *No Ordinary Time: Franklin and Eleanor Roosevelt: The Home Front in World War II.* New York: Simon & Schuster, 1994.

Gould, Jean. *A Good Fight: The Story of F.D.R.'s Conquest of Polio.* New York: Dodd, Mead, 1960.

Graebner, Walter. *My Dear Mister Churchill.* Boston: Houghton Mifflin, 1965.

Graham, Katharine. *Katharine Graham's Washington.* New York: Alfred A. Knopf, 2002.

Grigg, John. *1943: The Victory That Never Was.* New York: Hill and Wang, 1980.

Gunther, John. *Roosevelt in Retrospect: A Profile in History.* New York: Harper & Brothers, 1950.

Halle, Kay. *Irrepressible Churchill: Stories, Sayings and Impressions of Winston Churchill.* Cleveland: World Publishing Company, 1966.

————, ed. *The Grand Original: Portraits of Randolph Churchill by His Friends.* Boston: Houghton Mifflin, 1971.

Hanfstaengl, Ernst. *Hitler: The Missing Years.* New York: Arcade Publishing, 1994.

Harriman, W. Averell, and Elie Abel. *Special Envoy to Churchill and Stalin, 1941–1946.* New York: Random House, 1975.

Harvey, John, ed. *The Diplomatic Diaries of Oliver Hardy, 1937–1940.* New York: St. Martin's Press, 1970.

Hassett, William D. *Off the Record with F.D.R., 1942–1945.* New Brunswick, N.J.: Rutgers University Press, 1958.

Higgins, Trumbull. *Winston Churchill and the Second Front, 1940–1943.* New York: Oxford University Press, 1957.

Hitchens, Christopher. *Blood, Class and Nostalgia: Anglo-American Ironies.* New York: Farrar, Straus & Giroux, 1990.

Hitler, Adolf. *Mein Kampf.* New York: Reynal & Hitchcock, 1940.

Hodgkin, E. C., ed. *Letters from Tehran: A British Ambassador in World War II, Persia.* New York: I. B. Tauris & Co., 1991.

Holloway, David. *Stalin and the Bomb: The Soviet Union and Atomic Energy, 1939–1956.* New Haven, Conn.: Yale University Press, 1994.

Holmes, Richard, ed. *The Oxford Companion to Military History.* Oxford: Oxford University Press, 2001.

Hoopes, Townsend, and Douglas Brinkley. *FDR and the Creation of the U.N.* New Haven, Conn.: Yale University Press, 1997.

Hopkins, Robert. *Witness to History: Recollections of a World War II Photographer.* Seattle, Wash.: Castle Pacific Publishing, 2002.

Howard, Michael. *The Mediterranean Strategy in the Second World War.* New York: Praeger, 1968.

Ickes, Harold L. *The Secret Diary of Harold L. Ickes.* Vols. 2 and 3. New York: Simon & Schuster, 1954. Vol. 2: *The Inside Struggle, 1936–1939.* Vol. 3: *The Lowering Clouds, 1939–1941.*

Ismay, Hastings Lionel. *The Memoirs of General Lord Ismay.* New York: Viking Press, 1960.

James, Robert Rhodes. *Churchill: A Study in Failure, 1900–1939.* New York: World, 1970.

———, ed. *Winston S. Churchill: His Complete Speeches.* Vols. 6, 7, and 8. New York: Chelsea House, 1974. Vol. 6: *1935–1942.* Vol. 7: *1943–1949.* Vol. 8: *1950–1963.*

Jenkins, Roy. *Churchill: A Biography.* New York: Farrar, Straus & Giroux, 2001.

John G. Waite Associates, Architects. *The President As Architect: Franklin D. Roosevelt's Top Cottage.* Albany, N.Y.: Mount Ida Press, 2001.

Johnson, David Alan. *The Battle of Britain and the American Factor, July–October, 1940.* Conshohocken, Pa.: Combined Press, 1998.

Keegan, John. *The Second World War.* New York: Penguin, 1990.

———. *Winston Churchill.* Penguin Lives Series. New York: Viking Press, 2002.

Kempton, Murray. *Rebellions, Perversities, and Main Events.* New York: Times Books, 1994.

Kennedy, Paul, ed. *Grand Strategies in War and Peace.* New Haven, Conn.: Yale University Press, 1991.

Kershaw, Ian. *Hitler, 1889–1936: Hubris.* New York: W. W. Norton, 1999.

———. *Hitler, 1936–1945: Nemesis.* New York: W. W. Norton, 2000.

Kimball, Warren F. *Forged in War: Roosevelt, Churchill and the Second World War.* New York: Morrow, 1997.

———. *The Juggler: Franklin Roosevelt As Wartime Statesman.* Princeton, N.J.: Princeton University Press, 1991.

———. *The Most Unsordid Act: Lend-Lease, 1939–1941.* Baltimore: Johns Hopkins University Press, 1969.

————. *Swords or Ploughshares?: The Morgenthau Plan for Defeated Nazi Germany, 1943–1946*. Philadelphia: Lippincott, 1976.

————, ed. *Churchill and Roosevelt: The Complete Correspondence*. 3 vols. Princeton, N.J.: Princeton University Press, 1984.

Kintrea, Frank. " 'Old Peabo' and the School." *American Heritage,* October/November 1980.

Kleeman, Rita Halle. *Gracious Lady: The Life of Sara Delano Roosevelt*. New York: D. Appleton–Century, 1935.

Langer, William L., and S. Everett Gleason. *The Challenge to Isolation, 1937–1940*. New York: Harper & Brothers, 1952.

————. *The Undeclared War, 1940–1941*. New York: Harper & Brothers, 1953.

Langhorne, Elizabeth. *Nancy Astor and Her Friends*. New York: Praeger Publishers, 1974.

Larrabee, Eric. *Commander in Chief: Franklin Delano Roosevelt, His Lieutenants, and Their War*. New York: Harper & Row, 1987.

Lash, Joseph P. *Eleanor and Franklin*. New York: W. W. Norton, 1971.

————. *Eleanor: The Years Alone*. New York: W. W. Norton, 1972.

————. *Roosevelt and Churchill, 1939–1941: The Partnership That Saved the West*. New York: W. W. Norton, 1976.

————. *A World of Love: Eleanor Roosevelt and Her Friends, 1943–1962*. Garden City, N.Y.: Doubleday, 1984.

Lasser, William. *Benjamin V. Cohen: Architect of the New Deal*. New Haven, Conn.: Yale University Press, 2002.

Leahy, William. *I Was There*. New York: Whittlesey House, 1950.

Leslie, Anita. *Lady Randolph Churchill: The Story of Jennie Jerome*. New York: Charles Scribner's Sons, 1969.

————. *The Remarkable Mr. Jerome*. New York: Henry Holt, 1954.

Lerner, Max. *Public Journal: Marginal Notes on Wartime America*. New York: Viking Press, 1945.

Leuchtenburg, William E. *The FDR Years: On Roosevelt and His Legacy*. New York: Columbia University Press, 1995.

Lindley, Ernest K. *Franklin D. Roosevelt: A Career in Progressive Democracy*. New York: Blue Ribbon Books, 1931.

Lukacs, John. *Churchill: Visionary, Statesman, Historian*. New Haven, Conn.: Yale University Press, 2002.

————. *The Duel: 10 May–31 July 1940: The Eighty-Day Struggle Between Churchill and Hitler*. New York: Ticknor and Fields, 1991.

————. *Five Days in London, May 1940*. New Haven, Conn.: Yale University Press, 1999.

Lyttleton, Oliver. *The Memoirs of Lord Chandos*. London: Bodley Head, 1962.

MacKenzie, Norman, ed. *The Letters of Sidney and Beatrice Webb.* Vol. 3: *Pilgrimage, 1912–1947.* Cambridge, Eng.: Cambridge University Press, 1978.

MacKenzie, Norman, and Jeanne MacKenzie, eds. *The Diary of Beatrice Webb.* Vols. 3 and 4. Cambridge, Mass.: Belknap Press of Harvard University Press, 1984–1985. Vol. 3: *1905–1924, "The Power to Alter Things,"* 1984. Vol. 4: *1924–1943, "The Wheel of Life,"* 1985.

Macmillan, Harold. *War Diaries: Politics and War in the Mediterranean, January, 1943–May, 1945.* New York: St. Martin's Press, 1984.

Manchester, William. *The Glory and the Dream: A Narrative History of America, 1932–1972.* Boston: Little, Brown, 1974.

————. *The Last Lion: Winston Spencer Churchill.* 2 vols. Boston: Little, Brown, 1983–1988. Vol. 1: *Visions of Glory, 1874–1932,* 1983. Vol. 2: *Alone, 1932–1940,* 1988.

Marchant, James, ed. *Winston Spencer Churchill: Servant of Crown and Commonwealth.* London: Cassell, 1954.

Martin, John. *Downing Street: The War Years.* London: Bloomsbury, 1991.

McCullough, David. *Truman.* New York: Simon & Schuster, 1992.

McIntire, Ross, in collaboration with George Creel. *White House Physician.* New York: G. P. Putnam's Sons, 1946.

Moran, Lord. *Churchill, Taken from the Diaries of Lord Moran: The Struggle for Survival, 1940–1965.* Boston: Houghton Mifflin, 1966.

Morgan, Frederick. *Overture to Overlord*. Garden City, N.Y.: Doubleday, 1950.

Morgan, Ted. *Churchill: Young Man in a Hurry, 1874–1915*. New York: Simon & Schuster, 1983.

Morgenthau, Henry, III. *Mostly Morgenthaus: A Family History*. New York: Tick-nor and Fields, 1991.

Morison, Elting E., ed. *Letters of Theodore Roosevelt*. Vols. 3, 5, and 7. Cambridge, Mass.: Harvard University Press, 1951, 1952, 1954.

Morton, H. V. *Atlantic Meeting: An Account of Mr. Churchill's Voyage in H.M.S.* Prince of Wales, *in August, 1941, and the Conference with President Roosevelt Which Resulted in the Atlantic Charter.* New York: Dodd, Mead, 1943.

Mosley, Oswald. *My Life.* New Rochelle, N.Y.: Arlington House, 1972.

Murray, Williamson, and Allan R. Millett. *A War to Be Won: Fighting the Second World War.* Cambridge, Mass.: Belknap Press of Harvard University Press, 2000.

Muskie, Stephen O. *Campobello: Roosevelt's "Beloved Island."* Camden, Maine: Down East Books, 1982.

Neufeld, Michael J. and Michael Berenbaum, eds. *The Bombing of Auschwitz: Should the Allies Have Attempted It?* New York: St. Martin's Press, 2000.

Newton, Verne, ed. *FDR and the Holocaust.* New York: St. Martin's Press, 1996.

Nicholas, H. G., ed. *Washington Despatches, 1941–1945: Weekly Political Reports from the British Embassy.* Chicago: University of Chicago Press, 1981.

Nicolson, Nigel, ed. *Diaries and Letters of Harold Nicolson.* 3 vols. London: Collins, 1966–1968.

Novick, Peter. *The Holocaust in American Life.* Boston: Houghton Mifflin, 1999.

Ogden, Christopher. *The Life of the Party: The Biography of Pamela Digby Churchill Hayward Harriman.* Boston: Little, Brown, 1994.

Parker, R.A.C., ed. *Winston Churchill: Studies in Statesmanship.* Washington, D.C.: Brassey's, 1995.

Pawle, Gerald. *The War and Colonel Warden. Based on the Recollections of C. R. Thompson, Personal Assistant to the Prime Minister, 1940–1945.* New York: Alfred A. Knopf, 1963.

Perkins, Frances. *The Roosevelt I Knew.* New York: Viking Press, 1946.

Persico, Joseph E. *Roosevelt's Secret War: FDR and World War II Espionage.* New York: Random House, 2001.

Phillips, Harlan B. *Felix Frankfurter Reminisces.* New York: Reynal & Company, 1960.

Pilpel, Robert H. *Churchill in America, 1895–1961: An Affectionate Portrait.* New York: Harcourt Brace Jovanovich 1976.

Pogue, Forrest C. *George C. Marshall: Education of a General, 1880–1939.* London: MacGibbon & Kee, 1964.

Polmar, Norman and Thomas B. Allen. *World War II: America at War, 1941–1945.* New York: Random House, 1991.

————. *World War II: The Encyclopedia of the War Years, 1941–1945.* New York: Random House, 1996.

Price, Claire. "Churchill Takes Up Where He Left Off." *The New York Times Magazine,* October 1, 1939.

Reilly, Michael F., as told to William J. Slocum. *Reilly of the White House.* New York: Simon & Schuster, 1947.

Reporting World War II. 2 vols. New York: Library of America, 1995.

Reynolds, David. *The Creation of the Anglo-American Alliance, 1937–41: A Study in Competitive Co-operation.* Chapel Hill, N.C.: University of North Carolina Press, 1981.

————. *From Munich to Pearl Harbor: Roosevelt's America and the Origins of the Second World War.* Chicago: Ivan R. Dee, 2001.

Reynolds, David, Warren F. Kimball, and A. O. Chubarian, eds. *Allies at War: The Soviet, American, and British Experience, 1939–1945.* New York: St. Martin's Press, 1994.

Rhodes, Richard. *The Making of the Atomic Bomb.* New York: Simon & Schuster, 1986.

Rigdon, William. *White House Sailor.* Garden City, N.Y.: Doubleday, 1962.

Roberts, Andrew. *Eminent Churchillians.* New York: Simon & Schuster, 1994.

————. *"The Holy Fox": A Biography of Lord Halifax.* London: Weidenfeld and Nicolson, 1991.

Roosevelt, Eleanor. *On My Own: The Years Since the White House.* New York: Harper & Brothers, 1958.

———. *This I Remember.* New York: Harper & Brothers, 1949.

———. *This Is My Story.* New York: Harper & Brothers, 1937.

Roosevelt, Elliott. *As He Saw It.* New York: Duell, Sloan and Pearce, 1946.

———, ed. *F.D.R.: His Personal Letters.* Vols. 1, 2, 3, and 4. New York: Duell, Sloan and Pearce, 1947–1950.

Roosevelt, James, and Bill Libby. *My Parents: A Differing View.* Chicago: Playboy Press, 1976.

Roosevelt, James, and Sidney Shalett. *Affectionately, F.D.R.: A Son's Story of a Lonely Man.* New York: Harcourt, Brace, 1959.

Roosevelt, Sara, as told to Isabel Leighton and Gabrielle Forbush. *My Boy Franklin.* New York: R. Long & R. R. Smith, 1933.

Rose, N. A., ed. *Baffy: The Diaries of Blanche Dugdale, 1936–1947.* London: Valentine, Mitchell, 1973.

Rosenman, Samuel I. *Working with Roosevelt.* New York: Harper & Brothers, 1952.

Rubenstein, William D. *The Myth of Rescue: Why the Democracies Could Not Have Saved More Jews from the Nazis.* New York: Routledge, 1997.

Sainsbury, Keith. *Churchill and Roosevelt at War: The War They Fought and the Peace They Hoped to Make.* New York: New York University Press, 1994.

———. *The Turning Point: Roosevelt, Stalin, Churchill, and Chiang-Kai-Shek, 1943: The Moscow, Cairo, and Teheran Conferences.* New York: Oxford University Press, 1985.

Schapsmeier, Edward L. and Frederick H. Schapsmeier. *Prophet in Politics: Henry A. Wallace and the War Years, 1940–1965.* Ames: Iowa State University Press, 1970.

Schlesinger, Arthur M., Jr. *The Age of Roosevelt.* 3 vols. Boston: Houghton Mifflin, 1957–1960.

———. *The Imperial Presidency.* Boston: Houghton Mifflin, 1973.

———. *A Life in the Twentieth Century: Innocent Beginnings, 1917–1950.* Boston: Houghton Mifflin, 2000.

Schlup, Leonard C., and Donald W. Whisenhunt, eds. *"It Seems to Me": Selected Letters of Eleanor Roosevelt.* Lexington: University Press of Kentucky, 2001.

Sherwood, Robert E. *Roosevelt and Hopkins: An Intimate History.* New York: Harper & Brothers, 1948.

Shirer, William L. *Berlin Diary: The Journal of a Foreign Correspondent, 1934–1941.* New York: Alfred A. Knopf, 1941.

———. *The Rise and Fall of the Third Reich: A History of Nazi Germany.* New York: Simon & Schuster, 1960.

Shogan, Robert. *Hard Bargain: How FDR Twisted Churchill's Arm, Evaded the Law, and Changed the Role of the American Presidency.* New York: Charles Scribner's Sons, 1995.

Shoumatoff, Elizabeth. *FDR's Unfinished Portrait: A Memoir.* Pittsburgh: University of Pittsburgh Press, 1990.

Smith, A. Merriman. *Thank You, Mr. President: A White House Notebook.* New York: Harper & Brothers, 1946.

Smith, Amanda, ed. *Hostage to Fortune: The Letters of Joseph P. Kennedy.* New York: Viking Press, 2001.

Smith, Bradley F. *The Shadow Warriors: OSS and the Origins of the C.I.A.* New York: Basic Books, 1983.

Smith, Richard Norton. *Thomas E. Dewey and His Times.* New York: Simon & Schuster, 1982.

Smith, Sally Bedell. *Reflected Glory: The Life of Pamela Churchill Harriman.* New York: Simon & Schuster, 1996.

Snow, C. P. *Variety of Men.* New York: Charles Scribner's Sons, 1967.

Soames, Mary. *A Churchill Family Album: A Personal Anthology.* London: A. Lane, 1982.

———. *Clementine Churchill: The Biography of a Marriage.* Boston: Houghton Mifflin, 1979.

———, ed. *Winston and Clementine: The Personal Letters of the Churchills.* Boston: Houghton Mifflin, 1999.

Somerville, Mollie. *Eleanor Roosevelt As I Knew Her.* McLean, Va.: EPM Publications, 1996.

Speer, Albert. *Inside the Third Reich: Memoirs.* New York: Macmillan, 1970.

Stafford, David. *Roosevelt and Churchill: Men of Secrets.* London: Little, Brown, 1999.

Steel, Ronald. *Walter Lippmann and the American Century.* Boston: Little, Brown, 1980.

Stimson, Henry L., and McGeorge Bundy. *On Active Service in Peace and War.* New York: Harper & Brothers, 1948.

Streit, Clarence K. *Union Now with Britain.* New York: Harper & Brothers, 1941.

Stettinius, Edward R., Jr. *Roosevelt and the Russians: The Yalta Conference.* Garden City, N.Y.: Doubleday & Company, 1949.

Strout, Richard L. *TRB: Views and Perspectives on the Presidency.* New York: Macmillan, 1979.

Sykes, Christopher. *Nancy: The Life of Lady Astor.* New York: Harper & Row, 1972.

Taylor, A.J.P. *The Origins of the Second World War.* New York: Atheneum, 1962.

Taylor, A.J.P., et al. *Churchill: Four Faces and the Man.* London: Allen Lane, 1969.

Thompson, Kenneth W. *Winston Churchill's World View: Statesmanship and Power.* Baton Rouge: Louisiana State University Press, 1983.

Thompson, W. H. *I Was Churchill's Shadow.* London: Christopher Johnson, 1951.

Thorne, Christopher G. *Allies of a Kind: The United States, Britain and the War Against Japan, 1941–1945.* New York: Oxford University Press, 1978.

Tittle, Walter. *Roosevelt As an Artist Saw Him.* New York: Robert M. McBride and Company, 1948.

Trollope, Anthony. *The Last Chronicle of Barset.* New York: Oxford University Press, 1989.

Truman, Margaret, ed. *Where the Buck Stops: The Personal and Private Writings of Harry S Truman.* New York: Warner Books, 1989.

Tugwell, Rexford. *The Democratic Roosevelt: A Biography of Franklin D. Roosevelt.* Garden City, N.Y.: Doubleday, 1957.

Tully, Grace. *F.D.R.: My Boss.* New York: Charles Scribner's Sons, 1949.

Tyerman, Christopher. *A History of Harrow School, 1324–1991.* New York: Oxford University Press, 2000.

Ward, Geoffrey C. *Before the Trumpet: Young Franklin Roosevelt, 1882–1905.* New York: Harper & Row, 1985.

———. *A First-Class Temperament: The Emergence of Franklin Roosevelt.* New York: Harper & Row, 1989.

———, ed. *Closest Companion: The Unknown Story of the Intimate Friendship Between Franklin Roosevelt and Margaret Suckley.* Boston: Houghton Mifflin, 1995.

Weigley, Russell F. *The American Way of War: A History of United States Military Strategy and Policy.* New York: Macmillan, 1973.

Weinberg, Gerhard L. *A World at Arms: A Global History of World War II.* Cambridge, Eng.: Cambridge University Press, 1994.

Welles, Benjamin. *Sumner Welles: FDR's Global Strategist: A Biography.* New York: St. Martin's Press, 1997.

West, J. B., with Mary Lynn Kotz. *Upstairs at the White House: My Life with the First Ladies.* New York: Coward, McCann & Geoghegan, 1973.

West, Mark I. *Roald Dahl*. New York: Twayne Publishers, 1992.

Wheeler-Bennett, John Wheeler. *Special Relationships: America in Peace and War*. London: Macmillan, 1975.

————, ed. *Action This Day: Working with Churchill*. London: Macmillan, 1968.

Winant, John Gilbert. *A Letter from Grosvenor Square: An Account of a Stewardship*. Boston: Houghton Mifflin, 1947.

Wood, E. Thomas. *Karski: How One Man Tried to Stop the Holocaust*. New York: John Wiley & Sons, 1994.

Wyman, David S. *The Abandonment of the Jews: America and the Holocaust, 1941–1945*. New York: New Press, 1998.

Young, Kenneth, ed. *The Diaries of Sir Robert Bruce Lockhart*. Vol. 1: *1915–1938*. London: Macmillan, 1973.

OFFICIAL DOCUMENTS AND PUBLICATIONS

Public Papers and Addresses of Franklin D. Roosevelt. Compiled by Samuel Rosenman. 13 vols. New York: Russell and Russell, 1938–1950.

United States Department of State. *Foreign Relations of the United States: The Conferences at Cairo and Tehran, 1943*. Department of State Publication 7187. Washington, D.C.: U.S. Government Printing Office, 1961.

————. *Foreign Relations of the United States: The Conferences at Malta and Yalta, 1945*. Department of State

Publication 6199. Washington, D.C.: U.S. Government Printing Office, 1955.

————. *Foreign Relations of the United States: The Conference at Quebec, 1944.* Department of State Publication 8627. Washington, D.C.: U.S. Government Printing Office, 1972.

————. *Foreign Relations of the United States: The Conferences at Washington and Quebec, 1943.* Department of State Publication 8552. Washington, D.C.: U.S. Government Printing Office, 1970.

————. *Foreign Relations of the United States: The Conferences at Washington, 1941–1942, and Casablanca, 1943.* Department of State Publication 8414. Washington, D.C.: U.S. Government Printing Office, 1968.

War Records of Prime Minister Winston Churchill. Public Record Office, Kew Gardens, England, and Churchill Archives Centre, Churchill College, Cambridge, England.

MAGAZINES, NEWSPAPERS, AND JOURNALS

American Heritage

Collier's

Diplomatic History

Finest Hour

Harper's

Life

The Times (London)

New York Herald-Tribune

The New York Times

The New Yorker

Newsweek

Saturday Evening Post

Scribner's

Smithsonian

Time

Transactions of the Royal Historical Society

The Washington Post

Washington Star

PHOTOGRAPH CREDITS

Corbis   288
Franklin D. Roosevelt Library   300
Franklin D. Roosevelt Library   312
Corbis   323
Franklin D. Roosevelt Library   336
Franklin D. Roosevelt Library   336
Franklin D. Roosevelt Library   348
Franklin D. Roosevelt Library   364

INDEX

JON MEACHAM is the managing editor of *Newsweek*. Born in Chattanooga in 1969, he is a graduate of The University of the South in Sewanee, Tennessee. The editor of *Voices in Our Blood: America's Best on the Civil Rights Movement,* Meacham lives in New York City with his wife and son.